OUTBOARD MOTOR MAINTENANCE & TUNE-UP MANUAL

(1st Edition — Volume 1)
Covers Motors Below 30 Horsepower
MAINTENANCE SECTIONS

INTERTEC PUBLISHING CORPORATION
P.O. Box 12901, Overland Park Kansas 66212

Cover photograph courtesy of Evinrude Motors

INTRODUCTION

The Outboard Motor Maintenance Manual contains the specifications and procedures necessary for someone with average mechanical ability to properly maintain an outboard motor contained herein.

Additional maintenance information for general applications is found in the Boat & Motor Facts, Fixes and Tips manual published by Intertec Publishing. This manual provides maintenance information on a wide variety of marine equipment, including outboard motors.

If extensive service information is required, such as overhaul of the engine and lower unit, the Outboard Motor Service Manual published by Intertec Publishing is recommended. The Outboard Motor Service Manual is noted in the maintenance sections where additional service information may be helpful.

SAFETY NOTES

Safety notes are interspersed throughout the manual to highlight information which the reader should be aware of when servicing an outboard motor. The safety information is contained in a box under a CAUTION or WARNING head which is highlighted by a color panel.

⚠CAUTION

A CAUTION indicates that personal injury or damage to equipment may result due to hazards or improper service practices.

⚠WARNING

A WARNING specifies unsafe operations or hazards that can cause serious personal injury or death.

Due to a variety of possible situations and unforeseen circumstances, safety notes cannot alert the reader to all hazards. The reader must exercise caution and be alert for unsafe conditions when operating or maintaining an outboard motor.

DUAL DIMENSIONS

This service manual provides specifications in both the U.S. Customary and Metric (SI) systems of measurement. The first specification is given in the measuring system perceived by us to be the preferred system when servicing a particular component, while the second specification (given in parenthesis) is the converted measurement. For instance, a specification of "0.011 inch (0.28 mm)" would indicate that we feel the preferred measurement, in this instance, is the U.S. system of measurement and the metric equivalent of 0.011 inch is 0.28 mm.

CHRYSLER

US MARINE CORP.
105 Marine Drive
Hartford, Wisconsin 53027

3.5 AND 3.6 HP
(PRIOR TO 1978)

3.5 HP MODELS

Year Produced	Model
1969	3039, 3049, 3139

3.6 HP MODELS

Year Produced	Model
1970	32HA, 32BA, 33HA, 33BA
1971 & 1972	32HB, 32BB, 33HB, 33BB
1973, 1974, 1976 & 1977	32HC, 32BC, 33HC, 33BC

Specifications

	3.5 HP	3.6 HP
Hp/rpm	3.5/4500	3.6/4500
Bore	2-1/16 in.	2-1/16 in.
	(52.4 mm)	(52.4 mm)
Stroke	1-9/16 in.	1-9/16 in.
	(39.7 mm)	(39.7 mm)
Number of cylinders	1	1
Displacement	5.18 cu. in.	5.18 cu. in.
	(85 cc)	(85 cc)
Compression at cranking speed (average)	65-75 psi	65-75 psi
	(449-517 kPa)	(449-517 kPa)
Spark plug	Champion H8J	Champion H8J
Electrode gap	0.030 in.	0.030 in.
	(0.76 mm)	(0.76 mm)
Breaker point gap	0.020 in.	0.020 in.
	(0.51 mm)	(0.51 mm)
Carburetor:		
Make	Tillotson	Tillotson
Model	MD124A	CO-1A
Adjustment	See Text	See Text
Fuel:oil ratio	16:1	25:1*

*Fuel to oil ratio should be increased to 16:1 for the first three hours of running (break-in) and for severe service.

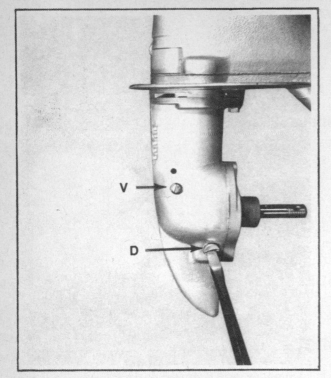

Fig. C1-1—View showing location of vent screw (V) and drain/fill screw (D) on 3.5 and 3.6 hp models.

Maintenance

LUBRICATION

ENGINE. The engine is lubricated by oil mixed with the fuel. The recommended fuel:oil ratio for normal operation is 16:1 for 3.5 hp models and 25:1 for 3.6 hp models. During engine break-in of 3.6 hp models, the fuel:oil ratio should be 16:1.

The manufacturer recommends the use of no-lead automotive gasoline although regular and premium grades may be used. The gasoline octane rating must be 85 or higher.

LOWER UNIT. The lower unit gears and bearings are lubricated by oil contained in the gearcase. Only a noncorrosive, EP90 outboard gear oil should be used. The gearcase should be drained and refilled every 100 hours or every six months, and fluid maintained at the level of the upper (vent) plug hole.

The outboard motor must be upright when draining or filling gearcase. Remove both plugs (V and D—Fig. C1-1) on port side of gearcase when draining or filling. To fill with lubricant, force lubricant into lower plug hole (D) until lubricant reaches lower edge of upper plug hole (V). Install new gaskets on plugs, if necessary. Install upper plug (V) before removing lubricant dispenser so fluid remains in gearcase, then remove dispenser and install lower plug (D).

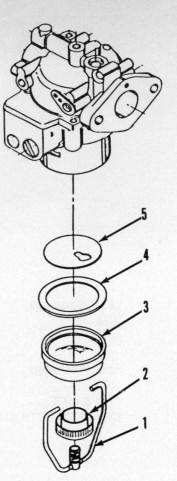

Fig. C1-2—Exploded view of carburetor sediment bowl components used on 3.5 hp models.

1. Bail
2. Nut
3. Sediment bowl
4. Gasket
5. Screen

FUEL SYSTEM

FUEL FILTER. All models are equipped with a mesh fuel filter which is integral with the fuel tank fuel fitting. The fuel filter should be inspected and cleaned at least once each season, or more frequently if fuel stoppage due to filter blockage by foreign material is a problem. Empty the fuel tank or be prepared to catch fuel before unscrewing the fuel fitting.

CARBURETOR. The carburetor on 3.5 hp models is equipped with a sediment bowl to trap foreign material. To remove sediment bowl, unscrew nut (2—Fig. C1-2), detach bail (1) and remove bowl (3) and screen (5). Clean bowl and screen and reinstall using a new gasket (4), if necessary.

FUEL TANK. It may be necessary to remove the fuel tank for cleaning or for access to underlying engine components. The manual starter is attached to the fuel tank on all models. On 3.5 hp models the fuel tank is also the engine cover

Illustrations Courtesy Chrysler

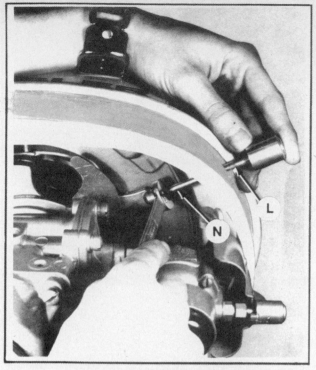

Fig. C1-3—*Loosen jam nut (N) before unscrewing speed control lever (L). Tighten the jam nut after installing control lever to prevent loosening of lever.*

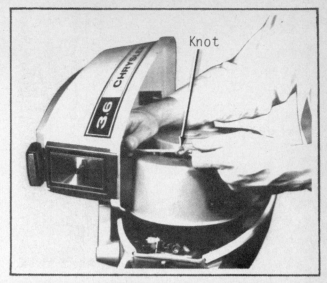

Fig. C1-4—*On 3.6 hp models, tie a knot in the starter rope so the starter rope will not wind into the starter when the rope handle is detached.*

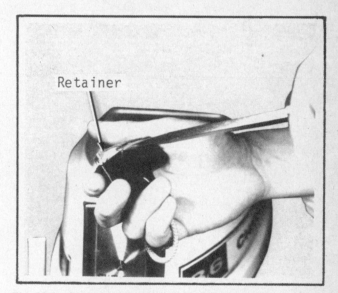

Fig. C1-5—*Pry out the retainer in the rope handle for access to the rope end.*

while on 3.6 hp models a separate engine cover surrounds the power head.

To remove the fuel tank on 3.5 hp models, loosen the speed control lever jam nut shown in Fig. C1-3 and unscrew the speed control lever. Be prepared to catch fuel, then disconnect fuel line from the fuel valve and plug the fuel line. Unscrew the four screws on the underside of the fuel tank securing it to the power head and remove the fuel tank. Reinstall the fuel tank by reversing the removal procedure. Be sure the speed control lever and fuel line are securely attached.

To remove the fuel tank on 3.6 hp models, unscrew the screw(s) securing the engine cover. Unscrew the gas cap and pull out the cap retaining chain and wire retainer. Lift the engine cover up and shift it to one side so there is access to the starter rope. Disconnect spark plug lead and ground lead to engine to prevent accidental starting. Pull out the starter rope at the starter housing and tie a knot so the rope cannot rewind into the starter as shown in Fig. C1-4. Pry the rope retainer out of the rope handle as shown in Fig. C1-5. Remove the rope handle then the engine cover. Be prepared to catch fuel, then disconnect and plug the fuel line. Unscrew four screws securing the fuel tank then lift off the fuel tank. Reinstall the fuel tank by reversing the removal procedure. Be sure the fuel line is securely attached.

STARTER

The manual starter is attached to the top of the fuel tank. To remove the starter on 3.5 hp models, unscrew fasteners and lift off starter. To remove the starter on 3.6 hp models, first remove the engine cover as outlined in the FUEL TANK section, then unscrew the fasteners retaining the starter and lift off the starter.

To disassemble the starter, proceed as follows: Remove the rope handle on 3.5 hp models or untie the knot on 3.6 hp models and allow the rope to wind into the starter (if the rewind spring or rope is broken this step is unnecessary). Remove "E" ring (15—Fig. C1-6). Remove friction shoe assembly along with washers as shown in Fig. C1-6.

Chrysler 3.5 & 3.6 Hp

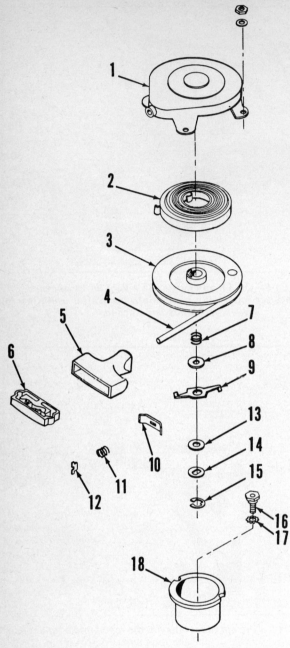

Fig. C1-6 — Exploded view of the manual starter used on 3.6 hp models. The starter on 3.5 hp models is similar except spring (7) is located between washers (13 and 14) and washer (14) has a large outside diameter.

1. Starter housing
2. Rewind spring
3. Rope pulley
4. Rope
5. Handle
6. Retainer
7. Spring
8. Fiber washer
9. Lever
10. Friction shoe
11. Spring
12. Retainer
13. Fiber washer
14. Steel washer
15. "E" ring
16. Flywheel retaining screw
17. Serrated washer
18. Starter cup

Remove remaining washer, and on 3.6 hp models, the spring. Carefully lift out rope pulley while being careful not to dislodge the rewind spring. If the rewind spring must be removed, position the starter housing so the spring side is towards the floor or bench then tap the starter housing against the floor or bench so the spring dislodges and uncoils.

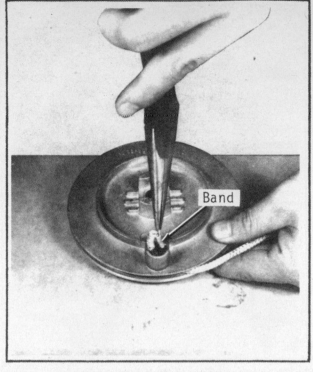

Fig. C1-7 — To install starter rope end, double the rope end over and push the banded end back into the cavity.

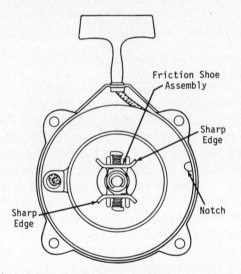

Fig. C1-8 — View of starter showing proper installation of friction shoe assembly. Note position of sharp edges on friction shoes.

⚠WARNING

Care should be exercised when working with or around a coiled starter rewind spring as sudden uncoiling can cause injury. Safety eyewear and gloves are recommended.

To install the rewind spring, hook outer end of spring around post in starter housing and wind

Illustrations Courtesy Chrysler

spring into housing in a counterclockwise direction from outer spring end. If a new spring is installed, position spring assembly in housing then carefully remove coil retaining bands. Lubricate spring with grease.

Rope length should be 48 inches (122 cm). The starter rope is secured to the pulley by a metal band at the rope end. Thread the unbanded end of the starter rope into pulley until the banded end protrudes as shown in Fig. C1-7. Fold the banded end over as shown so the rope is doubled over. Pull the rope taut so the doubled-over rope end is seated in the pulley.

Lubricate the shaft in the starter housing with a light coat of grease. Install the rope pulley in the starter housing while engaging inner spring end in the slot in the pulley. Hold the rope in pulley notch (Fig. C1-8) during installation. Assemble the remaining components on the pulley as shown in Fig. C1-6. Note that on 3.5 hp models spring (7) is located between washers (13 and 14) and washer (14) has a large OD. The friction shoe assembly must be installed so the sharp edges are positioned as shown in Fig. C1-8. Install "E" ring (15 — Fig. C1-6) in groove in shaft.

With the rope in notch (Fig. C1-8), rotate the pulley three full turns counterclockwise and pass the rope end through the rope outlet. Tie a knot in the rope on 3.6 hp models or attach the rope handle on 3.5 hp models. Pull the rope and check starter action. With the rope pulled out as far as possible, it should be possible to rotate the pulley an additional ⅛ to ⅜ of a turn. This additional rotation ensures that the rewind spring is not fully extended. If the pulley will not rotate the additional amount, recheck the rope length.

Reinstall the starter on the gas tank and install the engine cover on 3.6 hp models.

COOLING SYSTEM

The power head is air-cooled by a fan integral with the flywheel which forces air through cooling fins on the cylinder.

On 3.5 hp motors, a cooling tube is located in the lower unit. This tube picks up water from behind the propeller, below the anti-cavitation plate and directs it into the exhaust portion of the lower housing. The 3.6 hp motors are equipped with a rubber impeller type water pump which pumps water into the exhaust housing. Periodically inspect the water inlet for blockage.

PROPELLER

Power is transmitted from the propeller shaft to the propeller by a drive pin which is designed to shear when the propeller contacts an obstruction. The drive pin (shear pin) is made of stainless steel with a diameter of 5/32 inch and a length of 1-3/16

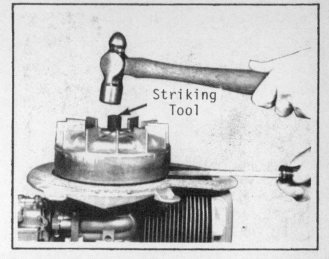

Fig. C1-9 — "Pop" the flywheel loose by carefully prying up against the flywheel while striking the crankshaft end as outlined in text.

inches. The correct drive pin must be used to protect the drive components from damage.

The standard propeller is designed for left-hand rotation and has two blades. Propeller diameter is 7½ inches (19 cm) and pitch is 4½ inches (11.4 cm).

⚠WARNING

When working on or around the propeller the spark plug lead should be disconnected and grounded to the engine to prevent accidental starting if the propeller is rotated.

To remove the propeller, detach the cotter pin then unscrew the propeller nut. Drive the shear pin out of the propeller and propeller shaft. Pull the propeller off the propeller shaft.

Reinstall the propeller by reversing the removal procedure. Apply a coating of water-resistant grease to the propeller shaft before installing the propeller.

Tune-Up

IGNITION SYSTEM

All models are equipped with a conventional flywheel magneto type ignition system. All ignition components except the spark plug are located underneath the flywheel.

To adjust breaker point gap, the flywheel must be removed. To remove the flywheel, first remove the fuel tank as outlined in the previous FUEL TANK section. Unscrew the fywheel retaining

Chrysler 3.5 & 3.6 Hp

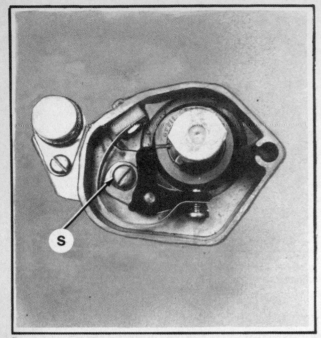

Fig. C1-10—Align index mark on point cam with breaker point follower arm when measuring breaker point gap. Loosen screw (S) to adjust gap.

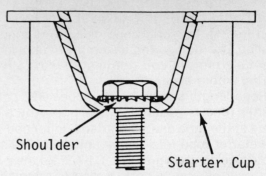

Fig. C1-11—The hole in the starter cup must pilot on the shoulder of the flywheel retaining screw during assembly.

screw and remove the starter cup. A band type wrench should be used to hold the flywheel during screw loosening. Screw a cap screw of the correct diameter and pitch into the end of the crankshaft so the screw head bears against only the end of the crankshaft (it may be necessary to use spacers between the screw head and crankshaft end), or install Chrysler tool T2919. Using a suitable prying tool, lightly pry up against the flywheel while moderately striking the screw or tool T2919 in the crankshaft end. See Fig. C1-9. The flywheel should "pop" free.

⚠WARNING

Be sure suitable tools are used to withdraw the flywheel. Damage resultant from the misapplication of force or the use of incorrect tools may cause engine damage, engine malfunction or personal injury.

Remove the flywheel and inspect it for cracks or other damage. Be sure to inspect the tapered center portion of the flywheel as well. A damaged flywheel must be discarded as it may fly apart at high engine rpm.

To check the breaker point gap, install the flywheel retaining screw in the end of the crankshaft then rotate the crankshaft clockwise by turning the screw. Rotate the crankshaft so the in-

dex mark on the breaker cam is aligned with the breaker point follower arm as shown in Fig. C1-10. The breaker point gap should be 0.020 inch (0.5 mm). Loosen breaker point retaining screw (S) to adjust breaker point gap. After tightening screw (S), rotate the crankshaft and recheck point gap. Lubricate the cam wiper felt with a small amount of breaker point cam lubricant. Do not apply too much lubricant as it may be thrown off the cam onto the breaker points causing misfiring.

Be sure the tapered mating surfaces of the crankshaft and flywheel are clean and dry, then install the flywheel. Install the flywheel retaining screw and starter cup. Note that the starter cup hole must index on the shoulder of the flywheel screw as shown in Fig. C1-11. Tighten the flywheel retaining screw to 25 ft.-lbs. (34 N·m). Reinstall the fuel tank.

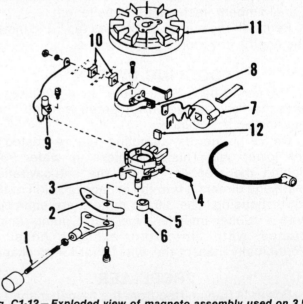

Fig. C1-12—Exploded view of magneto assembly used on 3.5 hp models.

1. Speed control lever	5. Cam	9. Condenser
2. Throttle cam	6. Key	10. Insulators
3. Armature plate	7. Coil	11. Flywheel
4. Friction screw	8. Breaker points	12. Oil wick

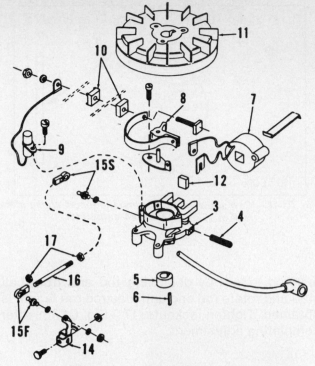

Fig. C1-13—*Exploded view of magneto assembly and throttle control used on 3.6 hp models.*

3. Armature plate
4. Friction screw
5. Breaker cam
6. Key
7. Coil
8. Breaker points
9. Condenser
10. Insulators
11. Flywheel
12. Felt wick
14. Throttle cam
15. Rod ends
16. Control rod
17. Locknuts

SPEED CONTROL LINKAGE

The speed control lever is connected to the magneto stator plate. The carburetor throttle is also actuated by the speed control lever. Moving the speed control lever advances or retards ignition as well as opening and closing the throttle. It is therefore important to synchronize linkage movement for best performance.

3.5 Hp Models

To adjust the speed control linkage on 3.5 hp models, proceed as follows: Verify that throttle link (20—Fig. C1-15) is in the inner hole (B) of throttle shaft (19). Move the speed control lever so it is centered over the idle mixture adjusting screw as shown in Fig. C1-14. Follower arm (21—Fig. C1-15) should just contact the throttle control cam (2—Fig. C1-12) and begin to open the carburetor throttle. If not, loosen clamp screw (S) and shorten or length link (20).

3.6 Hp Models

To check and adjust the speed control linkage on 3.6 hp models, the fuel tank should be removed. Move the speed control lever from low to high speed while noting at what point throttle cam (14—Fig. C1-13) just contacts cam follower roller (21—C1-16). A mark (T—Fig. C1-17) is located on the throttle cam and should be at the center of the

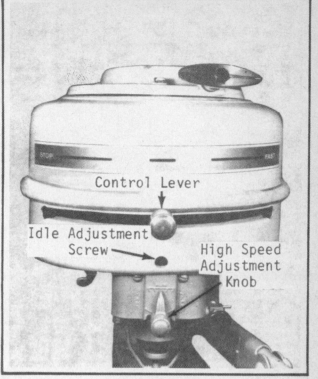

Fig. C1-14—*View of 3.5 hp model showing location of speed control lever, idle mixture screw and high speed mixture adjustment knob.*

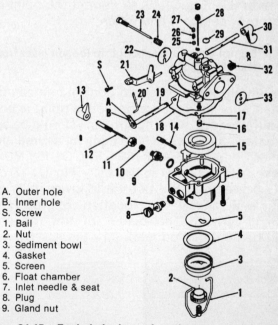

Fig. C1-15—*Exploded view of carburetor used on 3.5 hp motors.*

A. Outer hole
B. Inner hole
S. Screw
1. Bail
2. Nut
3. Sediment bowl
4. Gasket
5. Screen
6. Float chamber
7. Inlet needle & seat
8. Plug
9. Gland nut
10. Packing
11. Nut
12. Main adjustment needle
13. Knob
14. Float shaft
15. Float
16. Plug
17. Main nozzle
18. Gasket
19. Throttle shaft
20. Link
21. Follower
22. Choke plate
23. Idle mixture needle
24. Spring
25. Friction pin
26. Spring
27. Plug
28. Idle tube
29. Expansion plug
30. Lever
31. Shaft
32. Spring
33. Throttle plate

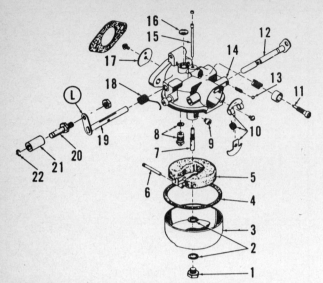

Fig. C1-16—Exploded view of carburetor used on 3.6 hp models.

1. Retaining screw	9. Main jet	16. Welch plug
2. Gasket	10. Choke	17. Throttle plate
3. Float bowl	11. Idle mixture needle	18. Return spring
4. Gasket	12. Choke shaft	19. Throttle shaft
5. Float	13. Choke detent ball	20. Follower
6. Float pin	14. Carburetor body	21. Roller
7. Main nozzle	15. Bypass tube	22. Clip
8. Inlet valve		

roller when they just touch. Bend the throttle shaft lever (L—Fig. C1-16) to correct the point of contact between cam and roller.

NOTE: Do not bend lever enough to loosen lever from end of carburetor throttle shaft.

The length of the magneto control link can be adjusted after the carburetor pickup point is correct. Initial length of the control link should be approximately 3½ inches (89 mm) measured between rod ends (15F and 15S—Fig. C1-13). Move the speed control lever so mark (T—Fig. C1-17) on cam is centered at the throttle follower roller as shown and check the location of rod end (15S—Fig. C1-13). The center of the rod end should be centered on mark (M—Fig. C1-17). Ad-

Fig. C1-17—View of aligning marks used when adjusting or checking speed control linkage synchronization on 3.6 hp models.

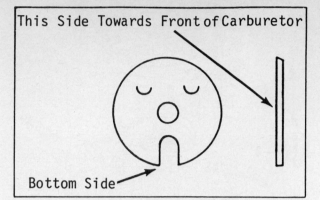

Fig. C1-18—View showing correct installation of choke plate used in Tillotson MD124A carburetor.

just rod length by detaching rod end from ball stud and rotate rod end until desired rod length is obtained. Tighten locknuts (17—Fig. C1-13), after completing adjustment.

CARBURETOR
3.5 Hp Models

A Tillotson MD124A float type carburetor is used on 3.5 hp models. Refer to Fig. C1-15 for an exploded view.

ADJUSTMENT. The carburetor is equipped with high and low speed mixture adjustment screws. Refer to Fig. C1-14 for location of adjustment screws.

To adjust mixture screws, initially turn both screws (the high speed screw has a knob attached to the screw) out from a lightly seated position. Start the engine and run it until it reaches normal operating temperature. Set the speed control lever to the lowest speed position the engine will run. Turn the idle mixture screw clockwise until the engine starts to misfire, note the screw position, then turn the screw counterclockwise until the engine again misfires. Note the screw's position then turn the screw so it is midway between the two misfiring positions.

To adjust the high speed mixture screw, run the engine at full throttle then use the same procedure as described for the idle mixture screw adjustment. Turn the high speed screw clockwise and then counterclockwise to find the misfiring points. Then position the high speed screw midway between the misfiring points. If the knob pointer is not vertical, loosen the knob retaining set screw and reposition the knob.

Note that a slight adjustment of the carburetor may be necessary with the engine under load or different operating conditions.

Illustrations Courtesy Chrysler

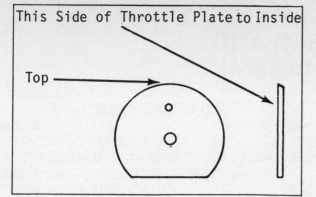

Fig. C1-19—View showing correct installation of throttle plate used in Tillotson MD124A or CO-1A carburetors.

Fig. C1-20—Float level (A) of Tillotson CO-1A carburetor should be 13/32 inch (10.3 mm).

OVERHAUL. Note the following points when overhauling the carburetor. Reinstall the throttle and choke plates as shown in Figs. C1-18 and C1-19. The plate edge is angled so the plates must be installed correctly for proper carburetor operation. Be sure plates do not stick or bind when throttle or choke shaft is rotated. When installing the float, be sure that slot in float lever engages the groove in the fuel inlet needle.

To check float level, the fuel bowl must be removed from the carburetor then inverted. With the bowl held upside down, the lowest free end of the float should be even with or approximately 1/64 inch (0.4 mm) below fuel bowl gasket surface. Adjust the float level by bending the valve fork on float.

3.6 Hp Model

A Tillotson CO-1A float type carburetor is used on 3.6 hp models. Refer to Fig. C1-16 for an exploded view.

ADJUSTMENT. The idle mixture may be adjusted after removing the engine cover. Initial setting of the idle mixture screw (11—Fig. C1-16) is one turn out from a lightly seated position. Follow the procedure in the previous 3.5 hp model section to adjust the idle mixture screw. The 3.6 hp models must be immersed in water when running to prevent damage to the water pump impeller.

High speed mixture is controlled by main jet (9). Main jet standard size (0.037 in.) will normally be correct for operation from sea level to 3000 feet (0 to 914 m) altitude. Main jet size 0.035 inch is recommended from 3000 to 6000 feet (914 to 1829 m) altitude and size 0.033 inch is recommended for altitudes above 6000 feet (1829 m).

OVERHAUL. Note the following points when overhauling the carburetor. Choke detent ball (13—Fig. C1-16) and spring are located behind the choke shaft and will be loose when shaft is withdrawn. Hold the ball and spring in place in the carburetor using a suitable pin or rod while inserting the choke shaft. Install the upper choke plate, spring and lower choke plate (10) so spring tension forces the upper choke plate against the upper tab of the lower choke plate. The upper choke plate must be installed so the open ends of the pivot loops are toward the front of the carburetor. The tab portion above the screw hole on the lower choke plate must be in front of the upper choke plate.

Install the throttle plate as shown in Fig. C1-19. The plate edge is angled so the plate must be installed correctly for proper carburetor operation. Rotate the throttle shaft to be sure the throttle plate does not stick or bind.

To check float level, invert the carburetor and measure the distance from the float to the gasket surface as shown in Fig. C1-20. Distance (A) should be 13/32 inch (10.3 mm). Adjust float level by bending tang on float arm.

Install fuel bowl (3—Fig. C1-16) so indented portion is towards front of carburetor.

CHRYSLER
3.5 (1980 to 1984) AND
4.0 HP (1977 to 1984)

3.5 HP MODELS

Year Produced	Model
1980	32 H0D
1981	32 H1D
1982	32 H2E
1983	32 H3
1984	32 H4

4.0 HP MODELS

Year Produced	Model
1977	42HB,42BB,43HB,47HB,47BB
1978	42H8C,42B8C,42H8D,42B8D,42H8E,42B8E, 47H8C,47B8C,47H8D,47B8D,47H8E,47B8E
1979	42H9F,42B9F,47H9F,47B9F
1980	42H0G,42B0G,43H0A,47HOG,47B0G
1981	42H1H,42B1H,43H1B,43B1B
1982	42H2J,42B2J
1983	42H3
1984	42H4

Specifications

HP/rpm	3.5/4500
	4.0/5250
Bore	2 in.
	(50.8 mm)
Stroke	1-19/32 in.
	(40.5 mm)
Number of cylinders	1
Displacement	5.0 cu.in.
	(82 cc)
Compression at cranking speed (average, with recoil starter)	110-125 psi
	(759-862 kPa)
Spark Plug:	
Champion	L86 (Canada RL86)
Electrode gap	0.030 in.
	(0.76 mm)
Breaker point gap	0.020 in.
	(0.5 mm)
Fuel:oil ratio	50:1

Maintenance

LUBRICATION

ENGINE. The engine is lubricated by oil mixed with the fuel. The recommended fuel:oil ratio for normal operation is 50:1. During engine break-in the fuel:oil ratio should be 25:1.

The manufacturer recommends the use of no-lead automotive gasoline although regular and premium grades may be used. The gasoline octane rating must be 85 or higher.

LOWER UNIT. The lower unit gears and bearings are lubricated by oil contained in the gear-case. Only a noncorrosive, EP90 outboard gear oil should be used. The gearcase should be drained and refilled every 100 hours or every six months, and fluid maintained at the level of the upper (vent) plug hole.

The outboard motor must be upright when draining or filling gearcase. Remove both plugs (V and D — Fig. C2-1) on port side of gearcase when draining or filling. To fill with lubricant, force lubricant into lower plug hole (D) until lubricant reaches lower edge of upper plug hole (V). Install new gaskets on plugs, if necessary. Install upper plug (V) before removing lubricant dispenser so fluid remains in gearcase, then remove dispenser and install lower plug (D).

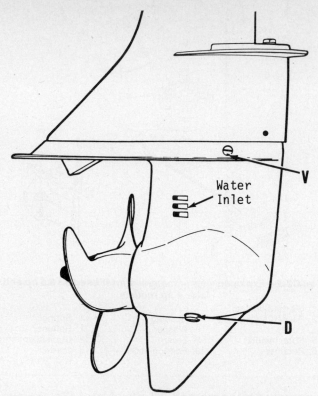

Fig. C2-1 — View showing location of water inlet ports, vent plug (V) and fill/drain plug (D).

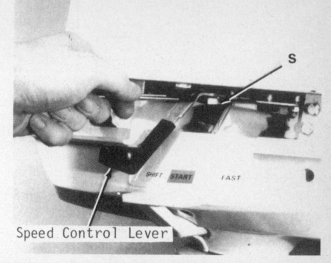

Fig. C2-2 — Unscrew retaining screw (S) to remove speed control lever.

After approximately every 60 days of use, a good quality water-resistant grease should be injected in all grease fittings.

FUEL SYSTEM

FUEL FILTER. All models are equipped with a mesh fuel filter which is integral with the fuel tank fuel fitting. The fuel filter should be inspected and cleaned at least once each season, or more frequently if fuel stoppage due to foreign material is a problem. Empty the fuel tank or be prepared to catch fuel before unscrewing the fuel fitting.

FUEL TANK. It may be necessary to remove the fuel tank for cleaning or for access to underlying engine components. The manual starter is attached to the fuel tank on all models. On 3.5 hp models the fuel tank is exposed while on 4 hp models the fuel tank and engine are underneath an engine cover.

To remove the fuel tank proceed as follows: On 4 hp models, remove the fuel cap assembly then remove the screws which secure the engine cover. On 4 hp models, pull out the starter rope, lift off the engine cover, tie a knot in the starter rope next to the starter, remove the rope handle and then remove the engine cover.

On all models, drain fuel from the fuel tank. Unscrew the two screws securing the fuel tank bracket to the intake manifold (10 — Fig. C2-12).

Unscrew the front legs of the fuel tank from the bottom support plate. Unscrew the two screws securing the rear of the fuel tank to the engine. Remove the screw (S — Fig. C2-2) which secures the speed control lever to the ignition stator plate and remove lever. Rotate the stator plate clockwise as far as it will go. Lift off the fuel tank.

Reinstall the fuel tank by reversing the removal procedure. Note that the stator plate must be in the same position during installation as it was when the tank was removed. Note that spacers are used between the front tank legs and the support plate.

SHIFT LINKAGE

All 4 hp models may be shifted from neutral to forward and vice versa. The shift lever is connected to an upper shift rod which is coupled to the lower shift rod in the gearcase.

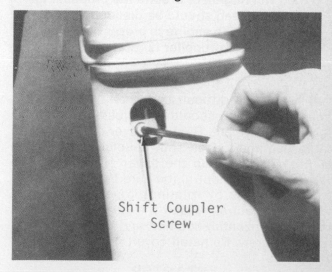

Fig. C2-3 — The shift coupler screw is accessible after removing the cover on the motor leg. Refer to text for shift linkage adjustment.

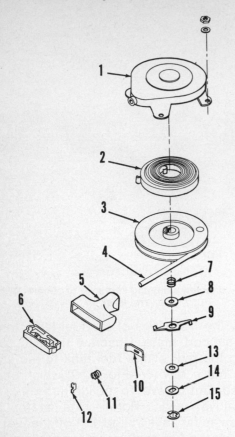

Fig. C2-4 — Exploded view of manual starter used on early 4 hp models.

1. Starter housing	6. Retainer	11. Spring
2. Rewind spring	7. Spring	12. Retainer
3. Pulley	8. Fiber washer	13. Fiber washer
4. Rope	9. Lever	14. Steel washer
5. Rope handle	10. Friction shoe	15. "E" ring

⚠ WARNING

When working on or around the propeller the spark plug lead should be disconnected and grounded to the engine to prevent accidental starting if the propeller is rotated.

If shifting is difficult or the unit won't stay in gear, the linkage should be adjusted or checked for misadjustment. Remove cover on port side of motor leg and loosen shift coupler screw shown in Fig. C2-3. Pull up the lower shift rod so the lower unit is in neutral (be sure to pull up all the way and check by rotating propeller to be sure unit is in neutral). Place the gear shift lever in neutral (horizontal) position and tighten the shift coupler screw. Reinstall cover.

STARTER

The manual starter is attached to the top of the fuel tank. To remove the starter on 3.5 hp models,

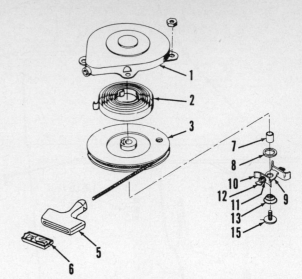

Fig. C2-5 — Exploded view of manual starter used on 3.5 hp and later 4 hp models.

1. Starter housing		
2. Rewind spring	7. Bushing	11. Spring
3. Pulley	8. Washer	12. Retainer
5. Rope handle	9. Lever	13. Conical spring
6. Retainer	10. Friction shoe	15. Screw

unscrew fasteners and lift off starter. To remove the starter on 4 hp models, first remove the engine cover as outlined in the FUEL TANK section, then unscrew the fasteners retaining the starter and lift off the starter.

To disassemble the starter, proceed as follows: Remove the rope handle on 3.5 hp models or untie the knot on 4 hp models and allow the rope to wind into the starter (if the rewind spring or rope is broken this step is unnecessary). Remove "E" ring or screw (15 — Fig. C2-4 or C2-5). Remove friction shoe assembly along with remaining components on pulley shown in Fig. C2-4 or C2-5. Carefully lift out rope pulley while being careful not to dislodge the rewind spring. If the rewind spring must be removed, position the starter housing so the spring side is towards the floor or bench then tap the starter housing against the floor or bench so the spring dislodges and uncoils.

⚠ WARNING

Care should be exercised when working with or around a coiled starter rewind spring as sudden uncoiling can cause injury. Safety eyewear and gloves are recommended.

To install the rewind spring, hook outer end of spring around post in starter housing and wind spring into housing in a counterclockwise direc-

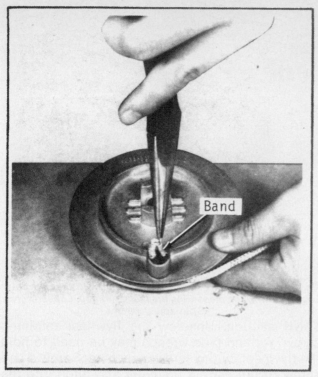

Fig. C2-6 — To install a banded starter rope end, double the rope end over and push the banded end back into the cavity.

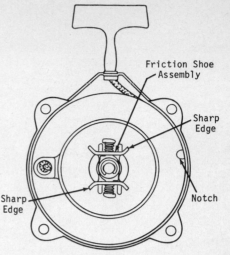

Fig. C2-7 — View of starter showing proper installation of friction shoe assembly. Note position of sharp edges on friction shoes.

tion from outer spring end. If a new spring is installed, position spring assembly in housing then carefully remove coil retaining bands. Lubricate spring with grease.

Rope length should be 48 inches (122 cm). If the rope has a banded end, install rope as follows: Thread the unbanded end of the starter rope into the pulley until the banded end protrudes as shown in Fig. C2-6. Fold the banded end over as shown so the rope is doubled over. Pull the rope taut so the doubled-over rope end is seated in the pulley.

If the rope is unbanded, pass the rope through the rope hole, tie a knot in the rope and then pull the rope taut into the rope cavity of the pulley.

Lubricate the shaft in the starter housing with a light coat of grease. Install the rope pulley in the starter housing while engaging inner spring end in the slot in the pulley. Hold the rope in pulley notch (Fig. C2-7) during installation. Assemble the remaining components on the pulley as shown in Fig. C2-4 or C2-5. The friction shoe assembly must be installed so the sharp edges are positioned as shown in Fig. C2-7. Install "E" ring (15 — Fig. C2-4) in groove in shaft on early models or retaining screw (15 — Fig. C2-5) on later models.

With the rope in notch (Fig. C2-7), rotate the pulley three full turns counterclockwise and pass the rope end through the rope outlet. Tie a knot in the rope on 4 hp models or attach the rope handle on 3.5 hp models. Pull the rope and check starter action. With the rope pulled out as far as possible,

it should be possible to rotate the pulley an additional ⅛ to ⅜ of a turn. This additional rotation ensures that the rewind spring is not fully extended. If the pulley will not rotate the additional amount, recheck the rope length.

Reinstall the starter on the gas tank and install the engine cover on 4 hp models.

COOLING SYSTEM

All models are equipped with an impeller type water pump located in the lower unit that circulates water through the power head.

⚠ CAUTION

Do not operate outboard motor unless the lower unit is immersed in water, otherwise, the water pump impeller will be damaged.

If cooling system problems are encountered, first check the water inlet (see Fig. C2-1) for material which may be blocking the inlet. If the water pump must be inspected, refer to the Outboard Motor Service Manual.

PROPELLER

Power is transmitted from the propeller shaft to the propeller by a drive pin which is designed to shear when the propeller contacts an obstruction. Be sure the correct drive pin (shear pin) is installed or the lower unit may be damaged if an obstruction is struck.

All models are equipped with a three-blade, right-hand drive propeller. For standard

Illustrations Courtesy Chrysler

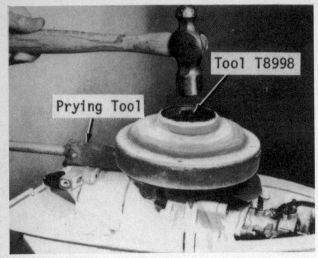

Fig. C2-8—"Pop" the flywheel loose by carefully prying up against the flywheel while striking the crankshaft end as outlined in text.

Fig. C2-9—Align index mark on point cam with breaker point follower arm when measuring breaker point gap. Loosen screw (S) to adjust gap.

length—15 inch (38 cm) motor leg—models the standard propeller diameter is 7¼ inches (18.4 cm) and the pitch is 6½ inches (16.5 cm). For long leg—20 inch (50.8 cm) motor leg—models the standard propeller diameter is 7¼ inches (18.4 cm) and the pitch is 5½ inches (14 cm).

⚠️WARNING

When working on or around the propeller the spark plug lead should be disconnected and grounded to the engine to prevent accidental starting if the propeller is rotated.

To remove the propeller, detach the cotter pin then unscrew the propeller nut. Drive the shear pin out of the propeller and propeller shaft. Pull the propeller off the propeller shaft.

Reinstall the propeller by reversing the removal procedure. Apply a coating of water-resistant grease to the propeller shaft before installing the propeller.

Tune-Up

IGNITION SYSTEM

All models are equipped with a conventional flywheel magneto type ignition system. All ignition components except the spark plug are located underneath the flywheel.

To adjust breaker point gap the flywheel must be removed. To remove the flywheel, first remove the fuel tank as outlined in the previous FUEL

TANK section. Unscrew the flywheel retaining screw. A band type wrench may be used to hold the flywheel during screw loosening. Screw a cap screw of the correct diameter and pitch into the end of the crankshaft so the screw head bears against only the end of the crankshaft (it may be necessary to use spacers between the screw head and crankshaft end), or install Chrysler tool T8998. Using a suitable prying tool, lightly pry up against the flywheel while moderately striking the screw or tool T8998 in the crankshaft end. See Fig. C2-8. The flywheel should "pop" free.

⚠️WARNING

Be sure suitable tools are used to withdraw the flywheel. Damage resultant from the misapplication of force or the use of incorrect tools may result in engine damage, engine malfuncion or personal injury.

Remove the flywheel and inspect it for cracks or other damage. Be sure to inspect the tapered center portion of the flywheel as well. A damaged flywheel must be discarded as it may fly apart at high engine rpm.

To check the breaker point gap, install the flywheel retaining screw in the end of the crankshaft then rotate the crankshaft clockwise by turning the screw. Rotate the crankshaft so the index mark on the breaker cam is aligned with the breaker point follower arm as shown in Fig. C2-9. The breaker point gap should be 0.020 inch (0.5 mm). Loosen breaker point retaining screw (S) to adjust breaker point gap. After tightening screw

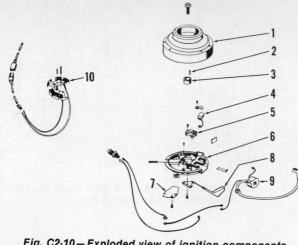

Fig. C2-10—Exploded view of ignition components.

1. Flywheel
2. Key
3. Breaker cam
4. Condenser
5. Breaker points
6. Stator plate
7. Cam
8. Speed control lever
9. Ignition coil
10. Alternator stator

(S), rotate the crankshaft and recheck point gap. Lubricate the cam wiper felt with a small amount of breaker point cam lubricant. Do not apply too much lubricant as it may be thrown off the cam onto the breaker points causing misfiring.

Be sure the tapered mating surfaces of the crankshaft and flywheel are clean and dry, then install the flywheel. Tighten the flywheel retaining screw to 15-20 ft.-lbs. (20-27 N·m). Reinstall the fuel tank.

SPEED CONTROL LINKAGE.

The speed control lever is connected to the magneto stator plate to advance or retard ignition timing. Throttle linkage is synchronized to open the throttle as magneto timing is advanced.

To check speed control linkage, remove the fuel tank. Turn speed control lever until throttle cam shown in Fig. C2-11 contacts cam follower. Index mark on throttle cam should be in center of cam follower when cam contacts follower. If mark is not aligned with cam follower centerline, loosen throttle cam retaining screw and relocate cam. Recheck synchronization after relocating cam.

Idle speed is adjustable only on 4 hp models after 1977. On these models an adjusting screw bears against the speed control lever at idle. Turn the idle speed screw so the engine idles at 800-1200 rpm when the screw contacts the speed control lever.

CARBURETOR

All models are equipped with the Walbro LMB float type carburetor shown in Fig. C2-12.

ADJUSTMENT. The idle mixture is adjusted by turning the idle mixture adjustment screw (7 — Fig. C2-12) on all models. The high speed mixture on 1977 4 hp models is determined by the position of high speed mixture screw (31) which is turned using lever (32). On all other models the high speed mixture is controlled by high speed jet (24).

Initial setting of idle mixture screw is one turn out from a lightly seated position. The idle mixture adjustment screw can be turned by inserting a screwdriver through the hole in the starboard side of the lower engine cover. Before adjusting idle mixture, run the engine until normal operating temperature is reached. The outboard motor lower unit must be immersed in water when the engine is running to prevent damage to the water pump impeller.

With the engine running at idle speed, turn the idle mixture screw (7 — Fig. C2-12) clockwise until the engine starts to misfire. Note the screw's position. Turn the screw counterclockwise until the engine again misfires and note the screw's position. Turn the screw so it is midway between the two misfiring positions.

To adjust the high speed mixture adjustment screw on 1977 4 hp models, run the engine at full throttle then use the same procedure as described for the idle mixture screw adjustment. Turn the adjustment lever (32) clockwise and then counterclockwise to find the misfiring points. Then position the lever midway between the misfiring points. If the lever does not point straight forward, remove then reattach the lever to the adjustment screw (31).

High speed mixture on all models except the 1977 4 hp models is controlled by main jet (24).

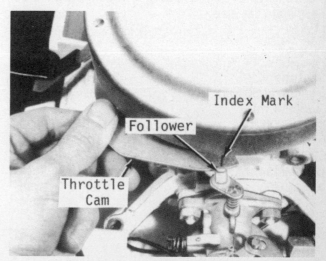

Fig. C2-11—The centerline of the cam follower should align with the index mark on the throttle cam when follower contacts the cam. See text.

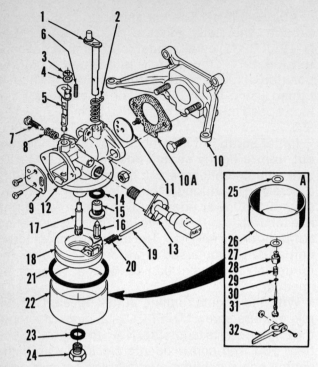

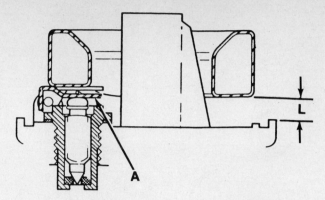

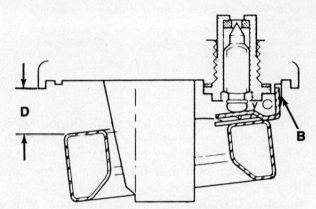

Fig. C2-12 — Exploded view of Walbro LMB carburetor. On 1977 4 hp models components (25 through 32) are used; the reed valve assembly is also attached to the front side of intake manifold (10).

Fig. C2-13 — Float level (L) should be ⅛ inch (3.2 mm). Adjust float level by bending tab (A).

Fig. C2-14 — Float drop (D) should be 5/16 inch (8 mm). Adjust float drop by bending tab (B).

1. Throttle shaft	17. Nozzle
2. Spring	18. Float
3. "E" ring	19. Float pin
4. Washer	20. Spring
5. Choke shaft	21. Gasket
6. Stop spring	22. Fuel bowl
7. Idle mixture screw	23. Gasket
8. Spring	24. High speed jet
9. Choke plate	25. Gasket
10. Intake manifold	26. Fuel bowl
10A. Gasket	27. Gasket
11. Throttle plate	28. Needle seat
12. Body	29. Spring
13. Fuel valve	30. "O" ring
14. Gasket	31. High speed mixture screw
15. Fuel inlet seat	32. Lever
16. Fuel inlet valve	

The following table will assist in selecting the correct main jet size.

	Main Jet Size	
Altitude	**3.5 Hp**	**4 Hp**
Sea Level-3000 ft. .... (0-914 m)	0.039	0.038
3000-5000 ft. .... (914-1524 m)	0.038	0.037
5000-7000 ft. .... (1524-2134 m)	0.037	0.036
Above 7000 ft. .... (Above 2134 m)	0.036	0.035

OVERHAUL. Refer to Fig. C2-12 for an exploded view of the carburetor. Note the following points when overhauling the carburetor. Install throttle plate (11) so the stamped number side is towards the engine and the three holes are towards the idle mixture screw side of the carburetor. Install the choke plate (9) so the stamped number side is towards carburetor intake and the oblong slot is on fuel inlet side of carburetor. Install float spring (20) so spring assists float in closing fuel inlet valve. Float level (L—Fig. C2-13) is measured with the carburetor inverted. Float level (L) should be ⅛ inch (3.2 mm) and is adjusted by bending tab (A). Float drop (D—Fig. C2-14) is measured with carburetor in normal upright position. Float drop should be 5/16 inch (8 mm) and is adjusted by bending tab (B).

CHRYSLER 4.9 AND 5 HP
(1974, 1975 and 1976)

Specifications

Hp/rpm	4.9/4500
	5/4750
Bore	1 ¾ in.
	(44.5 mm)
Stroke	1 9/16 in.
	(39.7 mm)
Number of cylinders	2
Displacement	7.52 cu. in.
	(123 cc)
Compression at cranking speed (average):	
Models BA, HA	60-70 psi
	(414-483 kPa)
Models BB, HB	70-80 psi
	(483-552 kPa)
Models BC, BD, HC, HD	90-100 psi
	(621-690 kPa)
Spark plug:	
Champion	L10
Electrode gap	0.030 in.
	(0.76 mm)
Breaker point gap	0.020 in.
	(0.51 mm)
Ignition timing	See text
Carburetor make	Amal
Fuel:oil ratio:	
Normal	48:1
Break-in & severe service	24:1

Maintenance

LUBRICATION

ENGINE. The engine is lubricated by oil mixed with the fuel. For normal service after break-in, mix 1/6 pint of two-stroke engine oil with each gallon of gasoline. For severe service and during break-in, the recommended ratio is one third (⅓) pint of oil per gallon of gasoline. Manufacturer recommends use of no-lead automotive gasoline although regular or premium gasoline may be used if octane rating is 85 or higher. Gasoline and oil should be thoroughly mixed.

The lower unit gears and bearings are lubricated by oil contained in the gearcase. Only a noncorrosive, leaded, EP90 outboard gear oil should be used. The gearcase fluid level should be checked every 30 hours and fluid maintained at the level of the upper (vent) plug hole. Change lubricant after every 100 hours of operation.

The outboard motor must be upright when draining or filling the gearcase. Remove both plugs (V and D-Fig. C3-1) on port side of gearcase when draining or filling. To fill with lubricant, force lubricant into lower plug hole (D) until lubricant reaches lower edge of upper plug hole (V). Install new gaskets on plugs, if necessary. Install

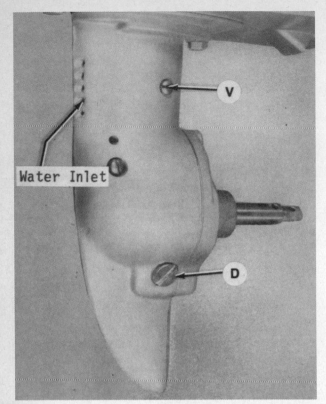

Fig. C3-1 — View showing location of water inlet ports, vent plug (V) and fill/drain plug (D).

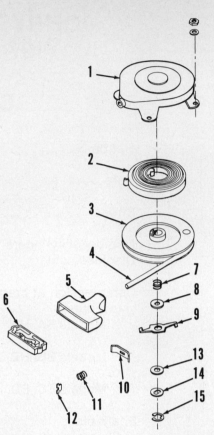

Fig. C3-2 — Exploded view of manual starter.

1. Starter housing	6. Retainer	11. Spring
2. Rewind spring	7. Spring	12. Retainer
3. Pulley	8. Fiber washer	13. Fiber washer
4. Rope	9. Lever	14. Steel washer
5. Rope handle	10. Friction shoe	15. "E" ring

upper plug (V) before removing lubricant dispenser so fluid remains in gearcase, then remove dispenser and install lower plug (D).

FUEL SYSTEM

FUEL FILTER. All models are equipped with a mesh fuel filter which is integral with the fuel tank fuel fitting. The fuel filter should be inspected and cleaned at least once each season, or more frequently if fuel stoppage due to foreign material is a problem. Empty the fuel tank or be prepared to catch fuel before unscrewing the fuel fitting.

FUEL TANK. It may be necessary to remove the fuel tank for cleaning or for access to underlying engine components. The manual starter is attached to the fuel tank on all models.

To remove the fuel tank, unscrew the gas cap and pull out the cap retaining chain and wire retainer. Unscrew the cover screw located above the choke knob then unscrew the two screws securing the rear of the upper engine cover to the lower cover. Lift off upper engine cover so there is access to the starter rope. Disconnect spark plug lead and ground lead to engine to prevent accidental starting. Pull out the starter rope at the starter housing and tie a knot so the rope cannot rewind into the starter. Pry the rope retainer out of the rope handle, remove the rope handle and then remove the upper engine cover. Turn fuel valve to

closed position. Disconnect the fuel line. Unscrew the four screws securing the fuel tank and remove the fuel tank.

Reinstall the fuel tank by reversing the removal procedure. Be sure the fuel line is securely attached.

STARTER

To remove the starter, first remove the engine cover as outlined in the FUEL TANK section, then unscrew the fasteners retaining the starter and lift off the starter.

To disassemble the starter, proceed as follows: Untie the knot and allow the rope to wind into the starter (if the rewind spring or rope is broken this step is unnecessary). Remove "E" ring (15 — Fig. C3-2). Remove friction shoe assembly along with washers. Remove remaining washer and the spring. Carefully lift out rope pulley while being careful not to dislodge the rewind spring. If the rewind spring must be removed, position the starter housing so the spring side is towards the floor or bench. Tap the starter housing against the floor or bench so the spring dislodges and uncoils.

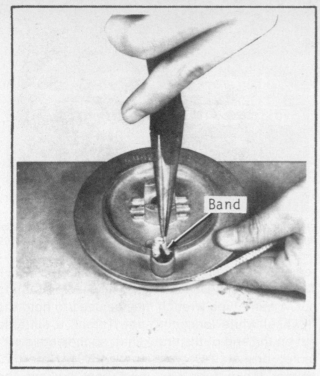

Fig. C3-3 — To install rope, double the rope end over and push the banded end back into the cavity.

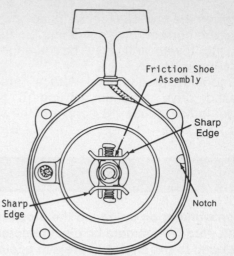

Fig. C3-4 — View of starter showing proper installation of friction shoe assembly. Note position of sharp edges on friction shoes.

> **⚠WARNING**
>
> **Care should be exercised when working with or around a coiled starter rewind spring as sudden uncoiling can cause injury. Safety eyewear and gloves are recommended.**

To install the rewind spring, hook outer end of spring around post in starter housing and wind spring into housing in a counterclockwise direction from outer spring end. If a new spring is installed, position spring assembly in housing then carefully remove coil retaining bands. Lubricate spring with grease.

Rope length should be 48 inches (122 cm). The starter rope is secured to the pulley by a metal band at the rope end. Thread the unbanded end of the starter rope into the pulley until the banded end protrudes as shown in Fig. C3-3. Fold the banded end over as shown so the rope is doubled over. Pull the rope taut so the doubled-over rope end is seated in the pulley.

Lubricate the shaft in the starter housing with a light coat of grease. Install the rope pulley in the starter housing while engaging inner spring end in the slot in the pulley. Hold the rope in pulley notch (Fig. C3-4) during installation. Assemble the remaining components on the pulley as shown in Fig. C3-2. The friction shoe assembly must be installed so the sharp edges are positioned as shown in Fig. C3-4. Install "E" ring (15—Fig. C3-2) in groove in shaft.

With the rope in notch (Fig. C3-4) rotate the pulley three full turns counterclockwise and pass the rope end through the rope outlet. Tie a knot in the rope. Pull the rope and check starter action. With the rope pulled out as far as possible, it should be possible to rotate the pulley an additional 1/8 to 3/8 of a turn. This additional rotation ensures that the rewind spring is not fully extended. If the pulley will not rotate the additional amount, recheck the rope length.

Reinstall the starter on the gas tank and install the engine cover.

COOLING SYSTEM

All models are equipped with an impeller type water pump located in the lower unit that circulates water through the power head.

> **⚠CAUTION**
>
> **Do not operate outboard motor unless the lower unit is immersed in water, otherwise, the water pump impeller will be damaged.**

If cooling system problems are encountered, first check the water inlet (see Fig. C3-1) for material which may be blocking the inlet. If the water pump must be inspected, refer to the Outboard Motor Service Manual.

PROPELLER

Power is transmitted from the propeller shaft to the propeller by a drive pin which is designed to shear when the propeller contacts an obstruction. Be sure the correct drive pin (shear pin) is installed or the lower unit may be damaged if an obstruction is struck.

All models are equipped with a three-blade, right-hand drive propeller. Standard propeller diameter is 7½ inches (18.4 cm) and the pitch is 6 inches (15.2 cm).

⚠WARNING

When working on or around the propeller the spark plug lead should be disconnected and grounded to the engine to prevent accidental starting if the propeller is rotated.

To remove the propeller, detach the cotter pin then remove the propeller spinner. Drive the shear pin out of the propeller and propeller shaft. Pull the propeller off the propeller shaft.

Reinstall the propeller by reversing the removal procedure. Apply a coating of water-resistant grease to the propeller shaft before installing the propeller.

Tune-Up

IGNITION SYSTEM

All models are equipped with a conventional flywheel magneto type ignition system. All ignition components except the spark plugs are located underneath the flywheel.

Two sets of breaker points are used with each breaker point set controlling ignition for one cylinder. To adjust breaker point gap, the flywheel must be removed. To remove the flywheel, first

Fig. C3-5 — The flywheel may be "popped" loose by carefully prying up against the flywheel while striking the crankshaft end as outlined in text.

Fig. C3-6 — Align index mark on point cam with breaker point follower arm of each breaker point set when measuring breaker point gap.

remove the fuel tank as outlined in the FUEL TANK section. Unscrew the flywheel retaining nut. A band type wrench may be used to hold the flywheel while loosening nut. Thread a suitable nut on the end of the crankshaft so the end is protected or install Chrysler tool T18091. Note that neither the nut or tool must bear against the flywheel. Using a suitable prying tool, lightly pry up against the flywheel while moderately striking the nut or tool T18091. See Fig. C3-5. The flywheel should "pop" free.

⚠WARNING

Be sure suitable tools are used to remove the flywheel. Damage resultant from the misapplication of force or the use of incorrect tools may cause engine damage, engine malfunction or personal injury.

Remove the flywheel and inspect it for cracks or other damage. Be sure to inspect the tapered center portion of the flywheel as well. A damaged flywheel must be discarded as it may fly apart at high engine rpm.

To check the breaker point gap, install the flywheel retaining nut and use the nut to turn the crankshaft clockwise. Rotate the crankshaft so the index mark on the breaker cam is aligned with the breaker point follower arm as shown in Fig. C3-6. Rotate the crankshaft so the mark is aligned with each follower arm. The breaker point gap for each set of breaker points should be 0.020 inch (0.51 mm). Loosen the breaker point retaining screw to adjust point gap. After tightening retaining screw, rotate the crankshaft and recheck

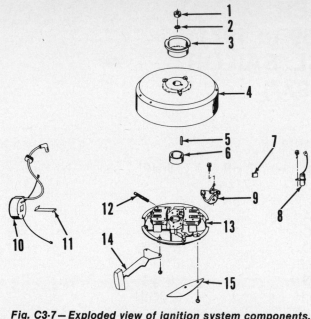

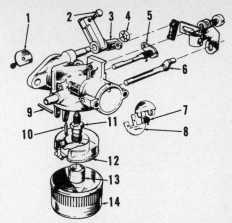

Fig. C3-7—Exploded view of ignition system components.

1. Nut	6. Breaker cam	11. Clip
2. Serrated washer	7. Felt	12. Friction screw
3. Starter cup	8. Condenser	13. Stator plate
4. Flywheel	9. Breaker points	14. Speed control lever
5. Key	10. Ignition coil	15. Cam plate

Fig. C3-9—Exploded view of Amal carburetor. Refer to Fig. C3-10 for installation of throttle plate (1).

1. Throttle plate	6. Choke shaft	
2. Speed control screw	7. Spring	11. Main jet
3. Throttle lever	8. Choke plate	12. Float
4. Lockwasher	9. Float pin	13. Fuel filter
5. Throttle shaft	10. Inlet fuel valve	14. Float bowl

point gap. Lubricate the cam wiper felt with a small amount of breaker point cam lubricant. Do not apply too much lubricant as it may be thrown off the cam into the breaker points causing misfiring.

Be sure the tapered mating surfaces of the crankshaft and flywheel are clean and dry, then install the flywheel. Tighten the flywheel retaining nut to 35-40 ft.-lbs. (48-54 N·m).

SPEED CONTROL LINKAGE.

The speed control lever is connected to the magneto stator plate to adavnce or retard the ignition timing. Throttle linkage is synchronized to open the throttle as magneto timing is advanced. It is very important that the throttle linkage be properly synchronized for best performance.

To synchronize linkage, remove upper engine cover. Position speed control lever so that mark (Fig. C3-8) on stator plate is aligned with crankcase parting line. Turn adjusting screw (S) until throttle lever just contacts cam plate on underside of stator plate.

CARBURETOR

All models are equipped with an Amal float type carburetor. Refer to Fig. C3-9 for an exploded view of carburetor.

Idle mixture and float level are nonadjustable. Refer to SPEED CONTROL LINKAGE for adjustment of throttle linkage. Standard main jet (11—Fig. C3-9) size is 52CC. Throttle plate (1) must be installed so that punch mark (P—Fig. C3-10) on throttle plate is to the top and facing the flange end of the carburetor.

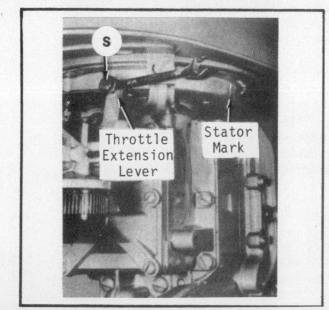

Fig. C3-8—Turn screw (S) so throttle lever just contacts cam plate when stator mark is aligned with crankshaft parting line.

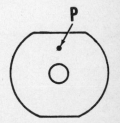

Fig. C3-10—install throttle plate (1—Fig. C3-9) with punch mark (P) to top and facing flange end of carburetor.

CHRYSLER
5 AND 7 HP (1969 to 1971)
6 AND 8 HP INCL. SAILOR
(1971 to 1977)

Year Produced	5 HP	6 HP	7 HP	8 HP
1969	5*‡	.....	7*‡	.....
1970	5*§A	.....	7*§A	.....
1971	.....	6*§A	.....	8*§A
1972	.....	6*§C	.....	8*§C
1973	.....	6*§D	.....	8*§C,D
1974	.....	6*§E,F	.....	8*§E,F
1975	.....	6*§G	.....	8*§G
1976 & 1977	.....	6*§G,H 60HA, B (Sailor)	.....	8*§G,H

*Variation Code: 0—Standard Shaft, 1—Long Shaft, 2—Standard Shaft, 3—Long Shaft.

‡Production Code Before 1970, 1, 3 & 5—U.S.A. Models, 2, 4 & 6—Canada Models.

§Production Code After 1970, H—U.S.A. Models, B—Canada Models.

Specifications

	5 & 6 HP	7 & 8 HP
Hp/rpm	5/4750 6/5000	7/4750 8/5000
Bore.........................	1⅞ in. (47.6 mm)	2 in. (50.8 mm)
Stroke	1⅝ in. (41.3 mm)	1⅝ in. (41.3 mm)
Number of cylinders	2	2
Displacement...................	8.99 cu. in. (147 cc)	10.2 cu. in. (167 cc)
Compression at cranking speed (average)	5 hp, 75-85 psi (518-586 kPa) 6 hp, 85-95 psi (586-655 kPa)	7 hp, 90-100 psi (621-690 kPa) 8 hp, 100-110 psi (690-759 kPa)
Spark plug:		
Champion	L4J	L4J
Electrode gap	0.030 in. (0.76 mm)	0.030 in. (0.76 mm)
Breaker point gap	0.020 in. (0.51 mm)	0.020 in. (0.51 mm)
Carburetor make	See Text	See Text
Fuel:oil ratio:		
Normal	48:1	48:1
Break-in....................	24:1	24:1

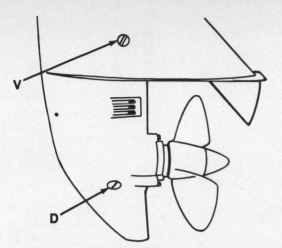

Fig. C4-1 — View showing location of vent plug (V) and fill/drain plug (D) on all models except Sailor models.

Maintenance

LUBRICATION

ENGINE. The engine is lubricated by oil mixed with the fuel. The recommended fuel:oil ratio for normal operation is 48:1. During engine break-in the fuel:oil ratio should be 24:1.

The manufacturer recommends the use of no-lead automotive gasoline although regular and premium grades may be used. The gasoline octane rating must be 85 or higher.

LOWER UNIT. The lower unit gears and bearings are lubricated by oil contained in the gearcase. Only noncorrosive, leaded, EP90 outboard gear oil should be used. The gearcase fluid level should be checked after every 30 hours of operation. Oil level must be maintained at the level of the upper (vent) plug hole. Change lubricant after every 100 hours of operation.

The outboard motor must be upright when draining or filling gearcase. Remove the vent and drain plugs shown in Fig. C4-1 or C4-2 when draining or filling. To fill with lubricant, force lubricant into lower plug hole (D) until lubricant reaches lower edge of upper plug hole (V). Install new gaskets on plugs, if necessary. Install upper plug (V) before removing lubricant dispenser so fluid remains in gearcase, then remove dispenser and install lower plug (D).

At least twice each season inject a good quality grease into all grease fittings.

FUEL SYSTEM

FUEL PUMP. A diaphragm type fuel pump is mounted on the side of power head cylinder block and ported to the upper crankcase. Pressure and vacuum pulsations from the crankcase are di-

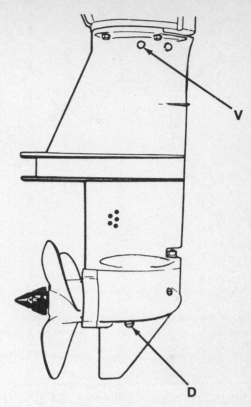

Fig. C4-2 — View showing location of vent (V) and fill/drain plug (D) on Sailor models.

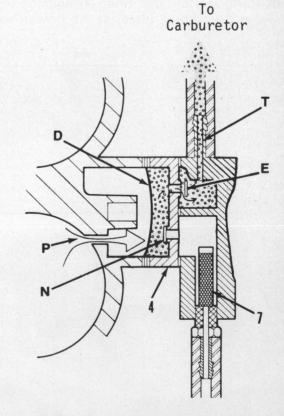

Fig. C4-3 — Schematic view of diaphragm type fuel pump used on all models. The check valves are of the reed type.

D. Diaphragm
E. Output reed valve
N. Inlet reed valve
P. Pressure port
T. Outlet
4. Reed plate
7. Inlet fitting & filter

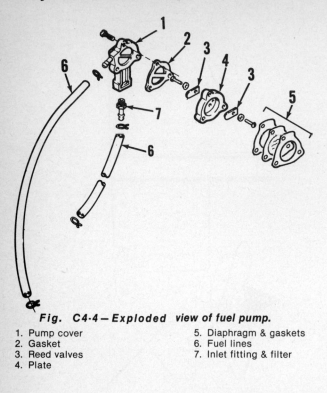

Fig. C4-4 — Exploded view of fuel pump.

1. Pump cover
2. Gasket
3. Reed valves
4. Plate
5. Diaphragm & gaskets
6. Fuel lines
7. Inlet fitting & filter

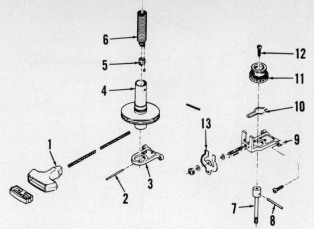

Fig. C4-5 — View of manual starter components used on later 6 and 8 hp models. Early models do not use starter interlock (13).

1. Pull handle
2. Spring pin
3. Lower bracket
4. Start spool & shaft
5. Spring retainer
6. Rewind spring
7. Spring arbor
8. Pinion pin
9. Upper bracket
10. Pinion spring
11. Starter pinion gear
12. Screw
13. Starter interlock

rected through the port (P — Fig. C4-3) to the rear of the diaphragm (D). When the power head piston moves upward in its cylinder, vacuum in the crankcase draws the diaphragm inward and fuel enters the pump through filter (7) and the inlet reed valve (N) in reed plate (4). As power head forces the diaphragm outward into fuel chamber, fuel passes through the outlet reed valve (E) into outlet (T).

Defective or questionable parts should be renewed. Pump valves (3 — Fig. C4-4) should seat lightly and squarely on reed plate (4). The diaphragm should be renewed if air leaks or cracks are found, or if deterioration is evident.

STARTER

Refer to Fig. C4-5 for exploded view of manual starter assembly common to all models.

To disassemble, remove motor top cowl and flywheel. Refer to IGNITION section for flywheel removal procedure. Remove screw (12 — Fig. C4-5) and install rewind key (tool 2985) in top of spring arbor (7) where screw (12) was installed (see Fig. C4-6). Tighten rewind key and then apply a slight amount of counterclockwise force so that pinion pin (8 — Fig. C4-5) may be removed. Use caution as rewind spring (6) is now free to unwind and will spin the arbor (7) and the rewind key. Slowly allow rewind key to turn and unwind the recoil spring. Pinion, arbor and spring may be lifted free of starter at this time.

Starter rope may be removed after removing upper bracket (9) and starter spool (4). Wind rope in spool counterclockwise as viewed from top of spool.

Rewind spring should be greased before reinstallation. Assemble arbor (7), spring (6) and spring retainer (5) and install in spool. Grease inside of pinion gear (11) and install on top of arbor. Use rewind key to turn arbor and rewind spring

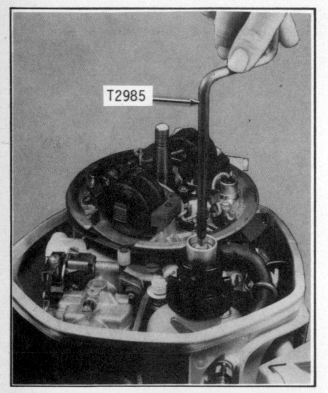

Fig. C4-6 — Rewind key (tool T2985) is used to unwind and wind the starter rewind spring.

3½-4 turns counterclockwise as viewed from the top. Align holes in spool, arbor and slot in pinion gear and partially install pin (8). Remove rewind key while holding end of pin and then complete installation of pin. Install screw (12) in top of starter.

COOLING SYSTEM

All models are equipped with an impeller type water pump located in the lower unit that circulates water through the power head.

⚠ CAUTION

Do not operate outboard motor unless the lower unit is immersed in water, otherwise, the water pump impeller will be damaged.

If cooling system problems are encountered, first check the water inlet for material which may be blocking the inlet. If the water pump must be inspected, refer to the Outboard Motor Service Manual.

PROPELLER

Power is transmitted from the propeller shaft to the propeller by splines on the shaft. The propeller is retained on the shaft by a pin which contacts the propeller and shaft. Be sure to use the correct pin.

All models except Sailor are equipped with a two-blade propeller. Sailor models are equipped with a three-blade propeller. All propellers are right-hand rotating. Propeller standard sizes are listed in the following table:

	Diameter	Pitch
5 & 6 hp (except Sailor)	7 in. (17.8 cm)	4¾ in. (12 cm)
6 hp Sailor	10½ in. (26.7 cm)	7 in. (17.8 cm)
7 & 8 hp	7½ in. (19 cm)	6¼ in. (15.9 cm)

⚠ WARNING

When working on or around the propeller the spark plug lead should be disconnected and grounded to the engine to prevent accidental starting if the propeller is rotated.

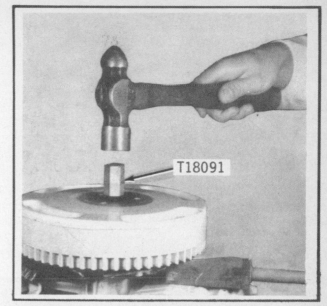

Fig. C4-7—The flywheel may be "popped" loose by carefully prying up against the flywheel while striking the tool or nut as outlined in text.

To remove the propeller, detach the cotter pin and remove the propeller spinner. Drive out the propeller retaining pin and pull the propeller off the shaft.

Reinstall the propeller by reversing the removal procedure. Apply a coating of water-resistant grease to the propeller shaft before installing the propeller.

Tune-Up

IGNITION SYSTEM

All models are equipped with a conventional flywheel magneto type ignition system. All ignition components except the spark plugs are located underneath the flywheel.

Two sets of breaker points are used with each breaker point set controlling ignition for one cylinder. To adjust breaker point gap the flywheel must be removed. Remove power head cover and unscrew flywheel retaining nut. A band type wrench may be used to hold the flywheel while loosening nut. Thread a suitable nut on the end of the crankshaft so the end is protected or install tool T18091. Note that neither the nut or tool must bear against the flywheel. Using a suitable prying tool, lightly pry up against the flywheel while moderately striking the nut or tool T18091. See Fig. C4-7. The flywheel should "pop" free.

Fig. C4-8—Align index mark on point cam with breaker point follower arm of each breaker point set when measuring breaker point gap.

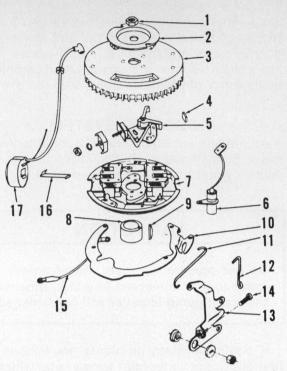

Fig. C4-9—Exploded view of ignition system components.

1. Nut	7. Base plate	13. Control lever
2. Starter collar	8. Point cam	14. Idle stop screw
3. Flywheel	9. Woodruff key	15. Ground wire
4. Felt wiper	10. Throttle cam	16. Wedge spring
5. Breaker points	11. Throttle link	17. Coil/plug lead
6. Condenser	12. Speed control link	

⚠WARNING

Be sure suitable tools are used to remove the flywheel. Damage resultant from the misapplication of force or the use of incorrect tools may cause engine damage, engine malfunction or personal injury.

Remove the flywheel and inspect it for cracks or other damage. Be sure to inspect the tapered center portion of the flywheel as well. A damaged flywheel must be discarded as it may fly apart at high engine rpm.

To check the breaker point gap, install the flywheel retaining nut and use the nut to turn the crankshaft clockwise. Rotate the crankshaft so the index mark on the breaker cam is aligned with the breaker point follower arm as shown in Fig. C4-8. Rotate the crankshaft so the mark is aligned with each follower arm. The breaker point gap for each set of breaker points should be 0.020 inch (0.51 mm). Loosen the breaker point retaining screw to adjust point gap. After tightening retaining screw, rotate the crankshaft and recheck point gap. Lubricate the cam wiper felt with a small amount of breaker point cam lubricant. Do not apply too much lubricant as it may be thrown off the cam onto the breaker points causing misfiring.

Be sure the tapered mating surfaces of the crankshaft and flywheel are clean and dry, then install the flywheel. Tighten the flywheel retaining nut to 40 ft.-lbs. (54 N·m).

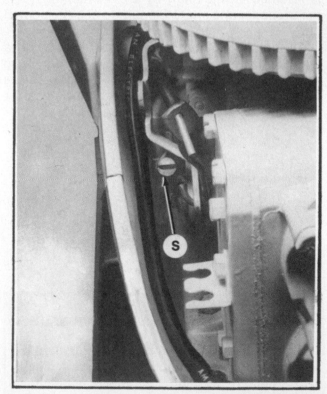

Fig. C4-10—View of idle speed screw. Adjust screw as outlined in text.

Illustrations Courtesy Chrysler

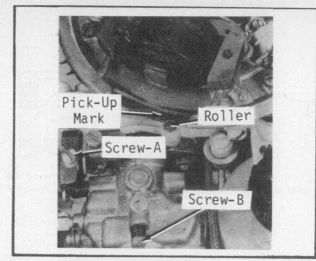

Fig. C4-11 — View of throttle pickup point timing. Adjust pick-up point by turning screw (A). Refer to text for procedure.

SPEED CONTROL LINKAGE.

The speed control lever or grip is connected to the magneto stator plate to advance or retard the ignition timing. Throttle linkage is synchronized to open the throttle as magneto timing is advanced. It is very important that the throttle linkage be properly synchronized for best performance.

Throttle pickup point is adjusted in the following manner: With engine turned off, turn idle speed stop screw (S—Fig. C4-10) until pickup mark on throttle cam plate is to starboard side of cam follower roller as shown in Fig. C4-11. Turn speed control grip slowly until throttle cam touches roller on throttle cam follower. Continue to turn speed control grip until carburetor throttle shaft (22—Fig. C4-12 or 17—Fig. C4-15) begins to move. Pickup mark on throttle cam should be even with or no more than 1/32 inch (0.79 mm) from roller at this time. Turn screw (A—Fig. C4-11) to adjust throttle pickup point. Make final adjustment of idle speed stop screw (S—Fig. C4-10) with engine running to obtain idle speed of 700 rpm in forward gear.

CARBURETOR

All 5 And 7 Hp Models, And 6 Hp Models Prior to 1972

All 5 and 7 hp models, and 6 hp models prior to 1972 are equipped with a Tillotson type MD carburetor. Refer to Fig. C4-12 for an exploded view of carburetor.

ADJUSTMENT. The idle mixture may be adjusted after removing the engine cover. Initial setting of the idle mixture screw (see Fig. C4-16 for location) is one turn out from a lightly seated posi-

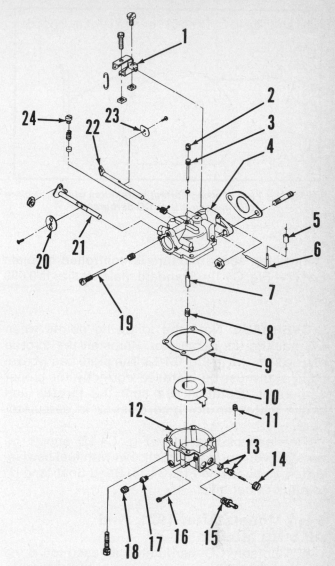

Fig. C4-12 — Exploded view of Tillotson MD type carburetor.

1. Adjusting arm	13. Inlet valve
2. Idle plug screw	14. Plug
3. Idle tube	15. Fuel connector
4. Throttle body	16. Float pin
5. Throttle cam roller	17. Main jet
6. Throttle cam follower	18. Plug screw
7. Nozzle	19. Idle screw
8. Main nozzle plug	20. Choke plate
9. Gasket	21. Choke shaft
10. Float	22. Throttle shaft
11. Set screw	23. Throttle plate
12. Float bowl	24. Choke detent plug

tion. To adjust idle mixture screw, run motor until operating temperature is obtained. The outboard motor lower unit must be immersed in water when running to prevent damage to the water pump impeller.

Shift unit into forward gear and run at slowest, smooth engine speed. Turn the idle mixture screw clockwise until the engine starts to misfire, note the screw's position, then turn the screw counterclockwise until the engine again misfires. Note the screw's position. Turn the screw so it is midway between the two misfiring positions.

Chrysler 5, 6, 7 & 8 Hp

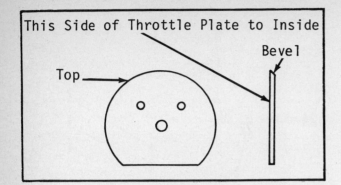

Fig. C4-13 — View showing correct installation of throttle plate on Tillotson MD or CO carburetor.

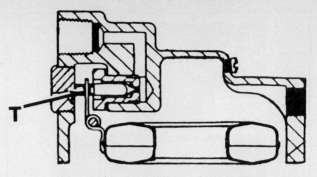

Fig. C4-14 — With fuel bowl inverted, the float should be parallel to the fuel bowl gasket surface. Bend tang (T) to adjust float.

The high speed mixture is controlled by main jet (17 — Fig. C4-12). Standard main jet size is 0.039 inch.

OVERHAUL. Note the following points when overhauling the carburetor. Reinstall the throttle plate as shown in Fig. C4-13. The plate has a bevel edge and must be installed correctly for proper carburetor operation. Be sure the throttle and choke plates do not bind or stick in carburetor bore.

Free end of float (10 — Fig. C4-12) should be parallel with surface of fuel bowl with fuel bowl inverted as shown in Fig. C4-14. Bend float tang (T) to adjust float level.

6 Hp Models After 1971, And All 8 Hp Models

A Tillotson CO carburetor is used on 6 hp models after 1971 and on all 8 hp models. Refer to Fig. C4-15 for an exploded view of carburetor.

ADJUSTMENT. Refer to previous adjustment section for 5 and 7 hp models equipped with Tillotson MD carburetor and follow procedure outlined. Note location of idle mixture screw in Fig. C4-16.

Standard main jet size is 0.037 inch on CO6A, 0.032 inch on CO6B and 0.033 inch on CO6C. Standard main jet size for 8 hp models is 0.049 inch on CO4A, 0.047 inch on CO4B and 0.045 inch on C04C, CO4D and CO6C.

OVERHAUL. Note the following points when overhauling the carburetor. Choke detent ball (14 — Fig. C4-15) and spring are located behind the choke shaft and will be loose when shaft is withdrawn. Hold the ball and spring in place in the carburetor using a suitable pin or rod while inserting the choke shaft. Install the upper choke plate, spring and lower choke plate (15), so spring tension forces the upper choke plate against the up-

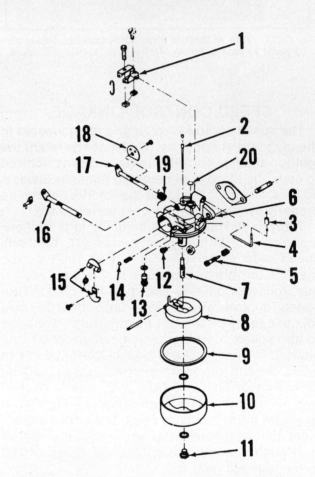

Fig. C4-15 — Exploded view of Tillotson CO type carburetor.

1. Adjusting arm
2. Bypass tube
3. Throttle cam roller
4. Throttle cam follower
5. Idle screw
6. Throttle body
7. Main nozzle
8. Float
9. Gasket
10. Float bowl
11. Retaining screw
12. Main jet
13. Inlet valve
14. Choke friction ball
15. Choke assy.
16. Choke shaft
17. Throttle shaft
18. Throttle plate
19. Throttle return spring
20. Welch plug

per tab of the lower choke plate. The upper choke plate must be installed so the open ends of the pivot loops are toward the front of the carburetor. The tab portion above the screw hole on the lower

Illustrations Courtesy Chrysler

Fig. C4-16 — View showing location of idle mixture screw (5) on Tillotson CO carburetor. The idle mixture screw on Tillotson MD carburetors is located at (L) at front of carburetor.

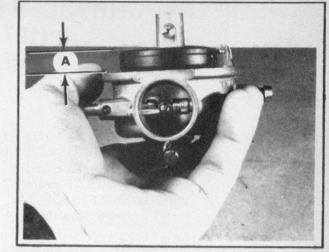

Fig. C4-17 — Float level (A) should be 13/32 inch (10.3 mm) on Tillotson CO carburetor.

choke plate must be in front of the upper choke plate.

Install the throttle plate as shown in Fig. C4-13. The plate edge is angled so the plate must be installed correctly for proper carburetor operation. Rotate the throttle shaft to be sure the throttle plate does not stick or bind.

To check float level, invert the carburetor and measure the distance from the float to the gasket surface as shown in Fig. C4-17. Distance (A) should be 13/32 inch (10.3 mm). Adjust float level by bending tang on float arm.

Install fuel bowl so indented portion is towards front of carburetor.

CHRYSLER 6, 7.5 AND 8 HP
(1978-1984)
(Incl. Sailor)

6 HP MODELS

Year Produced	Model
1978	62H8J,62B8J,67H8A,67B8A
1979	60H9C,60B9C,61H9B,62H9K, 62H9L,64H9E,67H9B,67H9C
1980	60H0D,60B0D,61H0C,61B0C, 64H0F,65H0A,65B0A
1981	64H1G,64B1G
1982	64H2H,64B2H

7.5 HP MODELS

Year Produced	Model
1979	70H9A,70B9A,71H9A,71B9A,72H9B, 72B9B,75H9A,75B9A,77H9A,77B9A
1980	72H0C,72B0C,77H0B,77B0B
1981	71H1B,71B1B,72H1D, 72B1D,77H1C,77B1C
1982	71H2C,71B2C,72H2E,72B2E
1983	71H3D,71B3D,72H3F,72B3F
1984	71H4,71B4,72H4,72B4

8 HP MODELS

Year Produced	Model
1978	82H8J,82B8J,87H8A,87B8A

Specifications

	6 & 7.5 HP	8 HP
Hp/rpm	6/4750 7.5/4750	8/5250
Bore	2.0 in. (51 mm)	2.0 in. (51 mm)
Stroke	1 19/32 in. (40.2 mm)	1 19/32 in. (40.2 mm)
Number of cylinders	2	2
Displacement	10.0 cu. in. (164 cc)	10.0 cu. in. (164 cc)
Compression at cranking speed (average)	115-130 psi (794-897 kPa)	115-130 psi (794-897 kPa)
Spark plug:		
Champion	L86	L86
Electrode gap	0.030 in. (0.76 mm)	0.030 in. (0.76 mm)
Ignition: Type:		
Models 64H9E,64H0F 64H1G,64B1G,64H2H, 64B2H	Breaker Point	.....
All other models	Breakerless	Breakerless
Breaker point gap — (models so equipped)	0.020 in. (0.5 mm)	......
Fuel:oil ratio:		
Normal	50:1	50:1
Break-in	25:1	25:1

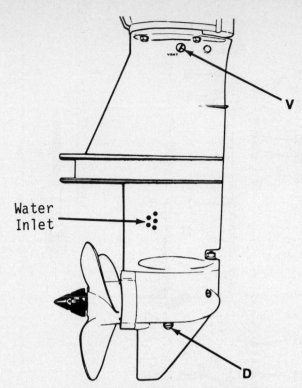

Fig. C5-1 — Drawing showing location of water inlet, vent plug (V) and fill/drain plug (D) on Sailor models.

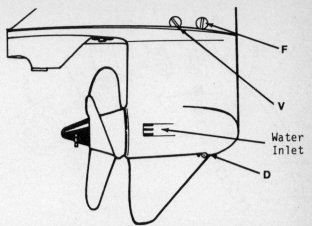

Fig. C5-2 — Drawing showing location of water inlet, drain plug (D), fill plug (F) and vent plug (V).

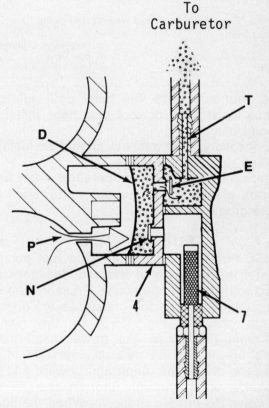

Fig. C5-3 — Cross-sectional view of diaphragm type fuel pump used on all models. Check valves are of the reed type.

D. Diaphragm	
E. Output reed valve	T. Outlet
N. Inlet reed valve	4. Reed plate
P. Pressure port	7. Inlet fitting & filter

Maintenance

LUBRICATION

ENGINE. The engine is lubricated by oil mixed with the fuel. The recommended fuel:oil ratio for normal operation is 50:1. During engine break-in the fuel:oil ratio should be 25:1.

The manufacturer recommends the use of no-lead automotive gasoline although regular and premium grades may be used. The gasoline octane rating must be 85 or higher.

LOWER UNIT. The lower unit gears and bearings are lubricated by oil contained in the gearcase. Only noncorrosive, leaded, EP90 outboard gear oil should be used. Check gearcase oil level after every 30 hours of operation. Refill and drain gearcase oil after 100 hours of operation or every six months. Oil level must be maintained at the level of the upper (vent) plug hole.

The outboard motor must be upright when draining or filling gearcase. Sailor models are equipped with vent and fill/drain plugs as shown in Fig. C5-1. All other models are equipped with three plugs, vent (V — Fig. C5-2), fill (F) and drain (D).

To drain lubricant, remove vent and fill/drain plugs on Sailor models or fill and drain plugs on other models.

To fill the gearcase on Sailor models, remove the vent and drain plugs. Force lubricant into lower plug hole (D — Fig. C5-1) until lubricant reaches lower edge of upper plug hole (V). Install upper plug (V) before removing lubricant dispenser so fluid remains in gearcase, then remove dispenser and install lower plug (D).

To fill the gearcase on all models except Sailor, remove fill plug (F — Fig. C5-2) and vent plug (V).

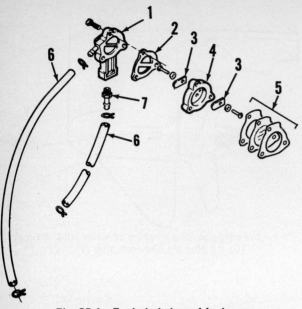

Fig. C5-4 — Exploded view of fuel pump.

1. Pump housing
2. Gasket
3. Pump valve (2 used)
4. Plate
5. Diaphragm & gasket
6. Fuel lines
7. Inlet fitting & filter

Force lubricant into fill hole until lubricant reaches lower edge of vent plug hole. Install fill and vent plugs.

If necessary, new gaskets should be installed on plugs to prevent leakage.

After every thirty days of operation, apply water resistant grease to the manual starter shaft and the pin groove in the gear.

FUEL SYSTEM

FUEL PUMP. A diaphragm type fuel pump is mounted on the side of the cylinder block and ported to the upper crankcase. Pressure and vacuum pulsations from the crankcase are directed through port (P—Fig. C5-3) to the rear of diaphragm (D). When the power head piston moves upward in its cylinder, vacuum in the crankcase draws the diaphragm inward and fuel enters the pump through filter (7) and the inlet reed valve (N) in reed plate (4). When the piston moves down in cylinder, crankcase pressure increases and the fuel pump diaphragm is forced outward into fuel chamber, and fuel passes through the outlet reed valve (E) into outlet (T).

Defective or questionable parts should be renewed. Pump valves (3—Fig. C5-4) should seat lightly and squarely on reed plate (4). The diaphragm should be renewed if air leaks or cracks are found, or if deterioration is evident.

STARTER

All models are equipped with the manual starter shown in Fig. C5-5. Starter gear (11) engages the flywheel ring gear. Starter interlock

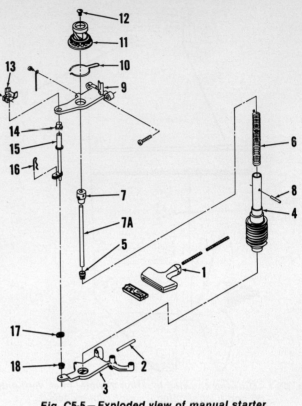

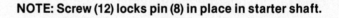

Fig. C5-5 — Exploded view of manual starter.

1. Rope handle
2. Pin
3. Lower bracket
4. Spool
5. Spring retainer
6. Rewind spring
7. Spring drive
8. Pin
9. Upper bracket
10. Pinion spring
11. Starter gear
12. Screw
13. Starter interlock
14. Bushing
15. Interlock shaft
16. Cotter pin
17. Spring washer
18. Bushing

(13) prevents starter gear rotation except when unit is in neutral.

To disassemble starter, remove starter interlock (13) and screw (12).

NOTE: Screw (12) locks pin (8) in place in starter shaft.

Fig. C5-6 — Use rewind key tool T3139-1 as outlined in text when disassembling or reassembling manual starter.

Thread the special "T" handle tool T3139-1 in threaded hole from which screw (12) was removed (see Fig. C5-6). Tighten the tool securely, then carefully push pin (8 — Fig. C5-5) out of pinion and starter spool. Allow tool and spring drive (7) to turn until rewind spring (6) is unwound, then use the tool to withdraw rewind spring (6) and drive (7) from center of starter spool (4). Guide post (7A) and spring retainer (5) can be lifted out after rewind spring is removed.

Rewind spring, gear (11) or associated parts can be renewed at this time. To renew starter rope, remove brackets securing spool.

Thread the new rope through hole in end of spool and install rope retainer approximately ½ inch (12.7 mm) from end. Wind rope on spool and install spool, brackets and rope guide. Install rewind spring assembly and gear (11). Use "T" handle tool to turn rewind spring counterclockwise eight turns. Align holes in gear (11), spool (4) and spring drive (7) and insert pin (8). Remove tool and install screw (12). Rewind spring cavity of starter spool should be partially filled with Lubriplate or a similar grease.

COOLING SYSTEM

All models are equipped with an impeller type water pump located in the lower unit that circulates water through the power head.

⚠CAUTION

Do not operate outboard motor unless the lower unit is immersed in water, otherwise, the water pump impeller will be damaged.

Fig. C5-7—*Pry up against the flywheel and strike the tool or nut to "pop" the flywheel loose. See text.*

If cooling system problems are encountered, first check the water inlet (see Fig. C5-1 or C5-2) for material which may be blocking the inlet. If the water pump must be inspected, refer to the Outboard Motor Service Manual.

PROPELLER

Power is transmitted from the propeller shaft to the propeller by splines on the shaft. The propeller is retained on the shaft by a pin which contacts the propeller and shaft. Be sure to use the correct pin.

⚠WARNING

When working on or around the propeller the spark plug lead should be disconnected and grounded to the engine to prevent accidental starting if the propeller is rotated.

To remove the propeller, detach the cotter pin and remove the propeller spinner. Drive out the propeller retaining pin and pull the propeller off the shaft.

Reinstall the propeller by reversing the removal procedure. Apply a coating of water-resistant grease to the propeller shaft before installing the propeller.

Tune-Up

IGNITION SYSTEM

Some 6 hp models are equipped with a breaker point ignition system while all other models are equipped with the Magnapower breakerless, capacitor discharge ignition system. Models with a breaker point ignition system have all ignition components except spark plugs under the flywheel. Magnapower equipped models may be identified by the ignition modules attached to the engine.

Breaker Point Models

BREAKER POINT GAP. Two sets of breaker points are used with each breaker point set controlling ignition for one cylinder. To adjust breaker point gap, the flywheel must be removed. Remove the power head cover and unscrew the flywheel retaining nut. A band type wrench may be used to hold the flywheel while loosening the nut. Thread a suitable nut on the end of the crankshaft so the end is protected, or install tool T2909 as shown in Fig. C5-7. Note that neither the nut or tool must bear against the flywheel. Using a suitable prying

Fig. C5-8 — Align index mark on point cam with breaker point follower arm of each breaker point set when measuring breaker point gap.

tool, lightly pry up against the flywheel while moderately striking the nut or tool T2909. See Fig. C5-7. The flywheel should "pop" free.

⚠WARNING

Be sure suitable tools are used to remove the flywheel. Damage resultant from the misapplication of force or the use of incorrect tools may cause engine damage, engine malfunction or personal injury.

Remove the flywheel and inspect it for cracks or other damage. Be sure to inspect the tapered center portion of the flywheel as well. A damaged flywheel must be discarded as it may fly apart at high engine rpm.

To check the breaker point gap, install the flywheel retaining nut and use the nut to turn the crankshaft clockwise. Rotate the crankshaft so

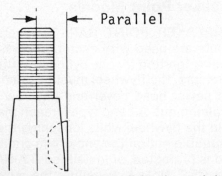

Fig. C5-9 — The flywheel key must be parallel to the crankshaft centerline as shown.

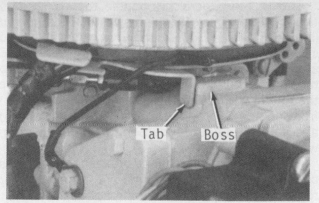

Fig. C5-10 — Full ignition advance occurs when the stator plate tab contacts boss on cylinder block.

the index mark on the breaker cam is aligned with the breaker point follower arm as shown in Fig. C5-8. Rotate the crankshaft so the mark is aligned with each follower arm. The breaker point gap for each set of breaker points should be 0.020 inch (0.51 mm). Loosen the breaker point retaining screw to adjust point gap. After tightening retaining screw, rotate the crankshaft and recheck point gap. Lubricate the cam wiper felt with a small amount of breaker point cam lubricant. Do not apply too much lubricant as it may be thrown off the cam onto the breaker points causing misfiring.

Be sure the tapered mating surfaces of the crankshaft and flywheel are clean and dry. The flywheel key must be positioned as shown in Fig. C5-9. Install flywheel and rope pulley; note that pulley must index in holes in flywheel. Tighten flywheel retaining nut to 40 ft.-lbs. (54 N·m).

IGNITION TIMING. Full throttle and full advance should occur simultaneously. Full advance

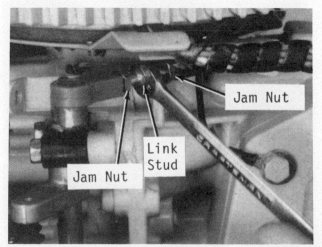

Fig. C5-11 — View showing location of stator control link. Adjust link length as outlined in IGNITION TIMING section.

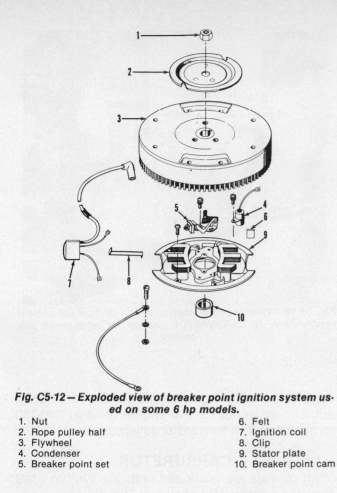

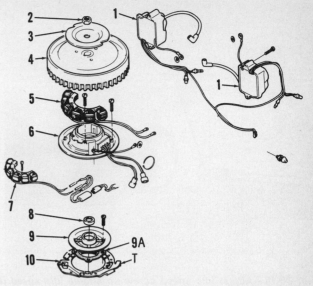

Fig. C5-12 — Exploded view of breaker point ignition system used on some 6 hp models.

1. Nut
2. Rope pulley half
3. Flywheel
4. Condenser
5. Breaker point set
6. Felt
7. Ignition coil
8. Clip
9. Stator plate
10. Breaker point cam

Fig. C5-13 — Exploded view of ignition components. Cam ring tab (T) is full advance stop.

1. CD coil module
2. Nut
3. Rope collar
4. Flywheel
5. Ignition stator
6. Stator plate
7. Alternator stator
8. Seal
9. Seal housing
9A. Gasket
10. Cam ring

is limited by the stator plate tab contacting a boss on the cylinder block as shown in Fig. C5-10. To check ignition timing, shift unit to forward gear and turn the speed control grip to full throttle. The stator plate tab should just contact the cylinder block boss at full throttle. If not, then the length of the stator control link must be adjusted. To adjust link length, loosen jam nuts and rotate link stud (see Fig. C5-11). Retighten jam nuts and recheck adjustment.

Magnapower Models

The Magnapower ignition system does not use breaker points and no maintenance is required. Follow the procedure outlined for breaker point models to set ignition timing. Refer to the Outboard Motor Service Manual for Magnapower ignition system service.

SPEED CONTROL LINKAGE.

The speed control lever is connected to the ignition stator plate to advance or retard ignition timing. Throttle linkage is synchronized to open throttle as ignition timing is advanced.

Refer to IGNITION TIMING section and check full advance adjustment prior to synchronizing throttle and ignition timing as follows: Turn throttle grip so timing mark on stator plate cam is aligned with cam follower (Fig. C5-15) within 1/32 inch (0.8 mm). Turn adjustment screw so cam follower just contacts cam. Turn throttle grip several times and recheck adjustment.

Idle speed is adjusted by turning the idle speed adjustment screw located adjacent to the speed

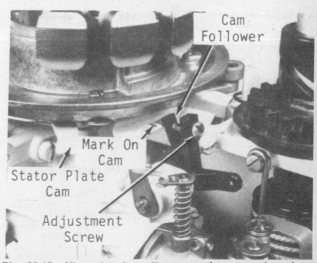

Fig. C5-15 — View showing alignment of cam mark and cam follower. Refer to SPEED CONTROL LINKAGE.

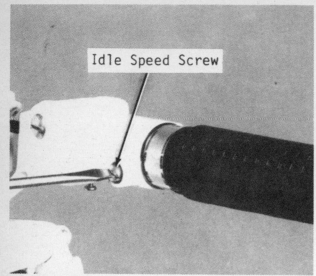

Fig. C5-16 — Adjust idle speed screw so engine idle speed is 600-750 rpm with outboard motor in forward gear.

Fig. C5-18 — View showing location of idle mixture adjustment screw. Refer to CARBURETOR section for adjustment procedure.

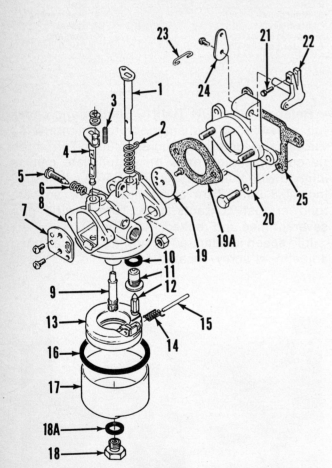

Fig. C5-17 — Exploded view of Walbro LMB carburetor used on all models.

1. Throttle shaft	10. Washer	18A. Gasket
2. Spring	11. Valve seat	19. Throttle plate
3. Spring	12. Fuel inlet valve	19A. Gasket
4. Choke shaft	13. Float	20. Intake manifold
5. Idle mixture screw	14. Spring	21. Screw
6. Spring	15. Float pin	22. Cam follower
7. Choke plate	16. Gasket	23. Throttle link
8. Body	17. Float bowl	24. Throttle lever
9. Nozzle	18. Main jet	25. Gasket

control grip (see Fig. C5-16). Turn the idle speed adjustment screw so the engine idles at 600-750 rpm with unit in forward or reverse gear.

CARBURETOR

All models are equipped with the Walbro LMB float type carburetor shown in Fig. C5-17.

ADJUSTMENT. The idle mixture is adjusted by turning the idle mixture adjustment screw shown in Fig. C5-18. Initial setting of idle mixture screw is one turn out from a lightly seated position. Before performing idle mixture adjustment, run the engine until normal operating temperature is reached. The outboard motor lower unit must be immersed in water when the engine is running to prevent damage to the water pump impeller.

Shift outboard motor to forward gear and adjust engine speed to slowest, smooth speed. Turn the

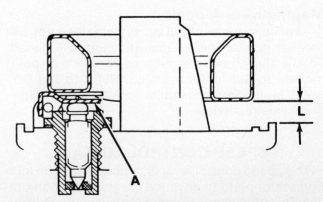

Fig. C5-19 — Float level (L) should be ⅛ inch (3.2 mm). Adjust float level by bending tab (A).

Illustrations Courtesy Chrysler

idle mixture screw clockwise until the engine starts to misfire, note the screw position, then turn the screw counterclockwise until the engine again misfires. Note the screw's position. Turn the idle mixture screw so it is midway between the two misfiring positions.

The high speed mixture is controlled by main jet (18—Fig. C5-17). The following tables will assist in selecting the correct main jet size.

6 HP

Altitude	Jet Size	Part Number
Sea Level-3000 ft. . . . . . . (0-914 m)	0.039	10096
3000-5000 ft. . . . . (914-1524 m)	0.038	10093
5000-7000 ft. . . . . (1524-2134 m)	0.037	10086
Above 7000 ft. . . . . (Above 2134 m)	0.036	10094

7.5 AND 8 HP

Altitude	Jet Size	Part Number
Sea Level-3000 ft. . . . . . . (0-914 m)	0.041	10089
3000-5000 ft. . . . . (914-1524 m)	0.040	10097
5000-7000 ft. . . . . (1524-2134 m)	0.039	10096
Above 7000 ft. . . . . (Above 2134 m)	0.038	10093

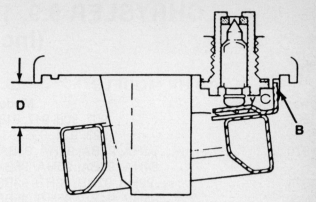

Fig. C5-20 — Float drop (D) should be 5/16 inch (8 mm). Adjust float drop by bending tab (B).

OVERHAUL. Refer to Fig. C5-17 for an exploded view of the carburetor. Note the following points when overhauling the carburetor. Install throttle plate (19) so the stamped number side is towards the engine and the three holes are toward the idle mixture screw side of the carburetor. Install the choke plate (7) so the stamped number side is towards the carburetor intake and the oblong slot is on the fuel inlet side of the carburetor. Install float spring (14) so spring assists float in closing fuel inlet valve. Float level (L—Fig. C5-19) is measured with the carburetor inverted. Float level (L) should be 1/8 inch (3.2 mm) and is adjusted by bending tab (A). Float drop (D—Fig. C5-20) is measured with carburetor in normal upright position. Float drop should be 5/16 inch (8 mm) and is adjusted by bending tab (B).

CHRYSLER 9.9, 10, 12, 12.9 AND 15 HP
(Incl. Sailor)

9.9 HP MODELS

Year Produced	Model
1969	907, 908, 917, 918, 923, 924, 933, 934
1970	92HA, 92BA, 93HA, 93BA, 94HA, 94BA, 95HA, 95BA
1971	92HB, 92BB, 93HB, 93BB 94HB, 94BB, 95HB, 95BB
1972	92HD, 92BD, 93HD, 93BD, 94HD, 94BD, 95HD, 95BD
1973	92HE, 92BE, 93HE, 93BE, 94HE, 94BE, 95HE, 95BE
1979	91H9A, 91B9A, 92H9F, 92B9F, 93H9F, 93B9F, 98H9A, 98B9A, 99H9A, 99B9A
1980	91H0B, 91B0B, 92H0G, 92B0G, 93H0G, 93B0G, 95H0G, 95B0F
1981	92H1H, 92B1H, 95H1G, 95B1G, 98H1B, 98B1B
1982	92H2J, 92B2J, 95H2H, 95B2H, 98H2C, 98B2C
1983	91H3C, 91B3C, 92H3K, 92B3K, 95H3J, 95B3J
1984	91H4, 92H4, 95H4

10 HP MODELS

Year Produced	Model
1974	102HA, 102BA, 102HB, 102BB, 103HA, 103BA, 103HB, 103BB, 104HA, 104BA, 104HB, 104BB, 105HA, 105BA, 105HB, 105BB
1975	102HC, 102BC, 103HC, 103BC, 104HC, 104BC, 105HC, 105BC
1976	100HA (Sailor), 100BA (Sailor), 102HC, 102BC, 102HD, 102BD, 103HC, 103BC, 103HD, 103BD, 108HA, 108BA, 109HA, 109BA
1977	100HA (Sailor), 100BA (Sailor), 102HD, 102BD, 103HD, 103BD, 108HA, 108BA, 109HA, 109BA

10 HP MODELS (Cont.)

Year Produced	Model
1978	101H8A (Sailor), 101B8A (Sailor), 102H8E, 102B8E, 103H8E, 103B8E, 108H8B, 108B8B, 109H8B, 109B8B

12 HP MODELS

Year Produced	Model
1979	121H9A, 121B9A, 122H9E, 122B9E, 123H9E, 123B9E, 125H9E, 125B9E, 128H9A, 128B9A, 129H9A, 129B9A

12.9 HP MODELS

Year Produced	Model
1971	122HA, 122BA, 123HA, 123BA, 124HA, 124BA, 125HA, 125BA
1972	122HC, 122BC, 123HC, 123BC, 124HC, 124BC, 125HC, 125BC
1973	122HD, 122BD, 123HD, 123BD, 124HD, 124BD, 125HD, 125BD

15 HP MODELS

Year Produced	Model
1974	152HA, 152BA, 153HA, 153BA, 154HA, 154BA, 155HA, 155BA
1975	152HB, 152BB, 153HB, 153BB, 154HB, 154BB, 155HB, 155BB
1976	152HB, 152BB, 152HC, 152BC, 153HB, 153BB, 153HC, 153BC, 158HA, 158BA, 159HA, 159BA
1977	152HC, 152BC, 153HC, 153BC, 158HA, 158BA, 159HA, 159BA
1978	152H8D, 152B8D, 153H8D, 153B8D, 158H8B, 158B8B, 159H8B, 159B8B
1979	152H9E, 152B9E, 153H9E, 153B9E, 158H9C, 158B9C, 159H9C, 159B9C
1980	152H0F, 152B0F, 153H0F, 153B0F
1981	152H1G, 152B1G, 152H1H
1982	152H2H, 152B2H
1983	152H3J, 152B3J, 158H3D, 158B3D
1984	152H4, 158H4

Specifications

	9.9 & 10 HP	12.9 HP	12 & 15 HP
Hp/rpm	9.9/4750 10/4750	12.9/5000	12/4750 15/5100
Bore	2-3/16 in. (55 mm)	2-3/16 in. (55 mm)	2¼ in. (57 mm)

Specifications (Cont.)

Stroke	1-¾ in. (44 mm)	1-13/16 in. (46 mm)	1-15/16 in. (49 mm)
Number of cylinders	2	2	2
Displacement	13.15 cu. in. (216 cc)	13.62 cu. in. (223 cc)	15.41 cu. in. (252 cc)
Compression at cranking speed (average)	105-125 psi (725-863kPa)	120-130 psi (828-897kPa)	125-135 psi (863-931kPa)
Spark plug:			
Champion	L4J	L4J	L4J
Electrode gap	0.030 in. (0.76 mm)	0.030 in. (0.76 mm)	0.030 in. (0.76 mm)
Breaker point gap	See Text	0.020 in. (0.5 mm)	See Text
Ignition timing	See Text	See Text	See Text
Carburetor make	See Text	See Text	See Text
Fuel:oil ratio:			
Normal	50:1	50:1	50:1
Break-in	25:1	25:1	25:1

Maintenance

LUBRICATION

ENGINE. The engine is lubricated by oil mixed with the fuel. The recommended fuel:oil ratio for normal operation is 50:1. During engine break-in the fuel:oil ratio should be 25:1.

The manufacturer recommends the use of no-lead automotive gasoline although regular and premium grades may be used. The gasoline octane rating must be 85 or higher.

LOWER UNIT. The lower unit gears and bearings are lubricated by oil contained in the gearcase. Only noncorrosive, leaded, EP90 outboard gear oil should be used. The gearcase fluid level should be checked after every 30 hours of operation. Oil level must be maintained at the level of the upper (vent) plug hole. Change fluid after every 100 hours of operation or every six months.

The outboard motor must be upright when draining or filling gearcase. Remove the vent and drain plugs shown in Fig. C6-1 or C6-2 when drain-

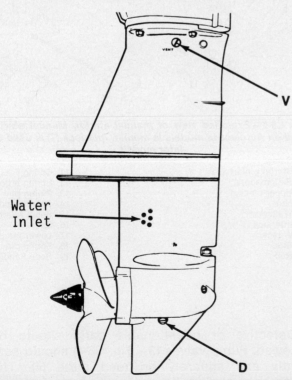

Fig. C6-1 — View showing location of vent plug (V) and fill/drain plug (D) on Sailor models.

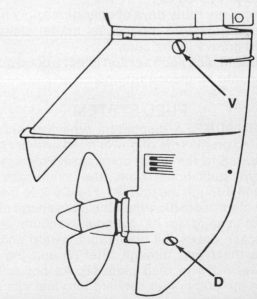

Fig. C6-2 — View showing location of vent plug (V) and fill/drain plug (D) on all models except Sailor.

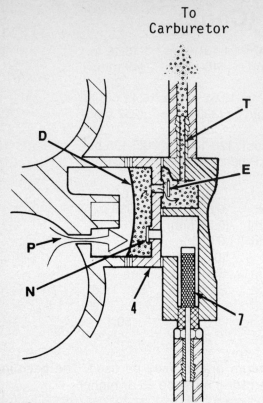

To
Carburetor

Fig. C6-3—Schematic view of diaphragm type fuel pump used
on all models. The check valves are reed type.

D. Diaphragm
E. Output reed valve
N. Inlet reed valve
P. Pressure port

T. Outlet
4. Reed plate
7. Inlet fitting & filter

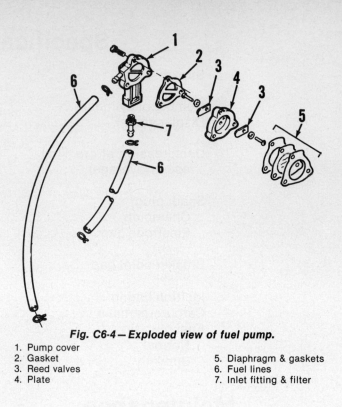

Fig. C6-4—Exploded view of fuel pump.

1. Pump cover
2. Gasket
3. Reed valves
4. Plate

5. Diaphragm & gaskets
6. Fuel lines
7. Inlet fitting & filter

ing or filling. To fill with lubricant, force lubricant into lower plug hole (D) until lubricant reaches lower edge of upper plug hole (V). Install new gaskets on plugs, if necessary. Install upper plug (V) before removing lubricant dispenser so fluid remains in gearcase, then remove dispenser and install lower plug (D).

After every thirty days of operation apply water-resistant grease to the manual starter shaft and the pin groove in the gear.

At least twice each season inject a good quality grease into all grease fittings.

FUEL SYSTEM

FUEL PUMP. A diaphragm type fuel pump is mounted on the side of power head cylinder block and ported to the upper crankcase. Pressure and vacuum pulsations from the crankcase are directed through the port (P—Fig. C6-3) to the rear of the diaphragm (D). When the power head piston moves upward in its cylinder, vacuum in the crankcase draws the diaphragm inward and fuel enters the pump through filter (7) and the inlet reed valve (N) in reed plate (4). As power head forces the diaphragm outward into fuel chamber, fuel passes through the outlet reed valve (E) into outlet (T).

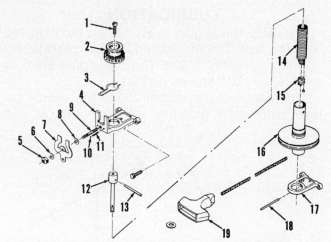

Fig. C6-5—Exploded view of manual starter. Manual starter
used on Autolectric models is similar. Interlock (7) is used on
later models.

1. Screw
2. Starter pinion gear
3. Pinion spring
4. Upper bracket
5. Nut
6. Washer
7. Interlock
8. Washer
9. Stud
10. Ball

11. Spring
12. Spring arbor
13. Pinion pin
14. Rewind spring
15. Spool retainer
16. Spool
17. Lower bracket
18. Spring pin
19. Rope handle

Defective or questionable parts should be renewed. Pump valves (3—Fig. C6-4) should seat lightly and squarely on reed plate (4). The diaphragm should be renewed if air leaks or cracks are found, or if deterioration is evident.

Fig. C6-6 — Rewind key (tool T2985) is used to unwind and wind the starter rewind spring.

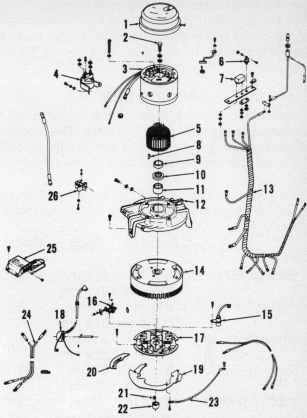

Fig. C6-7 — View of electric starter used on Autolectric models.

1. Cover	14. Flywheel
2. Armature bolt	15. Condenser
3. Starter housing	16. Breaker points
4. Starter relay	17. Stator plate
5. Armature	18. Ignition coil assy.
6. Rectifier diode	19. Throttle cam plate
7. Circuit breaker	20. Interlock switch cam
8. Woodruff key	21. Woodruff key
9. Spacer	22. Point cam
10. Bearing	23. Ground lead
11. Spacer	24. Battery cable
12. Starter support	25. Voltage regulator
13. Wiring harness	26. Interlock switch

STARTER

Refer to Fig. C6-5 for an exploded view of manual starter. The manual starter used on electric start models is of similar construction.

To disassemble starter, first remove engine cover and flywheel. Refer to IGNITION section for flywheel removal procedure. Remove screw (1 — Fig. C6-5) and install rewind key (tool T2985) in top of spring arbor (12) where screw (1) was located (see Fig. C6-6). Tighten rewind key until it bottoms; then turn tool handle slightly counterclockwise to relieve rewind spring tension and push out pin (13 — Fig. C6-5). Use caution as rewind spring (14) is now free to unwind and spin the arbor (12) and rewind key. Slowly allow rewind key to turn and unwind the rewind spring. Pinion, arbor and spring may be lifted free of starter after spring unwinds. Rope and rewind spool (16) may be removed after removal of rope handle and bracket (4). Note presence of detent balls (10) and springs (11) if interlock plate (7) is detached from bracket.

Note the following when reassembling manual starter: Wind rope in spool in a counterclockwise direction as viewed from the top. The rewind spring should be greased before installation. With spool, rope, rope handle and upper bracket installed, assemble arbor (12), spring (14) and spring retainer (15) into spool (16). Grease inside of pinion gear (2) and install gear on top of arbor. Use

rewind key (tool T2985) to turn arbor and rewind spring 3½-4 turns counterclockwise as viewed from the top. Align holes in spool, arbor and slot in pinion gear and partially install pin (8). Remove rewind key while holding end of pin, then fully insert pin. Install screw (1).

COOLING SYSTEM

All models are equipped with an impeller type water pump located in the lower unit that circulates water through the power head.

⚠CAUTION

Do not operate outboard motor unless the lower unit is immersed in water, otherwise, the water pump impeller will be damaged.

If cooling system problems are encountered, first check the water inlet for material which may be blocking the inlet. If the water pump must be inspected, refer to the Outboard Motor Service Manual.

PROPELLER

Power is transmitted from the propeller shaft to the propeller by splines on the shaft. The propeller is retained on the shaft by a pin which contacts the propeller and shaft. Be sure to use the correct pin.

All propellers are right-hand rotating. Standard propeller sizes are listed in the following table:

	Diameter	Pitch	Blades
9.9 hp			
Prior to 1979	8¼ in. (20.9 cm)	8¼ in. (20.9 cm)	2
1979-1981	8½ in. (21.6 cm)	8¼ in. (20.9 cm)	2
After 1981	8 in. (20.3 cm)	8¼ in. (20.9 cm)	3
All Autolectric	8½ in. (21.6 cm)	8¼ in. (20.9 cm)	2
All Sailor Models	10-3/8 in. (26.3 cm)	10 in. (25.4 cm)	3
10 Hp			
Standard Models	8¼ in. (20.9 cm)	8¼ in. (20.9 cm)	2
Sailor Models	10-3/8 in. (26.3 cm)	10 in. (25.4 cm)	3
12 Hp			
Standard Models	8 in. (20.3 cm)	9 in. (22.8 cm)	3
Sailor Models	10-3/8 in. (26.3 cm)	10 in. (25.4 cm)	3
12.9 Hp	8⅛ in. (20.6 cm)	8¼ in. (20.9 cm)	2
15 Hp	8 in. (20.3 cm)	9 in. (22.8 cm)	3

⚠WARNING

When working on or around the propeller the spark plug leads should be disconnected and grounded to the engine to prevent accidental starting if the propeller is rotated.

To remove the propeller, detach the cotter pin and remove the propeller spinner. Drive out the propeller retaining pin and pull the propeller off the shaft.

Reinstall the propeller by reversing the removal procedure. Apply a coating of water-resistant grease to the propeller shaft before installing the propeller.

Fig. C6-8 – Tool T2984 is used to pull the Autolectric armature off the crankshaft.

AUTOLECTRIC STARTER-GENERATOR

Some models are equipped with the Autolectric starter-generator shown in the exploded view in Fig. C6-7. The unit functions as an electric starter to start the engine and as a generator to charge the battery. It is necessary to remove the Autolectric unit to perform some service procedures, such as checking breaker point gap. Refer to the following section for removal and installation procedures of the Autolectric starter-generator.

REMOVE AND REINSTALL. Disconnect the battery cables from the battery then remove the top motor cover. Detach cover (1 – Fig. C6-7). Remove starter relay (4). Detach brush springs and remove brushes. Disconnect red lead from diode (6) terminal and gray lead from voltage regulator (25). Unscrew three screws securing starter-generator housing (3) and lift off housing. Unscrew armature retaining screw (2). Use tool T2984 or an equivalent to pull the armature off the crankshaft (see Fig. C6-8). Remove key (8—Fig. C6-7) and spacer (9). Remove circut breaker with bracket (7). Remove voltage regulator (25) and starter interlock switch (26). Disconnect battery cable from support (12). Remove three screws securing support and remove support. If the flywheel is to be removed, remove spacer (11).

Fig. C6-9 — The flywheel may be "popped" loose by carefully prying up against the flywheel while striking the tool or nut as outlined in text.

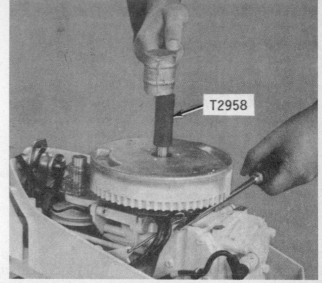

Fig. C6-10 — Tool T2958 should be used to protect the crankshaft end of Autolectric models when dislodging the flywheel.

Install the Autolectric starter-generator by reversing the disassembly procedure and noting the following points: There should be zero clearance between the flywheel, spacer (11) and bearing (10). It may be necessary to drive bearing (10) down to remove any clearance. Tighten armature retaining screw (2) to 20-25 ft.-lbs. (28-34 N·m). Be sure wires attached to light terminal in cover (1) are arranged so the wires cannot contact armature when cover is installed.

Tune-Up

IGNITION SYSTEM

The models in this section may be equipped with a breaker point ignition system or with the Magnapower breakerless, capacitor discharge ignition system. Models with a breaker point ignition system have all ignition components except spark plugs under the flywheel. Magnapower equipped models may be identified by the ignition modules attached to the engine.

Breaker Point Models

BREAKER POINT GAP. Two sets of breaker points are used with each breaker point set controlling ignition for one cylinder. To adjust the breaker point gap, the flywheel must be removed.

On Autolectric models, the starter-generator assembly must be removed for access to the flywheel. Refer to AUTOLECTRIC STARTER-GENERATOR section for removal procedure.

On all models except Autolectric models, unscrew the flywheel retaining nut. A band type wrench may be used to hold the flywheel while loosening the nut. On Autolectric models, install sleeve tool T2958 on the end of the crankshaft. On all other models, thread a suitable nut on the end of the crankshaft so the end is protected or install tool T2909. Note that the nut or tool must not bear against the flywheel. On all models, use a suitable prying tool and lightly pry up against the flywheel while moderately striking the nut or tool. See Fig. C6-9 or C6-10. The flywheel should "pop" free.

⚠️**WARNING**

Be sure suitable tools are used to remove the flywheel. Damage resultant from the misapplication of force or the use of incorrect tools may cause engine damage, engine malfunction or personal injury.

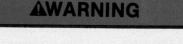

Fig. C6-11 — Align index mark on point cam with breaker point follower arm of each breaker point set when measuring breaker point gap.

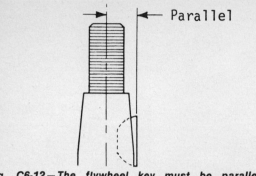

Fig. C6-12 — The flywheel key must be parallel to the crankshaft centerline as shown.

Remove the flywheel and inspect it for cracks or other damage. Be sure to inspect the tapered center portion of the flywheel as well. A damaged flywheel must be discarded as it may fly apart at high engine rpm.

To check the breaker point gap, install the flywheel retaining nut or armature screw and use it to turn the crankshaft clockwise. Rotate the crankshaft so the index mark on the breaker cam is aligned with the breaker point follower arm as shown in Fig. C6-11. Rotate the crankshaft so the mark is aligned with each follower arm to set point gap for each breaker point set. The breaker point gap for each set of breaker points should be 0.020 inch (0.51 mm). Loosen the breaker point retaining screw to adjust point gap. After tightening retaining screw, rotate the crankshaft and recheck point gap. Lubricate the cam wiper felt with a small amount of breaker point cam lubricant. Do not apply too much lubricant as it may be thrown off the cam onto the breaker points causing misfiring.

Fig. C6-17 — View showing location of idle speed screw on models prior to 1982.

Fig. C6-18 — Pickup mark on throttle cam should be no more than 1/32 inch (0.8 mm) from roller centerline when throttle shaft begins to move.

Be sure the tapered mating surfaces of the crankshaft and flywheel are clean and dry. The flywheel key must be positioned as shown in Fig. C6-12.

After installing flywheel on Autolectric models, refer to AUTOLECTRIC STARTER-GENERATOR section and install starter-generator assembly.

On all other models, install flywheel and rope pulley; note that pulley must index in holes in flywheel. Tighten flywheel nut to 45 ft.-lbs (61 N·m).

Magnapower Models

The Magnapower ignition system does not use breaker points and no maintenance is required. Ignition timing is not adjustable. Refer to the Outboard Motor Service Manual for Magnapower ignition system service.

SPEED CONTROL LINKAGE

The speed control lever (or grip) is attached to the magneto stator plate and moving the speed control will advance or retard the ignition timing. Throttle linkage is synchronized to open the carburetor throttle as magneto timing is advanced. It is very important that the speed control linkage be properly synchronized for best performance. Adjust linkage with motor not running.

On models prior to 1982, adjustment is as follows: Adjust idle stop screw (Fig. C6-17) until pickup mark (Fig. C6-18) is to left side of throttle roller as viewed from front side of motor. Turn speed control handle slowly toward the fast position until throttle roller touches cam plate on magneto. Continue turning handle until throttle shaft just begins to move. Pickup mark on throttle cam should be no more than 1/32 inch (0.8 mm)

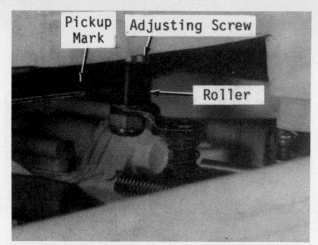

Fig. C6-19 — On models after 1981, pickup mark on throttle cam should be in the center of throttle roller when throttle shaft begins to move.

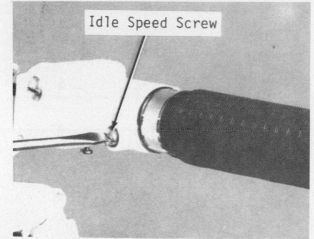

Fig. C6-20 — The idle speed screw is located adjacent to speed control grip on models after 1981.

from throttle roller centerline at this time. Turn adjusting screw (Fig. C6-18) to change point of throttle opening.

On models after 1981, turn speed control handle slowly toward the fast position and observe pickup mark (Fig. C6-19) on throttle cam. Throttle shaft should just begin to move when pickup mark is centered with throttle roller. Turn adjusting screw, if required, to change point of throttle opening.

Adjust idle speed with engine running at normal operating temperature and motor in forward gear. Idle stop screw location on models prior to 1982 is shown in Fig. C6-17 and on models after 1981 is shown in Fig. C6-20. Turn idle stop screw to obtain idle speed of 700 rpm with lower unit in forward or reverse gear.

CARBURETOR
9.9 Hp Models Prior to 1971

A Tillotson MD type carburetor is used on 9.9 hp models prior to 1971. Refer to Fig. C6-21 for an exploded view of carburetor.

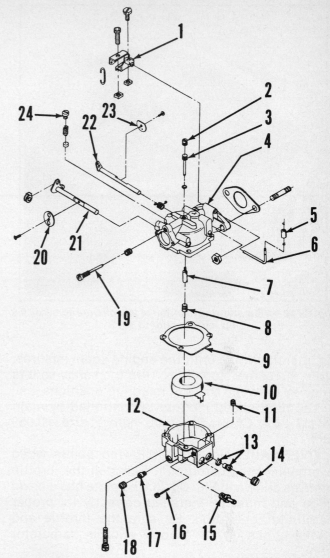

Fig. C6-21 — Exploded view of Tillotson MD carburetor.

1. Adjusting arm	13. Inlet valve
2. Idle plug screw	14. Plug
3. Idle tube	15. Fuel connector
4. Throttle body	16. Float pin
5. Throttle cam roller	17. Main jet
6. Throttle cam follower	18. Plug screw
7. Nozzle	19. Pilot air screw
8. Main nozzle plug	20. Choke plate
9. Gasket	21. Choke shaft
10. Float	22. Throttle shaft
11. Set screw	23. Throttle plate
12. Float bowl	24. Choke detent plug

ADJUSTMENT. The idle mixture may be adjusted after removing the engine cover. Initial setting of the idle mixture screw (see Fig. C6-22) is one turn out from a lightly seated position. To adjust idle mixture screw, run motor until operating temperature is obtained. The outboard motor lower unit must be immersed in water when running to prevent damage to the water pump impeller.

Shift unit into forward gear and run at slowest, smooth engine speed. Turn the idle mixture screw clockwise until the engine starts to misfire, note the screw's position, then turn the screw

Chrysler 9.9, 10, 12, 12.9 & 15 Hp

Fig. C6-22 — View showing location of idle mixture screw on 9.9 hp models prior to 1971.

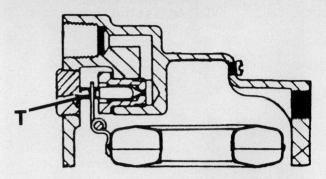

Fig. C6-24 — With fuel bowl inverted, the float should be parallel to the fuel bowl gasket surface. Bend tang (T) to adjust float.

counterclockwise until the engine again misfires. Note the screw's position. Turn the screw so it is midway between the two misfiring positions.

The high speed mixture is controlled by main jet (17 — Fig. C6-21). Standard main jet size is 0.059 inch.

OVERHAUL. Note the following points when overhauling the carburetor. Reinstall the throttle plate as shown in Fig. C6-23. The plate has a bevel edge and must be installed correctly for proper carburetor operation. Be sure the throttle and choke plates do not bind or stick in carburetor bore.

Free end of float (10 — Fig. C6-21) should be parallel with surface of fuel bowl with fuel bowl inverted as shown in Fig. C6-24. Bend float tang (T) to adjust float level.

9.9 And 15 Hp Models After 1981

A Walbro LMB type carburetor is used on 9.9 and 15 hp models after 1981. Refer to Fig. C6-25 for an exploded view of carburetor.

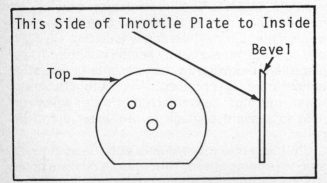

Fig. C6-23 — View showing correct installation of throttle plate on Tillotson MD or CO carburetor.

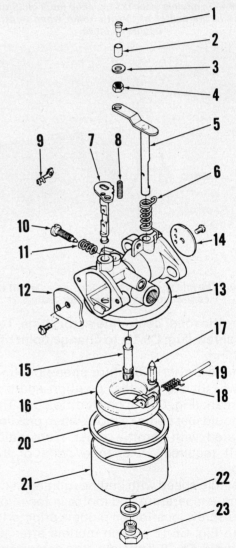

Fig. C6-25 — Exploded view of Walbro LMB carburetor.

1. Adjusting screw
2. Throttle roller
3. Washer
4. Nut
5. Throttle shaft
6. Spring
7. Choke shaft
8. Spring
9. Clip
10. Idle mixture screw
11. Spring
12. Choke plate
13. Throttle body
14. Throttle plate
15. Main nozzle
16. Float
17. Inlet valve
18. Spring
19. Float shaft
20. Gasket
21. Float bowl
22. Gasket
23. Main jet assy.

Illustrations Courtesy Chrysler

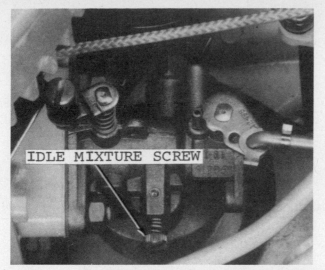

Fig. C6-26 — View showing location of idle mixture screw on 9.9 and 15 hp models after 1981.

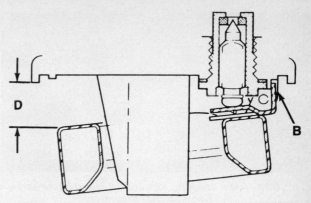

Fig. C6-28 — Float drop (D) on Walbro LMB carburetor should be 5/16 inch (8 mm). Bend tang (B) to adjust float drop.

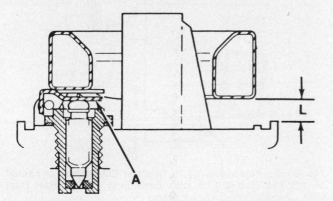

Fig. C6-27 — Float level (L) on Walbro LMB carburetor should be 1/8 inch (3.2 mm). Bend tang (A) to adjust float level.

ADJUSTMENT. The idle mixture may be adjusted after removing the engine cover. Initial setting of idle mixture screw (see Fig. C6-26) is one turn open from a lightly seated position. To adjust idle mixture, follow procedure previously outlined for 9.9 hp models prior to 1971.

High speed mixture is controlled by main jet (23 — Fig. C6-25). Standard main jet size is 0.046 inch for carburetor model LMB-228. Standard main jet size for carburetor LMB-229 is 0.0625 inch.

OVERHAUL. Refer to Fig. C6-25 for an exploded view of the carburetor. Note the following points when overhauling the carburetor. Install throttle plate (14) so the stamped number side is toward the engine and the three holes are toward the idle mixture screw side of the carburetor. Install the choke plate (12) so the stamped number side is toward the carburetor intake and the oblong slot is on the fuel inlet side of the carburetor. Install float spring (18) so spring assists float in closing fuel inlet valve. Float level (L—Fig. C6-27) is measured with the carburetor inverted. Float level

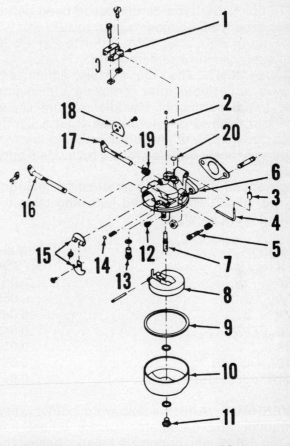

Fig. C6-29 — Exploded view of Tillotson CO carburetor.

1. Adjusting arm	11. Retaining screw
2. Bypass tube	12. Main jet
3. Throttle cam roller	13. Inlet valve
4. Throttle cam follower	14. Choke friction ball
5. Pilot air screw	15. Choke assy.
6. Throttle body	16. Choke shaft
7. Main nozzle	17. Throttle shaft
8. Float	18. Throttle plate
9. Gasket	19. Throttle return spring
10. Float bowl	20. Welch plug

(L) should be 1/8 inch (3.2 mm) and is adjusted by bending tab (A). Float drop (D—Fig. C6-28) is measured with carburetor in normal upright position. Float drop should be 5/16 inch (8 mm) and is adjusted by bending tab (B).

Fig. C6-30 — View showing location of idle mixture screw on Tillotson CO carburetor.

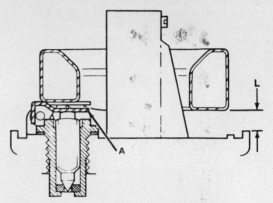

Fig. C6-31 — Float level (L) on Tillotson CO carburetor should be 13/32 inch (10.3 mm). Bend tang (A) to adjust float level.

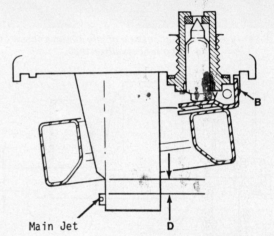

Fig. C6-32 — Float drop (D) on Tillotson CO carburetor should be 1/32-1/16 inch (0.8-1.6 mm). Bend tang (B) to adjust float drop.

All Other Models

A Tillotson CO type carburetor is used on all models except 9.9 hp models prior to 1971 and 9.9 and 15 hp models after 1981. Refer to Fig. C6-29 for an exploded view of carburetor.

ADJUSTMENT. The idle mixture adjustment screw is accessible after removing the engine cover. Initial setting of the idle mixture screw (see Fig. C6-30) is one turn open from a lightly seated position. To adjust idle mixture, follow procedure previously outlined for 9.9 hp models prior to 1971.

High speed mixture is controlled by main jet (12 — Fig. C6-29). Refer to the following table for standard main jet sizes:

Carburetor Model No.	Main Jet Size
CO-3A	0.051
CO-5A	0.055
CO-7A	0.047
CO-7B, CO-7C	0.045
CO-8A	0.053
CO-10A, CO-10B	0.055
CO-11A	0.045

OVERHAUL. Note the following points when overhauling the carburetor. Choke detent ball (14 — Fig. C6-29) and spring are located behind the choke shaft and will be loose when shaft is withdrawn. Hold the ball and spring in place in the carburetor using a suitable pin or rod while inserting the choke shaft. Install the upper choke plate, spring and lower choke plate (15) so spring tension forces the upper choke plate against the upper tab of the lower choke plate. The upper choke plate must be installed so the open ends of the pivot loops are toward the front of the carburetor. The tab portion above the screw hole on the lower choke plate must be in front of the upper choke plate.

Install the throttle plate as shown in Fig. C6-23. The plate edge is angled so the plate must be installed correctly for proper carburetor operation. Rotate the throttle shaft to be sure the throttle plate does not stick or bind.

To check float level, invert the carburetor and measure distance (L — Fig. C6-31) from the float to the carburetor body. Distance should be 13/32 inch (10.3 mm). Adjust float level by bending float arm tang (A).

Float drop is measured from bottom of free end of float to top of main jet as shown in Fig. C6-32. Float drop (D) should be 1/32-1/16 inch (0.8-1.6 mm). Adjust float drop by bending float arm tang (B).

CHRYSLER 20 HP (1969-1976)

Year Produced	Models
1969	2003, 2004, 2013, 2014, *2023, *2024, *2033, *2034
1970	202HA, BA, 203HA, BA, *204HA, *BA, *205HA, *BA
1971	202HB, BB, 203HB, BB, *204HB, *BB, *205HB, *BB
1972	202HD, BD, 203HD, BD, *204HD, *BD, *205HD, *BD
1973	202HD, 202BD, 202HE, 202BE, 203HD, 203BD, 203HE, 203BE, *204HE, *204BE, *205HD, *205BD, *205HE, *205BE
1974	202HF, 202BF, 203HF, 203BF, *204HF, *204BF, *205HF, *205BF
1975 & 1976	202HG, 202BG, 203HB, 203BG, *204HG, *204BG, *205HG, *205BG

*Electric starting models.

Specifications

Hp/rpm 20/5000
Bore . . . . 2-7/16 in.
(61.9 mm)
Stroke . . . . 2-9/64 in.
(54.4 mm)
Number of cylinders 2
Displacement . . . . 19.98 cu. in.
(327.4 cc)
Compression at cranking speed (average) . . . . 115-125 psi
(794-862 kPa)
Spark plug:
  Champion L4J
  Electrode gap . . . . 0.030 in.
  (0.76 mm)
Breaker point gap . . . . 0.020 in.
(0.51 mm)
Ignition timing . . . . See Text
Carburetor:
  Make . . . . Tillotson
  Model . . . . MD
Fuel:oil ratio . . . . 50:1†
†Fuel:oil ratio 25:1 for severe service.

Maintenance

LUBRICATION

ENGINE. The engine is lubricated by oil mixed with the fuel. The recommended fuel:oil ratio for normal operation is 50:1. During engine break-in the fuel:oil ratio should be 25:1.

The manufacturer recommends the use of no-lead automotive gasoline although regular and premium grades may be used. The gasoline octane rating must be 85 or higher.

LOWER UNIT. The lower unit gears and bearings are lubricated by oil contained in the gearcase. Only noncorrosive, leaded, EP90 outboard gear oil should be used. The gearcase fluid level should be checked after every 30 hours of operation. Oil level must be maintained at the level of the upper (vent) plug hole. Change fluid after every 100 hours of operation or every six months.

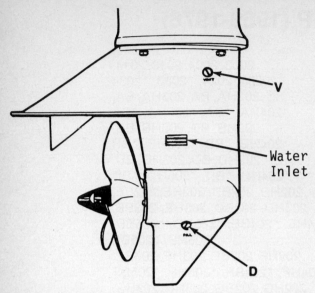

Fig. C7-1 — View showing location of vent plug (V) and fill/drain plug (D).

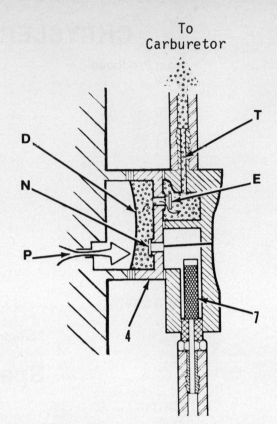

Fig. C7-2 — Schematic view of diaphragm type fuel pump used on all models. The check valves are reed type.

D. Diaphragm
E. Output reed valve   P. Pressure port   4. Reed plate
N. Inlet reed valve   T. Outlet   7. Inlet fitting & filter

The outboard motor must be upright when draining or filling gearcase. Remove the vent and drain plugs shown in Fig. C7-1 when draining or filling. To fill with lubricant, force lubricant into lower plug hole (D) until lubricant reaches lower edge of upper plug hole (V). Install new gaskets on plugs, if necessary. Install upper plug (V) before removing lubricant dispenser so fluid remains in gearcase, then remove dispenser and install lower plug (D).

At least twice each season, apply water resistant grease to the manual starter shaft and the pin groove in the gear.

At least twice each season inject a good quality grease into all grease fittings.

FUEL SYSTEM

FUEL PUMP. A diaphragm type fuel pump is mounted on the side of power head cylinder block and ported to the upper crankcase. Pressure and vacuum pulsations from the crankcase are directed through the port (P — Fig. C7-2) to the rear of the diaphragm (D). When the power head piston moves upward in its cylinder, vacuum in the crankcase draws the diaphragm inward and fuel enters the pump through filter (7) and the inlet reed valve (N) in reed plate (4). As power head forces the diaphragm outward into fuel chamber, fuel passes through the outlet reed valve (E) into outlet (T).

Defective or questionable parts should be renewed. Pump valves (3 — Fig. C7-2A) should seat lightly and squarely on reed plate (4). The diaphragm should be renewed if air leaks or cracks are found, or if deterioration is evident.

SHIFT LINKAGE

The shift linkage may be adjusted to synchronize the shift control with the engagement of gears in the gearcase. To adjust the shift linkage, proceed as follows:

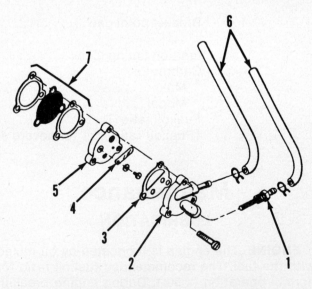

Fig. C7-2A — Exploded view of fuel pump.

1. Inlet fitting & filter
2. Pump cover
3. Gasket
4. Reed valves
5. Plate
6. Fuel lines
7. Diaphragm & gaskets

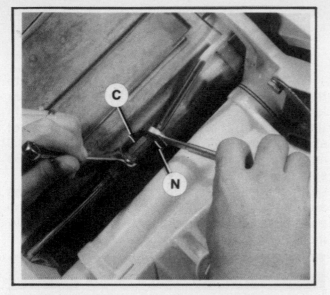

Fig. C7-3 — The shift linkage is adjusted by rotating shift rod coupler (C) as outlined in text.

To adjust the shift linkage the motor leg covers must be detached. Remove the motor top cover and unscrew the motor leg retaining screw directly behind the cylinder head. Unscrew the five screws holding the motor leg cover halves together; do not lose the nuts which are now loose in the port cover. Remove the starboard cover for access to shift rod coupler (C — Fig. C7-3).

⚠WARNING

To prevent accidental starting while rotating the propeller, disconnect the spark plug leads and properly ground leads to engine.

Loosen jam nut (N — Fig. C7-3). Position the shift control in neutral. Rotate shift rod coupler (C) so the propeller rotates freely thereby indicating the lower unit gears are in neutral. Hold the coupler to prevent rotation then tighten jam nut (N) against coupler (C). Reassemble the motor leg covers and check operation of shift mechanism.

STARTER

Fig C7-4 shows an exploded view of the manual starter assembly. Starter pinion (3) engages a starter ring gear on the flywheel.

To disassemble the starter, first remove the engine cover and flywheel. Refer to IGNITION section for flywheel removal procedure. Remove screw (6 — Fig. C7-4) in top of starter shaft.

NOTE: This screw locks pin (2) in place.

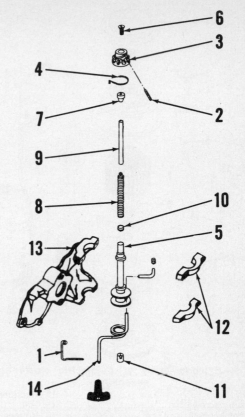

Fig. C7-4 — Exploded view of manual starter assembly.

1. Rope guide	6. Lock screw	
2. Drive pin	7. Spring drive	11. Retainer extension
3. Pinion	8. Recoil spring	12. Bearing caps
4. Pinion spring	9. Guide post	13. Inlet manifold
5. Starter spool	10. Retainer	14. Rope

Thread the special "T" handle tool (T3139) in threaded hole from which screw (6) was removed. Tighten the tool until it bottoms; then turn tool handle slightly counterclockwise to relieve recoil spring tension, and push out pin (2). Allow the tool and spring drive (7) to turn clockwise to unwind the recoil spring (8). Pull up on tool to remove the recoil spring and components. Guide post (9) and spring retainer (10) can be lifted out after recoil spring is removed.

Recoil spring, pinion (3) or associated parts can be renewed at this time. To renew the starter rope, remove clamps (12) then remove the spool. Thread rope through hole in lower end of spool (5) and install the rope retainer approximately ½ inch (12.7 mm) from end of rope. Pull tight, then fully wind the rope onto spool and reinstall assembly. Make certain that retainer extension (11) is in place. With recoil spring and drive pinion (3) installed, use the "T" handle tool to wind the recoil spring counterclockwise eight turns. Align the holes in pinion (3), spool (5) and spring drive (7), then install the drive pin (2). Remove the tool and secure the pin with the locking screw (6). Recoil spring

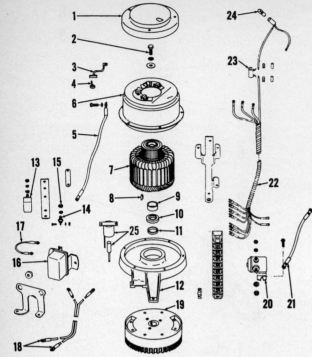

Fig. C7-5 — Exploded view of Autolectric starter-generator assembly.

1. Cover
2. Armature screw
3. Brushes (4 used)
4. Brush spring
5. Starter lead wire
6. Housing & field assy.
7. Armature
8. Key
9. Spacer
10. Bearing
11. Spacer
12. Support housing
13. Circuit breaker
14. Rectifier
15. Nut
16. Voltage regulator
17. Regulator ground
18. Battery cables
19. Flywheel
20. Starter relay
21. Ground wire
22. Wiring harness
23. Resistor
24. Dome light
25. Choke solenoid

cavity should be partially filled with Lubriplate or similar grease when reassembling.

If tension of pinion spring (4) is incorrect, the pinion (3) may remain extended and prevent full speed operation.

COOLING SYSTEM

All models are equipped with an impeller type water pump located in the lower unit that circulates water through the power head.

⚠️CAUTION

Do not operate outboard motor unless the lower unit is immersed in water, otherwise, the water pump impeller will be damaged.

If cooling system problems are encountered, first check the water inlet for material which may be blocking the inlet. If the water pump must be

inspected, refer to the Outboard Motor Service Manual.

PROPELLER

Power is transmitted from the propeller shaft to the propeller by splines on the shaft. The propeller is retained on the shaft by a pin which contacts the propeller and shaft. The pin is made of stainless steel with a diameter of 3/16 inch (4.8 mm) and a length of 1-5/16 inches (33.3 mm). Be sure to use the correct pin.

The propeller is designed for right hand rotation and is equipped with three blades. Standard propeller size is 8½ inch (21.6 cm) diameter and 8½ inch (21.6 cm) pitch.

⚠️WARNING

When working on or around the propeller the spark plug leads should be disconnected and grounded to the engine to prevent accidental starting if the propeller is rotated.

To remove the propeller, detach the cotter pin and remove the propeller spinner. Drive out the propeller retaining pin and pull the propeller off the shaft.

Reinstall the propeller by reversing the removal procedure. Apply a coating of water-resistant grease to the propeller shaft before installing the propeller.

AUTOLECTRIC STARTER-GENERATOR

Some models are equipped with the Autolectric starter-generator shown in the exploded view in Fig. C7-5. The unit functions as an electric starter to start the engine and as a generator to charge the battery.

It is necessary to remove the Autolectric unit to perform some service procedures, such as checking breaker point gap. Refer to the following section for removal and installation procedures of the Autolectric starter-generator. Be sure wiring is connected properly or components may be damaged.

REMOVE AND REINSTALL. Disconnect the battery cables from the battery and remove the top motor cover. Detach cover (1 — Fig. C7-5). Disconnect red wire lead from starter-generator housing. Disconnect gray starter-generator wire from voltage regulator. Disconnect red/black wire from rectifier. Detach wire clamp securing starter-generator wires to power head. Remove brushes

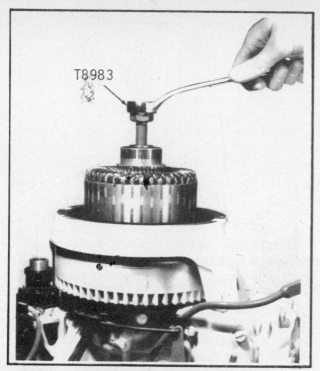

Fig. C7-7 — Tool T8983 is used to pull the Autolectric armature off the crankshaft.

Fig. C7-9 — Tool T2958 should be used to protect the crankshaft end of Autolectric models when dislodging the flywheel. flywheel.

Fig. C7-8 — The flywheel may be "popped" loose by carefully prying up against the flywheel while striking the tool or nut as outlined in text.

and brush springs. Remove screws securing starter-generator housing and remove housing (6). Unscrew armature retaining screw (2), then remove lockwasher and washer. Use tool T8983 or an equivalent to pull the armature off the crankshaft (see Fig. C7-7). Remove key (8 — Fig. C7-5) and spacer (9). Remove three screws securing support and remove support (12). If the flywheel is to be removed, remove spacer (11).

Install the Autolectric starter-generator by reversing the disassembly procedure and noting the following points: There should be zero clearance between the flywheel, spacer (11) and bearing (10). It may be necessary to drive bearing (10) down to remove any clearance. Tighten armature retaining screw (2) to 15-25 ft.lbs. (20-34 N·m). Be sure wires attached to light terminal in cover (1) are arranged so the wires cannot contact armature when cover is installed.

Tune-Up

IGNITION SYSTEM

All models are equipped with a conventional flywheel magneto type ignition system. All ignition components except the spark plugs are located underneath the flywheel.

Two sets of breaker points are used with each breaker point set controlling ignition for one cylinder. To adjust the breaker point gap, the flywheel must be removed.

On Autolectric models, the starter-generator assembly must be removed for access to the flywheel. Refer to AUTOLECTRIC STARTER-GENERATOR section for removal procedure.

On all models except Autolectric models, unscrew the flywheel retaining nut. A band type wrench may be used to hold the flywheel while loosening the nut. On Autolectric models, install sleeve tool T2958 on the end of the crankshaft. On all other models, thread a suitable nut on the end of the crankshaft so the end is protected or install tool T2909. Note that the nut or tool must not bear against the flywheel. On all models, use a suitable prying tool and lightly pry up against the flywheel

Fig. C7-10 — Align index mark on point cam with breaker point follower arm of each breaker point set when measuring breaker point gap.

while moderately striking the nut or tool. See Fig. C7-8 or C7-9. The flywheel should "pop" free.

⚠ **WARNING**

Be sure suitable tools are used to remove the flywheel. Damage resultant from the misapplication of force or the use of incorrect tools may cause engine damage, engine malfunction or personal injury.

Remove the flywheel and inspect it for cracks or other damage. Be sure to inspect the tapered center portion of the flywheel as well. A damaged flywheel must be discarded as it may fly apart at high engine speed.

To check the breaker point gap, install the flywheel retaining nut or armature screw and use it to turn the crankshaft clockwise. Rotate the crankshaft so the index mark on the breaker cam is aligned with the breaker point follower arm as shown in Fig. C7-10. Rotate the crankshaft so the mark is aligned with each follower arm to set point gap for each breaker point set. The breaker point gap for each set of breaker points should be 0.020 inch (0.51 mm). Loosen the breaker point retaining screw, rotate the crankshaft and recheck point gap. Lubricate the cam wiper felt with a small amount of breaker point cam lubricant. Do not apply too much lubricant as it may be thrown off the cam onto the breaker points causing misfiring.

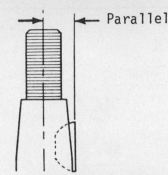

Fig. C7-11 — The flywheel key must be parallel to the crankshaft centerline as shown.

Be sure the tapered mating surfaces of the crankshaft and flywheel are clean and dry. The flywheel key must be positioned as shown in Fig. C7-11.

After installing flywheel on Autolectric models, refer to AUTOLECTRIC STARTER-GENERATOR section and install starter-generator assembly.

On all other models, install flywheel and rope pulley, note that pulley must index in holes in flywheel. Tighten flywheel nut to 45 ft.-lbs. (61 N·m).

SPEED CONTROL LINKAGE

The speed control lever or grip is connected to the magneto stator plate to advance or retard the ignition timing. Throttle linkage is synchronized to open the throttle as magneto timing is advanced. It is very important that the throttle linkage is properly synchronized for best performance.

Fig. C7-12 — View showing location of idle mixture screw (I), clamp screw (S), cam follower (1) and cam (2).

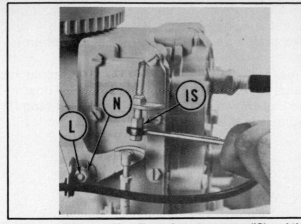

Fig. C7-13 — Idle speed is adjusted at stop screw (IS) and throttle friction is adjusted by turning inside bellcrank nut (N). Tighten outside nut (L) to maintain correct throttle friction.

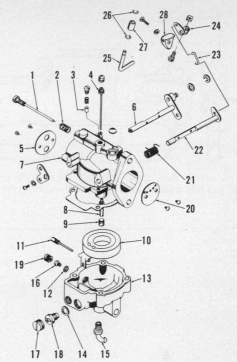

Fig. C7-14 — Exploded view of Tillotson MD carburetor and cam follower linkage.

1. Idle mixture screw	16. Main (high speed) jet
2. Spring	17. Plug
3. Choke detent	18. Fuel inlet needle seat
4. Idle tube	19. Plug
5. Choke valve	20. Throttle plate
6. Choke shaft	21. Spring
7. Body	22. Throttle shaft
8. Main nozzle	23. Link
9. Plug	24. Lever
10. Float	25. Cam follower
11. Float shaft	26. Retaining rings
12. Gasket	27. Roller
13. Body	28. Bracket
14. Gasket	
15. Fuel inlet fitting	

To synchronize the linkage, refer to Fig. C7-12. With the engine not running, loosen the clamping screw (S) in throttle control bellcrank. Move the speed control grip of lever until the scribe mark on throttle cam (2) is aligned with center of cam follower (1). Move cam follower until it just contacts cam at the scribe mark, then tighten screw (S). As speed control grip or lever is moved further to the "Fast" position, the throttle valve should start to open.

The idle speed stop screw (IS — Fig. C7-13) should be adjusted to provide 800-1000 rpm in neutral. Throttle friction is adjusted by turning the inside nut (N) and adjustment is maintained by tightening locknut (L).

FUEL SYSTEM

A Tillotson MD type carburetor is used on all models. Refer to Fig. C7-14 for an exploded view of carburetor.

ADJUSTMENT. The idle mixture may be adjusted after removing the engine cover. Initial setting of the idle mixture screw (I — Fig. C7-12) is one turn out from a lightly seated position. To adjust idle mixture screw, run motor until operating temperature is obtained. The outboard motor lower unit must be immersed in water when running to prevent damage to the water pump impeller.

Shift unit into forward gear and run at slowest, smooth engine speed. Turn the idle mixture screw clockwise until the engine starts to misfire, note the screw's position, then turn the screw counterclockwise until the engine again misfires. Note the screw's position. Turn the screw so it is midway between the two misfiring positions.

The high speed mixture is controlled by main jet (16 — Fig. C7-14). Standard main jet size is 0.069

inch for 1971 and earlier models or 0.067 inch for 1972 and later models. Standard main jet size should be correct below 5000 feet (1524 m).

OVERHAUL. Note the following points when overhauling the carburetor. Reinstall the throttle plate as shown in Fig. C7-15. The plate has a bevel

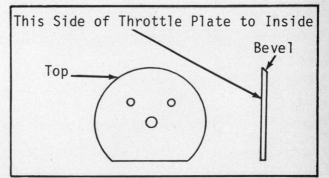

Fig. C7-15 — View showing correct installation of throttle plate on Tillotson MD carburetor.

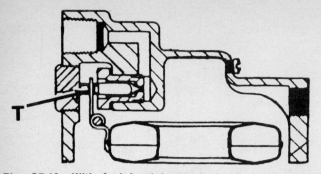

Fig. C7-16—With fuel bowl inverted, the float should be parallel to the fuel bowl gasket surface. Bend tang (T) to adjust float.

edge and must be installed correctly for proper carburetor operation. Be sure the throttle and choke plates do not bind or stick in carburetor bore.

Free end of float (10—Fig. C7-14) should be parallel with surface of fuel bowl with fuel bowl inverted as shown in Fig. C7-16. Bend float tang (T) to adjust float level.

CHRYSLER 20 AND 25 HP

20 HP MODELS

Year Produced	Model
1978	202B8H, 202B8J, 203B8H, 203B8J, 206B8A, 207B8A
1979	202H9K, 202B9K, 203H9K, 203B9K, 206H9B, 206B9B, 207H9B, 207B9B
1980	202H0L, 202B0L, 203H0L, 203B0L
1981	202H1M, 202B1M, 203H1M, 203B1M, 206H1C, 206B1C, 207H1C, 207B1C
1982	202H2N, 202B2N

25 HP MODELS

Year Produced	Model
1973, 1974, 1975, 1976, 1977	252HA, 252BA, 252HB, 242BB, 253HA, 253BA, 253HB, 253BB, 254HA, 254BA, 254HB, 254BB, 255HA, 255BA, 255HB, 255BB, 256HA, 256BA, 257HA, 257BA
1978	252H8C, 252H8D, 253H8C, 253H8D, 256H8C, 257H8C
1981	252H1E, 252B1E
1982	252H2F, 252B2F
1983	252H3G, 252B3G, 257H3D, 257B3D
1984	252H4, 252B4

Specifications

Hp/rpm 20/4750
25/5000

Bore .... 2-13/16 in.
(71.4 mm)

Stroke .... 2.3 in.
(58.4 mm)

Number of cylinders 2

Displacement .... 28.57 cu. in.
(468 cc)

Compression at cranking speed (average) .... 95-105 psi
(656-724 kPa)

Spark plug:
  Champion L4J
  Electrode gap .... 0.030 in.
(0.76 mm)

Breaker point gap (models so equipped) .... 0.020 in.*
(0.51 mm)

Ignition timing .... See Text

Carburetor:
  Make .... Tillotson
  Model .... WB

Fuel:oil ratio .... 50:1†

*Breaker point gap is 0.015 inch (0.38 mm) for models 256HA, 256BA, 257HA and 257BA.

†Fuel:oil ratio should be 25:1 for break-in period.

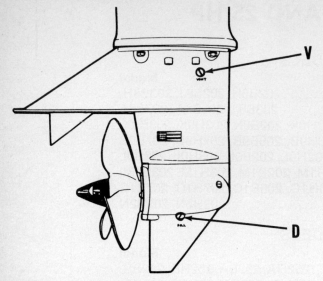

Fig. C8-1 — View showing location of vent (V) and drain (D) plugs.

Fig. C8-3 — Apply grease to electric starter shaft in area shown above.

Maintenance

LUBRICATION

ENGINE. The engine is lubricated by oil mixed with the fuel. The recommended fuel:oil ratio for normal operation is 50:1. During engine break-in the fuel:oil ratio should be 25:1.

The manufacturer recommends the use of no-lead automotive gasoline although regular and premium grades may be used. The gasoline octane rating must be 85 or higher.

LOWER UNIT. The lower unit gears and bearings are lubricated by oil contained in the gearcase. Only noncorrosive, leaded, EP90 outboard gear oil should be used. The gearcase fluid level should be checked after every 30 hours of opera-

tion. Oil level must be maintained at the level of the upper (vent) plug hole. Change fluid after every 100 hours of operation or every six months.

The outboard motor must be upright when draining or filling gearcase. Remove the vent and drain plugs shown in Fig. C8-1 when draining or filling. To fill with lubricant, force lubricant into lower plug hole (D) until lubricant reaches lower edge of upper plug hole (V). Install new gaskets on plugs, if necessary. Install upper plug (V) before removing lubricant dispenser so fluid remains in gearcase, then remove dispenser and install lower plug (D).

Depending on usage, remove the manual starter and apply water-resistant grease to the rubbing surfaces of the pawls and pawl plate. See Fig. C8-2.

On models equipped with an electric starter, the starter shaft should be lubricated after every thirty days with a water-resistant grease. It is necessary to remove the manual starter for access to the electric starter shaft. Apply grease to area shown in Fig. C8-3.

After every sixty days of operation, inject a good quality grease into all grease fittings and apply grease to control linkage rubbing surfaces.

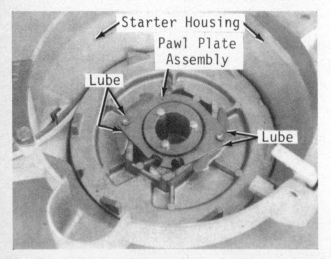

Fig. C8-2 — Lubricate rubbing surfaces of starter pawls and pawl plate by applying water-resistant grease to areas shown above.

FUEL SYSTEM

FUEL PUMP. All models are equipped with a diaphragm type fuel pump. Diaphragm (D—Fig. C8-4) is actuated by crankcase pulsations directed through passages (PV) and (PP). Valves (C) allow fuel to pass in one direction only. The two fuel pump stages operate alternately.

NOTE: Either stage operating independently may permit the motor to run, but not at peak performance.

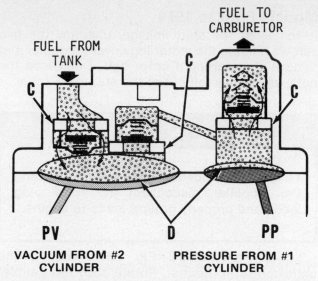

FUEL TO CARBURETOR

FUEL FROM TANK

C

C

C

C

PV

D

PP

VACUUM FROM #2 CYLINDER

PRESSURE FROM #1 CYLINDER

Fig. C8-4—Diagram showing operation of fuel pump. Diaphragm (D) moves due to crankcase pulsations directed through passages (PV) and (PP). Valves (c) allow fuel to pass in one direction only.

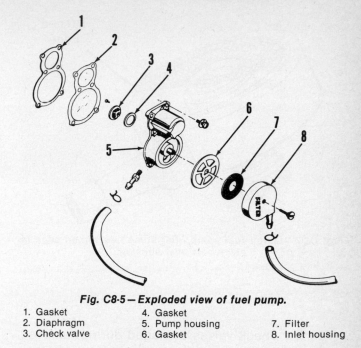

Fig. C8-5—Exploded view of fuel pump.

1. Gasket	4. Gasket
2. Diaphragm	5. Pump housing
3. Check valve	6. Gasket
	7. Filter
	8. Inlet housing

A filter screen (7—Fig. C8-5) is located in inlet housing (8). If fuel blockage is suspected due to a clogged or stopped filter screen, remove inlet housing for access to filter screen. Install filter screen so turned edge is away from inlet housing as shown in Fig. C8-7.

TESTING. A fuel pressure gage may be connected in the fuel line between the fuel pump and carburetor to determine if the fuel pump is operating properly. Note that the fuel tank should not be more than 24 inches (61 cm) lower than the fuel pump. Be sure fuel tank is vented properly before test.

OVERHAUL. To overhaul the fuel pump, disconnect both hoses from the pump. Unscrew the six screws retaining the fuel pump, then separate the pump body (5—Fig. C8-5), diaphragm (2) and gasket (1) from the motor. Remove inlet housing (8) and gasket (6). The center check valve (see Fig. C8-6) can be removed after unscrewing the two retaining screws. The upper check valve can be removed by pulling out with a hooked tool. The lower check valve can be driven out by inserting a rod through the hole in the opposite side of the body.

⚠ CAUTION

Do not operate outboard motor unless the lower unit is immersed in water, otherwise, the water pump impeller will be damaged.

Start then run outboard motor at engine speed listed in following table. Fuel pump should produce pressures listed.

Engine Rpm	Fuel Pressure
600	1 psi (6.9 kPa)
2500-3000	1.5 psi (10.4 kPa)
4500	2.5 psi (17.2 kPa)

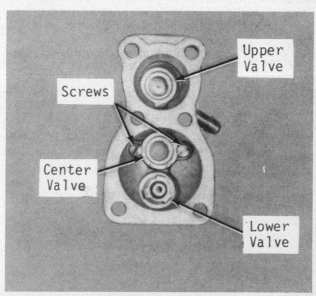

Upper Valve

Screws

Center Valve

Lower Valve

Fig. C8-6—Fuel pump check valves must be installed as shown for proper operation.

Illustrations Courtesy Chrysler

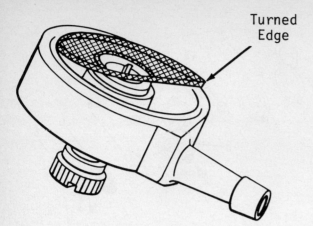

Turned Edge

Fig. C8-7—Install fuel pump filter screen so turned edge is away from inlet housing.

Renew check valves damaged during removal. Inspect the diaphragm for tears, holes and other damage.

When reassembling pump, note correct position of check valves as shown in Fig. C8-6. When installing check valves, apply pressure only to outer ring of valve. Install filter screen (7—Fig. C8-5) so turned edge is away from inlet housing as shown in Fig. C8-7. Install gasket (6—Fig. C8-5) so slot in gasket matches key on body tube. Install inlet housing (8) so keyway in housing mates with key on housing tube.

PUDDLE DRAIN VALVE

A puddle drain valve is located in the hose from the bottom of the crankcase cover to the bottom of the transfer port cover. The puddle valve is designed to remove puddled fuel from the crankcase, thus providing smooth operation at all speeds and lessening the possibility of spark plug fouling.

To check operation of the puddle valve, disconnect hose ends and blow through each end of hose. Puddle valve should pass air when blowing through crankcase cover end of hose but not when blowing through transfer port end of hose. Remove puddle valve from hose if it does not operate correctly. Install a new puddle valve in hose approximately one inch from end of hose. The small hole in the puddle valve must be towards the short end of hose. Attach hose to engine with puddle valve end of hose connected to crankcase cover.

SHIFT LINKAGE

The shift linkage may be adjusted to synchronize the shift control with the engagement of gears in the gearcase.

Models Prior to 1979

To adjust the shift linkage, unscrew the five screws holding the motor leg covers together and remove the starboard cover half. Don't lose the nuts which may fall out of the starboard cover.

⚠WARNING

To prevent accidental starting while rotating the propeller, disconnect the spark plug leads and properly ground leads to engine.

Loosen jam nut (N—Fig. C8-8). Position the shift control in neutral. Rotate shift rod coupler (C) so the propeller rotates freely thereby indicating the lower unit gears are in neutral. Hold the coupler to prevent rotation, then tighten jam nut (N) against coupler (C). Reassemble the motor leg covers and check operation of shift mechanism.

Models After 1978

To adjust the shift linkage, detach the lower shock mount covers (M—Fig. C8-9) on each side of the motor leg. Remove the lower thrust shock mount (T—Fig. C8-10). Remove six screws (S—Fig. C8-9) holding the front and rear motor leg covers together and remove the rear cover. Remove side shock mounts (Fig. C8-11) on each side of motor leg. Engage the reverse lock, then pull the lower unit back far enough to allow the front motor leg cover to slide down and out.

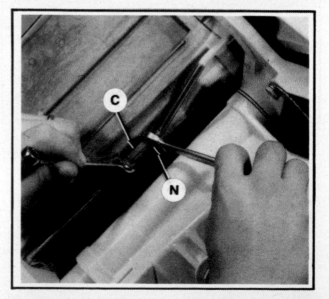

Fig. C8-8—After loosening jam nut (N), shift rod coupler (C) is rotated to adjust shift linkage on models prior to 1979.

Illustrations Courtesy Chrysler

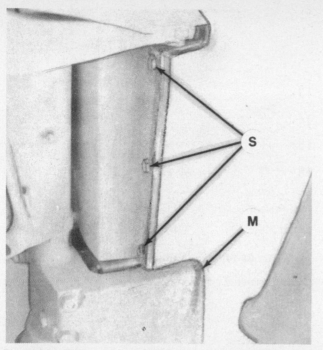

Fig. C8-9 — View showing location of lower shock mount covers (M) and screws (S) securing motor leg covers. There are three screws (S) on each side.

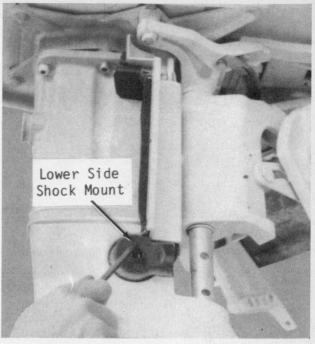

Fig. C8-11 — View of lower side shock mount.

⚠WARNING

To prevent accidental starting while rotating the propeller, disconnect the spark plug leads and properly ground leads to engine.

Position shift control so lower unit is in neutral (the propeller rotates freely). While rotating propeller, move the shift control towards forward gear and stop at point where clutch dogs just begin to contact forward gear. Mark the lower shift rod (R — Fig. C8-12) in relation to the motor leg. Move the shift control towards reverse and

mark the lower shift rod just as the clutch dogs begin to contact the reverse gear. Measure the distance between the two marks on the lower shift rod and make a mark to indicate halfway between forward and reverse which is neutral.

Loosen jam nut (N). Position the shift control so the lower shift rod (R) mark indicates the lower unit gears are positioned in neutral. The shift detent ball should now be fully seated in the neutral hole (N — Fig. C8-13) of the shift lever. If the ball

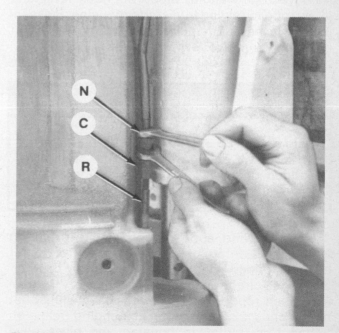

Fig. C8-12 — View of shift rod and coupler used on models after 1978. Refer to text for shift linkage adjustment.

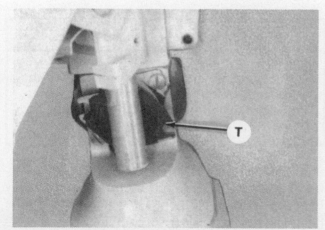

Fig. C8-10 — View of lower shock mount (T).

Fig. C8-13 — Lower unit gears should be in neutral when shift detent ball is seated in neutral hole (N) of shift lever.

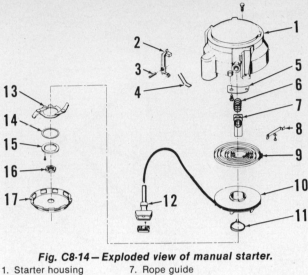

Fig. C8-14 — Exploded view of manual starter.

1. Starter housing	7. Rope guide	13. Pawl plate
2. Interlock lever	8. Housing liner	14. Shims
3. Pin	9. Rewind spring	15. Retainer
4. Spring	10. Rope & pulley	16. Nut
5. Plate	11. Spring	17. Starter cup
6. Spring	12. Handle	

does not seat properly, rotate shift rod coupler (C—Fig. C8-12) until it does so. Hold the coupler to prevent rotation, then tighten jam nut (N) against coupler (C).

Reassemble covers and shock mounts by reversing disassembly procedure. Check operation of shift mechanism.

STARTER

Refer to Fig. C8-14 for an exploded view of manual starter. To disassemble starter, remove starter from engine (the ignition components bracket must be removed on electric start models). Unscrew retainer (15) screws and remove retainer, shims (14), pawl plate (13) and spring (11). Remove rope handle, press interlock lever and allow rope to rewind into starter housing. Press interlock lever and remove rope and pulley (10). If necessary, remove rewind spring.

⚠WARNING

Care should be exercised when working with or around a coiled starter rewind spring as sudden uncoiling can cause injury. Safety eyewear and gloves are recommended.

Install rewind spring in housing with spring wound in counterclockwise direction from outer end of spring. Wind rope on pulley in counterclockwise direction as viewed with pulley in housing. Insert rope through slot of pulley with about nine inches (22.9 cm) of rope extending from slot. Install rope pulley in housing and place pawl spring (11) on rope pulley with ends pointing up.

Install pawl plate (13) with pawl side toward pulley and engage slots with pawl spring (11) ends. Install shims (14) and retainer (15). Sufficient shims (14) should be installed to remove excessive end play in assembly. Shims are available in thicknesses of 0.006 (silver), 0.007 (brass) and 0.010 inch (black). Turn rope pulley approximately two turns clockwise to preload rewind spring and pass end of rope through rope guide of starter housing. Attach rope handle and pull rope until it is fully extended. It should still be possible to rotate rope pulley a slight amount after rope is extended to prevent damage to rewind spring.

COOLING SYSTEM

All models are equipped with an impeller type water pump located in the lower unit that circulates water through the power head.

⚠CAUTION

Do not operate outboard motor unless the lower unit is immersed in water, otherwise, the water pump impeller will be damaged.

If cooling system problems are encountered, first check the water inlet for material which may be blocking the inlet. If the water pump must be inspected, refer to the Outboard Motor Service Manual.

Illustrations Courtesy Chrysler

Fig. C8-15—Loosen flywheel by carefully prying up against the flywheel while striking the tool or nut as outlined in text.

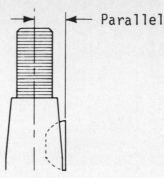

Fig. C8-16—View showing proper installation of flywheel key in crankshaft.

PROPELLER

Power is transmitted from the propeller shaft to the propeller by splines on the shaft. The propeller is retained on the shaft by a pin which contacts the propeller and shaft. Be sure to use the correct pin.

The propeller is designed for right-hand rotation, and is equipped with three blades. Standard propeller size for models prior to 1979 is 8½ inch (21.6 cm) diameter and 10 inch (25.4 cm) pitch. Standard propeller size for models after 1978 is 10⅜ inch (26.4 cm) diameter and 12½ inch (31.8 cm) pitch.

Tune-Up

IGNITION SYSTEM

All manual start models are equipped with a breaker point ignition system. Models equipped with an electric starter prior to 1978 are also equipped with a breaker point ignition system. Models equipped with an electric starter after 1977 are equipped with the Magnapower breakerless, capacitor discharge ignition system. All ignition components except the spark plugs are located under the flywheel on models equipped with a breaker point ignition system. Magnapower equipped models may be identified by the ignition modules attached to the engine.

Breaker Point Models

BREAKER POINT GAP. Two sets of breaker points are used with each breaker point set controlling ignition for one cylinder.

To adjust breaker point gap, the manual starter and flywheel must be removed. To remove the flywheel proceed as follows: Unscrew the flywheel retaining nut (a band type wrench may be used to hold the flywheel while loosening the nut). Thread a suitable nut on the end of the crankshaft so the end is protected or install tool T2910. Note that neither the nut or tool must bear against the flywheel. Using a suitable prying tool, lightly pry up against the flywheel while moderately striking the nut or tool T2910. See Fig. C8-15. The flywheel should "pop" free.

⚠WARNING

Be sure suitable tools are used to remove the flywheel. Damage resultant from the misapplication of force or the use of incorrect tools may cause engine damage, engine malfunction or personal injury.

Remove the flywheel and inspect it for cracks or other damage. Be sure to inspect the tapered center portion of the flywheel as well. A damaged flywheel must be discarded as it may fly apart at high engine speed.

To check the breaker point gap, install the flywheel retaining nut and use the nut to turn the crankshaft clockwise. Rotate the crankshaft until the breaker point gap is maximum (follower arm contacts high point of cam) and make a mark on the cam opposite the follower arm rub block. After setting gap for one set of points, rotate crankshaft and align mark with follower arm rub block of remaining breaker point set. Both sets of breaker points should be adjusted exactly alike. Breaker point gap should be 0.020 inch (0.51 mm).

Lubricate the cam wiper felt with a small amount of breaker point cam lubricant. Do not apply too much lubricant as it may be thrown off the cam onto the breaker points causing misfiring.

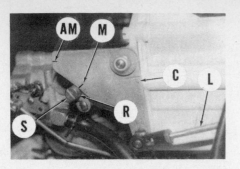

Fig. C8-17 — View of throttle cam and linkage. Refer to text for adjustment.

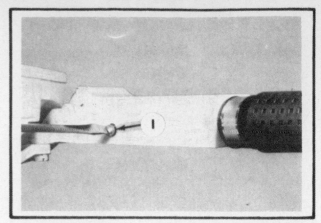

Fig. C8-19 — Idle speed on manual start models is adjusted by turning idle speed screw (I) in steering handle.

Be sure the tapered mating surfaces of the crankshaft and flywheel are clean and dry. The flywheel key must be positioned as shown in Fig. C8-16. Tighten flywheel retaining nut to 45 ft.-lbs. (61 N·m).

Magnapower Models

The Magnapower ignition system does not use breaker points and no maintenance is required. Ignition timing is not adjustable. Refer to the Outboard Motor Service Manual for Magnapower ignition system service.

SPEED CONTROL LINKAGE.

Ignition timing and throttle opening on all models must be synchronized so that throttle is opened as timing is advanced.

To synchronize linkage, disconnect link (L— Fig. C8-17) from throttle cam (C) and with throttle closed, turn eccentric screw (S) until roller (R) is exactly centered over mark (M) on throttle cam. Reconnect link (L) to magneto and rotate magneto stator ring until it is against full advance stop. Upper mark (AM) on throttle cam should now be aligned with roller (R). Disconnect link (L) and turn

link ends to adjust length of link so that mark (AM) and roller are aligned when stator is at full advance. Turn throttle stop screw (S—Fig. C8-18) in steering handle shaft on models with manual starter so that screw contacts wall (W) of handle just as stator plate reaches full advance stop.

Idle speed in forward gear should be 550-650 rpm on manual start models. Adjust idle speed of manual start models by turning idle speed screw (I—Fig. C8-19) on side of steering handle. Idle speed in forward gear should be 650-750 rpm on electric start models. Adjust idle speed of electric start models by turning idle speed screw (I—Fig. C8-19A) adjacent to exhaust port cover.

CARBURETOR

All models are equipped with a Tillotson WB carburetor. Refer to Fig. C8-20 for an exploded view of the carburetor.

ADJUSTMENT. The idle mixture adjustment screw is accessible after removing the motor cover. Initial setting of the idle mixture screw (see

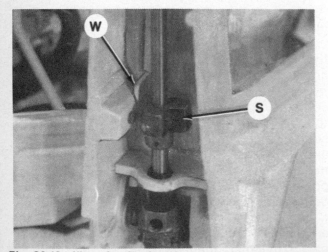

Fig. C8-18 — View showing location of throttle stop screw on models with a manual starter.

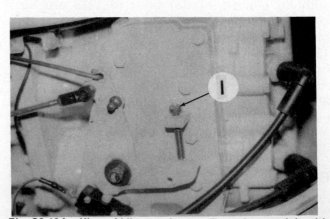

Fig. C8-19A — View of idle speed screw (I) used on models with electric starter. Idle speed should be 650-750 rpm with unit in forward gear.

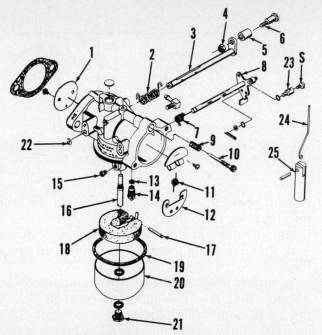

Fig. C8-20 — *Exploded view of Tillotson WB carburetor.*

1. Throttle plate
2. Spring
3. Throttle shaft
4. Nut
5. Roller
6. Eccentric screw
7. Spring
8. Choke shaft
9. Spring
10. Idle mixture screw
11. Spring
12. Choke plate
13. Gasket
14. Fuel inlet valve
15. High speed jet
16. Main nozzle
17. Float pin
18. Float
19. Gasket
20. Fuel bowl
21. Screw
22. "E" ring
23. Swivel
24. Rod
25. Choke plunger

Fig. C8-21) is 1¼ turns out from a lightly seated position. To adjust idle mixture screw, run motor until operating temperature is obtained. The outboard motor lower unit must be immersed in water when running to prevent damage to the water pump impeller.

Shift unit into forward gear and run at slowest, smooth engine speed. Turn the idle mixture screw clockwise until the engine starts to misfire, note the screw's position, then turn the screw counterclockwise until the engine again misfires. Note the screw's position. Turn the screw so it is midway between the two misfiring positions.

NOTE: When turning idle mixture screw, wait ten seconds after turning screw each ⅛ turn to allow recirculation system to function, otherwise puddled fuel may affect idle mixture.

If the engine "pops" or dies when the throttle is opened rapidly from idle, then the mixture is too lean. Enrichen the mixture by turning the mixture screw counterclockwise in small increments until smooth acceleration is obtained.

High speed mixture is controlled by main jet (15 — Fig. C8-20). Refer to the following table for the recommended main jet size.

Altitude	Jet Size	Part Number
Sea Level-1250 ft. (0-381 m)	0.066	014188
1250-3750 ft. (381-1143 m)	0.064	0.14108
3750-6250 ft. (1143-1905 m)	0.062	014187
6250-8250 ft. (1905-2515 m)	0.060	014186

On electric start models there should be a clearance of 0.010-0.014 inch (0.26-0.33 mm) between the lower edge of choke plate (12 — Fig. C8-20) and carburetor bore when the choke is activated. Plunger (25) should be bottomed in the choke solenoid when measuring clearance. Loosen screw (S) and move connecting rod (24) in connector (23) to obtain desired clearance. Make certain that choke plate is free and returns to full open position.

OVERHAUL. Note the following points when overhauling the carburetor. Install the choke plate

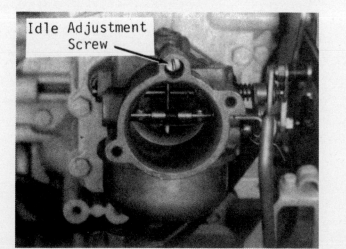

Fig. C8-21 — *View showing location of idle mixture screw.*

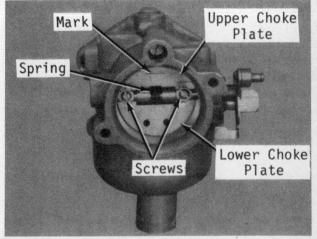

Fig. C8-22 — *Choke plate components should be installed as shown above.*

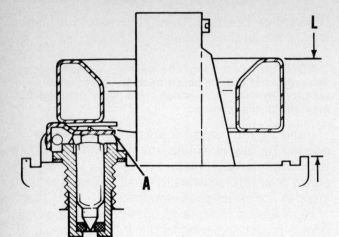

Fig. C8-23—Float level (L) on Tillotson WB carburetor should be 13/32 inch (10.3 mm). Bend tang (A) to adjust float level.

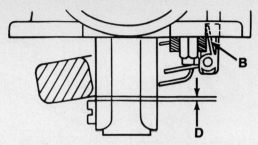

Fig. C8-24 — Float drop (D) on Tillotson WB should be 1/32-1/16 inch (0.8-1.6 mm). Bend tang (B) to adjust float drop.

and shaft assembly as shown in Fig. C8-22. Note that the mark on the upper choke plate should face out. The ends of the spring should be behind the choke plates so spring tension forces the upper choke plate against the tabs of the lower choke plate. Choke return spring (7 — Fig. C8-20) should hold the choke open.

Install throttle plate (1) so marked side is out and notched end is up when throttle plate is in closed position. Operate throttle and be sure throttle plate does not stick or bind.

Install float pin (17) by inserting smooth end first, then continue insertion until grooved end is flush with side of mounting boss.

To check float level, invert the carburetor and measure distance (L — Fig. C8-23) from the float to the carburetor body. Distance should be 13/32 inch (10.3 mm). Adjust float level by bending float arm tang (A).

Float drop is measured from bottom of free end of float to top of main jet as shown in Fig. C8-24. Float drop (D) should be 1/32-1/16 inch (0.8-1.6 mm). Adjust float drop by bending float arm tang (B).

ESKA

THE ESKA COMPANY
2400 Kerper Blvd.
Dubuque, Iowa 52001

ESKA 1.2 AND 2.5 HP

Year Produced	1.2 hp	2.5 hp
1977	14058A	14089A
1978	.....	14089B
1979	.....	14089C

Specifications

	1.2 hp	2.5 hp
Bore	1.19 in.	1.61 in.
	(30.2 mm)	(40.9 mm)
Stroke	1.19 in.	1.495 in.
	(30.2 mm)	(38 mm)
Number of cylinders	1	1
Displacement	1.39 cu. in.	3.05 cu. in.
	(22.8 cc)	(50 cc)
Spark plug:		
Champion	RJ8J	RJ8J
Electrode gap	0.025 in.	0.025 in.
	(0.6 mm)	(0.6 mm)
Breaker point gap	0.012-0.015 in.	0.012-0.015 in.
	(0.3-0.38 mm)	(0.3-0.38 mm)
Fuel:oil ratio	32:1	32:1

Fig. E1-1—Drain lubricant from gearcase by removing gearcase cover. Fill gearcase by directing lubricant through fill plug (F) hole until lubricant is even with hole with outboard motor in upright position.

Maintenance

LUBRICATION

The power head is lubricated by oil mixed with the fuel. Recommended fuel:oil ratio is 32:1. Oil should be BIA certified TC-W.

Lower unit is lubricated by oil contained in gearcase. To fill gearcase, remove fill screw (F—Fig. E1-1) and fill gearcase with unit upright until lubricant flows out of fill screw hole. Lubricant should be SAE 90 outboard gear lubricant.

FUEL SYSTEM

Periodically inspect the fuel lines and connections for leakage and damage. With the engine stopped, periodically remove the drain screw on the bottom of the carburetor float bowl and drain the fuel into a suitable container. Note that on 1.2

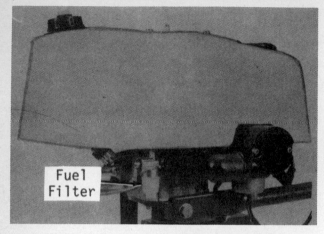

Fig. E1-2 — View showing location of fuel filter.

hp models the bottom screw retains the float bowl to the carburetor. Inspect the drained fuel. If an excessive amount of dirt or other foreign matter is observed in the fuel, clean the fuel system as needed.

A combination fuel shut-off valve and filter unit is located beneath the fuel tank as shown in Fig. E1-2. Periodically unscrew the filter cup and inspect the cup and filter. Renew the filter if damaged or if filter cannot be cleaned. Inspect filter at least twice each season or more frequently if necessary.

EXHAUST SYSTEM

The muffler cover shown in Fig. E1-3 should be removed periodically so the exhaust system can be inspected. If carbon deposits are evident, they should be removed by scraping with a wooden scraper or other suitable tool. Rotate the crankshaft so the piston covers the exhaust port to prevent entrance of carbon into the cylinder. Care should be exercised when scraping to prevent damage to engine components.

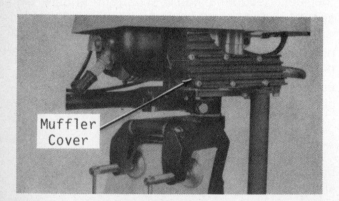

Fig. E1-3 — Remove the muffler cover to inspect the exhaust port for carbon deposits.

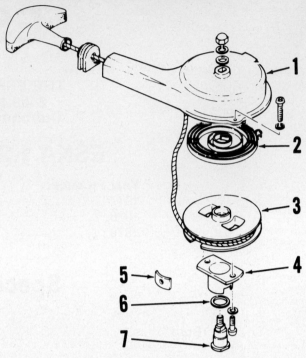

Fig. E1-4 — Exploded view of rewind starter used on 1.2 hp models.

1. Housing
2. Rewind spring
3. Rope pulley
4. Drive coupling
5. Rope guide
6. Washer
7. Pulley shaft

MANUAL STARTER

Both models are equipped with a pawl type rewind starter. The starter may be removed after unscrewing the mounting screws and lifting up the starter.

To disassemble the starter, pull the starter rope out and hold the pulley so the rope does not rewind. Direct the rope through the notch in the outer edge of the pulley, then allow the pulley to rotate without rewinding the rope until spring tension is released. Refer to Fig. E1-4 or E1-5 and disassemble the starter while exercising caution when removing the rewind spring.

⚠WARNING

Care should be exercised when working with or around a coiled starter rewind spring as sudden uncoiling can cause injury. Safety eyewear and gloves are recommended.

Reassemble the starter by reversing the disassembly procedure and referring to Fig. E1-4 or E1-5. Rewind spring on 1.2 hp models must be wound in a counterclockwise direction from the outer spring end when installing spring in starter housing (1). Rewind spring on 2.5 hp models must

Illustrations Courtesy Eska

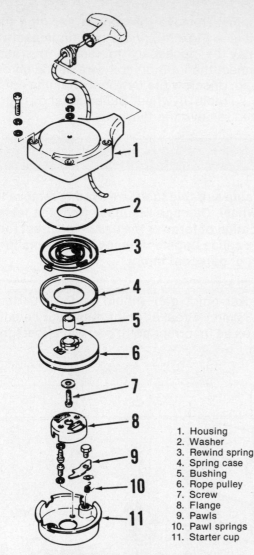

Fig. E1-6 — *Remove the air shroud for access to the flywheel.*

1. Housing
2. Washer
3. Rewind spring
4. Spring case
5. Bushing
6. Rope pulley
7. Screw
8. Flange
9. Pawls
10. Pawl springs
11. Starter cup

Fig. E1-5 — *Exploded view of rewind starter used on 2.5 hp models.*

be wound in a clockwise direction in spring case (4). The rope should be wrapped around the rope pulley in a counterclockwise direction on 1.2 hp models when viewed with pulley installed. On 2.5 hp models, wrap the rope around the pulley in a clockwise direction as viewed with the pulley installed.

COOLING SYSTEM

The power head is air-cooled by a fan built into the flywheel. The fan shroud must be in place and power head cooling fins must be clean and unbroken or engine may overheat. Manufacturer recommends renewing power head cylinder if 10 percent of cooling fins are missing or cracked.

PROPELLER

A left-hand rotating propeller is used on 1.2 hp models while a right-hand rotating propeller is used on 2.5 hp models.

Power is transmitted from the propeller shaft to the propeller by a drive pin which is designed to shear when the propeller contacts an obstruction. Be sure the correct drive pin (shear pin) is installed or the lower unit may be damaged if an obstruction is struck.

To remove the propeller, first disconnect the spark plug lead and properly ground the lead to the engine.

⚠ WARNING

When working on or around the propeller the spark plug lead should be disconnected and grounded to the engine to prevent accidental starting if the propeller is rotated.

Detach the cotter pin and slide the propeller off the propeller shaft. Inspect the shear pin and renew if necessary. Before reinstalling the propeller, apply water-resistant grease to the propeller shaft.

Tune-Up

IGNITION SYSTEM

All models are equipped with a flywheel magneto ignition system. Refer to the following sections for adjustment of breaker point gap and ignition timing.

Eska 1.2 & 2.5 Hp

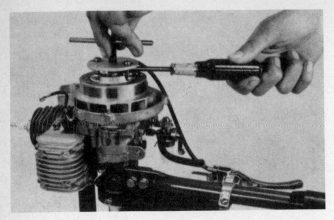

Fig. E1-7 — Use a suitable pulling tool to remove the flywheel.

BREAKER POINT GAP. To check or adjust breaker point gap, the flywheel must be removed. To remove the flywheel, first remove the manual starter, fuel tank cap and engine cover. Be prepared to catch fuel, then disconnect fuel line between fuel tank and fuel valve. Detach fuel tank. On 2.5 hp models, remove the starter cup (11—Fig. E1-5) and pawl assembly. On both models, disconnect the spark plug lead from the spark plug. Remove the screws securing the air shroud (see Fig. E1-6); note that an impact driver tool may be necessary to loosen the screws. Disconnect the ignition coil wire as the shroud is removed. Unscrew the flywheel retaining nut, then use a suitable flywheel puller as shown in Fig. E1-7 and remove the flywheel.

> ## ⚠️WARNING
>
> **Be sure suitable tools are used to remove the flywheel. Damage resultant from the misapplication of force or the use of incorrect tools may cause engine damage, engine malfunction or personal injury.**

Breaker point gap should be 0.012-0.015 inch (0.3-0.38 mm). Breaker point gap must be set correctly as an incorrect point gap will affect ignition timing.

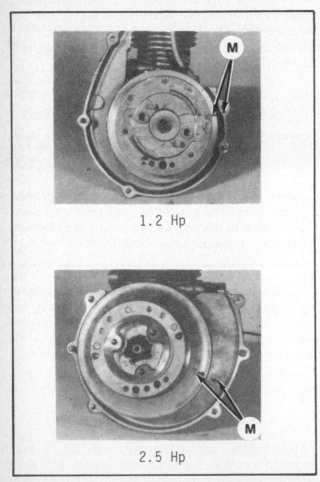

1.2 Hp

2.5 Hp

Fig. E1-8 — Views showing location of ignition timing marks (M).

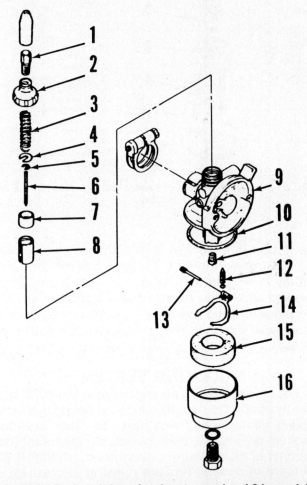

Fig. E1-9 — Exploded view of carburetor used on 1.2 hp models.

1. Cable guide		
2. Cap	7. Throttle stop	12. Fuel inlet valve
3. Spring	8. Throttle slide	13. Float pin
4. Clip retainer	9. Body	14. Float arm
5. Clip	10. Gasket	15. Float
6. Jet needle	11. Main jet	16. Float bowl

Illustrations Courtesy Eska

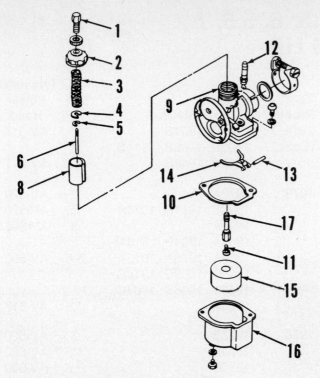

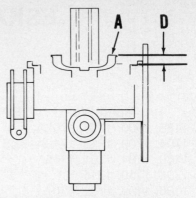

Fig. E1-11—Distance (D) above gasket surface should be 0.138 inch (3.5 mm) on 1.2 hp models.

Fig. E1-10—Exploded view of carburetor used on 2.5 hp models. Refer to Fig. E1-8 for parts identification except for: 17. Needle jet.

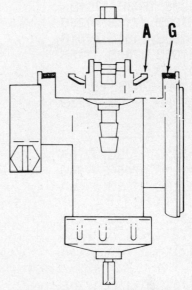

Fig. E1-12—Carburetor float arm (A) on 2.5 hp models should be level with gasket (G).

Reinstall the flywheel by reversing the removal procedure.

IGNITION TIMING. To check or adjust ignition timing, remove the air shroud as outlined in the BREAKER POINT GAP section. Connect an ohmmeter or continuity checker to the wire lead from the breaker points and to ground on the engine. Rotate the flywheel clockwise and note when the breaker points open. The breaker points should open when the "M" mark on the periphery of the flywheel is aligned with the mark on the crankcase as shown in Fig. E1-8.

If ignition timing is incorrect, remove the flywheel as outlined in the BREAKER POINT GAP section. Loosen the two screws retaining the stator plate (not the breaker point screws) and rotate the stator plate to adjust ignition timing. Tighten screws and recheck ignition timing. Reassemble components.

CARBURETOR

Both models are equipped with a variable venturi, float type carburetor as shown in Fig. E1-9 or E1-10.

ADJUSTMENT. The idle mixture is not adjustable. Midrange air:fuel ratio is controlled by the position of jet needle (6) in main jet (11) or needle jet (17). As the throttle slide is raised to admit more air through the carburetor, the jet needle will be withdrawn from the main jet or needle jet allowing more fuel to flow into the carburetor bore. Relocating the jet needle clip (5) on the jet

needle (6) will change the air:fuel ratio. Moving the clip to a higher groove in the jet needle will lean the air:fuel mixture; placing the clip in a lower groove will richen the mixture. Full throttle mixture is controlled by the size of the main jet.

Normal position of the jet needle clip (5) is in the third groove from the top on the jet needle (6). Main jet size is #50 for 1.2 hp models and #74 for 2.5 hp models.

OVERHAUL. Overhaul of the carburetor is evident after inspecting the carburetor and referral to Fig. El-9 or El-10. Be sure the throttle cable end properly engages throttle slide (8). Note that clip retainer (4) holds the jet needle clip and jet needle assembly in position in the throttle slide. Carefully insert the throttle slide assembly so the groove in the side of the slide engages the pin in the throttle slide bore of the carburetor body.

The float arm on 1.2 hp models should be 0.138 inch (3.5 mm) above the carburetor body measured as shown in Fig. El-11. The float arm on 2.5 hp models should be level with the float bowl gasket as shown in Fig. El-12.

ESKA 3, 3.5, 4.5, 5, 5.5, 7 AND 7.5 HP

Year Produced	Model No.	HP	Tecumseh Power Head
1969	1188, 1700, 1703, 1703A, 1704, 1709, 1713, 1713A	3.5	AV-520
	1189, 1194, 1701, 1705, 1706, 1710, 1715	5	AV-600
	1186, 1199, 1702, 1707, 1708, 1711, 1717	7	AV-750
1970	1188, 1703B, 1704B, 1709B, 1713B, 1723B	3.5	AV-520
	1189B, 1194B, 1701B, 1705B, 1706B, 1715B, 1733B	5	AV-600
	1199, 1702B, 1707B, 1708B, 1717B, 1723B, 1734B	7	AV-750
1971	1703C, 1713C, 1770A	3.5	AV-520
	1701C, 1705C, 1706C, 1715C, 1733C, 1766A, 1771A	5	AV-600
	1702C, 1708C, 1721A, 1727A, 1745A, 1747A, 1767A, 1772A, 1777A	7	AV-750
1972	1703D, 1713D, 1770B, 1788A, 1791A	3.5	AV-520
	1705D, 1706D, 1715D, 1766B, 1771B, 1784A, 1789A	5	AV-600
	1727B, 1746A, 1747B, 1756A, 1767B, 1772B, 1776A, 1790A	7	AV-817
1973	1929A, 1945A	3.5	AV-520
	1903A	4.5	AV-520
	1705E, 1908A, 1913A, 1928A, 1930A	5	AV-600
	1747C, 1931A	7	AV-817
	1905A, 1909A, 1914A, 1932A, 1966A	7.5	AV-817
1974	1929B, 1945B	3.5	AV-520
	1903B	4.5	AV-520
	1705F, 1908B, 1913B, 1928B, 1930B	5	AV-600

Year Produced	Model No.	HP	Tecumseh Power Head
1974 (Cont.)	1747D, 1931B	7	AV-817
	1905B, 1909B, 1914B, 1932B, 1944B	7.5	AV-817
1975	1973A	3	AV-520
	1903C, 1941B, 1974A	4.5	AV-520
	1997A	5	AV-600
	1904A, 1904B, 1910A, 1969A, 1970A, 1975A	5.5	AV-600
	1905C, 1909C, 1914C, 1944C, 1966C, 1967C, 1976A	7.5	AV-817
1976	1973B	3	AV-520
	1974B	4.5	AV-520
	1975B	5.5	AV-600
	1944D, 1976B	7.5	AV-817
1977	1403B	3.5	AV-520
	14035B, 14036B	5	AV-600
	14037B, 14038A, 14059A	7.5	AV-817
1978	14034C	3.5	AV-520
	14035C, 14106A	5	AV-600
	14107A, 14108A	7.5	AV-817
1979	14034D	3.5	AV-520
	14035D, 14160B	5	AV-600
	14107B, 14108B	7.5	AV-817
1980	14139A	3.5	AV-520
	14140A	5	AV-600
	14141A	7.5	AV-817
1981	14178A, 14183A	3.5	AV-520
	14035E, 14140B, 14179B, 14189A	5	AV-600
	14141B, 14180A	7.5	AV-817
1982	14178B, 14183B	3.5	AV-520
	14140C, 14179B	5	AV-600
	14141C, 14180B	7.5	AV-817
1983, 1984, 1985	14207	3.5	AV-520
	14208	5	AV-600
	14209	7.5	AV-817

These motors are also sold as Explorer, Federal, Goldenjet, Hanimex, Hiawatha, Pathfinder, Seaco, Seacruiser-Grant, Sea King, Sea Hawk, Sears, Skipper, Sportfisher and Wizard models.

Specifications

	AV520	AV600	AV750	AV817
Bore	2.09 in.	2.09 in.	2.375 in.	2.437 in.
	53 mm	53 mm	60.3 mm	61.9 mm
Stroke	1.50 in.	1.76 in.	1.68 in.	1.75 in.
	38.1 mm	44.7 mm	42.7 mm	44.4 mm
Number of cylinders....	1	1	1	1
Displacement	5.16 cu. in.	6.05 cu. in.	7.50 cu. in.	8.17 cu. in.
	84.6 cc	99.1 cc	122.9 cc	133.9 cc
Spark plug:				
Champion	J13Y*	J13Y*	J13Y*	J13Y*
AC	45S	45S	45S	45S
Electrode gap	0.030 in.	0.030 in.	0.030 in.	0.030 in.
	0.76 mm	0.76 mm	0.76 mm	0.76 mm
Conventional magneto:				
Breaker point gap	See Text	See Text	See Text	See Text
Piston position max.				
advance timing	See Text	See Text	See Text	See Text
Solid state magneto:				
Max. advance timing .	See Text	See Text	See Text	See Text
Fuel:oil ratio	See Text	See Text	See Text	See Text

*Recommended spark plug for models after 1976 is Champion RJ13Y.

The engine model number (AV520, AV600, AV750 or AV817) is for easy reference only to the general construction. If service parts are required, the type number MUST be used. The type number is stamped in the blower housing or on a tag attached to the engine. A correct type number will usually consist of three numbers, a dash followed by two more numbers (such as 643-09). When servicing power head, make certain that identification tag is reinstalled.

Maintenance

LUBRICATION

ENGINE. The engine is lubricated by oil mixed with regular grade gasoline. Recommended fuel to oil ratio is 16:1 for 1969 model motors. Oil used should be a good grade of oil intended for use in outboard motors. Fuel and oil should be mixed in a ratio of 24:1 for 1970 through 1973 model motors. Fuel:oil ratio of 32:1 may be used on 1974 and later models if oil used is BIA certified TC-W. If BIA certified TC-W oil is not available, use a good grade of outboard motor oil in a 24:1 fuel to oil mixture on 1974 and later models.

The lower unit gears and bearings are lubricated by oil contained in the gearcase. SAE 90 outboard gear lubricant should be used. Lubricant should be checked at least every 20 hours of operation and maintained at level of the upper vent plug (U—Fig. E2-1) when motor is in upright position. The gearcase should be drained and filled with new oil at least once each season.

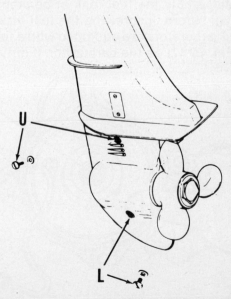

Fig. E2-1 — View of gearcase showing location of vent plug (U) and drain/fill plug (L). The drain/fill plug is located on the starboard side of models not equipped with a neutral gear.

Eska 3, 3.5, 4.5, 5, 5.5, 7 & 7.5 Hp

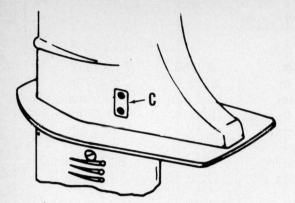

Fig. E2-2 — Remove cover (C) for access to shift rod screw on models so equipped.

Remove both plugs (U and L) and lay motor on side to drain the gearcase.

Motor should be in upright position when filling gearcase with lubricant. Insert filler tube in lower plug (L) opening and fill until lubricant is at level of upper plug (U) opening. Install upper plug, then remove filler tube and install lower plug. Use new gaskets on plugs if necessary to provide a water tight seal.

Every 60 days lubricate exposed screw threads or rubbing surfaces with water-resistant lithium grease or oil. Inject grease into grease fitting(s) on swivel bracket. Models may be equipped with one or two grease fittings which may be located in the side or on the underside of the swivel bracket.

FUEL SYSTEM

Periodically inspect the fuel lines and connections for leakage and damage. Some models are equipped with a fuel filter attached to the fuel line fitting on the fuel tank. Before removing the fuel tank filter, empty the fuel tank or be prepared to catch fuel before unscrewing the fuel fitting.

Some carburetors are equipped with a fuel filter (25S — Fig. E2-17) on the carburetor. If dirty fuel is

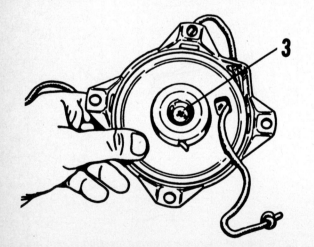

Fig. E2-3 — View of underside of manual starter. Retainer screw (3) should be tightened to 45-55 in.-lbs. (5.1-6.2 N·m).

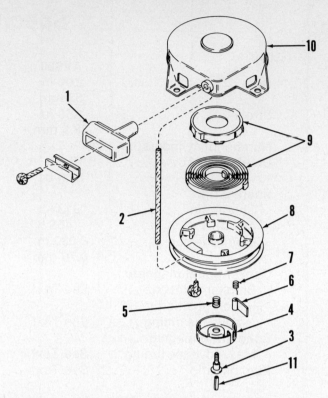

Fig. E2-4 — Exploded view of starter. Refer to Fig. E2-5 for installation of parts (5, 6 & 7).

1. Handle
2. Rope
3. Retainer screw
4. Retainer housing
5. Brake spring
6. Starter dog
7. Dog return spring
8. Pulley
9. Spring & keeper
10. Housing
11. Centering pin

suspected of causing poor engine performance, remove the fuel pump and inspect the fuel filter on the carburetor. Clean or renew the filter if dirty.

SHIFT LINKAGE

Some models are equipped with a forward/neutral or a forward/neutral/reverse lower unit. It may be necessary to adjust the shift linkage so the desired gear is properly engaged.

To adjust shift linkage, remove cover (C — Fig. E2-2) and loosen the screw fastening the upper and lower shift rods together; DO NOT drop screw into gearcase. Move gear shift lever to neutral position.

⚠WARNING

To prevent accidental starting while rotating the propeller, disconnect the spark plug lead and properly ground lead to engine.

The propeller should rotate freely thereby indicating the lower unit gears are in neutral. If pro-

Illustrations Courtesy Eska

peller does not rotate, reposition the lower shift rod by moving it up or down so lower unit is in neutral. Tighten screw securing shift rods together. Operate gear shift and check for proper gear engagement.

STARTER

The rope for the recoil starter can be renewed without disassembling the starter. Remove the starter assembly from motor, pull rope out fully and hold pulley to prevent rewinding. Refer to Fig. E2-3. Remove old rope and install new rope, making certain that the inner knot is in pocket on underside of pulley. If the old rope was broken, preload the recoil spring by turning the pulley approximately 6 turns before installing new rope.

If the starter does not engage immediately when rope is pulled, make certain that retainer screw (3 — Fig. E2-4) is tightened to 44-55 in.-lbs. (5.1-6.2 N·m) torque.

To overhaul the starter, first remove the rope, then allow the pulley (8) to unwind slowly. Remove retainer screw (3), then lift parts out of housing (10).

NOTE: Spring and keeper (9) are available only as a unit.

When assembling, grease spring (9) lightly then position spring and keeper (9) and pulley (8) in housing (10). Install brake spring (5), starter dog return spring (7) and starter dog (6) as shown in Fig. E2-5. Install retainer screw (3 — Fig. E2-4) and tighten to 45-55 in.-lbs. (5.1-6.2 N·m) torque. Preload the rewind spring by turning the pulley approximately six turns counterclockwise before installing the rope. Refer to Fig. E2-3.

COOLING SYSTEM

The power head is air-cooled by a fan built into the flywheel. Be sure the shroud is in place and the cooling fins are clean and undamaged or engine may overheat.

The lower motor leg is water-cooled. On all models except 3 hp models, a water pump in the gearcase pumps water through a water tube to the exhaust plate beneath the engine. On 3 hp

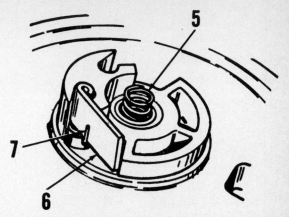

Fig. E2-5 — When assembling, make certain that parts (5, 6 & 7) are assembled as shown. End of dog return spring (7) should pull dog in.

models, forward motion forces water up the water tube. If overheating is suspected and water does not exit from the water outlet holes, check for obstruction of water inlet. Refer to the Outboard Motor Service Manual if water pump or water tube must be inspected as the gearcase must be removed.

PROPELLER

Power is transmitted from the propeller shaft to the propeller by a drive pin which is designed to shear when the propeller contacts an obstruction. The correct drive pin must be used to protect the drive components from damage.

The standard propeller has two blades on models with no gear shift; all other models use a propeller with three blades. The propeller on models with full-range gearshift (forward, neutral, reverse) is designed for right–hand rotation. The propeller on all other models is designed for left hand rotation.

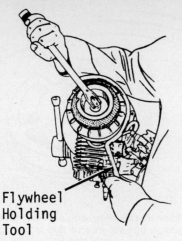

Flywheel
Holding
Tool

Fig. E2-6 — The flywheel may be held using Tecumseh tool 670217 while unscrewing the flywheel retaining nut.

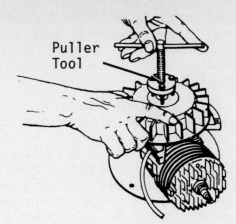

Puller
Tool

Fig. E2-8 — If the flywheel is equipped with tapped holes, a suitable puller tool may be used to remove the flywheel.

To remove the propeller, detach the cotter pin then unscrew the propeller nut. Remove propeller and shear pin.

Before installing the propeller, apply a coating of water-resistant grease to the propeller shaft.

Tune-Up

IGNITION SYSTEM

Two types of ignition system have been used. Some models are equipped with a conventional breaker point type flywheel magneto ignition system. Some models are equipped with a solid-state breakerless flywheel magneto system. The breaker point gap is adjusted on models so equipped as outlined in the following paragraphs. Refer to the SPEED CONTROL LINKAGE section for ignition timing adjustment procedure.

To adjust the breaker point gap on models equipped with breaker points, the flywheel must

be removed. To remove the flywheel, first remove the top engine cover, if so equipped. Remove the manual starter, then drain and remove the fuel tank while being careful not to spill fuel.

⚠ WARNING

To prevent accidental starting, disconnect and properly ground the spark plug lead to the engine.

To remove the flywheel, prevent flywheel rotation by holding the flywheel with Tecumseh tool 670217 as shown in Fig. E2-6 or a strap wrench as shown in Fig. E2-7. Hold the flywheel with the wrench and unscrew the flywheel retaining nut. Use a suitable flywheel puller as shown in Fig. E2-8 or knock-off nut. DO NOT attempt to dislodge flywheel by prying up against flywheel.

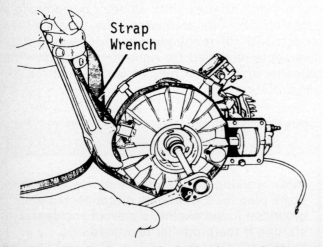

Strap
Wrench

Fig. E2-7 — The flywheel may be held using a suitable strap wrench while unscrewing the flywheel retaining nut.

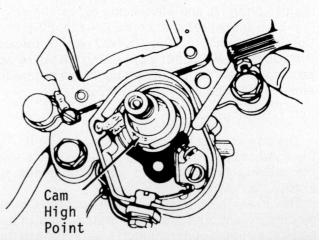

Cam
High
Point

Fig. E2-9 — The breaker point follower arm must rest against the high point of the cam when measuring breaker point gap.

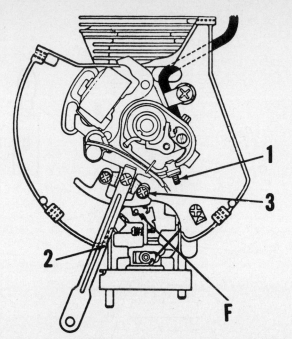

Fig. E2-10 — *View showing speed controls and points of adjustment for motors with pressed in fuel inlet type carburetors and breaker point magneto. Refer to text.*

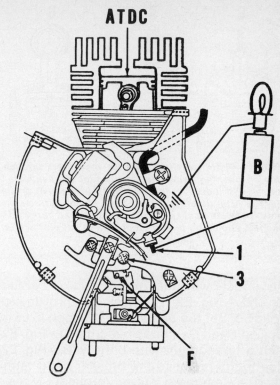

Fig. E2-11 — *View showing speed controls and points of adjustments for motors with fuel inlet located on cover plate and breaker point magneto. Piston position (ATDC) should be set as described in Fig. E2-12.*

⚠WARNING

Be sure suitable tools are used to remove the flywheel. Damage resultant from the misapplication of force or the use of incorrect tools may cause engine damage, engine malfunction or personal injury.

Inspect the flywheel key and renew it if damaged. Be sure to install the correct key.

Remove the cover on the breaker point box for access to the breaker points. Measure the breaker point gap when the point follower arm is contacting the highest point of the breaker point cam (see Fig. E2-9).

Breaker point gap should be 0.018 inch (0.46 mm) for type numbers 642-01 through 642-07B, 642-08A through 642-10, 643-01 through 643-05A, 643-06 through 643-09, and 643-15. Breaker point gap for all other engines should be 0.020 inch (0.51 mm). It is important that breaker point gap is correct and breaker points are in good condition before adjusting the speed control linkage. Ignition timing and throttle opening must be synchronized correctly to provide best operation. Refer to SPEED CONTROL LINKAGE section for checking ignition timing.

During reassembly, tighten the flywheel retaining nut to 25 ft.-lbs. (34 N·m).

SPEED CONTROL LINKAGE.

The ignition timing is advanced by the speed control lever and the throttle is operated by a cam attached to the magneto stator plate. The ignition timing and throttle opening must be synchronized to provide correct operation. Refer to the appropriate following paragraphs for timing the ignition and synchronizing the throttle opening.

MODELS WITH BREAKER POINTS. Before attempting to set ignition timing, make certain that breaker points are in good condition and gap at maximum opening is correct as described in the IGNITION SYSTEM paragraphs. The flywheel must be removed and wires from coil and condenser must be disconnected from breaker point terminal (1 — Fig. E2-10 or E2-11).

On models with fuel inlet fitting pressed into carburetor (26 & 26F — Fig. E2-17), check throttle pickup as follows: Move speed control lever until side is aligned with edge of shroud base (2 — Fig. E2-10). The follower (F) should be almost touching the cam.

NOTE: There should be slight clearance (thickness of paper) between cam and follower.

If clearance between follower and cam is incorrect, loosen screw (3), move idle end of cam as required, then tighten screw (3). Make certain that there is only a slight amount of clearance.

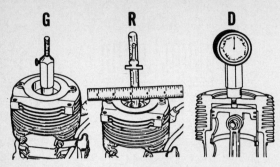

Fig. E2-12 — Piston position can be measured through the spark plug opening using the timing gage (G) available from Tecumseh Products Co. (part 670124), a ruler (R) or dial indicator (D). After determining top dead center, turn crankshaft counterclockwise to set piston before top dead center (BTDC). Crankshaft should be turned clockwise to set piston after top dead center (ATDC).

On models with fuel inlet fitting on carburetor plate (26L — Fig. E2-17), check the throttle pickup as follows: Set the piston at 0.003 inch (0.08 mm). **After** Top Dead Center as described in Fig. E2-12. Attach a timing light with battery (B — Fig. E2-11) or continuity meter to the breaker point terminal (1) and to magneto stator (ground). Move the speed control lever to starboard (clockwise) until the timing light glows (continuity exists through breaker points). Move the speed control lever toward fast position until the breaker points just open (light goes out).

NOTE: Do not move speed control lever too far. The cam follower (F) should just contact cam as the timing light goes out (breaker points open). If follower contacts cam before breaker points open or if there is clearance between follower and cam when breaker points open, loosen screw (3) and move the idle end of cam as required, then tighten screw (3).

On all models, refer to Fig. E2-12 and the following table then position piston at correct timing position:

Type Number	TIMING BTDC
639-06	0.095 in. (2.41 mm)
640-12 thru 640-19A	0.115 in. (2.92 mm)
642-01 thru 642-07B	0.100 in. (2.54 mm)
642-07C	0.085 in. (2.16 mm)
642-08	0.110 in. (2.79 mm)
642-08A thru 642-10	0.100 in. (2.54 mm)
642-13 thru 642-16C	0.085 in. (2.16 mm)
642-16D	0.078 in. (1.98 mm)

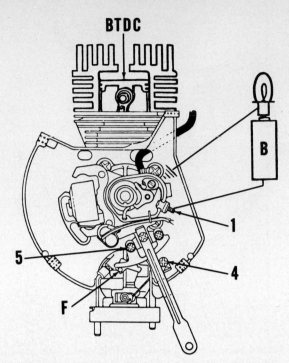

E2-13 — View showing controls and points of adjustment for adjusting maximum ignition advance and maximum throttle opening. The cam and/or carburetor may be damaged if cam attempts to open throttle further than possible.

Type Number	TIMING BTDC
642-17 thru 642-19	0.085 in. (2.16 mm)
642-19A	0.078 in. (1.98 mm)
642-20	0.085 in. (2.16 mm)
642-20A thru 642-22	0.078 in. (1.98 mm)
642-23	0.085 in. (2.16 mm)
642-24	0.085 in. (2.16 mm)
642-25	0.078 in. (1.98 mm)
642-26	0.085 in. (2.16 mm)
642-27 thru 642-28A	0.078 in. (1.98 mm)
642-29	0.085 in. (2.16 mm)
642-30 thru 642-35	0.078 in. (1.98 mm)
643-01 thru 643-14	0.090 in. (2.29 mm)
643-14A, 643-14B, 643-14C	0.085 in. (2.16 mm)
643-15	0.090 in. (2.29 mm)
643-15A thru 643-32A	0.085 in. (2.16 mm)

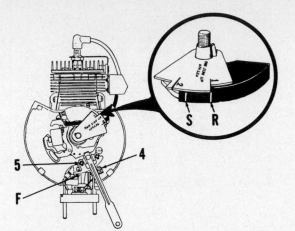

E2-14—Refer to text for adjustment of controls. View shows high speed position. Insert shows location of starting trigger (S) and run trigger (R) in relation to the special tool.

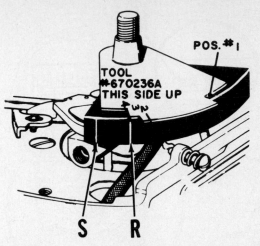

Fig. E2-15—Refer to text for adjustment of the idle pickup. Changing the position of idle speed end of cam will affect high speed adjustment which should be rechecked.

Attach a timing light with battery (B—Fig. E2-13) or continuity meter to the breaker point terminal (1) and to magneto stator plate (ground). Move the speed control lever clockwise until the timing light glows (breaker points closed). Move the speed control lever toward fast position (counterclockwise) until the breaker points just open (light goes out).

NOTE: It may be necessary to loosen the stop bracket (4) in order to allow enough movement to open breaker points. Also, make certain that follower (F) is not binding against cam.

The speed control lever should contact stop bracket (4) just as breaker points open. If incorrect, loosen the retaining screw and reposition stop bracket (4).

After the maximum advance stop (4) is correctly set, move the speed control lever against stop bracket (4) and check the cam follower (F). The follower should have opened the throttle completely, but make certain that cam and follower are not binding. If throttle is not completely open or if follower is binding, loosen screw (5), reposition the high speed end of cam as required then tighten screw (5).

The low speed (throttle pickup) adjustments should be checked again after setting the high speed adjustments. Changes at either end of the throttle cam will affect the location of the other end slightly. Position of cam is correct only after both low and high speed ends check satisfactory.

MODELS WITH SOLID STATE MAGNETOS. The flywheel must be removed and a special tool (part number 670236A for AV600 and AV750 models and part number 670238A for AV817 models) available from Tecumseh Products Co. must be used.

To set the maximum ignition advance, refer to following table and set the piston to the proper

BTDC position per instructions in Fig. E2-12.

Model Number	TIMING BTDC
AV600	0.085 in. (2.16 mm)
AV750	0.095 in. (2.41 mm)
AV817	
Type 640-02 thru 640-06B	0.118 in. (3.0 mm)
Type 640-07 thru 640-21	0.115 in. (2.92 mm)

Position the proper Tecumseh special tool over the flywheel key in crankshaft as shown in Fig. E2-14, then move controls to maximum speed position (counterclockwise). The run trigger (R) should be aligned with edge "1" of special tool as shown in the inset. If incorrect, loosen stop bracket (4) and reposition as necessary to stop movement of speed control when run trigger is aligned with edge "1". After stop (4) is correctly positioned, check the cam follower (F) with controls in maximum speed position. The follower should have opened throttle completely, but make certain that cam and follower are not binding. If throttle is not completely open or if follower is binding, loosen screw (5), reposition the high speed end of cam as required then tighten screw (5).

To check the throttle pickup point, set the piston to the same BTDC position as for high speed adjustment. (see previous ignition timing table). Move the speed control until the run trigger (R—Fig. E2-15) is aligned with the "2" mark on the special tool for AV750 models or the "4" mark on the tool for AV600 models. Special tool 670238A, used to check AV817 models, has only "2" mark for throttle pickup point check. With speed con-

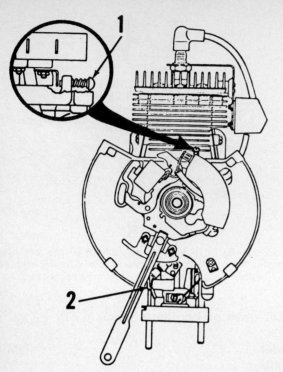

Fig. E2-16—The stop (ground) screw (1) should be adjusted as described in text to stop motor after lever is past shroud bracket (2).

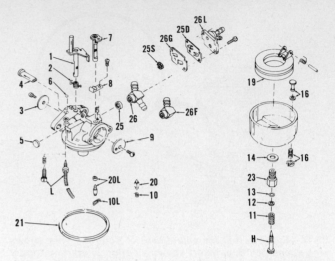

Fig. E2-17—Exploded view of Tecumseh carburetor. On gravity feed models, fitting (26F) is used. On early fuel pump models, pumping element (4), outlet check valve (25), inlet check valve and fitting (26) are used. On latest models with fuel pump, check valves (25D), inlet cover (26L) and screen (25S) are used.

H. High speed mixture needle	13. "O" ring
L. Idle mixture needle	14. Washer
1. Throttle shaft	16. Bowl drain
2. Throttle spring	19. Float
3. Throttle plate	20. Inlet needle
4. Pumping element	20L. Inlet needle & seat
5. Welch plug	21. Seating ring
6. Lead shot	23. Bowl retainer
7. Choke shaft	25. Outlet check valve
8. Detent	25D. Check valves
9. Choke plate	25S. Screen
10. Spring	26. Inlet check valve & fitting
10L. Clip	26F. Inlet fitting
11. Spring	26G. Gasket
12. Washer	26L. Inlet cover

trol in this position, the cam should be just touching the follower (F—Fig. E2-14). Make certain that throttle has not yet moved, but is touching cam. If incorrect loosen screw and reposition the idle speed end of cam as required.

The throttle cam should be rechecked for full throttle opening after adjusting idle pickup. Changes at either end of cam will affect the location of the other end slightly. Position of cam is correct only after both low and high speed ends check satisfactorily.

After the high speed stop and throttle cam are accurately adjusted, move the speed control lever clockwise until lever is past the shroud bracket (2—Fig. E2-16). Turn the ground (stop) screw (1) in until it contacts the stop plate on stator. The ignition will be grounded and motor will stop when the stop plate touches screw (1).

CARBURETOR

All models are equipped with a Tecumseh float type carburetor similar to the carburetor shown in Fig. E2-17.

ADJUSTMENT. All models are equipped with an idle mixture screw (L—Fig. E2-17). The screw may be rotated by turning the knob on the screw or on some models by turning the knob on the control panel. Some models are also equipped with an adjustable high speed mixture screw (H). Clockwise rotation of either the idle or high speed mixture screw will lean the mixture. The outboard motor must be immersed in water when running to prevent damage to the water pump impeller.

To adjust mixture screws, initially turn both screws, if so equipped, out from a lightly seated position. Start the engine and run it until it reaches normal operating temperature. Set speed control to slow speed position. Turn the idle mixture screw clockwise until the engine starts to misfire, not the screw position, then turn the screw counterclockwise until the engine again misfire, note the screw position, then turn the screw so it is midway between the two misfiring positions. If necessary, richen the idle mixture so the engine accelerates cleanly under load without misfiring.

To adjust the high speed mixture screw on models so equipped, use the same procedure as used to adjust the idle mixture screw.

A high altitude modification kit is available for some models with a fixed high speed jet. The kit provides better engine performance by changing the high speed mixture to a mixture suitable for high altitude operation.

OVERHAUL. Several variations of the basic carburetor have been used. Refer to the following procedures which apply to the particular carburetor being serviced.

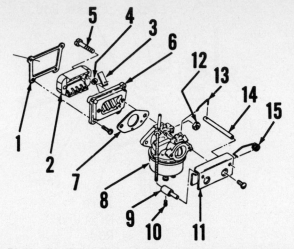

Fig. E2-18 — Exploded view of the reed valve used on AV750 models. Carburetor and reed valve must be removed and installed as a unit.

1. Gasket
2. Reed stop
3. Reed petals
4. Washer
5. Carburetor attaching screw
6. Reed plate
7. Gasket
8. Carburetor
9. Idle adjustment knob
10. Set screw
11. Control panel
12. Nut
13. Choke link
14. Choke rod
15. Stop spring

Note that on models with an AV750 engine, the reed valve unit and carburetor must be removed together from the engine. The carburetor is secured to the reed valve plate by screws entering from the backside of the plate. See Fig. E2-18.

Disassembly of carburetor will depend upon extent of service required. Parts (4, 13, 16, 20, 20L, 21, 25, 25D, 26, 26F and 26G — Fig. E2-17) may be damaged by most commercial carburetor cleaning solvents and must be removed. The gravity feed inlet fitting (26F) and early type check valves (25 and 26) are pressed into carburetor body. The fitting (26 or 26F) should be pulled out of bore, then carefully drill outlet check valve (25) with a 9/64-inch drill to a depth of 1/8-inch (3.2 mm) as shown in Fig. E2-19.

Fig. E2-20 — The 8-32 tap can be used as a puller to remove the outlet check valve from early fuel pump carburetors.

NOTE: Do not drill too far or carburetor body will be damaged.

Thread an 8-32 tap into the outlet check valve, then use the proper size nut and flat washer to convert tap into a puller as shown in Fig. E2-20. Pull check valve out by tightening nut.

Inlet needle (20 — Fig. E2-17) has a Viton tip that seats directly into carburetor body on some models or into a renewable Viton seat (20L) on later models. Seat (20L) may be removed by inserting a small wire hook through hole and pulling seat out of brass liner. Viton seat should be renewed if removed from carburetor body. New seat should be installed with grooved side toward carburetor body, away from needle (20) as shown in Fig. E2-21.

On all models, install throttle plate (3) with stamped lines facing out (toward engine) and at 12 and 3 o'clock positions as shown in Fig. E2-22. If the choke plate (9) is provided with stamped mark, the mark should be toward inside of carburetor and flat should be toward fuel inlet fitting

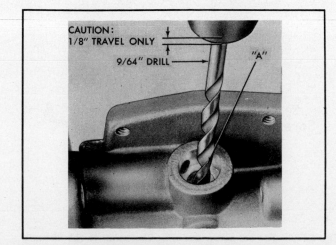

E2-19 — View showing method of removing early type check valve (25 — Fig. E2-17).

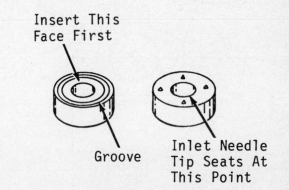

Fig. E2-21 — The Viton seat used on some carburetors must be installed correctly to operate properly. Install seat so grooved side enters carburetor first.

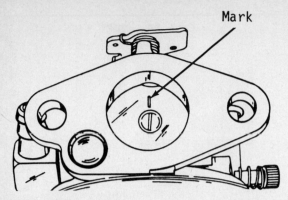

Fig. E2-22 — Mark on throttle plate should be at 12 o'clock position as shown. Some models may have a second mark which should be located at 3 o'clock position.

(26, 26F or 26L). If choke plate is not marked, the flat side should be down toward float bowl.

Float setting should be 0.200-0.220 inch (5.08-5.59 mm), measured with body and float assembly inverted, between free end of float and rim of carburetor body. Preferred method for checking float level is to use Tecumseh float gage 670253A as shown in Fig. E2-23. When installing fuel bowl, the flat under side should be located

Fig. E2-23 — Float height may be set using Tecumseh tool 670253A. Position gage at a right angle to float pin.

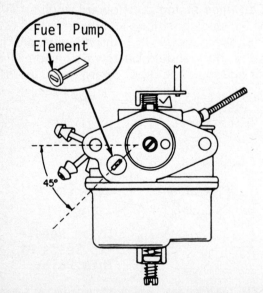

Fig. E2-24 — Fuel pump element (4 — Fig. E2-17) should be installed at a 45° angle as shown.

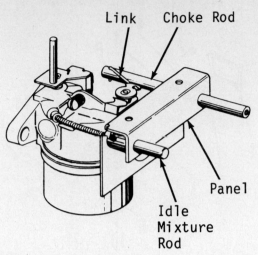

Fig. E2-25 — View of assembled control panel and carburetor.

below the fuel inlet (26, 26F or 26L).

The fuel pumping element (4) is a rubber boot which expands and contracts due to changes in crankcase pressure. The pumping element should be installed at 45° angle as shown in Fig. E2-24. Incorrect installation may interfere with pumping action.

Inspect check valves (25D — Fig. E2-17) on models so equipped. Renew check valves if curled, frayed or damaged.

On AV750 models, coat threads of carburetor retaining screws with Loctite before assembling.

When reinstalling the carburetor control panel on models so equipped, note the following: Refer to Figs. E2-18, E2-25 and E2-26 for views of panel assembly. With set screw loose in collar surrounding idle mixture control rod, rotate control rod so idle mixture screw is one turn out from closed position. Rotate collar so set screw is at 6 o'clock position (down) and tighten set screw. The idle mixture control rod should rotate ½ turn in either direction before contacting spring end. Check control operation after assembly.

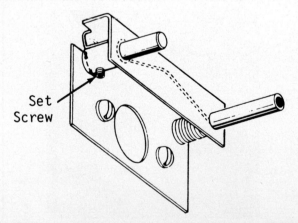

Fig. E2-26 — The set screw securing the collar to the idle mixture control rod should be at 6 o'clock position when idle mixture screw is open one turn.

Illustrations Courtesy Eska

ESKA TWO-CYLINDER MODELS

Year Produced	Model	HP
1973	1925A	9.5
	1906A, 1911A, 1916A	
	1933A, 1967A	9.9
	1926A, 1934A	14.0
	1907A, 1912A, 1917A, 1968A	15.0
1974	1925B	9.5
	1906B, 1911B, 1916B, 1933B	9.9
	1926B	14.0
	1907B, 1912B, 1917B, 1967A	15.0
1975	1906C, 1906D, 1978A, 1978B	9.9
	1907C, 1968C, 1979A	15.0
1976	1978C	9.9
	1979C	15.0
1977	14039	9.9
	14040	15.0
1978	14109A	9.9
	14110A	15.0
1979	14109B, 14136B	9.9
	14110B, 14137B	15.0
1980	14152A	9.9
	14153A	15.0
1981	14152B, 14181B	9.9
	14153B, 14182A	15.0
1982	14152C, 14181B, 14199A, 14204A	9.9
	14153C, 14182C	15.0
1983, 1984 & 1985	14210	9.9
	14211	15.0

These motors are also sold as Explorer, Hanimex, Seaco, Seacruiser-Grant, Sea Hawk, Sears and Wizard models.

Specifications

Bore.................................2.375 in. (60.3 mm)
Stroke ....1.68 in. (42.7 mm)
Number of cylinders 2
Displacement....................14.82 cu. in. (242.8 cc)
Spark plug:
  Champion........................J13Y*
  Electrode gap....................0.030 in. (0.76 mm)
Ignition type ....Solid State
Max. advance timing—BTDC..........0.125 in. (3.18 mm)
Fuel:oil ratio ....50:1†

*Recommended spark plug for models after 1976 is Champion RJ13Y.

†Fuel:oil ratio should be increased to 32:1 if BIA certified TC-W oil is not used.

The engine model number, BV-1500, indicates basic engine configuration and displacement; B-Two cylinder, V-vertical crankshaft, 1500-15.00 cubic inch displacement. If service parts are required, the type number MUST be used. The type number is on a metal tag attached to one of the exhaust cover screws. Typical type numbers are 380 or 380A. When servicing power head, make certain that identification tag is reinstalled.

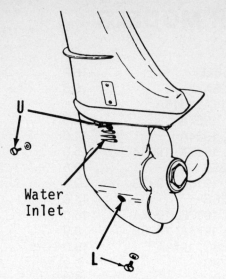

Fig. E3-1 — View of gearcase showing location of vent plug (U), fill/drain plug (L) and water inlet.

Maintenance

LUBRICATION

ENGINE. The power head is lubricated by oil mixed with regular grade, leaded gasoline. Recommended fuel-to-oil ratio is 50:1 when using oils that are BIA certified TC-W. If BIA certified TC-W oil is not available, use a good grade of oil intended for use in outboard motors mixed in a 32:1 ratio with regular grade gasoline.

LOWER UNIT. The lower unit gears and bearings are lubricated by approximately 6 ounces (177 cc) of oil contained in gearcase. SAE 90 outboard gear lubricant should be used. Lubricant should be maintained at level of upper, vent plug (U—Fig. E3-1) when motor is in upright position. Check lubricant level after every 20 hours of operation. The gearcase should be drained and filled with new lubricant at least once each year. Remove both plugs (U and L) to drain gearcase. If excessive water is noted when draining, seals and gaskets should be renewed as outlined in the Outboard Motor Service Manual. Motor should be in

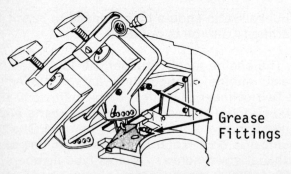

Fig. E3-2 — Lubricate the swivel bracket by injecting grease through grease fittings.

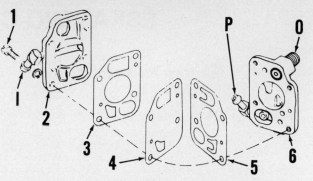

Fig. E3-3 — Exploded view of fuel pump used on engines with type numbers 381, 381A, 381B and 381C.

I. Fuel inlet	1. Screw	4. Diaphragm
O. Fuel outlet	2. Cover	5. Check valve
P. Pulse line	3. Gasket	6. Body

upright position when refilling gearcase. Insert filler tube in fill/drain plug opening (L) and squeeze tube until lubricant reaches level of vent plug opening (U). Install and tighten upper plug then remove filler tube and install lower plug. Make sure that gaskets on plugs are in good condition.

Every 60 days lubricate exposed screw threads or rubbing surfaces with water-resistant lithium grease or oil. Inject grease into grease fittings on swivel bracket (see Fig. E2-2). Apply grease to manual starter spiral shaft.

FUEL SYSTEM

Periodically inspect the fuel lines and connections for leakage and damage.

Some carburetors are equipped with a fuel filter (20 — Fig. E3-13) on the carburetor. If dirty fuel is suspected of causing poor engine performance, remove the fuel pump and inspect the fuel filter on the carburetor. Clean or renew the filter if dirty.

FUEL PUMP. Models with engines with type numbers 381, 381A, 381B and 381C are equipped with a diaphragm type fuel pump. The outlet of the fuel pump is threaded and the pump outlet screws into the side of the carburetor.

The pump operates due to pressure and vacuum pulsations received from the engine crankcase through the pulse line. The crankcase pulsations actuate the diaphragm in the fuel pump which draws fuel from the fuel tank and forces fuel to the carburetor. Two flap type check valves prevent reverse fuel flow.

The carburetor must be removed before the fuel pump can be unscrewed from the carburetor. Refer to Fig. E3-3 for an exploded view of pump. Unscrew the four retaining screws and separate the pump components for access to internal components. Inspect the diaphragm and check valves for wear, fraying and other damage. When installing the fuel pump on the carburetor, coat pipe threads of fuel pump with antiseize compound.

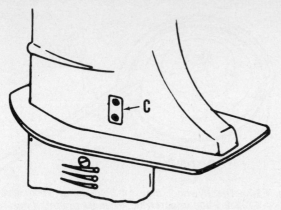

Fig. E3-4 — Remove cover (C) for access to shift rod screw.

SHIFT LINKAGE

It may be necessary to adjust the shift linkage so the desired gear is properly engaged.

To adjust shift linkage, remove cover (C — Fig. E3-4) and loosen the screw fastening the upper and lower shift rods together; DO NOT drop screw into gearcase. Move gear shift lever to neutral position.

⚠WARNING

To prevent accidental starting while rotating the propeller, disconnect the spark plug lead and properly ground lead to engine.

The propeller should rotate freely in both directions thereby indicating the lower unit gears are in neutral. If propeller does not rotate, reposition the lower shift rod by moving it up or down. Three "clicks" should be heard as the lower unit is shifted from forward to neutral to reverse, or vice versa. The middle click indicates the unit is in neutral. Tighten screw securing the shift rods together. Operate gear shift lever and check for proper gear engagement.

STARTER

The majority of manual starter service may be performed with starter still attached to power head; however, starter may be removed as an assembly if engine work is to be performed.

To remove starter assembly, tie a slip knot in rope next to guide (G — Fig. E3-5) on starter bracket. Remove rope handle then remove screws securing mount bracket (11) to power head.

Starter should be installed so teeth of starter gear are at least 1/16 inch (1.6 mm) below base of flywheel teeth. If starter is installed too close to flywheel, gears will bind and starter will be

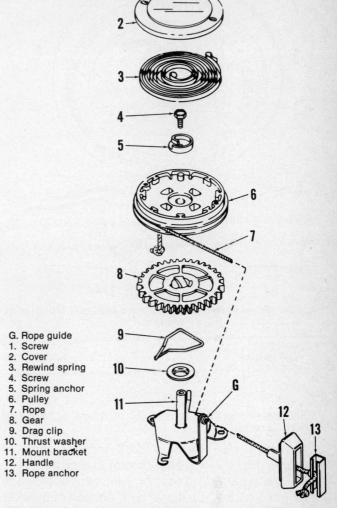

G. Rope guide
1. Screw
2. Cover
3. Rewind spring
4. Screw
5. Spring anchor
6. Pulley
7. Rope
8. Gear
9. Drag clip
10. Thrust washer
11. Mount bracket
12. Handle
13. Rope anchor

Fig. E3-5 — Exploded view of manual starter assembly typical of all models.

damaged by engine operation. Test installation of starter with spark plugs removed to be sure gears disengage completely. Starter mount bracket has a slotted hole to allow gear engagement adjustment.

To disassemble starter for service, remove handle and allow rope to be pulled onto starter so rewind spring tension is relieved. Remove cover (2) only after spring tension has been released. Rewind spring can be renewed.

⚠WARNING

Care should be exercised when working with or around a coiled starter rewind spring as sudden uncoiling can cause injury. Safety eyewear and gloves are recommended.

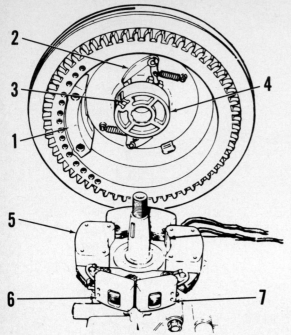

Fig. E3-6 — View of solid-state magneto assembly typical of all models.

1. Magnet
2. Flyweight
3. Trigger magnet
4. Sleeve assy.

5. Ignition module
6. High speed coil
7. Low speed coil

To remove pulley wheel (6), remove screw and spring hub (5).

Standard size rope is 5/32 inch (4 mm) in diameter and 69 inches (175 cm) in length.

Before assembling starter, lubricate both sides of thrust washer (10), spiral axle portion of bracket (11) and pulley spiral with an EP lithium grease. Screw used to retain spring anchor (5) should be tightened to 35-45 in.-lbs. (3.95-5.08 N·m) torque. Screw must be tight enough to prevent spring anchor from turning and releasing rewind spring tension.

COOLING SYSTEM

All models are equipped with an impeller type water pump located in the lower unit that circulates water through the power head.

⚠CAUTION

Do not operate outboard motor unless the lower unit is immersed in water, otherwise, the water pump impeller will be damaged.

If cooling system problems are encountered, first check the water inlet (see Fig. E3-1) for

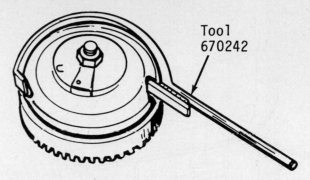

Fig. E3-7 — The flywheel may be held using Tecumseh tool 670242 while unscrewing flywheel retaining nut.

material which may be blocking the inlet. If the water pump must be inspected, refer to the Outboard Motor Service Manual.

PROPELLER

Power is transmitted from the propeller shaft to the propeller by a drive pin which is designed to shear when the propeller contacts an obstruction. The propeller is equipped with a cushion hub to lessen impact. Be sure the correct drive pin (shear pin) is installed or the lower unit may be damaged if an obstruction is struck.

All models are equipped with a three-blade, right-hand propeller.

⚠WARNING

When working on or around the propeller the spark plug lead should be disconnected and grounded to the engine to prevent accidental starting if the propeller is rotated.

To remove the propeller, detach the cotter pin then unscrew the propeller nut. Remove propeller and shear pin.

Before installing the propeller, apply a coating of water-resistant grease to the propeller shaft.

Tune-Up

IGNITION SYSTEM

All models are equipped with a breakerless, solid-state ignition system. Servicing the ignition system is not normally required. Refer to Fig. E3-6 for identification of ignition system components. Refer to the following section for ignition timing adjustment procedure.

IGNITION TIMING. If stator, flywheel, advance weights or trigger magnet have been changed,

Illustrations Courtesy Eska

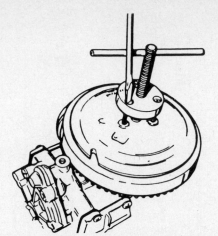

Fig. E3-8 — Use a suitable flywheel puller to remove flywheel.

then ignition timing should be checked. If the stator plate is moved without prior marking, check ignition timing. If ignition timing is believed incorrect, use the following procedure for checking ignition timing.

⚠WARNING

To prevent accidental starting, disconnect and properly ground the spark plug lead to the engine.

The flywheel must be removed to check or adjust ignition timing. Remove the engine top cover. Prevent flywheel rotation using Tecumseh tool 670242 (see Fig. E3-7) or a suitable strap wrench. Unscrew the flywheel retaining nut and use a suitable puller as shown in Fig. E3-8 to remove the flywheel.

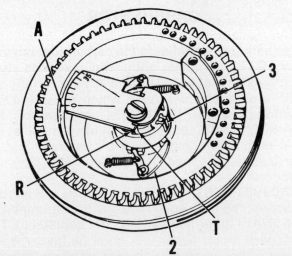

Fig. E3-9 — Install Tecumseh tool 670243 and check advancer sleeve movement as outlined in text.

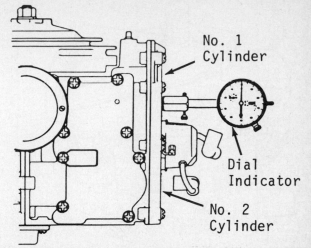

Fig. E3-10 — Install a dial indicator in the spark plug hole for number 1 cylinder and check ignition timing as outlined in text.

⚠WARNING

Be sure suitable tools are used to remove the flywheel. Damage resultant from the misapplication of force or the use of incorrect tools may cause engine damage, engine malfunction or personal injury.

Full movement range of advancer mechanism must be checked first. Position Tecumseh tool 670243 in trigger sleeve assembly in flywheel. Tabs (T — Fig. E3-9) of tool should engage ribs (R) in trigger sleeve. Place a pencil mark (A) on flywheel adjacent to "O" degree mark on tool. Grasp advance mechanism flyweights (2) and pull them out fully against their stop. Do not use tool to turn trigger assembly. Observe and record degree mark on special tool adjacent to pencil mark on flywheel.

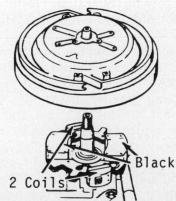

Fig. E3-11 — Late type ignition system is identified by black ignition modules and only two coils. Early type ignition system has four coils, or it has only two coils but the ignition modules are orange.

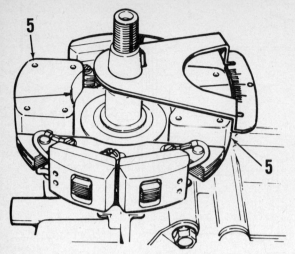

Fig. E3-12 — The stator assembly is timed using Tecumseh tool 670244 as outlined in text.

To determine the correct position of the stator assembly, the piston in number 1 cylinder (top cylinder) must be positioned in the cylinder at the point where ignition occurs. To determine piston position, remove the spark plugs and install a dial indicator as shown in Fig. E3-10 in the number 1 (top) cylinder spark plug hole. Determine top dead center for the piston and zero the dial indicator for piston TDC (temporarily reinstall the flywheel so it can be used to rotate the crankshaft). Refer to Fig. E3-11 and determine if ignition is an early or late version (late version has only two coils and the ignition modules are black). Rotate the flywheel in a clockwise direction and position the piston at 0.125 inch (3.18 mm) BTDC if equipped with early version of ignition system. Position the piston at 0.107 inch (2.72 mm) BTDC if equipped with late version of ignition system.

Place Tecumseh timing tool 670244 on crankshaft. Make sure tool is fully seated on crankshaft and Woodruff key (Fig. E3-12). Make sure crankshaft is not moved from desired position during timing operation. Refer to degree measurement obtained when checking advance mechanism.

If trigger sleeve assembly movement was 30°, set stator so that mark on ignition module is aligned with "0" degree mark on tool. If trigger sleeve movement was greater than 30°, turn stator **clockwise** past "0" degree mark, the number of degrees that trigger sleeve assembly moved more then 30°. For example, if trigger sleeve movement was 33°, stator should be turned clockwise until 3° mark on timing tool is aligned with mark on ignition module. If trigger sleeve movement was only 28°, turn stator 2° counterclockwise from point when line on ignition module and "0" degree mark on timing tool align.

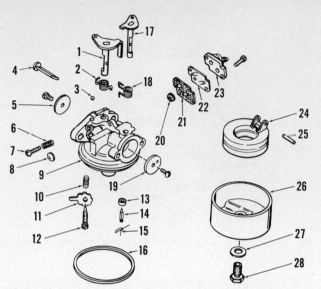

Fig. E3-13 — Exploded view of typical carburetor used on all models. Fuel pump components (4, 21, 22 and 23) are not used if engine is equipped with fuel pump shown in Fig. E3-3.

1. Throttle shaft
2. Return spring
3. Lead shot
4. Pump element
5. Throttle plate
6. Spring
7. Idle speed screw
8. Welch plug
9. Body
10. Spring
11. Star wheel
12. Idle mixture screw
13. Viton needle seat
14. Inlet needle
15. Clip
16. Gasket
17. Choke shaft
18. Return spring
19. Choke plate
20. Screen
21. Gasket
22. Check valve
23. Cover
24. Float
25. Pin
26. Fuel bowl
27. Gasket
28. Main jet

When assembling components, apply a small amount of E.P. lithium grease on portion of crankshaft adjacent to trigger sleeve assembly. Make sure that no grease is on crankshaft taper when reassembling unit. Tighten flywheel nut to 30-35 ft.-lbs. (41-47 N·m).

SPEED CONTROL LINKAGE

The speed control linkage only controls throttle position. No adjustment is required. Periodically inspect linkage for worn or damaged components which may cause binding.

CARBURETOR

All models are equipped with a Tecumseh float type carburetor similar to the carburetor shown in Fig. E3-13. Models with engines with type numbers 381, 381A, 381B and 381C are equipped with a separate fuel pump which is serviced as outlined in FUEL SYSTEM section of the MAINTENANCE section. On all other models, the fuel pump is attached to the carburetor and is serviced as outlined in the carburetor overhaul section.

ADJUSTMENT. The idle mixture is adjustable, however, the high speed mixture is determined by the size of an orifice which is not adjustable. The outboard motor lower unit must be immersed in water when running to prevent damage to water pump impeller.

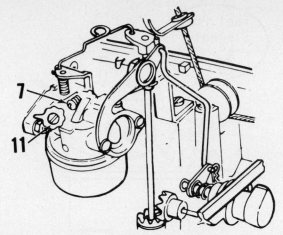

Fig. E3-14 — View showing location of idle speed screw (7) and idle mixture star wheel (11).

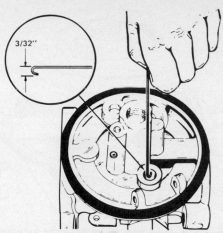

Fig. E3-16 — Viton inlet needle seat (13 — Fig. E3-13) may be removed by pushing a small hook through seat and pulling.

To adjust idle mixture, press star wheel (11 — Fig. E3-13) in and hold it in this position while adjusting screw (12). Turn mixture screw (12) in until it is lightly seated then back out one turn. Hold star wheel (11) in and turn it so that projection is at 12 o'clock position (straight up), then let it out to engage screw (12). Start and run motor until operating temperature is reached. Place motor in forward gear and turn speed control grip fully to slow speed position. Turn star wheel, without pushing in, slowly out (counterclockwise) until engine speed decreases from rich mixture. Turn star wheel back in until engine is idling smoothly. Adjust idle speed screw (7 — Fig. E3-14) to obtain slowest possible smooth idle speed (approximately 750-1000 rpm). Mixture should be rich enough to provide smooth acceleration from idle to full throttle and not misfire when decelerating.

To adjust maximum throttle opening in neutral and reverse on models prior to 1978, shift motor to neutral and turn speed control grip until throttle bracket is touching locknut lever (L — Fig. E3-15). Engine speed should be 2500-3500 rpm. If engine speed is not within limits, loosen set screw and reposition lever (A).

OVERHAUL. When disassembling carburetor for service, note location of identification marks on choke shutter (19 — Fig. E3-13) and throttle shutter (5). Carburetors may be cleaned in commercial solvents after complete disassembly and removal of all rubber or nylon parts and gaskets. After cleaning, all passages should be cleared with compressed air.

Viton inlet needle seat (13) should not be removed unless renewal is intended. To remove seat (13), fashion a small hook from a paper clip, insert hook through seat and pull seat out of brass sleeve (Fig. E3-16). Do not try to remove brass sleeve. New Viton inlet needle seat may be driven into brass sleeve with a 5/32 inch (4 mm) flat punch after lubricating sleeve with a drop of light oil. Seat must be installed with grooved side (G — Fig. E3-17) down. Make sure the needle seat is completely seated in brass sleeve (S).

Float setting should be 0.185-0.235 inch (4.7-6.0 mm) for carburetors used on type 380 through

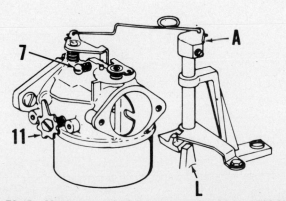

Fig. E3-15 — Maximum speed in neutral should be 2500-3500 rpm. Speed is adjusted by repositioning lever (A) when throttle bracket is against lockout lever (L).

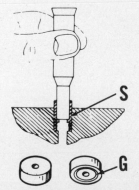

Fig. E3-17 — Use a 5/32 inch (4 mm) flat punch to install new inlet needle seat. Install seat with grooved side (G) down.

Illustrations Courtesy Eska

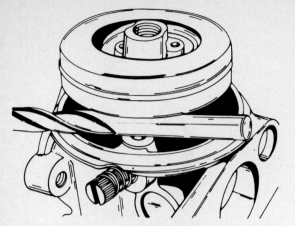

Fig. E3-18 — Float level should be checked by placing an appropriate size drill bit between float and carburetor body. Refer to text for proper size drill bit.

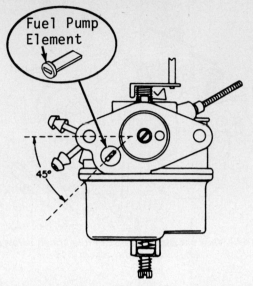

Fig. E3-19 — Fuel pump element (4 — Fig. E3-13) should be installed at a 45° angle as shown.

380C and 382 through 382D engines and 0.155-0.217 inch (3.9-5.5 mm) for carburetors used on type 381 through 381C, 383 through 383C and 385 engines. Preferred method for checking float setting is to place an appropriate size drill bit between carburetor body and float assembly (Fig. E3-18). Recommended drill bit sizes are #4 (0.209 inch) for carburetor used on type 380 through 380C and 382 through 382D engines and #13 (0.185 inch) for carburetor used on type 381 through 381C, 383 through 383C and 385 engines.

On models with an attached fuel pump (components 4, 21, 22 and 23 — Fig. E3-13), the fuel pumping element (4) is a rubber boot which expands and contracts due to changes in crankcase pressure. The pumping element should be installed at a 45° angle as shown in Fig. E3-19. Incorrect installation may interfere with pumping action. Inspect check valves (22 — Fig. E3-13) and renew if flap valves are curled, frayed or damaged.

When installing fuel pump on carburetor of units with separate fuel pump, coat pipe threads of fuel pump with an antiseize compound.

FORCE

US MARINE CORP.
105 Marine Drive
Hartford, Wisconsin 53027

4 HP MODELS

Specifications

HP/rpm 4.0/5250
Bore . . . . .2 in.
(50.8 mm)
Stroke. . . . . .1-19/32 in.
(40.5 mm)
Number of cylinders 1
Displacement. . . . . .5.0 cu. in.
(82 cc)
Compression at cranking speed
(average, with recoil starter) . . . . . . .110-125 psi
(759-862 kPa)
Spark plug:
Champion . . . . .L86 (Canada RL86)
Electrode gap . . . . .0.030 in.
(0.76 mm)
Breaker point gap .0.020 in.
(0.5 mm)
Fuel:oil ratio 50:1

MAINTENANCE

LUBRICATION

ENGINE. The engine is lubricated by oil mixed with the fuel. The recommended fuel:oil ratio for normal operation is 50:1. During engine break-in the fuel:oil ratio should be 25:1.

The manufacturer recommends the use of no-lead automotive gasoline although regular and premium grades may be used. The gasoline octane rating must be 85 or higher.

LOWER UNIT. The lower unit gears and bearings are lubricated by oil contained in the gearcase. Only a noncorrosive, EP90 outboard gear oil should be used. The gearcase should be drained and refilled every 100 hours or every six months, and fluid maintained at the level of the upper (vent) plug hole.

The outboard motor must be upright when draining or filling gearcase. Remove both plugs (V and D—Fig. F1-1) on port side of gearcase when draining or filling. To fill with lubricant, force lubricant into lower plug hole (D) until lubricant reaches lower edge of upper plug hole (V). Install

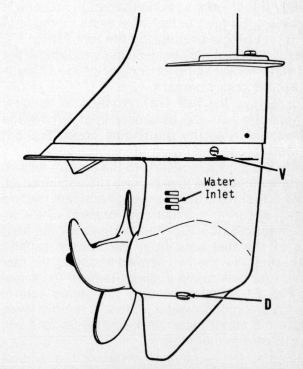

Fig. F1-1 — View showing location of water inlet ports, vent plug (V) and fill/drain plug (D).

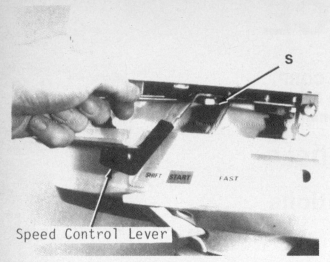

Fig. F1-2—Unscrew retaining screw (S) to remove speed control lever.

new gaskets on plugs, if necessary. Install upper plug (V) before removing lubricant dispenser so fluid remains in gearcase, then remove dispenser and install lower plug (D).

After approximately every 60 days of use, a good quality water-resistant grease should be injected in all grease fittings.

FUEL SYSTEM

FUEL FILTER. All models are equipped with a mesh fuel filter which is integral with the fuel tank fuel fitting. The fuel filter should be inspected and cleaned at least once each season, or more frequently if fuel stoppage due to foreign material is a problem. Empty the fuel tank or be prepared to catch fuel before unscrewing the fuel fitting.

FUEL TANK. It may be necessary to remove the fuel tank for cleaning or for access to underlying engine components.

To remove the fuel tank proceed as follows: Remove the fuel cap assembly then remove the screws which secure the engine cover. Pull out the starter rope and lift off the engine cover. Tie a knot in the starter rope next to the starter, remove the rope handle and then remove the engine cover.

Drain fuel from the fuel tank. Unscrew the two screws securing the fuel tank bracket to the intake manifold (10—Fig. F1-12). Unscrew the front legs of the fuel tank from the bottom support plate. Unscrew the two screws securing the rear of the fuel tank to the engine. Remove the screw (S—Fig. F1-2) which secures the speed control lever to the ignition stator plate and remove lever. Rotate the stator plate clockwise as far as it will go. Lift off the fuel tank.

Reinstall the fuel tank by reversing the removal procedure. Note that the stator plate must be in the same position during installation as it was

when the tank was removed. Note that spacers are used between the front tank legs and the support plate.

SHIFT LINKAGE

All models may be shifted from neutral to forward and vice versa. The shift lever is connected to an upper shift rod which is coupled to the lower shift rod in the gearcase.

⚠WARNING

When working on or around the propeller the spark plug lead should be disconnected and grounded to the engine to prevent accidental starting if the propeller is rotated.

If shifting is difficult or the unit won't stay in gear, the linkage should be adjusted or checked for misadjustment. Remove cover on port side of motor leg and loosen shift coupler screw shown in Fig. F1-3. Pull up the lower shift rod so the lower unit is in neutral (be sure to pull up all the way and check by rotating propeller to be sure unit is in neutral). Place the gear shift lever in neutral (horizontal) position and tighten the shift coupler screw. Reinstall cover.

STARTER

The manual starter is attached to the top of the fuel tank. To remove the starter, first remove the engine cover as outlined in the FUEL TANK section, then unscrew the fasteners retaining the starter and lift off the starter.

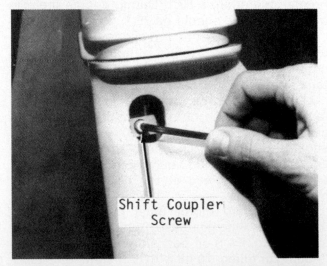

Fig. F1-3—The shift coupler screw is accessible after removing the cover on the motor leg. Refer to text for shift linkage adjustment.

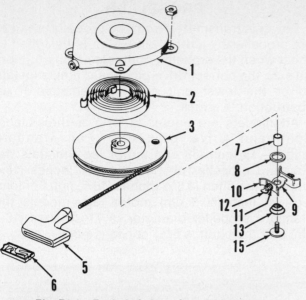

Fig. F1-4 — Exploded view of manual starter.

1. Starter housing
2. Rewind spring
3. Pulley
5. Rope handle
6. Retainer
7. Bushing
8. Washer
9. Lever
10. Friction shoe
11. Spring
12. Retainer
13. Conical spring
15. Screw

To disassemble the starter, proceed as follows: Untie the knot in the rope and allow the rope to wind into the starter (if the rewind spring or rope is broken this step is unnecessary). Remove "E" ring or screw (15 — Fig. F1-4). Remove friction shoe assembly along with remaining components on pulley shown in Fig. F1-4. Carefully lift out rope

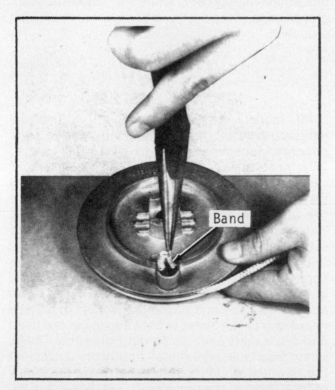

Fig. F1-6 — To install a banded starter rope end, double the rope end over and push the banded end back into the cavity.

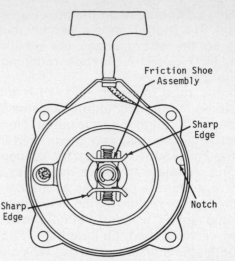

Fig. F1-7 — View of starter showing proper installation of friction shoe assembly. Note position of sharp edges on friction shoes.

pulley while being careful not to dislodge the rewind spring. If the rewind spring must be removed, position the starter housing so the spring side is towards the floor or bench then tap the starter housing against the floor or bench so the spring dislodges and uncoils.

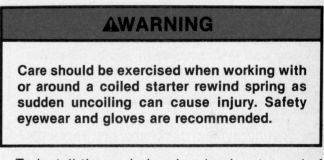

⚠WARNING

Care should be exercised when working with or around a coiled starter rewind spring as sudden uncoiling can cause injury. Safety eyewear and gloves are recommended.

To install the rewind spring, hook outer end of spring around post in starter housing and wind spring into housing in a counterclockwise direction from outer spring end. If a new spring is installed, position spring assembly in housing then carefully remove coil retaining bands. Lubricate spring with grease.

Rope length should be 48 inches (122 cm). If the rope has a banded end, install rope as follows: Thread the unbanded end of the starter rope into the puley until the banded end protrudes as shown in Fig. F1-6. Fold the banded end over as shown so the rope id doubled over. Pull the rope taut so the doubled-over rope end is seated in the pulley.

If the rope is unbanded, pass the rope through the rope hole, tie a knot in the rope end then pull the rope taut into the rope cavity of the pulley.

Lubricate the shaft in the starter housing with a light coat of grease. Install the rope pulley in the starter housing while engaging inner spring end in the slot in the pulley. Hold the rope in pulley notch (Fig. F1-7) during installation. Assemble the remaining components on the pulley as shown in Fig. F1-4. The friction shoe assembly must be installed so the sharp edges are positioned as shown in Fig. F1-7. Install retaining screw (15 — Fig. F1-4).

With the rope in notch (Fig. F1-7) rotate the pulley three full turns counterclockwise and pass the rope end through the rope outlet. Tie a knot in the rope. Pull the rope and check starter action. With the rope pulled out as far as possible, it should be possible to rotate the pulley an additional 1/8 to 3/8 of a turn. This additional rotation ensures that the rewind spring is not fully extended. If the pulley will not rotate the additional amount, recheck the rope length.

Reinstall the starter on the gas tank and install the engine cover.

COOLING SYSTEM

All models are equipped with an impeller type water pump located in the lower unit that circulates water through the power head.

⚠CAUTION

Do not operate outboard motor unless the lower unit is immersed in water, otherwise, the water pump impeller will be damaged.

If cooling system problems are encountered, first check the water inlet (see Fig. F1-1) for material which may be blocking the inlet. If the water pump must be inspected, refer to the Outboard Motor Service Manual.

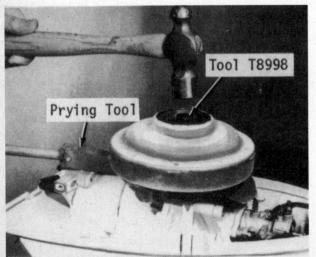

Fig. F1-8 — "Pop" the flywheel loose by carefully prying up against the flywheel while striking the crankshaft end as outlined in text.

PROPELLER

Power is transmitted from the propeller shaft to the propeller by a drive pin which is designed to shear when the propeller contacts an obstruction. Be sure the correct drive pin (shear pin) is installed or the lower unit may be damaged if an obstruction is struck.

All models are equipped with a three-blade, right-hand drive propeller. For standard length — 15 inch (38 cm) motor leg — models the standard propeller diameter is 7¼ inches (18.4 cm) and the pitch is 6½ inches (16.5 cm). For long leg — 20 inch (50.8 cm) motor leg — models the standard propeller diameter is 7¼ inches (18.4 cm) and the pitch is 5½ inches (14 cm).

⚠WARNING

When working on or around the propeller the spark plug lead should be disconnected and grounded to the engine to prevent accidental starting if the propeller is rotated.

To remove the propeller, detach the cotter pin then unscrew the propeller nut. Drive the shear pin out of the propeller and propeller shaft. Pull the propeller off the propeller shaft.

Reinstall the propeller by reversing the removal procedure. Apply a coating of water-resistant grease to the propeller shaft before installing the propeller.

Tune-Up

IGNITION SYSTEM

All models are equipped with a flywheel magneto type ignition system. All ignition components except the spark plug are located underneath the flywheel.

To adjust breaker point gap, the flywheel must be removed. To remove the flywheel, first remove the fuel tank as outlined in the previous FUEL TANK section. Unscrew the flywheel retaining screw. A band type wrench may be used to hold the flywheel during screw loosening. Screw a cap screw of the correct diameter and pitch into the end of the crankshaft so the screw head bears against only the end of the crankshaft (it may be necessary to use spacers between the screw head and crankshaft end), or install Force tool T8998. Using a suitable prying tool, lightly pry up against the flywheel while moderately striking the screw or tool T8998 in the crankshaft end. See Fig. F1-8. The flywheel should "pop" free.

Illustrations Courtesy Force

Remove the flywheel and inspect it for cracks or other damage. Be sure to inspect the tapered center portion of the flywheel as well. A damaged flywheel must be discarded as it may fly apart at high engine rpm.

To check the breaker point gap, install the flywheel retaining screw in the end of the crankshaft then rotate the crankshaft clockwise by turning the screw. Rotate the crankshaft so the index mark on the breaker cam is aligned with the breaker point follower arm as shown in Fig. F1-9. The breaker point gap should be 0.020 inch (0.5 mm). Loosen breaker point retaining screw (S) to adjust breaker point gap. After tightening screw (S), rotate the crankshaft and recheck point gap. Lubricate the cam wiper felt with a small amount of breaker point cam lubricant. Do not apply too much lubricant as it may be thrown off the cam onto the breaker points causing misfiring.

Be sure the tapered mating surfaces of the crankshaft and flywheel are clean and dry then install the flywheel. Tighten the flywheel retaining screw to 15-20 ft.-lbs. (20-27 N·m). Reinstall the fuel tank.

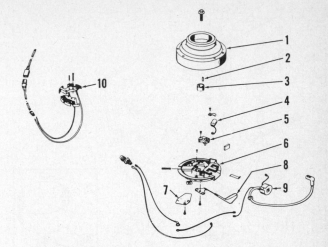

Fig. F1-10 — Exploded view of ignition components.

1. Flywheel
2. Key
3. Breaker cam
4. Condenser
5. Breaker points
6. Stator plate
7. Cam
8. Speed control lever
9. Ignition coil
10. Alternator stator

SPEED CONTROL LINKAGE

The speed control lever is connected to the magneto stator plate to advance or retard ignition timing. Throttle linkage is synchronized to open the throttle as magneto timing is advanced.

To check speed control linkage, remove the fuel tank. Turn speed control lever until throttle cam shown in Fig. F1-11 contacts cam follower (F). Mark (M) on throttle cam should be in center of cam follower when cam contacts follower. If mark is not aligned with cam follower centerline, loosen throttle cam retaining screw and relocate cam. Recheck synchronization after relocating cam.

Idle speed is adjustable. An adjusting screw bears against the speed control lever at idle. Turn the idle speed screw so the engine idles at

Fig. F1-9 — Align index mark on point cam with breaker point follower arm when measuring breaker point gap. Loosen screw (S) to adjust gap.

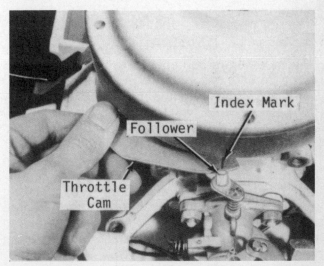

Fig. F1-11 — The centerline of the cam follower should align with the index mark on the throttle cam when follower contacts the cam. See text.

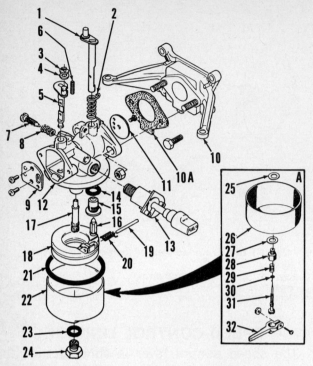

Fig. F1-12—Exploded view of Walbro LMB carburetor.

1 . Throttle shaft	17. Nozzle
2 . Spring	18. Float
3 . "E" ring	19. Float pin
4 . Washer	20. Spring
5 . Choke shaft	21. Gasket
6 . Stop spring	22. Fuel bowl
7 . Idle mixture screw	23. Gasket
8 . Spring	24. High speed jet
9 . Choke plate	25. Gasket
10. Intake manifold	26. Fuel bowl
10A. Gasket	27. Gasket
11. Throttle plate	28. Needle seat
12. Body	29. Spring
13. Fuel valve	30. "O" ring
14. Gasket	31. High speed mixture
15. Fuel inlet seat	screw
16. Fuel inlet valve	32. Lever

800-1200 rpm when the screw contacts the speed control lever.

CARBURETOR

All models are equipped with the Walbro LMB float type carburetor shown in Fig. F1-12.

ADJUSTMENT. The idle mixture is adjusted by turning the idle mixture adjustment screw (7 — Fig. F1-12) on all models. The high speed mixture is controlled by high speed jet (24).

Initial setting of idle mixture screw is one turn out from a lightly seated position. The idle mixture adjustment screw can be turned by inserting a screwdriver through the hole in the starboard side of the lower engine cover. Before adjusting idle mixture, run the engine until normal operating temperature is reached.

NOTE: The outboard motor lower unit must be immersed in water when the engine is running to prevent damage to the water pump impeller.

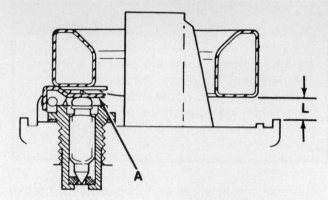

Fig. F1-13 — Float level (L) should be 1/8 inch (3.2 mm). Adjust float level by bending tab (A).

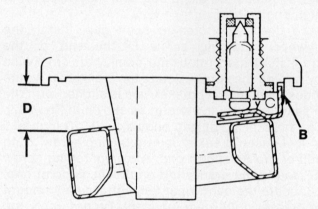

Fig. F1-14 — Float drop (D) should be 5/16 inch (8 mm). Adjust float drop by bending tab (B).

With the engine running at idle speed, turn the idle mixture screw (7 — Fig. F1-12) clockwise until the engine starts to misfire. Note the screw's position. Turn the screw counterclockwise until the engine again misfires and note the screw's position. Turn the screw so it is midway between the two misfiring positions.

High speed mixture is controlled by main jet (24). The following table will assist in selecting the correct main jet size.

Altitude	Main Jet Size
Sea Level-3000 ft.	0.038
(0-914 m)	
3000-5000 ft.	0.037
(914-1524 m)	
5000-7000 ft.	0.036
(1524-2134 m)	
Above 7000 ft.	0.035
(Above 2134 m)	

OVERHAUL. Refer to Fig. F1-12 for an exploded view of the carburetor. Note the following points when overhauling the carburetor. Install throttle plate (11) so the stamped number side is towards the engine and the three holes are towards the idle mixture screw side of the carburetor. Install the choke plate (9) so the stamped number side is towards carburetor intake and the oblong slot is on fuel inlet side of carburetor. Install float spring (20) so spring assists float in closing fuel inlet valve. Float level (L — Fig. F1-13) is measured with the carburetor inverted. Float level (L) should be 1/8 inch (3.2 mm) and is adjusted by bending tab (A). Float drop (D — Fig. F1-14) is measured with carburetor in normal upright position. Float drop should be 5/16 inch (8 mm) and is adjusted by bending tab (B).

FORCE 9.9 AND 15 HP

Specifications

	9.9 HP	15 HP
Hp/rpm	9.9/4750	15/5100
Bore	2-3/16 in.	2¼ in.
	(55 mm)	(57 mm)
Stroke	1-3/4 in.	1-15/16 in.
	(44 mm)	(49 mm)
Number of cylinders	2	2
Displacement	13.15 cu. in.	15.41 cu. in.
	(216 cc)	(252 cc)
Compression at cranking speed (average)	105-125 psi	125-135 psi
	(725-863kPa)	(863-931kPa)
Spark plug:		
Champion	L4J	L4J
Electrode gap	0.030 in.	0.030 in.
	(0.76 mm)	(0.76 mm)
Breaker point gap	0.020 in.	0.020 in.
	(0.51 mm)	(0.51 mm)
Ignition timing	See Text	See Text
Carburetor make	Walbro LMB	Walbro LMB
Fuel:oil ratio:		
Normal	50:1	50:1
Break-in	25:1	25:1

Maintenance

LUBRICATION

ENGINE. The engine is lubricated by oil mixed with the fuel. The recommended fuel:oil ratio for normal operation is 50:1. During engine break-in the fuel:oil ratio should be 25:1.

The manufacturer recommends the use of no-lead automotive gasoline although regular and premium grades may be used. The gasoline octane rating must be 85 or higher.

LOWER UNIT. The lower unit gears and bearings are lubricated by oil contained in the gearcase. Only noncorrosive, leaded, EP90 outboard gear oil should be used. The gearcase fluid level should be checked after every 30 hours of operation. Oil level must be maintained at the level of the upper (vent) plug hole. Change fluid after every 100 hours of operation or every six months.

The outboard motor must be upright when draining or filling gearcase. Remove the vent and drain plugs shown in Fig. F2-1 when draining or filling. To fill with lubricant, force lubricant into lower plug hole (D) until lubricant reaches lower edge of upper plug hole (V). Install new gaskets on

plugs, if necessary. Install upper plug (V) before removing lubricant dispenser so fluid remains in gearcase, then remove dispenser and install lower plug (D).

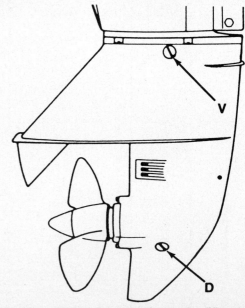

Fig. F2-1 — View showing location of vent plug (V) and fill/drain plug (D).

To
Carburetor

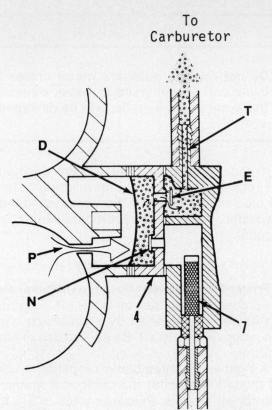

Fig. F2-2 — Schematic view of diaphragm type fuel pump used on all models. The check valves are reed type.

D. Diaphragm
E. Output reed valve   P. Pressure port   4. Reed plate
N. Inlet reed valve   T. Outlet   7. Inlet fitting & filter

After every thirty days of operation apply water-resistant grease to the manual starter shaft and the pin groove in the gear.

At least twice each season inject a good quality grease into all grease fittings.

FUEL SYSTEM

FUEL PUMP. A diaphragm type fuel pump is mounted on the side of power head cylinder block and ported to the upper crankcase. Pressure and vacuum pulsations from the crankcase are directed through the port (P — Fig. F2-2) to the rear of the diaphragm (D). When the power head piston moves upward in its cylinder, vacuum in the crankcase draws the diaphragm inward and fuel enters the pump through filter (7) and the inlet reed valve (N) in reed plate (4). As power head forces the diaphragm outward into fuel chamber, fuel passes through the outlet reed valve (E) into outlet (T).

Defective or questionable parts should be renewed. Pump valves (3 — Fig. F2-3) should seat lightly and squarely on reed plate (4). The diaphragm should be renewed if air leaks or cracks are found, or if deterioration is evident.

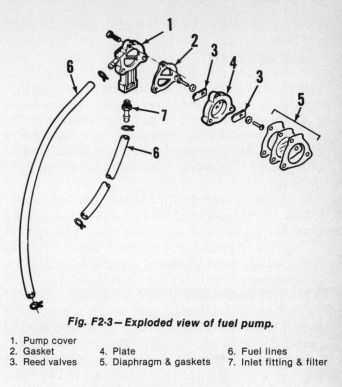

Fig. F2-3 — Exploded view of fuel pump.

1. Pump cover
2. Gasket   4. Plate   6. Fuel lines
3. Reed valves   5. Diaphragm & gaskets   7. Inlet fitting & filter

MANUAL STARTER

Refer to Fig. FD2-4 for an exploded view of manual starter. The manual starter used on electric start models is of similar construction.

To disassemble starter, first remove engine cover and flywheel. Refer to IGNITION section for flywheel removal procedure. Remove screw (1 — Fig. F2-4) and install rewind key (tool T2985) in top of spring arbor (12) where screw (1) was located (see Fig. F2-5). Tighten rewind key until it bottoms, then turn tool handle slightly

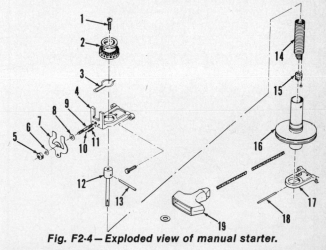

Fig. F2-4 — Exploded view of manual starter.

1. Screw
2. Starter pinion gear   8. Washer   14. Rewind spring
3. Pinion spring   9. Stud   15. Spool retainer
4. Upper bracket   10. Ball   16. Spool
5. Nut   11. Spring   17. Lower bracket
6. Washer   12. Spring arbor   18. Spring pin
7. Interlock   13. Pinion pin   19. Rope handle

counterclockwise to relieve rewind spring tension and push out pin (13 — Fig. F2-4). Use caution as rewind spring (14) is now free to unwind and spin the arbor (12) and rewind key. Slowly allow rewind key to turn and unwind the rewind spring. Pinion, arbor and spring may be lifted free of starter after spring unwinds. Rope and rewind spool (16) may be removed after removal of rope handle and bracket (4). Note presence of detent balls (10) and springs (11) if interlock plate (7) is detached from bracket.

Note the following when reassembling manual starter: Wind rope in spool in a counterclockwise direction as viewed from the top. The rewind spring should be greased before installation. With spool, rope, rope handle and upper bracket installed, assemble arbor (12), spring (14) and spring retainer (15) and install in spool. Grease inside of pinion gear (2) and install gear on top of arbor. Use rewind key (tool T2985) to turn arbor and rewind spring 3½-4 turns counterclockwise as viewed from the top. Align holes in spool, arbor and slot in pinion gear and partially install pin (8). Remove rewind key while holding end of pin, then fully insert pin. Install screw (1).

COOLING SYSTEM

All models are equipped with an impeller type water pump located in the lower unit that circulates water through the power head.

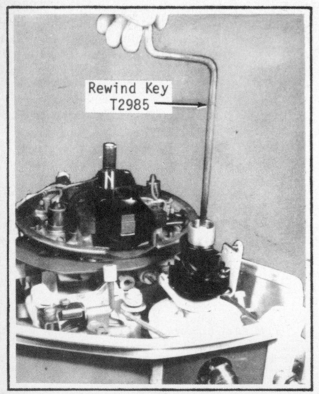

Fig. F2-5 — Rewind key (tool T2985) is used to unwind and wind the starter rewind spring.

If cooling system problems are encountered, first check the water inlet for material which may be blocking the inlet. If the water pump must be inspected, refer to the Outboard Motor Service Manual.

PROPELLER

Power is transmitted from the propeller shaft to the propeller by splines on the shaft. The propeller is retained on the shaft by a pin which contacts the propeller and shaft. Be sure to use the correct pin.

A right-hand, three-blade propeller is used on all models. Propeller diameter is 8 inches (20.3 cm) for all models. Propeller pitch is 8¼ inches (20.9 cm) for 9.9 hp models and 9 inches (22.8 cm) for 15 hp models.

To remove the propeller, detach the cotter pin and remove the propeller spinner. Drive out the propeller retaining pin and pull the propeller off the shaft.

Reinstall the propeller by reversing the removal procedure. Apply a coating of water-resistant grease to the propeller shaft before installing the propeller.

Tune-Up

IGNITION SYSTEM

All models are equipped with a conventional, flywheel magneto ignition system. All ignition components except spark plugs are located under the flywheel.

To set breaker point gap or service ignition components, the flywheel must be removed as

Fig. F2-6 — The flywheel may be "popped" loose by carefully prying up against the flywheel while striking the tool or nut as outlined in text.

Fig. F2-7 — Align index mark on point cam with breaker point follower arm of each breaker point set when measuring breaker point gap.

described in the following procedure: Prevent flywheel rotation by holding the flywheel with a suitable strap type wrench. Hold the flywheel and unscrew the flywheel retaining nut. Thread a suitable nut on the end of the crankshaft so the end is protected or install tool T2909. Note that the nut or tool must not bear against the flywheel. Use a suitable prying tool and lightly pry up against the flywheel while moderately striking the nut or tool. See Fig. F2-6. The flywheel should "pop" free.

⚠WARNING

Be sure suitable tools are used to remove the flywheel. Damage resultant from the misapplication of force or the use of incorrect tools may cause engine damage, engine malfunction or personal injury.

Remove the flywheel and inspect it for cracks or other damage. Be sure to inspect the tapered center portion of the flywheel as well. A damaged flywheel must be discarded as it may fly apart at high engine rpm.

To check the breaker point gap, install the flywheel retaining nut and use it to turn the crankshaft clockwise. Rotate the crankshaft so the index mark on the breaker cam is aligned with the breaker point follower arm as shown in Fig. F2-7. Rotate the crankshaft so the mark is aligned with each follower arm to set point gap for each breaker point set. The breaker point gap for each set of breaker points should be 0.020 inch (0.51

mm). Loosen the breaker point retaining screw to adjust point gap. After tightening retaining screw, rotate the crankshaft and recheck point gap. Lubricate the cam wiper felt with a small amount of breaker point cam lubricant. Do not apply too much lubricant as it may be thrown off the cam onto the breaker points causing misfiring.

Be sure the tapered mating surfaces of the crankshaft and flywheel are clean and dry. The flywheel key must be positioned as shown in Fig. F2-8. Install flywheel and rope pulley; note that pulley must index in holes in flywheel. Tighten flywheel nut to 45 ft.-lbs. (61 N·m).

SPEED CONTROL LINKAGE

The speed control lever (or grip) is attached to the magneto stator plate and moving the speed control will advance or retard the ignition timing. Throttle linkage is synchronized to open the carburetor throttle as magneto timing is advanced. It is very important that the speed control linkage be

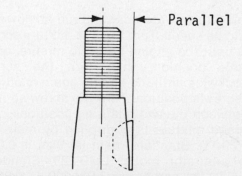

Fig. F2-8 — The flywheel key must be parallel to the crankshaft centerline as shown.

Fig. F2-9 — Pickup mark on throttle cam should be in the center of throttle roller when throttle shaft begins to move.

Fig. F2-10 — The idle speed screw is located adjacent to speed control grip.

properly synchronized for best performance. Adjust linkage with motor not running.

Turn speed control handle slowly toward the fast position and observe pickup mark (Fig. F2-9) on throttle cam. Throttle shaft should just begin to move when pickup mark is centered with throttle roller. Turn adjusting screw, if required, to change point of throttle opening.

Adjust idle speed with engine running at normal operating temperature and motor in forward gear. Idle stop screw location is shown in Fig. F2-10. Turn idle stop screw to obtain idle speed of 700 rpm with lower unit in forward or reverse gear.

CARBURETOR

All models are equipped with a Walbro LMB type carburetor. Refer to Fig. F2-11 for an exploded view of carburetor.

ADJUSTMENT. The idle mixture may be adjusted after removing the engine cover. Initial setting of the idle mixture screw (see Fig. F2-12) is one turn out from a lightly seated position. To adjust idle mixture screw, run motor until operating temperature is attained.

NOTE: The outboard motor lower unit must be immersed in water when running to prevent damage to the water pump impeller.

Shift unit into forward gear and run at slowest, smooth engine speed. Turn the idle mixture screw clockwise until the engine starts to misfire, note the screw's position, then turn the screw counterclockwise until the engine again misfires. Note the screw's position. Turn the screw so it is midway between the two misfiring positions.

High speed mixture is controlled by main jet (23 — Fig. F2-11). Standard main jet size is 0.046 inch for carburetor model LMB-228. Standard main jet size for carburetor LBM-229 is 0.0625 inch.

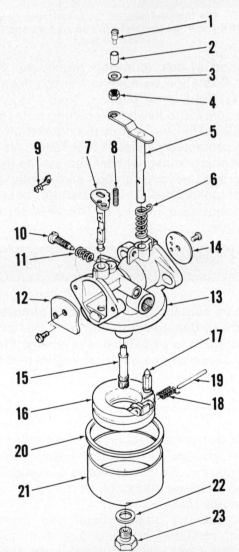

Fig. F2-11 — Exploded view of Walbro LMB carburetor.

1. Adjusting screw	9. Clip	
2. Throttle roller	10. Idle mixture screw	17. Inlet valve
3. Washer	11. Spring	18. Spring
4. Nut	12. Choke plate	19. Float shaft
5. Throttle shaft	13. Throttle body	20. Gasket
6. Spring	14. Throttle plate	21. Float bowl
7. Choke shaft	15. Main nozzle	22. Gasket
8. Spring	16. Float	23. Main jet assy.

Fig. F2-12 — View showing location of idle mixture screw.

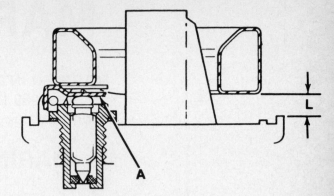

Fig. F2-13 — Float level (L) on Walbro LMB carburetor should be 1/8 inch (3.2 mm). Bend tang (A) to adjust float level.

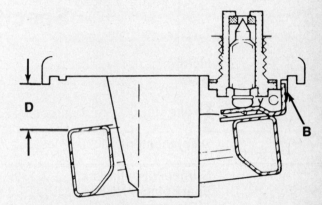

Fig. F2-14 — Float drop (D) on Walbro LMB carburetor should be 5/16 inch (8 mm). Bend tang (B) to adjust float drop.

OVERHAUL. Refer to Fig. F2-11 for an exploded view of the carburetor. Note the following points when overhauling the carburetor. Install throttle plate (14) so the stamped number side is towards the engine and the three holes are towards the idle mixture screw side of the carburetor. Install the choke plate (12) so the stamped number side is towards the carburetor intake and the oblong slot is on the fuel inlet side of the carburetor. Install float spring (18) so spring assists float in closing fuel inlet valve. Float level (L—Fig. F2-13) is measured with the carburetor inverted. Float level (L) should be 1/8 inch (3.2 mm) and is adjusted by bending tab (A). Float drop (D—Fig. F2-14) is measured with carburetor in normal upright position. Float drop should be 5/16 inch (8 mm) and is adjusted by bending tab (B).

MARINER

MARINER INTERNATIONAL CO.
1939 Pioneer Rd.
Fond du Lac, Wisconsin 54935

MARINER 2 HP

NOTE: Metric fasteners are used throughout outboard motor.

Specifications

Hp/rpm 2/5000
Bore . . . . .39 mm
                                   (1.54 in.)
Stroke . . . . .36 mm
                                   (1.42 in.)
Displacement . . . . .43 cc
                                   (2.6 cu. in.)
Number of cylinders 1
Spark plug — NGK B6HS*
   Electrode gap . . . . .0.5-0.6 mm
                                  (0.020-0.024 in.)
Breaker point gap . . . . .0.25-0.45 mm†
                                  (0.010-0.018 in.)
Ignition timing . . . . .See Text
Carburetor make . . . . .TK
Idle speed . . . . .900-1100 rpm‡
Fuel:oil ratio 50:1
Gearcase oil capacity . . . . .45 mL
                                   (1.5 oz.)

*Recommended spark plug on models with serial number 6A1-000101 and above is NGK B5HS.
†Recommended breaker point gap on models with serial number 6A1-000101 and above is 0.30-0.40 mm (0.012-0.016 in.).
‡Recommended idle speed on models with serial number 6A1-000101 and above is 1150-1250 rpm.

Maintenance

LUBRICATION

ENGINE. The engine is lubricated by oil mixed with the fuel. The fuel should be regular leaded, low lead or unleaded gasoline with a minimum pump octane rating of 86. Recommended oil is Quicksilver Formula 50-D Outboard Lubricant or a BIA certified two-stroke motor oil. The recommended fuel:oil ratio for normal operation is 50:1.

During engine break-in, the fuel:oil ratio should be increased to 25:1.

The manufacturer's recommended break-in period is defined as follows: For the first five minutes of operation the engine should not exceed its slowest possible cruising speed. After five minutes, slowly increase the engine speed to half throttle (2500-3500 rpm) for the first three hours of operation. Running the engine at or near full throttle for extended periods is not recommended until after ten hours of operation.

Illustrations Courtesy Mariner

LOWER UNIT. The lower unit gears and bearings are lubricated by oil contained in the gearcase. The recommended oil is Mariner Super Duty Gear Lube or a suitable EP 90 outboard gear oil. The gearcase oil capacity is 45 milliliters (1.5 oz.). The gearcase should be refilled after every 50 hours of operation and the lubricant renewed after every 100 hours of operation or more frequently if needed.

The gearcase on one-plug gearcases is drained and filled through the same plug port. The plug is identified as "OIL FILL."

To drain the oil, remove oil plug (1—Fig. M1-1) from gearcase housing. Lay the motor with the plug opening down and allow the lubricant to drain into a suitable container.

To fill the gearcase with oil, lay the motor with the plug opening up. Add oil through plug opening (B—Fig. M1-2) until the oil begins to overflow, then reinstall and tighten oil plug (1—Fig. M1-1).

The gearcase on two-plug models is drained and filled through the same plug port (D—Fig. M1-3). An oil level (vent) port (L) is used to indicate the full oil level of the gearcase and to ease in oil drainage.

To drain the oil, place the outboard motor in a vertical position. Remove drain plug (D) and oil level plug (L), and allow the lubricant to drain into a suitable container.

To fill the gearcase with oil, place the outboard motor in a vertical position. Add oil through drain plug (D) opening with an oil feeder until the oil begins to overflow from oil level plug (L) port. Reinstall oil level plug (L) with a new gasket, if needed, and tighten. Remove oil feeder, then reinstall drain plug (D) with a new gasket, if needed, and tighten.

PIVOT POINTS AND SLIDES. Lubricate all pivot points and linkage slides with a good quality marine type multipurpose grease as frequently as needed to keep the components operating freely and properly.

Fig. M1-1—View showing location of the lower unit drain and fill plug (1) on one plug models. The plug is identified as "OIL FILL."

FUEL SYSTEM

Periodically inspect the fuel tank and fuel lines for damage. Renew components if needed.

Keep the external surface of the carburetor clean and all connections and sealing surfaces tight.

On early models, the float bowl is equipped with drain plug (D—Fig. M1-4). After closing the fuel valve, occasionally remove drain plug (D) and allow the fuel to drain off into a suitable container. Inspect fuel for any foreign matter. If an excessive amount of foreign matter is found, extensive cleaning of the fuel system is needed.

On all models, a fuel strainer is used in the fuel valve. Clean fuel strainer periodically and renew fuel valve if excessive blockage is noted.

Fig. M1-2—On one plug models, fill lower unit gearcase with a suitable oil through plug opening (B) until the oil begins to overflow.

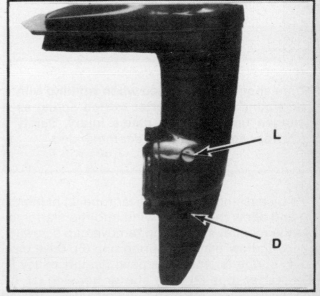

Fig. M1-3—View showing lower unit gearcase drain and fill plug (D) and oil level (vent) plug (L) on two plug models.

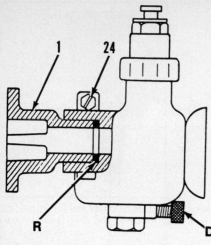

Fig. M1-4 — *View showing carburetor float bowl drain plug (D) supplied on early models. Cap screw (24) is used to tighten clamp securing carburetor on reed plate (1) spigot end. "O" ring (R) should create an airtight fit between components.*

STARTER

When starter rope (2—Fig. M1-6) is pulled, pulley (4) will rotate. As pulley (4) rotates, the drive pawl (5) moves outward to mesh with the starter cup and crank the engine.

When starter rope (2) is released, pulley (4) is rotated in the reverse direction by force from rewind spring (3). As pulley (4) rotates, the starter rope is rewound and drive pawl (5) is disengaged from the starter cup.

The manual starter must be disassembled to renew starter rope (2) or any other internal starter component.

To overhaul the manual starter, proceed as follows: Remove the engine's bottom and side covers. Remove the scews securing the manual starter to the power head and withdraw.

⚠WARNING

Care should be exercised when working with or around a coiled starter rewind spring as sudden uncoiling can cause injury. Safety eyewear and gloves are recommended.

To disassemble, untie starter rope (2) at handle (10) and allow the rope to wind into the starter. Invert the manual starter and remove cap screw (8), then withdraw plate (7), spring clip (6), drive pawl return spring (9) and drive pawl (5). Lift pulley (4) with starter rope (2) from starter housing (1). BE CAREFUL when removing pulley (4) as rewind spring (3) may be dislodged.

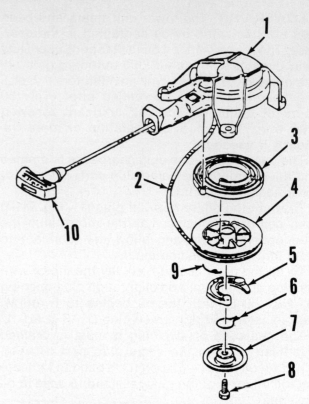

Fig. M1-6 — *Exploded view of manual rewind starter.*

1. Starter housing
2. Starter rope
3. Rewind spring
4. Pulley
5. Drive pawl
6. Spring clip
7. Plate
8. Cap screw
9. Return spring
10. Handle

NOTE: Should pulley (4) not lift free from rewind spring (3), insert a suitable screwdriver blade through hole in pulley (4) to hold rewind spring (3) securely in housing (1).

Untie starter rope (2) and remove rope from pulley (4) if renewal is required. To remove rewind spring (3), use suitable hand protection and extract rewind spring (3) from housing (1). Allow rewind spring to uncoil in a safe area.

Inspect all components for excessive wear or any other damage and renew if needed.

To reassemble, first apply a coating of a suitable water-resistant grease to rewind spring area of housing (1). Install rewind spring (3) in housing (1) so spring coils wind in a counterclockwise direction from the outer end. Make sure the spring's outer hook is properly secured in starter housing. Wind starter rope (2) onto pulley (4) approximately 3 turns counterclockwise when viewed from the flywheel side. Direct remaining starter rope (2) length through notch in pulley (4).

NOTE: Lubricate all friction surfaces with a suitable water-resistant grease during reassembly.

Assemble pulley (4) to starter housing making sure that slot in pulley's drum properly engages hook end in rewind spring (3). Thread starter rope (2) through housing (1) and handle (10) and secure.

Install drive pawl (5), return spring (9), spring clip (6) and plate (7). Apply a suitable thread fastening solution on cap screw (8) threads and securely tighten. Turn pulley (4) 2-3 turns counterclockwise when viewed from the flywheel side, then release starter rope (2) from pulley (4) notch and allow rope to slowly wind onto pulley.

NOTE: Do not apply any more tension on rewind spring (3) than is required to draw starter handle (10) back into the proper released position.

Remount manual starter assembly, then complete reassembly.

COOLING SYSTEM

Ports (I — Fig. M1-7) located on both sides of the lower unit are used as the water inlets for the cooling system. The ports must be kept clean of all foreign matter to ensure efficient operation of the cooling system.

⚠CAUTION

Do not operate outboard motor unless the lower unit is immersed in water, otherwise, the water pump impeller will be damaged.

PROPELLER

The standard propeller has three blades, a diameter of 184 mm (7¼ in.) and a pitch of 114 mm (4½ in.).

⚠WARNING

Disconnect spark plug lead and properly ground lead before performing any propeller service, otherwise, accidental starting can occur if propeller shaft is rotated.

To remove the propeller, remove cotter pin (2 — Fig. M1-8) and withdraw propeller (1) from propeller shaft (4).

Inspect propeller (1) and shear pin (3) for excessive wear and renew if excessive wear or damage is noted.

Apply a water-resistant grease to the propeller bore, then install propeller (1) on propeller shaft (4) and retain with a new cotter pin (2).

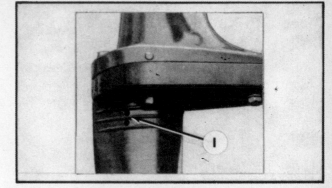

Fig. M1-7 — Cooling system water inlet ports (I) are located on both sides of the lower unit.

Tune-Up

IGNITION SYSTEM

The standard spark plug is NGK B6HS on models prior to serial number 6A1-000101 and NGK B5HS on models with serial number 6A1-000101 and above. Recommended electrode gap is 0.5-0.6 mm (0.020-0.024 in.).

The breaker point gap should be 0.25-0.45 mm (0.010-0.018 in.) on models prior to serial number 6A1-000101 and 0.30-0.40 mm (0.012-0.016 in.) on models with serial number 6A1-000101 and above. Breaker point gap can be inspected and adjusted through the opening in flywheel (1 — Fig. M1-9). To inspect and, if needed, adjust the breaker point gap, first remove the screws securing the engine cover or covers and remove. On early models, remove cap screws (5) and withdraw starter pulley (3) and flywheel cover (2). On later models, remove

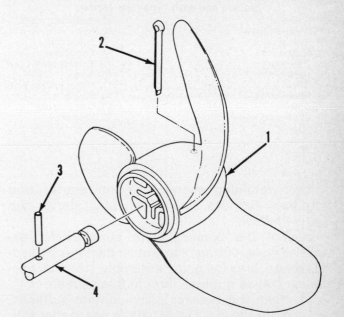

Fig. M1-8 — Propeller (1) is mounted on propeller shaft (4) and is retained by cotter pin (2). Shear pin (3) is renewed only after withdrawing propeller (1) from propeller shaft (4).

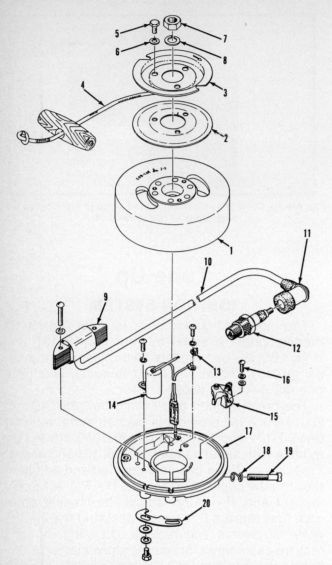

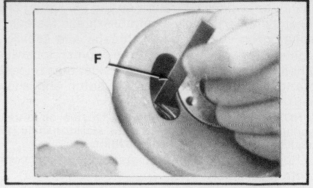

Fig. M1-10 — View showing the use of a point file (F) to clean the breaker point contact surfaces.

Fig. M1-11 — View showing the use of a feeler gage (G) to check the clearance between the breaker point contact surfaces.

Fig. M1-9 — Exploded view of magneto assembly typical of all models and early type rope starter.

1. Flywheel
2. Flywheel cover
3. Starter pulley
4. Starter rope
5. Cap screw
6. Lockwasher
7. Nut
8. Lockwasher
9. Coil
10. Spark plug lead
11. Spark plug boot
12. Spark plug
13. Lubricator
14. Condenser
15. Breaker point assy.
16. Screw
17. Magneto base plate
18. Spring
19. Clamp screw
20. Stop plate

screws retaining manual rewind starter and withdraw. Remove screws retaining starter cup and withdraw.

Inspect the breaker point surfaces for excessive wear, pitting or any other damage. If needed, renew breaker point assembly (15) and condenser (14) as outlined later in this section.

To clean the breaker point contact surfaces, use a point file (F—Fig. M1-10) or sandpaper with a grit rating of 400 to 600. After polishing, wipe the contact surfaces clean with a dry cloth and lightly

grease the breaker point arm and lubricator (13—Fig. M1-9) with a suitable lubricant.

Turn the flywheel until the breaker point contact surfaces are placed at their widest position, then reach through the flywheel opening with a feeler gage (G—Fig. M1-11) of the appropriate size and check the distance between the point surfaces. If the distance is not within the recommended limits, loosen the point set securing screw (16—Fig. M1-9) and adjust the point set until the correct gap is obtained. Tighten the point set securing screw (16) and recheck the breaker point gap. Repeat the adjustment procedure, if needed, until the correct breaker point gap is obtained.

To renew breaker point assembly (15) and condenser (14), proceed as follows: Using a suitable flywheel holding tool (H—Fig. M1-12) to prevent flywheel rotation, remove securing nut (7—Fig. M1-9) using suitable tools (T—Fig. M1-12). Remove flywheel from crankshaft end using a suitable puller assembly (P—Fig. M1-13). Note flywheel key located in crankshaft end slot.

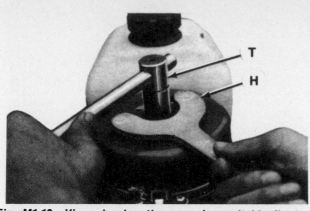

Fig. M1-12—View showing the use of a suitable flywheel holding tool (H) to prevent flywheel rotation during removal of securing nut (7—Fig. M1-9) with suitable tools (T).

Fig. M1-14—View showing the installation of a dial indicator in the spark plug hole to obtain correct piston positioning for timing ignition system. Refer to text.

⚠**WARNING**

Be sure suitable tools are used to remove the flywheel. Damage resultant from the misapplication of force or the use of incorrect tools may cause engine damage, engine malfunction or personal injury.

With reference to Fig. M1-9, renew breaker point assembly (15) and condenser (14). Adjust the breaker point gap to the recommended setting as outlined in a previous paragraph. Make sure the securing screws are properly tightened. Be sure the flywheel key is properly positioned in the crankshaft end, then reinstall flywheel (1). Install lockwasher (8) and nut (7). Tighten securing nut (7) to 30-34 N·m (22-25 ft.-lbs.) on models prior to serial number 6A1-000101 and 39-49 N·m (29-36 ft.-lbs.) on models with serial number 6A1-000101 and above.

To obtain the correct ignition timing on models prior to serial number 6A1-000101, proceed as follows: Install a suitable degree wheel on the flywheel or a dial indicator in the spark plug hole (Fig. M1-14). Position the piston at 18°-24° BTDC or 1.2-2.0 mm (0.047-0.079 in.) BTDC. Loosen screws securing magneto stop plate (20—Fig. M1-9) and move speed control lever to full throttle position.

Disconnect the white wire leading to the stop switch at connector (C—Fig. M1-16). Using a suitable continuity tester (M), connect one tester lead to the white wire (W) leading to the breaker point assembly and the other tester lead to the ground wire (J) leading from magneto base plate (17—Fig. M1-15). Rotate magneto base plate (17) counterclockwise until the breaker point contacts just begin to open (an open circuit is indicated on the continuity tester). Without disturbing magneto base plate (17), position stop plate (20) tab against bracket (21) stop plate. Tighten stop plate (20) securing screws. Recheck ignition timing and

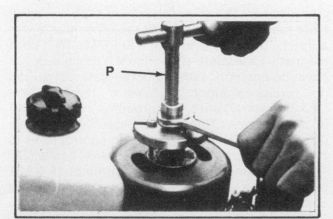

Fig. M1-13—Remove flywheel from crankshaft end using a suitable puller (P) assembly.

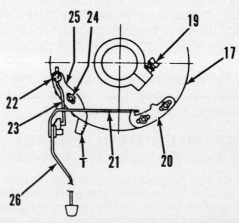

Fig. M1-15—Diagram showing speed control linkage used on models prior to serial number 6A1-000101. Refer to text for adjustment.

T. Adjuster plate tab
17. Magneto base plate
19. Clamp screw
20. Stop plate
21. Bracket
22. Swivel screw
23. Throttle link
24. Screw
25. Adjuster plate
26. Speed control lever

Mariner 2 Hp

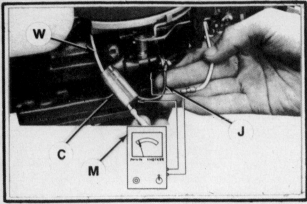

Fig. M1-16 — View showing the connection of a suitable continuity tester (M) for obtaining the correct ignition timing on models prior to serial number 6A1-000101. Refer to text.

C. Connector
J. Ground wire

M. Continuity tester
W. White wire

repeat adjustment procedure if needed, then adjust speed control linkage.

To obtain the correct ignition timing on models with serial number 6A1-000101 and above, proceed as follows: Install a suitable dial indicator in the spark plug hole (Fig. M1-14) and place piston at TDC. Properly synchronize indicator face with piston position. Disconnect the white wire leading to the stop switch at the connector located below the magneto base plate. Using a suitable continuity tester, connect one tester lead to the white wire leading to the breaker point assembly and the other tester lead to an engine ground. Rotate the flywheel counterclockwise until the continuity tester indicates the breaker points just close, then note the dial indicator. The dial indicator should read between 0.99 and 1.23 mm (0.039 and 0.049 in.). If not, adjust the breaker point gap. If indicator reads less than 0.99 mm (0.039 in.), increase breaker point gap. If indicator reads more than 1.23 mm (0.049 in.), decrease breaker point gap.

Adjust as needed until the correct ignition timing is attained, then remount starter cup, manual rewind starter and engine covers.

SPEED CONTROL LINKAGE
Models Prior To Serial No. 6A1-000101

NOTE: Be sure magneto stop plate (20 — Fig. M1-15) is properly adjusted as outlined in the previous IGNITION SYSTEM section before proceeding to adjustment of the speed control linkage.

Loosen swivel screw (22 — Fig. M1-15) so throttle link (23) is free in swivel and loosen adjuster plate screw (24). Rotate magneto base plate (17) counterclockwise until stop plate (20) tab contacts bracket (21) stop tab (full advance position).

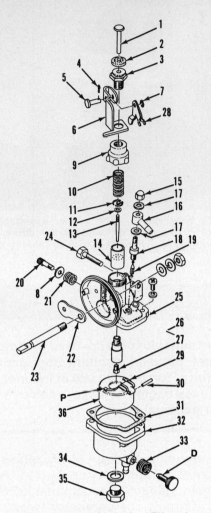

Fig. M1-17 — Exploded view of a typical TK carburetor used on all models.

D. Drain plug	12. Clip	
P. Float pad	13. Jet needle	25. Body
1. Throttle rod	14. Throttle valve	26. Main nozzle
2. Cover	15. Nut	27. Main jet
3. Nut	16. Fuel inlet	28. Throttle arm
4. Cotter pin	17. Washers	29. Float arm
5. Clevis pin	18. Fuel inlet seat	30. Float pin
6. Bracket	19. Fuel inlet valve	31. Gasket
7. Washer	20. Idle speed screw	32. Float bowl
8. Washer	21. Spring	33. Spring
9. Cap nut	22. Choke valve	34. Gasket
10. Spring	23. Choke shaft	35. Plug
11. Retainer	24. Cap screw	36. Float

Note that adjuster plate (25) tab (T) contacts carburetor throttle arm (28 — Fig. M1-17). With magneto base plate (17 — Fig. M1-15) held in full advance position, slide adjuster plate (25) so tab (T) forces against carburetor throttle arm (28 — Fig. M1-17) until the carburetor throttle valve is fully open. Tighten adjuster plate screw (24 — Fig. M1-15). Move the speed control lever to full throttle position and tighten swivel screw (22)

Adjust clamp screw (19) so a force of 19.6-24.5 N (4.4-5.5 lbs.) is required to move end of speed control lever (26).

An engine kill switch is mounted on the carburetor's control cover.

Illustrations Courtesy Mariner

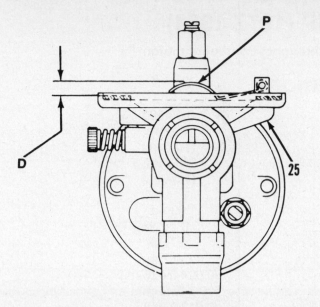

Fig. M1-18—With carburetor body (25) inverted as shown, distance (D) from the body's gasket surface to float pads (P) should be 3.5-4.5 mm (0.14-0.18 in.).

Fig. M1-19 — View showing the adjustment of engine idle speed screw (20). Some models are equipped with an access hole in the side cover. Refer to text.

Models After Serial No. 6A1-000100

The engine speed is regulated by the position of the throttle lever. As the throttle lever is raised or lowered, the carburetor's throttle valve (14 — Fig. M1-17) is operated via throttle rod (1). An engine kill switch is mounted on the carburetor's control cover.

CARBURETOR

ADJUSTMENT. Standard carburetor make is TK. Standard main jet (27 — Fig. M1-17) size is #64 for normal operation. Initial position of clip (12) in jet needle (13) is third notch from the top. Inserting clip (12) in a higher notch will lean mid-range mixture while inserting clip in a lower notch will richen mid-range mixture. Recommended idle speed with engine at normal operating temperature is 900-1100 rpm on models prior to serial number 6A1-000101 and 1150-1250 rpm on models with serial number 6A1-000101 and above.

Properly mount the outboard motor on a boat or a suitable test tank and immerse the lower unit. Connect a tachometer and set it on the appropriate range scale. Start the engine and allow it to warm up to normal operating temperature. Position the throttle control lever to the complete closed position, then adjust the engine idle speed screw (20 — Fig. M1-19) until the engine is idling within the recommended rpm range. Complete reassembly.

OVERHAUL. Remove all components as needed to remove control panel and expose carburetor assembly. Close fuel valve and remove all external components that will interfere with carburetor removal. Clean all external surfaces and remove accumulated dirt and grease. Loosen cap screw (24 — Fig. M1-17) and withdraw carburetor assembly. With reference to Fig. M1-17, disassemble the carburetor and note any discrepancies which must be corrected before reassembly. Remove all gaskets and "O" rings (label if needed for later reference) and set to the side.

Thoroughly clean all carburetor parts in a suitable solvent and inspect for excessive wear or any other damage. Note that plastic and rubber components should not be subjected to some cleaning solutions. Blow dry with clean compressed air. If compressed air is not available, use only lint-free cloths to wipe dry. Do not use a drill bit or wire to clean jets. Enlargement or damage of the calibrated holes may affect engine performance.

With reference to Fig. M1-17, reassemble the carburetor components with new gaskets and "O" rings. Note that the new gaskets should match up with those removed. If not, check with your parts supplier to be sure you have the correct gasket set. The "O" rings must fit properly and seal tight.

To determine the float level, invert the carburetor body (25 — Fig. M1-18) and measure distance (D) from the body's gasket surface to float pads (P). Distance (D) should be 3.5-4.5 mm (0.14-0.18 in.). Adjust the float level by bending float arm (29 — Fig. M1-17).

When reinstalling the carburetor, place a new "O" ring (R — Fig. M1-4) inside the carburetor bore, then install the carburetor on reed plate (1) spigot end. Lightly push the carburetor towards the reed plate until the "O" ring is properly seated against the spigot end, then tighten cap screw (24) until the carburetor retaining clamp is tight. Be sure the carburetor is in a vertical position. Completely reassemble the engine with the exception of the engine cover.

MARINER 3½ HP (1977-1981)

NOTE: Metric fasteners are used throughout outboard motor.

Specifications

Hp/rpm	3.5/4500
Bore	45 mm
	(1.77 in.)
Stroke	40 mm
	(1.57 in.)
Number of cylinders	1
Displacement	63 cc
	(3.8 cu. in.)
Spark plug—NGK	B7HS
Electrode gap	0.6-0.7 mm
	(0.024-0.028 in.)
Breaker point gap	0.3-0.45 mm
	(0.012-0.018 in.)
Ignition timing	See Text
Carburetor:	
Make	Mikuni
Model	BV18-14
Idle speed	1250-1350 rpm
Fuel:oil ratio	50:1
Gearcase oil capacity	80 mL
	(2.7 oz.)

Maintenance

LUBRICATION

ENGINE. The engine is lubricated by oil mixed with the fuel. The fuel should be regular leaded, low lead or unleaded gasoline with a minimum pump octane rating of 86. Recommended oil is Quicksilver Formula 50-D Outboard Lubricant or a BIA certified two-stroke motor oil. The recommended fuel:oil ratio for normal operation is 50:1. During engine break-in, the fuel:oil ratio should be increased to 25:1.

The manufacturer's recommended break-in period is defined as follows: For the first five minutes of operation the engine should not exceed its slowest possible cruising speed. After five minutes, slowly increase the engine speed to half throttle (2500-3500 rpm) for the first three hours of operation. Running the engine at or near full throttle for extended periods is not recommended until after ten hours of operation.

LOWER UNIT. The lower unit gears and bearings are lubricated by oil contained in the gearcase. The recommended oil is Mariner Super Duty Gear Lube or a suitable EP 90 outboard gear oil. The gearcase oil capacity is 80 milliliters (2.7 oz.). The gearcase should be refilled after every 50 hours of operation and the lubricant renewed after every 100 hours of operation or more frequently if needed. The gearcase is drained and filled through the same plug port (D—Fig. M2-1). An oil level (vent) port (L) is used to identify the full oil level of the gearcase and to ease in oil drainage.

To drain the oil, place the outboard motor in a vertical position. Remove drain plug (D) and oil level plug (L), and allow the lubricant to drain into a suitable container.

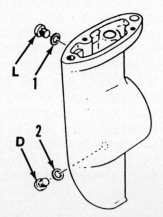

Fig. M2-1 — View showing lower unit gearcase drain and fill plug (D), oil level (vent) plug (L) and gaskets (1 and 2).

To fill the gearcase with oil, place the outboard motor in a vertical position. Add oil through drain plug (D) opening with an oil feeder until the oil begins to overflow from oil level plug (L) port. Reinstall oil level plug (L) with a new gasket (1), if needed, and tighten. Remove oil feeder, then reinstall drain plug (D) with a new gasket (2), if needed, and tighten.

PIVOT POINTS AND SLIDES. Lubricate all pivot points and linkage slides with a good quality marine type multipurpose grease as frequently as needed to keep the components operating freely and properly.

FUEL SYSTEM

FUEL FILTER. A fuel valve (Fig. M2-2) is located between the fuel tank and the carburetor. Its purpose is to control the flow of fuel and to prevent any foreign matter from entering the carburetor.

After draining the fuel tank through drain plug (P—Fig. M2-3), disconnect the fuel hoses and remove the fuel valve. With reference to Fig. M2-2 disassemble and clean the components after every 25-30 hours of use, or more frequent if excessive contaminates are noticed. Renew components if needed.

·CARBURETOR. The carburetor is fitted with a plunger type drain valve and a drain port at the base of the float bowl. The drain valve can be used to drain the fuel from the float bowl with the fuel valve in the "STOP" position or to check the float bowl fuel level with the fuel valve in the "OPEN" position. Refer to CARBURETOR in the Tune-Up section for checking float bowl fuel level.

An overflow hose connected between the float bowl outlet and the carburetor body inlet is used to prevent fuel overflow when the outboard motor is tilted at an angle of 85° or less.

FUEL TANK. It may be necessary to remove the fuel tank for cleaning or for access to underlying

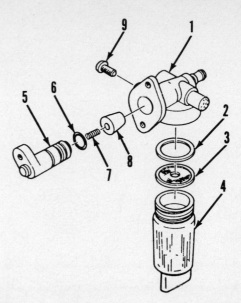

Fig. M2-2 — *Exploded view of fuel valve and filter assembly.*

1. Body	4. Cup	7. Spring
2. Gasket	5. Lever	8. Valve
3. Filter	6. "O" ring	9. Screw

engine components. The manual starter is attached to the top of the fuel tank. The fuel tank assembly serves as the top engine cover.

To remove the fuel tank, first remove the screws retaining the starter cover (2—Fig. M2-4) and withdraw the cover. Remove the remaining screw securing the manual starter case (3), then withdraw the manual starter assembly.

Turn the engine's apron cover fastener to the left and open the apron cover. Remove the screws retaining the aprons on both sides of the fuel tank and remove the aprons. Remove the fuel tank drain plug (P—Fig. M2-3) and allow the fuel to drain into a suitable container. Disconnect fuel hose between fuel tank and fuel valve. Remove four mounting nuts (1), washers (2) and damper assemblies (3), then withdraw fuel tank.

Installation is reverse order of removal.

STARTER

When starter rope (19—Fig. M2-4) is pulled, drum and pulley (5) will rotate. As drum and pulley (5) rotate, the three drive pawls (10) move apart thus meshing with starter cup (14) and cranking the engine.

When starter rope (19) is released, drum and pulley (5) is rotated in the reverse direction by force from rewind spring (4). As drum and pulley (5) rotates, the starter rope is rewound and drive pawls (10) are disengaged from starter cup (14).

The manual starter must be disassembled to renew starter rope (19) or any other internal starter component.

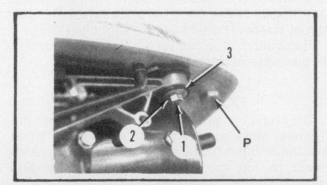

Fig. M2-3 — *View showing fuel tank drain plug (P). Fuel tank is secured in four locations to mounting brackets by nut (1), washer (2) and damper (3).*

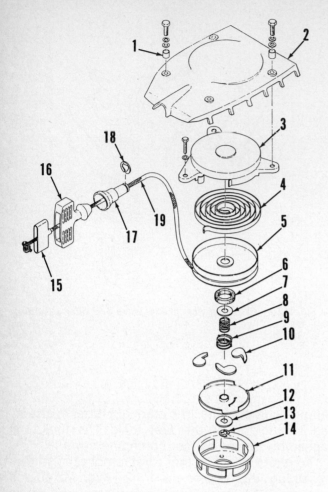

Fig. M2-4 — Exploded view of manual starter assembly.

1. Collar
2. Cover
3. Case
4. Rewind spring
5. Drum & pulley
6. Lubricator
7. Thrust washer
8. Spring
9. Pawl return spring
10. Pawls
11. Drive plate
12. Thrust washer
13. Clip
14. Starter cup
15. Anchor
16. Handle
17. Guide
18. Clip
19. Starter rope

To overhaul the manual starter, proceed as follows: Remove the screws retaining starter cover (2) and withdraw the cover. Remove the remaining screw securing the manual starter, then withdraw the manual starter.

> **⚠ WARNING**
>
> **Care should be exercised when working with or around a coiled starter rewind spring as sudden uncoiling can cause injury. Safety eyewear and gloves are recommended.**

To disassemble, untie starter rope (19) at handle (16) and allow the rope to wind into the starter.

Invert the unit and press on drive plate (11) to ease in removal of clip (13) and thrust washer (12). Remove drive plate (11), pawls (10), pawl return spring (9), drive plate spring (8), thrust washer (7) and lubricator (6). Turn drum and pulley (5) clockwise until rewind spring (4) is disengaged, then remove drum and pulley (5) with rewind spring (4) from case (3). BE CAREFUL when removing drum and pulley (5) as the rewind spring may be dislodged. Untie starter rope (19) and remove rope from drum and pulley (5) if renewal is required.

To renew rewind spring (4), use a piece of strong string or thin wire and make a loop with a diameter of 9.0-9.5 cm (3.54-3.74 in.). Enclose rewind spring (4) within the loop. Install rewind spring (4) in drum and pulley (5) with coils looping in a clockwise rotation from inner end, then remove the retaining string or wire. Hook the outer end of the spring in the drum slot.

To renew starter rope (19), first install rewind spring (4) in drum and pulley (5) as outlined in the previous paragraph. Install a new starter rope (19) into drum and pulley (5) with a knot on the inner end. Wind starter rope (19) around the pulley in a counterclockwise direction when viewed from the bottom. Leave approximately 40 cm (16 inches) of starter rope extending from the notch in drum and pulley (5) and install assembly in case (3). Install the rope end through guide (17), handle (16) and anchor (15) and secure with a knot. Turn drum and pulley (5) 4-5 full turns counterclockwise, then release starter rope (19) from pulley notch and allow rope to slowly wind onto pulley.

NOTE: Do not apply any more tension on rewind spring (4) than is required to draw starter handle back into the proper released position.

Install lubricator (6), thrust washer (7), drive plate spring (8), pawl return spring (9) and pawls (10). Hook one end of pawl return spring (9) in hole in drum and pulley (5) and the other end in slot of drive plate (11). Rotate drive plate (11) as needed and install. Press on drive plate (11) and install thrust washer (12) and secure with clip (13).

Remount manual starter assembly and cover (2) to complete reassembly.

COOLING SYSTEM

The engine is air-cooled by a fan built into the flywheel. Make sure that the flywheel cooling fins and the cylinder fins are unobstructed. Do not attempt to run the engine without the engine cylinder shroud, aprons and fuel tank in place.

A water tube (T — Fig. M2-5) in the drive shaft housing directs water through the lower unit to cool exiting exhaust gases. The water tube should be kept clean of any blockage.

PROPELLER

The standard propeller has three blades, a diameter of 190 mm (7½ in.) and a pitch of 100 mm (4 in.).

⚠WARNING

Disconnect spark plug lead and properly ground lead before performing any propeller service, otherwise, accidental starting can occur if propeller shaft is rotated.

To remove the propeller, remove cotter pin (2—Fig. M2-6) and withdraw propeller (1) from propeller shaft (4).

Inspect propeller (1) and shear pin (3) for excessive wear and renew if excessive wear or damage is noted.

Apply a water-resistant grease to the propeller bore, then install propeller (1) on propeller shaft (4) and retain with a new cotter pin (2).

Tune-Up

IGNITION SYSTEM

The standard spark plug is NGK B7HS with an electrode gap of 0.6-0.7 mm (0.024-0.028 in.).

The breaker point gap should be 0.3-0.45 mm (0.012-0.018 in.) and can be inspected and adjusted through the opening in flywheel (1—Fig. M2-7). To inspect and, if needed, adjust the breaker point gap, first remove the screws retaining starter cover (2—Fig. M2-4) and withdraw the cover. Remove the remaining screw securing the manual starter case (3), then withdraw the manual starter assembly.

Turn the engine's aft cover fastener to the left and open the aft cover. Remove the screws retaining the covers on both sides of the fuel tank and remove the covers. Remove the fuel tank drain plug (P—Fig. M2-3) and allow the fuel to drain into a suitable container. Disconnect fuel hose between fuel tank and fuel valve. Remove four mounting nuts (1), washers (2) and damper assemblies (3), then withdraw fuel tank. Remove cap screws (9—Fig. M2-7) and lockwashers (10) and withdraw starter pulley (14) and flywheel cover (11).

Inspect the breaker point surfaces for excessive wear, pitting or any other damage. If needed, renew breaker point assembly (3) and condenser (6) as outlined later in this section.

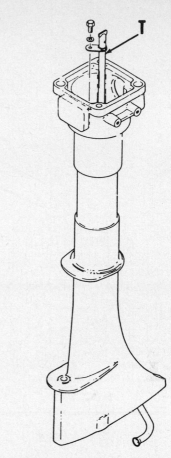

Fig. M2-5—Water tube (T) in the drive shaft housing directs water through the lower unit to cool exiting exhaust gases.

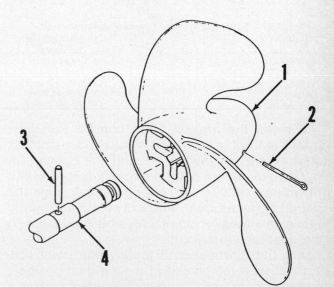

Fig. M2-6—Propeller (1) is mounted on propeller shaft (4) and is retained by cotter pin (2). Shear pin (3) is renewed only after withdrawing propeller (1) from propeller shaft (4).

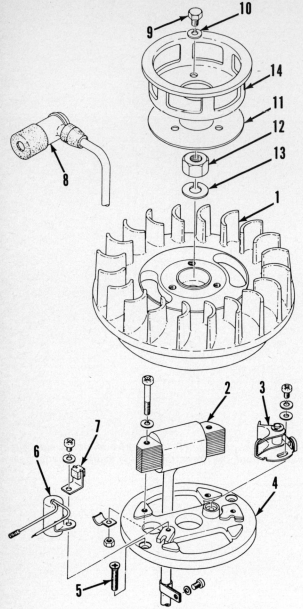

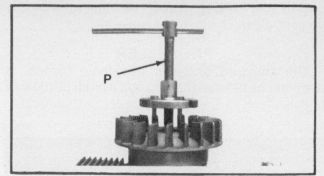

Fig. M2-8 — Remove flywheel from crankshaft end using a suitable puller assembly (P).

Fig. M2-7 — Exploded view of flywheel magneto unit.

1. Flywheel
2. Coil
3. Breaker point assy.
4. Magneto base plate
5. Screw
6. Condenser
7. Lubricator
8. Spark plug boot
9. Cap screw
10. Lockwasher
11. Flywheel cover
12. Nut
13. Lockwasher
14. Starter pulley

To clean the breaker point contact surfaces, rotate the flywheel until the breaker point contact surfaces are accessible through the opening in the flywheel. Use a point file or sandpaper with a grit rating of 400 to 600. After polishing, wipe the contact surfaces clean with a dry cloth and lightly grease the breaker point arm and lubricator (7) with a suitable lubricant.

Turn the flywheel until the breaker point contact surfaces are placed at their widest position, then reach through the flywheel opening with a feeler gage of the appropriate size and check the distance between the point surfaces. If the distance is not within the recommended limits, loosen the point set securing screw and adjust the point set until the correct gap is obtained. Tighten the point set securing screw and recheck the breaker point gap. Repeat the adjustment procedure, if needed, until the correct breaker point gap is obtained.

To renew breaker point assembly (3) and condenser (6), proceed as follows: Using a suitable flywheel holding tool to prevent flywheel rotation, remove securing nut (12) using suitable tools. Remove flywheel (1) from crankshaft end using a suitable puller assembly (P — Fig. M2-8). Note flywheel key located in crankshaft end slot.

> ### ⚠WARNING
>
> **Be sure suitable tools are used to remove the flywheel. Damage resultant from the misapplication of force or the use of incorrect tools may cause engine damage, engine malfunction or personal injury.**

With reference to Fig. M2-7, renew breaker point assembly (3) and condenser (6). Adjust the breaker point gap to the recommended setting as outlined in a previous paragraph. Make sure the securing screws are properly tightened. Be sure the flywheel key is properly positioned in the crankshaft end, then reinstall flywheel (1). Install lockwasher (13) and install and tighten securing nut (12) to 30-34 N·m (22-25 ft.-lbs.).

Magneto base plate (4) is fixed to the engine with tapered screws (5) and no timing adjustment is possible other than varying the breaker point gap. Breaker point contacts should open when piston is 16°-18° BTDC or 0.96-1.2 mm (0.038-0.047 in.) BTDC. Install a suitable degree wheel on the flywheel or a dial indicator in the spark plug hole to verify piston position when breaker point contacts open.

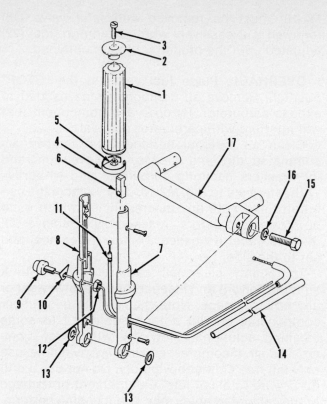

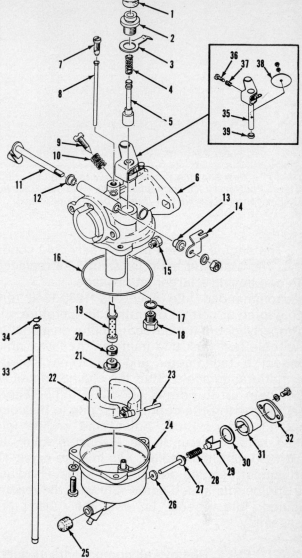

Fig. M2-9 — Exploded view of speed control linkage.

1. Twist grip
2. Friction cap
3. Screw
4. Indicator
5. Nut
6. Slider
7. Steering handle half
8. Steering handle half
9. Kill switch assy.
10. Stop plate
11. Throttle cable
12. Nut
13. Washer
14. Tube
15. Cap screw
16. Lockwasher
17. Frame

SPEED CONTROL LINKAGE

The engine speed is controlled by the position of the throttle linkage. A twist grip (1 — Fig. M2-9) at the end of the steering handle is used to regulate throttle linkage via throttle cable (11). An engine kill switch (9) is mounted on the steering handle below twist grip (1).

CARBURETOR

ADJUSTMENT. Standard carburetor is a Mikuni BV18-14. Standard main jet (15 — Fig. M2-10) size is #70 for normal operation. Adjustment of the main jet size may be required if the engine is operated under one of the following conditions:

1. The engine is run mostly at high speeds. The standard main jet should be replaced with one having a larger jet passage.

2. The engine is run mostly at low speeds. The standard main jet should be replaced with one having a smaller jet passage.

3. The engine is used in high altitude conditions. The standard main jet should be replaced with one having a smaller jet passage. The low at-

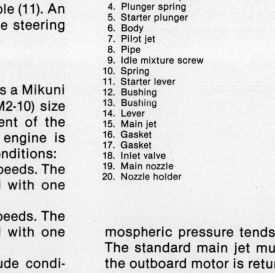

Fig. M2-10 — Exploded view of Mikuni BV18-14 carburetor.

1. Cover
2. Plunger cap
3. Starter lever plate
4. Plunger spring
5. Starter plunger
6. Body
7. Pilot jet
8. Pipe
9. Idle mixture screw
10. Spring
11. Starter lever
12. Bushing
13. Bushing
14. Lever
15. Main jet
16. Gasket
17. Gasket
18. Inlet valve
19. Main nozzle
20. Nozzle holder
21. Plug
22. Float
23. Float pin
24. Float bowl
25. Cap
26. Packing
27. Drain valve
28. Spring
29. Spring guide
30. Gasket
31. Drain cup
32. Plate
33. Overflow hose
34. Spring clamp
35. Throttle shaft
36. Idle speed screw
37. Spring
38. Throttle valve
39. Seal

mospheric pressure tends to richen the mixture. The standard main jet must be reinstalled when the outboard motor is returned to sea level conditions, or a lean condition will exist and possible engine damage may result.

Fig. M2-11 — View showing procedure for checking carburetor fuel level. Fuel level (L) in drain tube should be 23 mm (0.909 in.) below center of carburetor throttle bore. Refer to text.

4. The engine is used in extremely cold conditions. The standard main jet should be replaced with one having a larger jet passage.

Recommended idle speed is 1250-1350 rpm with engine at normal operating temperature.

Properly mount the outboard motor on a boat or a suitable test tank and immerse the lower unit. Connect a tachometer and set it on the appropriate range scale. Start the engine and allow it to warm up to normal operating temperature. Position the throttle control twist grip to the complete closed position. Adjust the engine idle speed screw (36) until the engine is idling at 1250-1350 rpm, then adjust idle mixture screw (9) until smooth engine operation is noted. Readjust the engine idle speed screw (36) until the recommended idle speed is obtained. Complete reassembly.

FUEL LEVEL. Remove all components as needed to expose carburetor inlet throttle bore as shown in Fig. M2-11. Place fuel valve in the "OPEN" position. Hold drain tube up and press float bowl drain cup (31 — Fig. M2-10). Fuel level (L — Fig. M2-11) in drain tube should be 23 mm (0.909 in.) below center of carburetor throttle bore.

If fuel level is incorrect, float bowl (24 — Fig.

M2-10) must be removed and inlet valve (18) renewed if excessively worn or tang on float (22) adjusted until the proper setting is obtained.

OVERHAUL. Place fuel valve in the "STOP" position. Remove all components as needed to expose carburetor. Remove any component that will interfere with carburetor removal.

Clean all external surfaces and remove accumulated dirt and grease. Remove nuts and lockwashers securing carburetor and withdraw. With reference to Fig. M2-10, disassemble the carburetor and note any discrepancies which must be corrected before reassembly. Remove all gaskets (label if needed for later reference) and set to the side.

Thoroughly clean all carburetor parts in a suitable solvent and inspect for excessive wear or any other damage. Note that plastic and rubber components should not be subjected to some cleaning solutions. Blow dry with clean compressed air. If compressed air is not available, use only lint-free cloths to wipe dry. Do not use a drill bit or wire to clean jets. Enlargement or damage of the calibrated holes may affect engine performance.

With reference to Fig. M2-10, reassemble the carburetor components with new gaskets. Note that the new gaskets should match up with those removed. If not, check with your parts supplier to be sure you have the correct gasket set.

When reinstalling the carburetor, place a new gasket between the carburetor and reed plate. Securely tighten the retaining nuts. Reconnect fuel supply line and check carburetor fuel level as outlined in a previous paragraph. Correct fuel level if needed. Completely reassemble the engine with the exception of the left apron. Initially adjust idle mixture screw (9 — Fig. M2-10) 1⅜ turns out from a lightly seated position.

Verify carburetor fuel level as outlined in the previous FUEL LEVEL section and note if fuel level adjustment is needed.

MARINER 5 HP (1977-1981)

NOTE: Metric fasteners are used throughout outboard motor.

Specifications

Hp/rpm	5/5000
Bore	50 mm
	(1.97 in.)
Stroke	47 mm
	(1.85 in.)
Number of cylinders	1
Displacement	92 cc
	(5.6 cu.in.)
Spark plug — NGK	B7HS
Electrode gap	0.5-0.6 mm)
	(0.20-0.024 in.)
Breaker point gap	0.30-0.40 mm
	(0.012-0.016 in.)
Ignition timing	See Text
Idle speed	1550-1650 rpm
Fuel:oil ratio	50:1
Gearcase oil capacity	80 mL
	(2.7 oz.)

Maintenance

LUBRICATION

ENGINE. The engine is lubricated by oil mixed with the fuel. The fuel should be regular leaded, low lead or unleaded gasoline with a minimum pump octane rating of 86. Recommended oil is Quicksilver Formula 50-D Outboard Lubricant or a BIA certified two-stroke motor oil. The recommended fuel:oil ratio for normal operation is 50:1. During engine break-in, the fuel:oil ratio should be increased to 25:1.

The manufacturer's recommended break-in period is defined as follows: For the first five minutes of operation the engine should not exceed its slowest possible cruising speed. After five minutes, slowly increase the engine speed to half throttle (2500-3500 rpm) for the first three hours of operation. Running the engine at or near full throttle for extended periods is not recommended until after ten hours of operation.

LOWER UNIT. The lower unit gears and bearings are lubricated by oil contained in the gearcase. The recommended oil is Mariner Super Duty Gear Lube or a suitable EP 90 outboard gear oil. The gearcase oil capacity is 80 milliliters (2.7 oz.). The gearcase should be refilled periodically and the lubricant renewed after every 50 hours of operation or more frequently if needed. The gearcase is drained and filled through the same plug port (D — Fig. M3-1). An oil level (vent) port (L) is used to indicate the full oil level of the gearcase and to ease in oil drainage.

To drain the oil, place the outboard motor in a vertical position. Remove drain plug (D) and oil

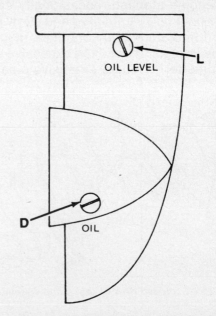

Fig. M3-1 — *View showing lower unit gearcase drain and fill plug (D) and oil level (vent) plug (L).*

Fig. M3-2 — The fuel hoses must be correctly connected to the fuel pump. The fuel supply hose connects to the fuel pump's inlet port, identified as "IN."

level plug (L), and allow the lubricant to drain into a suitable container.

To fill the gearcase with oil, place the outboard motor in a vertical position. Add oil through drain plug (D) opening with an oil feeder until the oil begins to overflow from oil level plug (L) port. Reinstall oil level plug (L) with a new gasket, if needed, and tighten. Remove oil feeder, then reinstall drain plug (D) with a new gasket, if needed, and tighten.

PIVOT POINTS AND SLIDES. Lubricate all pivot points and linkage slides with a good quality marine type multipurpose grease as frequently as needed to keep the components operating freely and properly.

FUEL SYSTEM

Periodically inspect the fuel lines and connections for damage. Renew components if needed. With the engine stopped, occasionally open the carburetor float bowl drain plug and allow the fuel to drain off into a suitable container. Inspect the fuel for any foreign matter. If an excessive amount of foreign matter is found, extensive cleaning of

the fuel system is needed. A filter screen is used in the fuel pump assembly.

Keep the external surface of the carburetor clean and all connections and sealing surfaces tight.

Refer to CARBURETOR in the Tune-Up section for checking float bowl fuel level.

FUEL PUMP. The fuel pump is operated by crankcase pressure changes from the up and down movement of the piston. When the crankcase pressure decreases (the piston is moving upward), the pump diaphragm is pulled toward the crankcase allowing fuel to enter the pump body and closing the discharge check valve. When the crankcase pressure increases (the piston is moving downward), the diaphragm is pushed outward discharging the fuel to the carburetor and closing the inlet check valve. This pulsating action allows for continuous fuel flow. The check valves are used to prevent reverse flow of the fuel.

The inlet port is identified as "IN" as shown in Fig. M3-2. The fuel hoses must be connected accordingly.

To overhaul, first remove the engine's top cover and disconnect the fuel tank supply hose at the outboard motor connector. Disconnect the fuel hoses at the fuel pump inlet and discharge nozzles and label if needed. Remove securing cap screws and withdraw fuel pump assembly.

With reference to Fig. M3-3, disassemble the fuel pump assembly. Inspect all components for damage and excessive wear and renew if needed. Clean filter screen (8) with a suitable cleaning solvent.

With reference to Fig. M3-3, reassemble the fuel pump assembly with new gaskets. Mount the fuel pump assembly to the crankcase with a new gasket and securely tighten the retaining cap screws.

NOTE: Fuel pump and engine malfunction will result if the fuel pump and all connections are not airtight.

Complete reassembly.

SHIFT LINKAGE

Direction of propeller rotation is determined by the position of the gear shift lever. The gear shift lever actuates gearcase components using shift linkage consisting of an upper and lower shift rod connected by an adjustment bracket. The tapered end of the lower shift rod controls the movement of the dog clutch on the propeller shaft. The positioning of the dog clutch on the propeller shaft determines whether forward, neutral or reverse directional movement is selected.

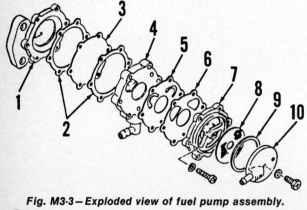

Fig. M3-3 — Exploded view of fuel pump assembly.

1. Base
2. Gaskets
3. Diaphragm
4. Body
5. Check valve
6. Gasket
7. Body
8. Screen
9. Gasket
10. Inlet cover

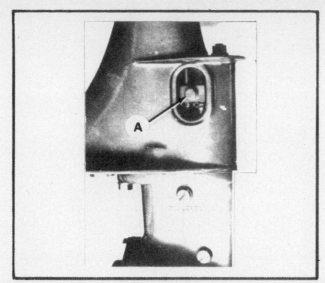

Fig. M3-4 — Adjustment cap screw (A) is used to adjust linkage. Refer to text.

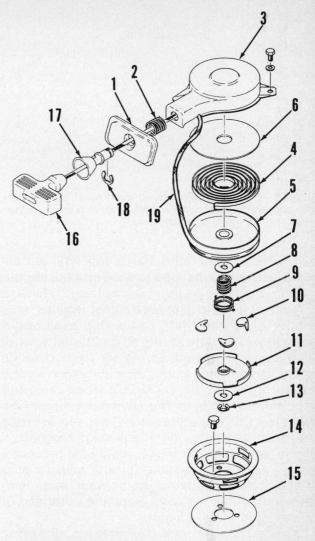

Fig. M3-5 — Exploded view of manual starter assembly.

1. Guide plate
2. Spring
3. Case
4. Rewind spring
5. Drum & pulley
6. Slide plate
7. Thrust washer
8. Spring
9. Pawl return spring
10. Pawl
11. Drive plate
12. Thrust washer
13. Clip
14. Starter cup
15. Flywheel cover
16. Handle
17. Guide
18. Clip
19. Starter rope

To adjust, remove adjustment cap screw (A — Fig. M3-4) cover. Loosen cap screw enough to allow lower shift rod to slide freely in adjustment bracket. Place shift lever in reverse detent position and lower shift rod in reverse position. Push down on adjustment bracket only with enough force to remove any slack in the linkage, then tighten adjustment cap screw (A). Check the adjustment by turning the propeller.

⚠WARNING

Disconnect spark plug lead and properly ground lead before performing any propeller service, otherwise, accidental starting can occur if propeller shaft is rotated.

Make sure neutral and forward properly engage. If not, repeat adjustment procedure, then reinstall cover.

STARTER

When starter rope (19—Fig. M3-5) is pulled, drum and pulley (5) will rotate. As drum and pulley (5) rotates, the three drive pawls (10) move apart thus meshing with starter cup (14) and cranking the engine.

When starter rope (19) is released, drum and pulley (5) is rotated in the reverse direction by force from rewind spring (4). As drum and pulley (5) rotates, the starter rope is rewound and drive pawls (10) are disengaged from starter cup (14).

The manual starter must be disassembled to renew starter rope (19) or any other internal starter component.

To overhaul the manual starter, proceed as follows: Remove the engine's top cover. Remove the screws retaining the manual starter to the air shroud and withdraw the starter assembly.

⚠WARNING

Care should be exercised when working with or around a coiled starter rewind spring as sudden uncoiling can cause injury. Safety eyewear and gloves are recommended.

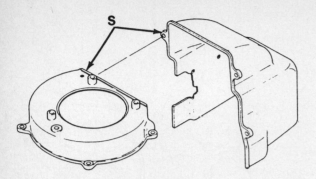

Fig. M3-6—Engine air shrouds (S) must be in place before operating engine or possible engine damage may result from overheating.

To disassemble, untie starter rope (19) at handle (16) and allow the rope to wind into the starter. Invert the unit and press on drive plate (11) to ease in removal of clip (13) and thrust washer (12). Remove drive plate (11), pawls (10), pawl return spring (9), drive plate spring (8) and thrust washer (7). Disengage rewind spring (4) from case (3) hook. Lift drum and pulley (5) with rewind spring (4) from case (3). BE CAREFUL when removing drum and pulley (5) as the rewind spring may be dislodged. Untie starter rope (19) and remove rope from drum and pulley (5) if renewal is required.

To renew rewind spring (4), install the prebound spring into drum and pulley (5) with coils looping in a clockwise rotation from inner end, then remove the retaining wire. Hook the outer end of the spring in the drum slot.

To renew starter rope (19), first install rewind spring (4) in drum and pulley (5) as outlined in the previous paragraph. Install a new starter rope (19) in drum and pulley (5) with a knot on the inner end. Wind starter rope (19) around the pulley two turns in a counterclockwise direction when viewed from the bottom. Direct remaining starter rope (19) length through notch in drum and pulley (5). Install the assembly into case (3). Make sure rewind spring (4) end engages case (3) hook. Thread starter rope (19) end through case and install external components (2, 1, 18, 17 and 16), then secure rope end in handle (16) with a knot. Turn drum and pulley (5) 2-3 turns counterclockwise, then release starter rope from pulley notch and allow rope to slowly wind onto pulley.

NOTE: Do not apply any more tension on rewind spring (4) than is required to draw starter handle (16) back into the proper released position.

Install thrust washer (7), drive plate spring (8), pawl return spring (9) and pawls (10). Hook one end of pawl return spring (9) in hole in drum and pulley (5) and the other end in slot of drive plate

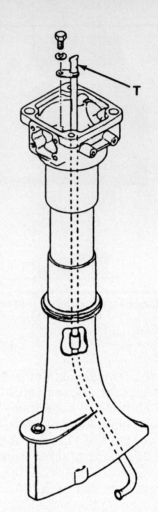

Fig. M3-7—Water tube (T) in the drive shaft housing directs water through the lower unit to cool exiting exhaust.

(11). Rotate drive plate (11) as needed and install. Press on drive plate (11) and install thrust washer (12) and secure with clip (13).

Remount manual starter assembly and engine's top cover to complete reassembly.

COOLING SYSTEM

The engine is air-cooled by a fan mounted on the flywheel. Make sure that the flywheel cooling fins and the cylinder fins are unobstructed. Do not attempt to run the engine without air shrouds (S—Fig. M3-6) in place.

A water tube (T—Fig. M3-7) in the drive shaft housing directs water through the lower unit to cool exiting exhaust gases. The water tube should be kept clean of any blockage.

PROPELLER

The standard propeller has three blades, a diameter of 184 mm (7¼ in.) and a pitch of 165 mm (6½ in.).

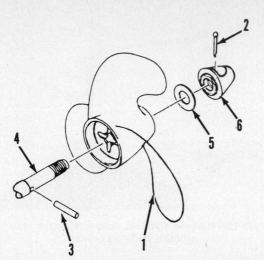

Fig. M3-8 — Propeller (1) is mounted on propeller shaft (4) and is retained by washer (5), spinner (6) and cotter pin (2). Shear pin (3) is renewed only after withdrawing propeller (1) from propeller shaft (4).

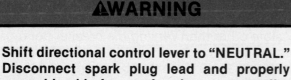

⚠**WARNING**

Shift directional control lever to "NEUTRAL." Disconnect spark plug lead and properly ground lead before performing any propeller service, otherwise, accidental starting can occur if propeller shaft is rotated.

To remove the propeller, remove cotter pin (2 — Fig. M3-8) and unscrew propeller spinner (6). Withdraw propeller (1) and washer (5) from propeller shaft (4).

Inspect propeller (1), propeller shaft (4) and shear pin (3) for damage and excessive wear and renew if needed.

Apply a water-resistant grease to the propeller bore, then install propeller (1) with washer (5) on propeller shaft (4) and retain with propeller spinner (6) and a new cotter pin (2).

Tune-Up

IGNITION SYSTEM

The standard spark plug is NGK B7HS with an electrode gap of 0.5-0.6 mm (0.020-0.024 in.).

The breaker point gap should be 0.3-0.4 mm (0.012-0.016 in.) and can be inspected and adjusted through the opening in flywheel (4 — Fig. M3-9). To inspect and, if needed, adjust the breaker point gap, first remove the engine's top cover. Remove the screws retaining the manual starter to the air shroud and withdraw the starter

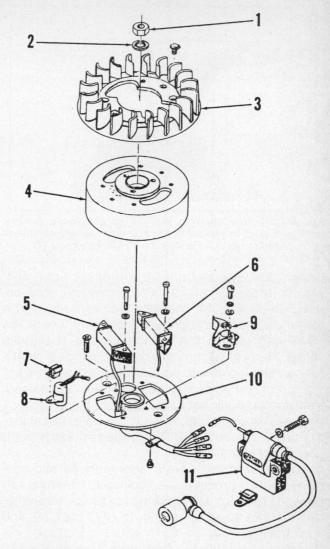

Fig. M3-9 — Exploded view of flywheel magneto unit.

1. Nut
2. Lockwasher
3. Fan
4. Flywheel
5. Lighting coil
6. Low voltage coil
7. Lubricator
8. Condenser
9. Breaker point assy.
10. Magneto base plate
11. Ignition coil

assembly. Remove the cap screws and lockwashers securing starter pulley (14 — Fig. M3-5) and flywheel cover (15) to the flywheel and withdraw.

Inspect the breaker point surfaces for excessive wear, pitting or any other damage. If needed, renew breaker point assembly (9 — Fig. M3-9) and condenser (8) as outlined later in this section.

To clean the breaker point contact surfaces, rotate the flywheel until the breaker point contact surfaces are accessible through the opening in flywheel (4). Use a point file or sandpaper with a grit rating of 400 to 600. After polishing, wipe the contact surfaces clean with a dry cloth and lightly grease the breaker point arm and lubricator (7) with a suitable lubricant.

Fig. M3-10— *View showing the use of a suitable flywheel holding tool (H) to prevent flywheel rotation during removal of securing nut (1—Fig. M3-9) with suitable tools (T).*

Fig. M3-11— *Remove flywheel from crankshaft end using a suitable puller assembly (P).*

Turn the flywheel until the breaker point contact surfaces are placed at their widest position, then reach through the flywheel opening with a feeler gage of the appropriate size and check the distance between the point surfaces. If the distance is not within the recommended limits, loosen the point set securing screw and adjust the point set until the correct gap is obtained. Tighten the point set securing screw and recheck the breaker point gap. Repeat the adjustment procedure, if needed, until the correct breaker point gap is obtained.

To renew breaker point assembly (9) and condenser (8), proceed as follows: Remove air shrouds (S—Fig. M3-6). Remove the six screws retaining fan (3—Fig. M3-9) to flywheel (4) and withdraw fan (3).

Using a suitable flywheel holding tool (H—Fig. M3-10) to prevent flywheel rotation, remove securing nut (1—Fig. M3-9) using suitable tools (T—Fig. M3-10). Remove flywheel (4—Fig. M3-9) from crankshaft end using a suitable puller assembly (P—Fig. M3-11). Note flywheel key located in crankshaft end slot.

⚠WARNING

Be sure suitable tools are used to remove the flywheel. Damage resultant from the misapplication of force or the use of incorrect tools may cause engine damage, engine malfunction or personal injury.

With reference to Fig. M3-9, renew breaker point assembly (9) and condenser (8). Adjust the breaker point gap to the recommended setting as outlined in a previous paragraph. Make sure the securing screws are properly tightened. Be sure the flywheel key is properly positioned in the crankshaft end, then reinstall flywheel (4). Install lockwasher (2) and install and tighten securing nut (1) to 39-49 N·m (29-36 ft.-lbs.).

Magneto base plate (10) is fixed to the engine with taperd screws and no timing adjustment is possible other than varying the breaker point gap. Breaker point contacts should open when piston is 15½°-20½° BTDC or 1.05-1.85 mm (0.041-0.073 in.) BTDC. Install a suitable degree wheel on the flywheel or a dial indicator in the spark plug hole to verify piston position when breaker point contacts open.

Complete reassembly.

Ignition coil. To check ignition coil (11—Fig. M3-9) located on the side of the engine cylinder air

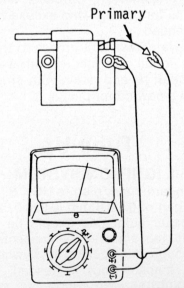

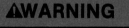

Fig. M3-12— *Connect ohmmeter leads as shown to measure the resistance in the primary side of the ignition coil. Refer to text.*

Illustrations Courtesy Mariner

Secondary

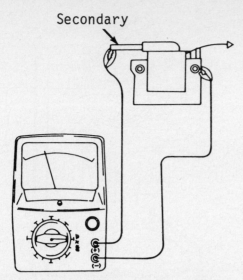

Fig. M3-13—Connect ohmmeter leads as shown to measure the resistance in the secondary side of the ignition coil. Refer to text.

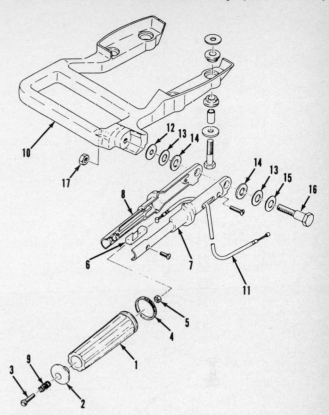

Fig. M3-14—Exploded view of speed control linkage.

1. Twist grip	
2. Friction cap	10. Frame
3. Screw	11. Throttle cable
4. Indicator	12. Washer
5. Nut	13. Washer
6. Slider	14. Washer
7. Steering handle half	15. Washer
8. Steering handle half	16. Bolt
9. Spring	17. Nut

shroud, use a suitable ohmmeter. Connect one tester lead to the coil's metal laminations, then connect the remaining tester lead alternately to the primary (Fig. M3-12) and secondary (Fig. M3-13) ignition coil leads. Resistance reading for primary circuit should be approximately 1.0 ohm while the secondary circuit resistance reading should be approximately 5900 ohms. Renew ignition coil (11—Fig. M3-9) if the meter readings are not within the proper range.

SPEED CONTROL LINKAGE

The engine speed is controlled by the position of the throttle linkage. A twist grip (1—Fig. M3-14) at the end of the steering handle is used to regulate the throttle linkage via throttle cable (11). Check linkage to make certain that carburetor throttle plate opens and closes fully according to the twist grip position and is correctly identified by indicator (4).

CARBURETOR

ADJUSTMENT. Standard main jet (24—Fig. 3-15) size is #82 for early models and #80 for later models when used under normal operation. Initial adjustment of idle mixture screw (3) is 1⅜ turns out from a lightly seated position. Recommended idle speed is 1550-1650 rpm with engine at normal operating temperature.

With the outboard motor properly mounted on boat or a suitable test tank, immerse the lower unit. Connect a tachometer and set it on the appropriate range scale. Start the engine and allow it to warm up to normal operating temperature.

Position the throttle control twist grip to the complete closed position. Adjust the engine idle speed screw (4) until the engine is idling at 1550-1650 rpm, then adjust idle mixture screw (3) until smooth engine operation is noted. Readjust the engine idle speed screw (4) until the recommended idle speed is obtained.

Recheck carburetor fuel level as previously outlined and adjust if needed.

Complete reassembly.

FUEL LEVEL. Remove the engine's top cover and the carburetor's silencer to expose carburetor inlet throttle bore as shown in Fig. M3-16. Connect a clear vinyl tube to the float bowl drain nozzle and hold the drain tube up. Open the float bowl drain plug. Run the engine at idle speed for a few minutes, then stop the engine. Fuel level in drain tube should be a distance (L) of 27-31 mm (1.063-1.220 in.) below center of carburetor throttle bore.

If fuel level is incorrect, float bowl (29—Fig. M3-15) must be removed and inlet valve (20)

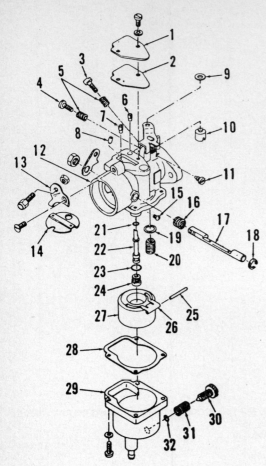

Fig. M3-15 — Exploded view of carburetor.

1. Top cover
2. Gasket
3. Idle mixture screw
4. Idle speed screw
5. Springs
6. Low speed jet
7. Low speed air jet
8. Main air jet
9. Washer
10. Cable connector
11. Throttle shaft screw
12. Carburetor body
13. Throttle cable plate
14. Choke plate
15. Main nozzle screw
16. Spring
17. Choke shaft
18. Snap ring
19. Gasket
20. Fuel inlet valve
21. Gasket
22. Main fuel nozzle
23. Gasket
24. Main jet
25. Float pin
26. Float arm
27. Float
28. Gasket
29. Float bowl
30. Drain plug
31. Spring
32. "O" ring

renewed if excessively worn or float arm (26) adjusted until the proper setting is obtained.

OVERHAUL. Remove any component that will interfere with carburetor removal. Clean all external surfaces and remove accumulated dirt and grease. Remove the cap screws securing the "L" shaped intake manifold and withdraw the intake manifold and carburetor as an assembly. Separate the carburetor from the intake manifold.

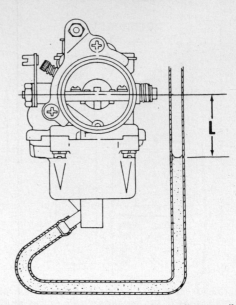

Fig. M3-16 — Fuel level in drain tube should be a distance (L) of 27-31 mm (1.063-1.220 in.) below center of carburetor throttle bore.

With reference to Fig. M3-15, disassemble the carburetor and note any discrepancies which must be corrected before reassembly. Remove all gaskets and "O" ring (label if needed for later reference) and set to the side.

Thoroughly clean all carburetor parts in a suitable solvent and inspect for excessive wear or any other damage. Note that plastic and rubber components should not be subjected to some cleaning solutions. Blow dry with clean compressed air. If compressed air is not available, use only lint-free cloths to wipe dry. Do not use a drill bit or wire to clean jets. Enlargement or damage of the calibrated holes may affect engine performance.

With reference to Fig. M3-15, reassemble the carburetor components with new gaskets and "O" ring. Note that the new gaskets should match up with those removed. If not, check with your parts supplier to be sure you have the correct gasket set. The "O" ring must fit properly and seal tight.

When reinstalling the carburetor, place a new gasket between the carburetor and intake manifold, and the intake manifold and cylinder port. Securely tighten the retaining cap screws and, if applicable, the nuts. Reconnect fuel supply line and carburetor linkage. Initially adjust idle mixture screw (3) 1⅜ turns out from a lightly seated position.

Verify carburetor fuel level as outlined in the previous FUEL LEVEL section and note if fuel level adjustment is needed.

MARINER 4 AND 5 HP (1982-1985)

NOTE: Metric fasteners are used throughout outboard motor.

Specifications

Hp/rpm	4/5000
	5/5000
Bore:	
4 hp	50 mm
	(1.98 in.)
5 hp	54 mm
	(2.14 in.)
Stroke:	
4 hp	42 mm
	(1.67 in.)
5 hp	45 mm
	(1.79 in.)
Number of cylinders	1
Displacement:	
4 hp	83 cc
	(5 cu. in.)
5 hp	103 cc
	(6.3 cu. in.)
Spark plug	NGK B7HS
Electrode gap	0.5-0.6 mm
	(0.020-0.024 in.)
Ignition type	CDI
Idle speed (in gear)	950-1050 rpm
Fuel:oil ratio	50:1
Gearcase oil capacity	105 mL
	(3.5 oz.)

Maintenance

LUBRICATION

ENGINE. The engine is lubricated by oil mixed with the fuel. The fuel should be regular leaded, low lead or unleaded gasoline with a minimum pump octane rating of 86. Recommended oil is Quicksilver Formula 50-D Outboard Lubricant or a BIA certified two-stroke motor oil. The recommended fuel:oil ratio for normal operation is 50:1. During engine break-in, the fuel:oil ratio should be increased to 25:1.

The manufacturer's recommended break-in period is defined as follows: For the first five minutes of operation the engine should not exceed its slowest possible cruising speed. After five minutes, slowly increase the engine speed to half throttle (2500-3500 rpm) for the first three hours of operation. Running the engine at or near full throttle for extended periods is not recommended until after ten hours of operation.

LOWER UNIT. The lower unit gears and bearings are lubricated by oil contained in the gear-case. The recommended oil is Mariner Super Duty Gear Lube or a suitable EP 90 outboard gear oil. The gearcase oil capacity is 105 milliliters (3.5

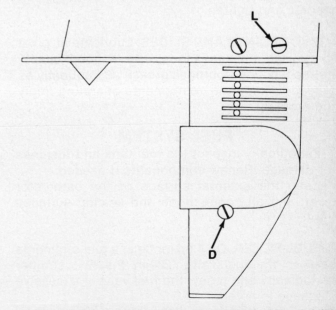

Fig. M4-1 — View showing lower unit gearcase drain and fill plug (D) and oil level (vent) plug (L).

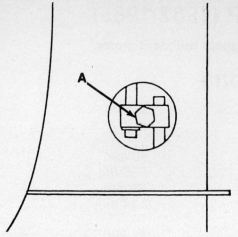

Fig. M4-2 — Adjustment cap screw (A) is used to adjust shift linkage. Refer to text.

oz.). The gearcase should be refilled periodically and the lubricant renewed after every 100 hours of operation or more frequently if needed. The gearcase is drained and filled through the same plug port (D — Fig. M4-1). An oil level (vent) port (L) is used to indicated the full oil level of the gearcase and to ease in oil drainage.

To drain the oil, place the outboard motor in a vertical position. Remove drain plug (D) and oil level plug (L), and allow the lubricant to drain into a suitable container.

To fill the gearcase with oil, place the outboard motor in a vertical position. Add oil through drain plug (D) opening with an oil feeder until the oil begins to overflow from oil level plug (L) port. Reinstall oil level plug (L) with a new gasket, if needed, and tighten. Remove oil feeder, then reinstall drain plug (D) with a new gasket, if needed, and tighten.

PIVOT POINTS AND SLIDES. Lubricate all pivot points and linkage slides with a good quality marine type multipurpose grease as frequently as needed to keep the components operating freely and properly.

FUEL SYSTEM

Periodically inspect the fuel tank and fuel ines for damage. Renew components if needed.

Keep the external surface of the carburetor clean and all connections and sealing surfaces tight.

FUEL FILTER. On 4 hp models, a fuel strainer is used in the fuel valve. Clean the fuel strainer periodically and renew the fuel valve if excessive blockage is noted.

On 5 hp models, a disposable type filter element is connected between the fuel supply line and the fuel pump inlet line. After every 50 hours of operation or more frequent if needed, remove the filter element and blow through the filter's inlet side with low air pressure and note the resistance. A minimal amount of resistance should be noted. If not, filter assembly should be renewed.

FUEL PUMP. The fuel pump is an integral part of the carburetor. Refer to CARBURETOR in the Tune-Up section for fuel pump overhaul.

NOTE: With the use of proper tools, the fuel pump assembly may be overhauled without carburetor removal.

SHIFT LINKAGE

Direction of propeller rotation is determined by the position of the gear shift lever. The gear shift lever actuates gearcase components using shift linkage consisting of an upper and lower shift rod connected by an adjustment bracket. The tapered end of the lower shift rod controls the movement of the dog clutch on the propeller shaft. The positioning of the dog clutch on the propeller shaft determines whether forward, neutral or reverse directional movement is selected.

To adjust, remove adjustment cap screw (A — Fig. M4-2) cover. Loosen cap screw (A) enough to allow the lower shift rod to slide freely in the adjustment bracket. Place the shift lever in the reverse detent position and the lower shift rod in the reverse position. Push down on the adjustment bracket only with enough force to remove any slack in the linkage, then tighten adjustment cap screw (A). Check the adjustment by turning the propeller.

⚠WARNING

Disconnect spark plug lead and properly ground lead before performing any propeller service, otherwise, accidental starting can occur if propeller shift.

Make sure neutral and forward properly engage. If not, repeat the adjustment procedure, then reinstall the adjustment cap screw's cover.

STARTER

When starter rope (10 — Fig. M4-3) is pulled, pulley (4) will rotate. As pulley (4) rotates, drive pawl (6) moves to engage with the flywheel, thus cranking the engine.

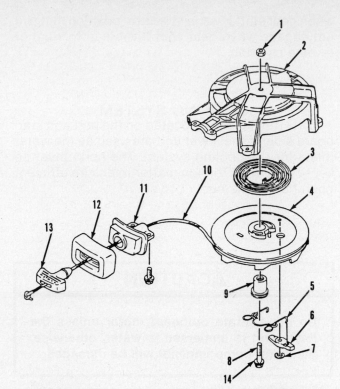

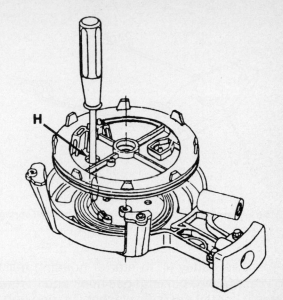

Fig. M4-4 — Pulley hole (H) is used during pulley withdrawal. Refer to text.

Fig. M4-3 — Exploded view of manual rewind starter.

1. Nut	8. Bolt
2. Starter housing	9. Shaft
3. Rewind spring	10. Starter rope
4. Pulley	11. Rope guide
5. Spring	12. Seal
6. Drive pawl	13. Handle
7. Clip	14. Washer

When starter rope (10) is released, pulley (4) is rotated in the reverse direction by force from rewind spring (3). As pulley (4) rotates, the starter rope is rewound and drive pawl (6) is disengaged from the flywheel.

A starter lockout assembly is used to prevent starter engagement when the gear shift lever is in the forward or reverse position.

The manual starter must be disassembled to renew starter rope (10) and rewind spring (3).

To overhaul the manual starter, proceed as follows: Remove the engine's top cover. Remove the screws retaining the manual starter to the engine. Remove the starter lockout cable at the starter housing. Note plunger and spring located at cable end, care should be used not to lose components should they fall free. Withdraw the starter assembly.

⚠WARNING

Care should be exercised when working with or around a coiled starter rewind spring as sudden uncoiling can cause injury. Safety eyewear and gloves are recommended.

Check pawl (6) for freedom of movement, excessive wear of engagement area and any other damage. Renew or lubricate pawl (6) with a suitable water-resistant grease and return starter to service if no other damage is noted.

To disassemble, remove clip (7) and withdraw pawl (6) and pawl spring (5). Untie starter rope (10) at handle (13) and allow the rope to wind into the starter. Remove bolt (8), washer (14) and shaft (9), then place a suitable screwdriver blade through hole (H — Fig. M4-4) to hold rewind spring (3 — Fig. M4-3) securely in housing (2). Carefully lift pulley (4) with starter rope (10) from housing (2). BE CAREFUL when removing pulley (4) as the rewind spring may be dislodged. Untie starter rope (10) and remove rope from pulley (4) if renewal is required. To remove rewind spring (3) from housing (2), invert housing so it sits upright on a flat surface, then tap the housing top until rewind spring (3) falls free and uncoils.

Inspect all components for damage and excessive wear and renew if needed.

To reassemble, first apply a coating of a suitable water-resistant grease to rewind spring area of housing (2). Install rewind spring (3) in housing (2) so spring coils wind in a counterclockwise direction from the outer end. Make sure the spring's outer hook is properly secured over starter housing (2) pin. Wind starter rope (10) onto pulley (4) approximately 2½ turns counterclockwise when viewed from the flywheel side. Direct remaining starter rope (10) length through notch in pulley (4).

NOTE: Lubricate all friction surfaces with a suitable water-resistant grease during reassembly.

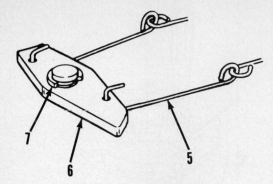

Fig. M4-5 — View showing proper installation of pawl spring (5), drive pawl (6) and clip (7).

Assemble pulley (4) to starter housing making sure that pulley's pin engages hook end in rewind spring (3). Install shaft (9), washer (14) and bolt (8). Apply Loctite 271 or 290 or an equivalent thread fastening solution on bolt (8) threads and install nut (1) and securely tighten.

Thread starter rope (10) through starter housing (2), rope guide (11) and handle (13) and secure with a knot. Turn pulley (4) two turns counterclockwise when viewed from the flywheel side, then release starter rope (10) from pulley notch and allow rope to slowly wind onto pulley.

NOTE: Do not apply any more tension on rewind spring (3) than is required to draw starter handle (13) back into the proper released position.

Install spring (5), pawl (6) and clip (7) as shown in Fig. M4-5. Remount manual starter assembly.

Adjust starter lockout assembly by turning adjusting nuts at cable end so starter will engage when gear shift lever is in neutral position, but will not engage when gear shift lever is in forward or reverse position.

COOLING SYSTEM
Ports (I — Fig. M4-6) located on the port and starboard side of the lower unit are used as the water inlets for the cooling system. The ports must be kept clean of all foreign matter to ensure efficient operation of the cooling system.

⚠CAUTION

Do not operate outboard motor unless the lower unit is immersed in water, otherwise, the water pump impeller will be damaged.

PROPELLER
The standard propeller on 4 hp models has three blades, a diameter of 190 mm (7½ in.) and a pitch of 203 mm (8 in.). The standard propeller on 5 hp models has three blades, a diameter of 184 mm (7¼ in.) and a pitch of 210 mm (8¼ in.). Optional propellers are available. Select a propeller that will allow the engine at full throttle to reach maximum operating rpm range (4500-5500).

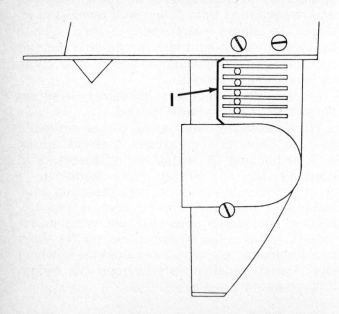

Fig. M4-6 — Cooling system water inlet ports (I) are located on both sides of the lower unit.

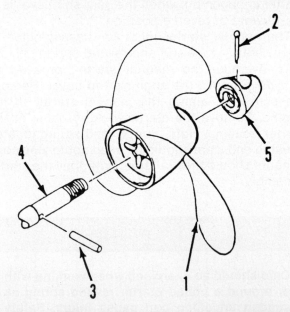

Fig. M4-7 — Propeller (1) is mounted on propeller shaft (4) and is retained by spinner (5) and cotter pin (2). Shear pin (3) is renewed only after withdrawing propeller (1) from propeller shaft (4).

Illustrations Courtesy Mariner

To remove the propeller, proceed as follows: Remove cotter pin (2 — Fig. M4-7) and unscrew propeller spinner (5). Withdraw propeller (1) from propeller shaft (4).

Inspect propeller (1), propeller shaft (4) and shear pin (3) for excessive wear and renew if excessive wear or damage is noted.

Apply a water-resistant grease to the propeller bore, then install propeller (1) on propeller shaft (4) and retain with propeller spinner (5) and a new cotter pin (2).

Tune-Up

IGNITION SYSTEM

Both the 4 and 5 hp models are equipped with a capacitor discharge ignition (CDI) system. Refer to the Outboard Motor Service Manual for testing and servicing the CD ignition system. If engine malfunction is noted and the ignition system is suspected, make sure the spark plug and all electrical wiring are in good condition and all electrical connections are tight before proceeding to troubleshooting the CD ignition system.

The standard spark plug on both the 4 and 5 hp models is NGK B7HS with an electrode gap of 0.5-0.6 mm (0.020-0.024 in.).

SPEED CONTROL LINKAGE

The engine speed is regulated by the position of the carburetor's throttle plate. The throttle plate is controlled by the twist grip via a control cable. When the twist grip is placed in the "FAST" position, stopper (TS — Fig. M4-8) on the carburetor's throttle arm should contact carburetor stop (CS). If not, reposition the control cable inner wire (W) length until the correct positioning is obtained.

CARBURETOR

The fuel pump and carburetor are a complete unit. Refer to the following OVERHAUL section for service procedures on both the fuel pump and carburetor.

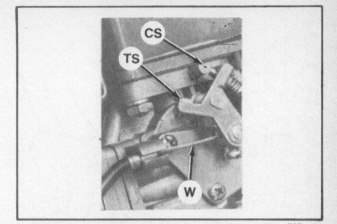

Fig. M4-8—View depicting control cable inner wire (W), carburetor stop (CS) and throttle arm stop (TS). Refer to text.

ADJUSTMENT. Use the standard carburetor jet sizes as recommended by the manufacturer for normal operation when used at altitudes of 2500 feet (760 mm) and less. Main jet (12—Fig. M4-9) size should be reduced from standard recommendation by one size for altitudes of 2500 to 5000 feet (760 to 1525 m), two sizes for altitudes 5000 to 7500 feet (1525 to 2285 m) and three sizes for altitudes of 7500 feet (2285 m) and up. Initial adjustment of idle mixture screw (5) is 1½ to 2 turns out from a lightly seated position on 4 hp models and 1 to 1½ turns out from a lightly seated position on 5 hp models. Recommended idle speed is 950-1050 rpm in gear with the engine at normal operating temperature.

With the outboard motor properly mounted on a boat or a suitable test tank, immerse the lower unit. Connect a tachometer and set it on the appropriate range scale. Start the engine and allow it to warm up to normal operating temperature. Position the throttle control twist grip to the complete closed position. Place the gear shift lever in the "Forward" position. Adjust the engine idle speed screw (8) until the engine is idling at 950-1050 rpm, then adjust idle mixture screw (5) until smooth engine operation is noted. Readjust the engine idle speed screw (8) until the recommended idle speed is obtained.

Reinstall engine's top cover.

OVERHAUL. The fuel pump is an integral part of the carburetor. With the use of proper tools, the fuel pump assembly may be overhauled without overhauling the complete carburetor. If the fuel pump is to be overhauled without carburetor removal, proceed as follows: Remove the engine's top cover. On 4 hp models, close the fuel valve and disconnect the fuel supply hose at the fuel pump inlet. On 5 hp models, disconnect the fuel tank supply hose at the outboard motor connector, then disconnect the fuel supply hose at the fuel pump inlet.

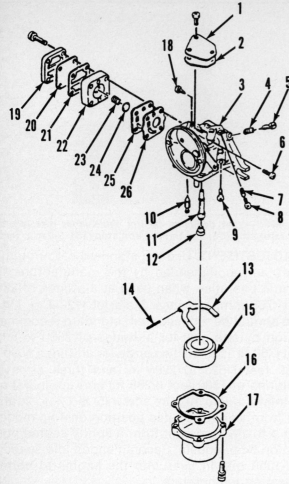

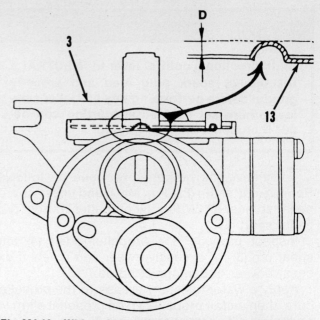

Fig. M4-10—With carburetor body (3) inverted, check float level by measuring distance (D) from carburetor body sealing surface to top of float lever (13) hump. Distance should be 1.5-2.5 mm (0.06-0.10 in.) and is adjusted by bending the arms of float lever (13).

Fig. M4-9 — Exploded view of carburetor/fuel pump assembly.

1. Cover plate	14. Pin
2. Gasket	15. Float
3. Carburetor body	16. Gasket
4. Spring	17. Float bowl
5. Idle mixture screw	18. Guide screw
6. Screw	19. Fuel pump cover
7. Spring	20. Diaphragm
8. Idle speed screw	21. Gasket
9. Pilot jet	22. Pump body
10. Needle valve	23. Spring
11. Main nozzle	24. Spring plate
12. Main jet	25. Diaphragm
13. Float lever	26. Gasket

With reference to Fig. M4-9, disassemble the fuel pump assembly. Inspect all components for damage and excessive wear and renew if needed. Clean components as needed with a suitable cleaning solution. Blow dry with clean compressed air. If compressed air is not available, use only lint-free cloths to wipe dry. Make sure all passages are clear of any obstructions.

With reference to Fig. M4-9, reassemble the fuel pump assembly with new gaskets. Securely tighten the retaining screws.

NOTE: Fuel pump and engine malfunction will result if the fuel pump and all connections are not airtight.

Complete reassembly.

Refer to the following for complete carburetor overhaul: Remove the engine's top cover. Remove the manual rewind starter assembly. Remove the two screws retaining the air intake cover and withdraw. Disconnect the choke rod from the carburetor choke lever clip. Loosen the screw securing the throttle control cable inner wire (6—Fig. M4-9), then extract the control cable and position the cable clear of carburetor assembly. On 4 hp models, close the fuel valve and disconnect the fuel supply hose at the fuel pump inlet. On 5 hp models, disconnect the fuel tank supply hose at the outboard motor connector, then disconnect the fuel supply hose at the fuel pump inlet. Clean all external surfaces and remove accumulated dirt and grease. Remove the two nuts and lockwashers securing the carburetor and withdraw the carburetor assembly.

With reference to Fig. M4-9, disassemble the complete carburetor assembly and note any discrepancies which must be corrected before reassembly. Remove all gaskets (label if needed for later reference) and set to the side.

Thoroughly clean all carburetor parts in a suitable solvent and inspect for damage and excessive wear. Note that plastic and rubber components should not be subjected to some cleaning solutions. Blow dry with clean compressed air. If compressed air is not available, use only lint-free cloths to wipe dry. Do not use a drill bit or wire to clean jets. Enlargement or damage of the calibrated holes may affect engine performance.

With reference to Fig. M4-9, reassemble the carburetor components with new gaskets. Note that the new gaskets should match up with those removed. If not, check with your parts supplier to be sure you have the correct gasket set.

To determine the float level, invert carburetor body (3—Fig. M4-10) with needle valve (10—Fig. M4-9) and float lever (13—Fig. M4-10) installed. Measure distance (D) from carburetor body sealing surface to top of float lever hump. Distance should be 1.5-2.5 mm (0.06-0.10 in.) and is adjusted by bending the arms of float lever (13).

When reinstalling the carburetor, place a new gasket between the carburetor and the intake manifold. Install the lockwashers and securely tighten the retaining nuts. Complete reassembly in the reverse of disassembly with the exception of the engine's top cover. Position the control cable inner wire (W—Fig. M4-8) so when the twist grip is placed in the "FAST" position, stopper (TS) on the carburetor's throttle arm contacts carburetor stop (CS). Initally adjust idle mixture screw (5—Fig. M4-11) 1½ to 2 turns out from a lightly

Fig. M4-11 — View depicting idle mixture screw (5) and idle speed screw (8).

seated position on 4 hp models and 1 to 1½ turns out from a lightly seated position on 5 hp models.

MARINER 8 HP (PRIOR TO 1979)

NOTE: Metric fasteners are used throughout outboard motor.

Specifications

Hp/rpm 8/5000
Bore . . . . .50 mm
(1.97 in.)
Stroke. . . . . .42 mm
(1.65 in.)
Number of cylinders 2
Displacement . . . . .164 cc
(10 cu. in.)
Spark plug—NGK. B7HS
    Electrode gap . . . . .0.5-0.6 mm
(0.020-0.024 in.)
Breaker point gap . . . . .0.30-0.40 mm
(0.012-0.016 in.)
Ignition timing . . . . .See Text
Idle speed . . . . .1150-1250 rpm
Fuel:oil ratio. 50:1
Gearcase oil capacity . . . . .230 mL
(7.8 oz.)

Maintenance

LUBRICATION

ENGINE. The engine is lubricated by oil mixed with the fuel. The fuel should be regular leaded, low lead or unleaded gasoline with a minimum pump octane rating of 86. Recommended oil is Quicksilver Formula 50-D Outboard Lubricant or a BIA certified two-stroke motor oil. The recommended fuel:oil ratio for normal operation is 50:1. During engine break-in, the fuel:oil ratio should be increased to 25:1.

The manufacturer's recommended break-in period is defined as follows: For the first five minutes of operation the engine should not exceed its slowest possible cruising speed. After five minutes, slowly increase the engine speed to half throttle (2500-3500 rpm) for the first three hours of operation.

Running the engine at or near full throttle for extended periods is not recommended until after ten hours of operation.

LOWER UNIT. The lower unit gears and bearings are lubricated by oil contained in the gearcase. The recommended oil is Mariner Super Duty Gear Lube or a suitable EP 90 outboard gear oil.

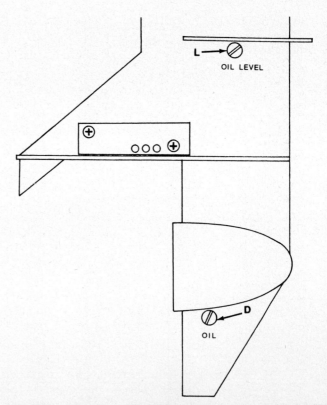

Fig. M5-1—View showing lower unit gearcase drain and fill plug (D) and oil level (vent) plug (L).

Illustrations Courtesy Mariner

The gearcase oil capacity is 230 milliliters (7.8 oz.). The gearcase should be refilled periodically and the lubricant renewed after every 50 hours of operation or more frequently if needed. The gearcase is drained and filled through the same plug port (D—Fig. M5-1). An oil level (vent) port (L) is used to indicate the full oil level of the gearcase and to ease in oil drainage.

To drain the oil, place the outboard motor in a vertical position. Remove drain plug (D) and oil level plug (L) and allow the lubricant to drain into a suitable container.

To fill the gearcase with oil, place the outboard motor in a vertical position. Add oil through drain plug (D) opening with an oil feeder until the oil begins to overflow from oil level plug (L) port. Reinstall oil level plug (L) with a new gasket, if needed, and tighten. Remove oil feeder, then reinstall drain plug (D) with a new gasket, if needed, and tighten.

PIVOT POINTS AND SLIDES. Lubricate all pivot points and linkage slides with a good quality marine type multipurpose grease as frequently as needed to keep the components operating freely and properly.

FUEL SYSTEM

Periodically inspect the fuel lines and connections for damage. Renew components if needed. With the engine stopped, occasionally open the carburetor's main body bowl drain plug and allow the fuel to drain off into a suitable container. Inspect the fuel for any foreign matter. If an excessive amount of foreign matter is found, extensive cleaning of the fuel system is needed. A filter screen is used in the fuel pump assembly and a strainer is placed in the fuel supply hose prior to entering the fuel pump inlet.

Keep the external surface of the carburetor clean and all connections and sealing surfaces tight.

FUEL PUMP. The fuel pump is operated by crankcase pressure changes from the up and down movement of the piston. When the crankcase pressure decreases (the piston is moving upward), the pump diaphragm is pulled toward the crankcase allowing fuel to enter the pump body and closing the discharge check valve. When the crankcase pressure increases (the piston is moving downward), the diaphragm is pushed outward discharging the fuel to the carburetor and closing the inlet check valve. This pulsating action allows for continuous fuel flow. The check valves are used to prevent reverse flow of the fuel.

The inlet port is identified as "IN" and the fuel hoses must be connected accordingly.

To overhaul, first remove the engine's top cover

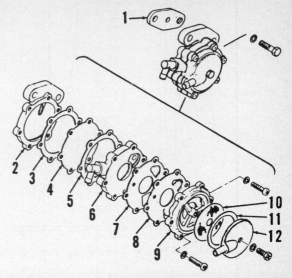

Fig. M5-2—Exploded view of fuel pump assembly.

1. Gasket	5. Gasket	9. Body
2. Base	6. Body	10. Screen
3. Gasket	7. Gasket	11. Gasket
4. Diaphragm	8. Check valve	12. Inlet

and disconnect the fuel tank supply hose at the outboard motor connector. Disconnect the fuel hoses at the fuel pump inlet and discharge nozzles and label if needed. Remove the securing cap screws and withdraw the fuel pump assembly.

With reference to Fig. M5-2, disassemble the fuel pump assembly. Inspect all components for damage and excessive wear and renew if needed. Clean filter screen (10) with a suitable cleaning solvent.

With reference to Fig. M5-2, reassemble the fuel pump assembly with new gaskets. Mount the fuel pump assembly to the crankcase with a new gasket (1) and securely tighten the retaining cap screws.

NOTE: Fuel pump and engine malfunction will result if the fuel pump and all connections are not airtight.

Complete reassembly.

SHIFT LINKAGE

Direction of propeller rotation is determined by the position of the gear shift lever. The gear shift lever actuates gearcase components using shift linkage consisting of an upper and lower shift rod connected by an adjustment bracket. The tapered end of the lower shift rod controls the movement of the dog clutch on the propeller shaft. The positioning of the dog clutch on the propeller shaft determines whether forward, neutral or reverse directional movement is selected.

To adjust, remove adjustment cap screw (A—Fig. M5-3) cover. Loosen cap screw enough to allow lower shift rod to slide freely in adjustment

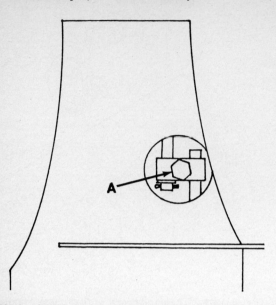

Fig. M5-3—Adjustment cap screw (A) is used to adjust shift linkage. Refer to text.

bracket. Place shift lever in reverse detent position and lower shift rod in reverse detent position. Push down on adjustment bracket only with enough force to remove any slack in the linkage, then tighten adjustment cap screw (A). Check adjustment by turning propeller.

⚠ WARNING

Disconnect spark plug leads and properly ground lead before performing any propeller service, otherwise, accidental starting can occur if propeller shaft is rotated.

Make sure neutral and forward properly engage. If not, repeat adjustment procedure, then reinstall cover.

STARTER

When starter rope (25—Fig. M5-4) is pulled, the manual starter assembly pivots around pivot bolt (2) and meshes starter gear (12) with the flywheel gear. As starter rope (25) is further pulled out, pulley (19) rotates, thus rotating drive plate (14) from friction caused by spring (16). The rotating drive plate (14) forces pawls (15) to move out and engage starter gear (12) recesses. The starter gear (12) is then rotated, thus causing the flywheel to rotate.

NOTE: Starter rope (25) must be drawn out slowly until resistance is felt, then pulled out quickly in a single motion. Damage to the starter will result if pawls (15) are not allowed to engage starter gear (12) recesses prior to sharply pulling starter rope (25).

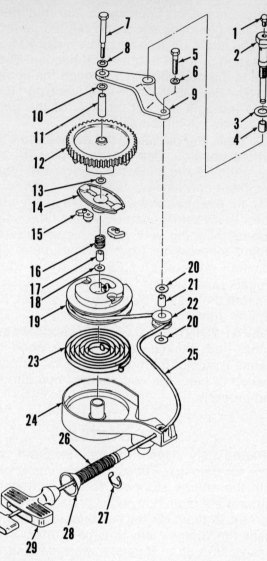

Fig. M5-4—Exploded view of manual starter assembly.

1. Grease fitting	16. Drive plate spring
2. Pivot bolt	17. Collar
3. Thrust washer	18. Washer
4. Collar	19. Pulley
5. Cap screw	20. Washer
6. Lockwasher	21. Collar
7. Cap screw	22. Pulley
8. Lockwasher	23. Rewind spring
9. Lever	24. Housing
10. Thrust washer	25. Starter rope
11. Distance collar	26. Spring
12. Starter gear	27. Clip
13. Thrust washer	28. Guide
14. Drive plate	29. Handle
15. Pawl	30. Anchor

When starter rope (25) is released, pulley (19) is rotated in the reverse direction by force from rewind spring (23). As pulley (19) rotates, the starter rope is rewound and drive pawls (15) are disengaged from starter gear (12). The manual starter assembly is pivoted away from the flywheel gear by pressure from spring (26).

The manual starter must be disassembled to renew starter rope (25) or any other internal starter component.

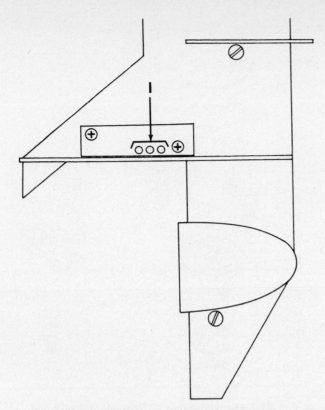

Fig. M5-5 — *Cooling system water inlet ports (I) are located on both sides of the lower unit.*

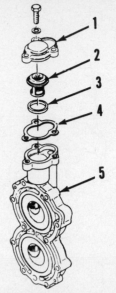

Fig. M5-5A — *Exploded view of the cooling system components located at the top of the engine's cylinder head (5).*

1. Cover
2. Thermostat
3. Spacer
4. Gasket
5. Cylinder head

To overhaul the manual starter, proceed as follows: Remove the engine's top cover. Untie starter rope (25) at anchor (30) and allow starter rope to slowly wind onto pulley (19). Tie a knot on the end of starter rope (25) to prevent it from being pulled into housing (24). Remove pivot bolt (2) and lift manual starter assembly from power head.

⚠WARNING

Care should be exercised when working with or around a coiled starter rewind spring as sudden uncoiling can cause injury. Safety eyewear and gloves are recommended.

To disassemble, remove cap screws (5 and 7) with washers (6 and 8). Withdraw lever (9) and starter gear (12) and distance collar (11) and thrust washers (10 and 13). Drive plate (14), pawls (15) and drive plate spring (16) can be serviced at this time. Drive plate spring (16) free length should be 131.6 mm (5.181 in.) with a minimum free length of 129.6 mm (5.102 in.) Inspect all components for damage and excessive wear and renew if needed.

Withdraw pulley (19) to renew rewind spring (23) if needed. BE CAREFUL when removing pulley (19) as rewind spring (23) may be dislodged.

Reassembly is the reverse order of disassembly. Apply a water-resistant grease to rewind spring (23) and pawls (15) during reassembly. Make sure that rewind spring (23) is correctly hooked in housing (24) and pulley (19). Starter rope (25) should be wound around pulley (19) six turns counterclockwise when viewed from starter gear (12) side. To assure the proper alignment of lever (9) with housing (24), install the manual starter assembly and pivot bolt (2) before tightening cap screws (5 and 7), tighten screws (5 and 7) to a torque of 4-6 N.m (3-4.5 ft.-lbs.).

COOLING SYSTEM

Ports (I-Fig. M5-5) located on both sides of the lower unit are used as the water inlets for the cooling system. The ports must be kept clean of all foreign matter to ensure efficient operation of the cooling system.

⚠CAUTION

Do not operate outboard motor unless the lower unit is immersed in water, otherwise, the water pump impeller will be damaged.

A thermostat positioned in the cylinder head is used to regulate the engine's operating temperature. Note that a thermostat that sticks or stays closed too long could cause engine overheating, resulting in poor engine operation and possible engine damage. A thermostat that opens too quickly or is stuck in the open position

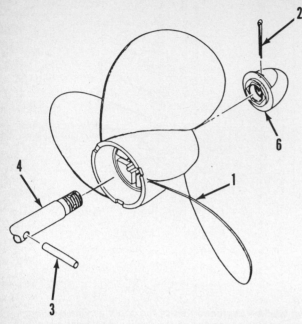

Fig. M5-6 — Propeller (1) is mounted on propeller shaft (4) and is retained by spinner (6) and cotter pin (2). Shear pin (3) is renewed only after withdrawing propeller (1) from propeller shaft (4).

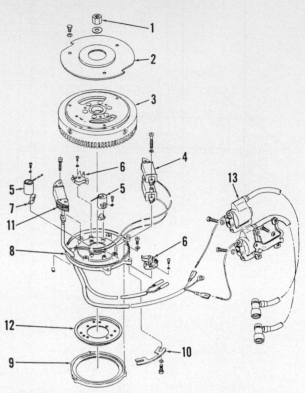

Fig. M5-7 — Exploded view of flywheel magneto unit.

1. Nut	8. Magneto base plate
2. Flywheel cover	9. Magneto base plate
3. Flywheel	retainer
4. Low voltage coil	10. Bracket
5. Condenser	11. Lighting coil
6. Breaker point assy.	12. Retainer
7. Lubricator	13. Ignition coil

will cause the engine not to reach its recommended operating temperature range, resulting in possible engine malfunction and poor engine efficiency. If thermostat malfunction is suspected, remove the thermostat cover located at the top of the cylinder head as shown in Fig. M5-5A to gain access to the thermostat.

Refer to the Outboard Motor Service Manual if more extensive service to the cooling system is required.

PROPELLER

The standard propeller has three blades, a diameter of 229 mm (9 in.) and a pitch of 178 mm (7 in.). A three-bladed propeller with a diameter of 229 mm (9 in.) and a pitch of 190 mm (7½ in.) or 229 mm (9 in.) is optionally available.

⚠️**WARNING**

Shift directional control lever to "NEUTRAL." Disconnect spark plug leads and properly ground leads before performing any propeller service, otherwise, accidental starting can occur if propeller shaft is rotated.

To remove the propeller, remove cotter pin (2—Fig. M5-6) and unscrew propeller spinner (6). Withdraw propeller (1) from propeller shaft (4).

Inspect propeller (1), propeller shaft (4) and shear pin (3) for damage and excessive wear. Renew if excessive wear or damage is noted.

Apply a water-resistant grease to the propeller bore, then install propeller (1) on propeller shaft (4) and retain with propeller spinner (6) and a new cotter pin (2).

Tune-Up
IGNITION SYSTEM

The standard spark plug is NGK B7HS with an electrode gap of 0.5-0.6 mm (0.020-0.024 in.).

The breaker point gap should be 0.3-0.4 mm (0.012-0.016 in.) and can be inspected and adjusted through the opening in flywheel (3—Fig. M5-7). Two breaker point assemblies (6) and two condensers (5) are used. To inspect and, if needed, adjust the breaker point gap, first remove the engine's top cover. Remove the three cap screws and lockwashers securing flywheel cover (2) to the flywheel and withdraw.

Inspect the breaker point surfaces for excessive wear, pitting or any other damage. If needed, renew breaker point assemblies (6) and condensers (5) as outlined later in this section.

Fig. M5-8 — View showing the use of a suitable flywheel holding tool (H) to prevent flywheel rotation during removal of securing nut (1 — Fig. M5-7) with suitable tools (T).

Fig. M5-9 — Remove flywheel from crankshaft end using a suitable puller assembly (P).

To clean the breaker point contact surfaces, rotate the flywheel until the breaker point contact surfaces are accessible through the opening in flywheel (3). Use a point file or sandpaper with a grit rating of 400 to 600. After polishing, wipe the contact surfaces clean with a dry cloth and lightly grease the breaker point arm and lubricator (7) with a suitable lubricant.

Turn the flywheel until the breaker point contact surfaces are placed at their widest position, then reach through the flywheel opening with a feeler gage of the appropriate size and check the distance between the point surfaces. If the distance is not within the recommended limits, loosen the point set securing screw and adjust the point set until the correct gap is obtained. Tighten the point set securing screw and recheck the breaker point gap. Repeat the adjustment procedure, if needed, until the correct breaker point gap is obtained. Follow the previously described procedure and adjust the other breaker point assembly.

To renew breaker point assemblies (6) and condensers (5), proceed as follows: Using a suitable flywheel holding tool (H—Fig. M5-8) to prevent flywheel rotation, remove securing nut (1—Fig. M5-7). Remove flywheel (3) from crankshaft end using a suitable puller assembly (P—Fig. M5-9). Note the flywheel key located in the crankshaft keyway.

⚠WARNING

Be sure suitable tools are used to remove the flywheel. Damage resultant from the misapplication of force or the use of incorrect tools may cause engine damage, engine malfunction or personal injury.

With reference to Fig. M5-7, renew breaker point assemblies (6) and condensers (5). Adjust the breaker point gap to the recommended setting as outlined in a previous paragraph. Make sure the securing screws are properly tightened. Be sure the flywheel key is properly positioned in the crankshaft end, then reinstall flywheel (3). Install lockwasher and install and tighten securing nut (1) to 30-34 N·m (22-25 ft.-lbs.).

To obtain the correct ignition timing: First adjust both breaker point assemblies (6) to the proper point gap as previously outlined. Remove both spark plugs. Use a point checker and attach the red tester lead to the grey wire coming from the magneto base plate (8) (top cylinder's low voltage coil lead). Connect the black tester lead to an engine ground.

NOTE: A suitable continuity tester can be used.

Fully open the throttle by pushing the magneto base plate to full advance position. Slowly turn the flywheel counterclockwise until the tester's pointer moves from "OPEN" to "CLOSE", then stop turning the flywheel. Check the alignment of the flywheel rotor's punch mark (P—Fig. M5-10) with the stopper's arrow (A). If not properly aligned, loosen cap screws retaining bracket (10) and

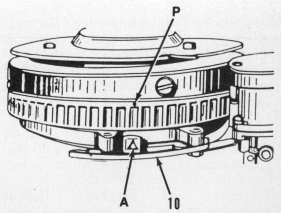

Fig. M5-10 — View showing punch mark (P) on flywheel rotor and arrow (A) on stopper used for setting ignition timing. Bracket (10) is used for top cylinder's adjustment. Refer to text.

Mariner 8 Hp (Prior to 1979)

Fig. M5-11 — A dial indicator is used to verify piston position.

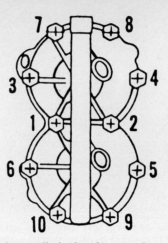

Fig. M5-12 — Tighten cylinder head screws in sequence shown.

adjust magento base plate (8—Fig. M5-7) until proper alignment is obtained, then tighten cap screws.

Attach the point checker's red tester lead to the orange wire coming from the magneto base plate (8) (bottom cylinder's low voltage coil lead). Make sure the black tester lead remains grounded to engine. Fully open the throttle by pushing the magneto base plate (8) to full advance position. Slowly turn the flywheel counterclockwise until the tester's pointer moved from "OPEN" to "CLOSE", then stop turning the flywheel. Check the alignment of punch mark (P—Fig. M5-10) on flywheel rotor with the arrow (A) on stopper. If not properly aligned, the full advance timing must be adjusted by varying the breaker point gap. Widening the gap advances the ignition timing and narrowing the gap slows the ignition timing.

To assure proper timing or if no punch marks are noted on the outside of the flywheel rotor, then a dial indicator must be used to verify piston position. Remove cylinder head and properly mount a dial indicator as shown in Fig. M5-11 in the top cylinder. Use a point checker and attach the red tester lead to the grey wire coming from the magneto base plate (8—Fig. M5-7). Connect the black tester lead to an engine ground.

Fully open the throttle by pushing the magneto base plate (8) to the full advance position. Slowly turn the flywheel counterclockwise until the tester's pointer moves from "OPEN" to "CLOSE", then stop turning the flywheel. Check the piston position reading on the dial indicator. The piston should be 2.1-2.8 mm (0.083-0.111 in.) BTDC. If not, loosen screws securing bracket (10—Fig. M5-10) and adjust the magneto base plate until the correct piston position is obtained when the tester's pointer moves from "OPEN" to "CLOSE", then tighten screws securing bracket (10). Repeat the procedure for the bottom cylinder. Attach the point checker's red tester lead to the orange wire coming from the magneto base plate (8—Fig.

M5-7). Make sure the black tester remains grounded to the engine. Adjust the full advance timing by varying the breaker point gap.

Reinstall cylinder head with a new gasket. Tighten cylinder head screws to an initial torque of 5.0 N·m (4.3 ft.-lbs.) using sequence shown in Fig. M5-12. Repeat sequence and tighten screws to a final torque of 10.7-12.8 N·m (7.9-9.4 ft.-lbs.).

Complete reassembly.

Ignition Coils. To check the ignition coils (13—Fig. M5-7) located on side of cylinders, use a suitable ohmmeter. Connect one tester lead to the coil's metal laminations, then connect the remaining tester lead alternately to the primary (Fig. M5-13) and secondary (Fig. M5-14) ignition coil leads. Resistance reading for primary circuit should be approximately 1.7 ohms while the

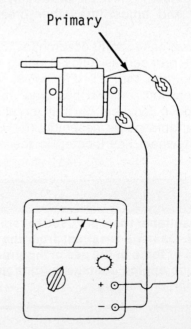

Fig. M5-13 — Connect ohmmeter leads as shown to measure resistance in the primary side of the ignition coil. Refer to text.

Illustrations Courtesy Mariner

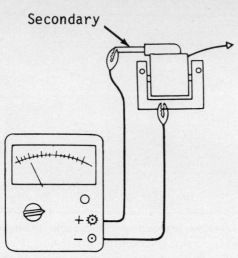

Fig. M5-14—Connect ohmmeter leads as shown to measure resistance in the secondary side of the ignition coil. Refer to text.

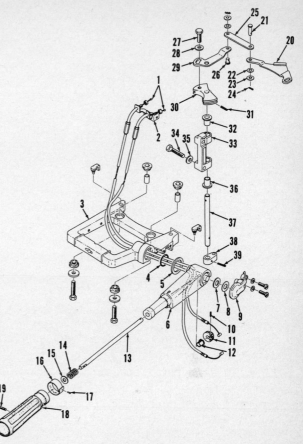

Fig. M5-15—View of speed control linkage components.

1. Control cables	14. Spring	27. Cap screw
2. Bracket	15. Washer	28. Flat washer
3. Handle bracket	16. Indicator	29. Link
4. "O" ring	17. Rivet	30. Pulley
5. Spacer	18. Twist grip	31. Pin
6. Steering handle	19. Screw	32. Bushing
7. Spacer	20. Throttle cam	33. Bracket
8. Spacer	21. Pivot pin	34. Cap screw
9. Cover	22. Wave washer	35. Flat washer
10. Pin	23. Flat washer	36. Bushing
11. Pulley	24. Clip	37. Shaft
12. Bushing	25. Link	38. End piece
13. Shaft	26. Pivot pin	39. Pin

secondary circuit resistance reading should be approximately 6000 ohms. Renew ignition coil(s) (13—Fig. M5-7) if the meter readings are not within the proper range.

SPEED CONTROL LINKAGE

As twist grip (18—Fig. M5-15) is rotated, the magneto base plate is rotated via cables (1) and associated linkage. Throttle cam (20) is mounted to the magneto base plate, thus operating carburetor throttle shaft in relation with the magneto base plate rotation.

Note that the adjustment of throttle cam (20) should only be made after the ignition timing has been correctly adjusted. When twist grip (18) is moved completely against the high speed stop, the carburetor throttle should be fully opened. MAKE SURE that the carburetor throttle does not reach the full open position before the ignition timing is fully advanced. The speed setting of twist grip (18) should be correctly identified by indicator (16).

CARBURETOR

ADJUSTMENT. Under normal operation, the following jet sizes are the standard recommendation: main jet (7—Fig. M5-16) #80 and pilot jet (3) #42. Initial adjustment of idle mixture screw (15) is ¾ to 1¼ turns out from a lightly seated position. Recommended idle speed is 1150-1250 rpm (900 rpm in gear) with engine at normal operating temperature.

With the outboard motor properly mounted on a boat or a suitable test tank, immerse the lower unit. Connect a tachometer and set it on the appropriate range scale. Start the engine and allow it to warm up to normal operating temperature. Position the throttle control twist grip to the com-

plete closed position. Adjust the engine idle speed screw (14) until the engine is idling at 1150-1250 rpm (900 rpm in gear), then adjust idle mixture screw (15) until smooth engine operation is noted. Readjust the engine idle speed screw (14) until the recommended idle speed is obtained.

Reinstall the engine's top cover.

OVERHAUL. Remove the engine's top cover. Disconnect all fuel hoses from the carburetor assembly. Unscrew plunger cap (18—Fig. M5-16) and withdraw the starter plunger assembly as shown in Fig. M5-17. Clean all external surfaces and remove accumulated dirt and grease. Remove the two nuts securing the carburetor and withdraw the carburetor assembly.

With reference to Fig. M5-16, disassemble the carburetor and note any discrepancies which

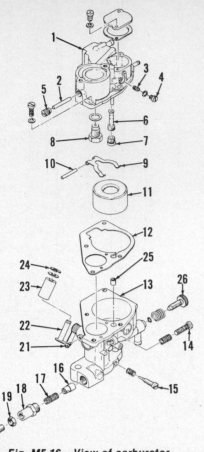

Fig. M5-16 — View of carburetor.

1. Top	14. Idle speed screw
2. Main nozzle	15. Idle mixture screw
3. Pilot jet	16. Starter plunger
4. Screw	17. Spring
5. Main nozzle plug	18. Plunger cap
6. Emulsion jet	19. Locknut
7. Main jet	20. Adjustment fitting
8. Inlet valve	21. Throttle shaft screw
9. Float lever	22. Throttle shaft
10. Float lever pin	23. Roller
11. Float	24. Snap ring
12. Gasket	25. Starter jet
13. Main body	26. Drain screw

Fig. M5-17 — View showing starter plunger assembly withdrawn.

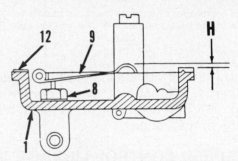

Fig. M5-18 — With carburetor top (1) inverted, float lever (9) height (H) above gasket (12) should be 0.5-1.5 mm (0.019-0.059 in.) with a good inlet valve (8) installed. Bend arms of float lever (9) evenly to adjust.

must be corrected before reassembly. Remove all gaskets (label if needed for later reference) and set to the side. Note that float lever pin (10) is staked in carburetor top (1).

Thoroughly clean all carburetor parts in a suitable solvent and inspect for damage and excessive wear. Note that plastic and rubber components should not be subjected to some cleaning solutions. Blow dry with clean compressed air. If compressed air is not available, use only lint-free cloths to wipe dry. Do not use a drill bit or wire to clean jets. Enlargement or damage of the calibrated holes may affect engine performance.

With reference to Fig. M5-16, reassemble the carburetor components with new gaskets. Note

that the new gaskets should match up with those removed. If not, check with your parts supplier to be sure you have the correct gasket set. Float lever pin (10) should be properly staked in carburetor top (1).

To determine the float level, invert carburetor top (1—Fig. M5-18) and measure height (H) of float lever (9) with a good inlet valve (8) and gasket (12) installed. Float lever height (H) should be 0.5-1.5 mm (0.019-0.059 in.) and is adjusted by bending the arms of float lever (9) evenly.

Starter plunger (16—Fig. M5-16) should be adjusted to just clear the starter bleed hole in the bottom of the carburetor body (13) when starter knob is pulled completely out. Adjustment is accomplished by loosening locknut (19) and turning adjustment fitting (20). Tighten locknut (19) after proper adjustment is obtained.

When reinstalling the carburetor, place new gasket(s) between the carburetor and manifold. Securely tighten the retaining nuts. Reconnect all fuel hoses at carburetor assembly. Attach starter plunger assembly as outlined in previous paragraph. Initially adjust idle mixture screw (15) ¾ to 1¼ turns out from a lightly seated position.

MARINER 8 HP (1979-1984)

NOTE: Metric fasteners are used throughout outboard motor.

Specifications

Hp/rpm 8/5000
Bore . . . . .50 mm
(1.97 in.)
Stroke. . . . . .42 mm
(1.65 in.)
Number of cylinders 2
Displacement . . . . .164 cc
(10 cu. in.)
Spark plug—NGK B7HS
Electrode gap . . . . .0.5-0.6 mm
(0.020-0.024 in.)
Breaker point gap . . . . .0.30-0.40 mm
(0.012-0.016 in.)
Ignition timing . . . . .See Text
Idle speed (in gear) . . . . .600-700 rpm
Fuel:oil ratio. 50:1
Gearcase oil capacity . . . . .230 mL
(7.8 oz.)

Maintenance

LUBRICATION

ENGINE. The engine is lubricated by oil mixed with fuel. The fuel should be regular leaded, low lead or unleaded gasoline with a minimum pump octane rating of 86. Recommended oil is Quicksilver Formula 50-D Outboard Lubricant or a BIA certified two-stroke motor oil. The recommended fuel:oil ratio for normal operation is 50:1. During engine break-in, the fuel:oil ratio should be increased to 25:1.

The manufacturer's recommended break-in period is defined as follows: For the first five minutes of operation the engine should not exceed its slowest possible cruising speed. After five minutes, slowly increase the engine speed to half throttle (2500-3500 rpm) for the first three hours of operation.

Running the engine at or near full throttle for extended periods is not recommended until after ten hours of operation.

LOWER UNIT. The lower unit gears and bearings are lubricated by oil contained in the gearcase. The recommended oil is Mariner Super Duty Gear Lube or a suitable EP 90 outboard gear oil. The gearcase oil capacity is 230 milliliters (7.8 oz.). The gearcase should be refilled periodically and the lubricant renewed after every 100 hours of operation or more frequently if needed. The gearcase is drained and filled through the same plug port (D—Fig. M6-1). An oil level (vent) port (L) is used to indicate the full oil level of the gearcase and to ease in oil drainage.

To drain the oil, place the outboard motor in a vertical position. Remove drain plug (D) and oil

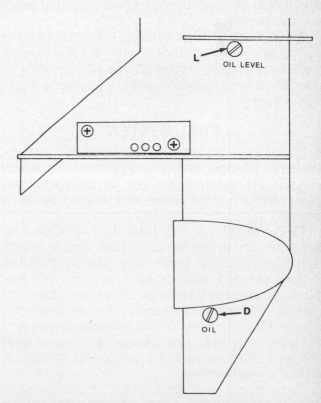

Fig. M6-1— *View showing lower unit gearcase drain and fill plug (D) and oil level (vent) plug (L).*

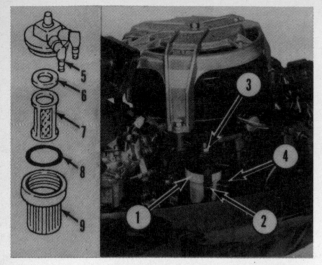

Fig. M6-2 — View showing location of fuel filter assembly and its components.

1. Fuel filter assy.
2. Fuel supply line
3. Mounting nut
4. Carburetor/fuel pump inlet line
5. Filter base
6. Gasket
7. Filter element
8. "O" ring
9. Cup

level plug (L), and allow the lubricant to drain into a suitable container.

To fill the gearcase with oil, place the outboard motor in a vertical position. Add oil through drain plug (D) opening with an oil feeder until the oil begins to overflow from oil level plug (L) port. Reinstall oil level plug (L) with a new gasket, if needed, and tighten. Remove oil feeder, then reinstall drain plug (D) with a new gasket, if needed, and tighten.

PIVOT POINTS AND SLIDES. Lubricate all pivot points and linkage slides with a good quality marine type multipurpose grease as frequently as needed to keep the components operating freely and properly.

FUEL SYSTEM

Periodically inspect the fuel lines and connections for damage. Renew components if needed.

Keep the external surface of the carburetor clean and all connections and sealing surfaces tight.

FUEL FILTER. A fuel filter assembly (1—Fig. M6-2) is connected between fuel supply line (2) and carburetor/fuel pump inlet line (4). With the engine stopped, occasionally unscrew the fuel filter cup (9) from filter base (5) and withdraw "O" ring (8), filter element (7) and gasket (6). Clean cup (9) and filter element (7) in a suitable solvent and blow dry with clean compressed air. Inspect filter element (7). If excessive blockage or damage is noted, renew element.

Reassembly is reverse order of disassembly. Renew gasket (6) and "O" ring (8) during reassembly.

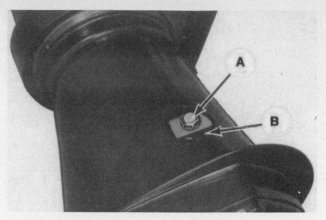

Fig. M6-3 — Adjustment cap screw (A) is used to adjust shift linkage in bracket (B).

FUEL PUMP. The fuel pump is an integral part of the carburetor. Refer to CARBURETOR in the Tune-Up section for fuel pump overhaul.

NOTE: The fuel pump assembly may be overhauled without carburetor removal.

SHIFT LINKAGE

Direction of propeller rotation is determined by the position of the gear shift lever. The gear shift lever actuates gearcase components using shift linkage consisting of an upper and lower shift rod connected by an adjustment bracket. The tapered end of the lower shift rod controls the movement of the dog clutch on the propeller shaft. The positioning of the dog clutch on the propeller shaft determines whether forward, neutral or reverse directional movement is selected.

To adjust, remove adjustment cap screw (A—Fig. M6-3) cover. Loosen cap screw enough to allow lower shift rod to slide freely in adjustment bracket (B). Place shift lever in reverse detent position and lower shift rod in reverse position. Push down on adjustment bracket (B) only with enough force to remove any slack in the linkage, then tighten adjustment cap screw (A). Check adjustment by turning propeller.

⚠WARNING

Disconnect spark plug leads and properly ground leads before performing any propeller service, otherwise, accidental starting can occur if propeller shaft is rotated.

Make sure neutral and forward properly engage. If not, repeat adjustment procedure, then install cover.

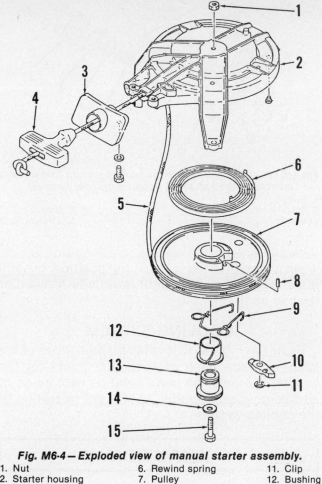

Fig. M6-4 — Exploded view of manual starter assembly.

1. Nut
2. Starter housing
3. Rope guide
4. Handle
5. Starter rope
6. Rewind spring
7. Pulley
8. Pin
9. Pawl spring
10. Pawl
11. Clip
12. Bushing
13. Shaft
14. Washer
15. Bolt

STARTER

When starter rope (5—Fig. M6-4) is pulled, pulley (7) will rotate. As the pulley (7) rotates, drive pawl (10) moves to engage with the flywheel, thus cranking the engine.

When starter rope (5) is released, pulley (7) is rotated in the reverse direction by force from rewind spring (6). As pulley (7) rotates, the starter rope is rewound and drive pawl (10) is disengaged from the flywheel.

A starter lockout assembly is used to prevent starter engagement when the gear shift lever is in the forward or reverse position.

The manual starter must be disassembled to renew starter rope (5) or rewind spring (6).

To overhaul the manual starter, proceed as follows: Remove the engine's top cover. Remove the screws retaining the manual starter to the engine. Remove the starter lockout cable at the starter housing. Note plunger and spring located at cable end; care should be used not to lose components should they fall free. Withdraw the starter assembly.

Fig. M6-5 — View showing proper installation of pawl spring (9), pawl (10) and clip (11). Pulley hole (H) is used during pulley withdrawal. Refer to text.

> **⚠ WARNING**
>
> **Care should be exercised when working with or around a coiled starter rewind spring as sudden uncoiling can cause injury. Safety eyewear and gloves are recommended.**

Check pawl (10) for freedom of movement and excessive wear of engagement area or any other damage. Renew or lubricate pawl (10) with a suitable water-resistant grease and return starter to service if no other damage is noted.

To disassemble, remove clip (11) and withdraw pawl (10) and pawl spring (9). Untie starter rope (5) at handle (4) and allow the rope to wind into the starter. Remove bolt (15), washer (14) and shaft (13), then place a suitable screwdriver blade through hole (H—Fig. M6-5) to hold rewind spring (6—Fig. M6-4) securely in housing (2). Carefully lift pulley (7) with starter rope (5) from housing (2). BE CAREFUL when removing pulley (7) as the rewind spring may be dislodged. Untie starter rope (5) and remove rope from pulley (7) if renewal is required. To remove rewind spring (6) from housing (2), invert housing so it sits upright on a flat surface, then tap the housing top until rewind spring (6) falls free and uncoils.

Inspect all components for damage and excessive wear and renew if needed.

To reassemble, first apply a coating of suitable water-resistant grease to rewind spring area of housing (2). Install rewind spring (6) in housing (2)

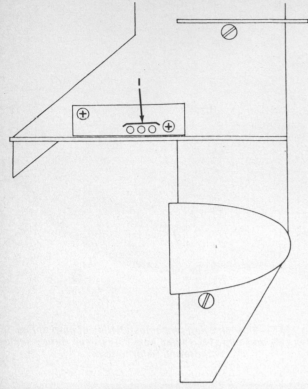

Fig. M6-6 — *Cooling system water inlet ports (I) are located on both sides of the lower unit.*

so spring coils wind in a counterclockwise direction from the outer end. Make sure the outer spring hook is properly secured over starter housing (2) pin. Wind starter rope (5) onto pulley (7) approximately 2½ turns counterclockwise when viewed from the flywheel side. Direct remaining starter rope (5) length through notch in pulley (7).

NOTE: Lubricate all friction surfaces with a suitable water-resistant grease during reassembly.

Assemble pulley (7) to starter housing making sure that pin (8) engages hook end in rewind spring (6). Install shaft (13), washer (14) and bolt (15). Apply Loctite 271 or 290 or an equivalent thread fastening solution on bolt (15) threads and install nut (1) and sucurely tighten.

Thread starter rope (5) through starter housing (2), rope guide (3) and handle (4) and secure with a knot. Turn pulley (7) 4-5 turns counterclockwise when viewed from the flywheel side, then release starter rope (5) from pulley notch and allow rope to slowly wind onto pulley.

NOTE: Do note apply any more tension on rewind spring (6) than is required to draw starter handle (4) back into the proper released position.

Install spring (9), pawl (10) and clip (11) as shown in Fig. M6-5. Remount manual starter assembly.

Adjust starter lockout assembly by turning adjusting nuts at cable end so starter will engage

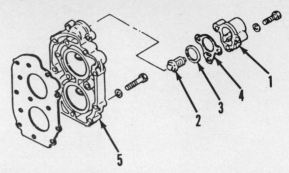

Fig. M6-6A — *Exploded view of the cooling system components located at the top of the engine's cylinder head (5).*

1. Housing
2. Thermostat
3. Spacer
4. Gasket
5. Cylinder head

when gear shift level is in neutral position, but will not engage when gear shift lever is in forward or reverse position.

COOLING SYSTEM

Ports (I — Fig. M6-6) located on both sides of the lower unit are used as the water inlets for the cooling system. The ports must be kept clean of all foreign matter to ensure efficient operation of the cooling system.

⚠CAUTION

Do not operate outboard motor unless the lower unit is immersed in water, otherwise, the water pump impeller will be damaged.

A thermostat positioned in the cylinder head is used to regulate the engine's operating temperature. Note that a thermostat that sticks or stays closed too long could cause engine overheating, resulting in poor engine operation and possible engine damage. A thermostat that opens too quickly or is stuck in the open position will cause the engine not to reach its recommended operating temperature range, resulting in possible engine malfunction and poor engine efficiency. If thermostat malfunction is suspected, remove thermostat housing located at the top of the cylinder head as shown in Fig. M6-6A to gain access to the thermostat.

Refer to the Outboard Motor Service Manual if more extensive service to the cooling system is required.

PROPELLER

The standard propeller has three blades, a diameter of 229 mm (9 in.) and a pitch of 178 mm (7 in.) Optional propellers are available. Select a pro-

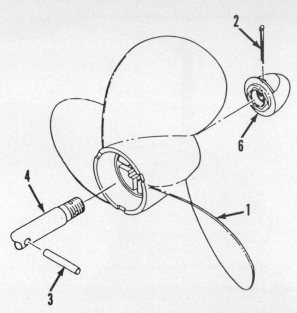

Fig. M6-7 — Propeller (1) is mounted on propeller shaft (4) and is retained by spinner (6) and cotter pin (2). Shear pin (3) is renewed only after withdrawing propeller (1) from propeller shaft (4).

peller that will allow the engine at full throttle to reach maximum operating rpm range (4500-5500 rpm).

⚠**WARNING**

Shift directional control lever to "NEUTRAL." Disconnect spark plug leads and properly ground leads before performing any propeller service, otherwise, accidental starting can occur if propeller shaft is rotated.

To remove the propeller, remove cotter pin (2 — Fig. M6-7) and unscrew propeller spinner (6). Withdraw propeller (1) from propeller shaft (4).

Inspect propeller (1), propeller shaft (4) and shear pin (3) for damage and excessive wear. Renew if excessive wear or damage is noted.

Apply a water-resistant grease to the propeller bore, then install propeller (1) on propeller shaft (4) and retain with propeller spinner (6) and a new cotter pin (2).

Tune-Up

IGNITION SYSTEM

The standard spark plug is NGK B7HS with an electrode gap of 0.5-0.6 mm (0.020-0.024 in.).

The breaker point gap should be 0.3-0.4 mm (0.012-0.016 in.) and can be inspected and adjusted through the opening in flywheel (3 — Fig. M6-8). Two breaker point assemblies (6) and two

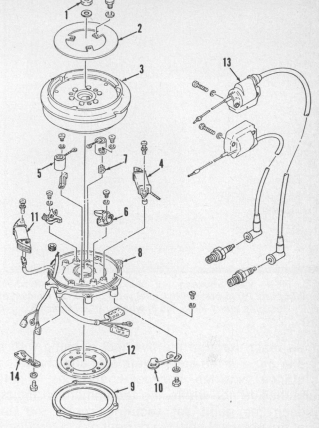

Fig. M6-8 — Exploded view of flywheel magneto unit.

1. Nut	8. Magneto base plate
2. Flywheel cover	9. Magneto base plate retainer
3. Flywheel	10. Bracket
4. Low voltage coil	11. Lighting coil
5. Condenser	12. Retainer
6. Breaker point assy.	13. Ignition coil
7. Lubricator	14. Throttle cam

condensers (5) are used. To inspect and, if needed, adjust the breaker point gap, first remove the engine's top cover. Remove the screws retaining the manual starter to the engine. Remove the starter lockout cable at the starter housing. Note plunger and spring located at cable end, care should be used not to lose components should they fall free. Withdraw the starter assembly. Remove the cap screws and lockwashers securing flywheel cover (2) to flywheel (3) and withdraw.

Inspect the breaker point surfaces for excessive wear, pitting or any other damage. If needed, renew breaker point assemblies (6) and condensers (5) as outlined later.

To clean the breaker point contact surfaces, rotate the flywheel until the breaker point contact surfaces are accessible through the opening in flywheel (3). Use a point file or sandpaper with a grit rating of 400 to 600. After polishing, wipe the contact surfaces clean with a dry cloth and lightly grease the breaker point arm and lubricator (7) with a suitable lubricant.

Turn the flywheel until the breaker point contact surfaces are placed at their widest position,

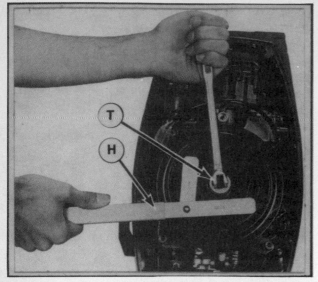

Fig. M6-9—View showing the use of a suitable flywheel holding tool (H) to prevent flywheel rotation during removal of securing nut (1 — Fig. M5-8) with suitable tools (T).

Fig. M6-10—Extract flywheel from crankshaft end using a suitable puller assembly (P) with the correct size cap screws (C).

then reach through the flywheel opening with a feeler gage of the appropriate size and check the distance between the point surfaces. If the distance is not within the recommended limits, loosen the point set securing screw and adjust the point set until the correct gap is obtained. Tighten the point set securing screw and recheck the breaker point gap. Repeat the adjustment procedure, if needed, until the correct breaker point gap is obtained. Repeat the adjustment procedure on the other breaker point assembly.

To renew breaker point assemblies (6) and condensers (5), proceed as follows: Using a suitable flywheel holding tool (H — Fig. M6-9) to prevent flywheel rotation, remove securing nut (1 — Fig. M6-8). Remove flywheel (3 — Fig. M6-8) from crankshaft end using a suitable puller assembly (P — Fig. M6-10) and the proper size cap screws (C). Note flywheel key located in crankshaft keyway.

⚠WARNING

Be sure suitable tools are used to remove the flywheel. Damage resultant from the misapplication of force or the use of incorrect tools may cause engine damage, engine malfunction or personal injury.

With reference to Fig. M6-8, renew breaker point assemblies (6) and condensers (5). Adjust the breaker point gap to the recommended setting as outlined in a previous paragraph. Make sure

the securing screws are properly tightened. Be sure the flywheel key is properly positioned in the crankshaft end, then reinstall flywheel (3). Install lockwasher and install and tighten securing nut (1) to 41-47 N·m (30-35 ft.-lbs.).

To obtain the correct ignition timing: First adjust both breaker point assemblies (6) to the proper point gap as previously outlined. Remove both spark plugs. Use a point checker and attach the red tester lead to the grey wire coming from magneto base plate (8) (top cylinder's low voltage coil lead). Connect the black tester lead to an engine ground.

NOTE: A suitable continuity tester can be used.

Install a dial indicator in the top cylinder spark plug port. Fully open the throttle by pushing the magneto base plate to full advance position. Slowly turn the flywheel counterclockwise until the tester's pointer moves from "OPEN" to "CLOSE", then stop turning the flywheel. Check the piston position reading on the dial indicator. The piston should be 2.1-2.7 mm (0.083-0.106 in.) BTDC. If not, loosen bracket (10) and adjust the magneto base plate (8) until the correct piston position is obtained when the tester's pointer moves from "OPEN" to "CLOSE", then tighten screws securing bracket (10). Repeat the procedure for the bottom cylinder. Attach the point checker's red tester lead to the orange wire coming from magneto base plate (8). Make sure the black tester lead remains grounded to engine. Adjust the full advance timing by varying the breaker point gap.

Primary

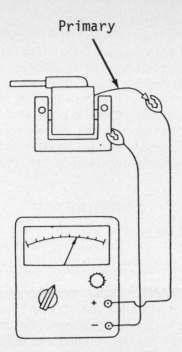

Fig. M6-11 — Connect ohmmeter leads as shown to measure resistance in the primary side of the ignition coil. Refer to text.

Secondary

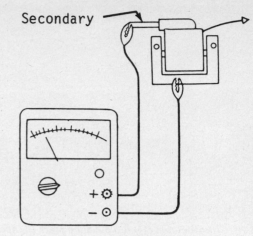

Fig. M6-12 — Connect ohmmeter leads as shown to measure resistance in the secondary side of the ignition coil. Refer to text.

Ignition Coils. To check ignition coils (13 — Fig. (M6-8) located on side of cylinders, use a suitable ohmmeter. Connect on tester lead to the coil's metal laminations, then connect the remaining tester lead alternately to the primary (Fig. M6-11) and secondary (Fig. M6-12) ignition coil leads. Resistance reading for primary wire connection should be 1.35-1.65 ohms, while the secondary wire connection resistance reading should be 4160-6240 ohms. Renew ignition coil or coils (13 — Fig. M6-8) if the meter readings are not within the proper range.

SPEED CONTROL LINKAGE

As twist grip (20 — Fig. M6-13) is rotated, the magneto base plate is rotated via cables (1) and associated linkage. Throttle cam (14 — Fig. M6-8) is mounted to magneto base plate (8), thus operating the carburetor throttle shaft in relation with magneto base plate (8) rotation.

To synchronize ignition and throttle control linkage, first make sure the ignition timing has been correctly adjusted. When twist grip (20 — Fig. M6-13) is moved completely against the high speed stop, the carburetor throttle should be fully opened. MAKE SURE that the carburetor throttle does not reach the full open position before the ignition timing is fully advanced.

To adjust the speed control linkage proceed as follows: Turn twist grip (20) to "FAST" position. Locate which cable (1) is relaxed and measure the cable slack. Cable slack should be 1-2 mm

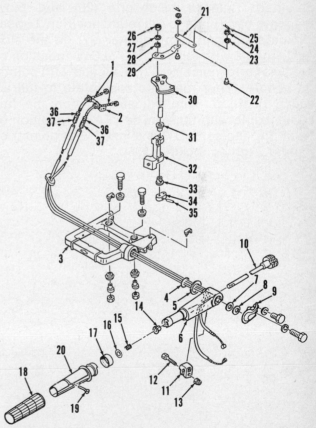

Fig. M6-13 — View of speed control linkage components.

1. Control cables	14. Bushing	26. Nut
2. Bracket	15. Spring	27. Lockwasher
3. Handle bracket	16. Washer	28. Flat washer
4. "O" ring	17. Indicator	29. Link
5. Spacer	18. Rubber cover	30. Pulley
6. Steering handle	19. Screw	31. Bushing
7. Spacer	20. Twist grip	32. Bracket
8. Spacer	21. Link	33. Bushing
9. Cover	22. Pivot pin	34. End piece
10. Throttle lever	23. Wave washer	35. Pin
11. Friction clamp	24. Flat washer	36. Locknuts
12. Bolt	25. Clip	37. Adjusters
13. Nut		

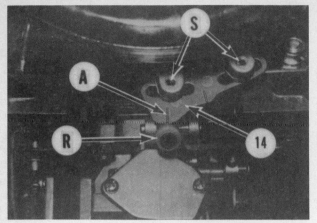

Fig. M6-14—Throttle cam (14) full advance mark (A) should be aligned with center of throttle roller (R) when twist grip is in the "FAST" position. Throttle cam (14) is adjusted by screws (S). Refer to text.

With twist grip (20) in "FAST" position, the center of the throttle roller (R—Fig. M6-14) should be aligned with full advance mark (A) on throttle cam (14). Loosen screws (S) and reposition throttle cam (14) if mark is not aligned.

With the twist grip still in the full throttle position, the carburetor throttle plate should be in the wide open position. If not, loosen screw (S—Fig. M6-15) and adjust throttle rod (4) in rod end (3) until wide open position is obtained, then retighten screw (S).

CARBURETOR

The fuel pump and carburetor are a complete unit. Refer to the following OVERHAUL section for service procedures on both the fuel pump and carburetor.

ADJUSTMENT. Under normal operation the following jet sizes are the standard recommendation for altitudes of 2500 feet (760 m) and less: main jet (21—Fig. M6-15) #80 and pilot jet (6) #46. Initial adjustment of idle mixture screw (8) is 1-7/8 to 2-3/8 tunrs out from a lightly seated position. Recommended idle speed is 600-700 rpm in gear with engine at normal operating temperature.

With the outboard motor properly mounted on a boat or a suitable test tank, immerse the lower unit. Connect a tachometer and set it on the appropriate range scale. Start the engine and allow it to warm up to normal operating temperature.

(0.04-0.08 in.). If not, loosen nuts at bracket (2) and adjust cable length until the proper cable slack is obtained. Release twist grip (20) and move magneto base plate to full retard position. Loosen locknuts (36) and turn adjuster (37) on the slow cable (cable with tension) so "SLOW" position on the twist grip indicator (17) is aligned with pointer on handle. Move magneto base plate to full advance position. Turn adjuster (37) on the fast cable (cable with tension) so "FAST" position on twist grip indicator (17) is aligned with pointer on handle. Tighten locknuts (36).

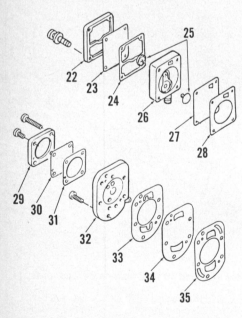

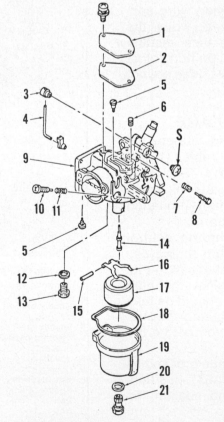

Fig. M6-15—Exploded view of carburetor. Fuel pump (22 through 29) is used on later models; fuel pump (29 through 35) was used on early models.

S. Screw	18. Gasket
1. Cover	19. Float bowl
2. Gasket	20. Gasket
3. Rod end	21. Main jet
4. Throttle rod	22. Fuel pump cover
5. Screw	23. Diaphragm
6. Pilot jet	24. Gasket
7. Spring	25. Check valve
8. Idle mixture screw	26. Pump body
9. Body	27. Diaphragm
10. Idle speed screw	28. Gasket
11. Spring	29. Fuel pump cover
12. Gasket	30. Diaphragm
13. Fuel inlet valve	31. Gasket
14. Main nozzle	32. Pump body
15. Pin	33. Diaphragm
16. Float lever	34. Diaphragm
17. Float	35. Gasket

Position the throttle control twist grip to the complete closed position. Place the gear shift lever in the "Forward" position. Adjust the engine idle speed screw (10) until the engine is idling at 600-700 rpm, then adjust idle mixture screw (8) until smooth engine operation is noted. Readjust the engine idle speed screw (10) until the recommended idle speed is obtained.

Reinstall the engine's top cover.

OVERHAUL. The fuel pump is an integral part of the carburetor. The fuel pump assembly may be overhauled without overhauling the complete carburetor. If the fuel pump is to be overhauled without carburetor removal, proceed as follows: Remove the engine's top cover and disconnect the fuel tank supply hose at the outboard motor connector. Disconnect the fuel supply hose at the fuel pump inlet.

With reference to Fig. M6-15, disassemble the fuel pump assembly. Inspect all components for excessive wear or any other damage and renew if needed. Clean components as needed with a suitable cleaning solution. Blow dry with clean compressed air. If compressed air is not available, use only lint-free cloths to wipe dry. Make sure all passages are clear of any obstructions.

With reference to Fig. M6-15, reassemble the fuel pump assembly with new gaskets. Securely tighten the retaining screws.

NOTE: Fuel pump and engine malfunction will result if the fuel pump and all connections are not airtight.

Complete reassembly.

Refer to the following for complete carburetor overhaul: Remove engine's top cover. Disconnect choke rod from carburetor choke level. Remove the two screws retaining air intake cover and withdraw cover. Disconnect the two crankcase recirculation hoses from the carburetor (label if needed). Disconnect the fuel tank supply hose at the outboard motor connector. Disconnect the fuel supply hose at the fuel pump inlet. Clean all external surfaces and remove accumulated dirt and grease. Remove the two nuts securing the carburetor and withdraw the carburetor assembly.

With reference to Fig. M6-15, disassemble the complete carburetor assembly and note any discrepancies which must be corrected before reassembly. Remove all gaskets (label if needed for later reference) and set to the side.

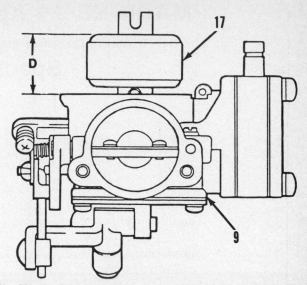

Fig. M6-16 — Distance (D) should be 20.5-22.5 mm (13/16-7/8 in.) from carburetor body (9) to base of float (17) for proper float level.

Thoroughly clean all carburetor parts in a suitable solvent and inspect for damage and excessive wear. Note that plastic and rubber components should be not be subjected to some cleaning solutions. Blow dry with clean compressed air. If compressed air is not available, use only lint-free cloths to wipe dry. Do not use a drill bit or wire to clean jets. Enlargement or damage of the calibrated holes may affect engine performance.

With reference to Fig. M6-15, reassemble the carburetor components with new gaskets. Note that the new gaskets should match up with those removed. If not, check with your parts supplier to be sure you have the correct gasket set.

To determine the float level, invert carburetor body (9—Fig. M6-16) and measure distance (D) from carburetor body (9) to base of float (17). Distance (D) should be 20.5-22.5 mm (13/16-7/8 in.) and is adjusted by bending the arms of float lever (16—Fig. M6-15) evenly.

When reinstalling the carburetor, place a new gasket between the carburetor and the intake manifold. Securely tighten the retaining nuts. Reconnect the two crankcase recirculation hoses and the fuel supply hose. Connect choke rod to carburetor choke lever. Install air intake cover and retain with the two screws. Initially adjust idle mixture screw (8) 1-7/8 to 2-3/8 turns out from a lightly seated position.

MARINER 9.9 AND 15 HP (1979-1985)

NOTE: Metric fasteners are used throughout outboard motor.

Specifications

Hp/rpm 9.9, 15/5500
Bore . . . . .56 mm
(2.20 in.)
Stroke . . . . .50 mm
(1.97 in.)
Number of cylinders 2
Displacement . . . . .246 cc
(15 cu. in.)
Spark plug — NGK B7HS
Electrode gap . . . . .0.5-0.6 mm
(0.020-0.024 in.)
Breaker point gap . . . . .0.3-0.4 mm*
(0.012-0.016 in.)
Igition timing . . . . .See Text
Idle speed (in gear) . . . . .600-700 rpm
Fuel:oil ratio. 50:1
Gearcase oil capacity . . . . .225 mL
(7.6 oz.)

*Later models are equipped with CD ignition.

Maintenance

LUBRICATION

ENGINE. The engine is lubricated by oil mixed with the fuel. The fuel should be regular leaded, low lead or unleaded gasoline with a minimum pump octane rating of 86. Recommended oil is Quicksilver Formula 50-D Outboard Lubricant or a BIA certified two-stroke motor oil. The recommended fuel:oil ratio for normal operation is 50:1. During engine break-in, the fuel:oil ratio should be increased to 25:1.

The manufacturer's recommended break-in period is defined as follows: For the first five minutes of operation the engine should not exceed its slowest possible cruising speed. After five minutes, slowly increase the engine speed to half throttle (2500-3500 rpm) for the first three hours of operation.

Running the engine at or near full throttle for extended periods is not recommended until after ten hours of operation.

LOWER UNIT. The lower unit gears and bearings are lubricated by oil contained in the gearcase. The recommended oil is Mariner Super Duty Gear Lube or a suitable EP 90 outboard gear oil. The gearcase oil capacity is 225 milliliters (7.6 oz.). The gearcase should be refilled periodically and the lubricant renewed after every 100 hours of operation or more frequently if needed. The gearcase is drained and filled through the same plug port (D—Fig. M7-1). An oil level (vent) port (L) is used to indicate the full oil level of the gearcase and to ease in oil drainage.

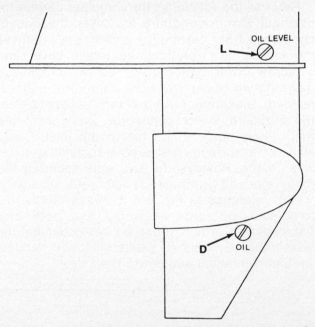

Fig. M7-1 — View showing lower unit gearcase drain and fill plug (D) and oil level (vent) plug (L).

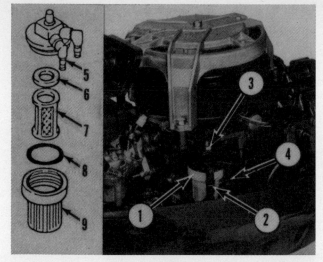

Fig. M7-2 — View showing location of fuel filter assembly and its components.

1. Fuel filter assy.
2. Fuel supply line
3. Mounting nut
4. Carburetor/fuel pump inlet line
5. Filter base
6. Gasket
7. Filter element
8. "O" ring
9. Cup

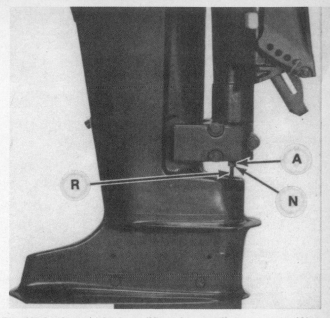

Fig. M7-3 — Loosen locknut (N) and turn adjustment nut (A) to alter length of upper and lower shift rod (R). Adjust nut (A) until proper engagement of reverse, neutral and forward is obtained, then retighten locknut (N).

To drain the oil, place the outboard motor in a vertical position. Remove drain plug (D) and oil level plug (L), and allow the lubricant to drain into a suitable container.

To fill the gearcase with oil, place the outboard motor in a vertical position. Add oil through drain plug (D) opening with an oil feeder until the oil begins to overflow from oil level plug (L) port. Reinstall oil level plug (L) with a new gasket, if needed, and tighten. Remove oil feeder, then reinstall drain plug (D) with a new gasket, if needed, and tighten.

PIVOT POINTS AND SLIDES. Lubricate all pivot points and linkage slides with a good quality marine type multipurpose grease as frequently as needed to keep the components operating freely and properly.

FUEL SYSTEM

Periodically inspect the fuel lines and connections for damage. Renew components if needed.

Keep the external surface of the carburetor clean and all connections and sealing surfaces tight.

FUEL FILTER. A fuel filter assembly (1 — Fig. M7-2) is connected between fuel supply line (2) and carburetor/fuel pump inlet line (4). With the engine stopped, occasionally unscrew the fuel filter cup (9) from filter base (5) and withdraw "O" ring (8), filter element (7) and gasket (6). Clean cup (9) and filter element (7) in a suitable solvent and blow dry with clean compressed air. Inspect filter element (7). If excessive blockage or damage is noted, renew element.

Reassembly is reverse order of disassembly. Renew gasket (6) and "O" ring (8) during reassembly.

FUEL PUMP. The fuel pump is an integral part of the carburetor. Refer to CARBURETOR in the Tune-Up section for fuel pump overhaul.

NOTE: The fuel pump assembly may be overhauled without carburetor removal.

SHIFT LINKAGE

Direction of propeller rotation is determined by the position of the gear shift lever. The gear shift lever actuates gearcase components using shift linkage consisting of an upper and lower shift rod connected by an adjustment bracket. The tapered end of the lower shift rod controls the movement of the dog clutch on the propeller shaft. The positioning of the dog clutch on the propeller shaft determines whether forward, neutral or reverse directional movement is selected.

To check shift linkage for proper adjustment, first place shift lever in reverse detent position. Check for proper engagement and propeller rotation by turning the propeller.

> **⚠WARNING**
>
> Disconnect spark plug leads and properly ground leads before performing any propeller service, otherwise, accidental starting can occur if propeller shaft is rotated.

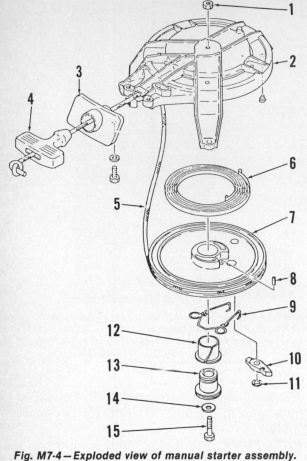

Fig. M7-4 — Exploded view of manual starter assembly.

1. Nut	6. Rewind spring	11. Clip
2. Starter housing	7. Pulley	12. Bushing
3. Rope guide	8. Pin	13. Shaft
4. Handle	9. Pawl spring	14. Washer
5. Starter rope	10. Pawl	15. Bolt

Check for proper engagement of neutral and forward.

To adjust, loosen locknut (N) and turn adjustment nut (A) until proper engagement of reverse, neutral and forward is obtained, then retighten locknut (N).

STARTER

When starter rope (5—Fig. M7-4) is pulled, pulley (7) will rotate. As pully (7) rotates, drive pawl (10) moves to engage with the flywheel, thus cranking the engine.

When starter rope (5) is released, pulley (7) is rotated in the reverse direction by force from rewind spring (6). As pulley (7) rotates, the starter rope is rewound and drive pawl (10) is disengaged from the flywheel.

A starter lockout assembly is used to prevent starter engagement when the gear shift lever is in the forward or reverse position.

The manual starter must be disassembled to renew starter rope (5) or rewind spring (6).

To overhaul the manual starter, proceed as

Fig. M7-5 — View showing proper installation of pawl spring (9), pawl (10) and clip (11). Pulley hole (H) is used during pulley withdrawal. Refer to text.

follows: Remove the engine's top cover. Remove the screws retaining the manual starter to the engine. Remove the starter lockout cable at the starter housing. Note plunger and spring located at the cable end, care should be used not to lose components should they fall free. Withdraw the starter assembly.

⚠WARNING

Care should be exercised when working with or around a coiled starter rewind spring as sudden uncoiling can cause injury. Safety eyewear and gloves are recommended.

Check pawl (10) for freedom of movement and excessive wear of engagement area or any other damage. Renew or lubricate pawl (10) with a suitable water-resistant grease and return starter to service if no other damage is noted.

To disassemble, remove clip (11) and withdraw pawl (10) and pawl spring (9). Untie starter rope (5) at handle (4) and allow the rope to wind into the starter. Remove bolt (15), washer (14) and shaft (13), then place a suitable screwdriver blade through hole (H—Fig. M7-5) to hold rewind spring (6—Fig. M7-4) securely in housing (2). Carefully lift pulley (7) with starter rope (5) from housing (2). BE CAREFUL when removing pulley (7) as the rewind spring may be dislodged. Untie starter rope (5) and

Fig. M7-6 — *Cooling system water inlet ports (I) are located on the bottom side of the antiventilation plate.*

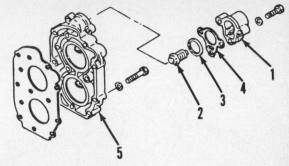

Fig. M7-6A — *Exploded view of the cooling system components located at the top of the engine's cylinder head (5).*
1. Housing
2. Thermostat
3. Spacer
4. Gasket
5. Cylinder head

remove rope from pulley (7) if renewal is required. To remove rewind spring (6) from housing (2), invert housing so it sets upright on a flat surface, then tap the housing top until the rewind spring (6) falls free and uncoils.

Inspect all components for damage and excessive wear and renew if needed.

To reassemble, first apply a coating of a suitable water-resistant grease to rewind spring area of housing (2). Install rewind spring (6) in housing (2) so spring coils wind in a counterclockwise direction from the outer end. Make sure the spring's outer hook is properly secured over starter housing (2) pin. Wind starter rope (5) onto pulley (7) approximately 2½ turns counterclockwise when viewed from the flywheel side. Direct remaining starter rope (5) length through notch in pulley (7).

NOTE: Lubricate all friction surfaces with a suitable water-resistant grease during reassembly.

Assemble pulley (7) to starter housing making sure that pin (8) engages hook end in rewind spring (6). Install shaft (13), washer (14) and bolt (15). Apply Loctite 271 or 290 or an equivalent thread fastening solution on bolt (15) threads and install nut (1) and securely tighten.

Thread starter rope (5) through starter housing (2), rope guide (3) and handle (4) and secure with a knot. Turn pulley (7) 4-5 turns counterclockwise when viewed from the flywheel side, then release starter rope (5) from pulley notch and allow rope to slowly wind onto pulley.

NOTE: Do not apply any more tension on rewind spring (6) than is required to draw starter handle (4) back into the proper released position.

Install spring (9), pawl (10) and clip (11) as shown in Fig. M7-5. Remount manual starter assembly.

Adjust starter lockout assembly by turning adjusting nuts at cable end so starter will engage when gear shift lever is in neutral position, but will not engage when gear shift lever is in forward or reverse position.

COOLING SYSTEM

Ports (I — Fig. M7-6) located on the bottom side of the antiventilation plate are used as the water inlet for the cooling system. The water passages in the port's cover must be kept clean of all foreign matter to ensure efficient operation of the cooling system.

⚠CAUTION

Do not operate outboard motor unless the lower unit is immersed in water, otherwise, the water pump impeller will be damaged.

A thermostat positioned in the cylinder head is used to regulate the engine's operating temperature. Note that a thermostat that sticks or stays closed too long could cause engine overheating, resulting in poor engine operation and possible engine damage. A thermostat that opens too quickly or is stuck in the open position will cause the engine not to reach its recommended operating temperature range, resulting in possible engine malfunction and poor engine efficiency. If thermostat malfunction is suspected, remove the thermostat housing located at the top of the cylinder head as shown in Fig. M7-6A to gain access to the thermostat.

Refer to the Outboard Motor Service Manual if more extensive service to the cooling system is required.

PROPELLER

Consult your local dealer or the manufacturer for the specifications pertaining to the standard

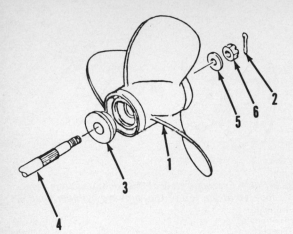

Fig. M7-7 — Thrust hub (3) and propeller (1) are mounted on propeller shaft (4) and are retained by washer (5), nut (6) and cotter pin (2). Tighten nut (6) to a torque of 14-22 N·m (10-16 ft.-lbs.).

propeller used on your model of outboard motor. Optional propellers are available. Select a propeller that will allow the engine at full throttle to reach a maximum operating rpm range (4500-5500 rpm).

> ### ⚠️WARNING
>
> Shift directional control lever to "NEUTRAL." Disconnect spark plug leads and properly ground leads before performing any propeller service, otherwise, accidental starting can occur if propeller shaft is rotated.

To remove the propeller, remove cotter pin (2—Fig. M7-7) and unscrew propeller retaining nut (6). Withdraw washer (5), propeller (1) and thrust hub (3) from propeller shaft (4).

Inspect all components for damage and excessive wear and renew if needed.

Apply Perfect Seal or a suitable equivalent to the propeller shaft splines, then install thrust hub (3), propeller (1) and washer (5) on propeller shaft (4). Install propeller retaining nut (6) and tighten to a torque of 14-22 N·m (10-16 ft.-lbs.). Install a new cotter pin (2).

Tune-Up

IGNITION SYSTEM

On early 9.9 and 15 hp models, a breaker point type ignition system is used. On late 9.9 and 15 hp models, a capacitor discharge ignition (CDI) system is used. Refer to the Outboard Motor Service Manual for testing and servicing the CD ignition system. If engine malfuction is noted and the ignition system is suspected, make sure spark

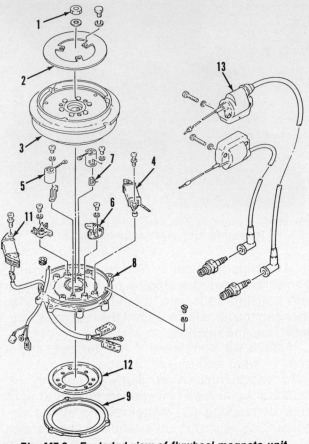

Fig. M7-8 — Exploded view of flywheel magneto unit.

1. Nut
2. Flywheel cover
3. Flywheel
4. Low voltage coil
5. Condenser
6. Breaker point assy.
7. Lubricator
8. Magneto base plate
9. Magneto base plate retainer
11. Lighting coil
12. Retainer
13. Ignition coil

plugs and all electrical wiring are in good condition and all electrical connections are tight before proceeding to troubleshooting the CD ignition system.

The standard spark plug on all models is NGK B7HS with an electrode gap of 0.5-0.6 mm (0.020-0.024 in.).

Breaker Point Ignition System

The breaker point gap should be 0.3-0.4 mm (0.012-0.016 in.) and can be inspected and adjusted through the opening in flywheel (3—Fig. M7-8). Two breaker point assembles (6) and two condensers (5) are used. To inspect and, if needed, adjust the breaker point gap, first remove the engine's top cover. Remove screws retaining the manual starter to the engine. Remove the starter lockout cable at the starter housing. Note plunger and spring located at cable end, care should be used not to lose components should they fall free. Withdraw the starter assembly. Remove the cap screws and lockwashers securing flywheel cover (2) to flywheel (3) and withdraw.

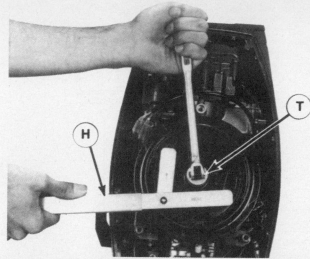

Fig. M7-9—View showing the use of a suitable flywheel holding tool (H) to prevent flywheel rotation during removal of securing nut (1 – Fig. M7-8) with suitable tools (T).

Inspect the breaker point surfaces for excessive wear, pitting or any other damage. If needed, renew breaker point assemblies (6) and condensers (5) as outlined later in this section.

To clean the breaker point contact surfaces, rotate the flywheel until the breaker point contact surfaces are accessible through the opening in flywheel (3). Use a point file or sandpaper with a grit rating of 400 to 600. After polishing, wipe the contact surfaces clean with a dry cloth and lightly grease the breaker point arm and lubricator (7) with a suitable lubricant.

Turn the flywheel until the breaker point contact surfaces are placed at their widest position, then reach through the flywheel opening with a feeler gage of the appropriate size and check the distance between the point surfaces. If the distance is not within the recommended limits, loosen the point set securing screw and adjust the point set until the correct gap is obtained. Tighten the point set securing screw and recheck the breaker point gap. Repeat the adjustment procedure, if needed, until the correct breaker point gap is obtained. Follow the previously described

Fig. M7-10—View showing magneto base plate and throttle cam. Refer to text for adjustment procedures.

C. Throttle cam
M. Magneto stop
S. Cap screws

1. Locknut
2. Adjustment screw

Fig. M7-11—Remove flywheel from crankshaft end using a suitable puller assembly (P) with the correct size cap screws (C).

procedure and adjust the other breaker point assembly.

To renew breaker point assemblies (6) and condensers (5), proceed as follows: Using a suitable flywheel holding tools (H—Fig. M7-9) to prevent flywheel rotation, remove securing nut (1—Fig. M7-8). Remove flywheel (3—Fig. M7-8) from crankshaft end using a suitable puller assembly (P—Fig. M7-11) and the proper size cap screws (C). Note flywheel key located in crankshaft keyway.

⚠WARNING

Be sure suitable tools are used to remove the flywheel. Damage resultant from misapplication of force or the use of incorrect tools may cause engine damage, engine malfunction or personal injury.

With reference to Fig. M7-8, renew breaker point assemblies (6) and condensers (5). Adjust the breaker point gap to the recommended setting as outlined in a previous paragraph. Make sure the securing screws are properly tightened. Be sure the flywheel key is properly positioned in the crankshaft end, then reinstall flywheel (3). Install lockwasher and tighten securing nut (1) to 75-82 N·m (55-60 ft.-lbs.).

To obtain the correct ignition timing: First adjust both breaker point assemblies (6) to the proper point gap as previously outlined. Remove both

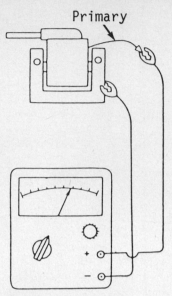

Fig. M7-12—Connect ohmmeter leads as shown to measure resistance in the primary side of the ignition coil. Refer to text.

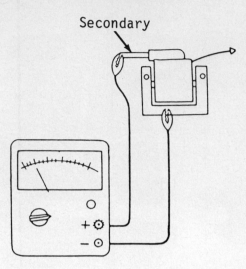

Fig. M7-13—Connect ohmmeter leads as shown to measure resistance in the secondary side of the ignition coil. Refer to text.

spark plugs. Use a point checker and attach the red tester lead to the grey wire (low voltage coil lead for top cylinder) coming from magneto base plate (8). Connect the black tester lead to an engine ground.

NOTE: A suitable continuity tester can be used.

To determine the correct position of the stator assembly, the piston in number 1 cylinder (top cylinder) must be positioned in the cylinder at the point where ignition occurs. To determine piston position, remove the spark plugs and install a dial indicator in the number 1 (top) cylinder spark plug hole. Determine top dead center for the piston and zero the dial indicator for piston TDC (temporarily reinstall the flywheel so it can be used to rotate the crankshaft). Fully open the throttle by pushing the magneto base plate to full advance position. Slowly turn the flywheel counterclockwise until the tester's pointer moves from "OPEN" to "CLOSE", then stop turning the flywheel. Check the piston position reading on the dial indicator. The piston should be 2.7-3.1 mm (0.106-0.122 in.) BTDC. If not, loosen cap screws (S—Fig. M7-10) and adjust throttle cam (C). Move throttle cam (C) towards magneto stop (M) to decrease magneto base plate movement and away from magneto stop (M) to increase magneto base plate movement. Continue adjustment procedure until the correct piston position is obtained when the tester's pointer moves from "OPEN" to "CLOSE", then tighten cap screw (s) securing throttle cam (C). Repeat the procedure for the bottom cylinder. Attach the point checker's red tester lead to the orange wire coming from the magneto base plate (8—Fig. M7-8). Make sure the black tester lead remains grounded to engine. Adjust

the full advance timing by varying the breaker point gap.

To check and, if needed, adjust ignition timing full retard (idle) setting, proceed as follows: Attach the point checker's red tester lead to the grey wire coming from magneto base plate (8) (top cylinder's low voltage coil lead). Connect the black tester lead to an engine ground. Push magneto base plate (8) to the full retard position. Slowly turn the flywheel clockwise until the tester's pointer moves from "CLOSE" to "OPEN". The timing pointer should be within the 3°-5° ATDC marking on the flywheel (3). If not, loosen locknut (1—Fig. M7-10) and turn the adjustment screw (2) until the correct degree reading ATDC is obtained when the tester's pointer moves from "CLOSE" to "OPEN", then tighten locknut (1).

Ignition Coils. To check ignition coils (13—Fig. (M7-8) located on side of cylinders, use a suitable ohmmeter. Connect one tester lead to the coil's metal laminations, then connect the remaining tester lead alternately to the primary (Fig. M7-12) and secondary (Fig. M7-13) ignition coil leads. Resistance reading for primary circuit should be 1.35-1.65 ohms, while the secondary circuit resistance reading should be 4150-6240 ohms. Renew ignition coil(s) (13—Fig. M7-8) if the meter readings are not within the proper range.

SPEED CONTROL LINKAGE
Models With Breaker Point Ignition System

As the twist grip is rotated, the magneto base plate is rotated via cables and associated linkage. Throttle cam (C—Fig. M7-14) is mounted to the

Fig. M7-14—During adjustment of reverse gear throttle limiting linkage, throttle roller (R) must align with throttle cam (C) mark (I). Refer to text.

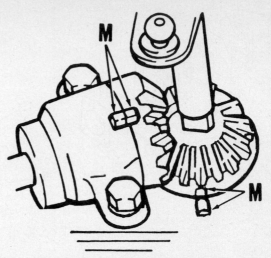

Fig. M7-16—Refer to text for adjustment of reverse gear throt-gear marks (M) should be aligned.

magneto base plate, thus operating the carburetor throttle shaft via roller (R) in relation with magneto base plate rotation.

To synchronize ignition and throttle control linkage, first make sure the ignition timing has been correctly adjusted. When the twist grip is moved completely against the high speed stop, the carburetor throttle should be fully opened. MAKE SURE that the carburetor throttle does not reach the full open position before the ignition timing is fully advanced.

To adjust the speed control linkage proceed as follows: Disconnect the adjustable link between the tower shaft and the magneto base plate. Turn the twist grip to the "FAST" position and note if marks (M—Fig. M7-16) are aligned. If marks do not align, remove gears and reinstall with marks properly aligned. With twist grip in "FAST" position, rotate magneto base plate to full advanced position, then install adjustable link between magneto base plate and tower shaft. Adjust length of link as required so link fits easily over mounting points. With twist grip still in the full throttle position, the carburetor throttle plate should be in the wide open position. If not, loosen screw (S—Fig. M7-17) and adjust throttle rod (4) in rod end (3) un-

til wide open position is obtained, then retighten screw (S).

Reverse gear throttle limiting linkage is used to prevent the possibility of full throttle operation when the gear shift lever is in the reverse position. To adjust linkage, place gear shift lever in the reverse position and turn the twist grip so throttle roller (R—Fig. M7-14) is aligned with throttle cam mark (I). Loosen stop bolt (B—Fig. M7-15) and move stop plate (P) so it contacts lever (L), then retighten bolt (B).

CARBURETOR

The fuel pump and carburetor are a complete unit. Refer to the following OVERHAUL section for service procedures on both the fuel pump and carburetor.

ADJUSTMENT. Use the standard carburetor jet sizes as recommended by the manufacturer for normal operation when used at altitudes of 2500 feet (760 m) and less. Main jet (21—Fig. M7-17) size should be reduced from standard recommendation by one size for altitudes of 2500 to 5000 feet (760 to 1525 m), two sizes for altitudes of 5000 to 7500 feet (1525 to 2285 m) and three sizes for altitudes of 7500 feet (2285 m) and up. Initial adjustment of idle mixture screw (8) is 1-7/8 to 2-3/8 turns out from a lightly seated position. Recommended idle speed is 600-700 rpm in gear with engine at normal operating temperature.

With the outboard motor properly mounted on a boat or a suitable test tank, immerse the lower unit. Connect a tachometer and set it on the appropriate range scale. Start the engine and allow it to warm up to normal operating temperature. Position the throttle control twist grip to the complete closed position. Place the gear shift lever in the "Forward" position. Adjust the engine idle speed screw (10) until the engine is idling at

Fig. M7-15—Refer to text for adjustment of reverse gear throttle stop plate (P).

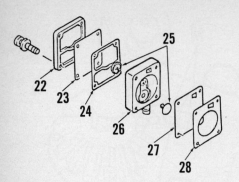

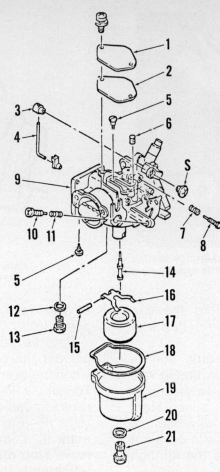

Fig. M7-17 — Exploded view of carburetor and fuel pump.

S. Screw	14. Main nozzle
1. Cover	15. Pin
2. Gasket	16. Float lever
3. Rod end	17. Float
4. Throttle rod	18. Gasket
5. Screw	19. Float bowl
6. Pilot jet	20. Gasket
7. Spring	21. Main jet
8. Idle mixture	22. Fuel pump
screw	cover
9. Body	23. Diaphragm
10. Idle speed	24. Gasket
screw	25. Check valve
11. Spring	26. Pump body
12. Gasket	27. Diaphragm
13. Fuel inlet valve	28. Gasket

600-700 rpm, then adjust idle mixture screw (8) until smooth engine operation is noted. Readjust the engine idle speed screw (10) until the recommended idle speed is attained.

Reinstall the engine's top cover.

OVERHAUL. The fuel pump is an integral part of the carburetor. The fuel pump assembly may be overhauled without overhauling the complete carburetor. If the fuel pump is to be overhauled without carburetor removal, proceed as follows: Remove the engine's top cover and disconnect the fuel tank supply hose at the outboard motor connector. Disconnect the fuel supply hose at the fuel pump inlet.

With reference to Fig. M7-17, disassemble the fuel pump assembly. Inspect all components for damage and excessive wear and renew if needed. Clean components as needed with a suitable cleaning solution. Blow dry with clean compressed air. If compressed air is not available, use only lint-free cloths to wipe dry. Make sure all passages are clear of any obstructions.

With reference to Fig. M7-17, reassemble the fuel pump assembly with new gaskets. Securely tighten the retaining screws.

NOTE: Fuel pump and engine malfunction will result it the fuel pump and all connections are not airtight.

Complete reassembly.

Refer to the following for complete carburetor overhaul: Remove engine's top cover. Disconnect choke lever and bushing from carburetor linkage. Remove the two screws retaining air intake cover

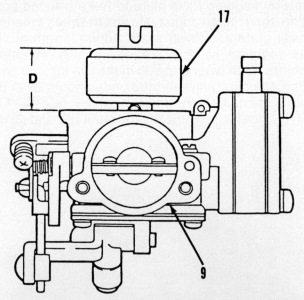

Fig. M7-18 — Distance (D) should be 20.5-22.5 mm (13/16-7/8 in.) from carburetor body (9) to base of float (17) for proper float level.

and withdraw cover. Disconnect the two crankcase recirculation hoses from the carburetor (label if needed). Disconnect the fuel tank supply hose at the outboard motor connector. Disconnect the fuel supply hose at the fuel pump inlet. Clean all external surfaces and remove accumulated dirt and grease. Remove the two nuts securing the carburetor and withdraw the carburetor assembly.

With reference to Fig. M7-17, disassemble the complete carburetor assembly and note any discrepancies which must be corrected before reassembly. Remove all gaskets (label if needed for later reference) and set to the side.

Thoroughly clean all carburetor parts in a suitable solvent and inspect for damage and excessive wear. Note that plastic and rubber components should not be subjected to some cleaning solutions. Blow dry with clean compressed air. If compressed air is not available, use only lint-free cloths to wipe dry. Do not use a drill bit or wire to clean jets. Enlargement or damage of the calibrated holes may affect engine performance.

With reference to Fig. M7-17, reassemble the carburetor components with new gaskets. Note that the new gaskets should match up with those removed. If not, check with your parts supplier to be sure you have the correct gasket set.

To determine the float level, invert carburetor body (9—Fig. M7-18) and measure distance (D) from carburetor body (9) to base of float (17). Distance (D) should be 20.5-22.5 mm (13/16-7/8 in.) and is adjusted by bending the arms of float lever (16—Fig. M7-17) evenly.

When reinstalling the carburetor, place a new gasket between the carburetor and the intake manifold. Securely tighten the retaining nuts. Reconnect the two crankcase recirculation hoses and the fuel supply hose. Connect choke lever and bushing to carburetor linkage. Install air intake cover and retain with the two screws. Initially adjust idle mixture screw (8) 1-7/8 to 2-3/8 turns out from a lightly seated position.

MARINER 15 HP (PRIOR TO 1979)

NOTE: Metric fasteners are used throughout outboard motor.

Specifications

Hp/rpm 15/5500
Bore . . . . .56 mm
(2.20 in.)
Stroke. . . . . .50 mm
(1.97 in.)
Number of cylinders 2
Displacement . . . . .246 cc
(15 cu. in.)
Spark plug—NGK B7HS
Electrode gap . . . . .0.5-0.6 mm
(0.020-0.024 in.)
Breaker point gap . . . . .0.3-0.4 mm
(0.012-0.016 in.)
Ignition timing . . . . .See Text
Idle speed . . . . .1450-1550 rpm
Fuel:oil ratio. 50:1

Maintenance

LUBRICATION

ENGINE. The engine is lubricated by oil mixed with the fuel. The fuel should be regular leaded, low lead or unleaded gasoline with a minimum pump octane rating of 86. Recommended oil is Quicksilver Formula 50-D Outboard Lubricant or a BIA certified two-stroke motor oil. The recommended fuel:oil ratio for normal operation is 50:1. During engine break-in, the fuel:oil ratio should be increased to 25:1.

The manufacturer's recommended break-in period is defined as follows: For the first five minutes of operation the engine should not exceed its slowest possible cruising speed. After five minutes, slowly increase the engine speed to half throttle (2500-3500 rpm) for the first three hours of operation.

Running the engine at or near full throttle for extended periods is not recommended until after ten hours of operation.

LOWER UNIT. The lower unit gears and bearings are lubricated by oil contained in the gearcase. The recommended oil is Mariner Super Duty Gear Lube or a suitable EP90 outboard gear oil. The gearcase should be refilled periodically and the lubricant renewed after every 50 hours of operation or more frequently if needed. The gearcase is drained and filled through the same plug port (D—Fig. M8-1). An oil level (vent) port (L) is used to indicate the full oil level of the gearcase and to ease oil drainage.

To drain the oil, place the outboard motor in a vertical position. Remove drain plug (D) and oil level plug (L), and allow the lubricant to drain into a suitable container.

To fill the gearcase with oil, place the outboard motor in a vertical position. Add oil through drain plug (D) opening with an oil feeder until the oil begins to overflow from oil level plug (L) port. Reinstall oil level plug (L) with a new gasket, if

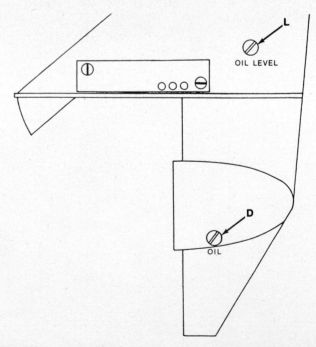

Fig. M8-1 — View showing lower unit gearcase drain and fill plug (D) and oil level (vent) plug (L).

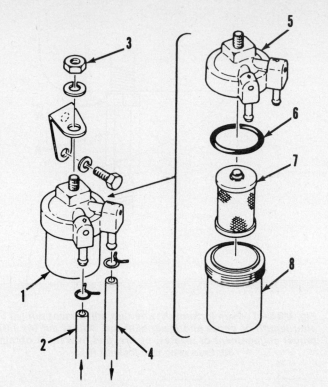

Fig. M8-2 — View showing fuel filter assembly, mounting bracket and fuel hoses.

1. Fuel filter assy.
2. Fuel supply line
3. Mounting nut
4. Fuel pump inlet line
5. Filter base
6. "O" ring
7. Filter element
8. Cup

needed, and tighten. Remove oil feeder, then reinstall drain plug (D) with a new gasket, if needed, and tighten.

PIVOT POINTS AND SLIDES. Lubricate all pivot points and linkage slides with a good quality marine type multipurpose grease as frequently as needed to keep the components operating freely and properly.

FUEL SYSTEM

Periodically inspect the fuel lines and connections for damage. Renew components if needed. With the engine stopped, occasionally open the carburetor float bowl drain plug and allow the fuel to drain off into a suitable container. Inspect the fuel for any foreign matter. If an excessive amount of foreign matter is found, extensive cleaning of the fuel system is needed.

Keep the external surface of the carburetor clean and all connections and sealing surfaces tight.

Refer to CARBURETOR in the Tune-Up section for checking float bowl fuel level.

FUEL FILTER. A fuel filter assembly (1 — Fig. M8-2) is connected between fuel supply line (2) and fuel pump inlet line (4). With the engine stopped, periodically unscrew fuel filter cup (8) from filter base (5) and withdraw filter element (7) and

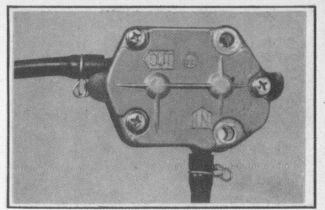

Fig. M8-3 — The fuel hoses must be correctly connected to the fuel pump. The fuel supply hose connects to the fuel pump's inlet port, identified as "IN."

"O" ring (6). Clean cup (8) and filter element (7) in a suitable solvent and blow dry with clean compressed air. Inspect filter element (7). If excessive blockage or damage is noted, renew element.

Reassembly is reverse order of disassembly. Renew "O" ring (6) during reassembly.

FUEL PUMP. The fuel pump is operated by crankcase pressure changes from the up and down movement of the piston. When the crankcase pressure decreases (the piston is moving upward), the pump diaphragm is pulled toward the crankcase allowing fuel to enter the pump chamber and closing the discharge check valve. When the crankcase pressure increases (the piston is moving downward), the diaphragm is pushed outward discharging the fuel to the carburetor and closing the inlet check valve. This pulsating action allows for continuous fuel flow. The check valves are used to prevent reverse flow of the fuel.

A spring is used to load the diaphragm, thus allowing the diaphragm to respond more quickly to crankcase pressure changes.

The inlet port is identified as "IN" and the discharge port is identified as "OUT" as shown in Fig. M8-3, the fuel hoses must be connected accordingly.

To overhaul, first remove the engine's top cover and disconnect the fuel tank supply hose at the outboard motor connector. Disconnect the fuel hoses at the fuel pump inlet and discharge nozzles and label if needed. Remove securing cap screws and withdraw fuel pump assembly.

With reference to Fig. M8-4, reassembly the fuel fuel pump assembly. Inspect all components for excessive wear or any other damage and renew if needed.

With reference to Fig. M8-4 reassemble the fuel pump assembly with new gaskets. Coat gasket (1) with a nonhardening type gasket sealer making

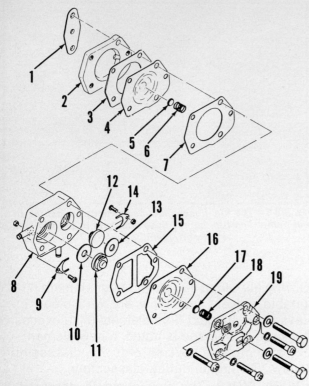

Fig. M8-4 — Exploded view of fuel pump. Diaphragms (4 and 16) are identical.

1. Gasket
2. Base
3. Gasket
4. Diaphragm
5. Spring plate
6. Spring
7. Gasket
8. Body
9. Retainer
10. Gasket
11. Outlet check valve
12. Inlet check valve
13. Gasket
14. Retainer
15. Gasket
16. Diaphragm
17. Spring plate
18. Spring
19. Cover

certain that passage in center is not plugged with gasket sealer. Mount the fuel pump assembly to the crankcase and securely tighten the retaining cap screws.

NOTE: Fuel pump and engine malfunction will result if the fuel pump and all connections are not airtight.

Complete reassembly.

SHIFT LINKAGE

Direction of propeller rotation is determined by the position of the gear shift lever. The gear shift lever actuates gearcase components using shift linkage consistng of an upper and lower shift rod connected by an adjustment bracket. The tapered end of the lower shift rod controls the movement of the dog clutch on the propeller shaft. The positioning of the dog clutch on the propeller shaft determines whether forward, neutral or reverse directional movement is selected.

To check shift linkage for proper adjustment, first place shift lever in reverse detent position. Check for proper engagement and propeller rotation by turning the propeller.

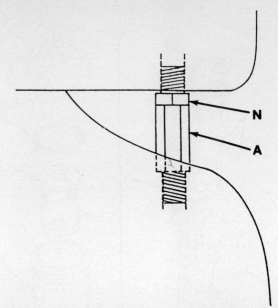

Fig. M8-5 — Loosen locknut (N) and turn adjustment nut (A) to alter length of upper and lower shift rod. Adjust nut (A) until proper engagement of reverse, neutral and forward is obtained, then retighten locknut (N).

> ⚠ **WARNING**
>
> **Disconnect spark plug leads and properly ground leads before performing any propeller service, otherwise, accidental starting can occur if propeller shaft is rotated.**

Check for proper engagement of neutral and forward.

To adjust, loosen locknut (N—Fig. M8-5) and turn adjustment nut (A) until proper engagement of reverse, neutral and forward is obtained, then retighten locknut (N).

STARTER

When starter rope (3—Fig. M8-6) is pulled, pulley (6) will rotate. As pulley (6) rotates, the three drive pawls (8) move apart thus meshing with starter cup (15) and cranking the engine.

When starter rope (3) is released, pulley (6) is rotated in the reverse direction by force from rewind spring (5). As pulley (6) rotates, starter rope (3) is rewound and drive pawls (8) are disengaged from starter cup (15).

The manual starter must be disassembled to renew starter rope (3) or any other internal starter component.

To overhaul the manual starter, proceed as follows: Remove the engine's top cover. Remove the screws retaining the manual starter to the engine, then withdraw the starter assembly.

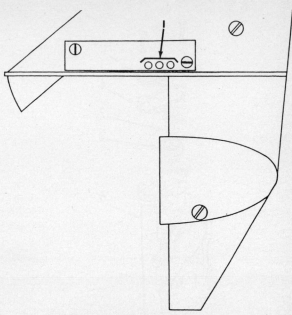

Fig. M8-7 — *Cooling system water inlet ports (I) are located on the starboard side of the lower unit.*

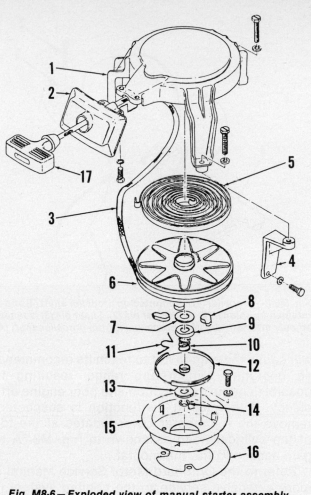

Fig. M8-6 — Exploded view of manual starter assembly.

1. Housing
2. Rope guide
3. Starter rope
4. Bracket
5. Rewind spring
6. Pulley
7. Thrust washer
8. Pawl
9. Thrust washer
10. Drive plate spring
11. Pawl return spring
12. Drive plate
13. Thrust washer
14. Clip
15. Starter cup
16. Flywheel cover
17. Handle

⚠️WARNING

Care should be exercised when working with or around a coiled starter rewind spring as sudden uncoiling can cause injury. Safety eyewear and gloves are recommended.

To disassemble, untie starter rope (3) at handle (17) and allow the rope to wind into the starter. Invert the unit and press on drive plate (12) to ease in removal of clip (14) and thrust washer (13). Remove drive plate (12), pawls (8) and pawl return springs (11). Lift pulley (6) with starter rope (3) from housing (1). BE CAREFUL when removing pulley (6) as the rewind spring may be dislodged. Remove starter rope (3) from pulley (6) if renewal

is required. Remove drive plate spring (10) and thrust washers (9 and 7). To remove rewind spring (5) from housing (1), invert housing so it sets upright on a flat surface, then tap the housing top until rewind spring (5) falls free and uncoils.

Inspect all components for damage and excessive wear and renew if needed.

To reassemble, first apply a coating of a suitable water-resistant grease to rewind spring area of housing (1). Install prebound rewind spring (5) in housing (1) so spring coils wind in a counter-clockwise direction from the outer end. Make sure the spring's outer hook is properly secured over starter housing (1) pin, then remove the retaining wire.

Install starter rope (3) in pulley (6) with a knot on the inner end. Wind starter rope (3) onto pulley (6) approximately two turns counterclockwise when viewed from the flywheel side. Direct remaining starter rope (3) length through notch in pulley (6).

NOTE: Lubricate all friction surfaces with a suitable water-resistant grease during reassembly.

Assemble pulley (6) with starter rope (3) to housing (1) making sure that rewind spring's (5) hooked end engages pulley (6).

Thread starter rope (3) end through housing (1) and rope guide (2), then secure rope end in handle (17) with a knot. Turn pulley (6) 4-5 turns counterclockwise when viewed from the flywheel side, then release starter rope (3) from pulley notch and allow rope to slowly wind onto pulley.

NOTE: Do not apply any more tension on rewind spring (5) than is required to draw starter handle (17) back into the proper released position.

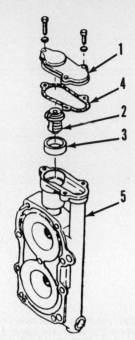

Fig. M8-7A — Exploded view of the cooling system components located at the top of the engine cylinder head (5).

1. Cover
2. Thermostat
3. Spacer
4. Gasket
5. Cylinder head

Install thrust washers (7 and 9) and drive plate spring (10). Install pawls (8) and pawl return springs (11). Hook drive plate (12) in return springs (11) and rotate drive plate (12) as needed to install. Press on drive plate (12) and install thrust washer (13) and secure with clip (14).

Remount the manual starter assembly and engine's top cover to complete reassembly.

COOLING SYSTEM

Ports (I—Fig. M8-7) located on the starboard side of the lower unit are used as the water inlets for the cooling system. The ports must be kept clean of all foreign matter to ensure efficient operation of the cooling system.

⚠CAUTION

Do not operate outboard motor unless the lower unit is immersed in water, otherwise, the water pump impeller will be damaged.

A thermostat positioned in the cylinder head is used to regulate the engine's operating temperature. Note that a thermostat that sticks or stays closed too long could cause engine overheating, resulting in poor engine operation and possible engine damage. A thermostat that opens too quickly or is stuck in the open position

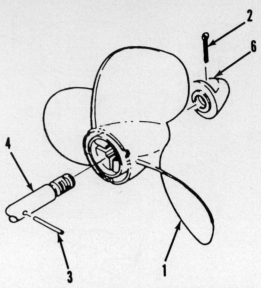

Fig. M8-8 — Propeller (1) is mounted on propeller shaft (4) and is retained by spinner (6) and cotter pin (2). Shear pin (3) is renewed only after withdrawing propeller (1) from propeller shaft (4).

will cause the engine not to reach its recommended operating temperature range, resulting in possible engine malfunction and poor engine efficiency. If thermostat malfunction is suspected, remove the thermostat cover located at the top of the cylinder head as shown in Fig. M8-7A to gain access to the thermostat.

Refer to the Outboard Motor Service Manual if more extensive service to the cooling system is required.

PROPELLER

The standard propeller has three blades, a diameter of 234 mm (9¼ in.) and a pitch of 230 mm (9 in.). Optional propellers are available. Select a propeller that will allow the engine at full throttle to reach maximum operating rpm range (4500-5500 rpm).

⚠WARNING

Shift directional control lever to "NEUTRAL." Disconnect spark plug leads and properly ground leads before performing any propeller service, otherwise, accidental starting can occur if propeller shaft is rotated.

To remove the propeller, remove cotter pin (2—Fig. M8-8) and unscrew propeller spinner (6). Withdraw propeller (1) from propeller shaft (4).

Inspect propeller (1), propeller shaft (4) and shear pin (3) for damage and excessive wear and renew if needed.

Apply a water-resistant grease to the propeller bore, then install propeller (1) to propeller shaft (4) and retain with propeller spinner (6) and a new cotter pin (2).

Tune-Up

IGNITION SYSTEM

The standard spark plug is NGK B7HS with an electrode gap of 0.5-0.6 mm (0.020-0.024 in.).

The breaker point gap should be 0.3-0.4 mm (0.012-0.016 in.) and can be inspected and adjusted through the opening in flywheel (3—Fig. M8-9). Two breaker point assemblies (6) and two condensers (5) are used. To inspect and, if needed, adjust the breaker point gap, first remove the engine's top cover. Remove the screws retaining the manual starter to the engine and withdraw the starter assembly. Remove the cap screws and lockwashers securing starter pulley (15—Fig. M8-6) and flywheel cover (16) to flywheel (3—Fig. M8-9) and withdraw.

Inspect the breaker point surfaces for excessive wear, pitting and any other damage. If needed, renew breaker point assemblies (6) and condensers (5) as outlined later.

To clean the breaker point contact surfaces, rotate the flywheel until the breaker point contact surfaces are accessible through the opening in flywheel (3). Use a point file or sandpaper with a grit rating of 400 to 600. After polishing, wipe the contact surfaces clean with a dry cloth and lightly grease the breaker point arm and lubricator (7) with a suitable lubricant.

Turn the flywheel until the breaker point contact surfaces are placed at their widest position, then reach through the flywheel opening with a feeler gage of the appropriate size and check the distance between the point surfaces. If the distance is not within the recommended limits, loosen the point set securing screw and adjust the point set until the correct gap is obtained.

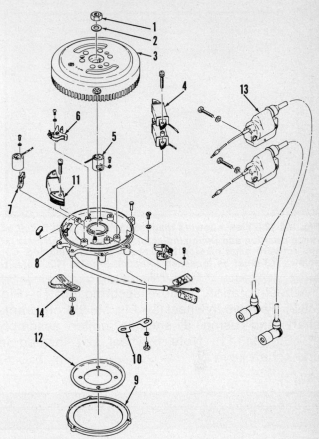

Fig. M8-9 — Exploded view of flywheel magneto unit.

1. Nut	8. Magneto base plate
2. Washer	9. Magneto base plate retainer
3. Flywheel	10. Bracket
4. Low voltage coil	11. Lighting coil
5. Condenser	12. Retainer
6. Breaker point assy.	13. Ignition coil
7. Lubricator	14. Throttle cam

Tighten the point set securing screw and recheck the breaker point gap. Repeat the adjustment procedure, if needed, until the correct breaker point gap is obtained. Repeat the adjustment procedure on the other breaker point assembly.

To renew breaker point assemblies (6) and condensers (5), proceed as follows: Using a suitable flywheel holding tool (H—Fig. M8-10) to prevent

Fig. M8-10 — View showing the use of a suitable flywheel holding tool (H) to prevent flywheel rotation during removal of securing nut (1—Fig. M8-9) with suitable tool (T).

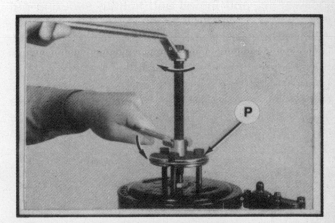

Fig. M8-11 — Remove flywheel from crankshaft end using a suitable puller assembly (P).

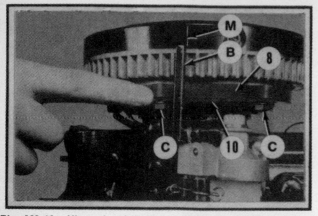

Fig. M8-12—View showing magneto base plate (8) in full advance position and timing indicators, flywheel timing mark (M) and forward edge of stop bracket (B), properly aligned. Cap screws (C) must be loosened to adjust bracket (10). Refer to text.

Fig. M8-13—View showing the installation of a dial indicator in the spark plug hole to obtain correct piston positioning for timing ignition system. Refer to text.

flywheel rotation, remove securing nut (1—Fig. M8-9). Remove flywheel (3—Fig. M8-9) from crankshaft end using a suitable puller assembly (P—Fig. M8-11). Note flywheel key located in crankshaft keyway.

⚠WARNING

Be sure suitable tools are used to remove the flywheel. Damage resultant from the misapplication of force or the use of incorrect tools may cause engine damage, engine malfunction or personal injury.

With reference to Fig. M8-9, renew breaker point assemblies (6) and condensers (5). Adjust the breaker point gap to the recommended setting as outlined in a previous paragraph. Make sure the securing screws are properly tightened. Be sure the flywheel key is properly positioned in the crankshaft end, then reinstall flywheel (3). Install lockwasher and install and tighten securing nut (1) to 69-78 N·m (51-58 ft.-lbs.).

To obtain the correct ignition timing, first adjust both breaker point assemblies (6) to the proper point gap as previously outlined. Remove both spark plugs. Use a point checker and attach the red tester lead to the grey wire coming from the magneto base plate (8) (top cylinder low voltage coil lead). Connect the black tester lead to an engine ground.

NOTE: A suitable continuity tester can be used.

Rotate the twist grip to full throttle position. Push the magneto base plate as shown in Fig. M8-12 to verify full advance position. Slowly turn

the flywheel counterclockwise until the tester's pointer moves from "OPEN" to "CLOSE", then note flywheel timing mark (M—Fig. M8-12). The flywheel timing mark should be aligned with the forward edge of stop bracket (B). If not, loosen cap screws (C) and adjust bracket (10). Continue the adjustment procedure until the flywheel timing mark aligns with the forward edge of the stop bracket when the tester's pointer moves from "OPEN" to "CLOSE", then tighten cap screws (C) securing bracket (10). Repeat the procedure for the bottom cylinder. Attach the point checker's red tester lead to the orange wire coming from magneto base plate (8—Fig. M8-9). Make sure the black tester lead remains attached to ground. Adjust the full advance timing by varying the breaker point gap.

NOTE: Replacement flywheels (3) do not have timing marks and must be marked according to piston position as outlined in the following paragraph.

If the ignition timing marks are questioned or a new flywheel is installed, the piston position must be determined. Install a dial indicator in the top cylinder spark plug hole as shown in Fig. M8-13. Set top piston at 2.5 mm (0.098 in.) BTDC and mark flywheel adjacent to forward edge of stop bracket. Attach the dial indicator to the bottom cylinder and mark flywheel in the same manner with the bottom piston at 2.5 mm (0.098 in.) BTDC.

To set ignition timing using a dial indicator, proceed as follows: With the flywheel being slowly turned counterclockwise, the piston should be 2.1-2.9 mm (0.082-0.114 in.) BTDC when the tester's pointer moves from "OPEN" to "CLOSE"

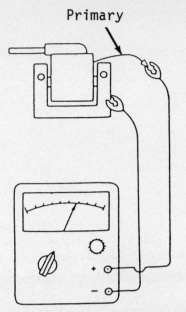

Primary

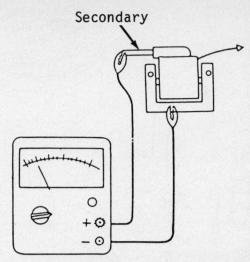

Secondary

Fig. M8-14—Connect ohmmeter leads as shown to measure resistance in the primary side of the ignition coil. Refer to text.

Fig. M8-15—Connect ohmmeter leads as shown to measure resistance in the secondary side of the ignition coil. Refer to text.

for top and bottom cylinder. Adjust full advance timing as previously outlined.

When the ignition timing adjustment is completed, check the speed control linkage adjustment as outlined in the following SPEED CONTROL LINKAGE section.

Ignition Coils. To check the ignition coils (13—Fig. M8-9) located on the side of cylinders, use a suitable ohmmeter. Connect one tester lead to the coil's metal laminations, then connect the remaining tester led alternately to the primary

(Fig. M8-14) and secondary (Fig. M8-15) ignition coil leads. Resistance reading for primary circuit should be 1.53-1.87 ohms, while the secondary circuit resistance reading should be 4800-7200 ohms. Renew the ignition coil(s) if the meter readings are not within the proper range.

SPEED CONTROL LINKAGE

The speed control handle components are connected by cables to a pulley adjacent to the engine. The pulley movement is transferred by linkage to rotate the magneto base plate and actuate the carburetor throttle so the ignition timing is advanced as the throttle opens.

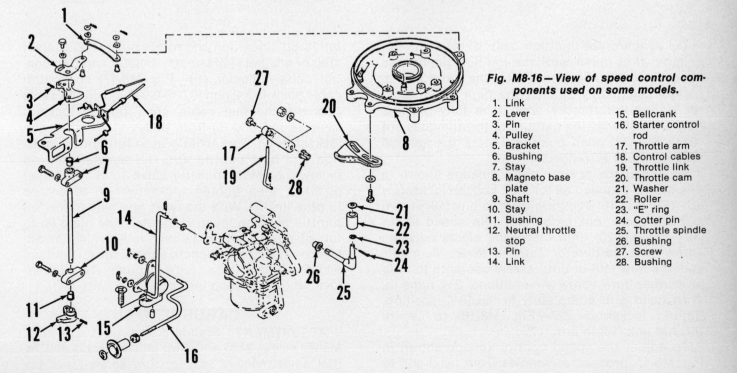

Fig. M8-16—View of speed control components used on some models.

1. Link
2. Lever
3. Pin
4. Pulley
5. Bracket
6. Bushing
7. Stay
8. Magneto base plate
9. Shaft
10. Stay
11. Bushing
12. Neutral throttle stop
13. Pin
14. Link
15. Bellcrank
16. Starter control rod
17. Throttle arm
18. Control cables
19. Throttle link
20. Throttle cam
21. Washer
22. Roller
23. "E" ring
24. Cotter pin
25. Throttle spindle
26. Bushing
27. Screw
28. Bushing

Mariner 15 Hp (Prior to 1979)

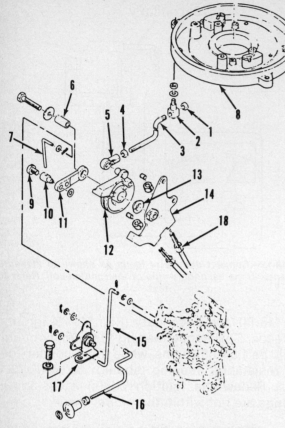

Fig. M8-17 — View of speed control components used on some models.

1. Nut
2. Swivel
3. Magneto control rod
4. Nut
5. Rod end
6. Sleeve
7. Throttle link
8. Magneto base plate
9. Screw
10. Swivel
11. Throttle arm
12. Pulley
13. Bushing
14. Bracket
15. Link
16. Starter control rod
17. Bellcrank
18. Control cables

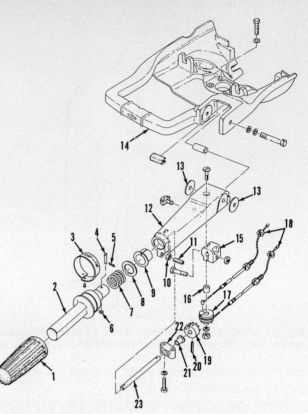

Fig. M8-18 — Exploded view of early type speed control components located in steering handle.

1. Rubber cover
2. Twist grip
3. Indicator
4. Pin
5. Clip
6. Washer
7. Spring
8. Washer
9. Bushing
10. Locknut
11. Throttle stop screw
12. Steering handle
13. Spacer
14. Bracket
15. Friction piece
16. Spacer
17. Pinion
18. Control cables
19. Drive gear
20. Pin
21. Bushing
22. Guide
23. Shaft

To synchronize ignition and throttle control linkage, first make sure the ignition timing has been correctly adjusted. When the twist grip is moved completely against the high speed stop, the carburetor throttle should be fully opened. MAKE SURE that the carburetor throttle does not reach the full open position before the ignition timing is fully advanced.

To adjust the speed control linkage shown in Fig. M8-16, proceed as follows: Loosen lockscrew (27 — Fig. M8-16) securing throttle link (19) in arm (17) and back out carburetor idle speed screw (10 — Fig. M8-20) until clearance exists between screw and carburetor throttle lever. Turn idle speed screw (10) in until screw contacts throttle lever, then turn screw an additional 2½ turns in. With twist grip completely in "SLOW" position, tighten lockscrew (27 — Fig. M8-16) to secure throttle link (19) in arm (17).

To adjust the speed control linkage shown in Fig. M8-17, proceed as follows: Turn twist grip to full throttle position and rotate pulley (12) against stop of bracket (14). Loosen locknut and turn control cable adjuster (18 — Fig. M8-17) so control cable slack is 1-2 mm (0.039-0.079 in.) on the cable opposite the pull cable, then tighten locknut. Remove rod end (5) from pulley (12) and loosen lockscrew (9). Turn twist grip to full throttle position and hold throttle arm (11) against stop on pulley (12). Move throttle valve to fully opened position, then tighten lockscrew (9) to secure throttle link (7). With the twist grip held in the full throttle position, push magneto base plate (8) to full advance position. Loosen locknut (4) and adjust rod end (5) on magneto control rod (3) until rod end (5) aligns with ball joint on pulley (12). Tighten locknut (4) and snap into position.

CARBURETOR

ADJUSTMENT. Standard main jet (16 — Fig. M8-20) size is #135 and pilot jet (13) size is #60. Initial adjustment of idle mixture screw (7) is 1¼

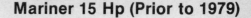

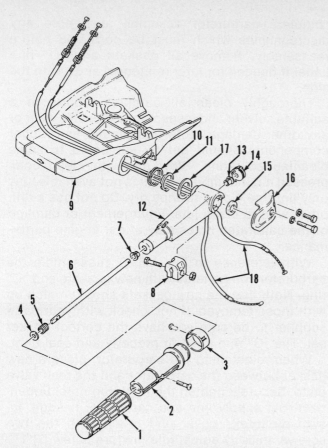

Fig. M8-19 — Exploded view of late type speed control components located in steering handle.

1. Rubber cover
2. Twist grip
3. Indicator
4. Washer
5. Spring
6. Shaft
7. Bushing
8. Friction piece
9. Bracket
10. Compression spring
11. Spring retainer
12. Steering handle
13. Bushing
14. Throttle cam
15. Spacer
16. Cover
17. Washer
18. Control cables

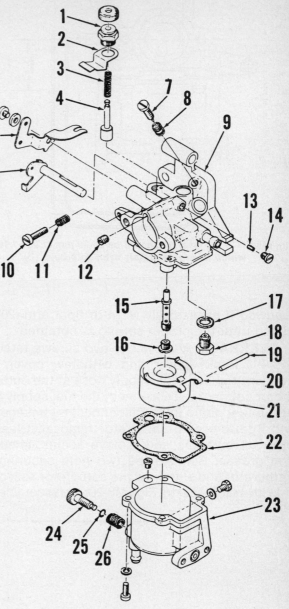

Fig. M8-20 — Exploded view of carburetor.

1. Nut
2. Plate
3. Spring
4. Choke plunger
5. Choke lever
6. Throttle shaft
7. Idle mixture mixture
8. Spring
9. Body
10. Idle speed screw
11. Spring
12. Low speed air jet
13. Pilot jet
14. Guide screw
15. Main nozzle
16. Main jet
17. Gasket
18. Fuel inlet valve
19. Float arm pin
20. Float arm
21. Float
22. Gasket
23. Float bowl
24. Drain plug
25. "O" ring
26. Spring

turns out from a lightly seated position. Recommended idle speed is 1450-1550 rpm with engine at normal operating temperature.

With the outboard motor properly mounted on a boat or a suitable test tank, immerse the lower unit. Connect a tachometer and set it on the appropriate range scale. Start the engine and allow it to warm up to normal operating temperature. Position the throttle control twist grip to the complete closed position. Adjust the engine idle speed screw (10) until the engine is idling at 1450-1550 rpm, then adjust idle mixture screw (7) until smooth engine operation is noted. Readjust the engine idle speed screw (10) until the recommended idle speed is obtained.

Recheck carburetor fuel level as previously outlined and adjust if needed.

Complete reassembly.

FUEL LEVEL. Remove the engine's top cover and position the outboard motor in an upright position. Connect a clear vinyl tube to the float bowl drain nozzle and hold the drain tube up. Open the float bowl drain plug. Run the engine at idle speed for a few minutes, then stop the engine. Fuel level (L — Fig. M8-21) should be 26-30 mm (1.024-1.181 in.) or approximately level with boss (B) on carburetor.

If fuel level is incorrect, float bowl (23 — Fig. M8-20) must be removed and inlet valve (18)

Mariner 15 Hp (Prior to 1979)

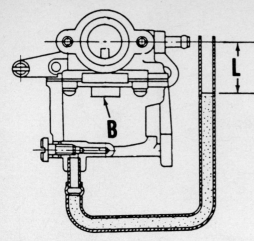

Fig. M8-21 — Fuel level (L) should be 26-30 mm (1.024-1.181 in.) which is approximately even with boss (B).

renewed if excessively worn or float arm (20) adjusted until the proper setting is obtained.

OVERHAUL. Remove the two screws retaining the air intake cover and withdraw cover. Disconnect the fuel tank supply hose at the outboard motor connector. Disconnect the fuel supply hose at the fuel pump inlet. Disconnect all linkage that will interfere with carburetor removal. Clean all external surfaces and remove accumulated dirt and grease. Remove the two nuts securing the carburetor and withdraw the carburetor assembly.

With reference to Fig. M8-20, disassemble the complete carburetor assembly and note any discrepancies which must be corrected before reassembly. Remove all gaskets and "O" ring (label if needed for later reference) and set to the side.

Thoroughly clean all carburetor parts in a suitable solvent and inspect for excessive wear or any other damage. Note that plastic and rubber components should not be subjected to some cleaning solutions. Blow dry with clean compressed air. If compressed air is not available, use only lint-free cloths to wipe dry. Do not use a drill bit or wire to clean jets. Enlargement or damage of the calibrated holes may affect engine performance.

With reference to Fig. M8-20, reassemble the carburetor components with new gaskets and "O" ring. Note that the new gaskets should match up with those removed. If not, check with your parts supplier to be sure you have the correct gasket set. The "O" ring must fit properly and seal tight.

When reinstalling the carburetor, place a new gasket between the carburetor and the reed valve plate. Securely tighten the retaining nuts. Reconnect fuel supply line and carburetor linkage. Install air intake cover and retain with the two screws. Initially adjust idle mixture screw (7) 1¼ turns out from a lightly seated position.

Verify carburetor fuel level as outlined in the previous FUEL LEVEL section and note if fuel level adjustment is needed.

Illustrations Courtesy Mariner

MARINER 20 (1979 AND PRIOR), 25 (1980-1984) AND 28 HP

NOTE: Metric fasteners are used throughout outboard motor.

Specifications

Hp/rpm	20/4500-5500
	25/4500-5500*
	28/4500-5500
Bore:	
20 hp	64 mm
	(2.52 in.)
25 & 28 hp	67 mm
	(2.64 in.)
Stroke	61 mm
	(2.40 in.)
Number of cylinders	2
Displacement:	
20 hp	392 cc
	(24 cu. in.)
25 & 28 hp	430 cc
	(26.2 cu. in.)
Spark plug — NGK:	
20 hp	B6HS
25 & 28 hp	B7HS
Electrode gap	0.5-0.6 mm†
	(0.020-0.024 in.)
Ignition	See Text
Idle speed:	
20 & 25 hp (early)	650-700 rpm
	(in gear)
25 hp (late)	650-750 rpm
	(in gear)
28 hp	1000-1100 rpm
Fuel:oil ratio	50:1

*For early 25 hp models, full throttle rpm range is 4700-5700.
†For 20 hp and early 25 hp models, electrode gap should be 0.6-0.7 mm (0.024-0.027 in.).

Maintenance

LUBRICATION

ENGINE. The engine is lubricated by oil mixed with the fuel. The fuel should be regular leaded, low lead or unleaded gasoline with a minimum pump octane rating of 86. Recommended oil is Quicksilver Formula 50-D Outboard Lubricant or a BIA certified two-stroke motor oil. The recommended fuel:oil ratio for normal operation is 50:1. During engine break-in, the fuel:oil ratio should be increased to 25:1.

The manufacturer's recommended break-in period is defined as follows: For the first five minutes of operation the engine should not exceed its slowest possible cruising speed. After five minutes, slowly increase the engine speed to half throttle (2500-3500 rpm) for the first three hours of operation. Running the engine at or near full throttle for extended periods is not recommended until after ten hours of operation.

LOWER UNIT. The lower unit gears and bearings are lubricated by oil contained in the gearcase. The recommended oil is Mariner Super Duty Gear Lube or a suitable EP 90 outboard gear oil. The gearcase should be refilled periodically and the lubricant renewed after every 50 hours of operation on 20 hp, early 25 hp and 28 hp models and after every 100 hours of operation on late 25 hp models or more frequently if needed. The gear-

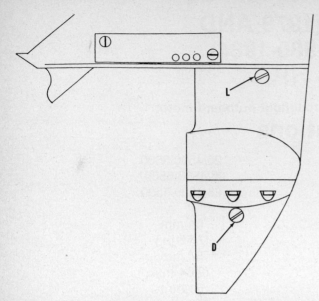

Fig. M9-1— *View showing lower unit gearcase drain and fill plug (D) and oil level (vent) plug (L) on 20 hp and early 25 hp models.*

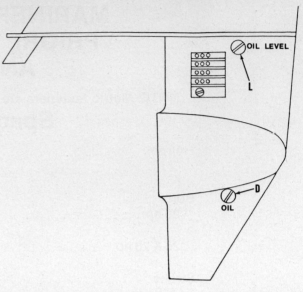

Fig. M9-2— *View showing lower unit gearcase drain and fill plug (D) and oil level (vent) plug (L) on late 25 hp and 28 hp models.*

case is drained and filled through the same plug port (D—Fig. M9-1 or D—Fig. M9-2). An oil level (vent) port (L) is used to indicate the full oil level of the gearcase and to ease oil drainage.

To drain the oil, place the outboard motor in a vertical position. Remove drain plug (D) and oil level plug (L), and allow the lubricant to drain into a suitable container.

To fill the gearcase with oil, place the outboard motor in a vertical position. Add oil through drain plug (D) opening with an oil feeder until the oil begins to overflow from oil level plug (L) port. Reinstall oil level plug (L) with a new gasket, if needed, and tighten. Remove oil feeder, then reinstall drain plug (D) with a new gasket, if needed, and tighten.

PIVOT POINTS AND SLIDES. Lubricate all pivot points and linkage slides with a good quality marine type multipurpose grease as frequently as needed to keep the components operating freely and properly.

FUEL SYSTEM

Periodically inspect the fuel lines and connections for damage. Renew components if needed. With the engine stopped, occasionally open the carburetor float bowl drain plug on 20 hp, early 25 hp and 28 hp models and allow the fuel to drain off into a suitable container. The float bowl must be removed on late 25 hp models to inspect for contaminants in float bowl. Inspect the fuel for foreign matter. If an excessive amount of foreign matter is found, extensive cleaning of the fuel system is needed.

Keep the external surface of the carburetor clean and all connections and sealing surfaces tight.

Float bowl fuel level can be checked by using a clear tube attached to the float bowl drain nozzle on 20 hp, early 25 hp and 28 hp models. Refer to CARBURETOR in the Tune-Up section for checking float bowl fuel level.

FUEL FILTER. A fuel filter assembly (1—Fig. M9-3) is connected between fuel supply line (2) and fuel pump inlet line (3). With the engine stopped, periodically unscrew fuel filter cup (7) from filter base (4) and withdraw filter element (6), "O" ring (5) and gasket (8) if applicable. Clean cup (7) and filter element (6) in a suitable solvent and blow dry with clean compressed air. Inspect filter

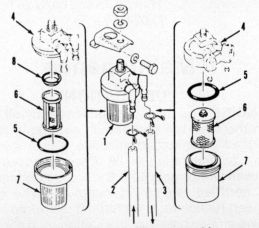

Fig. M9-3— *View showing fuel filter assembly, mounting bracket and fuel hoses. Both assemblies have been used.*

1. Fuel filter assy.
2. Fuel supply line
3. Fuel pump inlet line
4. Filter base
5. "O" ring
6. Filter element
7. Cup
8. Gasket

Fig. M9-4 — View shows early type fuel pump assembly. Connect fuel hoses as indicated by fuel pump cover for both early and late type fuel pump assemblies.

element (6). If excessive blockage or damage is noted, renew element.

Reassembly is reverse order of disassembly. Renew "O" ring (5) and gasket (8), if applicable, during reassembly.

FUEL PUMP. The fuel pump is operated by crankcase pressure changes from the up and down movement of the piston. When the crankcase pressure decreases (the piston is moving upward), the pump diaphragm is pulled toward the crankcase allowing fuel to enter the pump chamber and closing the inlet check valve. When the crankcase pressure increases (the piston is moving downward), the diaphragm is pushed outward discharging the fuel to the carburetor and closing the inlet check valve. This pulsating action allows for continuous fuel flow. The check valves are used to prevent reverse flow of the fuel.

NOTE: Early type fuel pump assembly uses umbrella type check valves and late type fuel pump assembly uses reed valve type check valves.

A spring is used to load the diaphragm, thus allowing the diaphragm to respond more quickly to crankcase pressure changes.

The inlet port is identified as "IN" and the discharge port is identified as "OUT" as shown in Fig. M9-4, the fuel hoses must be connected accordingly.

To overhaul, first remove the engine's top cover and disconnect the fuel tank supply hose at the outboard motor connector. Disconnect the fuel hoses at the fuel pump inlet and discharge nozzles and label if needed. Remove securing cap screws and withdraw fuel pump assembly.

With reference to Fig. M9-5, disassemble the fuel pump assembly. Inspect all components for excessive wear or any other damage and renew if needed.

With reference to Fig. M9-5, reassemble the fuel pump assembly with new gaskets. Coat gasket (1)

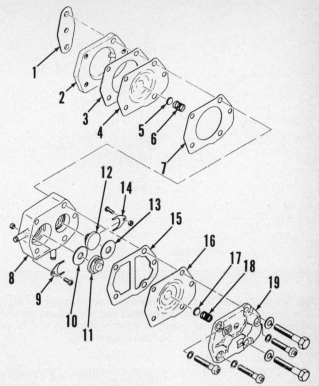

Fig. M9-5 — View showing early type fuel pump assembly. Late type fuel pump assembly can be identified by ribs on the inlet and outlet nozzle. Late type fuel pump uses reed valve type check valves instead of umbrella type check valves (11 and 12) as used on early type fuel pump.

1. Gasket
2. Base
3. Gasket
4. Diaphragm
5. Spring plate
6. Spring
7. Gasket
8. Body
9. Retainer
10. Gasket
11. Outlet check valve
12. Inlet check valve
13. Gasket
14. Retainer
15. Gasket
16. Diaphragm
17. Spring plate
18. Spring
19. Cover

with a nonhardening type gasket sealer making certain that passage in center is not plugged with gasket sealer. Mount the fuel pump assembly to the crankcase and securely tighten the retaining cap screws.

NOTE: Fuel pump and engine malfunction will result if the fuel pump and all connections are not airtight.

Complete reassembly.

SHIFT LINKAGE

Direction of propeller rotation is determined by the position of the gear shift lever. The gear shift lever actuates gearcase components using shift linkage consisting of an upper and lower shift rod connected by an adjustment nut (A — Fig. M9-6). The tapered end of the lower shift rod controls the movement of the dog clutch on the propeller shaft. The positioning of the dog clutch on the propeller shaft determines whether forward, neutral or reverse directional movement is selected.

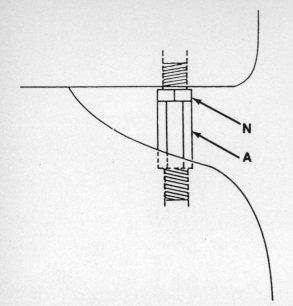

Fig. M9-6 — Loosen locknut (N) and turn adjustment nut (A) to alter length of upper and lower shift rod. Adjust nut (A) until proper engagement of reverse, neutral and forward is obtained, then tighten locknut (N).

To check shift linkage for proper adjustment, first place shift lever in reverse detent position. Check for proper engagement and propeller rotation by turning the propeller.

⚠️WARNING

Disconnect spark plug leads and properly ground leads before performing any propeller service, otherwise, accidental starting can occur if propeller shaft is rotated.

Check for proper engagement of neutral and forward.

To adjust, loosen locknut (N) and turn adjustment nut (A) until proper engagement of reverse, neutral and forward is obtained, then retighten locknut (N).

STARTER

When starter rope (5—Fig. M9-7) is pulled, pulley (7) will rotate. As pulley (7) rotates, drive pawl (10) moves to engage with the flywheel, thus cranking the engine.

When starter rope (5) is released, pulley (7) is rotated in the reverse direction by force from rewind spring (6). As pulley (7) rotates, the starter rope is rewound and drive pawl (10) is disengaged from the flywheel.

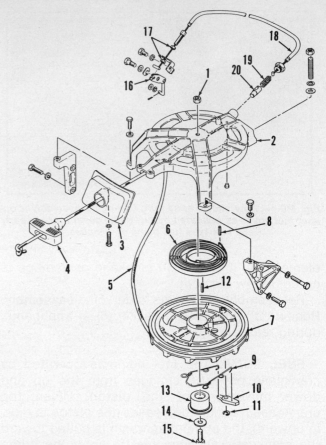

Fig. M9-7 — Exploded view of manual starter assembly.

1. Nut	11. Clip
2. Housing	12. Pin
3. Rope guide	13. Shaft
4. Handle	14. Washer
5. Starter rope	15. Bolt
6. Rewind spring	16. Lever & link
7. Pulley	17. Adjusting nuts
8. Pin	18. Starter lockout cable
9. Pawl spring	19. Spring
10. Pawl	20. Plunger

Safety plunger (20) engages lugs on pulley (7) to prevent starter engagement when the gear shift lever is in the forward or reverse position.

To overhaul the manual starter, proceed as follows: Remove the engine's top cover. Remove the screws retaining the manual starter to the engine. Remove starter lockout cable (18) at starter housing (2). Note plunger (20) and spring (19) located at the cable end, care should be used not to lose components should they fall free. Withdraw the starter assembly.

⚠️WARNING

Care should be exercised when working with or around a coiled starter rewind spring as sudden uncoiling can cause injury. Safety eyewear and gloves are recommended.

Check pawl (10) for freedom of movement and excessive wear of engagement area or any other damage. Renew or lubricate pawl (10) with a suitable water-resistant grease and return starter to service if no other damage is noted.

To disassemble, remove clip (11) and withdraw pawl (10) and pawl spring (9). Untie starter rope (5) at handle (4) and allow the rope to wind into the starter. Remove bolt (15), washer (14) and shaft (13), then place a suitable screwdriver blade through hole (H—Fig. M9-8) to hold rewind spring (6—Fig. M9-7) securely in housing (2). Carefully lift pulley (7) with starter rope (5) from housing (2). BE CAREFUL when removing pulley (7) as the rewind spring may be dislodged. Untie starter rope (5) and remove rope from pulley (7) if renewal is required. To remove rewind spring (6) from housing (2), invert housing so it sets upright on a flat surface, then tap the housing top until rewind spring (6) falls free and uncoils.

Inspect all components for damage and excessive wear and renew if needed.

To reassemble, first apply a coating of a suitable water-resistant grease to rewind spring area of housing (2). Install rewind spring (6) in housing (2) so spring coils wind in a counterclockwise direction from the outer end. Make sure the spring's outer hook is properly secured over starter housing pin (8). Wind starter rope (5) onto pulley (7) approximately 2½ turns counterclockwise when viewed from the flywheel side. Direct remaining starter rope (5) length through notch in pulley (7).

NOTE: Lubricate all friction surfaces with a suitable water-resistant grease during reassembly.

Assemble pulley (7) to starter housing making sure that pin (12) engages hook end in rewind spring (6). Install shaft (13), washer (14) and bolt (15). Apply Loctite or an equivalent thread fastening solution on bolt (15) threads and install nut (1) and securely tighten.

Thread starter rope (5) through starter housing (2), rope guide (3) and handle (4) and secure with a knot. Turn pulley (7) 2 to 3 turns counterclockwise when viewed from the flywheel side, then release starter rope (5) from pulley notch and allow rope to slowly wind onto pulley.

NOTE: Do not apply any more tension on rewind spring (6) than is required to draw starter handle (4) back into the proper released position.

Install spring (9), pawl (10) and clip (11) as shown in Fig. M9-8. Remount manual starter assembly.

Fig. M9-8 — View showing proper installation of pawl spring (9), pawl (10) and clip (11). Pulley hole (H) is used during pulley withdrawal. Refer to text.

Adjust starter lockout assembly by turning adjusting nuts (17—Fig. M9-7) at cable (18) end so starter will engage when gear shift lever is in neutral position, but will not engage when gear shift lever is in forward or reverse position. Plunger (20) end should recess in starter housing (2) 1 mm (0.04 in.) when gear shift lever is in neutral position.

COOLING SYSTEM

Ports (I—Fig. M9-9) located on the starboard side of the lower unit are used as the water inlet for the cooling system on 20 hp and early 25 hp models. Ports (I—Fig. M9-10) located on both sides of the lower unit are used as the water inlets for the cooling system on late 25 hp and 28 hp

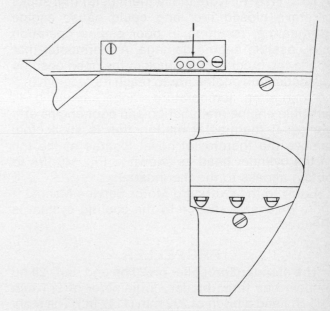

Fig. M9-9 — Cooling system water inlet ports (I) are located on the starboard side of the lower unit on 20 hp and early 25 hp models.

Mariner 20 (1979 & Prior), 25 (1980-1984) & 28 Hp

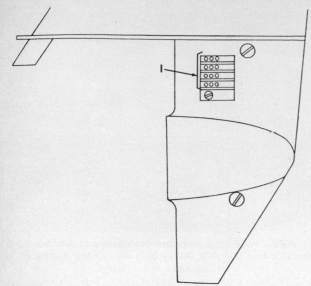

Fig. M9-10 — Cooling system water inlet ports (I) are located on both sides of the lower unit on late 25 hp and 28 hp models.

models. The ports must be kept clean of all foreign matter to ensure efficient operation of the cooling system.

⚠CAUTION

Do not operate outboard motor unless the lower unit is immersed in water, otherwise, the water pump impeller will be damaged.

A thermostat positioned in the cylinder head is used to regulate the engine operating temperature. The thermostat should start to open at 80°C (176°F). Note that a thermostat that sticks or stays closed too long could cause engine overheating, resulting in poor engine operation and possible engine damage. A thermostat that opens too quickly or is stuck in the open position will cause the engine not to reach its recommended operating temperature range, resulting in possible engine malfunction and poor engine efficiency. If thermostat malfunction is suspected, remove the thermostat cover located at the top of the cylinder head as shown in Fig. M9-10A to obtain access to the thermostat.

Refer to the Outboard Motor Service Manual if more extensive service to the cooling system is required.

PROPELLER

The standard propeller on 20 hp and early 25 hp models has three blades, a diameter of 241 mm (9½ in.) and a pitch of 292 mm (11½ in.). The standard propeller on late 25 hp and 28 hp models has three blades, a diameter of 251 mm (9⅞ in.) and a

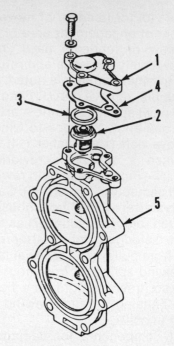

Fig. M9-10A — Exploded view of the cooling system components located at the top of the engine cylinder head (5). Models 20 and 25 hp are shown; 28 hp is similar.

1. Cover
2. Thermostat
3. Spacer
4. Gasket
5. Cylinder head

pitch of 267 mm (10½ in.). Optional propellers are available. Select a propeller that will allow the engine at full throttle to reach maximum operating rpm range (4700-5700 on early 25 hp models and 4500-5500 on all other models).

⚠WARNING

Shift directional control lever to "NEUTRAL." Disconnect spark plug leads and properly ground leads before performing any propeller service, otherwise, accidental starting can occur if propeller shaft is rotated.

To remove the propeller on 20 hp and early 25 hp models, proceed as follows: Remove cotter pin (2 — Fig. M9-11) and unscrew propeller spinner (5). Withdraw propeller (1) from propeller shaft (4).

Inspect propeller (1), propeller shaft (4) and shear pin (3) for damage and excessive wear and renew if needed.

Apply a water-resistant grease to the propeller bore, then install propeller (1) on propeller shaft (4) and retain with propeller spinner (5) and a new cotter pin (2).

To remove the propeller on late 25 hp and 28 hp models, proceed as follows: Remove cotter pin (2 — Fig. M9-12) and unscrew propeller retaining

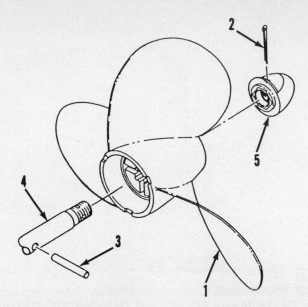

Fig. M9-11 — On 20 hp and early 25 hp models, propeller (1) is mounted on propeller shaft (4) and is retained by spinner (5) and cotter pin (2). Shear pin (3) is renewed only after withdrawing propeller (1) from propeller shaft (4).

nut (7). Withdraw washer (6), thrust hub (5), propeller (1) and thrust hub (3) from propeller shaft (4).

Inspect all components for damage and excessive wear and renew if needed.

Apply Perfect Seal or a suitable equivalent to the propeller shaft splines, then install thrust hub (3), propeller (1), thrust hub (5) and washer (6) on propeller shaft (4). Install propeller retaining nut (7) and tighten to a torque of 20-41 N·m (15-30 ft.-lbs.). Install a new cotter pin (2).

Tune-Up

IGNITION SYSTEM

On 20 hp, early 25 hp, 28 hp and some late 25 hp models, a breaker point type ignition system is us-

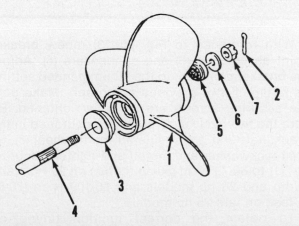

Fig. M9-12 — On late 25 hp and 28 hp models, thrust hubs (3 and 5) and propeller (1) are mounted on propeller shaft (4) and retained by washer (6), nut (7) and cotter pin (2). Tighten nut (7) to a torque of 20-41 N·m (15-30 ft.-lbs.).

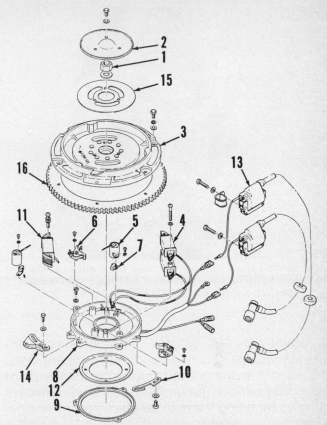

Fig. M9-13 — Exploded view of flywheel magneto unit. Toothed ring gear (16) is used on models with electric start.

1. Nut	9. Magneto base plate retainer
2. Flywheel cover	10. Bracket
3. Flywheel	11. Lighting coil
4. Low voltage coil	12. Retainer
5. Condenser	13. Ignition coil
6. Breaker point assy.	14. Throttle cam
7. Lubricator	15. Gasket
8. Magneto base plate	16. Ring gear

ed. On some late 25 hp models, a capacitor discharge ignition (CDI) system is used. Refer to the Outboard Motor Service Manual for testing and servicing the CD ignition system. If engine malfunction is noted and the ignition system is suspected, make sure the spark plugs and all electrical wiring are in good condition and all electrical connections are tight before proceeding to troubleshooting the CD ignition system.

The standard spark plug on 20 hp models is NGK B6HS with an electrode gap of 0.6-0.7 mm (0.024-0.027 in.). The standard spark plug on 25 hp and 28 hp models is NGK B7HS with an electrode gap of 0.6-0.7 mm (0.024-0.027 in.) on early 25 hp models and 0.5-0.6 mm (0.020-0.024 in.) on late 25 hp and 28 hp models.

To service models with breaker point type ignition system, proceed as follows: The breaker point gap should be 0.25-0.45 mm (0.010-0.018 in.) on 20 hp, early 25 hp and 28 hp models and 0.3-0.4 mm (0.012-0.016 in.) on late 25 hp models and can be inspected and adjusted through the opening in

Fig. M9-14 — View showing the use of a suitable flywheel holding tool (H) to prevent flywheel rotation during removal of securing nut (1 — Fig. M9-13) with suitable tools (T).

Fig. M9-15 — Remove flywheel from crankshaft end using a suitable puller assembly (P) with the correct size cap screws (C).

flywheel (3 — Fig. M9-13). Two breaker point assemblies (6) and two condensers (5) are used. To inspect and, if needed, adjust the breaker point gap, first remove the engine's top cover. Remove screws retaining the manual starter to the engine. Remove the starter lockout cable at the starter housing. Note plunger and spring located at cable end, care should be used not to lose components should they fall free. Withdraw the starter assembly. Remove the cap screws and lockwashers securing flywheel cover (2) to flywheel (3) and withdraw with gasket (15).

Inspect the breaker point surfaces for excessive wear, pitting or any other damage. If needed, renew breaker point assemblies (6) and condensers (5) as outlined later in this section.

To clean the breaker point contact surfaces, rotate the flywheel until the breaker point contact surfaces are accessible through the opening in flywheel (3). Use a point file or sandpaper with a grit rating of 400 to 600. After polishing, wipe the contact surfaces clean with a dry cloth and lightly grease the breaker point arm and lubricator (7) with a suitable lubricant.

Turn the flywheel until the breaker point contact surfaces are placed at their widest position, then reach through the flywheel opening with a feeler gage of the appropriate size and check the distance between the point surfaces. If the distance is not within the recommended limits, loosen the point set securing screw and adjust the point set until the correct gap is obtained. Tighten the point set securing screw and recheck the breaker point gap. Repeat the adjustment procedure, if needed, until the correct breaker point gap is obtained. Repeat the adjustment procedure on the other breaker point assembly.

To renew breaker point assemblies (6) and condensers (5), proceed as follows: Using a suitable flywheel holding tool (H — Fig. M9-14) to prevent flywheel rotation, remove securing nut (1 — Fig. M9-13). Remove flywheel (3 — Fig. M9-13) from the crankshaft end using a suitable puller assembly (P — Fig. M9-15) and the proper size cap screws (C). Note the flywheel key located in crankshaft keyway.

> ## ⚠WARNING
>
> Be sure suitable tools are used to remove the flywheel. Damage resultant from the misapplication of force or the use of incorrect tools may cause engine damage, engine malfunction or personal injury.

With reference to Fig. M9-13, renew breaker point assemblies (6) and condensers (5). Adjust the breaker point gap to the recommended setting as outlined in a previous paragraph. Make sure the securing screws are properly tightened. Be sure the flywheel key is properly positioned in the crankshaft end, then reinstall the flywheel (3). Install lockwasher and install and tighten securing nut (1) to 68-79 N·m (50-58 ft.-lbs.) on 20 hp, early 25 hp and 28 hp models and 95-109 N·m (70-80 ft.-lbs.) on late 25 hp models.

To obtain the correct ignition timing on magneto type ignition systems, first adjust both breaker point assemblies (6) to the proper point gap as previously outlined. Remove both spark

Fig. M9-16 — View showing magneto base plate in full advance position with bracket (10) against stop bracket (B). Flywheel timing mark (M) should be aligned with the forward edge of stop bracket (B) as shown in inset for correct timing during timing procedure as outlined in text. Cap screws (C) are used to adjust bracket (10).

plugs. Use a point checker and attach the red tester lead to a grey wire coming from magneto base plate (8) (top cylinder's low voltage coil lead). Connect the black tester lead to an engine ground.

NOTE: A suitable continuity tester can be used.

Rotate the twist grip to full throttle position. Verify magneto base plate (8) is in full advance position as shown in Fig. M9-16. Slowly turn the flywheel counterclockwise until the tester's pointer moves from "OPEN" to "CLOSE", then note the number one cylinder (top cylinder) flywheel timing mark (M—Fig. M9-16). The flywheel timing mark (M) should be aligned with the forward edge of stop bracket (B) as shown in inset. If not, loosen cap screws (C) and adjust bracket (10). Continue the adjustment procedure

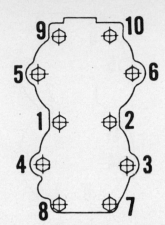

Fig. M9-18 — Tighten cylinder head screws on 20 hp and early 25 hp models in sequence shown.

until the flywheel timing mark aligns with the forward edge of the stop bracket when the tester's pointer moves from "OPEN" to "CLOSE", then tighten cap screws (C) securing bracket (10). Repeat the procedure for the bottom cylinder. Attach the point checker's red tester lead to the orange wire coming from magneto base plate (8—Fig. M9-13). Make sure the black tester lead remains grounded to engine. Adjust the full advance timing by varying the breaker point gap.

NOTE: Replacement flywheels (3) do not have timing marks and must be marked according to piston position as outlined in the following paragraph.

If the ignition timing marks are questioned or a new flywheel is installed, then a dial indicator must be used to verify piston position. Remove cylinder head and properly mount a dial indicator as shown in Fig. M9-17 in the top cylinder. Set top piston at 3.35 mm (0.132 in.) BTDC and mark flywheel adjacent to forward edge of stop bracket if timing mark is missing or incorrect. Attach the dial indicator to the bottom cylinder and mark the

Fig. M9-17 — A dial indicator is used to determine piston position.

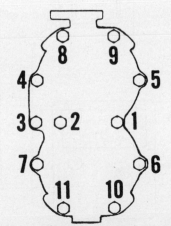

Fig. M9-19 — Tighten cylinder head screws on 28 hp models in sequence shown.

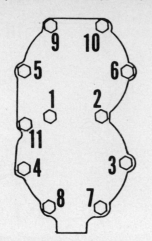

Fig. M9-20—Tighten cylinder head screws on late 25 hp models in sequence shown.

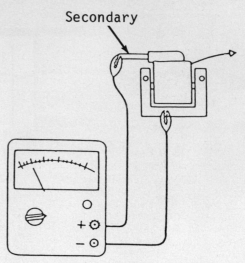

Fig. M9-22—Connect ohmmeter leads as shown to measure resistance in the secondary side of the ignition coil. Refer to text.

flywheel in the same manner with the bottom piston at 3.35 mm (0.132 in.) BTDC.

Proceed as follows if the dial indicator is used to set the ignition timing. With the flywheel being slowly turned counterclockwise, the piston should be 2.90-3.80 mm (0.114-0.150 in.) BTDC when the tester's pointer moves from "OPEN" to "CLOSE" for top and bottom cylinder. Adjust full advance timing as previously outlined.

When the ignition timing adjustment is completed, check the speed control linkage adjustment as outlined in the following SPEED CONTROL LINKAGE section.

Reinstall cylinder head with a new gasket. Tighten cylinder head screws to an initial torque of 14.7 N·m (11 ft.-lbs.) using sequence shown in Fig. M9-18 on 20 hp and early 25 hp models, Fig. M9-19 on 28 hp models and Fig. M9-20 on late 25

hp models. Repeat sequences and tighten screws to a final torque of 24.4-34 N·m (18-25 ft.-lbs.) on 20 hp, early 25 hp and late 25 hp models and 27.2-31.3 N·m (20-23 ft.-lbs.) on 28 hp models.

Complete reassembly.

Ignition Coils. To check the ignition coils (13—Fig. M9-13) located on the port and starboard side of cylinders, use a suitable ohmmeter. Connect one tester lead to the coil's metal laminations, then connect the remaining tester lead alternately to the primary (Fig. M9-21) and secondary (Fig. M9-22) ignition coil leads. Resistance reading for primary circuit should be 1.53-187 ohms on 20 hp, early 25 hp and 28 hp models and 1.34-1.63 ohms on late 25 hp models, while the secondary circuit resistance reading should be 4800-7200 ohms on 20 hp, early 25 hp and 28 hp models and 4160-6240 ohms on late 25 hp models. Renew the ignition coil(s) if the meter readings are not within the proper range.

SPEED CONTROL LINKAGE

The speed control handle components are connected by cables to a pulley adjacent to the engine. The pulley movement is transferred by linkage to rotate the magneto base plate and actuate the carburetor throttle so the ignition timing is advanced as the throttle opens.

All Models Except Late 25 Hp

To synchronize ignition and throttle control linkage, first make sure the ignition timing has been correctly adjusted. When the twist grip is moved completely against the high speed stop, the carburetor throttle should be fully opened. MAKE SURE that the carburetor throttle does not reach the full open position before the ignition timing is fully advanced.

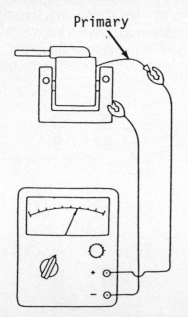

Fig. M9-21—Connect ohmmeter leads as shown to measure resistance in the primary side of the ignition coil. Refer to text.

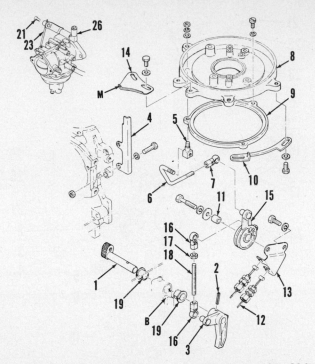

Fig. M9-23 — View of speed control components used on 28 hp models. Other models are similar.

1. Shaft
2. Pin
3. Throttle blockout lever
4. Stop bracket
5. Swivel
6. Link
7. Rod end
8. Magneto base plate
9. Retainer
10. Bracket
11. Sleeve
12. Control cables
13. Bracket
14. Throttle cam
15. Pulley
16. Rod end
17. Locknut
18. Link
19. Bushing
21. Screw
23. Link
26. Roller

Fig. M9-24 — View of blockout lever control rod (1), blockout lever (2) and magneto base plate control rod (3) used on late 25 hp models. Locknuts (N) and adjuster (A) are used to adjust cable slack. Refer to text.

To adjust the speed control linkage, proceed as follows: Turn twist grip to full throttle position. Loosen locknut and turn control cable (12—Fig. M9-23) adjuster so control cable slack is 1-2 mm (0.039-0.079 in.) on the cable opposite the pull cable, then tighten locknut. Remove rod end (7) from pulley (15). With the twist grip held in the full throttle position, push magneto base plate (8) to full advance position. Adjust rod end (7) on magneto control rod (6) until rod end (7) aligns with ball joint on pulley (15), then snap into position. Loosen locknut (17) and adjust rod end (16) on link (18) so throttle blockout lever (3) contacts bottom cowling stopper (B) when twist grip is turned to the full throttle position. Tighten locknut (17).

With twist grip in the full throttle position, mark on tab (M) of throttle cam (14) should be aligned with center of cam follower roller (26). To adjust, loosen retaining screws and reposition throttle cam (14) to center mark on roller (26). With twist grip in full throttle position, loosen lockscrew (21) and move carburetor throttle lever (23) to wide open position, then retighten lockscrew (21).

Late 25 Hp Models

NOTE: Ignition timing should be properly adjusted before proceeding to the speed control linkage adjustment.

ADJUSTMENT. Detach magneto base plate control rod (3—Fig. M9-24) and blockout lever control rod (1). Measure length of magneto base plate control rod from joint center to joint center and adjust to a length of 69.2-70.0 mm (2.58-2.90 in.), then reconnect control rod. Position gear shift lever in "NEUTRAL."

Turn twist grip to full throttle position. Loosen locknuts (N) and turn control cable adjustment (A) until cable slack is 1-2 mm (0.039-0.079 in.), then tighten locknuts.

With the twist grip held in the full throttle position, push magneto base plate to full advance position. Measure length of blockout lever control rod (3) from joint center to joint center and adjust to a length of 91.5 mm (3.6 in.), then reconnect control rod. Blockout lever (2) should contact bottom cowling stopper when twist grip is turned to the full throttle position with the magneto base plate fully advanced and the gear shift lever is in "NEUTRAL" position. If not, readjust blockout lever control rod (3) until the proper adjustment is obtained.

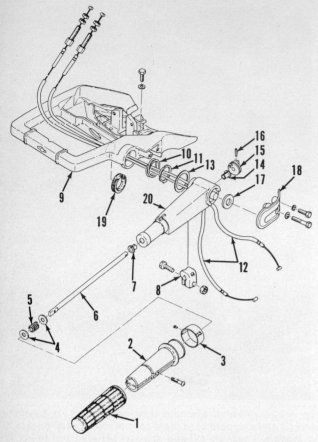

Fig. M9-25 — Exploded view of speed control components located in steering handle typical of all models.

1. Rubber cover	11. Spring retainer
2. Twist grip	12. Control cables
3. Indicator	13. Washer
4. Washers	14. Bushing
5. Spring	15. Throttle cam
6. Shaft	16. Pin
7. Bushing	17. Spacer
8. Friction piece	18. Cover
9. Bracket	19. Rubber grommet
10. Compression spring	20. Steering handle

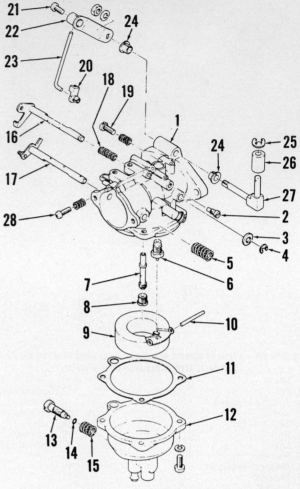

Fig. M9-26 — Exploded view of carburetor. Components 13, 14 and 15 are not used on late 25 hp models.

1. Body	15. Spring
2. Pilot jet	16. Throttle shaft
3. Washer	17. Choke shaft
4. Clip	18. Spring
5. Spring	19. Idle mixture screw
6. Fuel inlet valve	20. Link keeper
7. Main nozzle	21. Screw
8. Main jet	22. Throttle arm
9. Float	23. Link
10. Pin	24. Bushing
11. Gasket	25. Clip
12. Float bowl	26. Cam follower roller
13. Drain valve	27. Cam follower
14. "O" ring	28. Idle speed screw

CARBURETOR

ADJUSTMENT. On 20 hp and early 25 hp models under normal operation, the following jet sizes are the standard recommendation: main jet (8—Fig. M9-26) #140 and pilot jet (2) #60. On late 25 hp and 28 hp models, use the standard carburetor jet sizes as recommended by the manufacturer for normal operation when used at altitudes of 2500 feet and less. Main jet (8) size should be reduced from standard recommendation by one size for altitudes of 2500 to 5000 feet, two sizes for altitudes of 5000 to 7500 feet and three sizes for altitudes of 7500 feet and up. Initial adjustment of the idle mixture screw (19) is 1-1½ turns out from a lightly seated position on 20 hp and early 25 hp models, 1¼ to 1¾ turns out from a lightly seated position on 28 hp models and 1⅜ to 2 turns out from a lightly seated position on late 25 hp models. Recommended idle is 650-700 rpm (in gear) on 20 hp and early 25 hp models, 650-750

rpm (in gear) on late 25 hp models and 1000-1100 on 28 hp models with the engine at normal operating temperature.

With the outboard motor properly mounted on a boat or a suitable test tank, immerse the lower unit. Connect a tachometer and set it on the appropriate range scale. Start the engine and allow it to warm up to normal operating temperature. Position the throttle control twist grip to the complete closed position. Refer to previous paragraph for idle speed specifications and adjust engine idle speed screw (28). Then adjust idle mixture screw (19) until smooth engine operation is noted. Readjust the engine idle speed screw (28) until the recommended idle speed is obtained.

On 20 hp, early 25 hp and 28 hp models, check carburetor fuel level as outlined in the following FUEL LEVEL section and adjust if needed.

Complete reassembly.

FUEL LEVEL. To check carburetor fuel level on 20 hp, early 25 hp and 28 hp models, proceed as follows: Remove the engine's top cover and position the outboard motor in an upright position. Connect a clear vinyl tube to the float bowl drain nozzle and hold the drain tube up. Open the float bowl drain plug. Run the engine at idle speed for a few minutes, then stop the engine. Fuel level (L—Fig. M9-27) should be 29-33 mm (1.13-1.31 in.).

If fuel level is incorrect, float bowl (12—Fig. M9-26) must be removed and inlet valve (6) renewed if excessively worn or tab on float (9) adjusted until the proper setting is obtained.

OVERHAUL. Remove the screws retaining the air intake cover and withdraw cover. Disconnect the fuel tank supply hose at the outboard motor connector. Disconnect the fuel supply hose at the carburetor inlet. Disconnect all linkage that will interfere with carburetor removal. Clean all external surfaces and remove accumulated dirt and grease. Remove the two nuts securing the carburetor and withdraw the carburetor assembly.

With reference to Fig. M9-26, disassemble the complete carburetor assembly and note any discrepancies which must be corrected before reassembly. Remove all gaskets and "O" ring, if applicable, (label if needed for later reference) and set to the side.

Thoroughly clean all carburetor parts in a suitable solvent and inspect for damage and excessive wear. Note that plastic and rubber components should not be subjected to some cleaning solutions. Blow dry with clean compressed air. If compressed air is not available, use only lint-free cloths to wipe dry. Do not use a drill bit or wire to clean jets. Enlargement or damage of the calibrated holes may affect engine performance.

With reference to Fig. M9-26, reassemble the carburetor components with new gaskets and "O" ring, if applicable. Note that the new gaskets should match up with those removed. If not,

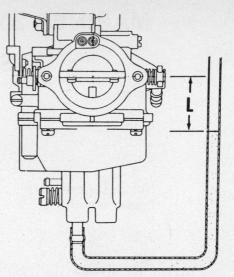

Fig. M9-27 — On 20 hp, early 25 hp and 28 hp models, fuel level (L) should be 29-33 mm (1.13-1.31 in.) below center of carburetor bore when viewed through a clear vinyl tube. Refer to text.

check with your parts supplier to be sure you have the correct gasket set. The "O" ring must fit properly and seal tight.

To determine the float level on late 25 hp models, invert carburetor body (1) and slowly raise float (9). Note whether float (9) is parallel with surface of carburetor body when needle of fuel inlet valve (6) just breaks contact with float (9) tang. If not, adjust float (9) tang until proper float level is obtained.

When reinstalling the carburetor, place a new gasket between the carburetor and the reed valve plate. Securely tighten the retaining nuts. Reconnect fuel supply line and carburetor linkage. Install air intake cover and retain with screws. Initially adjust idle mixture screw (19) 1-1½ turns out from a lightly seated position on 20 hp and early 25 hp models, 1¼ to 1¾ turns out from a lightly seated position on 28 hp models and 1⅜ to 2 turns out from a lightly seated position on late 25 hp models.

If applicable, verify carburetor fuel level as outlined in the previous FUEL LEVEL section and note if fuel level adjustment is needed.

MARINER 20 (1985) AND 25 (1985) HP

Specifications

Hp/rpm	20/4500-5500
	25/5000-6000
Bore	2.56 in.
	(65 mm)
Stroke	2.36 in.
	(60 mm)
Number of cylinders	2
Displacement	24.4 cu. in.
	(400 cc)
Spark plug	See Text
Idle Speed (in gear)	600-700
Fuel:oil ratio	50:1
Gearcase oil capacity	7.6 oz.
	(225 mL)

Maintenance

LUBRICATION

ENGINE. The engine is lubricated by oil mixed with the fuel. The fuel should be regular leaded, low lead or unleaded gasoline with a minimum pump octane rating of 86. Recommended oil is Quicksilver Formula 50-D Outboard Lubricant or a BIA certified two-stroke motor oil. The recommended fuel:oil ratio for normal operation is 50:1.

LOWER UNIT. The lower unit gears and bearings are lubricated by oil contained in the gearcase. The recommended oil is Quicksilver Super-Duty Gear Lubricant. The gearcase oil capacity is 7.6 oz. (225 mL) on all models. The gearcase oil level should be checked every 3 days and the lubricant renewed periodically. The gearcase is drained and filled through the same plug port (D—Fig. M10-1). An oil level (vent) port (L) is used to indicate the full oil level of the gearcase and to ease oil drainage.

To drain the oil, place the outboard motor in a vertical position. Remove drain plug (D) and oil level plug (L), and allow the lubricant to drain into a suitable container.

To fill the gearcase with oil, place the outboard motor in a vertical position. Add oil through drain plug (D) opening with an oil feeder until the oil begins to overflow from oil level plug (L) port. Reinstall oil level plug (L) with a new gasket, if needed, and tighten. Remove oil feeder, then reinstall drain plug (D) with a new gasket, if needed, and tighten.

PIVOT POINTS AND SLIDES. Lubricate all pivot points and linkage slides with a good quality marine type multipurpose grease as frequently as needed to keep the components operating freely and properly.

FUEL SYSTEM

Periodically inspect the fuel lines and connections for damage. Renew components if needed.

Keep the external surface of the carburetor clean and all connections and sealing surfaces tight.

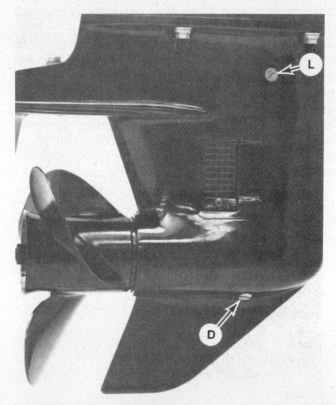

Fig. M10-1 — View showing lower unit drain and fill plug (D) and oil level (vent) plug (L).

Illustrations Courtesy Mariner

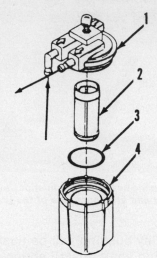

Fig. M10-2 — Exploded view of reusable type fuel filter.

1. Filter base
2. Filter element
3. Sealing ring
4. Filter cup

FUEL FILTER. A fuel filter assembly is connected between fuel supply line and carburetor/fuel pump inlet line. With the engine stopped, occasionally unscrew fuel filter cup (4 — Fig. M10-2) from filter base (1) and withdraw sealing ring (3) and filter element (2). Clean cup (4) and filter element (2) in a suitable solvent and blow dry with clean compressed air. Inspect filter element (2). If excessive blockage or damage is noted, renew element.

Reassembly is reverse order of disassembly. If needed, renew sealing ring (3) during reassembly.

A strainer (18 — Fig. M10-3) positioned behind inlet cover (16) on "BC" type carburetors, is used to provide additional filtering of foreign contaminants. To inspect, remove inlet cover (16) and strainer (18). Clean strainer (18) in a suitable solvent and blow dry with clean compressed air. Inspect strainer (18). If excessive blockage or damage is noted, then renew strainer (18). If needed, renew gasket (17).

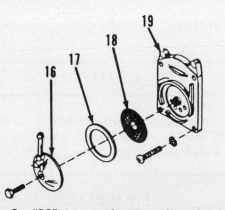

Fig. M10-3 — On "BC" type carburetor, view showing fuel strainer (18) located behind fuel pump inlet cover (16). Gasket (17) is used to seal between inlet cover (16) and pump cover (19).

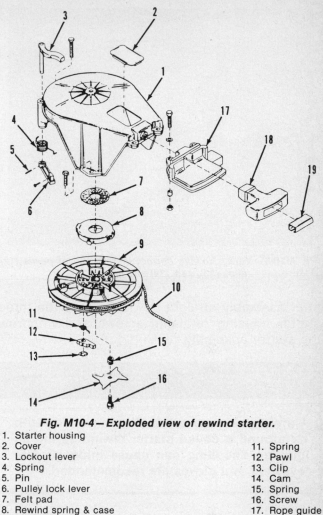

Fig. M10-4 — Exploded view of rewind starter.

1. Starter housing
2. Cover
3. Lockout lever
4. Spring
5. Pin
6. Pulley lock lever
7. Felt pad
8. Rewind spring & case
9. Pulley
10. Starter rope
11. Spring
12. Pawl
13. Clip
14. Cam
15. Spring
16. Screw
17. Rope guide
18. Handle
19. Anchor

FUEL PUMP. The fuel pump is an integral part of the carburetor. Refer to CARBURETOR in the Tune-Up section for fuel pump overhaul.

NOTE: The fuel pump assembly may be overhauled without carburetor removal.

STARTER

When starter rope (10 — Fig. M10-4) is pulled, pulley (9) will rotate. As pulley (9) rotates, the two drive pawls (12) move apart thus meshing with the flywheel and cranking the engine.

When starter rope (10) is released, pulley (9) is rotated in the reverse direction by force from rewind spring (8). As pulley (9) rotates, starter rope (10) is rewound and drive pawls (12) are disengaged from the flywheel.

A starter lockout assembly is used to prevent starter engagement when the gear shift control is in the forward or reverse position.

To overhaul the manual starter, proceed as follows: Remove the engine cover. Detach fuel filter assembly from starter housing by pulling

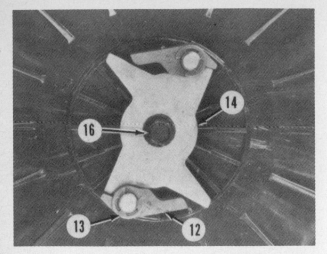

Fig. M10-5 — View showing correct installation of pawls (12), clips (13), cam (14) and screw (16).

Fig. M10-6 — Cooling system water inlet ports (I) are located on the port and starboard side of the lower unit.

filter assembly straight down. Remove the three starter housing retaining screws and withdraw the starter assembly.

⚠WARNING

Care should be exercised when working with or around a coiled starter rewind spring as sudden uncoiling can cause injury. Safety eyewear and gloves are recommended.

To disassemble, remove clips (13) and withdraw pawls (12) and springs (11). Untie starter rope (10) at anchor (19) and allow the rope to wind into the starter. Remove screw (16), cam (14) and spring (15). Carefully lift pulley (9) with starter rope (10) from housing (1). BE CAREFUL when removing pulley (9) as the rewind spring (8) may be dislodged. Remove starter rope (10) from pulley (9) if renewal is required. Separate rewind spring and case (8) from pulley (9). If renewal of rewind spring is required, use extreme caution when removing rewind spring from spring case (8).

Inspect all components for damage and excessive wear and renew if needed.

To reassemble, first apply a coating of a suitable water-resistant grease to rewind spring area of spring case (8). Install rewind spring in spring case (8) so spring coils wind in a clockwise direction from the outer end. Make sure the spring's outer hook is properly secured. Install rewind spring and case (8) into pulley (9). Wind starter rope (10) onto pulley (9) counterclockwise when viewed from the flywheel side. Assemble pulley (9) to starter housing (1) making sure rewind spring end properly engages notch in starter housing center shaft. When pulley (9) is seated

properly, pulley bushing will be flush with end of starter housing shaft. Install spring (15), cam (14) and secure with screw (16). Install springs (11), pawls (12) and clips (13) as shown in Fig. M10-5.

Rotate pulley (9 — Fig. M10-4) counterclockwise until starter rope (10) end is aligned with starter housing rope outlet. Thread starter rope (10) through starter housing (1), rope guide (17) and handle (18) and secure in anchor (19). Pull starter rope (10) out to full length while checking for freedom of travel, then allow starter rope (10) to rewind onto pulley (9). Starter handle (18) should be drawn back into the proper released position. If not, release starter rope (10) from handle (18) and rotate pulley (9) one complete turn counterclockwise (flywheel side) and reassemble.

NOTE: Do not apply any more tension on rewind spring (8) than is required to draw starter handle (18) back into the proper released position.

Remount manual starter assembly and complete reassembly.

COOLING SYSTEM
Ports (I — Fig. M10-6) located on the port and starboard side of the lower unit are used as the water inlets for the cooling system. The ports must be kept clean of all foreign matter to ensure efficient operation of the cooling system.

⚠CAUTION

Do not operate outboard motor unless the lower unit is immersed in water, otherwise, the water pump impeller will be damaged.

PROPELLER
Consult your local dealer or the manufacturer for the specifications pertaining to the standard propeller used on your model of outboard motor.

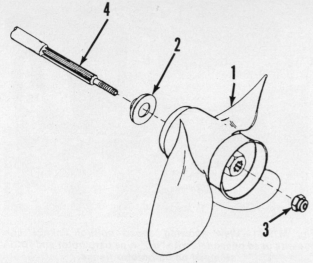

Fig. M10-7—Thrust hub (2) and propeller (1) are mounted on propeller shaft (4) and retained by nut (3).

Optional propellers are available. Select a propeller that will allow the engine at full throttle to reach maximum operating rpm range (4500-5500 on 20 hp models and 5000-6000 on 25 hp models).

⚠WARNING

Shift directional control lever to "NEUTRAL." Disconnect the spark plug leads and properly ground leads before performing any propeller service, otherwise, accidental starting can occur if propeller shaft is rotated.

To remove the propeller, unscrew propeller retaining nut (3—Fig. M10-7). Withdraw propeller (1) and thrust hub (2) from propeller shaft (4).

Inspect all components for damage and excessive wear and renew if needed.

Apply Perfect Seal or a suitable equivalent to the propeller shaft splines, then install thrust hub (2) and propeller (1). Install propeller retaining nut (3) and securely tighten.

Tune-Up

IGNITION SYSTEM

A capacitor discharge ignition (CDI) system is used. Refer to the Outboard Motor Service Manual for testing and servicing the CD ignition system. If engine malfunction is noted and the ignition system is suspected, make sure the spark plugs and all electrical wiring are in good condition and all electrical connections are tight before proceeding to troubleshooting the CD ignition system.

Fig. M10-8—View showing ground plate (P) attached to the negative ignition coil terminal.

On models with a ground plate (P—Fig. M10-8) attached to the negative ignition coil terminal, the standard spark plug is Champion L77J4. A Champion QL77J4 is recommended by the manufacturer should radio frequency interference suppression be required. Spark plug electrode gap should be 0.040 inch (1.02 mm). On models that are equipped with a ground wire attached to the negative ignition coil terminal, the standard spark plug is Champion L76V. A Champion QL76V is recommended by the manufacturer should radio frequency interference suppression be required. Renew surface gap spark plug if center electrode is more than 1/32 inch (0.79 mm) below the flat surface of the plug end.

SPEED CONTROL LINKAGE

The speed control twist grip, through the use of linkage, operates the stator plate to advance or retard the ignition timing. The carburetor throttle plate is synchronized to open as the timing is advanced.

Models With "BC" Type Carburetor And "BCIA" Stamped On Carburetor Flange

To synchronize ignition timing and throttle opening, proceed as follows: Mount the outboard

Fig. M10-9—On models with "BC" type carburetor, at full throttle the ignition timing is at full advance when three dots (D) align with timing mark (M) on starter housing. Refer to text for adjustment of speed control link (K) and throttle rod (T).

Mariner 20 (1985) & 25 (1985) Hp

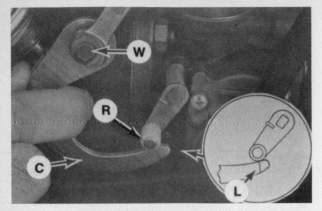

Fig. M10-10 — View showing throttle cam (C), throttle cam mark (L), throttle shaft roller (R) and screw (W) used on models with "BC" type carburetor. Refer to text for speed control linkage adjustment procedures.

Fig. M10-11 — View showing speed control linkage components used on models with "BC" type carburetor and "BCIA" stamped on carburetor flange.

B.	Timing dots			
C.	Throttle cam	R.	Roller	
L.	Throttle cam mark	T.	Throttle rod	
M.	Timing mark	V.	Throttle lever	
P.	Dashpot	IS.	Idle speed stop screw	

motor on a boat or a suitable test tank and immerse the lower unit. Remove the engine cover. Connect a power timing light to the top cylinder spark plug lead. With the engine in the forward gear and running at full throttle, three timing dots (D — Fig. M10-9) should be aligned with timing mark (M) on starter housing. To adjust full advance ignition timing, stop the engine and adjust length of link (K) by disconnecting and turning link end. Lengthening link will advance ignition timing. Recheck full throttle ignition timing, then stop engine.

Disconnect throttle rod (T) from throttle cam, loosen screw (W — Fig. M10-10) and move throttle cam (C) so mark (L) is aligned with roller (R) and cam just touches roller. Retighten screw (W). Start the engine, then advance throttle lever (V — Fig. M10-11) until two timing dots (B) on flywheel are aligned with timing mark (M). Adjust length of throttle rod (T) so when rod is attached to throttle cam (C), mark (L) is in contact with roller (R).

Idle speed is adjusted at stop screw (IS). Refer to the following CARBURETOR section for idle speed adjustment. Adjust position of dashpot (P) so dashpot plunger is fully depressed when the engine is idling at the recommended rpm.

Models With "BC" Type Carburetor And "BCIB" Or "BCIC" Stamped On Carburetor Flange

To synchronize ignition timing and throttle opening, proceed as follows: Mount the outboard motor on a boat or a suitable test tank and immerse the lower unit. Remove the engine cover. Connect a power timing light to the top cylinder spark plug lead. With the engine in forward gear and running at full throttle, three timing dots (D — Fig. M10-9) should be aligned with timing mark (M) on starter housing. To adjust full advance ignition timing, stop the engine and adjust length of link (K) by disconnecting and turning link

end. Lengthening link will advance ignition timing. Recheck full throttle ignition timing, then stop engine.

Disconnect throttle rod (T) from throttle cam, loosen screw (W — Fig. M10-10) and move throttle cam (C) so mark (L) is aligned with roller (R) and cam just touches roller. Retighten screw (W). Start the engine, then advance throttle lever (V — Fig. M10-12) until four timing dots (F) on flywheel are aligned with timing mark (M). Adjust length of throttle rod (T) so when rod is attached to throttle cam (C), mark (L) is in contact with roller (R).

Idle speed is adjusted at stop screw (IS). Refer to the following CARBURETOR section for idle speed adjustment. Adjust position of dashpot (P) so dashpot plunger is fully depressed when the engine is idling at the recommended rpm.

Fig. M10-12 — View showing speed control linkage components used on models with "BC" type carburetor and "BCIB" or "BCIC" stamped on carburetor flange.

C.	Throttle cam			
F.	Timing dots	R.	Roller	
L.	Throttle cam mark	T.	Throttle rod	
M.	Timing mark	V.	Throttle lever	
P.	Dashpot	IS.	Idle speed stop screw	

Fig. M10-13—On models with "WMC" type carburetor, at full throttle the ignition timing is at full advance when three dots (D) align with timing mark (M) on starter housing. Refer to text for adjustment of speed control link (K).

Models With "WMC" Type Carburetor

To synchronize ignition timing and throttle opening, proceed as follows: Mount the outboard motor on a boat or a suitable test tank and immerse the lower unit. Remove the engine cover. Connect a power timing light to the top cylinder spark plug lead. With the engine in the forward gear and running at full throttle, three timing dots (D—Fig. M10-13) should be aligned with timing mark (M) on starter housing. To adjust full advance ignition timing, stop the engine and adjust length of link (K) by disconnecting and turning link end. Lengthening link will advance ignition timing. Recheck full throttle ignition timing, then stop engine.

With the engine stopped, loosen screw (W—Fig. M10-14) and move throttle cam (C) so mark (L) is aligned with roller (R) and cam just touches roller.

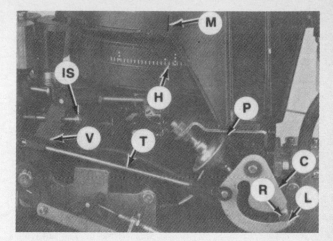

Fig. M10-15—View showing speed control linkage components used on models with "WMC" type carburetor.

C. Throttle cam
H. Flywheel timing mark
L. Throttle cam mark
M. Starter housing timing mark
P. Dashpot
R. Roller
T. Throttle rod
V. Throttle lever
IS. Idle speed screw

NOTE: Adjust idle speed screw (IS—Fig. M10-15), dashpot (P) and neutral rpm ratchet (N—Fig. M10-16) if needed to obtain desired setting.

Retighten screw (W—Fig. M10-14). Start the engine, then advance throttle lever (V—Fig. M10-15) until the 2° ATDC timing mark (H) (one mark to the right of single dot) is aligned with timing mark (M). Adjust length of throttle rod (T) so when rod is attached to throttle cam (C), mark (L) is in contact with roller (R).

Idle speed is adjusted at stop screw (IS). Refer to the following CARBURETOR section for idle speed adjustment. Adjust position of dashpot (P) so dashpot plunger is fully depressed when the engine is idling at the recommended rpm.

With a suitable tachometer attached, start the engine and rotate the throttle control to the

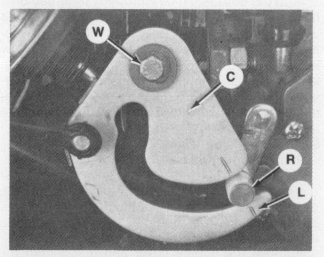

Fig. M10-14 — View showing throttle cam (C), throttle cam mark (L), throttle shaft roller (R) and screw (W) used on models with "WMC" type carburetor. Refer to text for speed control linkage adjustment procedures.

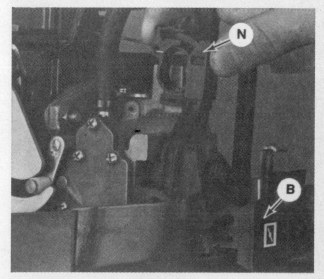

Fig. M10-16—View showing neutral rpm ratchet (N) and primer/fast idle knob (B) used on models with "WMC" type carburetor.

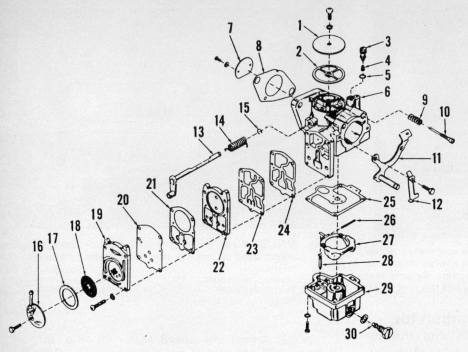

Fig. M10-17—Exploded view of "BC" type carburetor.

1. Cover
2. Gasket
3. Enrichment valve
4. Spring
5. Gasket
6. Body
7. Throttle plate
8. Gasket
9. Spring
10. Idle mixture screw
11. Plate
12. Choke knob detent
13. Throttle shaft roller
14. Spring
15. Snap ring
16. Inlet cover
17. Gasket
18. Strainer
19. Fuel pump cover
20. Diaphragm
21. Gasket
22. Pump body
23. Check valves
24. Gasket
25. Gasket
26. Float pin
27. Float
28. Fuel inlet valve
29. Float bowl
30. Main jet

"SLOW" position. Position the primer/fast idle knob (B—Fig. M10-16) in the middle detent position and adjust ratchet (N) until 1400-1700 rpm is obtained.

CARBURETOR
Models With "BC" Type Carburetor

The fuel pump and carburetor are a complete unit. Refer to the following OVERHAUL section for service procedures on both the fuel pump and carburetor.

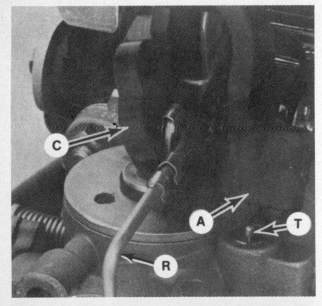

Fig. M10-18—View showning carburetor enrichment system used on "BC" type carburetor. Refer to text for adjustment procedures.

A. Enrichment arm
C. Enrichment valve cover
R. Enrichment rod
T. Enrichment valve stem

ADJUSTMENT. Standard main jet (30—Fig. M10-17) size is 0.067 inch (1.70 mm). Other main jet (30) sizes are available for adjusting the air:fuel mixture for altitude or other special conditions. Initial adjustment of idle mixture screw (10) is 1¼ turns out from a lightly seated position. Recommended idle speed is 600-700 rpm with engine at normal operating temperature and in gear.

All models are equipped with an enrichment valve (3) to enrichen the fuel mixture for cold starting. Raise enrichment valve cover (C—Fig. M10-18) if so equipped. With the choke knob turned fully clockwise, arm (A) should depress valve stem (T). Bend rod (R) to adjust position of arm (A).

With the outboard motor properly mounted on a boat or a suitable test tank, immerse the lower unit. Connect a tachometer and set it on the appropriate range scale. Start the engine and allow it to warm up to normal operating temperature. With the engine running at idle speed while in forward gear, turn idle mixture screw (10) until smooth engine operation is noted. Adjust engine idle speed screw (IS—Fig. M10-11 or M10-12) until 600-700 rpm is obtained.

Reinstall engine cover.

OVERHAUL. The fuel pump is an integral part of the carburetor. The fuel pump assembly may be overhauled without overhauling the complete carburetor. If the fuel pump is to be overhauled without carburetor removal, proceed as follows:

Remove the engine cover and disconnect the fuel tank supply hose at the outboard motor connector. Disconnect the fuel supply hose at the fuel pump inlet.

With reference to Fig. M10-17, disassemble the fuel pump assembly. Inspect all components for excessive wear or any other damage and renew if needed. Clean components as needed with a suitable cleaning solution. Blow dry with clean compressed air. If compressed air is not available, use only lint-free cloths to wipe dry. Make sure all passages are clear of any obstruction.

With reference to Fig. M10-17, reassemble the fuel pump assembly with new gaskets. Securely tighten the retaining screws.

NOTE: Fuel pump and engine malfunction will result if the fuel pump and all connections are not airtight.

Complete reassembly.

Refer to the following for complete carburetor overhaul: Remove the engine cover. Disconnect choke lever from choke knob. Disconnect the fuel tank supply hose at the outboard motor connector. Disconnect the fuel supply hose at the fuel pump inlet. If equipped with an electric starter, remove starter and unplug choke solenoid wire. Clean all external surfaces and remove accumulated dirt and grease. Remove the two nuts securing the carburetor and withdraw the carburetor assembly.

With reference to Fig. M10-17, disassemble the complete carburetor assembly and note any discrepancies which must be corrected before reassembly. Remove all gaskets (label if needed for later reference) and set to the side.

Thoroughly clean all carburetor parts in a suitable solvent and inspect for damage and excessive wear. Note that plastic and rubber components should not be subjected to some cleaning solutions. Blow dry with clean compressed air. If compressed air is not available, use only lint-free cloths to wipe dry. Do not use a drill bit or wire to clean jets. Enlargement or damage of the calibrated holes may affect engine performance.

With reference to Fig. M10-17, reassemble the carburetor components with new gaskets. Note that the new gaskets should match up with those removed. If not, check with your parts supplier to be sure you have the correct gasket set.

To determine the float level, invert carburetor float bowl (29 — Fig. M10-17) with fuel inlet valve (28) and float (27) installed. With float (27) hanging down as shown in Fig. M10-19, float end (L) should be even with or less than 1/32 inch (0.8 mm) below float bowl (29) edge. Bend float arm tang to adjust.

When reinstalling the carburetor, place a new gasket (8 — Fig. M10-17) between the carburetor and the adapter plate. Securely tighten the retaining nuts. Reassemble in the reverse order of disassembly with exception of the engine cover. In-

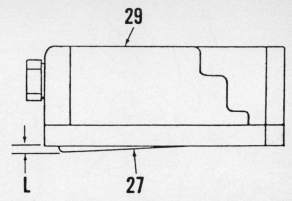

Fig. M10-19 — With float bowl (29) inverted as shown, float (27) level (L) should be even with or less than 1/32 inch (0.8 mm) below float bowl edge.

itally adjust idle mixture screw (10) 1¼ turns out from a lightly seated position.

Models With "WMC" Type Carburetor

The fuel pump and carburetor are a complete unit. Refer to the following OVERHAUL section for service procedures on both the fuel pump and carburetor.

ADJUSTMENT. Standard main jet (30 — Fig. M10-20) size is 0.046 inch (1.17 mm) on 20 hp models and 0.080 inch (2.03 mm) on 25 hp models. Other main jet (30) sizes are available for adjusting the air:fuel mixture for altitude or other special conditions. Initial adjustment of idle mixture screw (6) is 1¼ turns out from a lightly seated position. Recommended idle speed is 600-700 rpm with engine at normal operating temperature and in gear.

With the outboard motor properly mounted on a boat or a suitable test tank, immerse the lower unit. Connect a tachometer and set it on the appropriate range scale. Start the engine and allow it to warm up to normal operating temperature. With the engine running at idle speed while in forward gear, turn idle mixture screw (6) counterclockwise until the fuel mixture becomes too rich and the engine loads up and starts to misfire. Then turn idle mixture screw (6) clockwise until smooth engine operation is noted. Continue to turn screw (6) clockwise until the fuel mixture becomes too lean and the engine starts to slow down and misfire. At this point, turn idle mixture screw (6) to midpoint of too rich and too lean setting. Note that it is better to have the fuel mixture too rich than too lean. Adjust engine idle speed screw (IS — Fig. M10-15) until 600-700 rpm is obtained.

Reinstall engine top cover.

OVERHAUL. The fuel pump is an integral part of the carburetor. The fuel pump assembly may be overhauled without overhauling the complete car-

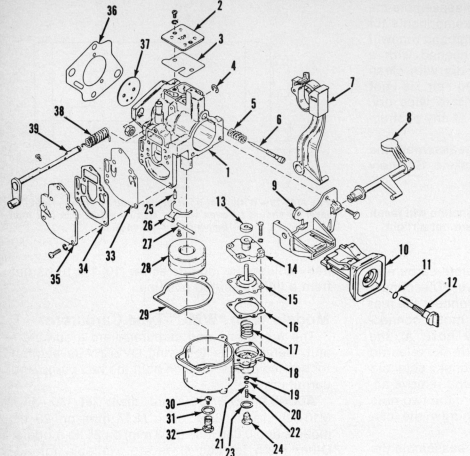

Fig. M10-20—Exploded view of "WMC" type carburetor.

1. Carburetor body
2. Cover
3. Gasket
4. Clip
5. Spring
6. Idle mixture screw
7. Neutral rpm ratchet
8. Enrichment lever
9. Enrichment bracket
10. Enrichment knob
11. "O" ring
12. Fast idle knob
13. Seal
14. Cover
15. Enrichment diaphragm
16. Gasket
17. Spring
18. Float bowl
19. Seat
20. Retainer
21. Check ball
22. Spring
23. Gasket
24. Plug
25. Inlet needle
26. Float arm
27. Float pin
28. Float
29. Gasket
30. Main jet
31. Gasket
32. Plug
33. Diaphragm
34. Gasket
35. Cover
36. Gasket
37. Throttle plate
38. Spring
39. Throttle shaft

buretor. If the fuel pump is to be overhauled without carburetor removal, proceed as follows:

Remove the engine cover and disconnect the fuel tank supply hose at the outboard motor connector.

With reference to Fig. M10-20, disassemble the fuel pump assembly. Inspect all components for excessive wear or any other damage and renew if needed. Clean components as needed with a suitable cleaning solution. Blow dry with clean compressed air. If compressed air is not available, use only lint-free cloths to wipe dry. Make sure all passages are clear of any obstruction.

With reference to Fig. M10-20, reassemble the fuel pump assembly with a new gasket. Securely tighten the retaining screws.

NOTE: Fuel pump and engine malfunction will result if the fuel pump and all connections are not airtight.

Complete reassembly.

Refer to the following for complete carburetor overhaul: Remove the engine's top cover. Disconnect the fuel tank supply hose at the outboard motor connector. Remove components as needed to separate the engine's bottom cover halves and withdraw. Disconnect the fuel supply hose at the

carburetor inlet. Clean all external surfaces and remove accumulated dirt and grease. Remove the two nuts securing the carburetor and withdraw the carburetor assembly. Detach idle wire at ratchet assembly (7—Fig. M10-20).

With reference to Fig. M10-20, disassemble the complete carburetor assembly and note any discrepancies which must be corrected before reassembly. Remove all gaskets (label if needed

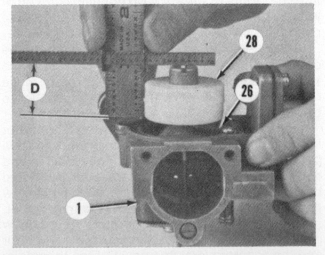

Fig. M10-21—With carburetor body (1) inverted, distance (D) should be 1 inch (25.4 mm) when measured as shown. Bend float arm (26) to adjust position of float (28).

for later reference), seal (13) and "O" ring (11), if needed, and set to the side.

Thoroughly clean all carburetor parts in a suitable solvent and inspect for excessive wear or any other damage. Note that plastic and rubber components should not be subjected to some cleaning solutions. Blow dry with clean compressed air. If compressed air is not available, use only lint-free cloths to wipe dry. Do not use a drill bit or wire to clean jets. Enlargement or damage of the calibrated holes may affect engine performance.

With reference to Fig. M10-20, reassemble the carburetor components with new gaskets. Note that the new gaskets should match up with those removed. if not, check with your parts supplier to be sure you have the correct gasket set.

To determine the float level, invert carburetor body (1 — Fig. M10-21) with fuel inlet valve (25 — Fig. M10-20), float arm (26 — Fig. M10-21) and float (28) installed. Measure distance (D) as shown in Fig. M10-21. Distance (D) should be 1 inch (25.4 mm). Bend float arm (26) to adjust.

When reinstalling the carburetor, place a new gasket (36 — Fig. M10-20) between the carburetor and the adapter plate. Securely tighten the retaining nuts. Reassemble in the reverse order of disassembly with the exception of the engine's top cover. Initially adjust idle mixture screw (6) 1¼ turns out from a lightly seated position.

MERCURY

**MERCURY MARINE
DIV. BRUNSWICK CORP.
Fond du Lac, Wisc. 54935**

MERC 2.2
Specifications

Hp	2.2
Bore	1.85 in.
	(47 mm)
Stroke	1.69 in.
	(43 mm)
Number of cylinders	1
Displacement	4.5 cu. in.
	(74.6 cc)
Spark plug — Champion	RL87YC
Electrode gap	0.040 in.
	(1 mm)
Breaker point gap	0.012-0.016 in.
	(0.3-0.4 mm)
Ignition timing	Fixed
Idle speed	900-1000 rpm
Fuel:oil ratio	50:1
Gearcase oil capacity	3 oz.
	(90 mL)

Maintenance

LUBRICATION

ENGINE. The engine is lubricated by oil mixed with the fuel. The fuel should be regular leaded, low lead or unleaded gasoline with a minimum pump octane rating of 86. Recommended oil is Quicksilver Formula 50-D Outboard Lubricant or a BIA certified two-stroke motor oil. The recommended fuel:oil ratio for normal operation is 50:1.

LOWER UNIT. The lower unit gears and bearings are lubricated by oil contained in the gearcase. The recommended oil is Quicksilver Super-Duty Gear Lubricant. The gearcase oil capacity is 3 ounces (90 mL). The gearcase should be refilled periodically and the lubricant renewed after every 30 days. The gearcase is drained and filled through the same plug port (D—Fig. MY1-1). An oil level (vent) port (L) is used to indicate the full oil level of gearcase and to ease oil drainage.

To drain the oil, place the outboard motor in a vertical position. Remove drain plug (D) and oil level plug (L), and allow the lubricant to drain into a suitable container.

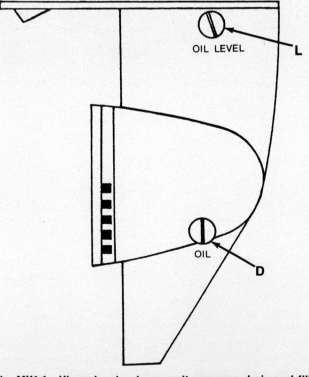

Fig. MY1-1 — View showing lower unit gearcase drain and fill plug (D) and oil level (vent) plug (L).

To fill the gearcase with oil, place the outboard motor in a vertical position. Add oil through drain plug (D) opening with an oil feeder until the oil begins to overflow from oil level plug (L) port. Reinstall oil level plug (L) with a new gasket, if needed, and tighten. Remove oil feeder, then reinstall drain plug (D) with a new gasket, if needed, and tighten.

PIVOT POINTS AND SLIDES. Lubricate all pivot points and linkage slides' with a good quality marine type multipurpose grease as frequently as needed to keep the components operating freely and properly.

FUEL SYSTEM

Periodically inspect the fuel tank and fuel line for damage. Renew components if needed. After closing the fuel valve, occasionally remove the carburetor float bowl drain plug and allow the fuel to drain off into a suitable container. Inspect fuel for any foreign matter. If an excessive amount of foreign matter is found, extensive cleaning of the fuel system is needed.

Keep the external surface of the carburetor clean and all connections and sealing surfaces tight.

FUEL TANK. It may be necessary to remove the fuel tank for cleaning or for access to underlying engine components.

To remove the fuel tank, first remove the spark plug access cover. Remove the screws retaining the port and starboard engine covers and then withdraw the covers. Close the fuel valve and disconnect the fuel hose from the fuel valve outlet. Remove the screws retaining the fuel tank and withdraw.

Installation is reverse order of removal.

STARTER

When starter rope (11—Fig. MY1-2) is pulled, pulley (3) will rotate. As pulley (3) rotates, ratchet (4) moves to engage with starter cup (13), thus cranking the engine.

When starter rope (11) is released, pulley (3) is rotated in the reverse direction by force from rewind spring (2). As pulley (3) rotates, the starter rope is rewound and ratchet (4) is disengaged from starter cup (13).

The manual starter must be disassembled to renew starter rope (11) or any other internal starter component.

To overhaul the manual starter, proceed as follows: Remove the screws retaining the engine's port and starboard side covers, then withdraw covers. Remove the screws retaining the manual starter assembly to the power head and withdraw.

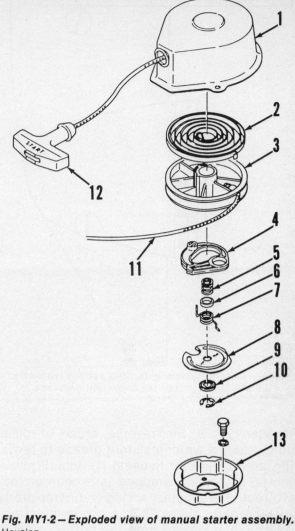

Fig. MY1-2 — Exploded view of manual starter assembly.

1. Housing		
2. Rewind spring	6. Sleeve	10. Clip
3. Pulley	7. Return spring	11. Starter rope
4. Ratchet	8. Friction plate	12. Handle
5. Spring	9. Thrust washer	13. Starter cup

> ⚠ **WARNING**
>
> **Care should be exercised when working with or around a coiled starter rewind spring as sudden uncoiling can cause injury. Safety eyewear and gloves are recommended.**

To disassemble, untie starter rope (11) at handle (12) and allow rope to wind into the starter. Invert the unit and remove clip (10), then withdraw thrust washer (9), friction plate (8), return spring (7), sleeve (6), spring (5) and ratchet (4). Remove pulley (3) while being careful not to dislodge rewind spring (2). Remove starter rope (11) from pulley (3) if renewal is required. If rewind spring (2) must be removed, care must be used to prevent spring from uncoiling dangerously.

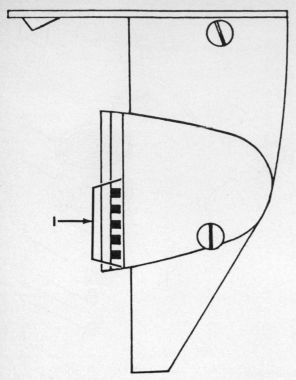

Fig. MY1-3 — Cooling system water inlet ports (I) are located on the starboard side of the lower unit gearcase.

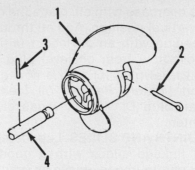

Fig. MY1-4 — Propeller (1) is mounted on propeller shaft (4) and is retained by cotter pin (2). Shear pin (3) is renewed only after withdrawing propeller (1) from propeller shaft (4).

water inlets for the cooling system. The ports must be kept clean of all foreign matter to ensure efficient operation of the cooling system.

⚠CAUTION

Do not operate outboard motor unless the lower unit is immersed in water, otherwise, the water pump impeller will be damaged.

PROPELLER

The standard propeller has two blades, a diameter of 7.4 inches (188 mm) and a pitch of 4.5 inches (114 mm).

⚠WARNING

Disconnect spark plug leads and properly ground leads before performing any propeller service, otherwise, accidental starting can occur if propeller shaft is rotated.

To remove the propeller, remove cotter pin (2 — Fig. MY1-4) and withdraw propeller (1) from propeller shaft (4).

Inspect propeller (1) and shear pin (3) for damage and excessive wear and renew if needed.

Apply a water-resistant grease to the propeller bore, then install propeller (1) on propeller shaft (4) and retain with a new cotter pin (2).

Tune-Up

IGNITION SYSTEM

The standard spark plug is Champion RL87YC with an electrode gap of 0.040 inch (1 mm).

The breaker point gap should be 0.012-0.016 inch (0.3-0.4 mm) and can be inspected and ad-

Reassembly is the reverse order of disassembly. Apply a water-resistant grease to rewind spring area of starter housing (1). Install rewind spring (2) with coils wrapped in a counterclockwise direction from outer spring end. Wrap starter rope (11) around pulley (3) in a counterclockwise direction when viewed from the bottom side. Install pulley (3) in starter housing (1) making sure pulley properly engages rewind spring (2). Thread rope end through starter housing (1) and secure on handle (12).

NOTE: Lubricate all friction surfaces with a suitable water-resistant grease during reassembly.

Install ratchet (4) so ratchet tooth points counterclockwise when viewed from the bottom side. Assemble remaining components. Apply tension to rewind spring (2) by engaging starter rope (11) in pulley (3) notch and turning pulley counterclockwise, then release starter rope (11) from pulley notch.

NOTE: Do not apply any more tension on rewind spring (2) than is required to draw starter handle (12) back into the proper released position.

Check starter action, then remount manual starter assembly and engine's side covers to complete reassembly.

COOLING SYSTEM

Ports (I—Fig. MY1-3) located on the starboard side of the lower unit gearcase are used as the

Fig. MY1-6—*View showing the use of a feeler gage (G) to check the clearance between the breaker point contact surfaces.*

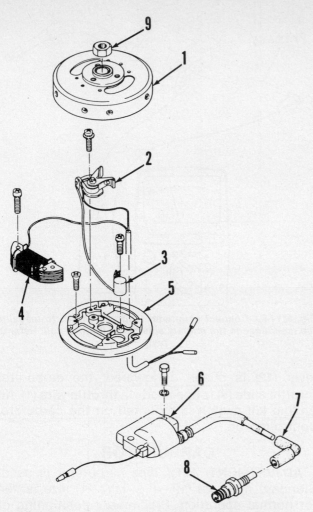

Fig. MY1-5—*Exploded view of flywheel magneto unit.*

1. Flywheel
2. Breaker point assy.
3. Condenser
4. Exciter coil
5. Magneto base plate
6. Ignition coil
7. Spark plug boot
8. Spark plug
9. Nut

justed through the opening in flywheel (1—Fig. MY1-5). To inspect and, if needed, adjust the breaker point gap, first remove the screws retaining the engine's port and starboard side covers, then withdraw covers. Remove the screws retaining the manual starter assembly to the power head and withdraw. Remove the screws and lockwashers securing starter pulley (13—Fig. MY1-2) to flywheel (1—Fig. MY1-5) and withdraw.

Inspect the breaker point surfaces for excessive wear, pitting or any other damage. If needed, renew breaker point assembly (2) and condenser (3) as outlined later in this section.

To clean the breaker point contact surfaces, use a point file or sandpaper with a grit rating of 400 to 600. After polishing, wipe the contact surfaces clean with a dry cloth and lightly grease the breaker point arm with a suitable lubricant.

Turn the flywheel until the breaker point contact surfaces are placed at their widest position,

then reach through the flywheel opening with a feeler gage (G—Fig. MY1-6) of the appropriate size and check the distance between the point surfaces. If the distance is not within the recommemded limits, loosen the point set securing screw and adjust the point set until the correct gap is obtained. Tighten the point set securing screw and recheck the breaker point gap. Repeat the adjustment procedure, if needed, until the correct breaker point gap is obtained.

To renew breaker point assembly (2—Fig. MY1-5) and condenser (3), proceed as follows: Using a suitable flywheel holding tool (H—Fig. MY1-7), remove securing nut (9—Fig. MY1-5). Remove flywheel (1—Fig. MY1-5) from crankshaft end using a suitable puller assembly (P—Fig. MY1-8) and suitable tools (T). Note flywheel key located in crankshaft keyway.

⚠WARNING

Be sure suitable tools are used to remove the flywheel. Damage resultant from the misapplication of force or the use of incorrect tools may cause engine damage, engine malfunction or personal injury.

With reference to Fig. MY1-5, renew breaker point assembly (2) and condenser (3). Adjust the breaker point gap to the recommended setting as outlined in a previous paragraph. Make sure the securing screws are properly tightened. Be sure the flywheel key is properly positioned in the crankshaft end, then reinstall flywheel (1). Tighten securing nut (9) to 30 ft.-lbs. (41 N·m).

Illustrations Courtesy Mercury

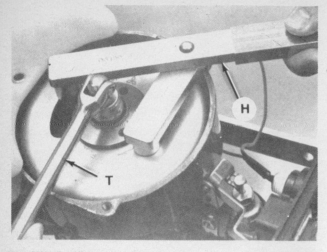

Fig. MY1-7—View showing the use of a suitable flywheel holding tool (H), to prevent flywheel rotation during removal of securing nut (9—Fig. MY1-5) with suitable tools (T).

Magneto base plate (5) is fixed to the engine with tapered screws and no timing adjustment is possible other than varying the breaker point gap between the recommended 0.012-0.016 inch (0.3-0.4 mm).

Ignition Coil. To check ignition coil (6—Fig. MY1-5) located on the side of the engine cylinder, use a suitable ohmmeter. Connect one tester lead to the coil's metal laminations, then connect the remaining tester lead alternately to the primary (Fig. MY1-9) and secondary (Fig. MY1-10) ignition coil leads. Resistance reading for primary circuit should be 0.81-1.09 ohms while the secondary circuit resistance reading should be 4250-5750 ohms. Renew ignition coil (6—Fig. MY1-5) if the meter readings are not within the proper range.

SPEED CONTROL LINKAGE

The engine speed is regulated by the position of throttle lever (12—Fig. MY1-11). As throttle

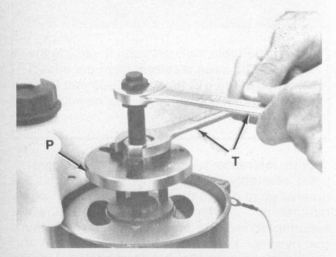

Fig. MY1-8—Remove flywheel (1—Fig. MY1-5) from crankshaft end using a suitable puller assembly (P) and suitable tools (T).

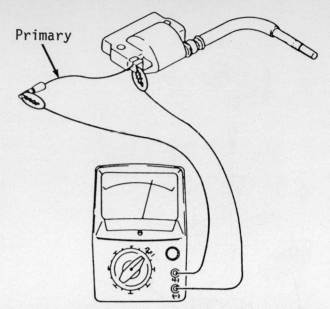

Fig. MY1-9—Connect ohmmeter leads as shown to measure the resistance in the primary side of the ignition coil. Refer to text.

lever (12) is raised or lowered, the carburetor throttle slide (9) is operated via throttle wire (1). An engine kill switch is mounted on the carburetor control cover.

CARBURETOR

ADJUSTMENT. A TK type carburetor is used. Standard main jet (19—Fig. MY1-11) size is #94 for normal operation. Preliminary positioning of clip (7) in jet needle (8) is second groove from the

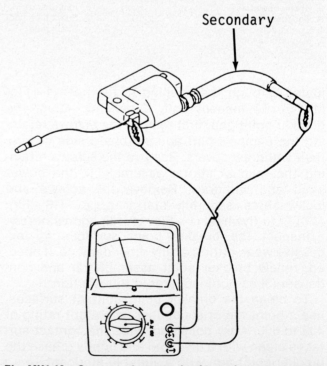

Fig. MY1-10—Connect ohmmeter leads as shown to measure the resistance in the secondary side of the ignition coil. Refer to text.

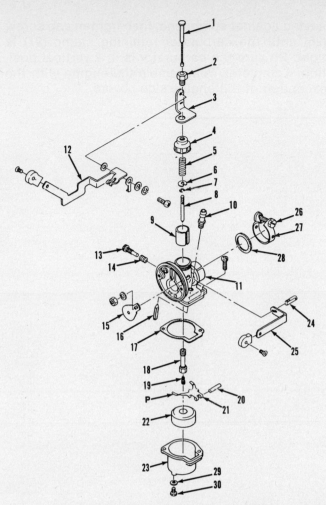

Fig. MY1-11—Exploded view of carburetor.

1. Throttle wire	16. Fuel inlet valve
2. Guide screw	17. Gasket
3. Bracket	18. Needle jet
4. Cap	19. Main jet
5. Spring	20. Float arm pin
6. Retainer	21. Float arm
7. Clip	22. Float
8. Jet needle	23. Float bowl
9. Throttle slide	24. Shaft
10. Fuel inlet	25. Choke lever
11. Body	26. Cap screw
12. Throttle lever	27. Clamp
13. Idle speed screw	28. Gasket
14. Spring	29. Gasket
15. Choke plate	30. Drain plug

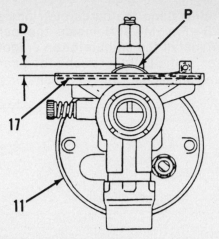

Fig. MY1-12—Float level is measured by inverting carburetor body (11) and measuring distance (D) from top of carburetor bowl gasket (17) to base of float arm pad (P). Bend float arms evenly to adjust.

OVERHAUL. Remove the engine's port and starboard side covers and position the outboard motor in an upright position. Close the fuel cock. Remove all components as needed to remove control panel and expose carburetor assembly. Disconnect fuel hose from carburetor inlet nozzle and remove any other component that will interfere with carburetor removal.

Clean all external surfaces and remove accumulated dirt and grease. Loosen cap screw (26) and withdraw carburetor assembly. With reference to Fig. MY1-11, disassemble the carburetor and note any discrepancies which must be corrected before reassembly. Remove all gaskets (label if needed for later reference) and set to the side.

Thoroughly clean all carburetor parts in a suitable solvent and inspect for excessive wear or any other damage. Note that plastic and rubber components should not be subjected to some cleaning solutions. Blow dry with clean compressed air. If compressed air is not available, use only lint-free cloths to wipe dry. Do not use a drill bit or wire to clean jets. Enlargement or damage of the calibrated holes may affect engine performance.

With reference to Fig. MY1-11, reassemble the carburetor components with new gaskets. Note that the new gaskets should match up with those removed. If not, check with your parts supplier to be sure you have the correct gasket set.

To determine the float level, invert carburetor body (11—Fig. MY1-12) and measure distance (D) from top of carburetor bowl gasket (17) to base of float arm pad (P). Distance should be 0.090 inch (2.3 mm) and is adjusted by bending float arm pads (P) evenly until the correct distance is obtained.

top. Inserting clip (7) in a higher notch will lean midrange mixture while inserting clip in a lower notch will richen midrange mixture. Recommended idle speed is 900-1000 rpm with engine at normal operating temperature.

Properly mount the outboard motor on a boat or suitable test tank and immerse the lower unit. Connect a tachometer and set it on the appropriate range scale. Start the engine and allow it to warm up to normal operating temperature. Position the throttle control lever to the complete closed position, then adjust the engine idle speed screw (13) until the engine is idling at 900-1000 rpm. Complete reassembly.

Merc 2.2 Hp

When reinstalling the carburetor, place a new gasket (28—Fig. MY1-11) inside the carburetor bore, then install the carburetor on spigot end of crankcase half. Lightly push the carburetor towards the crankcase until the gasket is properly seated against spigot end, then tighten cap screw (26) until the carburetor retaining clamp (27) is tight. Be sure the carburetor is in a vertical position. Completely reassemble the engine with the exception of the engine side covers.

MERC 4 (1979-1981)
MERC 40 (1976-1978)

Specifications

Hp 4
Bore . . . . .1.56 in.
(39.67 mm)
Stroke . . . . .1.44 in
(36.50 mm)
Number of cylinders 2
Displacement . . . . .5.5 cu. in.
(90.13 cc)
Spark plug — Champion L7J
    Electrode gap . . . . .0.050 in.
(1.27 mm)
Ignition . . . . .Breakerless
Idle speed (in gear) . . . . .600-700 rpm
Fuel:oil ratio. 50:1
Gearcase oil capacity . . . . .2¾ oz.
(81 mL)

Maintenance

LUBRICATION

ENGINE. The engine is lubricated by oil mixed with the fuel. The fuel should be regular leaded, low lead or unleaded gasoline with a minimum pump octane rating of 86. Recommended oil is Quicksilver Formula 50-D Outboard Lubricant or a BIA certified two-stroke motor oil. The recommended fuel:oil ratio for normal operation is 50:1.

LOWER UNIT. The lower unit gears and bearings are lubricated by oil contained in the gearcase. The recommended oil is Quicksilver Super-Duty Gear Lubricant. The gearcase oil capacity is 2¾ ounces (81 mL). The gearcase oil level should be checked every 30 days and the lubricant renewed periodically. The gearcase is drained and filled through the same plug port (D — Fig. MY2-1). An oil level (vent) port (L) is used to identify the full oil level of the gearcase and to ease oil drainage.

To drain the oil, place the outboard motor in a vertical position. Remove drain plug (D) and oil level plug (L), and allow the lubricant to drain into a suitable container.

To fill the gearcase with oil, place the outboard motor in a vertical position. Add oil through drain plug (D) opening with an oil feeder until the oil begins to overflow from oil level plug (L) port. Reinstall oil level plug (L) with a new gasket, if needed, and tighten. Remove oil feeder, then reinstall drain plug (D) with a new gasket, if needed, and tighten.

PIVOT POINTS AND SLIDES. Lubricate all pivot points and linkage slides with a good quality marine type multipurpose grease as frequently as needed to keep the components operating freely and properly.

FUEL SYSTEM

Periodically inspect the fuel tank and fuel lines for damage. Renew components if needed. After

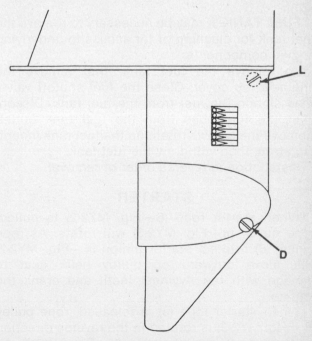

Fig. MY2-1—View showing lower unit gearcase drain and fill plug (D) and oil level (vent) plug (L).

Fig. MY2-2—View showing screws (S) retaining manual starter assembly to power head. Arrow indicates direction of rotation.

1. Cap screw	4. Starter pinion
2. Retainer	5. Clip
3. Spring holder	6. Starter rope

closing the fuel shutoff valve, occasionally remove the carburetor inlet fuel hose and nozzle, then withdraw the fuel strainer from the inlet port. Clean strainer in a suitable solvent and blow dry with clean compressed air. Inspect strainer. If excessive blockage or damage is noted, renew strainer. If an excessive amount of foreign matter is noted in strainer, extensive cleaning of the fuel system is needed.

Keep the external surface of the carburetor clean and all connections and sealing surfaces tight.

FUEL TANK. It may be necessary to remove the fuel tank for cleaning or for access to underlying engine components.

To remove the fuel tank, first remove the engine's top cover. Close the fuel shutoff valve, then siphon the fuel from the fuel tank. Disconnect the fuel hose from the fuel tank outlet. Remove the screws retaining the fuel tank mounting strap, then withdraw the fuel tank.

Installation is reverse order of removal.

STARTER

When starter rope (6—Fig. MY2-2) is pulled, rope pulley (8—Fig. MY2-3) will rotate. As rope pulley (8) rotates, starter pinion (4—Fig. MY2-2) will move outward on pulley helix gear to engage with the flywheel teeth and crank the engine.

When starter rope (6) is released, rope pulley (8—Fig. MY2-3) is rotated in the reverse direction by force from rewind spring (9—Fig. MY2-4). As pulley (8—Fig. MY2-3) rotates, starter pinion

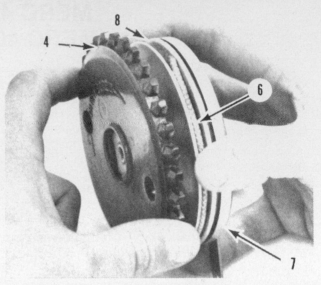

Fig. MY2-3—View shows the assembly of starter pinion (4), starter rope (6), housing (7) and rope pulley (8).

(4—Fig. MY2-2) will disengage from the flywheel teeth and be returned to the relaxed position by force from spring (10—Fig. MY2-5).

The manual starter must be disassembled to renew starter rope (6—Fig. MY2-2) or any other internal starter component.

To overhaul the manual starter, proceed as follows: Remove the engine's top cover. Untie starter rope (6—Fig. MY2-2) at the pull handle and allow the rope to wind into the starter. Remove the three screws (S) securing the manual starter to the power head and withdraw the assembly.

⚠WARNING

Care should be exercised when working with or around a coiled starter rewind spring as sudden uncoiling can cause injury. Safety eyewear and gloves are recommended.

NOTE: Cap screw (1) has left-hand threads. Rotate cap screw clockwise to remove and counterclockwise to install.

Remove cap screw (1) with flat washer. Remove pinion spring retainer (2) with clip, pinion spring holder (3), pinion spring, flat washers and shoulder washer. Withdraw starter pinion (4—Fig. MY2-3) from helix gear on pulley (8). Withdraw rope pulley (8) from housing (7). BE CAREFUL when removing rope pulley (8) to prevent possible injury from rewind spring (9—Fig. MY2-4). If renewal of starter rope (6—Fig. MY2-3) is required, the pins in rope pulley (8) must be driven out.

To remove rewind spring (9—Fig. MY2-4) from housing (7), place the assembly in a container slightly larger than housing (7) and enclosed on

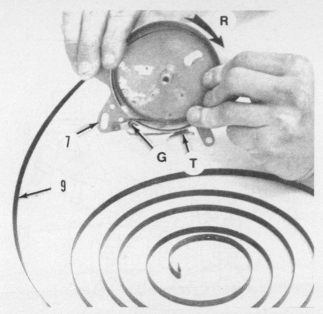

Fig. MY2-4 — View shows the installation of rewind spring (9) in housing (7). Attach outer end of rewind spring (9) to housing tab (T) and pass spring around guide (G). Hold spring in housing and rotate housing clockwise as shown at (R).

Fig. MY2-5—Distance (D) between spring holder (3) cutout and face of starter pinion (4) should be at least a distance (D) of 1/16 inch (1.6 mm). Refer to text for adjustment of distance (D). View identifies return spring (10).

all sides. Hold the housing by the mounting bracket and lightly tap the housing center shaft on the bottom of the container. Allow the rewind spring to uncoil, then detach spring end from housing mounting tab.

NOTE: If a container is not used, use suitable hand protection and extract rewind spring (9) from housing (7). Allow rewind spring to uncoil in a safe area.

Inspect all components for damage and excessive wear and renew if needed.

To reassemble, first apply a coating of a suitable water-resistant grease to rewind spring (9) area of housing (7). Attach outer end of rewind spring (9) to housing tab (T) and pass spring around guide (G). Hold spring in housing and rotate (R) housing clockwise. Rewind spring will coil counterclockwise into housing from the outer end.

To install starter rope (6—Fig. MY2-3) onto rope pulley (8), proceed as follows: Retain starter rope (6) end loop with the pin nearest rope pulley hub and stake pin in place. Wrap the starter rope twice around the pulley in a counterclockwise direction when viewed from the helix end. Insert the second pin into the pulley and stake pin in place. Coat housing center shaft with a suitable water-resistant grease, then install rope pulley (8). Make sure the inner end of rewind spring (9—Fig. MY2-4) properly engages rope pulley (8—Fig. MY2-3).

NOTE: DO NOT lubricate helix gear.

Install starter pinion (4) on helix gear. Complete reassembly and tighten cap screw (1—Fig. MY2-2)

to 30 in.-lbs. (3.39 N·m). Measure distance (D—Fig. MY2-5) from spring holder (3) cutout to face of starter pinion (4). Distance should be no less than 1/16 inch (1.6 mm). To adjust, install washers behind or ahead of shoulder washer until correct distance is obtained.

Remount manual starter and route starter rope (6—Fig. MY2-2) through front cowl and attach pull handle. Loop starter rope (6) around rope pulley in a counterclockwise direction if additional tension is needed on rewind spring.

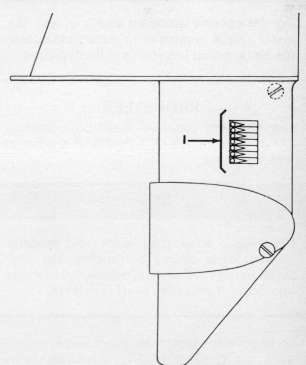

Fig. MY2-6 — Cooling system water inlet ports (I) are located on the port and starboard side of the lower unit.

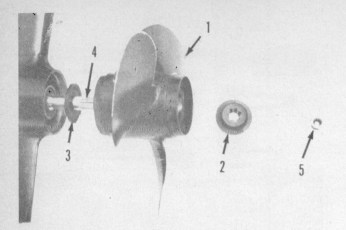

Fig. MY2-7 — Spacer (3), propeller (1) and splined washer (2) are mounted on propeller shaft (4) and retained by nut (5). Tighten nut (5) to a torque of 60 in.-lbs. (7 N·m).

NOTE: Do not apply any more tension on rewind spring that is required to draw starter handle back into the proper released position.

Complete reassembly.

COOLING SYSTEM

Ports (I—Fig. MY2-6) located on the port and starboard side of the lower unit gearcase are used as the water inlets for the cooling system. The ports must be kept clean of all foreign matter to ensure efficient operation of the cooling system.

⚠CAUTION

Do not operate outboard motor unless the lower unit is immersed in water, otherwise, the water pump impeller will be damaged.

PROPELLER

The standard propeller has three blades, a diameter of 8 inches (203 mm) and a pitch of 7 inches (178 mm).

⚠WARNING

Disconnect spark plug leads and properly ground leads before performing any propeller service, otherwise, accidental starting can occur if propeller shaft is rotated.

To remove the propeller, unscrew propeller retaining nut (5—Fig. MY2-7). Withdraw splined washer (2), propeller (1) and spacer (3) from propeller shaft (4).

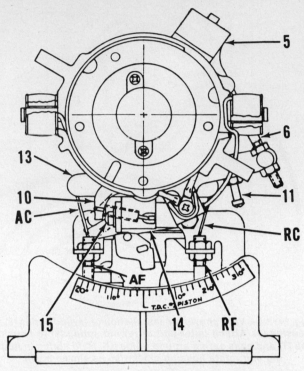

Fig. MY2-8 — Refer to text for speed control and ignition timing adjustments.

AF. Advance cable fitting
AC. Advance cable
RC. Retard cable
RF. Retard cable fitting
 5. Trigger ring
 6. Trigger ring rod

10. Ignition lever
11. Max. advance screw
13. Throttle lever
14. Throttle cam
15. Throttle cam screw

Inspect all components for damage and excessive wear and renew if needed.

Apply Perfect Seal or a suitable equivalent to the propeller shaft splines, then install spacer (3), propeller (1) and splined washer (2) on propeller shaft (4). Install propeller retaining nut (5) and tighten to a torque of 60 in.-lbs. (7 N·m).

Tune-Up

IGNITION SYSTEM

A "Thunderbolt" capacitor discharge ignition (CDI) system is used. Refer to the Outboard Motor Service Manual for testing and servicing the CD ignition system. If engine malfunction is noted and the ignition system is suspected, make sure the spark plugs and all electrical wiring are in good condition and all electrical connections are tight before proceeding to troubleshooting the CD ignition system.

The standard spark plug is Champion L7J with an electrode gap of 0.050 inch (1.27 mm).

IGNITION TIMING. The following ignition timing procedure must be followed from start to finish or incorrect timing may result.

Place twist grip in the complete closed position. The gap between throttle cam (14—Fig. MY2-8) and carburetor cam follower should be

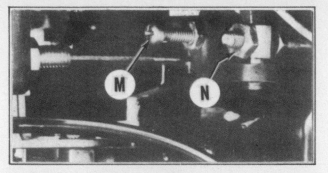

Fig. MY2-9—View showing location of maximum advance screw (M) and trigger rod nut (N).

0.005-0.015 inch (0.127-0.381 mm). If not, loosen cam screw (15), then move cam until the proper setting is obtained and retighten screw. Loosen nuts and turn retard cable fitting (RF) so 3-4 threads are exposed on cable housing end of fitting. Retighten nuts. Hold twist grip against idle stop and adjust advance cable fitting (AF) to just remove slack in advance cable (AC). Immerse lower unit in water and connect a power timing light to number one (top) spark plug. Connect a tachometer and set it on the appropriate range scale. Start and run engine until warm. With unit in gear, run engine at 1000-1500 rpm then quickly close throttle while noting ignition timing. Timing should momentarily retard to 18°-20° ATDC and then advance to 15°-18° ATDC at idle speed of 600 rpm. Turn link rod nuts (N — Fig. MY2-9) so ignition timing is 2° below advance reading. For instance, if timing fully retards to 18° ATDC then advances to 15° ATDC at 600 rpm, set ignition timing for idle at 17° ATDC. Maximum ignition timing should be 22°-26° BTDC and is adjusted by turning maximum advance screw (M).

Refer to the following SPEED CONTROL LINKAGE section and adjust carburetor throttle pickup point.

SPEED CONTROL LINKAGE

The throttle twist grip is connected to the throttle lever (13 — Fig. MY2-10) via two control cables and steering handle components. Throttle cam (14) is attached to throttle lever (13) and contacts carburetor cam follower. Ignition lever (10) rests on throttle lever (13) and both are supported by shoulder bolt (17). Rod (6) connects ignition lever (10) to trigger ring (5) and spring (12) attaches to ignition lever (10) and throttle lever. When the throttle twist grip is rotated for more speed, advance control cable (left cable) is pulled which rotates throttle lever (13) on shoulder bolt. Spring (12) forces ignition lever (10) to rotate with throttle lever (13) until ignition lever contacts maximum advance screw (11). Rod (6) forces trigger ring (5) to rotate as ignition lever rotates, thereby changing ignition timing.

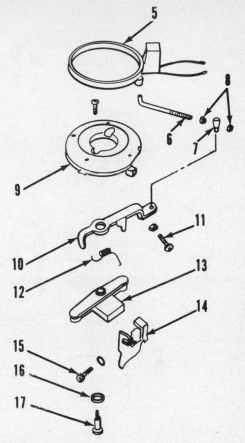

Fig. MY2-10—View of speed control linkage components.

5. Trigger ring	
6. Trigger ring rod	12. Spring
7. Swivel bolt	13. Throttle lever
8. Nuts	14. Throttle cam
9. Stator bracket	15. Throttle cam screw
10. Ignition lever	16. Washer
11. Max. advance screw	17. Shoulder bolt

Before adjusting throttle pickup point, refer to IGNITION TIMING under IGNITION SYSTEM section and check ignition timing. To adjust throttle pickup point, connect an ignition timing light to number one (top) spark plug. Run engine and note ignition timing when carburetor cam follower contacts throttle cam. Ignition timing should be 12°-16° ATDC. Loosen throttle cam screw (15) and adjust throttle cam position to obtain desired pickup point.

CARBURETOR

ADJUSTMENT. A Mercarb type carburetor is used. Standard main jet (13 — Fig. MY2-11) size is 0.041 inch (1.04 mm) for normal operation at elevations below 2500 feet (762 m). Preliminary adjustment of idle mixture screw (4) is 1½ turns out from a lightly seated position. Recommended idle speed is 600-700 rpm in gear with engine at normal operating temperature.

With the outboard motor properly mounted on a boat or a suitable test tank, immerse the lower unit. Connect a tachometer and set it on the ap-

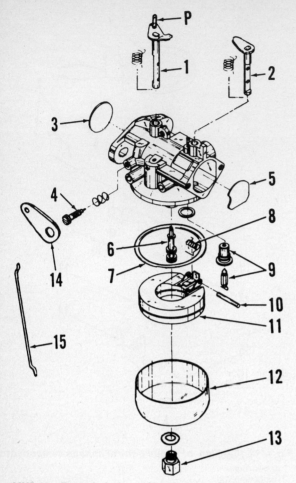

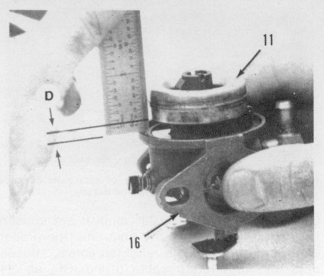

Fig. MY2-12—Float level is measured by inverting carburetor body (16) and measuring distance (D) from carburetor body surface to top of float (11). Refer to text.

Fig. MY2-11—Exploded view of carburetor. Remote idle mixture lever (14) and link (15) are used on later models.

P. Pickup pin
1. Throttle shaft
2. Choke shaft
3. Throttle plate
4. Idle mixture screw
5. Choke plate
6. Nozzle
7. Gasket
8. Spring
9. Fuel inlet valve
10. Float pin
11. Float
12. Float bowl
13. Main jet
14. Remote idle mixture lever
15. Link

propriate range scale. Start the engine and allow it to warm up to normal operating temperature. Position the throttle control twist grip to the complete closed position. Place the gear shift lever in the "Forward" position. Accelerate the engine to 1000 rpm, then adjust idle mixture screw (4) until smooth engine operation is noted. Idle engine at the recommended 600-700 rpm and note if smooth engine operation is still present. If not, make fine adjustment of idle mixture screw (4).

On models equipped with a remote idle mixture control, press lever (14) over idle mixture screw (4) so lever points in the 10 o'clock direction. Do not disturb the idle mixture screw setting.

Reinstall engine's top cover.

OVERHAUL. Remove engine's top cover. Remove screws retaining air intake cover and air intake assembly. Disconnect choke cable from carburetor and mounting bracket. Close fuel shut-off valve, then disconnect the fuel supply hose at the carburetor inlet. If equipped, remove remote idle lever (14) from idle mixture screw (4). Clean all external surfaces and remove accumulated dirt and grease. Remove the two nuts securing the carburetor and withdraw the carburetor assembly.

With reference to Fig. MY2-11, disassemble the carburetor and note any discrepancies which must be corrected before reassembly. Remove all gaskets (label if needed for later reference) and set to the side.

Thoroughly clean all carburetor parts in a suitable solvent and inspect for damage and excessive wear. Note that plastic and rubber components should not be subjected to some cleaning solutions. Blow dry with clean compressed air. If compressed air is not available, use only lint-free cloths to wipe dry. Do not use a drill bit or wire to clean jets. Enlargement or damage of the calibrated holes may affect engine performance.

With reference to Fig. MY2-11, reassemble the carburetor components with new gaskets. Note that the new gaskets should match up with those removed. If not, check with your parts supplier to be sure you have the correct gasket set.

To determine the float level, invert carburetor body (16—Fig. MY2-12) and measure distance (D) from carburetor body surface to top of float (11). Distance (D) should be 5/64 to 7/64 inch (2-2.8 mm). Adjust distance (D) by bending tang on float (11).

When reinstalling the carburetor, place a new gasket between carburetor and intake manifold. Securely tighten the retaining nuts. Complete reassembly in the reverse order of disassembly with the exception of the engine cover. Initially adjust idle mixture screw (4—Fig. MY2-11) 1½ turns out from a lightly seated position.

MERC 3.5, 3.6 AND 4.5
MERC 40 (1969-1974) AND 45

Specifications

Rated horsepower/rpm 3.5/4500-5000
                        3.6/4500-5000
                        4.0/4500-5500
                        4.5/4500-5500
Bore . . . . .2 in.
                        (50.8 mm)
Stroke . . . . .1 ¾ in.
                        (44.45 mm)
Number of cylinders 1
Displacement . . . . .5.5 cu. in
                        (90.1 cc)
Spark plug:
   Type . . . . .See Text
   Electrode gap . . . . .See Text
Ignition . . . . .See Text
Idle speed . . . . .See Text
Fuel:oil ratio 50:1
Fuel pump:
   Discharge pressure at WOT . . . . .2 psi
                        (14 kPa)
Gearcase oil capacity . . . . .See Text

Maintenance

LUBRICATION

ENGINE. The engine is lubricated by oil mixed with the fuel. The fuel should be regular leaded, low lead or unleaded gasoline with a minimum pump octane rating of 86. Recommended oil is Quicksilver Formula 50-D Outboard Lubricant or a BIA certified two-stroke motor oil. The recommended fuel:oil ratio for normal operation is 50:1.

LOWER UNIT. The lower unit gears and bearings are lubricated by oil contained in the gearcase. The recommended oil is Quicksilver Super-Duty Gear Lubricant. The gearcase oil capacity is 2¾ ounces (81 mL) on 3.5 and 3.6 models and 3¾ ounces (111 mL) on 4.5, 40 and 45 models. The gearcase oil level should be checked every 30 days and the lubricant renewed periodically. The gearcase is drained and filled through the same plug port (D—Fig. MY3-1 or Fig. MY3-2). An oil level (vent) port (L) is used to indicate the full oil level of the gearcase and to ease oil drainage.

To drain the oil, place the outboard motor in a vertical position. Remove drain plug (D) and oil level plug (L), and allow the lubricant to drain into a suitable container.

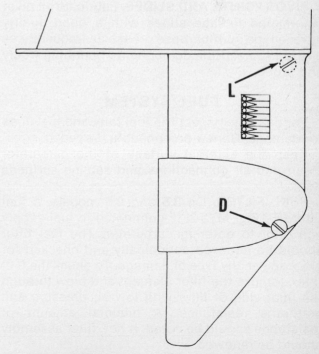

Fig. MY3-1—View showing lower unit gearcase drain and fill plug (D) and oil level (vent) plug (L) on 3.5 and 3.6 models. Note that oil level (vent) plug (L) is located on the port side of the lower unit.

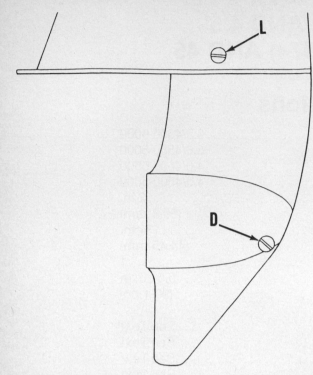

Fig. MY3-2—View showing lower unit gearcase drain and fill plug (D) and oil level (vent) plug (L) on 4.5, 40 and 45 models.

To fill the gearcase with oil, place the outboard in a vertical position. Add oil through drain plug (D) opening with an oil feeder until the oil begins to overflow from oil level plug (L) port. Reinstall oil level plug (L) with a new gasket, if needed, and tighten. Remove oil feeder, then reinstall drain plug (D) with a new gasket, if needed, and tighten.

PIVOT POINTS AND SLIDES. Lubricate all pivot points and linkage slides with a good quality marine type multipurpose grease as frequently as needed to keep the components operating freely and properly.

FUEL SYSTEM

Periodically inspect the fuel tank and fuel lines for damage. Renew components if needed.

Keep the external surface of the carburetor clean and all connections and sealing surfaces tight.

FUEL FILTER. On 3.5 and 3.6 models, a fuel filter (F—Fig. MY3-3) is connected in fuel supply line prior to entering carburetor. The fuel filter should be removed periodically and checked for blockage or any type of damage. To check the fuel filter, remove the filter element and blow through the inlet side of filter with low air pressure and note the resistance. A minimal amount of resistance should be noted. If not, filter assembly should be renewed.

On 40, 45 and 4.5 models, a strainer (3) contained in strainer cover (1) and mounted on top of carburetor bowl cover (5) is used to filter the fuel prior

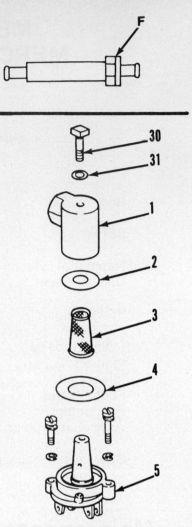

Fig. MY3-3—View showing a disposable type fuel filter (F) used on 3.5 and 3.6 models and a reusable type strainer (3) used on 4.5, 40 and 45 models.

F. Disposable type fuel filter	
1. Strainer cover	4. Gasket
2. Gasket	5. Bowl cover
3. Strainer	30. Cap screw
	31. Gasket

to it entering the carburetor float bowl. To inspect, remove cap screw (30) and withdraw strainer cover (1) and strainer (3). Clean strainer (3) in a suitable solvent and blow dry with clean compressed air. Inspect strainer (3). If excessive blockage or damage is noted, renew strainer. If needed, renew gaskets.

FUEL PUMP. The fuel pump is operated by crankcase pressure changes from the up and down movement of the piston. When the crankcase pressure decreases (the piston is moving upward), the pump diaphragm is pulled toward the crankcase allowing fuel to enter the pump body and closing the discharge check valve. When the crankcase pressure increases (the piston is moving downward), the diaphragm is pushed outward discharging the fuel to the carburetor and closing the inlet check valve. This pulsating action allows for continuous fuel flow.

Fig. MY3-4—View showing a Mikuni type fuel pump. The fuel pump is nonrepairable, so the complete fuel pump assembly must be renewed if malfunction is noted.

The check valves are used to prevent reverse flow of the fuel.

The fuel hoses must be connected according to fuel flow. The fuel supply line connected to the fuel pump inlet port and the line routed toward the fuel filter or carburetor assembly connected to the outlet port.

The Mikuni fuel pump shown in Fig. MY3-4 is not repairable. The complete fuel pump assembly must be renewed if malfunction is noted.

On models equipped with the fuel pump shown in Fig. MY3-5, proceed as follows to overhaul: Remove the engine's top cover and disconnect the fuel tank supply hose at the outboard motor connector. Disconnect the fuel hoses at the fuel pump inlet and outlet nozzles and label if needed. Remove any components that will obstruct in fuel pump removal, then remove the fuel pump assembly.

With reference to Fig. MY3-5, disassemble the fuel pump assembly. Inspect all components for damage and excessive wear and renew if needed.

With reference to Fig. MY3-5, reassemble the fuel pump assembly with new gaskets. Remount the fuel pump assembly and secure in place.

NOTE: Fuel pump and engine malfunction will result if the fuel pump and all connections are not airtight.

Complete reassembly.

FUEL TANK. It may be necessary to remove the fuel tank for cleaning or for access to underlying engine components.

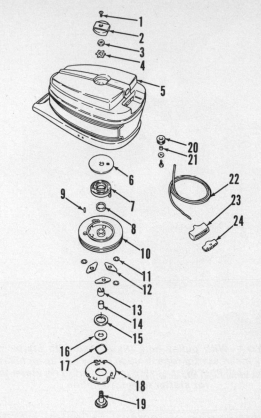

Fig. MY3-6—Exploded view of rewind starter assembly used on 4.5, 40 and 45 models.

1. Screw	13. Nylon bushing
2. Trim cap	14. Spacer
3. Nut	15. Retainer
4. Tab washer	16. Washer
5. Cover	17. Wave washer
6. Retainer washer	18. Pawl retainer plate
7. Rewind spring	19. Pulley shaft
8. Spring guide bushing	20. Pulley
9. Rope retainer pin	21. Spacer
10. Pulley	22. Starter rope
11. Wave washer	23. Handle
12. Pawl	24. Anchor

To remove the fuel tank, first remove the engine's top cover. Close the fuel shut-off valve. Disconnect the outlet hose at the fuel shut-off valve and connect a suitable length of hose to allow for tank drainage. Open fuel shut-off valve and allow the fuel to drain off into a suitable container. Disconnect the fuel hose from the fuel tank outlet. Remove the fuel tank mounting components, then withdraw the fuel tank.

Fig. MY3-5—Exploded view of diaphragm type fuel pump used on some models.

1. Base	
2. Check valve assy.	5. Gasket
3. Gasket	6. Diaphragm
4. Body	7. Gasket
	8. Cover

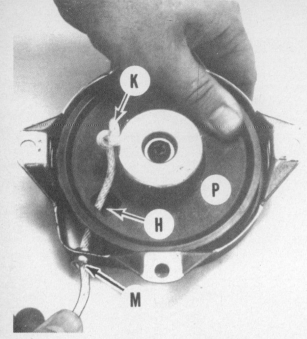

Fig. MY3-7—With pulley hole (H) aligned with starter cover hole (M), insert starter rope through pulley and cover holes and pull rope until knot (K) is seated in rope pulley (P). Refer to text for starter rope installation.

Reverse order of removal to install fuel tank, then refill.

STARTER
Models 4.5, 40 And 45

When starter rope (22 — Fig. MY3-6) is pulled, pulley (10) will rotate. As pulley (10) rotates, the three drive pawls (12) move apart thus meshing with the starter cup and cranking the engine.

When starter rope (22) is released, pulley (10) is rotated in the reverse direction by force from rewind spring (7). As pulley (10) rotates, starter rope (22) is rewound and drive pawls (12) are disengaged from the starter cup.

To overhaul the manual starter, first remove the engine's top cover (5).

⚠WARNING

Care should be exercised when working with or around a coiled starter rewind spring as sudden uncoiling can cause injury. Safety eyewear and gloves are recommended.

To disassemble, remove screw (1) and trim cap (2). Bend tabs of tab washer (4) away from nut (3). Insert a screwdriver in slot of pulley shaft (19) and loosen the left-hand thread nut (3). Allow screwdriver and pulley shaft (19) to turn clockwise until rewind spring (7) unwinds. Pry anchor (24) from starter handle (23) and remove anchor and

handle from starter rope (22). Remove nut (3), invert cover (5) and remove components (6 through 19) with starter rope (22). Make sure that rewind spring (7) remains in recess as pulley (10) is removed. Use suitable hand protection and extract rewind spring (7) from pulley (10). Allow rewind spring to uncoil in a safe area.

Inspect all components for damage and excessive wear and renew if needed.

NOTE: During reassembly, lubricate all friction surfaces with a suitable low temperature grease.

Assemble by reversing the disassembly procedure. Install spring guide bushing (8) on hub of pulley (10) with chamfered end of bushing toward pulley (10). Be sure that pawls (12) are all installed with the radius toward the outside and the identification mark (dot) away from pulley (10). Install wave washer retainer (15) with cup end out and position washer (16) and wave washer (17) in cup. Make certain that tang on spring retainer (6) engages slot in pulley shaft (19).

Position assembled manual starter with end of pulley shaft (19) through cover (5) and install tab washer (4) and nut (3). Pull free end of starter rope (22) through cover (5) and starter handle (23), then secure in anchor (24). Turn pulley shaft (19) counterclockwise until starter handle (23) is pulled into the proper released position, then continue to turn pulley shaft (19) an additional 1¼ turns. Tighten nut (3) and bend tabs of tab washer (4) to secure nut (3) in place. Install trim cap (2) and secure to cover (5) with screw (1). Pull starter rope (22) out to full length while checking for freedom of travel, then allow starter rope (22) to rewind onto pulley (10). Starter handle (23) should be drawn back into the proper released position.

Install engine's top cover (5) to complete reassembly.

Models 3.5 And 3.6

The manual rewind starter assembly cannot be serviced as individual components, with the exception of the starter rope. Should internal starter damage be noted, the complete manual starter must be renewed. Proceed as follows to service starter rope:

To renew the starter rope, first remove the engine's top cover and the nuts retaining the starter to the engine. Withdraw the manual starter assembly. If the starter rope is not broken, extract the rope anchor from the starter handle. Disconnect the starter rope from the anchor and allow the rope to wind into the starter. Unwind the starter rope from the rope pulley.

Tie a knot (K — Fig. MY3-7) in the end of the new starter rope. As viewed from the pulley side of the starter, rotate rope pulley (P) in a counterclock-

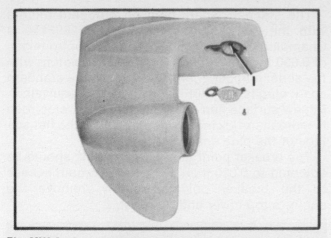

Fig. MY3-8—View showing port (I) located on the bottom side of the antiventilation plate used as the water inlet for the cooling system on 4.5, 40 and 45 models.

Fig. MY3-10—A typical view of a propeller setup used on all models. Thrust hub (3), propeller (1) and thrust hub (2) are mounted on propeller shaft (4) and retained by nut (5). Note that some models are equipped with a flat washer between thrust hub (3) and nut (5).

wise direction (against spring tension) until pulley (P) stops. Slowly allow pulley (P) to rotate clockwise until the rope hole in pulley (P) and starter cover are adjacent as shown in Fig. MY3-7. Thread unknotted end of rope through pulley hole (H) and starter cover hole (M) until knot (K) is seated in pulley (P). While keeping tension on starter rope, release pulley (P) and allow approximately 12 inches (30.5 cm) of rope to wind into the starter. Thread starter rope end through starter handle and secure in anchor. Release pulley (P) and allow the starter rope to completely wind into the starter.

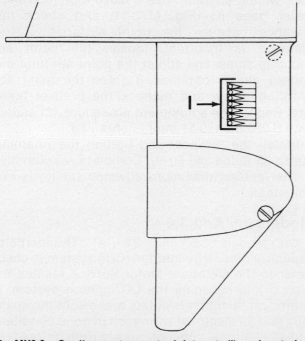

Fig. MY3-9—Cooling system water inlet ports (I) are located on the port and starboard side of the lower unit on 3.5 and 3.6 models.

When installing the starter, note that the slotted mounting ear slides under the fuel tank mounting tab. Before tightening the starter retaining nuts, pull the starter rope so starter dogs engage the starter cup thereby centering the starter. Tighten mounting nuts while maintaining tension on the rope.

COOLING SYSTEM

Port (I — Fig. MY3-8) located on the bottom side of the antiventilation plate is used as the water inlet for the cooling system on 4.5, 40 and 45 models. The water passages in the port cover must be kept clean of all foreign matter to ensure efficient operation of the cooling system.

Ports (I — Fig. MY3-9) located on the port and starboard side of the lower unit are used as the water inlets for the cooling system on 3.5 and 3.6 models. The ports must be kept clean of all foreign matter to ensure efficient operation of the cooling system.

⚠CAUTION

Do not operate outboard motor unless the lower unit is immersed in water, otherwise, the water pump impeller will be damaged.

PROPELLER

Consult your local dealer or the manufacturer for the specifications pertaining to the standard propeller used on your model of outboard motor. Optional propellers are available. Select a propeller that will allow the engine at full throttle to reach maximum operating rpm range (4500-5500).

Fig. MY3-11—View showing the use of a feeler gage (G) to check the clearance between the breaker point contact surfaces on 4.5, 40 and 45 models.

⚠WARNING

If applicable, shift directional control lever to "NEUTRAL." Disconnect the spark plug leads and properly ground leads before performing any propeller service, otherwise, accidental starting can occur if propeller shaft is rotated.

Shown in Fig. MY3-10 is a typical view of a propeller setup used on all models. Some models are equipped with a flat washer between thrust hub (3) and nut (5).

To remove the propeller, unscrew propeller retaining nut (5). Withdraw thrust hub (3), propeller (1) and thrust hub (2) from propeller shaft (4).

Inspect all components for damage and excessive wear and renew if needed.

Apply Perfect Seal or a suitable equivalent to the propeller shaft splines, then install thrust hub (2), propeller (1) and thrust hub (3) on propeller shaft (4). Install propeller retaining nut (5) and securely tighten.

Tune-Up

IGNITION SYSTEM
Models 4.5, 40 And 45

All models are equipped with a magneto ignition, however, late models (serial number 2771622 and later) are equipped with a "Thunderbolt Phase-Maker" electronic ignition magento. Refer to the Outboard Motor Service Manual for testing and servicing the ignition system except for servicing the breaker point assembly as outlined later in this section. If engine malfunction is noted and the ignition system is suspected, make sure the spark plug and all electrical wiring is in good condition and all electrical connections are tight before proceeding to troubleshooting the ignition system.

The standard spark plug on outboard motors with the serial number 2498136 to 2693114 is Champion L9J or AC M45FF with an electrode gap of 0.030 inch (0.76 mm). On outboard motors with the serial number 2771622 and later, the standard spark plug is AC V40FFK or a suitable equivalent. Renew surface gap spark plug if center electrode is more than 1/32 inch (0.79 mm) below the flat surface of the plug end.

The breaker point gap on all models should be adjusted to 0.020 inch (0.51 mm). To gain access to the breaker point assembly, remove the engine's top cover and flywheel.

⚠WARNING

Be sure suitable tools are used to remove the flywheel. Damage resultant from the misapplication of force or the use of incorrect tools may cause engine damage, engine malfunction or personal injury.

Inspect the breaker point surfaces for excessive wear, pitting and any other damage. If needed, renew breaker point assembly and condenser.

NOTE: The cam for the breaker point assembly is keyed to the crankshaft and should be installed with arrow up and indicating direction of rotation.

To adjust, rotate the crankshaft until the cam lobe places the breaker point contact surfaces at their widest position. Use a 0.020 inch (0.51 mm) feeler gage (G—Fig. MY3-11) and check the distance between the point surfaces. If the distance is incorrect, loosen the point set securing screw and adjust the point set until the correct gap is obtained. Tighten the point set securing screw and recheck the breaker point gap. Repeat the adjustment procedure, if needed, until 0.020 inch (0.51 mm) is obtained.

Install the flywheel and tighten the retaining nut to 35 ft.-lbs. (48 N·m). Complete reassembly.

The ignition maximum advance timing is not adjustable.

Models 3.5 And 3.6

On Models 3.5 and 3.6, a "Thunderbolt" capacitor discharge ignition (CDI) system is used. Refer to the Outboard Motor Service Manual for testing and servicing the CD ignition system. If engine malfunction is noted, make sure the spark plug and all electrical wiring are in good condition and all electrical connections are tight before proceeding to troubleshooting the CD ignition system.

Fig. MY3-12—On 40 model outboard motors, 1969 model year, the speed control linkage should be adjusted so throttle follower (20) just contacts cam (C) at 1000 rpm. Adjust by loosening screw (21) and repositioning throttle follower lever.

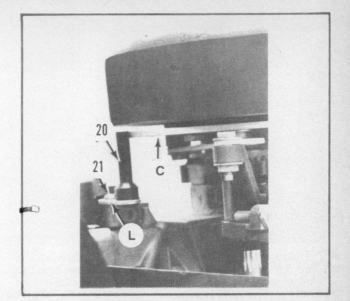

Fig. MY3-13—View of speed control cam (C), throttle follower (20), follower lever (L) and adjusting screw (21) used on Model 40 after 1969, and 4.5 and 45 models. Refer to text for adjustment.

The standard spark plug is Champion L81Y or Autolite AE22. A Champion QL81Y is recommended by the manufacturer should radio frequency interference suppression be required. Spark plug electrode gap should be 0.035 inch (0.89 mm).

Ignition timing is nonadjustable.

SPEED CONTROL LINKAGE
Models 4.5, 40 And 45

The speed control twist grip, through the use of linkage, operates the magneto stator plate to advance or retard the ignition timing. The carburetor throttle valve is synchronized to open as the timing is advanced. Before attempting to synchronize the throttle opening to the ignition advance, adjust the breaker point gap as outlined in the IGNITION SYSTEM section and the idle fuel mixture as outlined in the CARBURETOR section.

On Model 40 outboard motors, 1969 model year, run the engine until it reaches normal operating temperature. Engage the forward gear, then rotate the twist grip until the engine is operating at 1000 rpm. With the engine speed maintained at 1000 rpm, note the position of control cam (C—Fig. MY3-12). Control cam (C) should just contact throttle follower (20). Adjust by loosening screw (21) and repositioning throttle follower lever. Tighten screw (21) to secure adjustment.

On all other 4.5, 40 and 45 models, adjustment is performed with the engine stopped. Rotate the twist grip in the forward gear direction until the maximum speed setting is obtained. Use a feeler gage or a suitable tool and measure the play between throttle follower (20—Fig. MY3-13) and control cam (C). Throttle follower (20) should have almost completely opened the throttle with approximately 0.050 inch (1.27 mm) play remaining.

If incorrect, loosen screw (21) and reposition throttle follower lever (L).

To position control cam (C—Fig. MY3-14) for correct throttle pickup, first install a dial indicator assembly in the spark plug hole and properly zero the indicator needle with the piston at TDC. Rotate the crankshaft until the piston is exactly 0.005 inch (0.13 mm) ATDC. Attach a point checker or a continuity meter to the white wire coming from the breaker point assembly and to a suitable engine ground. Move the twist grip from the fast position toward the slow position until the point tester's pointer moves from "OPEN" to "CLOSE" or the continuity meter shows that the contact

Fig. MY3-14—View of control cam (C), retaining screws (S) and throttle follower (20). Refer to text for adjustment of throttle pickup on Model 40 after 1969, and 4.5 and 45 models.

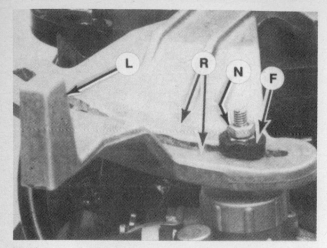

Fig. MY3-15 — View of carburetor and speed control lever (L) on 3.5 and 3.6 models. The carburetor throttle slide is pulled upward as ramp follower (F) rides up speed control lever ramp (R). Locknut (N) is used to secure adjustment of ramp follower (F). Refer to text for adjustment procedures.

points just close. With the piston at 0.005 inch (0.13 mm) ATDC and the contact points having just closed, the control cam (C) should be just touching (T) follower (20). If control cam (C) and follower (20) are not touching or if the throttle is partially open, loosen the two screws (S) attaching control cam (C) and reposition the control cam as required. Recheck the maximum throttle opening as previously outlined, very little adjustment is normally required.

Models 3.5 And 3.6

The ignition timing is advanced as speed control lever (L—Fig. MY3-15) attached to the stator base plate is moved towards the full throttle position. The carburetor throttle slide is pulled upward as ramp follower (F) rides up speed control lever ramp (R).

To synchronize the throttle opening with the speed control lever (L) movement, first adjust the engine idle speed as outlined in the following CARBURETOR section. Then position the speed control lever at its lowest idle position with the engine stopped. Loosen locknut (N) and adjust ramp follower (F) so the follower just touches speed control lever ramp (R). Do not rotate the throttle slide stud. Tighten locknut (N). Throttle slide should rise just as speed control lever moves from idle speed.

CARBURETOR
Models 4.5, 40 And 45

ADJUSTMENT. Standard carburetor is a Tillotson KB-10A. Standard main jet (16—Fig. MY3-16) size is 0.036 inch (0.91 mm) for normal operation. Other main jet sizes are available for adjusting the calibration for altitude or other special condi-

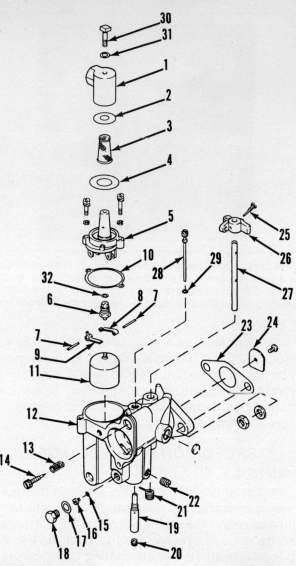

Fig. MY3-16—Exploded view of a Tillotson KB-10A carburetor.

1. Strainer cover	17. Gasket
2. Gasket	18. Plug
3. Strainer	19. Main nozzle
4. Gasket	20. Plug
5. Bowl cover	21. Spring
6. Inlet needle & seat	22. Plug
7. Pins	23. Gasket
8. Primary lever	24. Throttle valve
9. Secondary lever	25. Screw
10. Gasket	26. Throttle lever
11. Float	27. Throttle shaft
12. Body	28. Idle tube
13. Spring	29. Gasket
14. Idle mixture screw	30. Cap screw
15. Gasket	31. Gasket
16. Main jet	32. Gasket

tions. Preliminary adjustment of idle mixture screw (14) is one turn out from a lightly seated position. Recommended idle speed is 650-700 rpm with engine at normal operating temperature and in gear.

With the outboard motor properly mounted on a boat or a suitable test tank, immerse the lower unit. Connect a tachometer and set it on the appropriate range scale. Start the engine and allow it to warm up to normal operating temperature. With

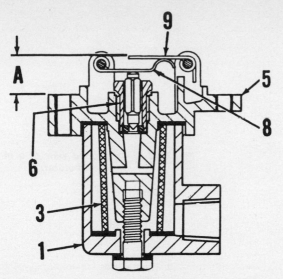

Fig. MY3-17—Cross-sectional view of float mechanism. Distance (A) should be 13/32 inch (10.32 mm). Refer to text for adjustment procedure and Fig. MY3-16 for parts indentification.

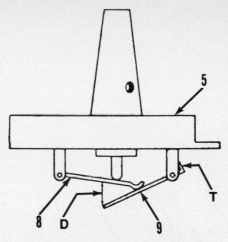

Fig. MY3-18—With bowl cover (5) upright, distance (D) between primary lever (8) and end of secondary lever (9) should be ¼ inch (6.4 mm). Bend tab (T) to adjust.

the engine running at idle speed while in forward gear, turn idle mixture screw (14) until smooth engine operation is noted. Adjust engine idle speed until 650-700 rpm is obtained.

Reinstall engine's top cover.

OVERHAUL. Remove engine's top cover. Remove choke and throttle linkage from carburetor. Disconnect the fuel supply hose at the carburetor inlet. Remove any other components that will interfere with carburetor removal. Clean all external surfaces and remove accumulated dirt and grease. Remove the two nuts securing the carburetor and withdraw the carburetor assembly.

With reference to Fig. MY3-16, disassemble the carburetor and note any discrepancies which must be corrected before reassembly. Remove all gaskets (label if needed for later reference) and set to the side.

Thoroughly clean all carburetor parts in a suitable solvent and inspect for damage and excessive wear. Note that plastic and rubber components should not be subjected to some cleaning solutions. Blow dry with clean compressed air. If compressed air is not available, use only lint-free cloths to wipe dry. Do not use a drill bit or wire to clean jets. Enlargement or damage of the calibrated holes may affect engine performance.

With reference to Fig. MY3-16, reassemble the carburetor components with new gaskets. Note that the new gaskets should match up with those removed. If not, check with your parts supplier to be sure you have the correct gasket set.

To determine the float level, invert bowl cover (5—Fig. MY3-17) with inlet needle and seat (6), primary lever (8) and secondary lever (9) installed. Measure distance (A) from carburetor body sur-

face to top of secondary lever (9). Distance (A) should be 13/32 inch (10.32 mm). Adjust distance (A) by bending curved end of primary lever (8). Turn bowl cover (5—Fig. MY3-18) upright and measure distance (D) between primary lever (8) and end of secondary lever (9). Distance (D) should be ¼ inch (6.4 mm). Bend tab (T) to adjust. The contact spring located in center of float (11—Fig. MY3-16) should extend 3/32 inch (2.38 mm) above top of float. Check to see if spring has been stretched or damaged.

Reinstall the carburetor with a new mounting gasket and securely tighten the retaining nuts. Complete reassembly in the reverse order of disassembly with the exception of the engine cover. Initially adjust idle mixture screw (14—Fig. MY3-16) one turn out from a lightly seated position.

Models 3.5 And 3.6

ADJUSTMENT. Standard carburetor is a Mikuni VM-16. Standard main jet (16—Fig. MY3-19) size is #150 for normal operation at elevations below 2500 feet (762 m). Preliminary positioning of clip (7) in jet needle (8) is the fourth groove from the top. On 3.5 models equipped with optional fuel pump, position clip (7) in third groove from the top. Inserting clip (7) in a higher notch will lean mid-range mixture while inserting clip n a lower notch will richen mid-range mixture. Preliminary adjustment of idle mixture screw (231) is two turns out from a lightly seated position. Recommended idle speed is 700-900 rpm with engine at normal operating temperature and in gear (3.5 models).

With the outboard motor properly mounted on a boat or a suitable test tank, immerse the lower unit. Connect a tachometer and set it on the appropriate range scale. Start the engine and allow it to warm up to normal operating temperature. If

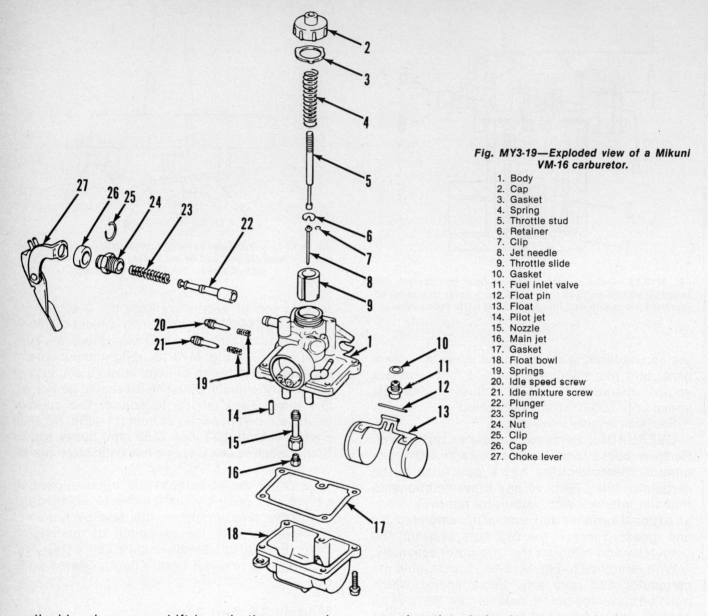

Fig. MY3-19—Exploded view of a Mikuni VM-16 carburetor.

1. Body
2. Cap
3. Gasket
4. Spring
5. Throttle stud
6. Retainer
7. Clip
8. Jet needle
9. Throttle slide
10. Gasket
11. Fuel inlet valve
12. Float pin
13. Float
14. Pilot jet
15. Nozzle
16. Main jet
17. Gasket
18. Float bowl
19. Springs
20. Idle speed screw
21. Idle mixture screw
22. Plunger
23. Spring
24. Nut
25. Clip
26. Cap
27. Choke lever

applicable, place gear shift lever in the engaged position. Move speed control lever to the slowest idle speed setting, then adjust idle speed screw (20) until the engine is at the recommended 700-900 rpm and note if smooth engine operation is present. If not, adjust idle mixture screw (21) until smooth engine operation is noted. Note that idle mixture screw (21) regulates an idle air passage and will lean the idle mixture when turned counterclockwise. Readjust idle speed screw (20) until the recommended idle speed is obtained.

Refer to the SPEED CONTROL LINKAGE section and adjust ramp follower (F—Fig. MY3-15) as outlined.

Reinstall engine's top cover.

OVERHAUL. Remove engine's top cover. On 3.5 models, move speed control lever to the "STOP" position, then remove the cap screw and washer securing the air intake cover and withdraw the cover assembly. Hold ramp follower (F—Fig. MY3-15) stationary, then loosen and remove locknut (N) and ramp follower (F). Move speed control lever to the full "FAST" position. Close fuel shut-off valve, then disconnect the fuel supply hose at the carburetor inlet. Clean all external surfaces and remove accumlated dirt and grease. Remove the two nuts and washers, if equipped, securing the carburetor and withdraw the carburetor assembly.

With reference to Fig. MY3-19, disassemble the carburetor and note any discrepancies which must be corrected before reassembly. Remove all gaskets (label if needed for later reference) and set to the side.

Thoroughly clean all carburetor parts in a suitable solvent and inspect for damage and excessive wear. Note that plastic and rubber components should not be subjected to some clean-

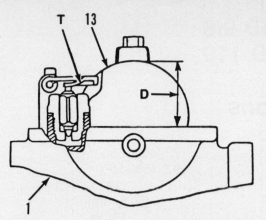

Fig. MY3-20—With carburetor body (1) inverted, distance (D) from carburetor body surface to top of float (13) should be 7/8 to 31/32 inch (22.2-24.6 mm). Adjust distance (D) by bending float arm tang (T).

Fig. MY3-21—View shows position of idle speed screw (20) and idle mixture screw (21).

ing solutions. Blow dry with clean compressed air. If compressed air is not available, use only lint-free cloths to wipe dry. Do not use a drill bit or wire to clean jets. Enlargement or damage of the calibrated holes may affect engine performance.

With reference to Fig. MY3-19, reassemble the carburetor components with new gaskets. Note that the new gaskets should match up with those removed. If not, check with your parts supplier to be sure you have the correct gasket set.

To determine the float level, invert carburetor body (1—Fig. MY3-20) and measure distance (D) from carburetor body surface to top of float (13). Distance (D) should be 7/8 to 31/32 inch (22.2-24.6 mm). Adjust distance (D) by bending float arm tang (T).

Reinstall the carburetor and secure with lockwashers, if equipped, and nuts. Complete reassembly in the reverse order of disassembly with the exception of the engine cover. Adjust speed control lever ramp (R—Fig. MY3-15) and ramp follower (F) so the carburetor throttle slide just starts to raise when the speed control handle is moved from the slowest idle speed setting. Initially adust idle mixture screw (21—Fig. MY3-21) two turns out from a lightly seated position.

MERC 7.5 AND 9.8
MERC 75 AND 110

Specifications

Hp/rpm:
- Merc 7.5 & 75 . . . . 7.5/4500-5500*
- Merc 9.8 & 110 . . . . 9.8/4500-5500*

Bore . . . . .2 in.
(50.8 mm)

Stroke . . . . 1 ¾ in.
(44.4 mm)

Number of cylinders 2

Displacement . . . . 10.9 cu. in.
(178.6 cc)

Spark plug . . . . .See Text

Ignition . . . . .See Text

Carburetor make:
- 1972 and earlier . . . . .Tillotson
- 1973 and later . . . . .Mercarb

Idle speed (in gear) . . . . 550-750 rpm

Fuel:oil ratio. 50:1

Fuel pump — nonintegral with carburetor:
- Discharge pressure at WOT . . . . .2 psi
(14 kPa)

Gearcase oil capacity . . . . 3 ¾ oz.§
(111 mL)

*Rated rpm on 7.5 models above serial number 5226934 and 9.8 models above serial number 5206549 is 5000-5800.
§Capacity on early 75 and 110 models is 3 ounces (90 mL).

Maintenance

LUBRICATION

ENGINE. The engine is lubricated by oil mixed with the fuel. The fuel should be regular leaded, low lead or unleaded gasoline with a minimum pump octane rating of 86. Recommended oil is Quicksilver Formula 50-D Outboard Lubricant or a BIA certified two-stroke motor oil. The recommended fuel:oil ratio for normal operation is 50:1.

LOWER UNIT. The lower unit gears and bearings are lubricated by oil contained in the gearcase. The recommended oil is Quicksilver Super-Duty Gear Lubricant. The gearcase oil capacity is 3 ounces (90 mL) on early 75 and 110 models and 3 ¾ ounces (111 mL) on late 75 ad 110 models and 7.5 and 9.8 models. The gearcase oil level should be checked every 30 days and the lubricant renewed periodically. The gearcase is drained and filled through the same plug port (D — Fig. MY4-1). An oil level (vent) port (L) is used to indicate the full oil level of the gearcase and to ease oil drainage.

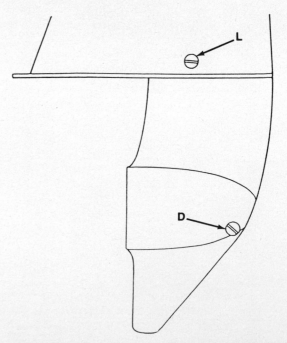

Fig. MY4-1 — View showing lower unit gearcase drain and fill plug (D) and oil level (vent) plug (L).

Illustrations Courtesy Mercury

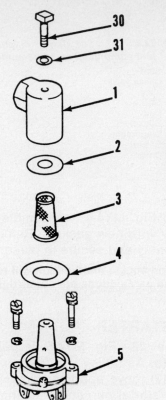

Fig. MY4-2—View showing reusable type fuel strainer (3) used on models with Tillotson type carburetors.

1. Strainer cover
2. Gasket
3. Strainer
4. Gasket
5. Bowl cover
30. Cap screw
31. Gasket

Fig. MY4-3—View showing fuel strainer (5) located behind fuel pump inlet cover (3) on models with Mercarb type carburetor.

1. Cap screw	3. Inlet cover	5. Strainer
2. Washer	4. Gasket	6. Pump cover

To drain the oil, place the outboard motor in a vertical position. Remove drain plug (D) and oil level plug (L), and allow the lubricant to drain into a suitable container.

To fill the gearcase with oil, place the outboard motor in a vertical position. Add oil through drain plug (D) opening with an oil feeder until the oil begins to overflow from oil level plug (L) port. Reinstall oil level plug (L) with a new gasket, if needed, and tighten. Remove oil feeder, then reinstall drain plug (D) with a new gasket, if needed, and tighten.

PIVOT POINTS AND SLIDES. Lubricate all pivot points and linkage slides with a good quality marine type multipurpose grease as frequently as needed to keep the components operating freely and properly.

FUEL SYSTEM

Periodically inspect the fuel lines and connections for damage. Renew components if needed.

Keep the external surface of the carburetor clean and all connections and sealing surfaces tight.

FUEL FILTER. On early 75 and 100 models equipped with a Tillotson type carburetor, a strainer (3—Fig. MY4-2) contained in strainer cover (1) and mounted on top carburetor bowl cover (5) is used to filter the fuel prior to it entering the carburetor float bowl. To inspect, remove cap screw (30) and withdraw strainer cover (1) and

strainer (3). Clean strainer (3) in a suitable solvent and blow dry with clean compressed air. Inspect strainer (3). If excessive blockage or damage is noted, renew strainer. If needed, renew gaskets.

On all models equipped with a Mercarb type carburetor, a strainer (5—Fig. MY4-3) positioned behind inlet fitting (3) is used to filter the fuel prior to it entering the fuel pump. To inspect, remove cap screw (1) and withdraw inlet fitting (3) and strainer (5). Clean strainer (5) in a suitable solvent and blow dry with clean compressed air. Inspect strainer (5). If excessive blockage or damage is noted, renew strainer. If needed, renew gaskets.

FUEL PUMP. On later models equipped with a Mercarb type carburetor (Fig. MY4-18), the fuel pump is an integral part of the carburetor. Refer to CARBURETOR in the Tune-Up section for fuel pump overhaul. The fuel pump assembly may be overhauled without carburetor removal.

On early models equipped with a Tillotson type carburetor (Fig. MY4-15), a fuel pump (Fig. MY4-4) that is nonintegral with the carburetor is used. The fuel pump is operated by crankcase pressure changes from the up and down movement of the piston. When the crankcase pressure decreases (the piston is moving upward), the pump diaphragm is pulled toward the crankcase allowing fuel to enter the pump body and closing the discharge check valve. When the crankcase pressure increases (the piston is moving downward), the diaphragm is pushed outward discharging the fuel to the carburetor and closing the inlet check valve. This pulsating action allows for continuous fuel flow. The check valves are used to prevent reverse flow of the fuel.

The fuel hoses must be connected according to fuel flow. The fuel supply line connected to the

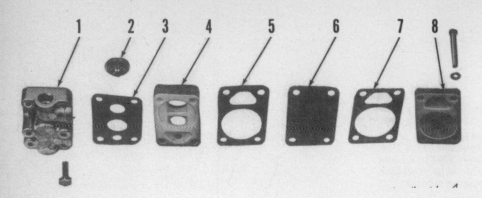

Fig. MY4-4 — Exploded view of diaphragm type fuel pump used on some models.

1. Base
2. Check valve assy.
3. Gasket
4. Body
5. Gasket
6. Diaphragm
7. Gasket
8. Cover

fuel pump inlet port and the line routed toward the carburetor assembly connected to the outlet port.

To overhaul the fuel pump, proceed as follows: Remove the engine's top cover and disconnect the fuel tank supply hose at the outboard motor connector. Disconnect the fuel hoses at the fuel pump inlet and outlet nozzles and label if needed. Remove any components that will obstruct in fuel pump removal, then remove the fuel pump assembly.

With reference to Fig. MY4-4, disassemble the fuel pump assembly. Inspect all components for damage and excessive wear and renew if needed.

With reference to Fig. MY4-4, reassemble the fuel pump assembly with new gaskets. Remount the fuel pump assembly and secure in place.

NOTE: Fuel pump and engine malfunction will result if the fuel pump and all connections are not airtight.

Complete reassembly.

STARTER

When starter rope (22 — Fig. MY4-5) is pulled, pulley (10) will rotate. As pulley (10) rotates, the three drive pawls (12) move apart thus meshing with the flywheel or starter cup and cranking the engine.

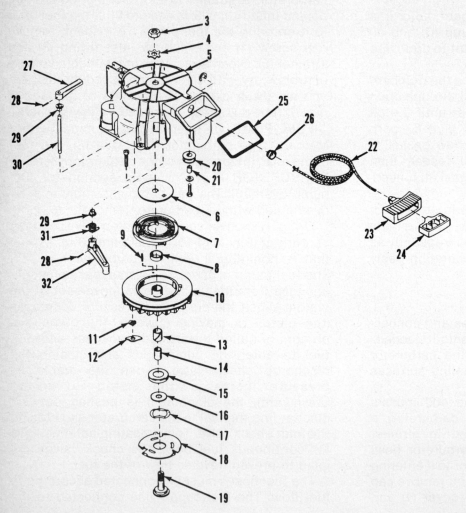
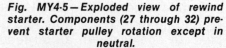

Fig. MY4-5 — Exploded view of rewind starter. Components (27 through 32) prevent starter pulley rotation except in neutral.

3. Nut
4. Tab washer
5. Housing
6. Retainer
7. Rewind spring
8. Bushing
9. Rope retainer pin
10. Pulley
11. Wave washer
12. Pawl
13. Nylon bushing
14. Spacer
15. Retainer
16. Washer
17. Wave washer
18. Plate
19. Pulley shaft
20. Pulley
21. Spacer
22. Starter rope
23. Handle
24. Anchor
25. Seal
26. Rope guide
27. Pulley lock lever
28. Pin
29. Bushing
30. Shaft
31. Spring
32. Actuator

Illustrations Courtesy Mercury

When starter rope (22) is released, pulley (10) is rotated in the reverse direction by force from rewind spring (7). As pulley (10) rotates, starter rope (22) is rewound and drive pawls (12) are disengaged from the flywheel or starter cup.

To overhaul the manual starter, first remove the engine's top cover. Remove the screws retaining the manual starter, then withdraw the starter assembly.

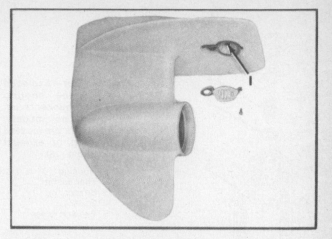

Fig. MY4-6 — View showing port (I) located on the bottom side of the antiventilation plate used as the water inlet for the cooling system.

⚠WARNING

Care should be exercised when working with or around a coiled starter rewind spring as sudden uncoiling can cause injury. Safety eyewear and gloves are recommended.

To disassemble, bend tabs of tab washer (4) away from nut (3). Insert a screwdriver in slot of pulley shaft (19) and loosen the left-hand thread nut (3). Allow screwdriver and pulley shaft (19) to turn clockwise until rewind spring (7) unwinds. Pry anchor (24) from starter handle (23) and remove anchors and handle from starter rope (22). Remove nut (3), invert starter housing (5) and remove manual starter components. Make sure that rewind spring (7) remains in recess as pulley (10) is removed. Use suitable hand protection and extract rewind spring (7) from pulley (10). Allow rewind spring to uncoil in a safe area.

Inspect all components for damage and excessive wear and renew if needed.

NOTE: During reasssembly, lubricate all friction surfaces with a suitable low temperature grease.

Assemble by reversing the disassembly procedure. Install spring guide bushing (8) on hub of pulley (10) with chamfered end of bushing toward pulley. Be sure that pawls (12) are all installed with the radius toward the outside and the identification mark (dot) away from pulley (10). Install wave washer retainer (15) with cup end out and position washer (16) and wave washer (17) in cup. Make certain that tang on spring retainer (6) engages slot in pulley shaft (19).

Position assembled manual starter with end of pulley shaft (19) through starter housing (5) and install tab washer (4) and nut (3). Pull free end of starter rope (22) through housing (5) and starter handle (23), then secure in anchor (24). Turn pulley shaft (19) counterclockwise until starter handle (23) is pulled into the proper released position, then continue to turn pulley shaft (19) an additional 1¼ turns. Tighten nut (3) and bend tabs of tab washer (4) to secure nut (3) in place. Pull starter rope (22) out to full length while checking

for freedom of travel, then allow starter rope (22) to rewind onto pulley (10). Starter handle (23) should be drawn back into the proper released position. Remount manual starter assembly and install engine top cover to complete reassembly.

COOLING SYSTEM

Port (I – Fig. MY4-6) located on the bottom side of the antiventilation plate is used as the water inlet for the cooling system. The water passages in the port cover must be kept clean of all foreign matter to ensure efficient operation of the cooling system.

⚠CAUTION

Do not operate outboard motor unless the lower unit is immersed in water, otherwise, the water pump impeller will be damaged.

On some models, a thermostat (2 – Fig. MY4-6A) positioned in exhaust cover (5) is used to regulate the engine's operating temperature. Note that a thermostat that sticks or stays closed too long could cause engine overheating, resulting in poor engine operation and possible engine damage. A thermostat that opens too quickly or is stuck in the open position will cause the engine not to reach its recommended operating temperature range, resulting in possible engine malfunction and poor engine efficiency. If thermostat malfunction is suspected, remove the thermostat housing (1) located at the top of exhaust cover (5) to gain access to thermostat (2).

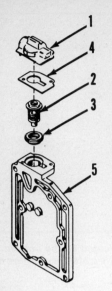

Fig. MY4-6A — Exploded view of the cooling system components used on some models. Components are located at the top of exhaust cover (5).

1. Housing
2. Thermostat
3. Spacer
4. Gasket
5. Exhaust cover

Refer to the Outboard Motor Service Manual if more extensive service to the cooling system is required.

PROPELLER

Consult your local dealer or the manufacturer for the specifications pertaining to the standard propeller used on your model of outboard motor. Optional propellers are available. Select a propeller that will allow the engine at full throttle to reach maximum operating rpm range (4500-5500).

⚠WARNING

Shift directional control lever to "NEUTRAL." Disconnect the spark plug leads and properly ground leads before performing any propeller service, otherwise, accidental starting can occur if propeller shaft is rotated.

Shown in Fig. MY4-7 is a typical view of a propeller setup used on all models. Some models are not equipped with flat washer (4) between splined washer (3) and nut (5).

To remove the propeller, unscrew propeller retaining nut (5). Withdraw flat washer (4), splined washer (3), propeller (1) and guide collar (2) from propeller shaft (6).

Inspect all components for damage and excessive wear and renew if needed.

Apply Perfect Seal or a suitable equivalent to the propeller shaft splines, then install guide collar (2), propeller (1), splined washer (3) and flat washer (4) on propeller shaft (6). Install propeller retaining nut (5) and securely tighten.

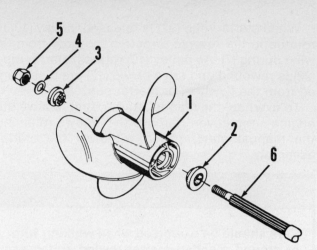

Fig. MY4-7 — A typical view of a propeller setup used on all models. Guide collar (2), propeller (1) and splined washer (3) are mounted on propeller shaft (6) and retained by flat washer (4) and nut (5). Note that some models are not equipped with a flat washer (4) between splined washer (3) and nut (5).

Tune-Up

IGNITION SYSTEM

All 75 models prior to serial number 3801458 and 110 models prior to serial number 3795658 are equipped with a magneto type ignition system, however, 75 models serial number 2810637-3801457 and 110 models serial number 2798057-3795657 are equipped with a "Thunderbolt Phase-Maker" electronic ignition magneto. Refer to the Outboard Motor Service Manual for testing and servicing the ignition system except for servicing the breaker point assemblies as outlined later in this section. If engine malfunction is noted and the ignition system is suspected, make sure the spark plugs and all electrical wiring are in good condition and all electrical connections are tight before troubleshooting the ignition system.

The standard spark plug is as follows:

Merc 75 (Before Ser. No. 2810637)
Type . . . . Champion L7J
Thread Reach. . . . . ½ inch
(12.7 mm)
Electrode Gap . . . . 0.030 inch
(0.76 mm)

Merc 75 (Ser. No. 2810637-3801457)
Use special surface gap AC type V40FFK, Champion type L78V or AC type VR40FF radio noise suppression spark plugs.

Merc 110 (Ser. No. 2508759-2708898)
Type . . . . Champion L4J
Thread Reach. . . . . ½ inch
(12.7 mm)
Electrode Gap . . . . 0.030 inch
(0.76 mm)

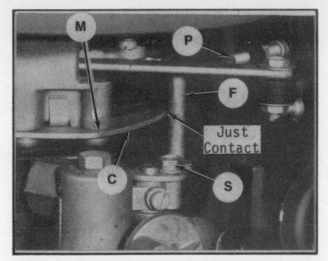

Fig. MY4-8—View of later type speed control linkage. One of the cam mounting screw holes (M) is slotted for adjustment.

C. Control cam
F. Follower
M. Cam slot
P. Maximum advance stop screw
S. Cap screw

Fig. MY4-9—View of neutral stop on early models. Later models are similar.

Merc 110 (Ser. No. 2798057-3795657)

Use special surface gap AC type V40FFK, Champion type L78V or AC type VR40FF radio noise suppression spark plugs.

Renew surface gap spark plug if center electrode is more than 1/32 inch (0.79 mm) below the flat surface of the plug end.

The breaker point gap on all models should be adjusted to 0.020 inch (0.51 mm). To gain access to the breaker point assemblies, remove the engine's top cover, the manual starter assembly and the flywheel.

⚠WARNING

Be sure suitable tools are used to remove the flywheel. Damage resultant from the misapplication of force or the use of incorrect tools may cause engine damage, engine malfunction or personal injury.

Inspect the breaker point surfaces for excessive wear, pitting or any other damage. If needed, renew breaker point assemblies and condensers.

To adjust, rotate the crankshaft until the breaker point contact surfaces are placed at their widest position. Use a 0.020 inch (0.51 mm) feeler gage and check the distance between the point surfaces. If the distance is incorrect, loosen the point set securing screw and adjust the point set until the correct gap is obtained. Tighten the point set securing the screw and recheck the breaker point gap. Repeat the adjustment procedure, if needed, until 0.020 inch (0.51 mm) is obtained. Repeat the adjustment procedure on the other breaker point assembly. Points should start to open 180° apart.

Install the flywheel and tighten the retaining nut to 35 ft.-lbs. (48 N·m). Complete reassembly. Refer to the following SPEED CONTROL LINKAGE section.

On Model 75 after serial number 3801457, Model 110 after serial number 3795657, Model 7.5 and Model 9.8, a "Thunderbolt" capacitor discharge ignition (CDI) system is used. Refer to the Outboard Motor Service Manual for testing and servicing the CD ignition system. If engine malfunction is noted, make sure the spark plugs and all electrical wiring are in good condition and all electrical connections are tight before troubleshooting the CD ingition system.

The standard spark plug is as follows:

Merc 75 (After Ser. No. 3801457)

Use special surface gap AC type V40FFM, Champion type L77V or AC type VR40FF radio noise suppression spark plugs.

Merc 110 (After Ser. No. 3795657)

Use special surface gap AC type V40FFM, Champion type L77V or AC type VR40FF radio noise suppression spark plugs.

Merc 7.5 (Before Ser. No. 5226935)

Use special surface gap spark plug AC V40FFK or Champion L78V.

Merc 7.5 (After Ser. No. 5226934)

Use special surface gap spark plug Champion L77J4. Champion QL77J4 may be used if radio frequency interference suppression is needed.

Merc 7.5, 9.8, 75 & 110

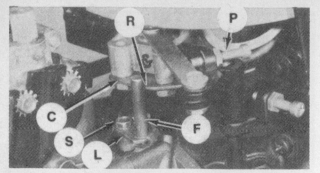

Fig. MY4-10—View of the speed control linkage typical of late models with point type magento.

C. Control cam
F. Follower
L. Lever

P. Maximum advance stop screw
R. 0.050 inch (1.27 mm)
S. Cap screw

Merc 9.8 (Before Ser. No. 5206550)

Use special surface gap spark plug AC V40FFK or Champion L78V.

Merc 9.8 (After Ser. No. 5206549)

Use special surface gap spark plug Champion L77J4. Champion QL77J4 may be used if radio frequency interference suppression is needed.

Renew surface gap spark plug if center electrode is more than 1/32 inch (0.79 mm) below the flat surface of the plug end.

SPEED CONTROL LINKAGE

The speed control twist grip, through the use of linkage, operates the stator plate to advance or retard the ignition timing. The carburetor throttle valve is synchronized to open as the timing is advanced. Several types of linkage are used. Refer to the appropriate following paragraphs for adjustment.

Models 75 (Before Ser. No. 2810637) And 110 (Ser. No. 1580203-2798056)

Before attempting to synchronize the throttle opening to the ignition advance, adjust breaker point gap on each set of breaker points as outlined in the previous IGNITION SYSTEM section and the idle fuel mixture as outlined in the following CARBURETOR section.

Start and run the engine until it reaches normal operating temperature. Engage the forward gear, then rotate the twist grip until the engine is operating at 1000-1100 rpm. With the engine speed maintained at 1000-1100 rpm, note the position of control cam (C—Fig. MY4-8). Control cam (C) should just contact throttle follower (F). Adjust by loosening screw (S) and repositioning throttle lever. Tighten screw (S) to secure adjustment. Note that on later models, magneto cam slot (M) is provided for a finer adjustment of pickup point.

The maximum advance stop screw (P) should be set so threaded end of screw extends ¼ inch (6.35 mm) through control lever.

The neutral stop (Fig. MY4-9) should be adjusted to provide a maximum speed of 2400-2700 rpm in neutral. Stop can be moved if needed after loosening screw (S). Start position on twist grip should be aligned at this setting.

Models 75 (Ser. No. 2810637-3801457) And 110 (Ser. No. 2798057-3795657)

Before attempting to synchronize the throttle opening to the ignition advance, adjust the breaker point gap on each set of breaker points as outlined in the previous IGNITION SYSTEM section.

Remove the top spark plug and install a suitable dial indicator. Zero indicator needle with piston TDC. Turn the crankshaft until the top piston is 0.193 inch (4.9 mm) BTDC. Attach a point checker or a continuity meter to the white wire coming from the breaker point assembly and to a suitable engine ground. Hold speed control twist grip against the maximum speed stop and adjust advance stop screw (P—Fig. MY4-10) until meter indicates that contact points just open by 0.193 inch (4.9 mm) BTDC.

With throttle set at maximum speed position, check play between follower (F) and cam (C). The follower should have almost opened the throttle completely with approximately 0.050 inch (1.27 mm) play (R) remaining. If incorrect, loosen screw (S) and reposition throttle follower lever (L).

Throttle pickup should occur 0.002 inch (0.05 mm) ATDC on Model 75 serial number 2810637-3488152 and Model 110 serial number 2798057-3482752. Throttle pickup should occur 0.007 inch (0.18 mm) ATDC on Model 75 serial number 3482752-3795657. To position cam for correct throttle pickup, rotate crankshaft until top piston is in specified position. Move the speed control twist grip toward the idle position until the point checker or continuity meter indicates that the points just open. With the crankshaft and speed controls set as described, cam (C—Fig. MY4-8) should just contact follower (F). If cam and follower are not touching or if throttle is partially open, loosen the two screws attaching cam (C) and reposition cam as required. Very little adjustment is normally necessary, however, the maximum throttle opening should be rechecked. Complete reassembly.

A power timing light may be used to check ignition timing and throttle pickup on models with degree markings on the engine cover support bracket. With the outboard motor properly mounted on a boat or a suitable test tank, im-

Fig. MY4-11—View showing timing mark (TM) on trigger coil housing and index mark (I) on crankcase end plate. Refer to text.

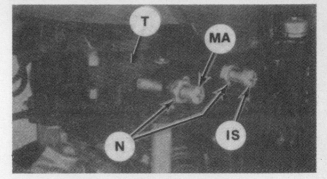

Fig. MY4-12—View of speed control linkage used on later models with CD type ignition.

N. Nuts
T. Throttle lever
IS. Idle speed stop screw

MA. Maximum advance
stop screw

merse the lower unit. Connect a power timing light to the top spark plug wire. Start the engine and allow it to warm up to normal operating temperature. The full advance position for all engines is 34° BTDC. Adjust maximum advance stop screw (P) if necessary. Move speed control twist grip toward the stop position while observing the flywheel timing mark with the timing light. Stop moving speed control twist grip when timing mark is 2° ATDC on Model 75 serial number 2810637-3488152 and Model 110 serial number 2798057-3482752 or when mark is 6° ATDC on Model 75 serial number 3488153-3801457 and Model 110 serial number 3482753-3795657. Throttle control cam (C) should just contact throttle follower (F) at this point. Loosen the two screws attaching cam (C) and reposition cam if necessary.

The neutral stop (Fig. MY4-9) should be adjusted to provide a maximum speed of 2400-2700 rpm in neutral. Stop can be moved if necessary after loosening screw (S). The "START" position on twist grip should be aligned when at 2400-2700 rpm. If not, loosen the Allen screw in bottom of twist grip and reposition.

Model 75 (Ser. No. 3801458 And Above) And Model 110 (Ser. No. 3795658 And Above)

To adjust speed control linkage, place outboard motor in forward gear and move speed control twist grip to maximum speed position. Timing mark (TM—Fig. MY4-11) on trigger coil holder should be aligned with timing index mark (I) on crankcase end plate. Turn maximum advance stop screw (MA—Fig. MY4-12) to align marks if necessary. Initial throttle pickup point is not adjustable.

To check timing with a power timing light, first properly mount outboard motor on a boat or a suitable test tank and immerse the lower unit. Connect a power timing light to the top spark plug wire. Start the engine and allow it to warm up to

normal operating temperature. Move speed control twist grip to maximum speed position. Timing mark on flywheel (M—Fig. MY4-13) should align with 30° BTDC on timing decal (D) of 75 models after 1975 and 35° BTDC on other models prior to 1978. Models after 1977 are not equipped with timing decal (D) so timing marks on flywheel and starter housing should be aligned. Adjust timing by turning maximun advance stop screw (MA—Fig. MY4-12). Be sure to tighten locknut (N) on screw (MA) when adjustment is completed.

The neutral stop (Fig. MY4-9) should be adjusted to provide a maximum speed of 2400-2700 rpm in neutral. Stop can be moved as necessary after loosening screw (S). The "START" position on twist grip should be aligned when at 2400-2700 rpm. If not, loosen Allen screw in bottom of twist grip and reposition.

Models 7.5 And 9.8

To adjust speed control mechanism, shift outboard motor to forward gear and rotate speed control twist grip to maximum speed position. Loosen control cable nuts (N—Fig. MY4-14). Move throttle lever (T—Fig. MY4-12) so timing mark on trigger

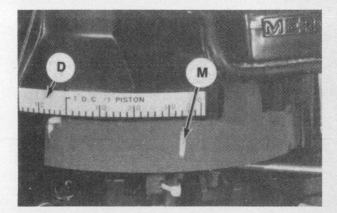

Fig. MY4-13—On models with CD type ignition, flywheel timing mark (M) should align with specified degree reading on timing decal (D) on models prior to 1978 and a timing mark on the starter housing on models after 1977. Refer to text.

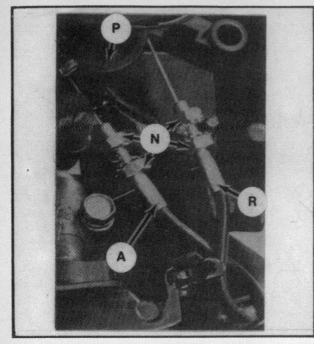

Fig. MY4-14—View of speed control cable used on 7.5 and 9.8 models.

A. Advance cable
N. Nuts
P. Pulley
R. Retard cable

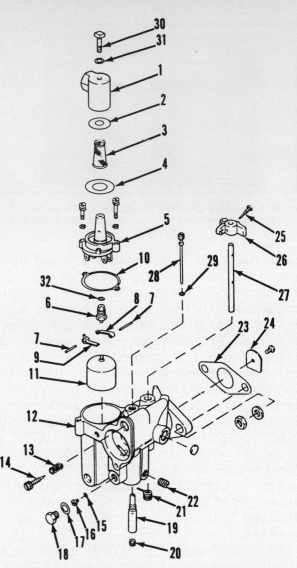

Fig. MY4-15—Exploded view of a Tillotson carburetor.

1. Strainer cover	17. Gasket
2. Gasket	18. Plug
3. Strainer	19. Main nozzle
4. Gasket	20. Plug
5. Bowl cover	21. Spring
6. Inlet needle & seat	22. Plug
7. Pins	23. Gasket
8. Primary lever	24. Throttle valve
9. Secondary lever	25. Screw
10. Gasket	26. Throttle lever
11. Float	27. Throttle shaft
12. Body	28. Idle tube
13. Spring	29. Gasket
14. Idle mixture screw	30. Cap screw
15. Gasket	31. Gasket
16. Main jet	32. Gasket

coil holder (TM—Fig. MY4-11) is aligned with timing mark (I) on crankcase end plate. Turn maximum advance screw (MA—Fig. MY4-12) so screw contacts throttle lever (T) just as timing marks are aligned. With throttle lever contacting maximum advance screw, pull advance control cable (A—Fig. MY4-14) toward speed control handle (do not apply excessive force) and tighten control cable nuts (N). Remove slack from retard control cable (R) using same procedure. Run engine until normal engine temperature is reached, then obtain an idle speed of 650-750 rpm by turning idle speed screw (IS—Fig. MY4-12). Stop engine, then with throttle lever (T) against idle speed screw (IS), adjust carburetor throttle lever so follower (F—Fig. MY4-8) just contacts throttle cam (C).

CARBURETOR
1972 And Prior 75 And 110 Models

ADJUSTMENT. Standard make of carburetor is a Tillotson. Carburetor model and standard main jet (16—Fig. MY4-15) size is as follows:

Merc 75 (Ser. No. 2529895-2721150)
Carburetor Model KB-9A
Std. Size Main Jet .0.034 in.
(0.86 mm)

Merc 75 (Ser. No. 2810637-3488152)
Carburetor Model KB-12A
Std. Size Main Jet .0.035 in.
(0.89 mm)

Merc 110 (Before Ser. No. 2475312)
Carburetor Model KB-5A
Std. Size Main Jet .0.049 in.
(1.24 mm)

Merc. 110 (Ser. No. 2508759-2708898)
Carburetor Model KB-8A
Std. Size Main Jet .0.049 in.
(1.24 mm)

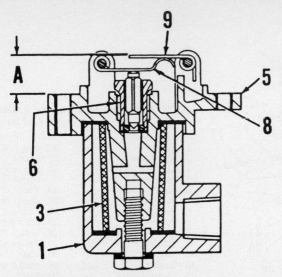

Fig. MY4-16—Cross-sectional view of float mechanism. Distance (A) should be 13/32 inch (10.32 mm). Refer to text for adjustment procedure and Fig. MY4-15 for parts identification.

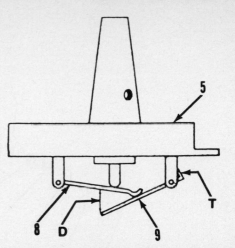

Fig. MY4-17—With bowl cover (5) upright, distance (D) between primary lever (8) and end of secondary lever (9) should be ¼ inch (6.4 mm). Bend tab (T) to adjust.

Merc 110 (Ser. No. 2798057-3482752)

Carburetor Model KB-11A
Std. Size Main Jet .... 0.047 in.
                                    (1.19 mm)

Other main jet sizes are available for adjusting the air:fuel mixture for altitude or other special conditions. Preliminary adjustment of idle mixture screw (14) is one turn out from a lightly seated position. Recommended idle speed is 650-750 rpm with engine at normal operating temperature and in gear.

With the outboard motor properly mounted on a boat or a suitable test tank, immerse the lower unit. Connect a tachometer and set it on the appropriate range scale. Start the engine and allow it to warm up to normal operating temperature. With the engine running at idle speed while in forward gear, turn idle mixture screw (14) until smooth engine operation is noted.

NOTE: On all Merc 110 models with a KB-5A carburetor, turning idle mixture screw (14) counterclockwise leans the mixture. On 75 and all other 110 models, turning idle mixture screw (14) clockwise leans the mixture.

Adjust engine idle speed until 650-750 rpm is obtained. Reinstall engine's top cover.

OVERHAUL. Remove engine's top cover. Remove choke and throttle linkage from carburetor. Disconnect the fuel supply hose at the carburetor inlet. Remove any other components that will interfere with carburetor removal. Clean all external surfaces and remove accumulated dirt and grease. Remove the two nuts securing the carburetor and withdraw the carburetor assembly.

With reference to Fig. MY4-15, disassemble the carburetor and note any discrepancies which must be corrected before reassembly. Remove all gaskets (label if needed for later reference) and set to the side.

Thoroughly clean all carburetor parts in a suitable solvent and inspect for damage and excessive wear. Note that plastic and rubber components should not be subjected to some cleaning solutions. Blow dry with clean compressed air. If compressed air is not available, use only lint-free cloths to wipe dry. Do not use a drill bit or wire to clean jets. Enlargement or damage of the calibrated holes may affect engine performance.

With reference to Fig. MY4-15, reassemble the carburetor components with new gaskets. Note that the new gaskets should match up with those removed. If not, check with your parts supplier to be sure you have the correct gasket set.

To determine the float level, invert bowl cover (5—Fig. MY4-16) with inlet needle and seat (6), primary lever (8) and secondary lever (9) installed. Measure distance (A) from carburetor body surface to top of secondary lever (9). Distance (A) should be 13/32 inch (10.32 mm). Adjust distance (A) by bending curved end of primary lever (8). Turn bowl cover (5—Fig. MY4-17) upright and measure distance (D) between primary lever (8) and end of secondary lever (9). Distance (D) should be ¼ inch (6.4 mm). Bend tab (T) to adjust. The contact spring located in center of float (11—Fig. MY4-15) should extend 3/32 inch (2.38 mm) above top of float. Check to see if spring has been stretched or damaged.

Reinstall the carburetor with a new mounting gasket and securely tighten the retaining nuts. Complete reassembly in the reverse order of disassembly with the exception of the engine cover. Initially adjust idle mixture screw (14—Fig. MY4-15) one turn out from a lightly seated position.

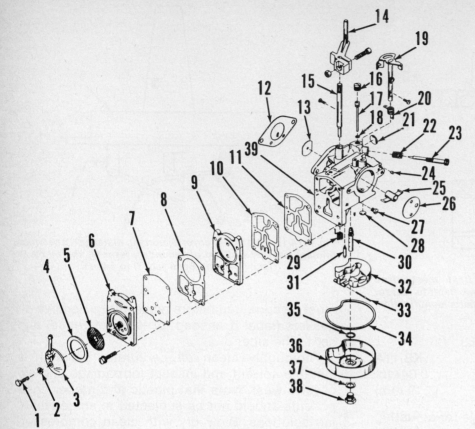

Fig. MY4-18—Exploded view of a Mercarb carburetor with an integral fuel pump.

1. Cap screw
2. Washer
3. Inlet cover
4. Gasket
5. Strainer
6. Pump cover
7. Diaphragm
8. Gasket
9. Pump body
10. Check valve diaphragm
11. Gasket
12. Gasket
13. Throttle plate
14. Throttle lever
15. Throttle shaft
16. Plug
17. Idle tube
18. Gasket
19. Choke shaft
20. Return spring
21. Welch plug
22. Spring
23. Idle mixture screw
24. Plug
25. Boost venturi
26. Choke plate
27. Main jet
28. Welch plug
29. Return spring
30. Main nozzle
31. Inlet needle
32. Float
33. Float pin
34. Gasket
35. Gasket
36. Float bowl
37. Gasket
38. Plug

All Other Models

The fuel pump and carburetor are a complete unit. Refer to the following OVERHAUL section for service procedures on both fuel pump and carburetor.

ADJUSTMENT. Standard make of carburetor is a Mercarb. Standard main jet (27 – Fig. MY4-18) size is as follows:

Merc 75 (Ser. No. 3588153-4131609)
Std. Size Main Jet .0.034 in.
(0.86 mm)

Merc 75 (Ser. No. 4131610-4397536)
Std. Size Main Jet .0.032 in.
(0.81 mm)

Merc 75 (Ser. No. 4397537 & up)
Std. Size Main Jet .0.045 in.
(1.14 mm)

Merc 110 (Ser. No. 3482753 & up)
Std. Size Main Jet .0.041 in.
(1.04 mm)

Merc 7.5
Std. Size Main Jet .0.040 in.
(1.02 mm)

Merc. 9.8
Std. Size Main Jet .0.039 in.
(0.99 mm)

Other main jet sizes are available for adjusting the calibration for altitude or other special conditions. Preliminary adjustment of idle mixture screw (23) is 1½ turns out from a lightly seated position. Recommended idle speed is 550-750 rpm with engine at normal operating temperature and in gear.

With the outboard motor properly mounted on a boat or a suitable test tank, immerse the lower unit. Connect a tachometer and set it on the appropriate range scale. Start the engine and allow it to warm up to normal operating temperature. With the engine running at idle speed while in forward gear, turn idle mixture screw (23) until smooth engine operation is noted. Adjust engine idle speed until 550-750 rpm is obtained.

Reinstall engine's top cover.

OVERHAUL. The fuel pump is an integral part of the carburetor. The fuel pump assembly may be overhauled without overhauling the complete carburetor. If the fuel pump is to be overhauled without carburetor removal, proceed as follows: Remove the engine's top cover and disconnect the fuel tank supply hose at the outboard

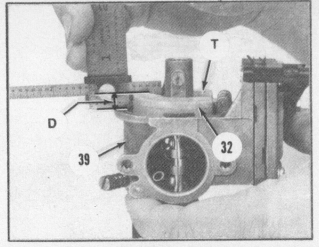

Fig. MY4-19—To determine float level, invert carburetor body (39) and measure distance (D) from carburetor body (39) to base of float (32). Distance (D) should be 15/64 to 17/64 inch (6-6.8 mm) and is adjusted by bending tang (T) on float arm.

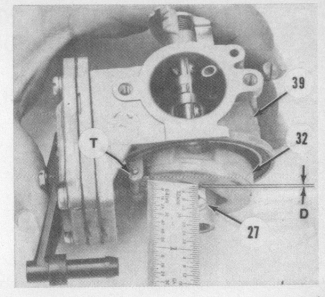

Fig. MY4-20—To determine float drop, turn carburetor body (39) upright and measure distance (D) from lowest portion of float (32) to highest point on main jet (27). Distance should be 1/32 to 1/16 inch (0.8-1.6 mm). Adjust by bending tang (T) at rear of float arm.

motor connector. Disconnect the fuel supply hose at the fuel pump inlet.

With reference to Fig. MY4-18, disassemble the fuel pump assembly. Inspect all components for excessive wear or any other damage and renew if needed. Clean components as needed with a suitable cleaning solution. Blow dry with clean compressed air. If compressed air is not available, use only lint-free cloths to wipe dry. Make sure all passages are clear of any obstruction.

With reference to Fig. MY4-18, reassemble the fuel pump assembly with new gaskets. Securely tighten the retaining screws.

NOTE: Fuel pump and engine malfunction will result if the fuel pump and all connections are not airtight.

Complete reassembly.

Refer to the following for complete carburetor overhaul: Remove engine's top cover. Disconnect choke cable from choke lever. Disconnect the fuel tank supply hose at the outboard motor connector. Disconnect the fuel supply hose at the fuel pump inlet. Clean all external surfaces and remove accumulated dirt and grease. Remove the two nuts securing the carburetor and withdraw the carburetor assembly.

With reference to Fig. MY4-18, disassemble the complete carburetor assembly and note any discrepancies which must be corrected before reassembly. Remove all gaskets (label if needed for later reference) and set to the side.

Thoroughly clean all carburetor parts in a suitable solvent and inspect for damage and ex-

cessive wear. Note that plastic and rubber components should not be subjected to some cleaning solutions. Blow dry with clean compressed air. If compressed air is not available, use only lint-free cloths to wipe dry. Do not use a drill bit or wire to clean jets. Enlargement or damage of the calibrated holes may affect engine performance.

With reference to Fig. MY4-18, reassemble the carburetor components with new gaskets. Note that the new gaskets should match up with those removed. If not, check with your parts supplier to be sure you have the correct gasket set.

To determine the float level, invert carburetor body (39—Fig. MY4-19) and measure distance (D) from carburetor body (39) to base of float (32). Distance (D) should be 15/64 to 17/64 inch (6-6.8 mm) and is adjusted by bending tang (T) on float arm.

Check the float drop by turning carburetor body (39—Fig. MY4-20) upright and measuring distance (D) from lowest portion of float (32) to highest point on main jet (27). Distance should be 1/32 to 1/16 inch (0.8-1.6 mm). Adjust float drop by bending tang (T) at rear of float arm.

When reinstalling the carburetor, place a new gasket (12—Fig. MY4-18) between the carburetor and the intake manifold. Securely tighten the retaining nuts. Reconnect the fuel supply hoses. Connect choke cable to choke lever. Initially adjust idle mixture screw (23) 1½ turns out from a lightly seated position.

MERC 20 (1979-1980)
MERC 200 (1969-1978)

Specifications

Rated horsepower	20
Maximum rpm	4800-5500
Bore	2-9/16 in.
	(65.02 mm)
Stroke	2-1/8 in.
	(53.98 mm)
Number of cylinders	2
Displacement	22 cu. in.
	(360.5 cc)
Spark plug:	
1969	Champion L4J
1970 and later	AC V40FFK
Electrode gap:	
1969	0.030 in.
	(0.76 mm)
1970 and later	Surface Gap
Breaker Point gap:	
1969-1972	0.020 in.
	(0.51 mm)
1973 and later	Breakerless Ignition
Carburetor make:	
1969-1972	Tillotson
1973 and later	Mercarb
Idle speed	See Text
Fuel:oil ratio	50:1
Fuel pump — nonintegral with carburetor:	
Discharge pressure at WOT	2 psi
	(14 kPa)
Gearcase oil capacity	6½ ozs.
	(192 mL)

Maintenance

LUBRICATION

ENGINE. The engine is lubricated by oil mixed with the fuel. The fuel should be regular leaded, low lead or unleaded gasoline with a minimum pump octane rating of 86. Recommended oil is Quicksilver Formula 50-D Outboard Lubricant or a BIA certified two-stroke motor oil. The recommended fuel:oil ratio for normal operation is 50:1.

LOWER UNIT. The lower unit gears and bearings are lubricated by oil contained in the gearcase. The recommended oil is Quicksilver Super-Duty Gear Lubricant. The gearcase oil capacity is 6½ ounces (192 mL) on all models. The gearcase oil level should be checked every 30 days and the lubricant renewed periodically. The gearcase is drained and filled through the same plug port (D—Fig. MY5-1). An oil level (vent) port (L) is used to indicate the full oil level of the gearcase and to ease oil drainage.

To drain the oil, place the outboard motor in a vertical position. Remove drain plug (D) and oil level plug (L), and allow the lubricant to drain into a suitable container.

To fill the gearcase with oil, place the outboard motor in a vertical position. Add oil through drain plug (D) opening with an oil feeder until the oil begins to overflow from oil level plug (L) port. Reinstall oil level plug (L) with a new gasket, if needed, and tighten. Remove oil feeder, then reinstall drain plug (D) with a new gasket, if needed, and tighten.

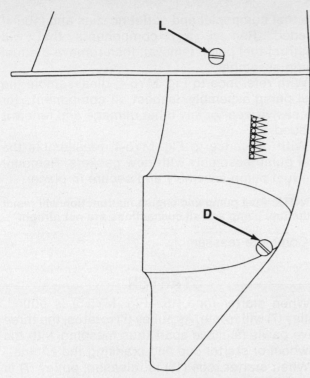

Fig. MY5-1—View showing lower unit gearcase drain and fill plug (D) and oil level (vent) plug (L).

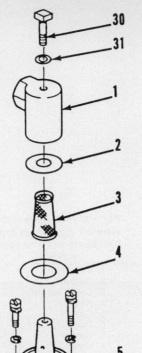

Fig. MY5-2—View showing reusable type fuel strainer (3) used on models with Tillotson type carburetors.

1. Strainer cover
2. Gasket
3. Strainer
4. Gasket
5. Bowl cover
30. Cap screw
31. Gasket

PIVOT POINTS AND SLIDES. Lubricate all pivot points and linkage slides with a good quality marine type multipurpose grease as frequently as needed to keep the components operating freely and properly.

FUEL SYSTEM

Periodically inspect the fuel lines and connections for damage. Renew components if needed.

Keep the external surface of the carburetor clean and all connections and sealing surfaces tight.

FUEL FILTER. On motors equipped with a Tillotson type carburetor, a strainer (3—Fig. MY5-2) contained in strainer cover (1) and mounted on top of carburetor bowl cover (5) is used to filter the fuel prior to it entering the carburetor float bowl. To inspect, remove cap screw (30) and withdraw strainer cover (1) and strainer (3). Clean strainer (3) in a suitable solvent and blow dry with clean compressed air. Inspect strainer (3). If excessive blockage or damage is noted, renew strainer. If needed, renew gaskets (2 and 4).

On models equipped with a Mercarb type carburetor, a strainer (5—Fig. MY5-3) positioned behind inlet fitting (3) is used to filter the fuel prior to it entering the fuel pump. To inspect, remove cap screw (1) and withdraw inlet fitting (3) and strainer (5). Clean strainer (5) in a suitable solvent and blow dry with clean compressed air. Inspect

strainer (5). If excessive blockage or damage is noted, renew strainer. If needed, renew gasket (4).

FUEL PUMP. On later models equipped with a Mercarb type carburetor (Fig. MY5-20), the fuel pump is an integral part of the carburetor. Refer to CARBURETOR in the Tune-Up section for fuel pump overhaul.

NOTE: The fuel pump assembly may be overhauled without carburetor removal.

On early models equipped with a Tillotson type carburetor (Fig. MY5-17), a fuel pump (Fig. MY5-4)

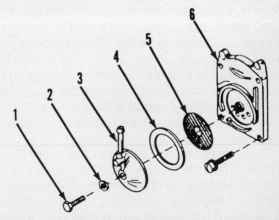

Fig. MY5-3—View showing fuel strainer (5) located behind fuel pump inlet cover (3) on models with Mercarb type carburetor.

1. Cap screw
2. Washer
3. Inlet cover
4. Gasket
5. Strainer
6. Pump cover

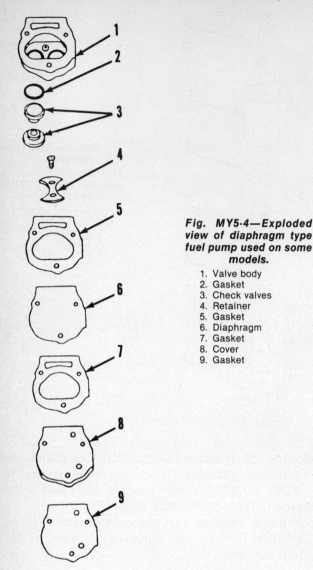

Fig. MY5-4—Exploded
view of diaphragm type
fuel pump used on some
models.

1. Valve body
2. Gasket
3. Check valves
4. Retainer
5. Gasket
6. Diaphragm
7. Gasket
8. Cover
9. Gasket

that is nonintegral with the carburetor is used. The fuel pump is operated by crankcase pressure changes from the up and down movement of the piston. When the crankcase pressure decreases (the piston is moving upward), the pump diaphragm is pulled toward the crankcase allowing fuel to enter the pump body and closing the discharge check valve. When the crankcase pressure increases (the piston is moving downward), the diaphragm is pushed outward discharging the fuel to the carburetor and closing the inlet check valve. This pulsating action allows for continuous fuel flow. The check valves are used to prevent reverse flow of the fuel.

The fuel hoses must be connected according to fuel flow. The fuel supply line connected to the fuel pump inlet port and the line routed toward the carburetor assembly connected to the outlet port.

To overhaul the fuel pump, proceed as follows: Remove the engine's top cover and disconnect the fuel tank supply hose at the outboard motor connector. Disconnect the fuel hoses at

the fuel pump inlet and outlet nozzles and label if needed. Remove any components that will obstruct fuel pump removal, then remove the fuel pump assembly.

With reference to Fig. MY5-4, disassemble the fuel pump assembly. Inspect all components for excessive wear or any other damage and renew if needed.

With reference to Fig. MY5-4, reassemble the fuel pump assembly with new gaskets. Remount the fuel pump assembly and secure in place.

NOTE: Fuel pump and engine malfunction will result if the fuel pump and all connections are not airtight.

Complete reassembly.

STARTER

When starter rope (18—Fig. MY5-5) is pulled, pulley (7) will rotate. As pulley (7) rotates, the three drive pawls (9) move apart thus meshing with the flywheel or starter cup and cranking the engine.

When starter rope (18) is released, pulley (7) is rotated in the reverse direction by force from rewind spring (6). As pulley (7) rotates, starter rope (18) is rewound and drive pawls (9) are disengaged from the flywheel or starter cup.

On early models, the manual starter assembly is integral with engine cover (25). On later models, a separate starter housing (3) is used.

To overhaul the manual starter, first remove the engine's top cover (25).

⚠**WARNING**

Care should be exercised when working with or around a coiled starter rewind spring as sudden uncoiling can cause injury. Safety eyewear and gloves are recommended.

To disassemble early type, remove screw (23) and trim cap (24). On later models, remove the screws retaining the manual starter assembly to the power head, then withdraw the starter assembly. On all models, bend tabs of tab washer (2) away from nut (1). Insert a screwdriver in slot of pulley shaft (16) and loosen the left-hand thread nut (1). Allow screwdriver and pulley shaft (16) to turn clockwise until rewind spring (6) unwinds. Pry anchor (20) from starter handle (19) and remove anchor and handle from starter rope (18). Remove nut (1), invert engine cover (25) or starter housing (3) and remove manual starter components. Make sure that rewind spring (6) remains in recess as pulley (7) is removed. Use suitable hand protec-

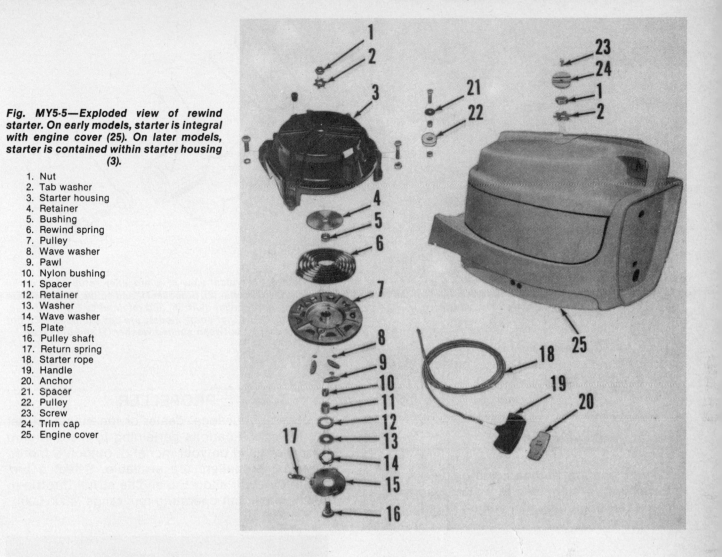

Fig. MY5-5—Exploded view of rewind starter. On early models, starter is integral with engine cover (25). On later models, starter is contained within starter housing (3).

1. Nut
2. Tab washer
3. Starter housing
4. Retainer
5. Bushing
6. Rewind spring
7. Pulley
8. Wave washer
9. Pawl
10. Nylon bushing
11. Spacer
12. Retainer
13. Washer
14. Wave washer
15. Plate
16. Pulley shaft
17. Return spring
18. Starter rope
19. Handle
20. Anchor
21. Spacer
22. Pulley
23. Screw
24. Trim cap
25. Engine cover

tion and extract rewind spring (6) from pulley (7). Allow rewind spring (6) to uncoil in a safe area.

Inspect all components for damage and excessive wear and renew if needed.

NOTE: During reassembly, lubricate all friction surfaces with a suitable low temperature grease.

Assemble by reversing the disassembly procedure. Install spring guide bushing (5) on hub of pulley (7) with chamfered end of bushing toward pulley. Be sure that pawls (9) are all installed with the radius toward the outside and the identification mark (dot) away from pulley (7). Install wave washer retainer (12) with cup end out and position washer (13) and wave washer (14) in cup. Make certain that tang on spring retainer (4) engages slot in pulley shaft (16).

Position assembled manual starter with end of pulley shaft (16) through starter housing (3) or engine cover (25) and install tab washer (2) and nut (1). Pull free end of starter rope (18) through housing (3) or engine cover (25) and starter handle (19), then secure in anchor (20). Turn pulley shaft (16) counterclockwise until starter handle (19) is pull-

ed into the proper released position, then continue to turn pulley shaft (16) an additional 1¼ turns. Tighten nut (1) and bend tabs of tab washer (2) to secure nut (1) in place. On early models, install trim cap (24) and secure to cover (25) with screw (23). Pull starter rope (18) out to full length while checking for freedom of travel, then allow starter rope (18) to rewind into pulley (7). Starter handle (19) should be drawn back into the proper released position. Remount manual starter assembly and install engine's top cover to complete reassembly.

COOLING SYSTEM

Port (I — Fig. MY5-6) located on the bottom side of the antiventilation plate is used as the water inlet for the cooling system on early 200 models. The water passages in the port cover must be kept clean of all foreign matter to ensure efficient operation of the cooling system.

Ports (I — Fig. MY5-7) located on the port and starboard side of the lower unit are used as the water inlets for the cooling system on late 200

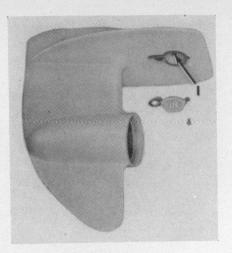

Fig. MY5-6—View showing port (I) located on the bottom side of the antiventilation plate used as the water inlet for the cooling system on early 200 models.

models and 20 models. The ports must be kept clean of all foreign matter to ensure efficient operation of the cooling system.

⚠CAUTION

Do not operate outboard motor unless the lower unit is immersed in water, otherwise, the water pump impeller will be damaged.

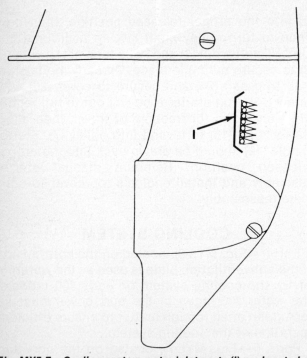

Fig. MY5-7—Cooling system water inlet ports (I) are located on the port and starboard side of the lower unit on late 200 models and 20 models.

Fig. MY5-8—A typical view of a propeller setup used on all models. Guide collar (2), propeller (1) and spline washer (3) are mounted on propeller shaft (6) and retained by flat washer (4) and nut (5). Note that some models are not equipped with flat washer (4) between splined washer (3) and nut (5).

PROPELLER

Consult your local dealer or the manufacturer for the specifications pertaining to the standard propeller used on your model of outboard motor. Optional propellers are available. Select a propeller that will allow the engine at full throttle to reach maximum operating rpm range (4800-500).

⚠WARNING

Shift directional control lever to "NEUTRAL." Disconnect the spark plug leads and properly ground leads before performing any propeller service, otherwise, accidental starting can occur if propeller shaft is rotated.

Shown in Fig. MY5-8 is a typical view of a propeller setup used on all models. Some models are not equipped with flat washer (4) between splined washer (3) and nut (5).

To remove the propeller, unscrew propeller retaining nut (5). Withdraw flat washer (4), splined washer (3), propeller (1) and guide collar (2) from propeller shaft (6).

Inspect all components for damage and excessive wear and renew if needed.

Apply Perfect Seal or a suitable equivalent to the propeller shaft splines, then install guide collar (2), propeller (1), splined washer (3) and flat washer (4) on propeller shaft (6). Install propeller retaining nut (5) and securely tighten.

Tune-Up

IGNITION SYSTEM

All 200 models prior to 1973 are equipped with a magneto type ignition system, however, 1972 models are equipped with a "Thunderbolt Phase-Maker" electronic ignition magneto. Refer to the Outboard Motor Service Manual for testing and servicing the ignition system except for servicing the breaker point assemblies as outlined later in this section. If engine malfunction is noted and the ignition system is suspected, make sure the spark plugs and all electrical wiring are in good condition and all electrical connections are tight before proceeding to troubleshooting the ignition system.

The standard spark plug is a Champion L4J with an electrode gap of 0.030 inch (0.76 mm) on models prior to 1970 and surface gap plug AC V40FFK on 1970-1972 models. Renew surface gap spark plug if center electrode is more than 1/32 inch (0.79 mm) below the flat surface of the plug end.

The breaker point gap on all models should be adjusted to 0.020 inch (0.51 mm). To gain access to the breaker point assemblies, remove the engine's top cover, the manual starter assembly and the flywheel.

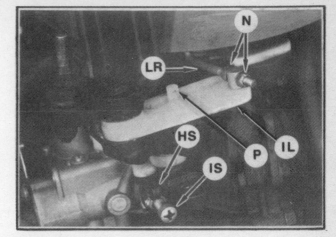

Fig. MY5-9—View of 1969 magneto advance (speed control) linkage. Refer to text for method of adjusting.

N. Nuts
P. Pin
HS. High speed stop screw
IL. Intermediate lever
IS. Idle speed stop screw
LR. Link rod

⚠WARNING

Be sure suitable tools are used to remove the flywheel. Damage resultant from the misapplication of force or the use of incorrect tools may cause engine damage, engine malfunction or personal injury.

Inspect surfaces of breaker points for excessive wear, pitting or any other damage. If needed, renew breaker point assemblies and condensers.

To adjust, rotate the crankshaft until the breaker point contact surfaces are placed at their widest position. Use a 0.020 inch (0.51 mm) feeler gage and check the distance between the point surfaces. If the distance is incorrect, loosen the point set securing screw and adjust the point set until the correct gap is obtained. Tighten the point set securing screw and recheck the breaker point gap. Repeat the adjustment procedure, if needed, until 0.020 inch (0.51 mm) is obtained. Repeat the adjustment procedure on the other breaker point assembly. Points should start to open 180 degrees apart.

On 1969 models, refer to the following SPEED CONTROL LINKAGE section. All other models, install the flywheel and tighten the retaining nut to 65 ft.-lbs. (88 N·m). Complete reassembly. Refer to the following SPEED CONTROL LINKAGE section.

On 1973 and later models a "Thunderbolt" capacitor discharge ignition (CDI) system is used. Refer to the Outboard Motor Service Manual for testing and servicing the CD ignition system. If engine malfunction is noted and the ignition system is suspected, make sure the spark plugs and all electrical wiring are in good condition and all electrical connections are tight before troubleshooting the CD ignition system.

The standard spark plug is surface gap plug AC V40FFK. Renew surface gap spark plug if center electrode is more than 1/32 inch (0.79 mm) below the flat surface of the plug end.

SPEED CONTROL LINKAGE

The speed control twist grip, through the use of linkage, operates the stator plate to advance or retard the ignition timing. The carburetor throttle valve is synchronized to open as the timing is advanced. Several types of linkage are used. Refer to the appropriate following paragraphs for adjustment.

1969 Models (Ser. No. 2550065-2827676)

Before attempting to synchronize the throttle opening to the ignition advance, adjust the breaker point gap on both sets of breaker points as outlined in the previous IGNITION SYSTEM section.

To determine the correct position of the stator assembly, the piston in number 1 cylinder (top cylinder) must be positioned in the cylinder at the point where ignition occurs. To determine piston

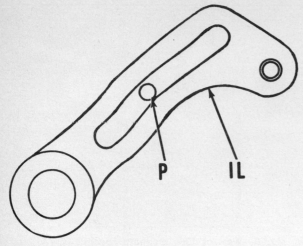

Fig. MY5-10—Pin (P) in intermediate lever (IL) groove must be positioned exactly as shown when adjusting link rod. Installed position of intermediate lever (IL) is shown in Fig. MY5-9.

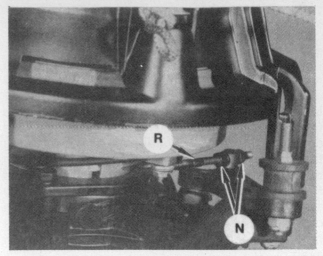

Fig. MY5-12—Ignition maximum advance is adjusted on 1970 and later models by turning nuts (N) on throttle control link rod (R). Refer to text.

position, remove the flywheel and spark plugs and install a dial indicator in the number 1 (top) cylinder spark plug hole. Determine top dead center for the piston and zero the dial indicator for piston TDC (temorarily reinstall the flywheel so it can be used to rotate the crankshaft). Rotate the crankshaft clockwise until the top piston is 0.300 inch (7.62 mm) BTDC. Shift to forward gear and turn the speed control twist grip until the breaker points for the top cylinder just open. Pin (P—Fig. MY5-9) in intermediate lever (IL) should be positioned exactly as shown in Fig. MY5-10. If the position of pin (P) is not correct, loosen nuts (N—Fig. MY5-9) and adjust length of link rod (LR) until pin (P) is correctly positioned in intermediate lever (IL) when points open as indicated by a point tester or a continuity meter.

Rotate the crankshaft clockwise until the top piston is 0.235 inch (5.97 mm) BTDC. Turn the speed control twist grip to full throttle (fast) position, then adjust the high speed stop screw (HS)

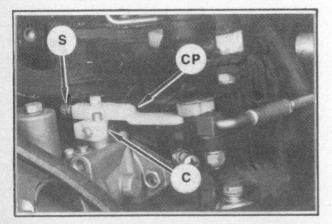

Fig. MY5-11—View of 1969 carburetor (speed control) linkage. Carburetor pickup is shown at CP, carburetor lever at (C) and maximum opening adjusting screw at (S). Refer to text for method of adjusting linkage.

until the point tester or continuity meter indicates the breaker points just open. Tighten locknut to secure position.

Turn the speed control twist grip until the lever is tight against stop screw (HS), then adjust screw (S—Fig. MY5-11) until carburetor throttle is completely open.

NOTE: DO NOT force linkage, allow 0.005-0.015 inch (0.13-0.38 mm) play in carburetor lever (C) to prevent damage to linkage.

Idle speed is adjusted at stop screw (IS—Fig. MY5-9). Refer to the following CARBURETOR section for idle speed adjustment.

1970-1972 Models (Ser. No. 2827677-3537530)

Before attempting to synchronize the throttle opening to the ignition advance, adjust the breaker point gap on both sets of breaker points as outlined in the previous IGNITION SYSTEM section.

The speed control linkage can be adjusted either with the engine running or with the engine stopped. Refer to the following paragraphs.

ENGINE STOPPED. To determine the correct position of the stator assembly, the piston in number 1 cylinder (top cylinder) must be positioned in the cylinder at the point where ignition occurs. To determine piston position, remove the flywheel and spark plugs and install a dial indicator in the number 1 (top) cylinder spark plug hole. Determine top dead center for the piston and zero the dial indicator for piston TDC (temporarily reinstall the flywheel so it can be used to rotate the crankshaft). Rotate the crankshaft until the top piston is 0.196 inch (4.98 mm) BTDC. Connect one lead of a point tester or a continuity

Illustrations Courtesy Mercury

Fig. MY5-13—View showing throttle follower (F), throttle pickup screw (P), high speed stop screw (HS) and idle speed stop screw (IS). Refer to text.

Fig. MY5-14—The maximum advance timing should occur at 33° BTDC on 1970 and later models.

meter to the white wire coming from the magneto stator and ground the other test lead. Shift to forward gear and turn the speed control twist grip to full throttle position. The points should just close when piston is at 0.196 inch (4.98 mm) BTDC and in maximum throttle position. If incorrect, turn the two self-locking nuts (N—Fig. MY5-12) on throttle control link rod (R) until tester indicates the points just close. Adjust nuts (N) in equal increments to keep nuts tight against swivel post.

Rotate the crankshaft until the top piston is 0.002 inch (0.05 mm) BTDC and turn speed control twist grip toward the slow speed position until the breaker points just open. Loosen locknut and turn throttle pickup screw (P—Fig. MY5-13) until screw just contacts the post on throttle follower (F).

Turn speed control twist grip to full throttle position and check clearance on throttle follower (F). If throttle follower (F) post does not have 0.035-0.048 inch (0.89-1.22 mm) play, adjust high speed stop screw (HS) until clearance (play) is correct.

Idle speed is adjusted at stop screw (IS). Refer to the following CARBURETOR section for idle speed adjustment.

ENGINE RUNNING. Connect a power timing light to the top spark plug lead and to an external power source. Start the outboard motor and operate at maximum advance setting. When timing light flashes, the flywheel timing mark should be aligned with the 33° BTDC mark (Fig. MY5-14) on starter frame. If incorrect, turn the two self-locking nuts (N—Fig. MY5-12) on throttle control link rod (R) until proper advance is obtained. Adjust nuts (N) in equal increments to keep nuts tight against swivel post.

Turn the speed control twist grip toward the slow speed position until the flywheel timing mark is between the 1° BTDC and the 4° ATDC

marks as shown in Fig. MY5-15. With the flywheel timing mark within this range, throttle pickup screw (P—Fig. MY5-13) should just contact the post on throttle follower (F). If incorrect, loosen locknut and turn throttle pickup screw (P) as required.

Stop engine and remove timing light. Turn speed control twist grip to full throttle position and check clearance on throttle follower (F). If throttle follower (F) post does not have 0.035-0.048 inch (0.89-1.22 mm) play, adjust high speed stop screw (HS) until clearance (play) is correct.

Idle speed is adjusted at stop screw (IS). Refer to the following CARBURETOR section for idle speed adjustment.

1973 And Later Models (Ser. No. 3537531 And Later)

ENGINE STOPPED. Remove engine cover and rewind starter assembly. Shift motor into "FORWARD" gear and turn speed control twist grip to full throttle position. Leading edge of trigger coil assembly (Fig. MY5-16) should align with full advance mark on stator bracket at this point. Adjust stop nuts on link rod to align trigger coil assembly with full advance mark if necessary.

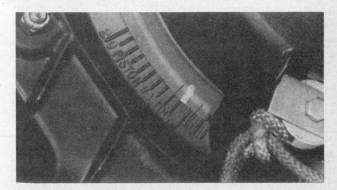

Fig. MY5-15—Throttle pickup should occur when ignition timing is within range of 1° BTDC and 4° ATDC on 1970-1972 models. On all later models, 2° BTDC and 2° ATDC on models below serial number 4102790 and 3°-7° BTDC on models above serial number 4102789. View shows 2° ATDC. Refer to text.

Merc 20 (1979-1980) & 200 (1969-1978)

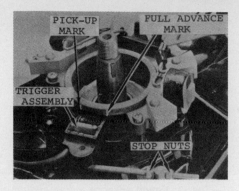

Fig. MY5-16—View of breakerless magneto stator assembly used on 1973 and later models. Flywheel is removed for clarity, marks are visible with flywheel installed.

Turn speed control twist grip as far as possible toward slow speed position. Observe trigger coil assembly while turning speed control twist grip back toward FAST position. Stop moving speed control twist grip when leading edge trigger coil is aligned with pickup mark on stator bracket. Throttle pickup screw (P—Fig. MY5-13) should just contact throttle follower (F). If incorrect, loosen locknut and turn throttle pickup screw (P) as required.

Turn speed control twist grip to full throttle position and check clearance on throttle follower (F). If throttle follower (F) post does not have 0.010-0.015 inch (0.25-0.38 mm) play, adjust high speed stop screw (HS) until clearance (play) is correct.

Idle speed is adjusted at stop screw (IS). Refer to the following CARBURETOR section for idle speed adjustment.

ENGINE RUNNING. Connect a power timing light to the top spark plug lead and to an external power source. Start the outboard motor and operate at maximum advance setting. When timing light flashes, the flywheel timing mark should be aligned with the 33° BTDC mark (Fig. MY5-14) on starter housing, or full advance timing mark (Fig. MY5-16) should align with timing pointer on models not equipped with degree marks. Full advance ignition timing is adjusted by turning the two self-locking stop nuts (Fig. MY5-16) on throttle control link rod. Adjust nuts in equal increments to keep nuts tight against swivel post.

Turn the speed control twist grip toward the slow speed position until the flywheel timing mark is between the 2° BTDC and 2° ATDC marks on models below serial number 4102790, between 3° and 7° BTDC marks on models above serial number 4102789, or pickup timing mark (Fig. MY5-16) is aligned with timing pointer on models not equipped with degree marks. With proper set-

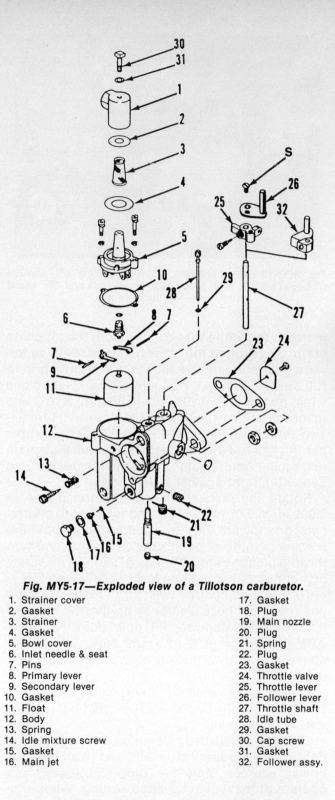

Fig. MY5-17—Exploded view of a Tillotson carburetor.

1. Strainer cover	17. Gasket
2. Gasket	18. Plug
3. Strainer	19. Main nozzle
4. Gasket	20. Plug
5. Bowl cover	21. Spring
6. Inlet needle & seat	22. Plug
7. Pins	23. Gasket
8. Primary lever	24. Throttle valve
9. Secondary lever	25. Throttle lever
10. Gasket	26. Follower lever
11. Float	27. Throttle shaft
12. Body	28. Idle tube
13. Spring	29. Gasket
14. Idle mixture screw	30. Cap screw
15. Gasket	31. Gasket
16. Main jet	32. Follower assy.

ting obtained, throttle pickup screw (P—Fig. MY5-13) should just contact the post on throttle follower (F). If incorrect, loosen locknut and turn throttle pickup screw (P) as required.

Stop engine and remove timing light. Turn speed control twist grip to full throttle position and check clearance on throttle follower (F). If throttle follower (F) post does not have 0.010-0.015 inch (0.25-0.38 mm) play, adjust high speed stop screw (HS) until clearance (play) is correct.

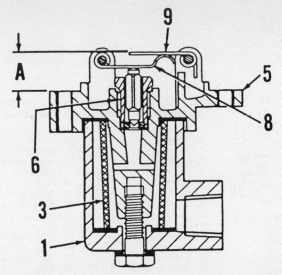

Fig. MY5-18—Cross-sectional view of float mechanism. Distance (A) should be 13/32 inch (10.32 mm). Refer to text for adjustment procedure and Fig. MY5-17 for parts identification.

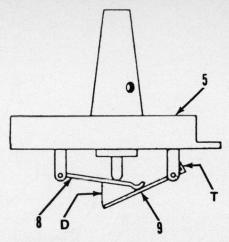

Fig. MY5-19—With bowl cover (5) upright, distance (D) between primary lever (8) and end of secondary lever (9) should be ¼ inch (6.4 mm). Bend tab (T) to adjust.

Idle speed is adjusted at stop screw (IS). Refer to the following CARBURETOR section for idle speed adjustment.

CARBURETOR
Models Prior To 1973

ADJUSTMENT. Standard make of carburetor is a Tillotson. Carburetor model and standard main jet (16—Fig. MY5-17) size is as follows:

Carburetor Model	Std. Main Jet Size
KA-20A	0.061 in. (1.55 mm)
KA-22A	0.059 in. (1.50 mm)
KA-22B	0.063 in. (1.60 mm)
KA-22C	0.065 in. (1.65 mm)
KA-23A	0.063 in. (1.60 mm)
KA-25A	0.059 in. (1.50 mm)

Other main jet sizes are available for adjusting the air:fuel mixture for altitude or other special conditions. Preliminary adjustment of idle mixture screw (14) is one turn out from a lightly seated position. Recommended idle speed is 600-700 rpm with engine at normal operating temperature and in gear.

With the outboard motor properly mounted on a boat or a suitable test tank, immerse the lower unit. Connect a tachometer and set it on the appropriate range scale. Start the engine and allow it to warm up to normal operating temperature.

With the engine running at idle while in forward gear, turn idle mixture screw (14) until smooth engine operation is noted.

Adjust engine idle speed until 600-700 rpm is obtained. Reinstall engine's top cover.

OVERHAUL. Remove the engine's top cover. Remove the choke and throttle linkage from the carburetor. Disconnect the fuel supply hose at the carburetor inlet. Remove any other components that will interfere with carburetor removal. Clean all external surfaces and remove accumulated dirt and grease. Remove the two nuts securing the carburetor and withdraw the carburetor assembly.

With reference to Fig. MY5-17, disassemble the carburetor and note any discrepancies which must be corrected before reassembly. Remove all gaskets (label if needed for later reference) and set to the side.

Thoroughly clean all carburetor parts in a suitable solvent and inspect for damage and excessive wear. Note that plastic and rubber components should not be subjected to some cleaning solutions. Blow dry with clean compressed air. If compressed air is not available, use only lint-free cloths to wipe dry. Do not use a drill bit or wire to clean jets. Enlargement or damage of the calibrated holes may affect engine performance.

With reference to Fig. MY5-17, reassemble the carburetor components with new gaskets. Note that the new gaskets should match up with those removed. If not, check with your parts supplier to be sure you have the correct gasket set.

To determine the float level, invert bowl cover (5—Fig. MY5-18) with inlet needle and seat (6), primary lever (8) and secondary lever (9) installed. Measure distance (A) from carburetor body surface to top of secondary lever (9). Distance (A) should be 13/32 inch (10.32 mm). Adjust distance (A) by bending curved end of primary lever (8). Turn

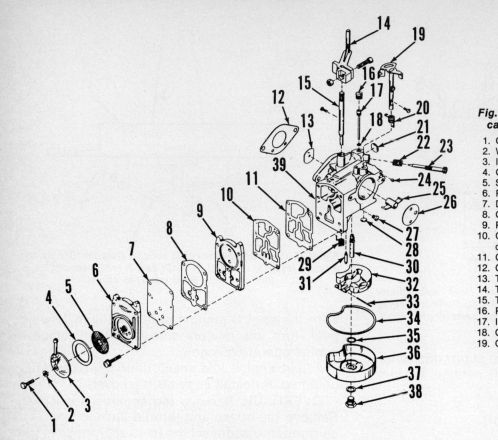

Fig. MY5-20—Exploded view of a Mercarb carburetor with an integral fuel pump.

1. Cap screw
2. Washer
3. Inlet cover
4. Gasket
5. Strainer
6. Pump cover
7. Diaphragm
8. Gasket
9. Pump body
10. Check valve diaphragm
11. Gasket
12. Gasket
13. Throttle plate
14. Throttle lever
15. Throttle shaft
16. Plug
17. Idle tube
18. Gasket
19. Choke shaft
20. Return spring
21. Welch plug
22. Spring
23. Idle mixture screw
24. Plug
25. Boost venturi
26. Choke plate
27. Main jet
28. Welch plug
29. Return spring
30. Main nozzle
31. Inlet needle
32. Float
33. Float pin
34. Gasket
35. Gasket
36. Float bowl
37. Gasket
38. Plug

bowl cover (5 — Fig. MY5-19) upright and measure distance (D) between primary lever (8) and end of secondary lever (9). Distance (D) should be ¼ inch (6.4 mm). Bend tab (T) to adjust. The contact spring located in center of float (11 — Fig. MY5-17) should extend 3/32 inch (2.38 mm) above top of float. Check to see if spring has been stretched or damaged.

Reinstall the carburetor with a new mounting gasket and securely tighten the retaining nuts. Complete reassembly in the reverse order of disassembly with the exception of the engine cover. Initially adjust idle mixture screw (14 — Fig. MY5-17) one turn out from a lightly seated position.

Models 1973 And Later

The fuel pump and carburetor are a complete unit. Refer to the following OVERHAUL section for service procedures on both the fuel pump and carburetor.

ADJUSTMENT. Standard main jet (27 — Fig. MY5-20) size is 0.057 inch (1.45 mm) on all models except motors with serial number 4102790-4351589, which is 0.053 inch (1.35 mm).

Other main jet sizes are available for adjusting the calibration for altitude or other special conditions. Preliminary adjustment of idle mixture screw (23) is 1½ turns out from a lightly seated

position. Recommended idle speed is 550-650 rpm with engine at normal operating temperature and in gear.

With the outboard motor properly mounted on a boat or a suitable test tank, immerse the lower unit. Connect a tachometer and set it on the appropriate range scale. Start engine and allow it to warm up to normal operating temperature. With the engine running at idle speed while in forward gear, turn idle mixture screw (23) until smooth engine operation is noted. Adjust engine idle speed until 550-650 rpm is obtained.

Reinstall engine's top cover.

OVERHAUL. The fuel pump is an integral part of the carburetor. The fuel pump assembly may be overhauled without overhauling the complete carburetor. If the fuel pump is to be overhauled without carburetor removal, proceed as follows: Remove the engine's top cover and disconnect the fuel tank supply hose at the outboard motor connector. Disconnect the fuel supply hose at the fuel pump inlet.

With reference to Fig. MY5-20, disassemble the fuel pump assembly. Inspect all components for damage and excessive wear and renew if needed. Clean components as needed with a suitable cleaning solution. Blow dry with clean compressed air. If compressed air is not available, use only lint-free cloths to wipe dry. Make sure all passages are clear of any obstruction.

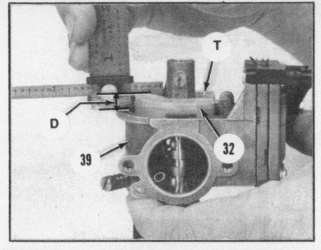

Fig. MY5-21—To determine float level, invert carburetor body (39) and measure distance (D) from carburetor body (39) to base of float (32). Distance (D) should be 15/64 to 17/64 inch (6-6.8 mm) and is adjusted by bending tang (T) on float arm.

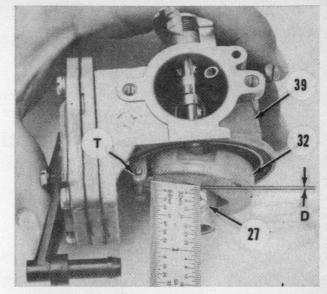

Fig. MY5-22—To determine float drop, turn carburetor body (39) upright and measure distance (D) from lowest portion of float (32) to highest point on main jet (27). Distance should be 1/32 to 1/16 inch (0.8-1.6 mm). Adjust by bending tang (T) at rear of float arm.

With reference to Fig. MY5-20, reassemble the fuel pump assembly with new gaskets. Securely tighten the retaining screws.

NOTE: Fuel pump and engine malfunction will result if the fuel pump and all connections are not airtight.

Complete reassembly.

Refer to the following for complete carburetor overhaul: Remove the engine's top cover. Disconnect the choke cable from the choke lever. Disconnect the fuel tank supply hose at the outboard motor connector. Disconnect the fuel supply hose at the fuel pump inlet. Clean all external surfaces and remove accumulated dirt and grease. Remove the two nuts securing the carburetor and withdraw the carburetor assembly.

With reference to Fig. MY5-20, disassemble the complete carburetor assembly and note any discrepancies which must be corrected before reassembly. Remove all gaskets (label if needed for later reference) and set to the side.

Thoroughly clean all carburetor parts in a suitable solvent and inspect for damage and excessive wear. Note that plastic and rubber components should not be subjected to some cleaning solutions. Blow dry with clean compressed air. If compressed air is not available, use only lint-free cloths to wipe dry. Do not use a drill bit or wire to clean jets. Enlargement or damage of the calibrated holes may affect engine performance.

With reference to Fig. MY5-20, reassemble the carburetor components with new gaskets. Note that the new gaskets should match up with those removed. If not, check with your parts supplier to be sure you have the correct gasket set.

To determine the float level, invert carburetor body (39 — Fig. MY5-21) and measure distance (D) from carburetor body (39) to base of float (32). Distance (D) should be 15/64 to 17/64 inch (6-6.8 mm) and is adjusted by bending tang (T) on float arm.

Check the float drop by turning carburetor body (39 — Fig. MY5-22) upright and measuring distance (D) from lowest portion of float (32) to highest point on main jet (27). Distance should be 1/32 to 1/16 inch (0.8-1.6 mm). Adjust float drop by bending tang (T) at rear of float arm.

When reinstalling the carburetor, place a new gasket (12 — Fig. MY5-20) between the carburetor and the intake manifold. Securely tighten the retaining nuts. Reconnect the fuel supply hoses. Connect choke cable to choke lever. Initially adjust idle mixture screw (23) 1½ turns out from a lightly seated position.

MERC 18 AND 25
(Prior To Serial No. 6416713)

NOTE: Metric and U.S. fasteners are used on outboard motor. Be sure correct fasteners and tools are used when servicing motor.

Specifications

Rated horsepower/rpm 18/5000-5500
25/5400-6000
Bore . . . . .2.56 in.
(65 mm)
Stroke . . . . .2.36 in.
(60 mm)
Number of cylinders 2
Displacement . . . . .24.4 cu. in.
(400 cc)
Spark plug:
  Type . . . . .Champion L77J4
  Electrode Gap . . . . .0.040 in.
(1.02 mm)
Ignition . . . . .Breakerless
Carburetor:
  Make . . . . .Tillotson
Fuel:oil ratio 50:1
Gearcase oil capacity . . . . .5½ oz.
(163 mL)

Maintenance

LUBRICATION

ENGINE. The engine is lubricated by oil mixed with the fuel. The fuel should be regular leaded, low lead or unleaded gasoline with a minimum pump octane rating of 86. Recommended oil is Quicksilver Formula 50-D Outboard Lubricant or a BIA certified two-stroke motor oil. The recommended fuel:oil ratio for normal operation is 50:1.

LOWER UNIT. The lower unit gears and bearings are lubricated by oil contained in the gearcase. The recommended oil is Quicksilver Super-Duty Gear Lubricant. The gearcase oil capacity is 5½ ounces (163 mL) on all models. The gearcase oil level should be checked every 30 days and the lubricant renewed periodically. The gearcase is drained and filled through the same plug port (D—Fig. MY6-1). An oil level (vent) is used to indicate the full oil level of the gearcase and to ease oil drainage.

To drain the oil, place the outboard motor in a vertical position. Remove drain plug (D) and oil

Fig. MY6-1—View showing lower unit gearcase drain and fill plug (D) and oil level (vent) plug (L).

level plug (l), and allow the lubricant to drain into a suitable container.

To fill the gearcase with oil, place the outboard motor in a vertical position. Add oil through drain plug (D) opening with an oil feeder until the oil begins to overflow from oil level plug (L) port. Reinstall oil level plug (L) with a new gasket, if needed, and tighten. Remove oil feeder, then reinstall drain plug (D) with a new gasket, if needed, and tighten.

POINT PIVOTS AND SLIDES. Lubricate all pivot points and linkage slides with a good quality marine type multipurpose grease as frequently as needed to keep the components operating freely and properly.

FUEL SYSTEM

Periodically inspect the fuel lines and connections for damage. Renew components if needed.

Keep the external surface of the carburetor clean and all connections and sealing surfaces tight.

FUEL FILTER. A fuel filter assembly is connected between fuel supply line and carburetor/fuel pump inlet line. With the engine stopped, occasionally unscrew fuel filter cap (4—Fig. MY6-2) from filter base (1) and withdraw sealing ring (3) and filter element (2). Clean cup (4) and filter element (2) in a suitable solvent and blow dry with clean compressed air. Inspect filter element (2). If excessive blockage or damage is noted, renew element.

Reassembly is reverse order of disassembly. If needed, renew sealing ring (3) during reassembly.

A strainer (18—Fig. MY6-3) positioned behind inlet cover (16) is used to provide additional filtering of foreign contaminates. To inspect, remove inlet cover (16) and strainer (18). Clean strainer (18) in a suitable solvent and blow dry with clean compressed air. Inspect strainer (18). If excessive blockage or damage is noted, renew strainer. If needed, renew gasket (17).

FUEL PUMP. The fuel pump is an integral part of the carburetor. Refer to CARBURETOR in the Tune-Up section for fuel pump overhaul. The fuel pump assembly may be overhauled without carburetor removal.

STARTER

When starter rope (10—Fig. MY6-4) is pulled, pulley (9) will rotate. As pulley (9) rotates, the two drive pawls (12) move apart thus meshing with the flywheel and cranking the engine.

When starter rope (10) is released, pulley (9) is rotated in the reverse direction by force from rewind spring (8). As pulley (9) rotates, starter rope

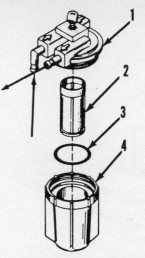

Fig. MY6-2 — Exploded view of reusable type fuel filter.
1. Filter base
2. Filter element
3. Sealing ring
4. Filter cup

(10) is rewound and drive pawls (12) are disengaged from the flywheel.

A starter lockout assembly is used to prevent starter engagement when the gear shift control is in the forward or reverse position.

To overhaul the manual starter, proceed as follows: Remove the engine's top cover. Detach fuel filter assembly from starter housing by pulling filter assembly straight down. Remove the three starter housing retaining screws and withdraw the starter assembly.

⚠WARNING

Care should be exercised when working with or around a coiled starter rewind spring as sudden uncoiling can cause injury. Safety eyewear and gloves are recommended.

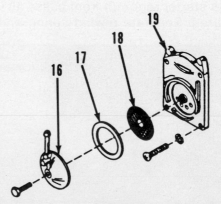

Fig. MY6-3—View showing fuel strainer (18) located behind fuel pump inlet cover (16). Gasket (17) is used to seal between inlet cover (16) and pump cover (19).

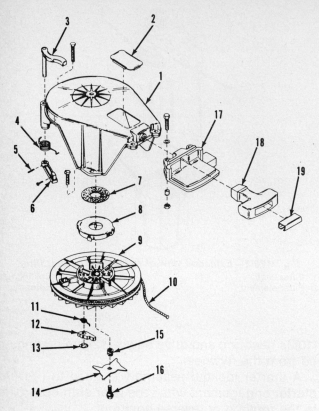

Fig. MY6-4—Exploded view of rewind starter.

1. Starter housing
2. Cover
3. Lockout lever
4. Spring
5. Pin
6. Pulley lock lever
7. Felt pad
8. Rewind spring & case
9. Pulley
10. Starter rope
11. Spring
12. Pawl
13. Clip
14. Cam
15. Spring
16. Screw
17. Rope guide
18. Handle
19. Anchor

To disassemble, remove clips (13) and withdraw pawls (12) and springs (11). Untie starter rope (10) at anchor (19) and allow the rope to wind into the starter. Remove screw (16), cam (14) and spring (15). Carefully lift pulley (9) with starter rope (10) from housing (1). BE CAREFUL when removing pulley (9) as rewind spring (8) may be dislodged. Remove starter rope (10) from pulley (9) if renewal is required. Separate rewind spring and case (8)

Fig. MY6-6—Cooling system water inlet ports (I) are located on the port and starboard side of the lower unit.

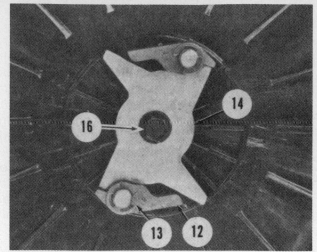

Fig. MY6-5—View showing correct installation of pawls (12), clips (13), cam (14) and screw (16).

from pulley (9). If renewal of rewind spring is required, use extreme caution when removing rewind spring from spring case (8).

Inspect all components for damage and excessive wear and renew if needed.

To reassemble, first apply a coating of a suitable water-resistant grease to rewind spring area of spring case (8). Install rewind spring in spring case (8) so spring coils wind in a clockwise direction from the outer end. Make sure the spring's outer hook is properly secured. Install rewind spring and case (8) into pulley (9). Wind starter rope (10) onto pulley (9) counterclockwise when viewed from the flywheel side. Assemble pulley (9) to starter housing (1) making sure rewind spring end properly engages notch in starter housing shaft. When pulley (9) is seated properly, pulley bushing will be flush with end of starter housing shaft. Install spring (15), cam (14) and secure with screw (16). Install springs (11), pawls (12) and clips (13) as shown in Fig. MY6-5.

Rotate pulley (9 — Fig. MY6-4) counterclockwise until starter rope (10) end is aligned with starter housing rope outlet. Thread starter rope (10) through starter housing (1), rope guide (17), handle (18) and secure in anchor (19). Pull starter rope (10) out to full length while checking for freedom of travel, then allow starter rope (10) to rewind onto pulley (9). Starter handle (18) should be drawn back into the proper released position. If not, release starter rope (10) from handle (18) and rotate pulley (9) one complete turn counterclockwise (flywheel side) and reassemble.

NOTE: Do not apply any more tension on rewind spring (8) than is required to draw starter handle (18) back into the proper released position.

Remount manual starter assembly and complete reassembly.

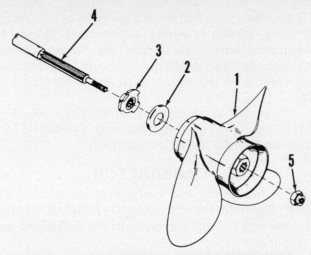

Fig. MY6-7—Thrust hub (3), cupped washer (2) and propeller (1) are mounted on propeller shaft (4) and retained by nut (5).

Fig. MY6-8—At full throttle, ignition timing is at full advance when three dots (D) align with timing mark (M) on starter housing. Refer to text for adjustment of speed control link (K) and throttle rod (T).

COOLING SYSTEM

Ports (I—Fig. MY6-6) located on the port and starboard side of the lower unit are used as the water inlets for the cooling system. The ports must be kept clean of all foreign matter to ensure efficient operation of the cooling system.

⚠CAUTION

Do not operate outboard motor unless the lower unit is immersed in water, otherwise, the water pump impeller will be damaged.

PROPELLER

Consult your local dealer or the manufacturer for the specifications pertaining to the standard propeller used on your model of outboard motor. Optional propellers are available. Select a propeller that will allow the engine at full throttle to reach maximum operating rpm range (5000-5500 on 18 hp models and 5400-6000 on 25 hp models).

⚠WARNING

Shift directional control lever to "NEUTRAL." Disconnect the spark plug leads and properly ground leads before performing any propeller service, otherwise, accidental starting can occur if propeller shaft is rotated.

To remove the propeller, unscrew propeller retaining nut (5—Fig. MY6-7). Withdraw propeller (1), cupped washer (2) and thrust hub (3) from propeller shaft (4).

Inspect all components for damage and excessive wear and renew if needed.

Apply Perfect Seal or a suitable equivalent to the propeller shaft splines, then install thrust hub (3), cupped washer (2) and propeller (1). Install propeller retaining nut (5) and securely tighten.

Tune-Up

IGNITION SYSTEM

A "Thunderbolt" capacitor discharge ignition (CDI) system is used. Refer to the Outboard Motor Service Manual for testing and servicing CD ignition system. If engine malfunction is noted, make sure the spark plugs and all electrical wiring are in good condition and all electrical connections are tight before proceeding to troubleshooting the CD ignition system.

The standard spark plug is Champion L77J4. A Champion QL77J4 is recommended by the manufacturer should radio frequency interference suppression be required. Spark plug electrode gap should be 0.040 inch (1.02 mm).

SPEED CONTROL LINKAGE

The speed control twist grip, through the use of linkage, operates the stator plate to advance or retard the ignition timing. The carburetor throttle plate is synchronized to open as the timing is advanced.

To synchronize ignition timing and throttle opening, proceed as follows: Mount the outboard motor on a boat or a suitable test tank and immerse the lower unit. Remove the engine cover.

Fig. 6-9—View of throttle cam (C), throttle cam lever (L), dashpot (P), screw (W) and throttle shaft roller (R). Refer to text for speed control linkage adjustment procedures.

Connect a power timing light to the top cylinder spark plug lead. With the engine in forward gear and running at full throttle, three timing dots (D—Fig. MY6-8) should be aligned with timing mark (M) on starter housing. To adjust full advance ignition timing, stop engine and adjust length of link (K) by disconnecting and turning link end. Lengthening link will advance ignition timing. Recheck full throttle ignition timing, then stop engine.

Disconnect throttle rod (T) from throttle cam, loosen screw (W—Fig. MY6-9) and move throttle cam (C) so mark (L) is aligned with roller (R) and cam just touches the roller. Retighten screw (W). Run the engine and open the speed control so two timing dots on flywheel are aligned with timing mark (M—Fig. MY6-8). Adjust length of throttle rod (T) so when rod is attached to throttle cam, mark (L—Fig. MY6-9) is within 1/16 inch (1.59 mm) of alignment with center of roller (R). Adjust position of dashpot (P) so dashpot plunger is fully depressed when roller (R) is located at end of throttle cam (C).

Idle speed is adjusted at stop screw (IS—Fig. MY6-11). Refer to the following CARBURETOR section for idle speed adjustment.

CARBURETOR

The fuel pump and carburetor are a complete unit. Refer to the following OVERHAUL section for service procedures on both the fuel pump and carburetor.

ADJUSTMENT. Standard make of carburetor is a Tillotson. Carburetor Model BC2A is used on 18 models and Model BC1A or BC1B is used on 25 models. Standard main jet (30—Fig. MY6-10) size is 0.046 inch (1.17 mm) on 18 models and 0.067 inch (1.70 mm) on 25 models. Other main jet (30) sizes are available for adjusting the calibration for altitude or other special conditions. Preliminary adjustment of idle mixture screw (10) is 1¼ turns out from a lightly seated position. Recommended idle speed is 600-700 rpm with engine at normal operating temperature and in gear.

All models are equipped with an enrichment valve (3) to enrichen the fuel mixture for cold starting. With choke knob turned fully clockwise, arm (A—Fig. MY6-11) should depress valve stem (T). Bend rod (R) to adjust position of arm (A).

With the outboard motor properly mounted on a boat or a suitable test tank, immerse the lower

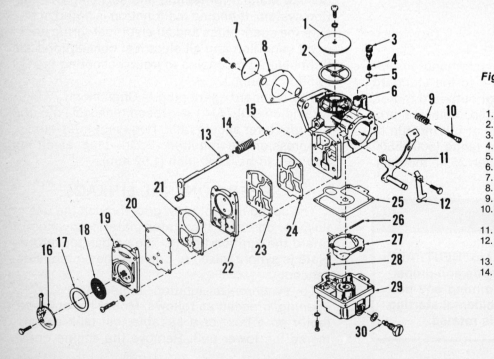

Fig. MY6-10—Exploded view of Tillotson carburetor used on all models.

1. Cover
2. Gasket
3. Enrichment valve
4. Spring
5. Gasket
6. Body
7. Throttle plate
8. Gasket
9. Spring
10. Idle mixture screw
11. Plate
12. Choke knob detent
13. Throttle shaft
14. Spring
15. Snap ring
16. Inlet cover
17. Gasket
18. Strainer
19. Fuel pump cover
20. Diaphragm
21. Gasket
22. Pump body
23. Check valves
24. Gasket
25. Gasket
26. Float pin
27. Float
28. Fuel inlet valve
29. Float bowl
30. Main jet

Fig. MY6-11—View of carburetor. Refer to text for adjustment of identified components.

A. Enrichment arm
R. Enrichment rod
T. Enrichment valve stem

IS. Idle speed screw
10. Idle mixture screw

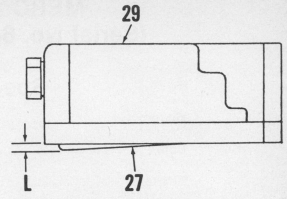

Fig. MY6-12— With float bowl (29) inverted as shown, float (27) level (L) should be even with or less than 1/32 inch (0.8 mm) below float bowl edge.

unit. Connect a tachometer and set it on the appropriate range scale. Start the engine and allow it to warm up to normal operating temperature. With the engine running at idle speed while in forward gear, turn idle mixture screw (10) until smooth engine operation is noted. Adjust engine idle speed screw (IS) until 600-700 rpm is obtained.

Reinstall engine top cover.

OVERHAUL. The fuel pump is an integral part of the carburetor. The fuel pump assembly may be overhauled without overhauling the complete carburetor. If the fuel pump is to be overhauled without carburetor removal, proceed as follows:

Remove the engine top cover and disconnect the fuel tank supply hose at the outboard motor connector. Disconnect the fuel supply hose at the fuel pump inlet.

With reference to Fig. MY6-10, disassemble the fuel pump assembly. Inspect all components for damage and excessive wear and renew if needed. Clean components as needed with a suitable cleaning solution. Blow dry with clean compressed air. If compressed air is not available, use only lint-free cloths to wipe dry. Make sure all passages are clear of any obstruction.

With reference to Fig. MY6-10, reassemble the fuel pump assembly with new gaskets. Securely tighten the retaining screws.

NOTE: Fuel pump and engine malfunction will result if the fuel pump and all connections are not airtight.

Complete reassembly.

Refer to the following for complete carburetor overhaul: Remove the engine's top cover. Disconnect choke lever from choke knob. Disconnect the fuel tank supply hose at the outboard motor connector. Disconnect the fuel supply hose at the

fuel pump inlet. Remove all components as needed to allow separation and removal of engine's lower covers. Remove securing screws and withdraw engine's lower covers. Clean all external surfaces and remove accumulated dirt and grease. Remove the two nuts securing the carburetor and withdraw the carburetor assembly.

With reference to Fig. MY6-10, disassemble the complete carburetor assembly and note any discrepancies which must be corrected before reassembly. Remove all gaskets (label if needed for later reference) and set to the side.

Thoroughly clean all carburetor parts in a suitable solvent and inspect for damage and excessive wear. Note that plastic and rubber components should not be subjected to some cleaning solutions. Blow dry with clean compressed air. If compressed air is not available, use only lint-free cloths to wipe dry. Do not use a drill bit or wire to clean jets. Enlargement or damage of the calibrated holes may affect engine performance.

With reference to Fig. MY6-10, reassemble the carburetor components with new gaskets. Note that the new gaskets should match up with those removed. If not, check with your parts supplier to be sure you have the correct gasket set.

To determine the float level, invert carburetor float bowl (29—Fig. MY6-10) with fuel inlet valve (28) and float (27) installed. With float (27) hanging down as shown in Fig. MY6-12, float end level (L) should be even with or less than 1/32 inch (0.8 mm) below float bowl (29) edge. Bend float arm tang to adjust.

When reinstalling the carburetor, place a new gasket (8—Fig. MY6-10) between the carburetor and the adapter plate. Securely tighten the retaining nuts. Reassemble in the reverse order of disassembly with the exception of the engine's top cover. Initially adjust idle mixture screw (10—Fig. MY6-11) 1¼ turns out from a lightly seated position.

MERC 18, 20 AND 25
(Serial No. 6416713 And Above)

Specifications

Hp/rpm 18,20/4500-5500
25/5000-6000
Bore . . . . .2.56 in.
(65 mm)
Stroke . . . . .2.36 in.
(60 mm)
Number of cylinders 2
Displacement . . . . .24.4 cu. in.
(400 cc)
Ignition type . . . . .Breakerless
Spark plug . . . . .See Text
Idle speed (in gear) 600-700
Fuel:oil ratio. 50:1
Gearcase oil capacity . . . . .7.6 oz.
(225 mL)

Maintenance

LUBRICATION

ENGINE. The engine is lubricated by oil mixed with the fuel. The fuel should be regular leaded, low lead or unleaded gasoline with a minimum pump octane rating of 86. Recommended oil is Quicksilver Formula 50-D Outboard Lubricant or a BIA certified two-stroke motor oil. The recommended fuel:oil ratio for normal operation is 50:1.

LOWER UNIT. The lower unit gears and bearings are lubricated by oil contained in the gearcase. The recommended oil is Quicksilver Super-Duty Gear lubricant. The gearcase oil capacity is 7.6 oz. (225 mL) on all models. The gearcase oil level should be checked every 30 days and the lubricant renewed periodically. The gearcase is drained and filled through the same plug port (D — Fig. MY7-1). An oil level (vent) port (L) is used to indicate the full oil level of the gearcase and to ease oil drainage.

To drain the oil, place the outboard motor in a vertical position. Remove drain plug (D) and oil level plug (L), and allow the lubricant to drain into a suitable container.

To fill the gearcase with oil, place the outboard motor in a vertical position. Add oil through drain plug (D) opening with an oil feeder until the oil begins to overflow from oil level plug (L) port. Reinstall oil level plug (L) with a new gasket, if needed, and tighten. Remove oil feeder, then reinstall drain plug (D) with a new gasket, if needed, and tighten.

PIVOT POINTS AND SLIDES. Lubricate all pivot points and linkage slides with a good quality marine type multipurpose grease as frequently as needed to keep the components operating freely and properly.

Fig. MY7-1 — View showing lower unit drain and fill plug (D) and oil level (vent) plug (L).

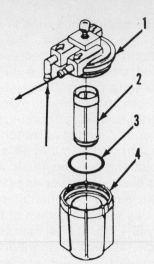

Fig. MY7-2 — Exploded view of reusable type fuel filter.

1. Filter base
2. Filter element
3. Sealing ring
4. Filter cup

FUEL SYSTEM

Periodically inspect the fuel lines and connections for damage. Renew components if needed.

Keep the external surface of the carburetor clean and all connections and sealing surfaces tight.

FUEL FILTER. A fuel filter assembly is connected between fuel supply line and carburetor/fuel pump inlet line. With the engine stopped, occasionally unscrew fuel filter cup (4 — Fig. MY7-2) from filter base (1) and withdraw sealing ring (3) and filter element (2). Clean cup (4) and filter element (2) in a suitable solvent and blow dry with clean compressed air. Inspect filter element (2). If excessive blockage or damage is noted, renew element.

Reassembly is reverse order of disassembly. If needed, renew sealing ring (3) during reassembly.

A strainer (18 — Fig. MY7-3) positioned behind inlet cover (16) on "BC" type carburetors, is used

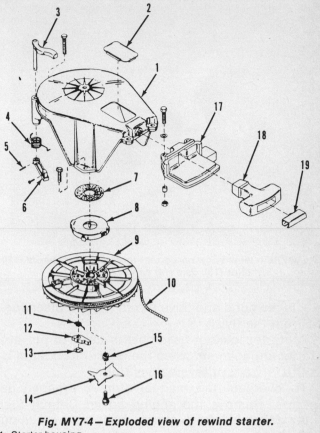

Fig. MY7-4 — Exploded view of rewind starter.

1. Starter housing
2. Cover
3. Lockout lever
4. Spring
5. Pin
6. Pulley lock lever
7. Felt pad
8. Rewind spring & case
9. Pulley
10. Starter rope
11. Spring
12. Pawl
13. Clip
14. Cam
15. Spring
16. Screw
17. Rope guide
18. Handle
19. Anchor

to provide additional filtering of foreign contaminates. To inspect, remove inlet cover (16) and strainer (18). Clean strainer (18) in a suitable solvent and blow dry with clean compressed air. Inspect strainer (18). If excessive blockage or damage is noted, renew strainer. If needed, renew gasket (17).

FUEL PUMP. The fuel pump is an integral part of the carburetor. Refer to CARBURETOR in the Tune-Up section for fuel pump overhaul. The fuel pump assembly may be overhauled without carburetor removal.

STARTER

When starter rope (10 — Fig. MY7-4) is pulled, pulley (9) will rotate. As pulley (9) rotates, the two drive pawls (12) move apart thus meshing with the flywheel and cranking the engine.

When starter rope (10) is released, pulley (9) is rotated in the reverse direction by force from rewind spring (8). As pulley (9) rotates, starter rope

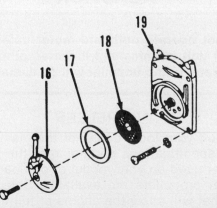

Fig. MY7-3 — On "BC" type carburetor, view showing fuel strainer (18) located behind fuel pump inlet cover (16). Gasket (17) is used to seal between inlet cover (16) and pump cover (19).

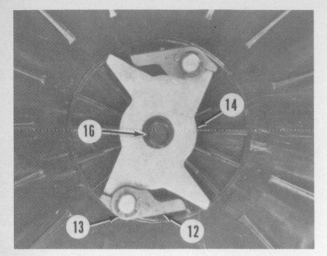

Fig. MY7-5—View showing correct installation of pawls (12), clips (13), cam (14) and screw (16).

(10) is rewound and drive pawls (12) are disengaged from the flywheel.

A starter lockout assembly is used to prevent starter engagement when the gear shift control is in the forward or reverse position.

To overhaul the manual starter, proceed as follows: Remove the engine cover. Detach fuel filter assembly from starter housing by pulling filter assembly straight down. Remove the three starter housing retaining screws and withdraw the starter assembly.

⚠WARNING

Care should be exercised when working with or around a coiled starter rewind spring as sudden uncoiling can cause injury. Safety eyewear and gloves are recommended.

To disassemble, remove clips (13) and withdraw pawls (12) and springs (11). Untie starter rope (10) at anchor (19) and allow the rope to wind into the starter. Remove screw (16), cam (14) and spring (15). Carefully lift pulley (9) with starter rope (10) from housing (1). BE CAREFUL when removing pulley (9) as rewind spring (8) may be dislodged. Remove starter rope (10) from pulley (9) if renewal is required. Separate rewind spring and case (8) from pulley (9). If renewal of rewind spring is required, use extreme caution when removing rewind spring from spring case (8).

Inspect all components for damage and excessive wear and renew if needed.

To reassemble, first apply a coating of a suitable water-resistant grease to rewind spring area of spring case (8). Install rewind spring in spring case (8) so spring coils wind in a clockwise direction from the outer end. Make sure the spring's outer hook is properly secured. Install rewind spring and case (8) into pulley (9). Wind starter rope (10) onto pulley (9) counterclockwise when viewed from the flywheel side. Assemble pulley (9) to starter housing (1) making sure rewind spring end properly engages notch in starter housing center shaft. When pulley (9) is seated properly, pulley bushing will be flush with end of starter housing shaft. Install spring (15), cam (14) and secure with screw (16). Install springs (11), pawls (12) and clips (13) as shown in Fig. MY7-5.

Rotate pulley (9—Fig. MY7-4) counterclockwise until starter rope (10) end is aligned with starter housing rope outlet. Thread starter rope (10) through starter housing (1), rope guide (17) and handle (18) and secure in anchor (19). Pull starter rope (10) out to full length while checking for freedom of travel, then allow starter rope (10) to rewind onto pulley (9). Starter handle (18) should be drawn back into the proper released position. If not, release starter rope (10) from handle (18) and rotate pulley (9) one complete turn counterclockwise (flywheel side) and reassemble.

NOTE: Do not apply any more tension on rewind spring (8) than is required to draw starter handle (18) back into the proper released position.

Remount manual starter assembly and complete reassembly.

COOLING SYSTEM

Ports (I—Fig. MY7-6) located on the port and starboard side of the lower unit are used as the water inlets for the cooling system. The ports must be kept clean of all foreign matter to ensure efficient operation of the cooling system.

⚠CAUTION

Do not operate outboard motor unless the lower unit is immersed in water, otherwise, the water pump impeller will be damaged.

PROPELLER

Consult your local dealer or the manufacturer for the specifications pertaining to the standard propeller used on your model of outboard motor. Optional propellers are available. Select a propeller that will allow the engine at full throttle to reach maximum operating rpm range (4500-5500 on 18 and 20 hp models and 5000-6000 on 25 hp models).

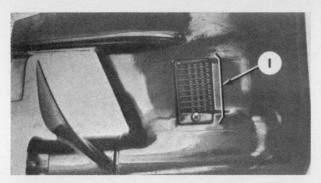

Fig. MY7-6 — Cooling system water inlet ports (I) are located on the port and starboard side of the lower unit.

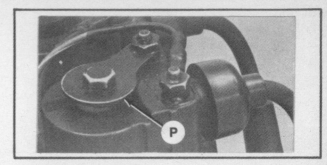

Fig. MY7-8 — View showing ground plate (P) attached to the negative ignition coil terminal.

Tune-Up

IGNITION SYSTEM

A capacitor discharge ignition (CDI) system is used. Refer to the Outboard Motor Service Manual for testing and servicing the CD ignition system. If engine malfunction is noted and the ignition system is suspected, make sure the spark plugs and all electrical wiring are in good condition and all electrical connections are tight before proceeding to troubleshooting the CD ignition system.

On models with a ground plate (P — Fig. MY7-8) attached to the negative ignition coil terminal, the standard spark plug is Champion L77J4. A Champion QL77J4 is recommended by the manufacturer should radio frequency interference suppression be required. Spark plug electrode gap should be 0.040 inch (1.02 mm). On models that are equipped with a ground wire attached to the negative ignition coil terminal, the standard spark plug is Champion L76V. A Champion QL76V is recommended by the manufacturer should radio frequency interference suppression be required. Renew surface gap spark plug if center electrode is more than 1/32 inch (0.79 mm) below the flat surface of the plug end.

⚠WARNING

Shift directional control lever to "NEUTRAL." Disconnect the spark plug leads and properly ground leads before performing any propeller service, otherwise, accidental starting can occur if propeller shaft is rotated.

To remove the propeller, unscrew propeller retaining nut (3 — Fig. MY7-7). Withdraw propeller (1) and thrust hub (2) from propeller shaft (4).

Inspect all components for damage and excessive wear and renew if needed.

Apply Perfect Seal or a suitable equivalent to the propeller shaft splines, then install thrust hub (2) and propeller (1). Install propeller retaining nut (3) and securely tighten.

SPEED CONTROL LINKAGE

The speed control twist grip, through the use of linkage, operates the stator plate to advance or retard the ignition timing. The carburetor throttle plate is synchronized to open as the timing is advanced.

Models With "BC" Type Carburetor And "BCIA" Stamped On Carburetor Flange

To synchronize ignition timing and throttle opening, proceed as follows: Mount the outboard motor on a boat or a suitable test tank and immerse the lower unit. Remove the engine cover. Connect a power timing light to the top cylinder spark plug lead. With the engine in the forward

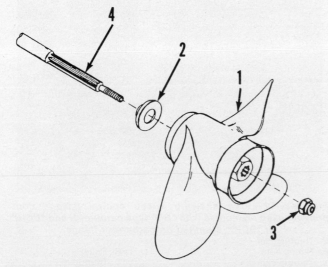

Fig. MY7-7 — Thrust hub (2) and propeller (1) are mounted on propeller shaft (4) and retained by nut (3).

Fig. MY7-9—On models with "BC" type carburetor, at full throttle the ignition timing is at full advance when three dots (D) align with timing mark (M) on starter housing. Refer to text for adjustment of speed control link (K) and throttle rod (T).

Fig. MY7-11—View showing speed control linkage components used on models "BC" type carburetor and 'BCIA' stamped on carburetor flange.

B. Timing dots	M. Timing mark	T. Throttle rod
C. Throttle cam	P. Dashpot	V. Throttle lever
L. Throttle cam mark	R. Roller	IS. Idle speed stop screw

gear and running at full throttle, three timing dots (D—Fig. MY7-9) should be aligned with timing mark (M) on starter housing. To adjust full advance ignition timing, stop the engine and adjust length of link (K) by disconnecting and turning link end. Lengthening link will advance ignition timing. Recheck full throttle ignition timing, then stop engine.

Disconnect throttle rod (T) from throttle cam, loosen screw (W—Fig. MY7-10) and move throttle cam (C) so mark (L) is aligned with roller (R) and cam just touches roller. Retighten screw (W). Start the engine, then advance throttle lever (V—Fig. MY7-11) until two timing dots (B) on flywheel are aligned with timing mark (M). Adjust length of throttle rod (T) so when rod is attached to throttle cam (C), mark (L) is in contact with roller (R).

Idle speed is adjusted at stop screw (IS). Refer to the following CARBURETOR section for idle speed adjustment. Adjust position of dashpot (P)

so dashpot plunger is fully depressed when the engine is idling at the recommended rpm.

Models With "BC" Type Carburetor and "BCIB" or BCIC" Stamped On Carburetor Flange

To synchronize ignition timing and throttle opening, proceed as follows: Mount the outboard motor on a boat or a suitable test tank and immerse the lower unit. Remove the engine's cover. Connect a power timing light to the top cylinder spark plug lead. With the engine in the forward gear and running at full throttle, three timing dots (D—Fig. MY7-9) should be aligned with timing mark (M) on starter housing. To adjust full ad-

Fig. MY7-12—View showing speed control linkage components used on models with "BC" type carburetor and "BCIB" or "BCIC" stamped on carburetor flange.

C. Throttle cam	
F. Timing dots	R. Roller
L. Throttle cam mark	T. Throttle rod
M. Timing mark	V. Throttle lever
P. Dashpot	IS. Idle speed stop screw

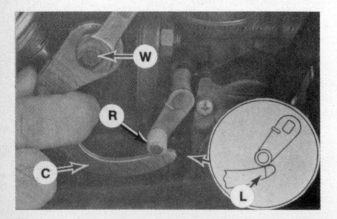

Fig. MY7-10—View showing throttle cam (C), throttle cam mark (L), throttle shaft roller (R) and screw (W) used on models with "BC" type carburetor. Refer to text for speed control linkage adjustment procedures.

Fig. MY7-13—On models with "WMC" type carburetor, at full throttle the ignition timing is at full advance when three dots (D) align with timing mark (M) on starter housing. Refer to text for adjustment of speed control link (K).

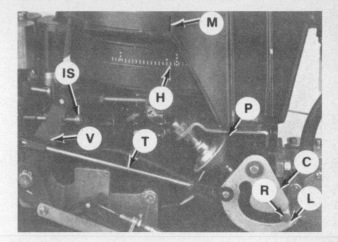

Fig. MY7-15—View showing speed control linkage components used on models with "WMC" type carburetor.

C. Throttle cam
H. Flywheel timing mark
L. Throttle cam mark
M. Starter housing timing mark
P. Dashpot
R. Roller
T. Throttle rod
V. Throttle lever
IS. Idle speed screw

vance ignition timing, stop the engine and adjust length of link (K) by disconnecting and turning link end. Lengthening link will advance ignition timing. Recheck full throttle ignition timing, then stop engine.

Disconnect throttle rod (T) from throttle cam, loosen screw (W—Fig. MY7-10) and move throttle cam (C) so mark (L) is aligned with roller (R) and cam just touches roller. Retighten screw (W). Start the engine, then advance throttle lever (V—Fig. MY7-12) until four timing dots (F) on flywheel are aligned with timing mark (M). Adjust length of throttle rod (T) so when rod is attached to throttle cam (C), mark (L) is in contact with roller (R).

Idle speed is adjusted at stop screw (IS). Refer to the following CARBURETOR section for idle speed adjustment. Adjust position of dashpot (P)

so dashpot plunger is fully depressed when the engine is idling at the recommended rpm.

Models With "WMC" Type Carburetor

To synchronize ignition timing and throttle opening, proceed as follows: Mount the outboard motor on a boat or a suitable test tank and immerse the lower unit. Remove the engine cover. Connect a power timing light to the top cylinder spark plug lead. With the engine in the forward gear and running at full throttle, three timing dots (D—Fig. MY7-13) should be aligned with timing mark (M) on starter housing. To adjust full advance ignition timing, stop the engine and adjust length of link (K) by disconnecting and turning link end. Lengthening link will advance ignition tim-

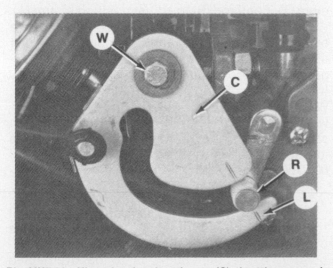

Fig. MY7-14—View showing throttle cam (C), throttle cam mark (L), throttle shaft roller (R) and screw (W) used on models with "WMC" type carburetor. Refer to text for speed control linkage adjustment procedures.

Fig. MY7-16—View showing neutral rpm ratchet (N) and primer/fast idle knob (B) used on models with "WMC" type carburetor.

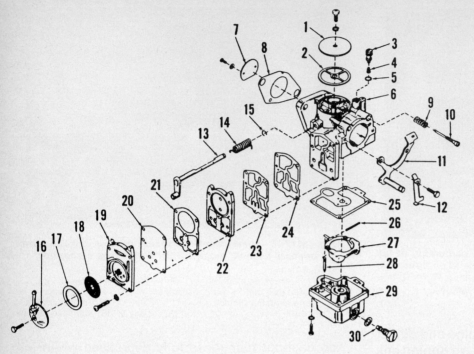

Fig. MY7-17 — Exploded view of "BC" type carburetor.

1. Cover	15. Snap ring
2. Gasket	16. Inlet cover
3. Enrichment valve	17. Gasket
4. Spring	18. Strainer
5. Gasket	19. Fuel pump cover
6. Body	20. Diaphragm
7. Throttle plate	21. Gasket
8. Gasket	22. Pump body
9. Spring	23. Check valves
10. Idle mixture screw	24. Gasket
11. Plate	25. Gasket
12. Choke knob detent	26. Float pin
13. Throttle shaft	27. Float
14. Spring	28. Fuel inlet valve
	29. Float bowl
	30. Main jet

ing. Recheck full throttle ignition timing, then stop engine.

With the engine stopped, loosen screw (W—Fig. MY7-14) and move throttle cam (C) so mark (L) is aligned with roller (R) and cam just touches roller.

NOTE: Adjust idle speed screw (IS—Fig. MY7-15), dashpot (P) and neutral rpm ratchet (N—Fig. MY7-16), if needed, to obtain desired setting.

Retighten screw (W—Fig. MY7-15). Start the engine, then advance throttle lever (V—Fig. MY7-15) until the 2° ATDC timing mark (H) (one mark to the right of single dot) is aligned with timing mark (M). Adjust length of throttle rod (T) so when rod is attached to throttle cam (C), mark (L) is in contact with roller (R).

Idle speed is adjusted at stop screw (IS). Refer to the following CARBURETOR section for idle speed adjustment. Adjust position of dashpot (P) so dashpot plunger is fully depressed when the engine is idling at the recommended rpm.

With a suitable tachometer attached, start the engine and rotate the throttle control to the "SLOW" position. Position the primer/fast idle knob (B—Fig. MY7-16) in the middle detent position and adjust ratchet (N) until 1400-1700 rpm is obtained.

CARBURETOR
Models With "BC" Type Carburetor

The fuel pump and carburetor are a complete unit. Refer to the following OVERHAUL section for service procedures on both the fuel pump and carburetor.

ADJUSTMENT. Standard main jet (30—Fig. MY7-17) size is 0.067 inch (1.70 mm). Other main jet (30) sizes are available for adjusting the calibration for altitude or other special conditions. Preliminary adjustment of idle mixture screw (10) is 1¼ turns out from a lightly seated position. Recommended idle speed is 600-700 rpm with engine at normal operating temperature and in gear.

All models are equipped with an enrichment valve (3) to enrichen the fuel mixture for cold starting. Raise enrichment valve cover (C—Fig. MY7-18), if so equipped. With the choke knob turned fully clockwise, arm (A) should depress valve stem (T). Bend rod (R) to adjust position of arm (A).

With the outboard motor properly mounted on a boat or a suitable test tank, immerse the lower unit. Connect a tachometer and set it on the appropriate range scale. Start the engine and allow it to warm up to normal operating temperature. With the engine running at idle speed while in forward gear, turn idle mixture screw (10) until smooth engine operation is noted. Adjust engine idle speed screw (IS—Fig. MY7-11 or MY7-12) until 600-700 rpm is obtained.

Reinstall engine cover.

OVERHAUL. The fuel pump is an integral part of the carburetor. The fuel pump assembly may be overhauled without overhauling the complete carburetor. If the fuel pump is to be overhauled without carburetor removal, proceed as follows:

Remove the engine cover and disconnect the fuel tank supply hose at the outboard motor

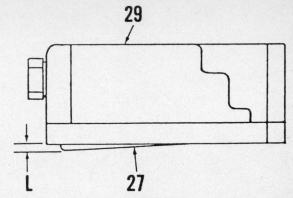

Fig. MY7-19—With float bowl (29) inverted as shown, float (27) level (L) should be even with or less than 1/32 inch (0.8 mm) below float bowl edge.

Fig. MY7-18—View showing carburetor enrichment system used on "BC" carburetor. Refer to text for adjustment procedures.

A. Enrichment arm
C. Enrichment valve cover
R. Enrichment rod
T. Enrichment valve stem

connector. Disconnect the fuel supply hose at the fuel pump inlet.

With reference to Fig. MY7-17, disassemble the fuel pump assembly. Inspect all components for damage and excessive wear and renew if needed. Clean components as needed with a suitable cleaning solution. Blow dry with clean compressed air. If compressed air is not available, use only lint-free cloths to wipe dry. Make sure all passages are clear of any obstruction.

With reference to Fig. MY7-17, reassemble the fuel pump assembly with new gaskets. Securely tighten the retaining screws.

NOTE: Fuel pump and engine malfunction will result if the fuel pump and all connections are not airtight.

Complete reassembly.

Refer to the following for complete carburetor overhaul: Remove the engine cover. Disconnect choke lever from choke knob. Disconnect the fuel tank supply hose at the outboard motor connector. Disconnect the fuel supply hose at the fuel pump inlet. If equipped with an electric starter, remove starter and unplug choke solenoid wire. Clean all external surfaces and remove accumulated dirt and grease. Remove the two nuts securing the carburetor and withdraw the carburetor assembly.

With reference to Fig. MY7-17, disassemble the complete carburetor assembly and note any discrepancies which must be corrected before reassembly. Remove all gaskets (label if needed for later reference) and set to the side.

Thoroughly clean all carburetor parts in a suitable solvent and inspect for damage and excessive wear. Note that plastic and rubber components should not be subjected to some cleaning solutions. Blow dry with clean compressed air. If compressed air is not available, use only lint-free cloths to wipe dry. Do not use a drill bit or wire to clean jets. Enlargement or damage of the calibrated holes may affect engine performance.

With reference to Fig. MY7-17, reassemble the carburetor components with new gaskets. Note that the new gaskets should match up with those removed. If not, check with your parts supplier to be sure you have the correct gasket set.

To determine the float level, invert carburetor float bowl (29—Fig. MY7-17) with fuel inlet valve (28) and float (27) installed. With float (27) hanging down as shown in Fig. MY7-19, float end level (L) should be even with or less than 1/32 inch (0.8 mm) below float bowl (29) edge. Bend float arm tang to adjust.

When reinstalling the carburetor, place a new gasket (8—Fig. MY7-17) between the carburetor and the adapter plate. Securely tighten the retaining nuts. Reassemble in the reverse order of disassembly with the exception of the engine cover. Initially adjust idle mixture screw (10) 1¼ turns out from a lightly seated position.

Models With "WMC" Type Carburetor

The fuel pump and carburetor are a complete unit. Refer to the following OVERHAUL section for service procedures on both the fuel pump and carburetor.

ADJUSTMENT. Standard main jet (30—Fig. MY7-20) size is 0.046 inch (1.17 mm) on 20 hp models and 0.080 inch (2.03 mm) on 25 hp models. Other main jet (30) sizes are available for adjusting the calibration for altitude or other special conditions. Preliminary adjustment of idle mixture screw (6) is 1¼ turns out from a lightly seated

Merc 18, 20 & 25 (Serial No. 6416713 & Above)

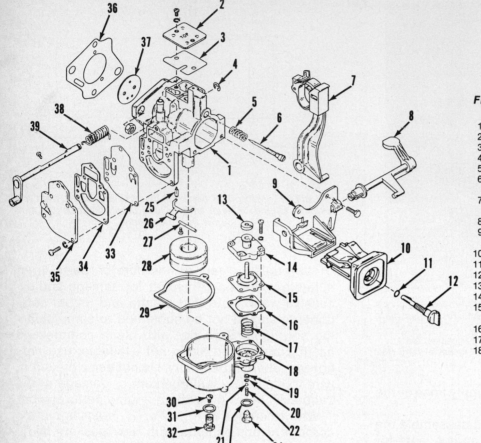

Fig. MY7-20—Exploded view of "WMC" type carburetor.

1. Carburetor body	19. Seat
2. Cover	20. Retainer
3. Gasket	21. Check ball
4. Clip	22. Spring
5. Spring	23. Gasket
6. Idle mixture screw	24. Plug
7. Neutral rpm ratchet	25. Inlet needle
8. Enrichment lever	26. Float arm
9. Enrichment bracket	27. Float pin
10. Enrichment knob	28. Float
11. "O" ring	29. Gasket
12. Fast idle knob	30. Main jet
13. Seal	31. Gasket
14. Cover	32. Plug
15. Enrichment diaphragm	33. Diaphragm
16. Gasket	34. Gasket
17. Spring	35. Cover
18. Float bowl	36. Gasket
	37. Throttle plate
	38. Spring
	39. Throttle shaft

position. Recommended idle speed is 600-700 rpm with engine at normal operating temperature and in gear.

With the outboard motor properly mounted on a boat or a suitable test tank, immerse the lower unit. Connect a tachometer and set it on the appropriate range scale. Start the engine and allow it to warm up to normal operating temperature. With the engine running at idle speed while in forward gear, turn idle mixture screw (6) counterclockwise until the fuel mixture becomes too rich and the engine loads up and starts to misfire. Then turn idle mixture screw (6) clockwise until smooth engine operation is noted. Continue to turn screw (6) clockwise until the fuel mixture becomes too lean and the engine starts to slow down and misfire. At this point, turn idle mixture screw (6) to mid point of too rich and too lean setting. Note that it is better to have the fuel mixture too rich than too lean. Adjust engine idle speed screw (IS—Fig. MY7-15) until 600-700 rpm is obtained.

Reinstall engine's top cover.

OVERHAUL. The fuel pump is an integral part of the carburetor. The fuel pump assembly may be overhauled without overhauling the complete car-

buretor. If the fuel pump is to be overhauled without carburetor removal, proceed as follows:

Remove the engine cover and disconnect the fuel tank supply hose at the outboard motor connector.

With reference to Fig. MY7-20, disassemble the fuel pump assembly. Inspect all components for damage and excessive wear and renew if needed. Clean components as needed with a suitable cleaning solution. Blow dry with clean compressed air. If compressed air is not available, use only lint-free cloths to wipe dry. Make sure all passages are clear of any obstruction.

With reference to Fig. MY7-20, reassemble the fuel pump assembly with a new gasket. Securely tighten the retaining screws.

NOTE: Fuel pump and engine malfunction will result if the fuel pump and all connections are not airtight.

Complete reassembly.

Refer to the following for complete carburetor overhaul: Remove engine top cover. Disconnect the fuel tank supply hose at the outboard motor connector. Remove components as needed to separate the engine bottom cover halves and withdraw. Disconnect the fuel supply hose at

Illustrations Courtesy Mercury

the carburetor inlet. Clean all external surfaces and remove accumulated dirt and grease. Remove the two nuts securing the carburetor and withdraw the carburetor assembly. Detach idle wire at ratchet assembly (7 — Fig. MY7-20).

With reference to Fig. MY7-20, disassemble the complete carburetor assembly and note any discrepancies which must be corrected before reassembly. Remove all gaskets (label if needed for later reference, seal (13) and "O" ring (11), if needed, and set to the side.

Thoroughly clean all carburetor parts in a suitable solvent and inspect for damage and excessive wear. Note that plastic and rubber components should not be subjected to some cleaning solutions. Blow dry with clean compressed air. If compressed air is not available, use only lint-free cloths to wipe dry. Do not use a drill bit or wire to clean jets. Enlargement or damage of the calibrated holes may affect engine performance.

With reference to Fig. MY7-20, reassemble the carburetor components with new gaskets. Note that the new gaskets should match up with those removed. If not, check with your parts supplier to be sure you have the correct gasket set.

To determine the float level, invert carburetor body (1 — Fig. MY7-21) with fuel inlet valve (25 — Fig. MY7-20), float arm (26 — Fig. MY7-21) and float (28) installed. Measure distance (D) as shown

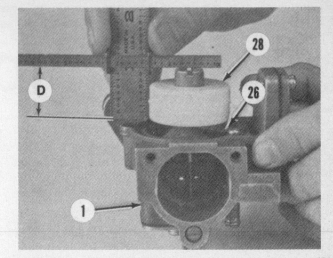

Fig. MY7-21—With carburetor body (1) inverted, distance (D) should be 1 inch (25.4 mm) when measured as shown. Bend float arm (26) to adjust position of float (28).

in Fig. MY7-21. Distance (D) should be 1 inch (25.4 mm). Bend float arm (26) to adjust.

When reinstalling the carburetor, place a new gasket (36 — Fig. MY7-20) between the carburetor and the adapter plate. Securely tighten the retaining nuts. Reassemble in the reverse order of disassembly with the exception of the engine top cover. Initially adjust idle mixture screw (6) 1¼ turns out from a lightly seated position.

OUTBOARD MARINE CORP.

EVINRUDE MOTORS
4143 N. 27th Street
Milwaukee, Wisconsin 53216

JOHNSON MOTORS
200 Sea-horse Drive
Waukegan, Illinois 60085

EVINRUDE 1½ AND 2 HP

Year Produced	1½ hp	2 hp
1969	1902	.....
1970	1002	.....
1971	.....	2102
1972	.....	2202
1973	.....	2302
1974	.....	2402
1975	.....	2502
1976	.....	2602
1977	.....	2702
1978	.....	2802
1979	.....	2902
1980	.....	E2RCS
1981	.....	E2RCIB
1982	.....	E2RCNE
1983	.....	E2RCTD
1984	.....	E2RCRS
1985	.....	E2RCOC

JOHNSON 1½ AND 2 HP

Year Produced	1½ hp	2 hp
1969	1R-69	.....
1970	1R-70	.....
1971	.....	2R71
1972	.....	2R72
1973	.....	2R73
1974	.....	2R74
1975	.....	2R75
1976	.....	2R76
1977	.....	2R77
1978	.....	2R78
1979	.....	2R79
1980	.....	2RCS
1981	.....	J2RCIB
1982	.....	J2RCNE
1983	.....	J2RCTD
1984	.....	J2RCRS
1985	.....	J2RCOC

Specifications

Hp/rpm:
1969-1970 .... 1½/4000
1971-1982 .... 2/4500
1983 .... 2/4200-4800
1984 .... 2/4500-5500
1985 .... 2/4000-5000
Bore .... 1.57 in.
(39.7 mm)
Stroke .... 1.38 in.
(34.9 mm)
Number of cylinders 1
Displacement .... 2.64 cu. in.
(43 cc)

Specifications (Cont.)

Sparkplug — Champion:
- 1969-1970 . . . . .J4J
- 1971-1984 . . . . .J6J
- 1985 . . . . .J6C
- Electrode gap . . . . .0.030 in.
  - (0.76 mm)
- Breaker point gap . . . . .0.020 in.
  - (0.51 mm)
- Carburetor make . . . . .Own
- Idle speed . . . . .650 rpm
- Fuel:oil ratio. 50:1*
- Gearcase oil capacity . . . . .1.28 oz.
  - (38 mL)

*On 1985 models, a 100:1 ratio can be used when Evinrude or Johnson outboard lubricant formulated for 100:1 fuel mix is used.

Maintenance

LUBRICATION

ENGINE. The engine is lubricated by oil mixed with the fuel. The fuel should be regular leaded or unleaded gasoline with a minimum pump octane rating of 86.

NOTE: On 1981 and later models, the manufacturer permits the above fuels to be used at a minimum pump octane rating of 67.

On models prior to 1985, recommended oil is Evinrude or Johnson 50/1 Lubricant or a BIA certified two-stroke motor oil. The recommended fuel:oil ratio for normal operation and engine break-in is 50:1.

On 1985 models, a fuel:oil ratio of 100:1 can be used when Evinrude or Johnson outboard lubricant formulated for 100:1 fuel mix is used. When any other BIA certified two-stroke motor oil is used or during engine break-in, the recommended fuel:oil ratio is 50:1.

The manufacturer's recommended break-in period is defined as follows: For the first fifteen minutes of operation the engine should not exceed its slowest possible cruising speed. After fifteen minutes, slowly increase the engine speed to ½ throttle for the next 45 minutes of operation. During that 45 minutes, short, full throttle accelerations (90 seconds) every five minutes are suggested. For the second hour, increase engine speed to ¾ throttle and periodically accelerate to full throttle. Run the engine at full throttle for 1 to 2 minutes before returning to ¾ throttle setting. Running the engine at or near full throttle for extended periods is not recommended until after 5 hours of operation.

LOWER UNIT. The lower unit gears and bearings are lubricated by oil contained in the gearcase. The recommended oil is OMC HI-VIS Gearcase Lube. The gearcase oil capacity is 1.28 oz. (38 mL). Gearcase oil level should be checked after every 50 hours of operation and gearcase should be drained and filled with new oil every 100 hours or once each season, whichever occurs first. The gearcase is drained and filled through the same plug port.

To drain the oil, remove oil plug (1 — Fig. OM1-1) from gearcase housing. Lay the motor with the plug opening down and allow the lubricant to drain into a suitable container.

To fill the gearcase with oil, lay the motor with the plug opening up. Add oil through plug opening until the oil begins to overflow, then reinstall oil plug (1) with a new gasket and tighten.

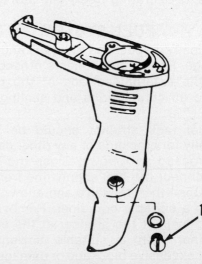

Fig. OM1-1 — View showing location of lower unit drain and fill plug (1).

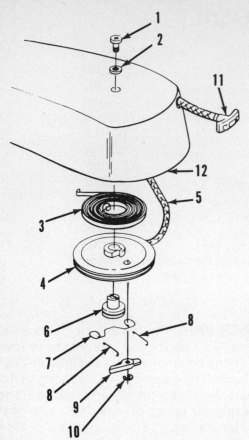

Fig. OM1-2 — Exploded view of manual rewind starter.

1. Screw	5. Starter rope	9. Drive pawl
2. Lockwasher	6. Spindle	10. Clip
3. Rewind spring	7. Friction spring	11. Handle
4. Pulley	8. Links	12. Cover

PIVOT POINTS AND SLIDES. Lubricate all pivot points and linkage slides with OMC TRIPLE-GUARD GREASE or a suitable equivalent every 60 days or more frequently if needed to keep the components operating freely and properly.

FUEL SYSTEM

Periodically inspect the fuel tank and fuel lines for damage. Renew components if needed.

Keep the external surface of the carburetor clean and all connections and sealing surfaces tight.

The fuel tank strainer should be inspected periodically for blockage or any other damage. To check, proceed as follows: Close the fuel valve and disconnect the fuel supply line from the carburetor. Open the fuel valve and allow the fuel to drain into a suitable container. Remove the fuel valve and inspect the strainer at the end. Clean the strainer with a suitable solvent. Renew strainer if excessive blockage or damage is noted. Apply a suitable sealant on fuel valve threads, then reinstall valve. Complete reassembly.

STARTER

When starter rope (5 — Fig. OM1-2) is pulled, pulley (4) will rotate. As pulley (4) rotates, drive pawl (9) moves to engage the flywheel, thus cranking the engine.

When starter rope (5) is released, pulley (4) is rotated in the reverse direction by rewind spring (3). As pulley (4) rotates, the starter rope is rewound and drive pawl (9) is disengaged from the flywheel.

The manual rewind starter assembly is an integral part of the engine cover. To overhaul the manual starter, proceed as follows: Remove the engine cover

---

⚠WARNING

Care should be exercised when working with or around a coiled starter rewind spring as sudden uncoiling can cause injury. Safety eyewear and gloves are recommended.

Check pawl (9) for freedom of movement and excessive wear of engagement area and damage. Renew or lubricate pawl (9) with OMC TRIPLE-GUARD GREASE or Lubriplate 777 and return starter to service if no other damage is noted.

To disassemble, remove clip (10) and withdraw pawl (9), links (8) and friction spring (7). Untie starter rope (5) at handle (11) and allow the rope to wind into the starter. Remove screw (1) and lockwasher (2), then withdraw spindle (6). Carefully lift pulley (4) with starter rope (5) from cover (12). BE CAREFUL when removing pulley (4) as rewind spring (3) may be dislodged. Remove rope (5) from pulley (4) if renewal is required. To remove rewind spring (3) from cover (12), invert cover so it sits upright on a flat surface, then tap the cover top until rewind spring (3) falls free and uncoils.

Inspect all components for damage and excessive wear and renew if needed.

To reassemble, first apply a coating of OMC TRIPLE-GUARD GREASE or Lubriplate 777 to rewind spring area of cover (12). Install rewind spring (3) in cover (12) so spring coils wind in a counterclockwise direction from the outer end.

NOTE: Lubricate all friction surfaces with OMC TRIPLE-GUARD GREASE or Lubriplate 777 during reassembly.

Install pulley (4) in cover (12). Make sure pulley hub properly engages hook on rewind spring (3). Wind starter rope (5) onto pulley (4) in a counterclockwise direction as viewed from the

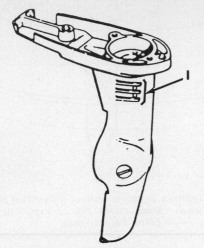

Fig. OM1-3 — *Cooling system water inlet ports (I) are located on both sides of the lower unit.*

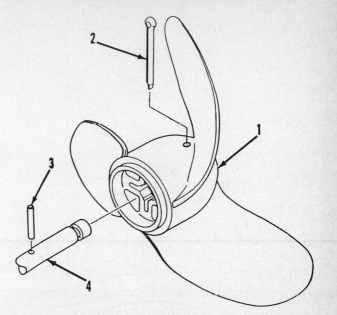

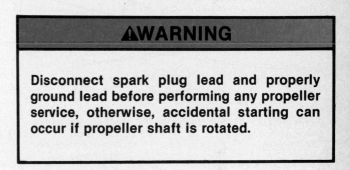

Fig. OM1-4 — *Propeller (1) is mounted on propeller shaft (4) and is retained by cotter pin (2). Shear pin (3) is renewed only after withdrawing propeller (1) from propeller shaft (4).*

flywheel side. Install spindle (6). Spray screw (1) threads with OMC Locquic Primer and apply OMC Screw Lock on screw threads, then install screw (1) with lockwasher (2) and securely tighten.

Turn pulley (4) 3½ turns counterclockwise when viewed from the flywheel side. Secure pulley position, then thread starter rope (5) through cover (12) opening and handle (11) and secure with a knot.

NOTE: Do not apply any more tension on rewind spring (3) than what is required to draw starter handle (11) back into the proper released position.

Install friction spring (7), links (8), pawl (9) and clip (10).

Remount engine cover (12).

COOLING SYSTEM

Ports (I — Fig. OM1-3) located on the port and starboard side of the lower unit are used as the water inlets for the cooling system. The ports must be kept clean of all foreign matter to ensure efficient operation of the cooling system.

⚠CAUTION

Do not operate outboard motor unless the lower unit is immersed in water, otherwise, the water pump impeller will be damaged.

PROPELLER

The standard propeller has three blades, a diameter of 7¼ inches (184 mm) and a pitch of 4½ inches (114 mm).

⚠WARNING

Disconnect spark plug lead and properly ground lead before performing any propeller service, otherwise, accidental starting can occur if propeller shaft is rotated.

To remove the propeller, remove the cotter pin (2 — Fig. OM1-4) and withdraw propeller (1) from propeller shaft (4).

Inspect propeller (1) and shear pin (3) for excessive wear and renew if excessive wear or damage is noted.

Apply OMC TRIPLE-GUARD GREASE to the propeller bore, then install propeller (1) on propeller shaft (4). Retain propeller with a new cotter pin (2).

Tune-Up

IGNITION SYSTEM

The standard spark plug is Champion J4J on 1969 and 1970 models, Champion J6J on 1971-1984 models and Champion J6C on 1985 models. The recommended electrode gap on all models is 0.030 inch (0.76 mm). The magneto breaker point gap should be 0.020 inch (0.51 mm) on used points and 0.022 inch (0.56 mm) on new points. The flywheel must be removed to service breaker point assembly (4 — Fig. OM1-5) and condenser (7).

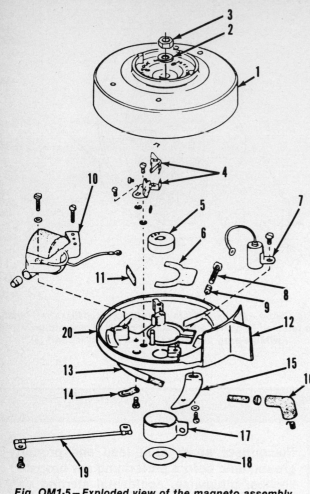

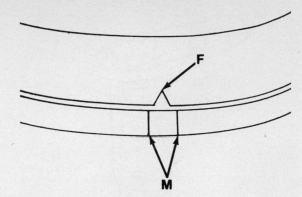

Fig. OM1-6—Ignition timing is correct if flywheel mark (F) is centered between timing marks (M) on magneto armature plate. Refer to text.

Fig. OM1-5—Exploded view of the magneto assembly.

1. Flywheel	11. Oiler wick
2. Lockwasher	12. Speed control lever
3. Nut	13. Spark plug lead
4. Breaker point assy.	14. Clip
5. Cam	15. Throttle cam
6. Gasket	16. Spark plug boot
7. Condenser	17. Bushing
8. Tension screw	18. Washer
9. Spring	19. Ground wire
10. Coil assy.	20. Magneto armature plate

To check the ignition timing, proceed as follows: With the outboard motor properly mounted on a boat or a suitable test tank, immerse the lower unit. Connect a tachometer and set it on the appropriate range scale. Connect a suitable timing light to the spark plug lead. Start the engine and adjust the speed control until the engine is running at 1000 rpm. Ignition timing is correct if flywheel mark (F—Fig. OM1-6) is centered between timing marks (M) on magneto armature plate. If ignition timing is not correct, then check and adjust breaker point gap or renew breaker point assembly as follows:

To remove flywheel (1—Fig. OM1-5), use a suitable flywheel holding tool and remove securing nut (3) and lockwasher (2) with suitable tools. Remove flywheel (1) from crankshaft end using a suitable puller assembly and suitable tools. Note flywheel key located in crankshaft keyway.

⚠WARNING

Be sure suitable tools are used to remove the flywheel. Damage resultant from the misapplication of force or the use of incorrect tools may cause engine damage, engine malfunction or personal injury.

Rotate the crankshaft until the breaker point contact surfaces are at their widest position. Then with a 0.020 inch (0.51 mm) feeler gage, check and adjust the point set until 0.020 inch (0.51 mm) gap is obtained.

NOTE: No service to the breaker point assembly is recommended by the manufacturer. The manufacturer recommends cleaning the contact surfaces with alcohol only. A strip of bias tape should be used between contact surfaces to remove any foreign matter.

If needed, renew breaker point assembly (4) and condenser (7). On new breaker point assembly (4), point gap should be set at 0.022 inch (0.56 mm).

After adjustment, make sure the breaker point assembly (4) and condenser (7) securing screws are properly tightened. Be sure the flywheel key is properly positioned in the crankshaft end, then reinstall flywheel (1). Install lockwasher (2) and install and tighten securing nut (3) to 22-25 ft.-lbs. (30-34 N·m). Check ignition timing as outlined earlier.

SPEED CONTROL LINKAGE

Speed control lever (12—Fig. OM1-5) rotates magneto armature plate (20) to advance the igni-

Fig. OM1-7—Refer to text when synchronizing the speed control linkage on models prior to 1978.

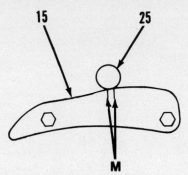

Fig. OM1-8—On models after 1977, cam follower roller (25) should be centered between marks (M) on cam (15) just as carburetor throttle opens. Refer to text.

tion timing. Cam (15) attached to the bottom of armature plate (20) is used to open the carburetor throttle as the ignition timing is advanced. The throttle opening and ignition timing cannot be properly synchronized if throttle cam (15) and related components are worn or damaged in any way. Renew components if needed.

To synchronize speed controls, first remove the engine cover. Move speed control lever (12) from the stop position until the carburetor throttle just begins to open. On models prior to 1978, the flat (port side) edge of the cam follower should be aligned with mark on cam (Fig. OM1-7). If incorrect, loosen throttle cam retaining screws and adjust throttle cam. On models after 1977, cam follower roller (25—Fig. OM1-8) should be centered between marks (M) on cam (15) just as carburetor throttle opens. Turn cam follower adjusting screw (24—Fig. OM1-9) to center roller on marks.

CARBURETOR

ADJUSTMENT. The carburetor is equipped with adjustment needles for both low and high speed mixture. Initial setting is 1¼ turns out from a lightly seated position for low speed mixture needle (L—Fig. OM1-9) and ½ to 1 turn out from a lightly seated position for high speed mixture needle (H). Needle should be adjusted after motor reaches normal operating temperature to provide best operation at idle and high speed. The high speed needle (H) should be adjusted for best operation at high speed before adjusting needle (L) for best operation at idle speed. Turning both needles clockwise leans the fuel mixture. Recommended idle speed with engine at normal operating temperature is 650 rpm.

With the outboard motor properly mounted on a boat or a suitable test tank, immerse the lower unit. Start the engine and allow it to warm up to normal operating temperature. Place the speed control lever at the "FAST" position. Adjust high

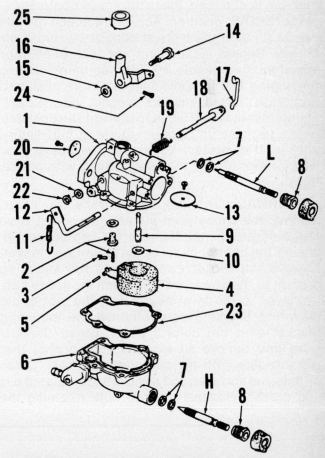

Fig. OM1-9—Exploded view of carburetor used on all models. Follower adjusting screw (24) and follower roller (25) are used on models after 1977.

H. High speed mixture needle	12. Choke shaft
L. Low speed mixture needle	13. Choke plate
	14. Shoulder screw
1. Carburetor body	15. Washer
2. Fuel inlet needle & seat	16. Cam follower
3. Needle-to-float clip	17. Link
4. Float	18. Throttle shaft
5. Pin	19. Return spring
6. Float bowl	20. Throttle plate
7. Packing	21. Washer
8. Packing nut	22. Throttle shaft retainer
9. High speed nozzle	23. Gasket
10. Gasket	24. Follower adjusting screw
11. Choke return spring	25. Roller

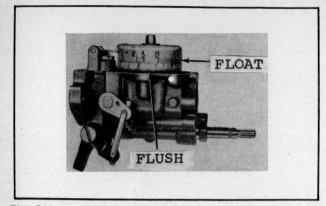

Fig. OM1-10—With fuel inlet needle closed, float should be flush with gasket surface of body as shown.

speed mixture needle (H) until the highest consistent rpm is obtained. Place the speed control lever at the "SLOW" position. Adjust low speed mixture needle (L) until the highest consistent rpm is obtained. Repeat adjustment procedure on high speed mixture needle (H). After adjustment, stop the engine and turn low speed mixture needle (L) and high speed mixture needle (H) ⅛ turn counterclockwise. This is to prevent the possibility of a too lean fuel mixture at low or high engine speeds. If necessary, reposition low speed knob with pointer up and high speed knob with pointer down.

OVERHAUL. Remove the engine's top cover. Remove the choke lever pin and low speed knob at the control panel. Remove the two screws retaining the control panel to the mounting bracket. Remove the two screws retaining the mounting bracket to the powerhead. Position the speed control lever so the lever aligns with the slot in the mounting bracket, then withdraw the mounting bracket with the control panel. Close the fuel valve and remove all external components that will interfere with the carburetor removal. Clean all external surfaces and remove accumulated dirt and grease. Remove the two nuts retaining the

carburetor and withdraw the carburetor.

With reference to Fig. OM1-9, disassemble the carburetor and note any discrepancies which must be corrected before reassembly. Remove all gaskets and set to the side for future reference.

Thoroughly clean all carburetor parts with a suitable solvent and inspect for damage and excessive wear.

NOTE: The manufacturer does not recommend submerging the parts in carburetor or parts cleaning solutions. An aerosol type carburetor cleaner is recommended. The float and other components made of plastic and rubber should not be subjected to some cleaning solutions. Safety eyewear and solvent resistant gloves are recommended.

Blow dry with clean compressed air. If compressed air is not available, use only lint-free cloths to wipe dry.

With reference to Fig. OM1-9, reassemble the carburetor components with new gaskets. Note that the new gaskets should match up with those removed. If not, check with your parts supplier to be sure you have the correct gasket set.

NOTE: DO NOT completely tighten packing nuts (8). Stop tightening packing nuts (8) when the mixture needles become difficult to rotate by hand.

To determine the float level, invert the carburetor body as shown in Fig. OM1-10. With the fuel inlet needle closed, the float should be parallel and flush with the carburetor float bowl gasket surface. Adjust the float level by bending arm on float (4 — Fig. OM1-9).

When reinstalling the carburetor, place a new gasket between the carburetor and the reed plate. Securely tighten the retaining nuts. Complete reassembly in the reverse order of disassembly. Initially adjust low speed mixture needle (L) 1¼ turns out from a lightly seated position. Initially adjust high speed mixture needle (H) ½ to 1 turn out from a lightly seated position.

EVINRUDE AND JOHNSON

4 HP

Year Produced	EVINRUDE Models	Year Produced	JOHNSON Models
1970 (Weedless Gearcase)	4006	1970 (Weedless Gearcase)	4W70
(Standard Gearcase)	4036	(Standard (Gearcase)	4R70
1971 (Weedless Gearcase)	4106	1971 (Weedless Gearcase)	4W71
(Standard Gearcase)	4136	(Standard Gearcase)	4R71
1972 (Weedless Gearcase)	4206	1972 (Weedless Gearcase)	4W72
(Standard Gearcase)	4236	(Standard Gearcase)	4R72
1973 (Weedless Gearcase)	4306	1973 (Weedless Gearcase)	4W73
(Standard Gearcase)	4336	(Standard Gearcase)	4R73
1974 (Weedless Gearcase)	4406	1974 (Weedless Gearcase)	4W74
(Standard Gearcase)	4436	(Standard Gearcase)	4R74
1975 (Weedless Gearcase)	4506	1975 (Weedless Gearcase)	4W75
(Standard Gearcase)	4536	(Standard Gearcase)	4R75
1976 (Weedless Gearcase)	4606	1976 (Weedless Gearcase)	4W76
(Standard Gearcase)	4636	(Standard Gearcase)	4R76
1977 (Weedless Gearcase)	4706	1977 (Weedless Gearcase)	4W77
(Standard Gearcase)	4736	(Standard Gearcase)	4R77
1978 (Weedless Gearcase)	4806	1978 (Weedless Gearcase)	4W78
(Standard Gearcase)	4836,4837	(Standard Gearcase)	4R78, 4RL78
1979 (Weedless Gearcase)	4904	1979 (Weedless Gearcase)	4W79
(Standard Gearcase)	4932,4933	(Standard Gearcase)	4R79,4RL79
1980 (Weedless Gearcase)	4WCS	1980 (Weedless Gearcase)	4WCS
(Standard Gearcase)	4RLCS	(Standard Gearcase)	4RLCS
1981 (Weedless Gearcase)	4WCI	1981 Weedless Gearcase)	4WCI
(Standard Gearcase)	4BRCI	(Standard Gearcase)	4BRCI
1982 (Weedless Gearcase)	4W	1982 (Weedless Gearcase)	4W
(Standard Gearcase)	4BR	(Standard Gearcase)	4BR
1983	4BR	1983	4BR
1984	4BR	1984	4BR
1985	4BR	1985	4BR

4.5 HP

Year Produced	EVINRUDE Models	Year Produced	JOHNSON Models
1980	5RCS	1980	5RCS
1981	5RCI	1981	5RCI
1982	5RH	1982	5RH
1983	5RHCT	1983	5RHCT

Specifications

Hp/rpm	4/4000-5000
	4.5/4500-5500
Bore	1.57 in.
	(39.7 mm)

Specifications Cont.

Stroke	1.38 in.
	(34.9 mm)
Number of cylinders	2
Displacement	5.28 cu. in.
	(87 cc)

Spark plug—Champion:
  4 hp models—
  1970 .... J4J
    Electrode gap .... 0.020 in.
                                         (0.51 mm)
  1971-1976 .... J6J
    Electrode gap .... 0.030 in.
                                         (0.76 mm)
  1977-1980 .... L77J4
    Electrode gap .... 0.040 in.
                                         (1.0 mm)
  1981-1985 .... L86
    Electrode gap .... 0.030 in.
                                         (0.76 mm)

  4.5 hp models—
  1980-1983 .... L77J4
    Electrode gap .... 0.040 in.
                                         (1.0 mm)

Ignition type:
  4 hp models—
  1970-1976 & 1981-1985 .... Breaker Point
    Breaker point gap .... 0.020 in.
                                      (0.51 mm)
  1977-1980 .... CD
  4.5 hp models .... CD
Carburetor make .... Own
Idle speed (in gear) .... 600 rpm
Fuel:oil ratio 50:1*
Fuel pump:
  Discharge pressure at 600 rpm ..... 1 psi
                                       (7 kPa)
  Discharge pressure at 2500-3000 rpm ... 1.5 psi
                                          (10 kPa)
  Discharge pressure at 4500 rpm ..... 2.5 psi
                                        (17 kPa)

*On 1985 models, a 100:1 ratio can be used when Evinrude or Johnson outboard lubricant formulated for 100:1 fuel mix is used.

Maintenance

LUBRICATION

ENGINE. The engine is lubricated by oil mixed with the fuel. The fuel should be regular leaded or unleaded gasoline with a minimum pump octane rating of 86.

NOTE: On 1981 and later models, the manufacturer permits the above fuels to be used at a minimum pump octane rating of 67.

On models prior to 1985, recommended oil is Evinrude or Johnson 50/1 Lubricant or a BIA certified two-stroke motor oil. The recommended

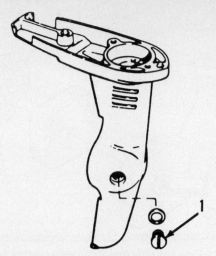

Fig. OM2-1—View showing location of lower unit drain and fill plug (1) on early 4 hp models.

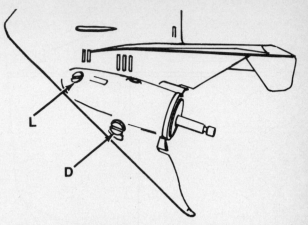

Fig. OM2-3—View showing lower unit gearcase drain and fill plug (D) and oil level (vent) plug (L) on weedless models.

fuel:oil ratio for normal operation and engine break-in is 50:1.

On 1985 models, a fuel:oil ratio of 100:1 can be used when Evinrude or Johnson outboard lubricant formulated for 100:1 fuel mix is used. When any other BIA certified two-stroke motor oil is used or during engine break-in, the recommended fuel:oil ratio is 50:1.

The manufacturer's recommended break-in period is defined as follows: For the first fifteen minutes of operation the engine should not exceed its slowest possible cruising speed. After fifteen minutes, slowly increase the engine speed to ½ throttle for the next 45 minutes of operation. During that 45 minutes, short, full throttle accelerations (90 seconds) every five minutes are suggested. For the second hour, increase engine speed to ¾ throttle and periodically accelerate to full throttle. Run the engine at full throttle for 1 to

2 minutes before returning to ¾ throttle setting. Running the engine at or near full throttle for extended periods is not recommended until after 5 hours of operation.

LOWER UNIT. The lower unit gears and bearings are lubricated by oil contained in the gearcase. The recommended oil is OMC HI-VIS Gearcase Lube. The gearcase oil level should be checked after every 50 hours of operation and the gearcase should be drained and filled with new oil every 100 hours or once each season, whichever occurs first.

On early 4 hp models, the gearcase is drained and filled through the same plug port. To drain the oil, remove oil plug (1 — Fig. OM2-1) from gearcase housing. Lay the motor with the plug opening down and allow the lubricant to drain into a suitable container.

To fill the gearcase with oil, lay the motor with the plug opening up. Add oil through plug opening until the oil begins to overflow, then reinstall oil plug (1) with a new gasket and tighten.

On late 4 hp models (Fig. OM2-2), weedless models (Fig. OM2-3) and 4.5 hp models (Fig. OM2-4), the gearcase oil is drained and filled through the same plug port (D). An oil level (vent) port (L) is used to indicate the full level of the gearcase with oil and to ease oil drainage.

To drain the oil, place the outboard motor in a vertical position. Remove drain plug (D) and oil level plug (L) and allow the lubricant to drain into a suitable container.

To fill the gearcase with oil, place the outboard motor in a vertical position. Add oil through drain plug (D) opening with an oil feeder until the oil begins to overflow from oil level plug (L) port. Reinstall oil level plug (L) with a new gasket, if needed, and tighten. Remove oil feeder, then reinstall drain plug (D) with a new gasket, if needed, and tighten.

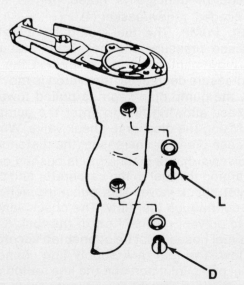

Fig. OM2-2—View showing lower unit gearcase drain and fill plug (D) and oil level (vent) plug (L) on late 4 hp models.

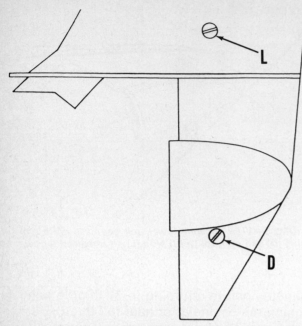

Fig. OM2-4— *View showing lower unit gearcase drain and fill plug (D) and oil level (vent) plug (L) on 4.5 hp models.*

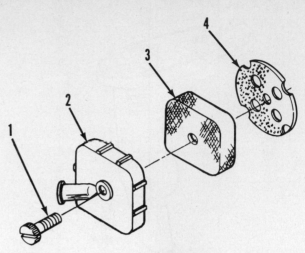

Fig. OM2-6— *View showing fuel strainer (3) located behind fuel pump inlet cover (2). Screw (1) retains inlet cover (2) and gasket (4) seals between inlet cover (2) and the pump cover.*

PIVOT POINTS AND SLIDES. Lubricate all pivot points and linkage slides with OMC TRIPLE-GUARD GREASE or a suitable equivalent every 60 days or more frequently if needed to keep the components operating freely and properly.

FUEL SYSTEM

Periodically inspect the fuel tank (4 hp models) and fuel lines for damage. Renew components if needed.

Keep the external surface of the carburetor clean and all connections and sealing surfaces tight.

FUEL FILTER. On models equipped with an outboard motor mounted fuel tank, the fuel tank strainer should be inspected periodically for blockage and damage. To check, proceed as follows: Close the fuel valve and disconnect the fuel supply line from the carburetor. Open the fuel valve and allow the fuel to drain into a suitable container. Remove the fuel valve and inspect the strainer at the end of the fuel valve. Clean the strainer with a suitable solvent and renew if excessive blockage or damage is noted. Apply a suitable sealant on fuel valve threads, then reinstall valve. Complete reassembly.

Fig. OM2-5— *View showing a disposable type filter element used on some models.*

Some models equipped with an outboard motor mounted fuel tank are also equipped with a disposable type filter element (Fig. OM2-5) between the fuel supply line and the carburetor inlet line. Periodically remove the filter element and blow through the filter's inlet side with low air pressure and note the resistance. A minimal amount of resistance should be noted. If not, filter assembly should be renewed.

On models equipped with a fuel pump, a strainer (3—Fig. OM2-6) positioned behind inlet cover (2) is used to filter the fuel prior to entering the fuel pump assembly. To inspect, remove screw (1) retaining inlet cover (2) and withdraw cover (2) with strainer (3). Clean strainer (3) in a suitable solvent and blow dry with clean compressed air. Inspect strainer (3). If excessive blockage or damage is noted, renew strainer (3). If needed, renew gasket (4).

FUEL PUMP. The fuel pump is operated by crankcase pressure changes from the up-and-down movement of the piston. When the crankcase pressure decreases (the piston is moving upward), the pump diaphragm is pulled toward the crankcase allowing fuel to enter the pump body and closing the discharge check valve. When the crankcase pressure increases (the piston is moving downward), the diaphragm is pushed outward discharging the fuel to the carburetor and closing the inlet check valve. This pulsating action provides continuous fuel flow. The check valves are used to prevent reverse flow of the fuel.

The fuel hoses must be connected according to fuel flow. The fuel tank supply line connects to the fuel pump inlet port and the line routed toward the carburetor assembly connects to the outlet port.

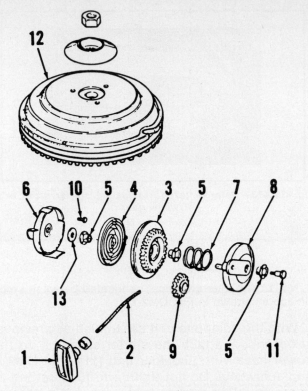

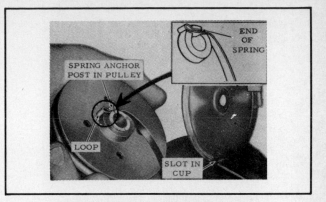

Fig. OM2-9—View showing installation of rewind spring inner end. Outer end catches on slot in cup.

STARTER

4 Hp Models Prior To 1979 And 4.5 Hp Models

The recoil starter used on these models is shown in Fig. OM2-7. The starter rotates the flywheel via gear teeth on pulley (3), idler (9) and lower edge of flywheel (12). Refer to the following paragraphs for removal, installation and adjustment.

To remove the starter, remove handle (1) and allow the starter assembly to unwind slowly.

NOTE: Hold pulley (3) to permit starter to unwind slowly. Care should be exercised when working with or around a coiled starter rewind spring as sudden uncoiling can cause injury. Safety eyewear and gloves are recommended.

Pull end of rewind spring (4) out rear slot as shown in Fig. OM2-8 as far as possible. Remove screws (10 and 11), then remove the starter assembly.

With reference to Fig. OM2-7, disassemble the starter assembly. Clean all components with a suitable solvent and inspect for damage and excessive wear and renew if needed.

Fig. OM2-7—View of manual rewind starter used on 4 hp models prior to 1979 and 4.5 hp models.

1. Handle	5. Bushing	9. Idler gear
2. Starter rope	6. Cup	10. Screw
3. Pulley	7. Spring	11. Shoulder bolt
4. Rewind spring	8. Idler gear arm	12. Flywheel

If fuel pump malfunction is noted, the fuel pump should be renewed as a complete assembly. Renew the mounting gasket and securely tighten the retaining screws.

NOTE: Fuel pump and engine malfunction will result if the fuel pump and all connections are not airtight.

Fig. OM2-8—Rewind spring should be withdrawn as shown before removing starter assembly.

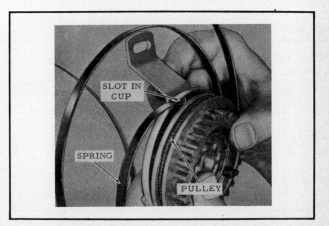

Fig. OM2-10—View showing assembly of pulley and cup with rewind spring coming through slot in cup.

Evinrude & Johnson 4 & 4.5 Hp

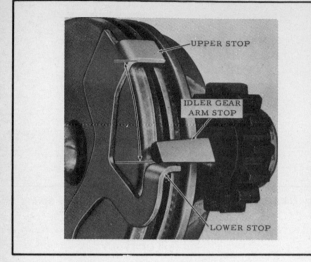

Fig. OM2-11—Idler arm must be between stops on cup as shown.

Fig. OM2-13—Refer to text for adjusting starter mesh with flywheel gear.

To reassemble, first wipe all metal parts with an oil dampened cloth and lightly coat bushing (5 — Fig. OM2-7) with OMC TRIPLE-GUARD GREASE. Insert starter rope (2) through the hole in pulley (3) with the knot inside the gear. Wind starter rope (2) in a clockwise direction in pulley groove as viewed from gear side of pulley (3). Hold starter rope (2) in pulley groove with a rubber band or tape and locate end of rewind spring (4) on pulley (3) as shown in Fig. OM2-9. Position washer (13 — Fig. OM2-7) on cup (6), then assemble pulley (3), starter rope (2) and rewind spring (4) to cup (6) with rewind spring end protruding from slot in cup (6) as shown in Fig. OM2-10. Install idler gear (9 — Fig. OM2-7) on shaft of idler gear arm (8), then assemble spring (7), idler gear (9) and arm (8) to the pulley and cup.

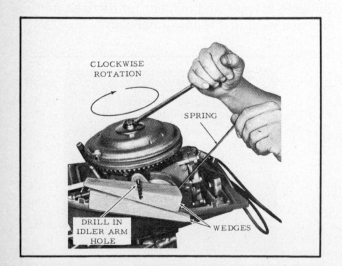

Fig. OM2-12—Refer to text for method of rewinding and preloading the rewind spring.

NOTE: The idler arm must be located between stops on cup as shown in Fig. OM2-11.

With the complete unit assembled as previously described, attach the starter assembly to the power head with shoulder bolt (11 — Fig. OM2-7) and screw (10). Do not tighten to final setting at this time. Make certain that washer (13) has not slipped and shoulder bolt (11) is through washer (13). To draw rewind spring (4) into cup (6), engage idler gear (9) with flywheel (12) gear and turn flywheel (12) in a clockwise direction until rewind spring (4) is drawn into cup (6). Refer to Fig. OM2-12. Disengage idler gear (9 — Fig. OM2-7) from flywheel (12) to relax rewind spring (4), then reengage idler gear (9) with flywheel (12) gear and turn flywheel (12) 2 turns clockwise to correctly preload rewind spring (4). Route starter rope (2) through the housing rope guide and attach starter handle (1).

To adjust idler gear (9) engagement, hold idler gear (9) into flywheel (12) teeth and make certain that stop (S — Fig. OM2-13) is against idler gear arm (8 — Fig. OM2-7). With the stop contacting the arm, tighten adjustment screw (10) and shoulder bolt (11).

4 Hp Models After 1978

When starter rope (5 — Fig. OM2-14) is pulled, pulley (4) will rotate. As pulley (4) rotates, drive pawl (9) moves to engage with the flywheel, thus cranking the engine.

When starter rope (5) is released, pulley (4) is rotated in the reverse direction by force from rewind spring (3). As pulley (4) rotates, the starter rope is rewound and drive pawl (9) is disengaged from the flywheel.

The manual rewind starter assembly is an integral part of the engine cover. To overhaul the manual starter, proceed as follows: Remove the engine cover.

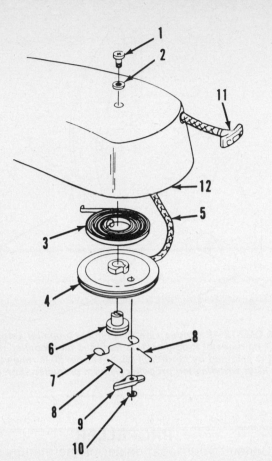

Fig. OM2-14—Exploded view of manual rewind starter used on 4 hp models after 1978.

1. Screw	5. Starter rope	9. Drive pawl
2. Lockwasher	6. Spindle	10. Clip
3. Rewind spring	7. Friction spring	11. Handle
4. Pulley	8. Links	12. Cover

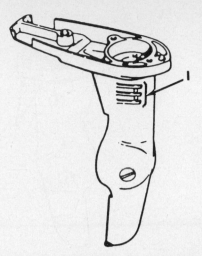

Fig. OM2-15 — On early 4 hp models, cooling system water inlet ports (I) are located n both sides of the lower unit.

⚠WARNING

Care should be exercised when working with or around a coiled starter rewind spring as sudden uncoiling can cause injury. Safety eyewear and gloves are recommended.

Check pawl (9) for freedom of movement and excessive wear of engagement area and damage. Renew or lubricate pawl (9) with OMC TRIPLE-GUARD GREASE or Lubriplate 777 and return starter to service if no other damage is noted.

To disassemble, remove clip (10) and withdraw pawl (9), links (8) and friction spring (7). Untie starter rope (5) at handle (11) and allow the rope to wind into the starter. Remove screw (1) and lockwasher (2), then withdraw spindle (6). Carefully lift pulley (4) with starter rope (5) from cover (12). BE CAREFUL when removing pulley (4) as rewind spring (3) may be dislodged. Remove rope (5) from

pulley (4) if renewal is required. To remove rewind spring (3) from cover (12), invert cover so it sets upright on a flat surface, then tap the cover top until rewind spring (3) falls free and uncoils.

Inspect all components for damage and excessive wear and renew if needed.

To reassemble, first apply a coating of OMC TRIPLE-GUARD GREASE or Lubriplate 777 to rewind spring area of cover (12). Install rewind spring (3) in cover (12) so spring coils wind in a counterclockwise direction from the outer end.

NOTE: Lubricate all friction surfaces with OMC TRIPLE-GUARD GREASE or Lubriplate 777 during reassembly.

Install pulley (4) in cover (12). Make sure pulley hub properly engages hook on rewind spring (3). Wind starter rope (5) onto pulley (4) in a counterclockwise direction as viewed from the flywheel side. Install spindle (6). Spray screw (1) threads with OMC Locquic Primer and apply OMC Screw Lock on screw threads, then install screw (1) with lockwasher (2) and securely tighten.

Turn pulley (4) 3½ turns counterclockwise when viewed from the flywheel side. Secure pulley position, then thread starter rope (5) through cover (12) opening and handle (11) and secure with a knot.

NOTE: Do not apply any more tension on rewind spring (3) than is required to draw starter handle (11) back into the proper released position.

Install friction spring (7), links (8), pawl (9) and clip (10).

Remount engine cover (12).

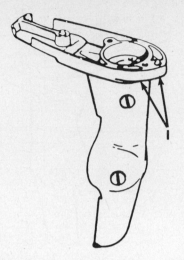

Fig. OM2-16—On late 4 hp models, cooling system water inlet ports (I) are located on both sides of the lower unit.

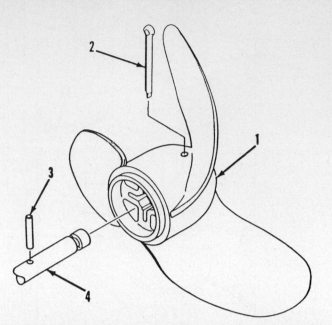

Fig. OM2-18—Exploded view of a typical propeller setup used on 4 hp models. Propeller (1) is mounted on propeller shaft (4) and is retained by cotter pin (2). Shear pin (3) is renewed only after withdrawing propeller (1) from propeller shaft (4).

COOLING SYSTEM

Ports (I—Fig. OM2-15) on early 4 hp models, (I—Fig. OM2-16) on late 4 hp models and (I—Fig. OM2-17) on weedless models are located on the port and starboard side of the lower unit and are used as the water inlets for the cooling system. A port located on the bottom side of the antiventilation plate is used as the water inlet for the cooling system on 4.5 hp models. The port or ports must be kept clean of all foreign matter to ensure efficient operation of the cooling system.

⚠ CAUTION

Do not operate outboard motor unless the lower unit is immersed in water, otherwise, the water pump impeller will be damaged.

PROPELLER

Consult your local dealer or the manufacturer for the specifications pertaining to the standard propeller used on your model of outboard motor. Optional propellers are available. Select a propeller that will allow the engine at full throttle to reach maximum operating rpm range (4000-5000 on 4 hp models and 4500-5500 on 4.5 hp models).

⚠ WARNING

Shift directional control lever to "NEUTRAL." Disconnect the spark plug leads and properly ground leads before performing any propeller service, otherwise, accidental starting can occur if propeller shaft is rotated.

Shown in Fig. OM2-18 is a view of a typical propeller setup used on 4 hp models. To remove the propeller, remove cotter pin (2) and withdraw propeller (1) from propeller shaft (4).

Inspect propeller (1) and shear pin (3) for excessive wear and renew if excessive wear or damage is noted.

Apply OMC TRIPLE-GUARD GREASE to the propeller bore, then install propeller (1) on propeller shaft (4) and retain with a new cotter pin (2).

Shown in Fig. OM2-19 is a view of a typical propeller setup used on 4.5 hp models. To remove the

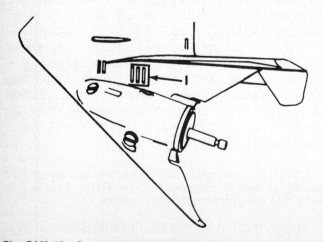

Fig. OM2-17—On weedless models, cooling system water inlet ports (I) are located on both sides of the lower unit.

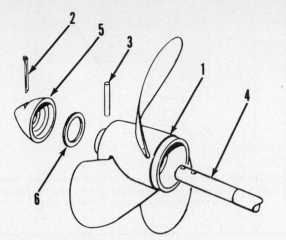

Fig. OM2-19 — Exploded view of a typical propeller setup used on 4.5 hp models. Refer to text.

1. Propeller
2. Cotter pin
3. Shear pin
4. Propeller shaft
5. Spinner
6. Thrust washer

propeller, remove cotter pin (2) and withdraw spinner (5). Remove shear pin (3), thrust washer (6) and withdraw propeller (1) from propeller shaft (4).

Inspect all components for damage and excessive wear and renew if needed.

Apply OMC TRIPLE-GUARD GREASE to propeller shaft (4), then install propeller (1), thrust washer (6) and shear pin (3). Install spinner (5) and secure with a new cotter pin (2).

Tune-Up

IGNITION SYSTEM

Breaker Point Type

The standard spark plug is Champion J4J with an electrode gap of 0.020 inch (0.51 mm) on 1970 models, Champion J6J with an electrode gap of 0.030 inch (0.76 mm) on 1971-1976 models and Champion L86 with an electrode gap of 0.030 inch (0.76 mm) on 1981-1985 models. The magneto breaker point gap should be 0.020 inch (0.51 mm) on used points and 0.022 inch (0.56 mm) on new points. The flywheel must be removed to service the breaker point assemblies and condensers.

To check the ignition timing, proceed as follows: With the outboard motor properly mounted on a boat or a suitable test tank, immerse the lower unit. Connect a tachometer and set it on the appropriate range scale. Connect a suitable timing light to the top cylinder spark plug lead. Start the engine and adjust the speed control until the engine is running at 1000 rpm. Ignition timing is correct if flywheel mark (F — Fig. OM2-20) is centered between timing marks (M) on magneto armature plate. Repeat the previous procedure with the timing light connected to the bot-

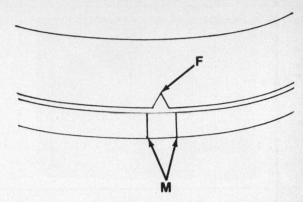

Fig. OM2-20 — Ignition timing is correct if flywheel mark (F) is centered between timing marks (M) on magneto armature plate. Refer to text.

tom cylinder spark plug lead. If ignition timing is not correct, then check and adjust breaker point gaps or renew breaker point assemblies as follows:

To remove the flywheel, use a suitable flywheel holding tool and remove the securing nut and lockwasher with suitable tools. Remove the flywheel from the crankshaft end using a suitable puller assembly and suitable tools. Note flywheel key located in the crankshaft keyway.

⚠WARNING

Be sure suitable tools are used to remove the flywheel. Damage resultant from the misapplication of force or the use of incorrect tools may cause engine damage, engine malfunction or personal injury.

Rotate the crankshaft until the breaker point contact surfaces are at their widest position. Then with a 0.020 inch (0.51 mm) feeler gage, check and adjust the point set until 0.020 inch (0.51 m) gap is obtained. Repeat the adjustment procedure on the other breaker point assembly.

NOTE: No service to the breaker point assemblies is recommended by the manufacturer. The manufacturer recommends cleaning the contact surfaces with alcohol only. A strip of bias tape should be used between contact surfaces to remove any foreign matter.

If needed, renew the breaker point assemblies and condensers. On a new breaker point assembly, point gap should be set at 0.022 inch (0.56 mm).

After adjustment, make sure the breaker point assemblies and condensers securing screws are properly tightened. Be sure the flywheel key is properly positioned in the crankshaft end, then

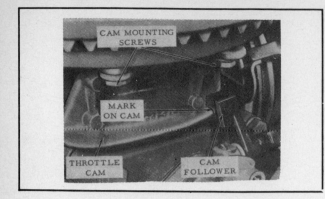

Fig. OM2-21—View of typical ignition and throttle synchronizing parts on models prior to 1978. Refer to text for adjusting procedures.

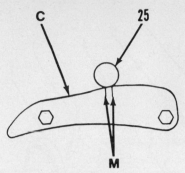

Fig. OM2-22—On models after 1977, cam follower roller (25) should be centered between marks (M) on cam (C) just as carburetor throttle opens. Refer to text.

reinstall the flywheel. Install the lockwasher, then install and tighten flywheel nut to 30-40 ft.-lbs. (40-54 N·m). Check ignition timing as outlined earlier.

CD Type

A capacitor discharge ignition (CDI) system is used. Refer to the Outboard Motor Service Manual for testing and servicing the CD ignition system. If engine malfunction is noted and the ignition system is suspected, make sure the spark plugs and all electrical wiring are in good condition and all electrical connections are tight before troubleshooting the CD ignition system.

The standard spark plug is Champion L77J4 with an electrode gap of 0.040 inch (1.0 mm).

SPEED CONTROL LINKAGE

The speed control lever rotates the armature plate to advance the ignition timing. The throttle cam attached to the bottom of the armature plate is used to open the carburetor throttle as the ignition is advanced. The throttle opening and ignition timing cannot be properly synchronized if the throttle cam and related components are worn or damaged in any way. Renew components if needed.

To synchronize speed controls, first remove the engine cover. Move the speed control lever from the stop position until the carburetor throttle just begins to open. On models prior to 1978, the mark on the throttle cam should be directly behind the starboard edge of the cam follower as shown in Fig. OM2-21. If incorrect, loosen throttle cam retaining screws and adjust throttle cam. On models after 1977, cam follower roller (25—Fig. OM2-22) should be centered between marks (M) on cam (C) just as carburetor throttle opens. Turn cam follower adjusting screw (24—Fig. OM2-23) to center roller on marks.

CARBURETOR

ADJUSTMENT. On models prior to 1978, the carburetor is equipped with adjustment needles for both low and high speed mixture. Initial setting is 1¼ turns out from a lightly seated position for low speed mixture needle (L—Fig. OM2-23) and ½ to 1 turn out from a lightly seated position for high speed mixture needle (H). Needle should be adjusted after motor reaches normal operating temperature to provide best operation at idle and high speed. The high speed needle (H) should be adjusted for best operation at high speed before adjusting needle (L) for best operation at idle speed. Turning both needles clockwise leans the fuel mixture.

On models after 1977, the carburetor is equipped with a low speed mixture adjustment needle, but uses a nonadjustable high speed jet. High speed air:fuel mixture is adjustable only by varying the orifice size of the high speed jet.

Recommended idle speed is 600 rpm with engine at normal operating temperature and in gear.

With the outboard motor properly mounted on a boat or a suitable test tank, immerse the lower unit. Start the engine and allow it to warm up to normal operating temperature.

On models prior to 1978, shift into "Forward" gear then place the speed control lever at the "FAST" position. Adjust high speed mixture needle (H). After adjustment, stop the engine and turned. Place the speed control lever at the "SLOW" position. Adjust low speed mixture needle (L) until the highest consistent rpm is obtained. Repeat adjustment procedure on high speed mixture needle (H). After adjustment, stop the enigne and turn low speed mixture needle (L) and high speed mixture needle (H) ⅛ turn counterclockwise. This is to prevent the possibility of a too lean fuel mixture at low or high engine speeds. If necessary, reposition low speed knob with pointer up and high speed knob with pointer down.

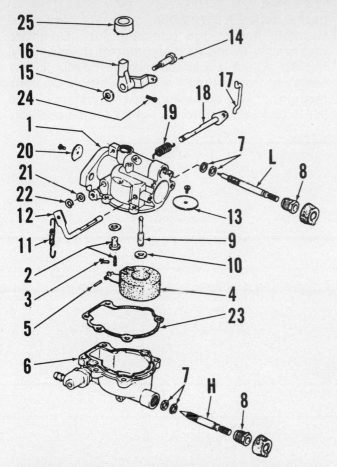

Fig. OM2-23—Exploded view of carburetor typical of the type used on all models. Follower adjusting screw (24) and follower roller (25) are used on models after 1977. The carburetor used on later 4 hp models and 4.5 hp models is equipped with a nonadjustable high speed jet in place of high speed adjustment needle (H) and a fuel shut-off valve is integral with the float bowl.

H. High speed mixture needle	12. Choke shaft
L. Low speed mixture needle	13. Choke plate
1. Carburetor body	14. Shoulder screw
2. Fuel inlet needle & seat	15. Washer
3. Needle-to-float clip	16. Cam follower
4. Float	17. Link
5. Pin	18. Throttle shaft
6. Float bowl	19. Return spring
7. Packing	20. Throttle plate
8. Packing nut	21. Washer
9. High speed nozzle	22. Throttle shaft retainer
10. Gasket	23. Gasket
11. Choke return spring	24. Follower adjusting screw
	25. Roller

On models after 1977, shift into forward gear and place the speed control in the slow position (approximately 700-800 rpm). Adjust low speed mixture needle (L) until the highest consistent rpm is obtained. Note that high speed air:fuel mixture is adjustable only by varying the high speed jet orifice size. After adjustment, stop the engine and turn low speed mixture needle (L) 1/16 turn counterclockwise. This is to prevent the possibility of a too lean fuel mixture at low engine speeds. If necessary, reposition low speed knob with pointer down.

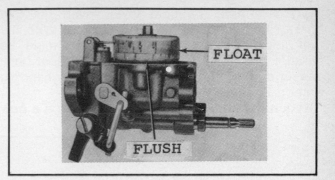

Fig. OM2-24—With fuel inlet needle closed, float should be flush with gasket surface of body as shown.

OVERHAUL. Remove the engine's top cover. Remove any linkage that will interfere with removal of the carburetor. Remove all components as needed to completely expose the carburetor. On models with an integral fuel tank, make sure the fuel line is properly plugged. Clean all external surfaces and remove accumulated dirt and grease. Remove the two nuts retaining the carburetor and withdraw the carburetor.

Shown in Fig. OM2-23 is an exploded view of the carburetor used on early 4 hp models. The carburetor used on later 4 hp models and 4.5 hp models is equipped with a nonadjustable high speed jet in place of high speed adjustment needle (H). A fuel shut-off valve is integral with the float bowl on later models.

With reference to Fig. OM2-23, disassemble the carburetor and note any discrepancies which must be corrected before reassembly. Remove all gaskets and "O" rings, if so equipped, and set to the side for future reference.

Thoroughly clean all carburetor parts with a suitable solvent and inspect for damage and excessive wear.

NOTE: The manufacturer does not recommend submerging the parts in carburetor or parts cleaning solutions. An aerosol type carburetor cleaner is recommended. The float and other components made of plastic and rubber should not be subjected to some cleaning solutions. Safety eyewear and solvent resistant gloves are recommended.

Blow dry with clean compressed air. If compressed air is not available, use only lint-free cloths to wipe dry.

With reference to Fig. OM2-23, reassemble the carburetor components with new gaskets. Note that the new gaskets should match up with those removed. If not, check with your parts supplier to be sure you have the correct gasket set.

NOTE: DO NOT completely tighten packing nuts (8). Stop tightening packing nuts (8) when the mixture needles become difficult to rotate by hand.

Evinrude & Johnson 4 & 4.5 Hp

To determine the float level, invert the carburetor body as shown in Fig. OM2-24. With the fuel inlet needle closed, the float should be parallel and flush with the carburetor float bowl gasket surface. Adjust the float level by bending arm on float (4 — Fig. OM2-23).

When reinstalling the carburetor, place a new gasket between the carburetor and the reed plate. Securely tighten the retaining nuts. Complete reassembly in the reverse order of disassembly. Initially adjust low speed mixture needle (L) 1¼ turns out from a lightly seated position. On early models, initially adjust high speed mixture needle (H) ½ to 1 turn out from a lightly seated position.

EVINRUDE AND JOHNSON
6 HP (1969-1979)

Year Produced	EVINRUDE Models	Year Produced	JOHNSON Models
1969	6902,6903	1969	6R69,6RL69
1970	6002,6003	1970	6R70,6RL70
1971	6102,6103	1971	6R71,6RL71
1972	6202,6203	1972	6R72,6RL72
1973	6302,6303	1973	6R73,6RL73
1974	6402,6403	1974	6R74,6RL74
1975	6504,6505	1975	6R75,6RL75
1976	6604,6605	1976	6R76,6RL76
1977	6704,6705	1977	6R77,6RL77
1978	6804,6805	1978	6R78,6RL78
1979	6904,6905	1979	6R79,6RL79

Specifications

Hp/rpm	6/4000-5000
Bore	1.94 in. (49.2 mm)
Stroke	1.50 in. (38.1 mm)
Number of cylinders	2
Displacement	8.84 cu. in. (145 cc)
Spark plug — Champion	
1969-1970	J4J
Electrode gap	0.030 in. (0.76 mm)
1971-1976	J6J
Electrode gap	0.030 in. (0.76 mm)
1977	L77J4
Electrode gap	0.040 in. (1.0 mm)
1978-1979	L78V
Electrode gap	Surface Gap
Ignition type:	
1969-1976	Breaker Point
Breaker point gap	0.020 in. (0.51 mm)
1977-1979	CD
Carburetor make	Own
Idle speed (in gear)	550 rpm
Fuel:oil ratio	50:1
Fuel pump:	
Discharge pressure at 600 rpm	1 psi (7 kPa)
Discharge pressure at 2500-3000 rpm	1.5 psi (10 kPa)
Discharge pressure at 4500 rpm	2.5 psi (17 kPa)

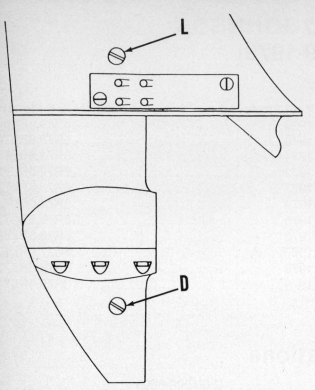

Fig. OM3-1—View showing lower unit gearcase drain and fill plug (D) and oil level (vent) plug (L).

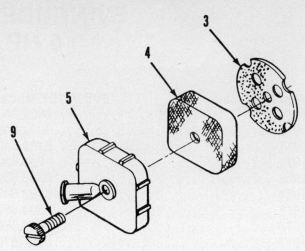

Fig. OM3-2—View showing fuel strainer (4) located behind fuel pump inlet cover (5). Screw (9) retains inlet cover (5) and gasket (3) seals between inlet cover (5) and the pump cover.

Maintenance

LUBRICATION

ENGINE. The engine is lubricated by oil mixed with the fuel. The fuel should be regular leaded or unleaded gasoline with a minimum pump octane rating of 86.

Recommended oil is Evinrude or Johnson 50/1 Lubricant or a BIA certified two-stroke motor oil. The recommended fuel:oil ratio for normal operation and engine break-in is 50:1.

The manufacturer's recommended break-in period is defined as follows: For the first fifteen minutes of operation the engine should not exceed its slowest possible cruising speed. After fifteen minutes, slowly increase the engine speed to ½ throttle for the next 45 minutes of operation. During that 45 minutes, short, full throttle accelerations (90 seconds) every five minutes are suggested. For the second hour, increase engine speed to ¾ throttle and periodically accelerate to full throttle. Run the engine at full throttle for 1 to 2 minutes before returning to ¾ throttle setting. Running the engine at or near full throttle for extended periods is not recommended until after 5 hours of operation.

LOWER UNIT. The lower unit gears and bearings are lubricated by oil contained in the gearcase. The recommended oil is OMC HI-VIS Gearcase Lube. The gearcase oil level should be checked after every 50 hours of operation and the gearcase should be drained and filled with new oil every 100 hours or once each season, whichever occurs first.

The gearcase is drained and filled through the same plug port (D—Fig. OM3-1). An oil level (vent) port (L) is used to indicate the full level of the gearcase oil and to ease oil drainage.

To drain the oil, place the outboard motor in a vertical position. Remove drain plug (D) and oil level plug (L) and allow the lubricant to drain into a suitable container.

To fill the gearcase with oil, place the outboard motor in a vertical position. Add oil through drain plug (D) opening with an oil feeder until the oil begins to overflow from oil level plug (L) port. Reinstall oil level plug (L) with a new gasket, if needed, and tighten. Remove oil feeder, then reinstall drain plug (D) with a new gasket, if needed, and tighten.

PIVOT POINTS AND SLIDES. Lubricate all pivot points and linkage slides with OMC TRIPLE-GUARD GREASE or a suitable equivalent every 60 days or more frequently if needed to keep the components operating freely and properly.

FUEL SYSTEM

Periodically inspect the fuel lines and connections for damage. Renew components if needed.

Keep the external surface of the carburetor clean and all connections and sealing surfaces tight.

FUEL FILTER. A strainer (4—Fig. OM3-2) positioned behind fuel pump inlet cover (5) is used to filter the fuel prior to entering the fuel pump assembly. To inspect, remove screw (9) retaining inlet cover (5) and withdraw cover (5) with strainer

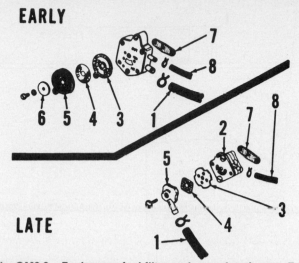

EARLY

LATE

Fig. OM3-3—Fuel pump, fuel filter and associated parts. Early type fuel pump is shown at top.

1. Inlet fuel line
2. Fuel pump
3. Gasket
4. Strainer
5. Cover
6. Washer
7. Gasket
8. Discharge fuel line

(4). Clean strainer (4) in a suitable solvent and blow dry with clean compressed air. Inspect strainer (4). If excessive blockage or damage is noted, renew strainer. If needed, renew gasket (3).

FUEL PUMP. The fuel pump is operated by crankcase pressure changes from the up-and-down movement of the piston. When the crankcase pressure decreases (the piston is moving upward), the pump diaphragm is pulled toward the crankcase allowing fuel to enter the pump body and closing the discharge check valve. When the crankcase pressure increases (the piston is moving downward), the diaphragm is pushed outward discharging the fuel to the carburetor and closing the inlet check valve. This pulsating action provides continuous fuel flow. The check valves are used to prevent reverse flow of the fuel.

The fuel hoses must be connected according to fuel flow. The fuel tank supply line connects to the fuel pump inlet port and the line routed toward the carburetor assembly connects to the outlet port.

Shown in Fig. OM3-3 are the early and late type fuel pumps used. If fuel pump malfunction is noted, the fuel pump should be renewed as a complete assembly. Renew the mounting gasket and securely tighten the retaining screws.

NOTE: Fuel pump and engine malfunction will result if the fuel pump and all connections are not airtight.

STARTER

The manual starter mounts on intake manifold (5—Fig. OM3-4) and starter rope (4) extends through the lower motor cover. The suggested

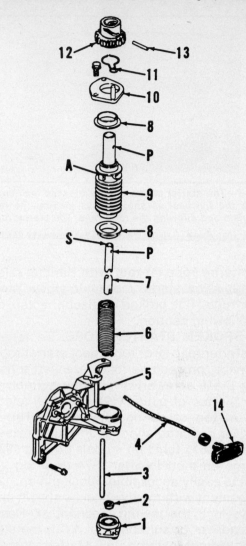

Fig. OM3-4—Exploded view of the manual rewind starter and associated parts. Intake manifold (5) contains the mounting bracket for the starter unit.

A. Attaching lug
P. Pin holes
S. Slot
1. Retainer plate
2. Bushing
3. Rope guide
4. Starter rope
5. Intake manifold
6. Rewind spring
7. Retainer
8. Bushing
9. Spool
10. Bearing head
11. Spring
12. Pinion
13. Roll pin
14. Starter handle

procedure for starter rope (4) renewal differs slightly from that required for starter overhaul, refer to the appropriate following sections for the recommended service procedures.

R&R WORN STARTER ROPE. To renew a worn starter rope (4—Fig. OM3-4), first remove the top engine cover and disconnect both spark plug high tension leads. Pull starter rope (4) until almost fully extended and starter rope end is accessible in spool (9). Block pinion (12) into engagement with the flywheel as shown in Fig. OM3-5 thus locking the rewind mechanism. With the starter securely locked, disconnect starter rope (4—Fig. OM3-4) from handle (14) and lug (A). Install a new starter rope (4) by reversing the removal procedure. While

Fig. OM3-5—*The starter pinion can be blocked into engagement with the flywheel as shown, thus locking the rewind mechanism and allowing the removal of the starter rope.*

pulling starter rope (4) taut with handle, release pinion (12). Allow starter rope (4) to slowly rewind. If starter rope (4) is broken or disconnected, refer to the following section.

R&R BROKEN STARTER ROPE. To renew a broken starter rope (4) or reconnect starter rope (4) after service, proceed as follows: Insert a heavy-duty flat blade screwdriver or other suitable tool through the top of pinion (12), spool (9) and into slot (S) in top of spring retainer (7). Turn the screwdriver or suitable tool counterclockwise approximately 16½ turns on models prior to 1975 or 12½ turns on models after 1974 until lug (A) in spool (9) is easily accessible. Block pinion (12) into engagement with the flywheel as shown in Fig. OM3-5 to lock the rewind mechanism. Remove the screwdriver or suitable tool. With the starter securely locked, install a new starter rope. With starter rope (4 — Fig. OM3-4) secured in lug (A) and handle (14), release pinion (12) and allow starter rope (4) to rewind.

OVERHAUL. To disconnect starter rope (4) for removal of the manual starter assembly, pull out starter rope (4) approximately 1 foot (30 cm) and tie a slip knot in starter rope (4) to prevent rewinding. Remove handle (14) from the starter rope end. Untie the slip knot and allow the starter rope to slowly wind onto spool (9) until rewind spring (6) is fully unwound. Remove the two cap screws securing upper bearing head (10) to intake manifold (5) and lift off items (6 through 13) as a unit. Drive out roll pin (13) and separate the components.

Wash the parts in a suitable solvent. Inspect and renew any parts that are damaged or worn. When assembling the starter, lubricate rewind spring (6) with a light grease. Note that pinion (12) and spool (9) should not be lubricated, but installed dry to prevent dust accumulation. Note the following during reassembly: Align holes (P) in spring retainer (7) and spool (9) with slots in pinion (12), and tap pin (13) through the holes and slots. Upper bearing head (10), spring (11) and upper

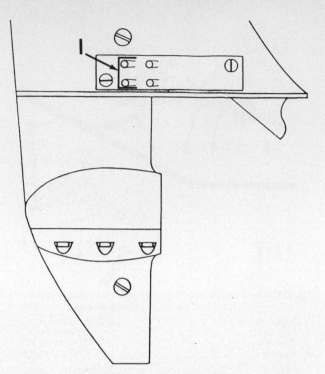

Fig. OM3-6—*Cooling system water inlet ports (I) are located on the port side of the lower unit.*

bushing (8) must be properly positioned before installing pinion (12). Make sure slot in lower end of spring retainer (7) engages inner end of rewind spring (6) and enters bushing (2).

Complete reassembly, then install starter rope (4) and adjust rewind spring (6) tension as previously outlined in R&R BROKEN STARTER ROPE section.

COOLING SYSTEM

Ports (I — Fig. OM3-6) located on the port side of the lower unit gearcase are used as the water inlets for the cooling system. The ports must be kept clean of all foreign matter to ensure efficient operation of the cooling system.

⚠️CAUTION

Do not operate outboard motor unless the lower unit is immersed in water, otherwise, the water pump impeller will be damaged.

A thermostat positioned in the cylinder head is used to regulate engine operating temperature. Note that a thermostat that sticks or stays closed too long could cause engine overheating, resulting in poor engine operation and possible engine damage. A thermostat that opens too quickly or is

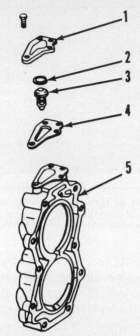

Fig. OM3-7—Exploded view showing the location of thermostat (3) in cylinder head (5).

1. Cover　　　　　　　　3. Thermostat
2. Seal　　　　　　　　 4. Gasket　　　　　5. Cylinder head

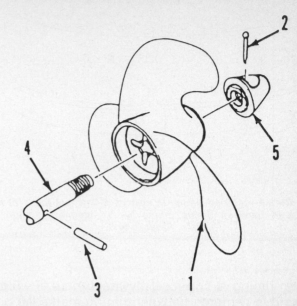

Fig. OM3-8—Propeller (1) is mounted on propeller shaft (4) and is retained by spinner (5) and cotter pin (2). Shear pin (3) is renewed only after withdrawing propeller (1) from propeller shaft (4).

stuck in the open position will cause the engine not to reach its recommended operating temperature range, resulting in possible engine malfunction and poor engine efficiency. The thermostat is calibrated to control the coolant temperature within the range of 145°-150°F (63°-66°C). If thermostat malfunction is suspected, remove the thermostat housing (1—Fig. OM3-7) located at the top of the cylinder head to obtain access to the thermostat (3).

Refer to the Outboard Motor Service Manual if more extensive service to the cooling system is required.

PROPELLER

Consult your local dealer or the manufacturer for the specifications pertaining to the standard propeller used on your model of outboard motor. Optional propellers are available. Select a propeller that will allow the engine at full throttle to reach maximum operating rpm range (4000-5000).

⚠WARNING

Shift directional control lever to "NEUTRAL." Disconnect the spark plug leads and properly ground leads before performing any propeller service, otherwise, accidental starting can occur if propeller shaft is rotated.

To remove the propeller, remove cotter pin (2—Fig. OM3-8) and unscrew spinner (5), then withdraw propeller (1) from propeller shaft (4).

Inspect propeller (1) and shear pin (3) for excessive wear and damage and renew if needed. Apply OMC TRIPLE-GUARD GREASE to the propeller bore, then install propeller (1) on propeller shaft (4). Screw spinner (5) onto propeller shaft (4) and retain with a new cotter pin (2).

Tune-Up

IGNITION SYSTEM

Breaker Point Type

The standard spark plug is Champion J4J with an electrode gap of 0.030 inch (0.76 mm) on 1969-1970 models and Champion J6J with an electrode gap of 0.030 inch (0.76 mm) on 1971-1976 models. The magneto breaker point gap should be 0.020 inch (0.51 mm) on used points and 0.022 inch (0.56 mm) on new points. The flywheel must be removed to service the breaker point assemblies and the condensers.

To check the ignition timing, proceed as follows: With the outboard motor properly mounted on a boat or a suitable test tank, immerse the lower unit. Connect a tachometer and set it on the appropriate range scale. Connect a suitable timing light to the top cylinder spark plug lead. Start the engine and adjust the speed control until the engine is running at 1000 rpm. Ig-

Evinrude & Johnson 6 Hp (1969-1979)

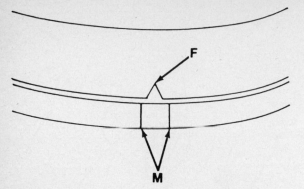

Fig. OM3-9—Ignition timing is correct if flywheel mark (F) is centered between timing marks (M) on magneto armature plate. Refer to text.

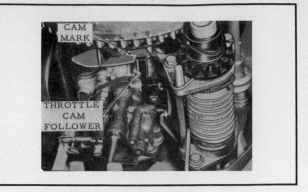

Fig. OM3-10—View of throttle cam index mark aligned with starboard side of cam follower on models prior to 1978.

nition timing is correct if flywheel mark (F—Fig. OM3-9) is centered between timing marks (M) on magneto armature plate. Repeat the previous procedure with the timing light connected to the bottom cylinder spark plug lead. If ignition timing is not correct, check and adjust breaker point gaps or renew breaker point assemblies as follows:

To remove the flywheel, use a suitable flywheel holding tool and remove the securing nut and lockwasher with suitable tools. Remove the flywheel from the crankshaft end using a suitable puller assembly and suitable tools. Note flywheel key located in the crankshaft keyway.

⚠ WARNING

Be sure suitable tools are used to remove the flywheel. Damage resultant from the misapplication of force or the use of incorrect tools may cause engine damage, engine malfunction or personal injury.

Rotate the crankshaft until the breaker point contact surfaces are at their widest position. Then with a 0.020 inch (0.51 mm) feeler gage, check and adjust the point set until 0.020 inch (0.51 mm) gap is obtained. Repeat the adjustment procedure on the other breaker point assembly.

NOTE: No service to the breaker point assemblies is recommended by the manufacturer. The manufacturer recommends cleaning the contact surfaces with alcohol only. A strip of bias tape should be used between contact surfaces to remove any foreign matter.

If needed, renew the breaker point assemblies and condensers. On a new breaker point assembly, point gap should be set at 0.022 inch (0.56 mm).

After adjustment, make sure the breaker point assemblies and condensers securing screws are properly tightened. Be sure the flywheel key is properly positioned in the crankshaft end, then reinstall the flywheel. Install the lockwasher, then install and tighten flywheel securing nut to 40-45 ft.-lbs. (54-61 N·m). Check ignition timing as previously outlined.

CD Type

A capacitor discharge ignition (CDI) system is used. Refer to the Outboard Motor Service Manual for testing and servicing the CD ignition system. If engine malfunction is noted and the ignition system is suspected, make sure the spark plugs and all electrical wiring are in good condition and all electrical connections are tight before troubleshooting the CD ignition system.

The standard spark plug is Champion L77J4 with an electrode gap of 0.040 inch (1.0 mm) on 1977 models and Champion L78V on 1978-1979 models. Champion L78V is a surface gap type spark plug and should be renewed if center electrode is more than 1/32 inch (0.79 mm) below the flat surface of the plug end.

SPEED CONTROL LINKAGE

The speed control lever rotates the armature plate to advance the ignition timing. The throttle cam attached to the bottom of the armature plate is used to open the carburetor throttle as the ignition is advanced. The throttle opening and ignition timing cannot be properly synchronized if the throttle cam and related components are worn or damaged in any way. Renew components if needed.

To synchronize speed controls, first remove the engine cover. Move the speed control lever from the stop position until the carburetor throttle just begins to open. On models prior to 1978, the mark on the throttle cam should be directly behind the starboard edge of the cam follower as shown in

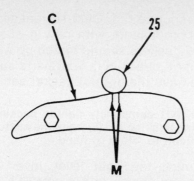

Fig. OM3-11—On models after 1977, cam follower roller (25) should be centered between marks (M) on cam (C) just as carburetor throttle opens. Refer to text.

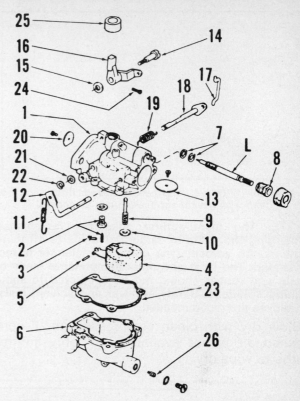

Fig. OM3-12—Exploded view of carburetor typical of the type used on all models. Follower adjusting screw (24) and follower roller (25) are used on models after 1977.

L. Low speed mixture needle	13. Choke plate
1. Carburetor body	14. Shoulder bolt
2. Fuel inlet needle & seat	15. Washer
3. Needle-to-float clip	16. Cam follower
4. Float	17. Link
5. Pin	18. Throttle shaft
6. Float bowl	19. Return spring
7. Packing	20. Throttle plate
8. Packing nut	21. Washer
9. High speed nozzle	22. Throttle shaft retainer
10. Gasket	23. Gasket
11. Choke return spring	24. Follower adjusting screw
12. Choke shaft	25. High speed jet.

Fig. OM3-10. If incorrect, loosen throttle cam retaining screws and adjust throttle cam. On models after 1977, cam follower roller (25—Fig. OM3-11) should be centered between marks (M) on cam (C) just as carburetor throttle opens. Turn cam follower adjusting screw (24—Fig. OM3-12) to center roller on marks.

CARBURETOR

ADJUSTMENT. The carburetor is equipped with an adjustment needle for the low speed mixture. The initial setting of low speed mixture needle (L—Fig. OM3-12) is 1½ turns out from a lightly seated position. The mixture needle should be adjusted after motor reaches normal operating temperature to provide the best operation at idle speed. Turning the needle clockwise leans the fuel mixture.

A nonadjustable high speed jet (26) is used to regulate the high speed air:fuel mixture. The orifice size of high speed jet (26) must be varied to adjust high speed air:fuel mixture. Standard high speed jet (26) sizes are as follows: 0.048 inch (1.22 mm) for 1969-1973 models, 0.044 inch (1.12 mm) for 1974-1975 models, 0.052 inch (1.32 mm) for 1976 models, 0.041 inch (1.04 mm) for 1977 models and 0.042 inch (1.07 mm) for 1978 and 1979 models. Other jet sizes are available for adjusting the calibration for altitude or other special conditions.

Recommended idle speed is 550 rpm with the engine at normal operating temperature and in gear.

With the outboard motor properly mounted on a boat or a suitable test tank, immerse the lower unit. Start the engine and allow it to warm up to normal operating temperature. Shift into forward gear and place the speed control in the slow position (approximately 700-750 rpm). Adjust low speed mixture needle (L) until the highest consistent rpm is obtained. Note that high speed air:fuel mixture is adjustable only by varying the size of

high speed jet orifice. After adjustment, stop the engine and turn low speed mixture needle (L) 1/16 turn counterclockwise. This is to prevent the possibility of a too lean fuel mixture at low engine speeds. If necessary, reposition low speed knob with pointer towards normal running position.

OVERHAUL. Remove the engine's top cover. Disconnect any linkage that will interfere with carburetor removal. Remove all components as needed to completely expose the carburetor. Clean all external surfaces and remove accumulated dirt and grease. Remove the two nuts retaining the carburetor and withdraw the carburetor.

With reference to Fig. OM3-12, disassemble the carburetor and note any discrepancies which must be corrected before reassembly. Remove all gaskets and set to the side for future reference.

Thoroughly clean all carburetor parts with a suitable solvent and inspect for damage and excessive wear.

Evinrude & Johnson 6 Hp (1969-1979)

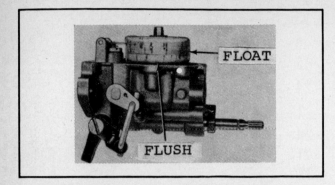

Fig. OM3-13 — With fuel inlet needle closed, float should be flush with gasket surface of body as shown.

NOTE: The manufacturer does not recommend submerging the parts in carburetor or parts cleaning solutions. An aerosol type carburetor cleaner is recommended. The float and other components made of plastic and rubber should not be subjected to some cleaning solutions. Safety eyewear and solvent resistant gloves are recommended.

Blow dry with clean compressed air. If compressed air is not available, use only lint-free cloths to wipe dry.

With reference to Fig. OM3-12, reassemble the carburetor components with new gaskets. Note that the new gaskets should match up with those removed. If not, check with your parts supplier to be sure you have the correct gasket set.

NOTE: DO NOT completely tighten packing nut (8). Stop tightening packing nut (8) when the mixture needle becomes difficult to rotate by hand.

To determine the float level, invert the carburetor body as shown in Fig. OM3-13. With the fuel inlet needle closed, the float should be parallel and flush with carburetor float bowl gasket surface. Adjust the float level by bending arm on float (4 — Fig. OM3-12).

When reinstalling the carburetor, place a new gasket between the carburetor and the intake manifold. Securely tighten the retaining nuts. Complete reassembly in the reverse order of disassembly. Initially adjust low speed mixture needle (L) 1½ turns out from a lightly seated position.

EVINRUDE AND JOHNSON
7.5 HP (1980-1983)
6 & 8 HP (1984-1985)

EVINRUDE MODELS

Year Produced	6 hp	7.5 hp	8 hp
1980	....	8RCS	....
1981	....	8RCI	....
1982	....	8RCN	....
1983	....	8RCT	....
1984	6RCR	....	8RCR
1985	6RCO	....	8RCO

JOHNSON MODELS

Year Produced	6 hp	7.5 hp	8 hp
1980	....	8RCS	....
1981	....	8RCI	....
1982	....	8RCN	....
1983	....	8RCT	....
1984	6RCR	....	8RCR
1985	6RCO	....	8RCO

Specifications

Hp/rpm	6/4500-5500
	7.5/4500-5500
	8/5000-6000
Bore	1.94 in.
	(49.2 mm)
Stroke	1.70 in.
	(43.2 mm)
Number of cylinders	2
Displacement	10 cu. in.
	(164 cc)
Spark plug—Champion	L77J4*
Electrode gap	0.040 in.
	(1.0 mm)
Ignition type	CD
Carburetor make	Own
Idle speed (in gear)	650 rpm
Fuel:oil ratio	50:1†
Fuel pump:	
Discharge pressure at 600 rpm	1 psi
	(7 kPa)
Discharge pressure at 2500-3000 rpm	1.5 psi
	(10 kPa)
Discharge pressure at 4500 rpm	2.5 psi
	(17 kPa)

*A Champion L78V is recommended for 6 and 8 hp models when used at sustained high speeds. Renew surface gap spark plug if center electrode is more than 1/32 inch (0.79 mm) below the flat surface of the plug end.

†On 1985 models, a 100:1 ratio can be used when Evinrude or Johnson outboard lubricant formulated for 100:1 fuel mix is used.

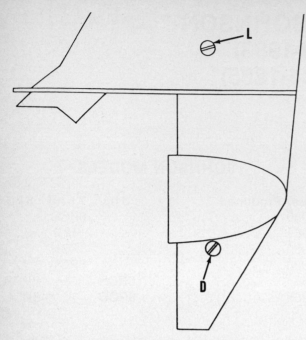

Fig. OM4-1 — *View showing lower unit gearcase drain and fill plug (D) and oil level (vent) plug (L).*

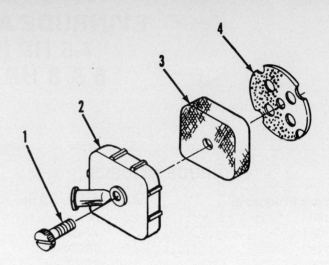

Fig. OM4-2 — *View showing fuel strainer (3) located behind fuel pump inlet cover (2). Screw (1) retains inlet cover (2) and gasket (4) seals between inlet cover (2) and the pump cover.*

Maintenance

LUBRICATION

ENGINE. The engine is lubricated by oil mixed with the fuel. The fuel should be regular leaded or unleaded gasoline with a minimum pump octane rating of 86.

NOTE: On 1981 and later models, the manufacturer permits the above fuels to be used at a minimum pump octane rating of 67.

On models prior to 1985, recommended oil is Evinrude or Johnson 50/1 Lubricant or a BIA certified two-stroke motor oil. The recommended fuel:oil ratio for normal operation and engine break-in is 50:1.

On 1985 models, a fuel:oil ratio of 100:1 can be used when Evinrude or Johnson outboard lubricant formulated for 100:1 fuel mix is used. When any other BIA certified two-stroke motor oil is used or during engine break-in, the recommended fuel:oil ratio is 50:1.

The manufacturer's recommended break-in period is defined as follows: For the first fifteen minutes of operation the engine should not exceed its slowest possible cruising speed. After fifteen minutes, slowly increase the engine speed to ½ throttle for the next 45 minutes of operation. During that 45 minutes, short, full throttle accelerations (90 seconds) every five minutes are suggested. For the second hour, increase engine speed to ¾ throttle and periodically accelerate to full throttle. Run the engine at full throttle for 1 to 2 minutes before returning to ¾ throttle setting. Running the engine at or near full throttle for extended periods is not recommended until after 5 hours of operation.

LOWER UNIT. The lower unit gears and bearings are lubricated by oil contained in the gearcase. The recommended oil is OMC HI-VIS Gearcase Lube. The gearcase oil level should be checked after every 50 hours of operation and the gearcase should be drained and filled with new oil every 100 hours or once each season, whichever occurs first.

The gearcase is drained and filled through the same plug port (D — Fig. OM4-1). An oil level (vent) port (L) is used to indicate the full oil level of the gearcase and to ease oil drainage.

To drain the oil, place the outboard motor in a vertical position. Remove drain plug (D) and oil level plug (L) and allow the lubricant to drain into a suitable container.

To fill the gearcase with oil, place the outboard motor in a vertical position. Add oil through drain plug (D) opening with an oil feeder until the oil begins to overflow from oil level plug (L) port. Reinstall oil level plug (L) with a new gasket, if needed, and tighten. Remove oil feeder, then reinstall drain plug (D) with a new gasket, if needed, and tighten.

PIVOT POINTS AND SLIDES. Lubricate all pivot points and linkage slides with OMC TRIPLE-GUARD GREASE or a suitable equivalent every 60 days or more frequently if needed to keep the components operating freely and properly.

FUEL SYSTEM

Periodically inspect the fuel lines and connections for damage. Renew components if needed.

Keep the external surface of the carburetor clean and all connections and sealing surfaces tight.

FUEL FILTER. A strainer (3—Fig. OM4-2) positioned behind fuel pump inlet cover (2) is used to filter the fuel prior to entering the fuel pump assembly. To inspect, remove screw (1) retaining inlet cover (2) and withdraw cover (2) with strainer (3). Clean strainer (3) in a suitable solvent and blow dry with clean compressed air. Inspect strainer (3). If excessive blockage or damage is noted, renew strainer. If needed renew gasket (4).

FUEL PUMP. The fuel pump is operated by crankcase pressure changes from the up-and-down movement of the piston. When the crankcase pressure decreases (the piston is moving upward), the pump diaphragm is pulled toward the crankcase allowing fuel to enter the pump body and closing the discharge check valve. When the crankcase pressure increases (the piston is moving downward), the diaphragm is pushed outward discharging the fuel to the carburetor and closing the inlet check valve. This pulsating action provides continuous fuel flow. The check valves are used to prevent reverse flow of the fuel.

The fuel hoses must be connected according to fuel flow. The fuel tank supply line connects to the fuel pump inlet port and the line routed toward the carburetor assembly connects to the outlet port.

If fuel pump malfunction is noted, the fuel pump should be renewed as a complete assembly. Renew the mounting gasket and securely tighten the retaining screws.

NOTE: Fuel pump and engine malfunction will result if the fuel pump and all connections are not airtight.

STARTER

The manual starter mounts on intake manifold (5—Fig. OM4-3) and starter rope (4) extends through the lower motor cover. A lockout lever mounted on top bearing head (10) is used to prevent engagement of pinion gear (12) when the throttle control lever is advanced past the "START" position. The suggested procedure for starter rope (4) renewal differs slightly from that required for starter overhaul, refer to the appropriate following sections for the recommended service procedures.

R&R WORN STARTER ROPE. To renew a worn starter rope (4—Fig. OM4-3), first remove the top engine cover and disconnect both spark plug high tension leads. Pull starter rope (4) until almost fully extended and the starter rope end is accessible

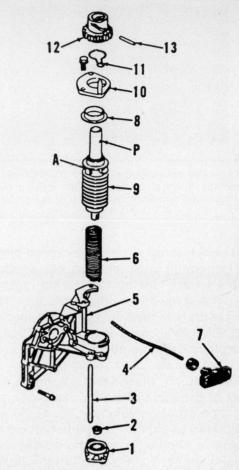

Fig. OM4-3 — Exploded view of the manual rewind starter and associated parts. Intake manifold (5) contains the mounting bracket for the starter unit. Refer to text.

A. Attaching lug
P. Pin hole
1. Retainer plate
2. Bushing
3. Rope guide
4. Starter rope
5. Intake manifold
6. Rewind spring
7. Handle
8. Bushing
9. Spool
10. Bearing head
11. Spring
12. Pinion
13. Roll pin

in spool (9). Insert a small punch through pin (13) or block pinion (12) into engagement with the flywheel as shown in Fig. OM4-4 thus locking the rewind mechanism. With the starter securely locked, disconnect starter rope (4—Fig. OM4-3) from handle (7) and lug (A). Install a new starter rope (4) by reversing the removal procedure. While pulling starter rope (4) taut with handle, release pinion (12). Allow starter rope (4) to slowly rewind. If starter rope (4) is broken or disconnected, refer to the following section.

R&R BROKEN STARTER ROPE. To renew a broken starter rope (4) or reconnect starter rope (4) after service, proceed as follows: Insert a heavy-duty flat blade screwdriver or other suitable tool through the top of pinion (12) and into the slot in top of spool (9). Turn the screwdriver or suitable tool counterclockwise approximately 12½ turns until lug (A) in spool (9) is easily accessible. Insert

Fig. OM4-4—The starter pinion can be blocked into engagement with the flywheel as shown, thus locking the rewind mechanism and allowing the removal of the starter rope.

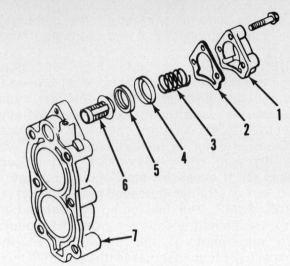

Fig. OM4-5—Exploded view showing the location of thermostat (6) in cylinder head (7).

1. Housing
2. Gasket
3. Spring
4. Retainer
5. Seal
6. Thermostat
7. Cylinder head

a small punch through pin (13) or block pinion (12) into engagement with the flywheel as shown in Fig. OM4-4 thus locking the rewind mechanism. Remove the screwdriver or suitable tool. With the starter securely locked, install a new starter rope (4—Fig. OM4-3) secured in lug (A) and handle (7), release pinion (12) and allow starter rope (4) to rewind.

OVERHAUL. To disconnect starter rope (4) for removal of the manual starter assembly, pull out starter rope (4) approximately 1 foot (30 cm) and tie a slip knot in starter rope (4) to prevent rewinding. Remove handle (7) from the starter rope. Untie the slip knot and allow the starter rope to slowly wind onto spool (9) until rewind spring (6) is fully unwound. Remove the two cap screws securing upper bearing head (10) to intake manifold (5) and lift off items (6 and 8 through 13) as a unit. Drive out roll pin (13) and separate the components.

Wash the parts in a suitable solvent. Inspect and renew any parts that are worn and/or damaged. When assembling the starter, lubricate rewind spring (6) with a light grease. Note that pinion (12) and spool (9) should not be lubricated, but installed dry to prevent dust accumulation. Note the following during reassembly: Align hole (P) in spool (9) with slots in pinion (12), then tap pin (13) through hole (P) and slots. Upper bearing head (10), spring (11) and upper bushing (8) must be properly positioned before installing pinion (12). Make sure slot in lower end of spool (9) engages inner end of rewind spring (6) and enters bushing (2).

Complete reassembly, then install starter rope (4) and adjust rewind spring (6) tension as previously outlined in R&R BROKEN STARTER ROPE section.

COOLING SYSTEM

A port located on the bottom side of the antiventilation plate is used as the water inlet for the cooling system. The port must be kept clean of all foreign matter to ensure efficient operation of the cooling system.

⚠CAUTION

Do not operate outboard motor unless the lower unit is immersed in water, otherwise, the water pump impeller will be damaged.

A thermostat positioned in the cylinder head is used to regulate engine operating temperature. Note that a thermostat that sticks or stays closed too long could cause engine overheating, resulting in poor engine operation and possible engine damage. A thermostat that opens too quickly or is stuck in the open position will cause the engine not to reach its recommended operating temperature range, resulting in possible engine malfunction and poor engine efficiency. If thermostat malfunction is suspected, remove the thermostat housing (1—Fig. OM4-5) located at the top of the cylinder head (7) to obtain access to the thermostat (6).

Refer to the Outboard Motor Service Manual if more extensive service to the cooling system is required.

PROPELLER

Consult your local dealer or the manufacturer for the specifications pertaining to the standard propeller used on your model of outboard motor. Optional propellers are available. Select a pro-

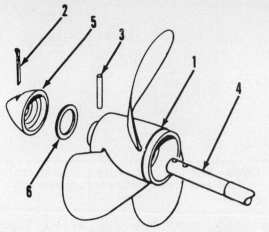

Fig. OM4-6 — Exploded view of a typical propeller setup used on all models.

1. Propeller
2. Cotter pin
3. Shear pin
4. Propeller shaft
5. Spinner
6. Thrust washer

peller that will allow the engine at full throttle to reach maximum operating rpm range (4500-5500 on 6 and 7.5 hp models and 5000-6000 on 8 hp models).

> ⚠️**WARNING**
>
> **Shift directional control lever to "NEUTRAL." Disconnect the spark plug leads and properly ground leads before performing any propeller service, otherwise, accidental starting can occur if propeller shaft is rotated.**

Shown in Fig. OM4-6 is a view of a typical propeller setup used on all models. To remove the propeller, remove cotter pin (2) and withdraw spinner (5). Remove shear pin (3), thrust washer (6) and withdraw propeller (1) from propeller shaft (4).

Inspect all components for damage and excessive wear and renew if needed.

Apply OMC TRIPLE-GUARD GREASE to propeller shaft (4), then install propeller (1), thrust washer (6) and shear pin (3). Install spinner (5) and secure with a new cotter pin (2).

Tune-Up

IGNITION SYSTEM

A capacitor discharge ignition (CDI) system is used. Refer to the Outboard Motor Service Manual for testing and servicing the CD ignition system. If engine malfunction is noted and the ignition system is suspected, make sure the spark plugs and all electrical wiring are in good condition and

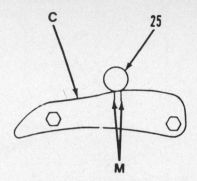

Fig. OM4-7 — Cam follower roller (25) should be centered between marks (M) on cam (C) just as carburetor throttle opens. Refer to text.

all electrical connections are tight before troubleshooting the CD ignition system.

The standard spark plug is Champion L77J4 with an electrode gap of 0.040 inch (1.0 mm). A Champion L78V is recommended for 6 and 8 hp models when used at sustained high speeds. Renew surface gap spark plug if center electrode is more than 1/32 inch (0.79 mm) below the flat surface of the plug end.

SPEED CONTROL LINKAGE

The speed control linkage rotates the armature plate to advance the ignition timing. The throttle cam attached to the bottom of the armature plate is used to open the carburetor throttle as the ignition is advanced. The throttle opening and ignition timing cannot be properly synchronized if the throttle cam and related components are worn or damaged in any way. Renew components if needed.

To synchronize speed controls, first remove the engine cover. Move the speed control from the stop position until the carburetor throttle just begins to open. At this point, the cam follower roller (25 — Fig. OM4-7) should be centered between marks (M) on cam (C). If not, turn cam follower adjusting screw (24 — Fig. OM4-8) to center roller on marks.

CARBURETOR

ADJUSTMENT. The carburetor is equipped with an adjustment needle for the low speed mixture. The initial setting of low speed mixture needle (L — Fig. OM4-8) is 1 turn out from a lightly seated position. The mixture needle should be adjusted after the motor reaches normal operating temperature to provide the best operation at idle speed. Turning the needle clockwise leans the fuel mixture.

A nonadjustable high speed jet (2) is used to regulate the high speed air:fuel mixture. The

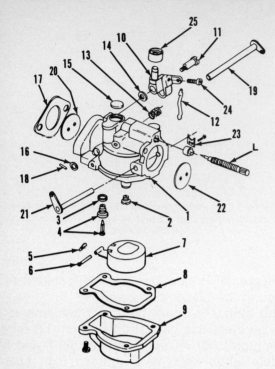

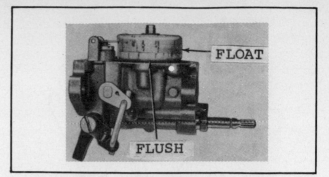

Fig. OM4-9—With fuel inlet needle closed, float should be flush with gasket surface of body as shown.

Fig. OM4-8—Exploded view of carburetor typical of the type used on all models.

L. Low speed mixture needle	13. Spring
1. Carburetor body	14. Washer
2. High speed jet	15. Plug
3. Gasket	16. Washer
4. Fuel inlet needle & seat	17. Gasket
5. Needle-to-float clip	18. Pin
6. Pin	19. Throttle shaft
7. Float	20. Throttle plate
8. Gasket	21. Choke shaft
9. Float bowl	22. Choke plate
10. Cam follower	23. Retainer
11. Shoulder screw	24. Follower adjusting screw
12. Link	25. Roller

orifice size of high speed jet (2) must be varied to adjust high speed air:fuel mixture. Consult your local dealer or the manufacturer for the standard size high speed jet (2) used on your model of outboard motor. Other jet sizes are available for adjusting the calibration for altitude or other special conditions.

Recommended idle speed is 650 rpm with the engine at normal operating temperature and in gear.

With the outboard motor properly mounted on a boat or a suitable test tank, immerse the lower unit. Start the engine and allow it to warm up to normal operating temperature. Shift into forward gear and place the speed control in the slow position (approximately 700-800 rpm). Adjust low speed mixture needle (L) until the highest consistent rpm is obtained. Note that high speed air:fuel mixture is adjustable only by varying the size of high speed jet orifice. After adjustment, stop the engine and turn low speed mixture needle (L) ⅛ turn counterclockwise. This is to prevent a too lean fuel mixture at low engine speeds. If

necessary, reposition low speed knob with pointer facing down.

OVERHAUL. Remove the engine's top cover. Disconnect any linkage that will interfere with carburetor removal. Remove all components as needed to completely expose the carburetor. Clean all external surfaces and remove accumulated dirt and grease. Remove the two nuts retaining the carburetor and withdraw the carburetor.

With reference to Fig. OM4-8, disassemble the carburetor and note any discrepancies which must be corrected before reassembly. Remove all gaskets and set to the side for future reference.

Thoroughly clean all carburetor parts with a suitable solvent and inspect for damage and excessive wear.

NOTE: The manufacturer does not recommend submerging the parts in carburetor or parts cleaning solutions. An aerosol type carburetor cleaner is recommended. The float and other components made of plastic and rubber should not be subjected to some cleaning solutions. Safety eyewear and solvent resistant gloves are recommended.

Blow dry with clean compressed air. If compressed air is not available, use only lint-free cloths to wipe dry.

With reference to Fig. OM4-8, reassemble the carburetor components with new gaskets. Note that the new gaskets should match up with those removed. If not, check with your parts supplier to be sure you have the correct gasket set.

To determine the float level, invert the carburetor body as shown in Fig. OM4-9. With the fuel inlet needle closed, the float should be parallel and flush with carburetor float bowl gasket surface. Adjust the float level by bending arm on float (4—Fig. OM4-8).

When reinstalling the carburetor, place a new gasket (17) between the carburetor and the intake manifold. Securely tighten the retaining nuts. Complete reassembly in the reverse order of disassembly. Initially adjust low speed mixture needle (L) 1 turn out from a lightly seated position.

EVINRUDE AND JOHNSON
9½ HP (1969-1973)

Year Produced	EVINRUDE Models	Year Produced	JOHNSON Models
1969	9922,9923	1969	9R69,9RL69
1970	9022,9023	1970	9R70,9RL70
1971	9122,9123	1971	9R71,9RL71
1972	9222,9223	1972	9R72,9RL72
1973	9322,9323	1973	9R73,9RL73

Specifications

Hp/rpm	9.5/4000-5000
Bore	2-5/16 in. (58.7 mm)
Stroke	1-13/16 in. (46.1 mm)
Number of cylinders	2
Displacement	15.2 cu. in. (249 cc)
Spark plug — Champion	J4J
Electrode gap	0.030 in. (0.76 mm)
Magneto point gap	0.020 in. (0.51 mm)
Carburetor make	Own
Idle speed (in gear)	550 rpm
Fuel:oil ratio	50:1
Fuel pump:	
Discharge pressure at 600 rpm	1 psi (7 kPa)
Discharge pressure at 2500-3000 rpm	1.5 psi (10 kPa)
Discharge pressure at 4500 rpm	2.5 psi (17 kPa)
Gearcase oil capacity	9.7 oz. (291 mL)

Maintenance

LUBRICATION

ENGINE. The engine is lubricated by oil mixed with the fuel. The fuel should be regular leaded or unleaded gasoline with a minimum pump octane rating of 86.

Recommended oil is Evinrude or Johnson 50/1 Lubricant or a BIA certified two-stroke motor oil. The recommended fuel:oil ratio for normal operation and engine break-in is 50:1.

The manufacturer's recommended break-in period is defined as follows: For the first fifteen minutes of operation the engine should not exceed its slowest possible cruising speed. After fifteen minutes, slowly increase the engine speed to ½ throttle for the next 45 minutes of operation. During that 45 minutes, short, full throttle accelerations (90 seconds) every five minutes are suggested. For the second hour, increase engine speed to ¾ throttle and periodically accelerate to full throttle. Run the engine at full throttle for 1 to 2 minutes before returning to ¾ throttle setting. Running the engine at or near full throttle for extended periods is not recommended until after 5 hours of operation.

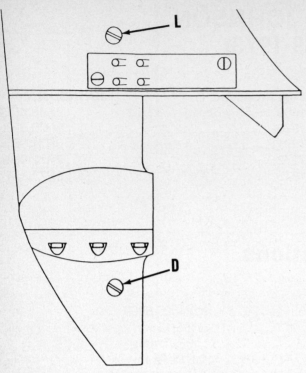

Fig. OM5-1 — View showing lower unit gearcase drain and fill plug (D) and oil level (vent) plug (L).

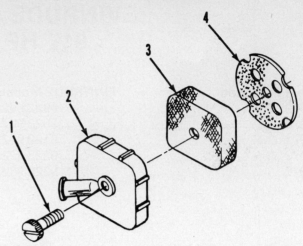

Fig. OM5-2 — View showing fuel strainer (3) located behind fuel pump inlet cover (2). Screw (1) retains inlet cover (2) and gasket (4) seals between inlet cover (2) and the pump cover.

LOWER UNIT. The lower unit gears and bearings are lubricated by oil contained in the gearcase. The recommended oil is OMC Sea-Lube Premium Blend Gearcase Lube or a suitable equivalent. The gearcase oil level should be checked after every 50 hours of operation and the gearcase should be drained and filled with new oil every 100 hours or once each season, whichever occurs first.

The gearcase is drained and filled through the same plug port (D — Fig. OM5-1). An oil level (vent) port (L) is used to indicate the full oil level of the gearcase and to ease oil drainage.

To drain the oil, place the outboard motor in a vertical position. Remove drain plug (D) and oil level plug (L) and allow the lubricant to drain into a suitable container.

To fill the gearcase with oil, place the outboard motor in a vertical position. Add oil through drain plug (D) opening with an oil feeder until the oil begins to overflow from oil level plug (L) port. Reinstall oil level plug (L) with a new gasket, if needed, and tighten. Remove oil feeder, then reinstall drain plug (D) with a new gasket, if needed, and tighten.

PIVOT POINTS AND SLIDES. Lubricate all pivot points and linkage slides with OMC Sea-Lube Anti-Corrosion Lubricant or a suitable equivalent every 60 days or more frequently if needed to keep the components operating freely and properly.

FUEL SYSTEM

Periodically Inspect the fuel lines and connections for damage. Renew components if needed.

Keep the external surface of the carburetor clean and all connections and sealing surfaces tight.

FUEL FILTER. A strainer (3 — Fig. OM5-2) positioned behind fuel pump inlet cover (2) is used to filter the fuel prior to entering the fuel pump assembly. To inspect, remove screw (1) retaining inlet cover (2) and withdraw cover (2) with strainer (3). Clean strainer (3) in a suitable solvent and blow dry with clean compressed air. Inspect strainer (3). If excessive blockage or damage is noted, renew strainer. If needed, renew gasket (4).

FUEL PUMP. The fuel pump is operated by crankcase pressure changes from the up-and-down movement of the piston. When the crankcase pressure decreases (the piston is moving upward), the pump diaphragm is pulled toward the crankcase allowing fuel to enter the pump body and closing the discharge check valve. When the crankcase pressure increases (the piston is moving downward), the diaphragm is pushed outward discharging the fuel to the carburetor and closing the inlet check valve. This pulsating action provides continuous fuel flow. The check valves are used to prevent reverse flow of the fuel.

The fuel hoses must be connected according to fuel flow. The fuel tank supply line connects to the fuel pump inlet port and the line routed toward the carburetor assembly connects to the outlet port.

If fuel pump malfunction is noted, the fuel pump should be renewed as a complete

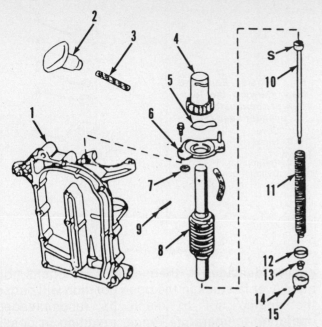

Fig. OM5-3—Exploded view of the manual rewind starter and associated parts. Inner exhaust cover (1) contains the mounting bracket for the starter unit. Refer to text.

S. Slot	8. Spool
1. Inner exhaust cover	9. Pin
2. Handle	10. Upper spring retainer
3. Starter rope	11. Rewind spring
4. Pinion	12. Outer bearing
5. Spring	13. Bushing
6. Upper bearing head	14. Set screw
7. Gasket	15. Lower spring retainer

Fig. OM5-4—The starter pinion can be blocked into engagement with the flywheel as shown, thus locking the rewind mechanism and allowing the removal of the starter rope.

assembly. Renew the mounting gasket and securely tighten the retaining screws.

NOTE: Fuel pump and engine malfunction will result if the fuel pump and all connections are not airtight.

STARTER

The manual starter mounts on inner exhaust cover (1—Fig. OM5-3) and starter rope (3) extends through the lower motor cover. The suggested procedure for starter rope (3) renewal differs slightly from that required for starter overhaul, refer to the appropriate following sections for the recommended service procedures.

R&R WORN STARTER ROPE. To renew a worn starter rope (3—Fig. OM5-3), first remove the top engine cover and disconnect both spark plug high tension leads. Pull starter rope (3) until almost fully extended and the starter rope end is accessible in spool (8). Block pinion (4) into engagement with the flywheel as shown in Fig. OM5-4 thus locking the rewind mechanism. With the starter securely locked, disconnect starter rope (3—Fig. OM5-3) from handle (2) and spool (8). Install a new starter rope (3) by reversing the removal procedure. While pulling starter rope (3) taut with handle, release pinion (4). Allow starter rope (3) to slowly rewind. If starter rope (3) is broken or disconnected, refer to the following section.

R&R BROKEN STARTER ROPE. To renew a broken starter rope (3) or reconnect starter rope (3) after service, proceed as follows: Insert a heavy-duty flat blade screwdriver or other suitable tool through the top of pinion (4), spool (8) and into slot (S) in top of spring retainer (10). Turn the screwdriver or suitable tool counterclockwise approximately 20½ turns until rope anchor in spool (8) is easily accessible. Block pinion (4) into engagement with the flywheel as shown in Fig. OM5-4 thus locking the rewind mechanism. Remove the screwdriver or suitable tool. With the starter securely locked, install a new starter rope. With starter rope (3—Fig. OM5-3) secured in spool (8) and handle (2), release pinion (4) and allow starter rope (3) to rewind.

OVERHAUL. To disconnect starter rope (3) for removal of the manual starter assembly, pull out starter rope (3) approximately 1 foot (30 cm) and tie a slip knot in starter rope (3) to prevent rewinding. Remove handle (2) from the starter rope end. Untie the slip knot and allow the starter rope to slowly wind onto spool (8) until rewind spring (11) is fully unwound. Remove the two cap screws securing upper bearing head (6) to inner exhaust cover (1). Drive out roll pin (9) and remove set screw (14), then separate the starter components.

Wash the parts in a suitable solvent. Inspect and renew any parts that are worn and/or damaged. When assembling the starter, lubricate rewind spring (11) with a light grease. Note that pinion (4) and spool (8) should not be lubricated, but installed dry to prevent dust accumulation. Note the following during reassembly: Place outer bearing (12), bushing (13) and lower spring retianer (15) on lower end of rewind spring (11) and lock the assembly by tightening set screw (14). Assemble pinion (4), spring (5) and bearing head (6) over upper end of spool. Insert upper spring retainer (10). Align pin holes in spring retainer (10) and spool (8) with engaging slots in pinion (4), then insert roll

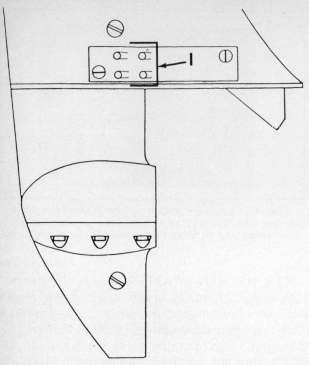

Fig. OM5-5 — Cooling system water inlet ports (I) are located on the port side of the lower unit.

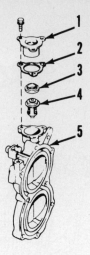

Fig. OM5-6 — Exploded view showing the location of thermostat (4) in cylinder head (5).
1. Cover
2. Gasket
3. Seal
4. Thermostat
5. Cylinder head

pin (9). The roll pin (9) should be positioned so split does not contact rubbing surfaces of pinion engaging slots. Assemble upper and lower starter components with a twisting motion to engage upper end of rewind spring (11) with retainer (10).

Complete reassembly, then install starter rope (3) and adjust rewind spring (11) tension as previously outlined in R&R BROKEN STARTER ROPE section.

COOLING SYSTEM

Ports (I — Fig. OM5-5) located on the port side of the lower unit gearcase are used as the water inlets for the cooling system. The ports must be kept clean of all foreign matter to ensure efficient operation of the cooling system.

⚠CAUTION

Do not operate outboard motor unless the lower unit is immersed in water, otherwise, the water pump impeller will be damaged.

A thermostat positioned in the cylinder head is used to regulate engine operating temperature. Note that a thermostat that sticks or stays closed too long could cause engine overheating, resulting in poor engine operation and possible engine damage. A thermostat that opens too quickly or is stuck in the open position will cause the engine not to reach its recommended operating temperature range, resulting in possible engine malfunction and poor engine efficiency. The thermostat is calibrated to control the coolant temperature within the range of 140°-145°F (60°-63°C). If thermostat malfunction is suspected, remove the thermostat housing (1 — Fig. OM5-6) located at the top of the cylinder head (5) to obtain access to the thermostat (4).

Refer to the Outboard Motor Service Manual if more extensive service to the cooling system is required.

PROPELLER

Consult your local dealer or the manufacturer for the specifications pertaining to the standard propeller used on your model of outboard motor. Optional propellers are available. Select a propeller that will allow the engine at full throttle to reach maximum operating rpm range (4000-5000).

⚠WARNING

Shift directional control lever to "NEUTRAL." Disconnect the spark plug leads and properly ground leads before performing any propeller service, otherwise, accidental starting can occur if propeller shaft is rotated.

To remove the propeller, remove cotter pin (2 — Fig. OM5-7) and unscrew spinner (5), then withdraw propeller (1) from propeller shaft (4).

Inspect propeller (1) and shear pin (3) for damage and excessive wear and renew if needed. Apply OMC Sea-Lube Anti-Corrosion Lubricant to the propeller bore, then install propeller (1) on pro-

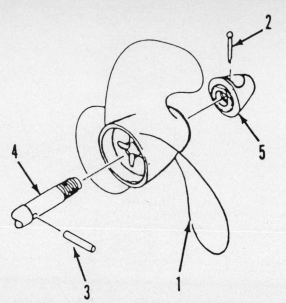

Fig. OM5-7— Propeller (1) is mounted on propeller shaft (4) and is retained by spinner (5) and cotter pin (2). Shear pin (3) is renewed only after withdrawing propeller (1) from propeller shaft (4).

peller shaft (4). Screw spinner (5) onto propeller shaft (4) and retain with a new cotter pin (2).

Tune-Up

IGNITION SYSTEM

The standard spark plug is Champion J4J with an electrode gap of 0.030 inch (0.76 mm). The magneto breaker point gap should be 0.020 inch (0.51 mm) on used points and 0.022 inch (0.56 mm) on new points. The flywheel must be removed to service the breaker point assemblies and the condensers.

To check the ignition timing, proceed as follows: With the outboard motor properly mounted on a boat or a suitable test tank, immerse the lower unit. Connect a tachometer and set it on the appropriate range scale. Connect a suitable timing light to the top cylinder spark plug lead. Start the engine and adjust the speed control until the engine is running at 1000 rpm. Ignition timing is correct if flywheel mark (F—Fig. OM5-8) is centered between timing marks (M) on magneto armature plate. Repeat the previous procedure with the timing light connected to the bottom cylinder spark plug lead. If ignition timing is not correct, check and adjust breaker point gaps or renew breaker point assemblies as follows:

To remove the flywheel, use a suitable flywheel holding tool and remove the securing nut and lockwasher with suitable tools. Remove the flywheel from the crankshaft end using a suitable puller assembly and suitable tools. Note flywheel key located in the crankshaft keyway.

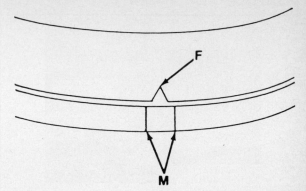

Fig. OM5-8—Ignition timing is correct if flywheel mark (F) is centered between timing marks (M) on magneto armature plate. Refer to text.

> ⚠ **WARNING**
>
> Be sure suitable tools are used to remove the flywheel. Damage resultant from the misapplication of force or the use of incorrect tools may cause engine damage, engine malfunction or personal injury.

Rotate the crankshaft until the breaker point contact surfaces are at their widest position. Then with a 0.020 inch (0.51 mm) feeler gage, check and adjust the point set until 0.020 inch (0.51 mm) gap is obtained. Repeat the adjustment procedure on the other breaker point assembly.

NOTE: No service to the breaker point assemblies is recommended by the manufacturer. The manufacturer recommends cleaning the contact surfaces with alcohol only. A strip of bias tape should be used between contact surfaces to remove any foreign matter.

If needed, renew the breaker point assemblies and condensers. On a new breaker point assembly, point gap should be set at 0.022 inch (0.56 mm).

After adjustment, make sure the breaker point assemblies and condensers securing screws are properly tightened. Be sure the flywheel key is properly positioned in the crankshaft end, then reinstall the flywheel. Install the lockwasher, then install and tighten flywheel securing nut to 40-45 ft.-lbs. (54-61 N·m). Check ignition timing as previously outlined.

SPEED CONTROL LINKAGE

The speed control lever rotates the magneto armature plate to advance the timing. The throttle lever is synchronized with the throttle plate to open the carburetor throttle as the ignition is advanced.

Evinrude & Johnson 9½ Hp (1969-1973)

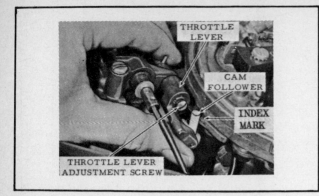

Fig. OM5-9 — The index mark on the armature plate cam should be aligned with the center of the cam follower when adjusting speed control linkage. The throttle lever adjustment screw holds the throttle lever to the throttle shaft.

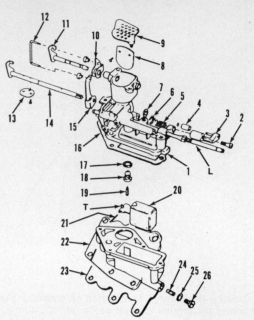

Fig. OM5-10 — Exploded view of carburetor typical of all models. Choke bellcrank and actuator lever are not shown.

L. Low speed mixture screw
T. Tab
1. Carburetor body
2. Adjustment screw
3. Throttle lever
4. Roller
5. Spring
6. Clip
7. Washer
8. Choke plate
9. Cover
10. Choke arm
11. Choke shaft
12. Link
13. Throttle plate
14. Throttle shaft
15. Throttle arm
16. Gasket
17. Gasket
18. Seat
19. Needle
20. Float
21. Pin
22. Float bowl
23. Gasket
24. High speed jet
25. Gasket
26. Plug

To synchronize the linkage, first remove the engine cover and move the speed control until the center of the cam follower is aligned with the index mark on the armature plate cam as shown in Fig. OM5-9. The cam, follower, and nylon roller on throttle lever should all be in contact and the carburetor throttle plate should be completely closed. If clearance exists or if the throttle plate has started to open, loosen throttle lever adjustment screw (Fig. OM5-9) and move the throttle lever until slack is removed or throttle is closed. Hold throttle shaft and lever and retighten screw, making sure adjustment is maintained. To further check the adjustment, turn speed control grip to the "FAST" position and check to make sure that the carburetor throttle plate is fully open.

CARBURETOR

ADJUSTMENT. The carburetor is equipped with an adjustment needle for the low speed mixture. The initial setting of low speed mixture needle (L — Fig. OM5-10) is ¾ turn out from a lightly seated position. The mixture needle should be adjusted after motor reaches normal operating temperature to provide the best operaton at idle speed. Turning the needle clockwise leans the fuel mixture.

A nonadjustable high speed jet (24) is used to regulate the high speed air:fuel mixture. The orifice size of high speed jet (24) must be varied to adjust high speed air:fuel mixture. Standard high speed jet (24) size is 0.048 inch (1.22 mm). Other jet sizes are available for adjusting the calibration for altitude or other special conditions.

Recommended idle speed is 550 rpm with the engine at normal operating temperature and in gear.

With the outboard motor properly mounted on a boat or a suitable test tank, immerse the lower unit. Start the engine and allow it to warm up to normal operating temperature. Shift into forward gear and place the speed control in the slow position (approximately 700-750 rpm). Adjust low speed mixture needle (L) until the highest consistent rpm is obtained. Note that high speed air:fuel mixture is adjustable only by varying the size of high speed jet orifice. After adjustment, stop the engine and turn low speed mixture needle (L) 1/16 turn counterclockwise. This is to prevent a too lean fuel mixture at low engine speeds. If necessary, reposition low speed knob with pointer facing midway between the lean and rich setting. Adjust idle speed knob at control handle pivot so engine is idling at 550 rpm in gear.

OVERHAUL. Remove the engine's top cover. Disconnect any linkage that will interfere with the carburetor removal. Remove all components as needed to completely expose the carburetor. Clean all external surfaces and remove accumulated dirt and grease. Remove the five screws retaining the carburetor and withdraw the carburetor.

With reference to Fig. OM5-10, disassemble the carburetor and note any discrepancies which must be corrected before reassembly. Remove all gaskets and set to the side for future reference.

NOTE: Threaded ends of choke and throttle plate attaching screws are staked during factory assembly. The manufacturer recommends that these screws not be removed when carburetor is cleaned and that a new carburetor body (1) be installed if parts are excessively worn or damaged in any other way.

Thoroughly clean all carburetor parts with a suitable solvent and inspect for damage and excessive wear.

NOTE: The manufacturer does not recommend submerging the parts in carburetor or parts cleaning solutions. An aerosol type carburetor cleaner is recommended. The float and other components made of plastic and rubber should not be subjected to some cleaning solutions. Safety eyewear and solvent resistant goves are recommended.

Blow dry with clean compressed air. If compressed air is not available, use only lint-free cloths to wipe dry.

With reference to Fig. OM5-10, reassemble the carburetor components with new gaskets. Note that the new gaskets should match up with those removed. If not, check with your parts supplier to be sure you have the correct gasket set.

To determine the float level, invert the carburetor body as shown in Fig. OM5-11. With the fuel inlet needle closed, the farthest edge of the float should be parallel with the carburetor body

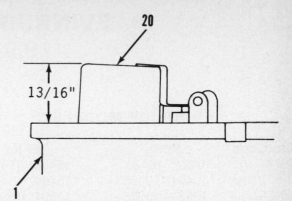

Fig. OM5-11 — With fuel inlet needle closed, the farthest edge of float (20) should be 13/16 inch (20.6 mm) from gasket surface of carburetor body (1).

and measure 13/16 inch (20.6 mm) from gasket surface of body. Adjust the float level by bending arm on float (20 — Fig. OM5-10). With carburetor body (1) in operating position and float (20) in open (drop) position, farthest corner of float (20) should measure 1-7/16 inches (36.5 mm) from gasket surface. Adjust by bending stop tab (T). Check to be sure float does not bind or rub.

When reinstalling the carburetor, place a new gasket (23) between the carburetor and the intake manifold. Securely tighten the retaining screws. Complete reassembly in the reverse order of disassembly. Initially adjust low speed mixture needle (L) ¾ turns out from a lightly seated position.

EVINRUDE AND JOHNSON
9.9 AND 15 HP

EVINRUDE MODELS

Year Produced	9.9 hp	15 hp
1974 ...	10424, 10425 *10454,*10455	15404, 15405 *15454,*15455
1975 ...	10524, 10525 *10554,*10555	15504, 15505 *15554,*15555
1976 ...	10624, 10625 *10654,*10655	15604, 15605 *15654,*15655
1977 ...	10724, 10725 *10754,*10755	15704, 15705 *10754,*15755
1978 ...	10824, 10825 *10835,*10855	15804, 15805 *15854,*15855
1979 ...	10924, 10925 *10935,*10955	15904, 15905 *15954,*15955
1980 ...	10RCS,10RLCS *10ELCS, *10ELCS	15RCS,15RLCS *15ECS,*15ELCS
1981 ...	10RCI,10RLCI *10ELCI,*10SELCI	15RCI,15RLC1 *15ECI
1982 ...	10RCN,10RLCN *10ELCN, *10SELCN	15RCN,15RLCN *15ECN
1983 ...	E10RCT,E10RLCT *E10SELCT	E15RCT,E15RLCT *E15ECT,*E15ELCT
1984 ...	E10RCR,E10RLCR *E10ELCR	E15RCR,E15RLCR *E15ECR,*E15ELCR
1985 ...	E10RCO, E10RLCO *E10ECO,*E10ELCO	E15RCO, E15RLCO *E15ECO,*E15ELCO

JOHNSON MODELS

Year Produced	9.9 hp	15 hp
1974	10R74, 10RL74 *10E74,*10EL74	15R74, 15RL74 *15E74,*15EL74
1975	10R75, 10RL75 *10E75,*10EL75	15R75, 15RL75 *15E75, 15EL75
1976	10R76, 10RL76 *10E76,*10EL76	15R76, 15RL76 *15E76,*15EL76
1977	10R77, 10RL77 *10E77,*10EL77	15R77, 15RL77 *15E77,*15EL77
1978	10R78, 10RL78 *10EL78,*10SEL78	15R78, 15RL78 *15E78,*15EL78
1979	10R79, 10RL79 *10EL79,*10SEL79	15R79, 15RL79 *15E79,*15EL79
1980	10RCS, 10RLCS *10ELCS, *10SELCS	15RCS, 15RLCS *15ECS,*15ELCS
1981	10RCI, 10RLCI *10ELCI, *10SELCI	15RCI, 15RLCI *15ECI
1982	10RCN, 10RLCN *10ELCN, *10SELCN	15RCN, 15RLCN *15ECN
1983	10RCT, 10RLCT *10SELCT	15RCT, 15RLCT *15ECT,*15ELCT
1984	10RCR, 10RLCR *10ELCR	15RCR, 15RLCR *15ECR,*15ELCR
1985	10RCO, 10RLCO *10ECO,*10ELCO	15RCO, 15RLCO *15ECO,*15ELCO

*Electric start models.

Specifications

Hp/rpm	9.9/5000-6000 15/5500-7000
Bore.......................................	2.188 in. (55.58 mm)
Stroke	1.760 in. (44.70 mm)
Number of cylinders	2
Displacement................................	13.2 cu. in. (216 cc)

Specifications (Cont.)

Spark plug—Champion:

1974-1976	UL4J
Electrode gap	0.030 in.
	(0.76 mm)
1977-1985	L77J4*
Electrode gap	0.040 in.
	(1.0 mm)

Ignition type:

1974-1976	Breaker Point
Breaker point gap	0.020 in.
	(0.51 mm)
1977-1985	CD
Carburetor make	Own
Idle speed (in gear)	650 rpm
Fuel:oil ratio	50:1†

Fuel pump:

Discharge pressure at 600 rpm	1 psi
	(7 kPa)
Discharge pressure at 2500-3000 rpm	1.5 psi
	(10 kPa)
Discharge pressure at 4500 rpm	2.5 psi
	(17 kPa)
Gearcase oil capacity	8.9 oz.
	(267 mL)

*A Champion L78V is recommended for 1985 models when used at sustained high speeds. Renew surface gap spark plug if center electrode is more than 1/32 inch (0.79 mm) below the flat surface of the plug end.

†On 1985 models, a 100:1 ratio can be used when Evinrude or Johnson outboard lubricant formulated for 100:1 fuel mix is used.

Maintenance

LUBRICATION

ENGINE. The engine is lubricated by oil mixed with the fuel. The fuel should be regular leaded or unleaded gasoline with a minimum pump octane rating of 86.

NOTE: On 1981 and later models, the manufacturer permits the above fuels to be used at a minimum pump octane rating of 67.

On models prior to 1985, recommended oil is Evinrude or Johnson 50/1 Lubricant or a BIA certified two-stroke motor oil. The recommended fuel:oil ratio for normal operation and engine break-in is 50:1.

On 1985 models, a fuel:oil ratio of 100:1 can be used when Evinrude or Johnson outboard lubricant formulated for 100:1 fuel mix is used. When any other BIA certified two-stroke motor oil is used or during engine break-in, the recommended fuel:oil ratio is 50:1.

The manufacturer's recommended break-in period is defined as follows: For the first fifteen minutes of operation the engine should not exceed its slowest possible cruising speed. After fifteen minutes, slowly increase the engine speed to ½ throttle for the next 45 minutes of operation. During that 45 minutes, short, full throttle accelerations (90 seconds) every five minutes are suggested. For the second hour, increase engine speed to ¾ throttle and periodically accelerate to full throttle. Run the engine at full throttle for 1 to 2 minutes before returning to ¾ throttle setting. Running the engine at or near full throttle for extended periods is not recommended until after 5 hours of operation.

LOWER UNIT. The lower unit gears and bearings are lubricated by oil contained in the gearcase. The recommended oil is OMC HI-VIS Gearcase Lube. The gearcase oil level should be

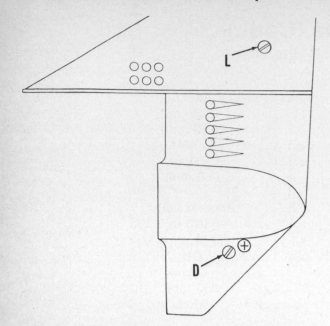

Fig. OM6-1—View showing lower unit gearcase drain and fill plug (D) and oil level (vent) plug (L).

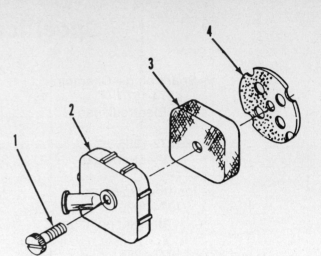

Fig. OM6-2—View showing fuel strainer (3) located behind fuel pump inlet cover (2). Screw (1) retains inlet cover (2) and gasket (4) seals between inlet cover (2) and the pump cover.

checked after every 50 hours of operation and the gearcase should be drained and filled with new oil every 100 hours or once each season, whichever occurs first.

The gearcase is drained and filled through the same plug port (D—Fig. OM6-1). An oil level (vent) port (L) is used to indicate the full oil level of the gearcase and to ease oil drainage.

To drain the oil, place the outboard motor in a vertical position. Remove drain plug (D) and oil level plug (L) and allow the lubricant to drain into a suitable container.

To fill the gearcase with oil, place the outboard motor in a vertical position. Add oil through drain plug (D) opening with an oil feeder until the oil begins to overflow from oil level plug (L) port. Reinstall oil level plug (L) with a new gasket, if needed, and tighten. Remove oil feeder, then reinstall drain plug (D) with a new gasket, if needed, and tighten.

PIVOT POINTS AND SLIDES. Lubricate all pivot points and linkage slides with OMC TRIPLE-GUARD GREASE or a suitable equivalent every 60 days or more frequently if needed to keep the components operating freely and properly.

FUEL SYSTEM

Periodically inspect the fuel lines and connections for damage. Renew components if needed.

Keep the external surface of the carburetor clean and all connections and sealing surfaces tight.

FUEL FILTER. A strainer (3—Fig. OM6-2) positioned behind fuel pump inlet cover (2) is used to filter the fuel prior to entering the fuel pump assembly. To inspect, remove screw (1) retaining inlet cover (2) and withdraw cover (2) with strainer (3). Clean strainer (3) in a suitable solvent and blow dry with clean compressed air. Inspect strainer (3). If excessive blockage or damage is noted, renew strainer. If needed, renew gasket (4).

FUEL PUMP. The fuel pump is operated by crankcase pressure changes from the up-and-down movement of the piston. When the crankcase pressure decreases (the piston is moving upward), the pump diaphragm is pulled toward the crankcase allowing fuel to enter the pump body and closing the discharge check valve. When the crankcase pressure increases (the piston is moving downward), the diaphragm is pushed outward discharging the fuel to the carburetor and closing the inlet check valve. This pulsating action provides continuous fuel flow. The check valves are used to prevent reverse flow of the fuel.

The fuel hoses must be connected according to fuel flow. The fuel tank supply line connects to the fuel pump inlet port and the line routed toward the carburetor assembly connects to the outlet port.

If fuel pump malfunction is noted, the fuel pump should be renewed as a complete assembly. Renew the mounting gasket and securely tighten the retaining screws.

NOTE: Fuel pump and engine malfunction will result if the fuel pump and all connections are not airtight.

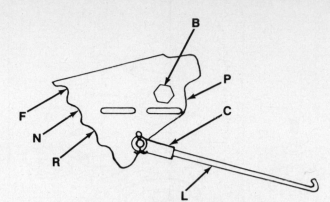

Fig. OM6-3—View showing shift plate (P) used on 1974 models. Refer to text for adjustment procedures.

B. Pivot bolt
C. Clevis
F. Forward notch

L. Shift link
N. Neutral notch

P. Shift plate
R. Reverse notch

SHIFT LINKAGE

1974 Model

To adjust shift linkage, first remove the fuel pump. Loosen screws retaining detent spring plate to side of engine. Spring plate is located adjacent to shift plate (P—Fig. OM6-3). Loosen shift plate pivot bolt (B) and detach shift link clevis (C) from shift plate (P). Retighten pivot bolt and rotate shift plate (P) clockwise until it contacts stop on intake manifold. Move shift detent so it is posi-

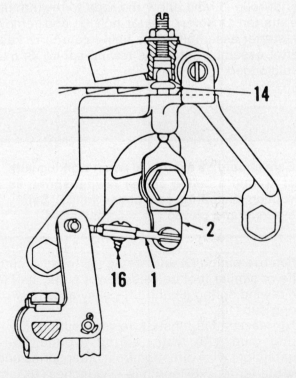

Fig. OM6-4—On 1974 models, interlock rod (14) must be centered on highest point of cam (2) when the outboard motor is placed in the neutral position. If not, loosen screw (16) and adjust length of link (1).

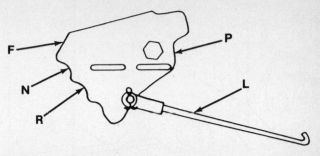

Fig. OM6-5—View showing shift plate (P) used on 1976-1981 models. Refer to text for adjustment procedures.

F. Forward notch
L. Shift link
N. Neutral notch

P. Shift plate
R. Reverse notch

tioned in reverse (R) position on shift plate (P), then tighten detent screws. Rotate shift plate (P) counterclockwise until detent is in neutral notch. Push in firmly on propeller shaft to remove end play and center outer shift lever in neutral position. Turn clevis (C) or nut on shift link (L) until clevis pin can be inserted easily into hole in shift plate (P). Install fuel pump.

Check for proper engagement of forward (F), neutral (N) and reverse (R) and propeller rotation by turning the propeller.

⚠️WARNING

Disconnect spark plug leads and properly ground before performing any propeller service, otherwise, accidental starting can occur if propeller shaft is rotated.

Place outboard motor in neutral and note position of interlock rod (14—Fig. OM6-4) on cam (2). If rod is not centered on highest point of cam, loosen link coupling screw (16) and adjust length of link (1) so rod is centered. Shift outboard motor to forward and back to neutral and check adjustment.

1976-1981 Models

Remove the fuel hose from the carburetor inlet. Remove cotter pin and washer from end of shift lever link (L—Fig. OM6-5) and detach link from shift lever. Position shift lever and shift plate (P) in reverse (R) position. Without exerting pressure on shift lever, adjust link (L) to align with hole in shift lever. Then shorten link (L) one full turn on 1976-1978 models and two full turns on 1979-1981 models for installation. Install link (L) in shift lever and complete reassembly.

Check for proper engagement of forward (F), neutral (N) and reverse (R) and propeller rotation by turning the propeller.

Evinrude & Johnson 9.9 & 15 Hp

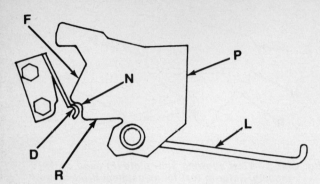

Fig. OM6-6—View showing shift plate (P) used on 1982-1985 models. Refer to text for adjustment procedures.

D. Detent
F. Forward position
L. Shift link

N. Neutral notch
P. Shift plate
R. Reverse position

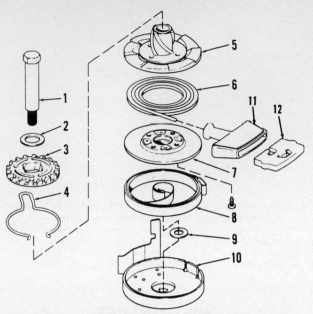

Fig. OM6-7—Exploded view of manual rewind starter.

1. Starter bolt
2. Washer
3. Pinion
4. Spring
5. Upper pulley half
6. Starter rope

7. Lower pulley half
8. Rewind spring
9. Washer
10. Spring cup
11. Handle
12. Anchor

⚠ WARNING

Disconnect spark plug leads and properly ground before performing any propeller service, otherwise, accidental starting can occur if propeller shaft is rotated.

1982-1985 Models

Remove the fuel hose from the carburetor inlet. Remove cotter pin and washer from end of shift lever link (L—Fig. OM6-6).

⚠ WARNING

Disconnect spark plug leads and properly ground leads before performing any propeller service, otherwise, accidental starting can occur if propeller shaft is rotated.

Move the directional shift lever to the forward (F) position and rotate the propeller shaft until the dog clutch lugs properly engage the drive gear lugs. Then slowly move the direction control lever toward the neutral position and note the position of detent (D) on shift plate (P) when the lugs disengage. Repeat the procedure with the directional shift lever in the reverse position. Detach link (L) from the shift lever and adjust link (L) until detent (D) is positioned at equal points on shift plate's forward and reverse ramps when lugs disengage. Install link (L) in shift lever and complete reassembly.

STARTER

To disassemble the starter, remove anchor (12—Fig. OM6-7) from handle (11) and remove starter rope (6) and allow the rope to rewind into the starter. Unscrew starter bolt (1) and remove the starter assembly while being careful to keep starter assembly intact as rewind spring (8) may be dislodged.

⚠ WARNING

Care should be exercised when working with or around a coiled starter rewind spring as sudden uncoiling can cause injury. Safety eyewear and gloves are recommended.

Remove pinion (3) and spring (4). Insert a putty knife or similar tool between lower pulley half (7) and rewind spring (8) and lift pulley assembly off spring cup (10).

To reassemble, install rewind spring (8) in spring cup (10) with spring wound in a counterclockwise direction from outer spring end. New starter rope (6) length is 71½ inches (182 cm) and wound around the rope pulley in a counterclockwise direction when viewed from the pinion end of the pulley. Be sure inner end of re-

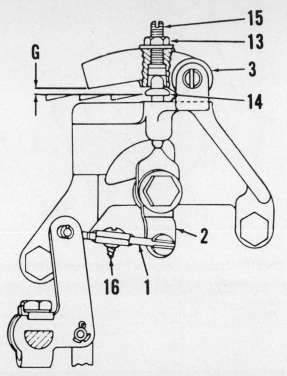

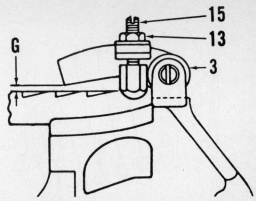

Fig. OM6-9—On 1975-1978 models, gap (G) between upper edge of rope pulley and end of pawl (3) should be 0.050-0.110 inch (1.27-2.79 mm) when the throttle control is in the "START" position. Refer to text for adjustment procedures.

G. Gap
3. Interlock pawl

13. Locknut
15. Screw

Fig. OM6-8—On 1974 models, gap (G) between upper edge of rope pulley and end of pawl (3) should be 0.070-0.100 inch (1.78-2.54 mm) when directional control lever is in neutral position. Refer to text for adjustment procedures.

G. Gap
1. Link
2. Cam

3. Interlock pawl
13. Locknut
14. Interlock rod

15. Screw
16. Screw

wind spring (8) engages spring anchor of lower pulley half (7) when pulley and spring are assembled. Complete remainder of reassembly and tighten starter bolt (1) to 18-20 ft.-lbs. (24-27 N·m).

Three types of starter interlocks have been used. On 1974 models, the starter interlock is designed to allow manual starter operation only when the outboard motor is in neutral. To adjust the interlock on 1974 models, place the outboard motor in the neutral position and loosen locknut (13—Fig. OM6-8). Turn cam screw (15) until there is 0.070-0.100 inch (1.78-2.54 mm) gap between starter interlock pawl (3) and upper pulley half (5—Fig. OM6-7).

NOTE: Refer to previous SHIFT LINKAGE section for adjustment of shift linkage before adjusting starter interlock if cam (2 — Fig. OM6-8) lobe is not centered on interlock rod (14) when the outboard motor is in neutral.

On 1975 through 1978 models, the starter interlock is designed to allow manual starter operation only when the throttle control is in the "STOP" position. To adjust interlock, the outboard motor should be in the neutral position and the throttle control in the "STOP" position. Loosen locknut (13—Fig. OM6-9) and turn adjusting screw (15) until there is 0.050-0.110 inch (1.27-2.79 mm) gap be-

tween starter interlock pawl (3) and upper pulley half (5—Fig. OM6-7).

On models after 1978, a pawl located on the throttle tower shaft prevents manual starter operation except when the throttle control is in the start position.

COOLING SYSTEM

Ports (I—Fig. OM6-10) located on the port and starboard side of the lower unit gearcase are used as the water inlets for the cooling system. The ports must be kept clean of all foreign matter to ensure efficient operation of the cooling system.

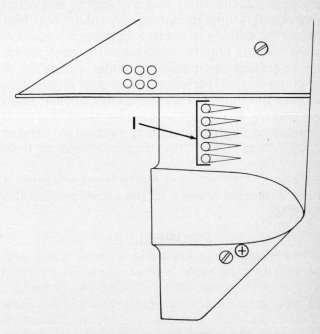

Fig. OM6-10—Cooling system water inlet ports (I) are located on the port and starboard side of the lower unit.

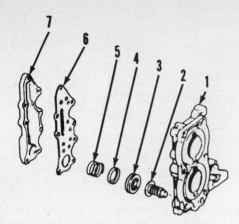

Fig. OM6-11—Exploded view showing the location of thermostat (2) in cylinder head (1).

1. Cylinder head
2. Thermostat
3. Seal
4. Retainer
5. Spring
6. Gasket
7. Cover

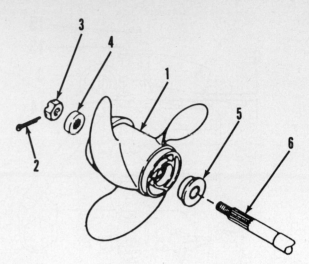

Fig. OM6-12—Exploded view of a typical propeller setup used on all models.

1. Propeller
2. Cotter pin
3. Nut
4. Thrust washer
5. Thrust bushing
6. Propeller shaft

⚠CAUTION

Do not operate outboard motor unless the lower unit is immersed in water, otherwise, the water pump impeller will be damaged.

A thermostat (2—Fig. OM6-11) positioned in the cylinder head is used to regulate engine operating temperature. Note that a thermostat that sticks or stays closed too long could cause engine overheating, resulting in poor engine operation and possible engine damage. A thermostat that opens too quickly or is stuck in the open position will cause the engine not to reach its recommended operating temperature range, resulting in possible engine malfunction and poor engine efficiency. The thermostat should start to open when the coolant temperature reaches 145°F (63°C). If thermostat (2) malfunction is suspected, remove cylinder head cover (7) to gain access to thermostat (2).

Refer to the Outboard Motor Service Manual if more extensive service to the cooling system is required.

PROPELLER

The standard propeller is a three blade propeller with a diameter of 9½ inches (241 mm) and a pitch of 10 inches (254 mm). Optional propellers are available. Select a propeller that will allow the engine at full throttle to reach maximum operating rpm range (5000-6000 on 9.9 hp models and 5500-7000 on 15 hp models).

⚠WARNING

Shift directional control lever to "NEUTRAL." Disconnect the spark plug leads and properly ground leads before performing any propeller service, otherwise, accidental starting can occur if propeller shaft is rotated.

To remove the propeller, remove cotter pin (2—Fig. OM6-12) and nut (3), then withdraw thrust washer (4), propeller (1) and thrust bushing (5) from propeller shaft (6).

Inspect all components for damage and excessive wear and renew if needed.

Apply OMC TRIPLE-GUARD GREASE to propeller shaft (6), then install thrust bushing (5), propeller (1) and thrust washer (4). Install nut (3) and tighten to 10 ft.-lbs. (13.6 N·m), then secure with a new cotter pin (2).

Tune-Up

IGNITION SYSTEM
Breaker Point Type

The standard spark plug is Champion UL4J with an electrode gap of 0.030 inch (0.76 mm). The magneto breaker point gap should be 0.020 inch (0.51 mm) on used points and 0.022 inch (0.56 mm) on new points. The flywheel must be removed to service the breaker point assemblies and the condensers.

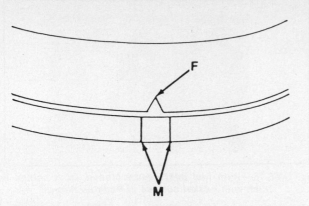

Fig. OM6-13—Ignition timing is correct if flywheel mark (F) is centered between timing marks (M) on magneto armature plate. Refer to text.

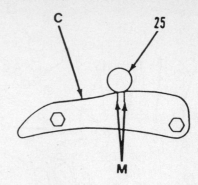

Fig. OM6-14—On models after 1978, cam follower roller (25) should be centered between marks (M) on cam (C) just as carburetor throttle opens. Refer to text.

To check the ignition timing, proceed as follows: With the outboard motor properly mounted on a boat or a suitable test tank, immerse the lower unit. Connect a tachometer and set it on the appropriate range scale. Connect a suitable timing light to the top cylinder spark plug lead. Start the engine and adjust the speed control until the engine is running at 1000 rpm. Ignition timing is correct if flywheel mark (F—Fig. OM6-13) is centered between timing marks (M) on magneto armature plate. Repeat the previous procedure with the timing light connected to the bottom cylinder spark plug lead. If ignition timing is not correct, check and adjust breaker point gaps or renew breaker point assemblies as follows:

To remove the flywheel, use a suitable flywheel holding tool and remove the securing nut and lockwasher with suitable tools. Remove the flywheel from the crankshaft end using a suitable puller assembly and suitable tools. Note flywheel key located in the crankshaft keyway.

⚠WARNING

Be sure suitable tools are used to remove the flywheel. Damage resultant from the misapplication of force or the use of incorrect tools may cause engine damage, engine malfunction or personal injury.

Rotate the crankshaft until the breaker point contact surfaces are at their widest position. Using a suitable feeler gage, check and adjust the point set until 0.020 inch (0.51 mm) gap is obtained. Repeat the adjustment procedure on the other breaker point assembly.

NOTE: No service to the breaker point assemblies is recommended by the manufacturer. The manufacturer recommends cleaning the contact surfaces with alcohol only. A strip of bias tape should be used between contact surfaces to remove any foreign matter.

If needed, renew the breaker point assemblies and condensers. On a new breaker point assembly, point gap should be set at 0.022 inch (0.56 mm).

After adjustment, make sure the breaker point assemblies and condensers securing screws are properly tightened. Be sure the flywheel key is properly positioned in the crankshaft keyway, then reinstall the flywheel. Install the lockwasher, then install and tighten flywheel securing nut to 45-50 ft.-lbs. (61-68 N·m). Check ignition timing as previously outlined.

CD Type

A capacitor discharge ignition (CDI) system is used. Refer to the Outboard Motor Service Manual for testing and servicing the CD ignition system. If engine malfunction is noted and the ignition system is suspected, make sure the spark plugs and all electrical wiring are in good condition and all electrical connections are tight before troubleshooting the CD ignition system.

The standard spark plug is Champion L77J4 with an electrode gap of 0.040 inch (1.0 mm). A Champion L78V is recommended for 1985 models when used at sustained high speeds. Renew surface gap spark plug if center electrode is more than 1/32 inch (0.79 mm) below the flat surface of the plug end.

SPEED CONTROL LINKAGE

The speed control linkage rotates the armature plate to advance the ignition timing. The throttle cam attached to the bottom of the armature plate is used to open the carburetor throttle as the ignition is advanced. The throttle opening and ignition timing cannot be properly synchronized if the throttle cam and related components are worn or

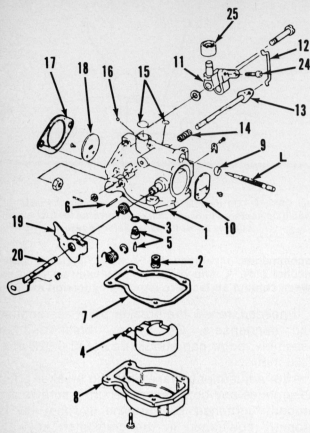

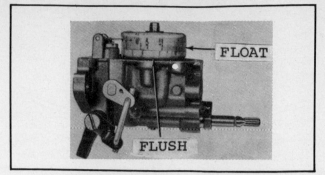

Fig. OM6-16—With fuel inlet needle closed, float should be flush with gasket surface of body as shown.

Fig. OM6-15—Exploded view of carburetor typical of the type used on all models.

L. Low speed mixture
   needle
1. Carburetor body
2. High speed jet
3. Gasket
4. Float
5. Fuel inlet needle & seat
6. Pin
7. Gasket
8. Float bowl
9. Retainer
10. Choke plate
11. Cam follower
12. Link
13. Throttle shaft
14. Spring
15. Welch plugs
16. Lead ball
17. Gasket
18. Throttle plate
19. Choke lever
20. Choke shaft
24. Follower adjusting
    screw
25. Roller

damaged in any way. Renew components if needed.

To synchronize speed controls, first remove the engine cover. Move the speed control from the stop position until the carburetor throttle just begins to open. At this point, on models prior to 1979, the cam follower roller (25—Fig. OM6-15) should be centered on "V" mark on cam plate. If not, loosen cam plate retaining screws and reposition plate. On models after 1978, the cam follower roller (25—Fig. OM6-14) should be centered between marks (M) on cam (C). If not, turn cam follower adjusting screw (24—Fig. OM6-15) to center roller on marks.

CARBURETOR

ADJUSTMENT. The carburetor is equipped with an adjustment needle for the low speed mixture.

The initial setting of low speed mixture needle (L—Fig. OM6-15) is 1 turn out from a lightly seated position. The mixture needle should be adjusted after the motor reaches normal operating temperature to provide the best operation at idle speed. Turning the needle clockwise leans the fuel mixture.

A nonadjustable high speed jet (2) is used to regulate the high speed air:fuel mixture. The orifice size of high speed jet (2) must be varied to adjust high speed air:fuel mixture. Consult your local dealer or the manufacturer for the standard size high speed jet (2) used on your model of outboard motor. Other jet sizes are available for adjusting the calibration for altitude or other special conditions.

Recommended idle speed is 650 rpm with the engine at normal operating temperature and in gear.

With the outboard motor properly mounted on a boat or a suitable test tank, immerse the lower unit. Start the engine and allow it to warm up to normal operating temperature. Shift into forward gear and place the speed control in the slow position (approximately 700-800 rpm). Adjust low speed mixture needle (L) until the highest consistent rpm is obtained. Note that high speed air:fuel mixture is adjustable only by varying the size of high speed jet orifice. After adjustment, stop the engine and turn low speed mixture needle (L) 1/8 turn counterclockwise. This is to prevent a too lean fuel mixture at low engine speeds. If necessary, reposition low speed knob with pointer facing down.

OVERHAUL. Remove the engine top cover. Disconnect any linkage that will interfere with the carburetor removal. Remove all components as needed to completely expose the carburetor. Clean all external surfaces and remove accumulated dirt and grease. Remove the two nuts retaining the carburetor and withdraw the carburetor.

With reference to Fig. OM6-15, disassemble the carburetor and note any discrepancies which must be corrected before reassembly. Remove all gaskets and set to the side for future reference.

Thoroughly clean all carburetor parts with a suitable solvent and inspect for damage and excessive wear.

NOTE: The manufacturer does not recommend submerging the parts in carburetor or parts cleaning solutions. An aerosol type carburetor cleaner is recommended. The float and other components made of plastic and rubber should not be subjected to some cleaning solutions. Safety eyewear and solvent resistant gloves are recommended.

Blow dry with clean compressed air. If compressed air is not available, use only lint-free cloths to wipe dry.

With reference to Fig. OM6-15, reasemble the carburetor components with new gaskets. Note that the new gaskets should match up with those removed. If not, check with your parts supplier to be sure you have the correct gasket set.

To determine the float level, invert the carburetor body as shown in Fig. OM6-16. With the fuel inlet needle closed, the float should be parallel and flush with the carburetor float bowl gasket surface. Adjust the float level by bending arm on float (4 — Fig. OM6-15).

When reinstalling the carburetor, place a new gasket (17) between the carburetor and the intake manifold. Securely tighten the retaining nuts. Complete reassembly in the reverse order of disassembly. Initially adjust low speed mixture needle (L) 1 turn out from a lightly seated position.

EVINRUDE AND JOHNSON
18, 20 AND 25 HP

EVINRUDE MODELS

Year Produced	18 hp	20 hp	25 hp
1969	18902, 18903	.....	25902, 25903
1970	18002, 18003	.....	25002, 25003
1971	18102, 18103	.....	25102, 25103
1972	18202, 18203	.....	25202, 25203
			*25252, *25253
1973	.....	.....	25302, 25303
			*25352, *25353
1974	.....	.....	25402, 25403
			*25452, *25453
1975	.....	.....	25502, 25503
			*25552, *25553
1976	.....	.....	25602, 25603
			*25652, *25653
1977	.....	.....	25702, 25703
			*25752, *25753
1978	.....	.....	25802, 25803
			*25852, *25853
1979	.....	.....	25904, 25905
			*25952, *25953
1980	.....	.....	25RCS, 25RLCS
			*25TECS, *25TELCS
1981	.....	.....	25RCI, 25RLCI
			25RWCI, 25WLCI
			*25ECI, *25ELCI
			*25TECI, *25TELCI
1982	.....	.....	25RCN, 25RLCN
			25RWCN, 25RWLCN
			*25ECN, *25ELCN
			*25TECN, *25TELCN
1983	....	.....	25RCT, 25RLCT
			*25ECT, *25ELCT
			*25TECT, *25TELCT
			25RWCT, 25RWLCT
1984	.....	.....	25RCR, 25RLCR
			*25TECR, *25TELCR
1985	.....	20CRCO, 20CRLCO	25RCO, 25RLCO
		*20ECO, *20ELCO	*25ECO, *25ELCO
			*25TECO, *25TELCO
			25WRCO, 25RWLCO

*Electric start models.

JOHNSON MODELS

Year Produced	20 hp	25 hp
1969	20R69, 20RL69	25R69, 25RL69
1970	20R70, 20RL70	25R70, 25RL70
1971	20R71, 20RL71	25R71, 25RL71
1972	20R72, 20RL72	25R72, 25RL72
		*25E72, *25EL72

JOHNSON MODELS (CONT.)

1973	. . . . .	25R73, 25RL73
		*25E73, *25EL73
1974	. . . . .	25R74, 25RL74
		*25E74, *25EL74
1975	. . . . .	25R75, 25RL75
		*25E75, *25EL75
1976	. . . . .	25R76, 25RL76
		*25E76, *25EL76
1977	. . . . .	25R77, 25RL77
		*25E77, *25EL77
1978	. . . . .	25R78, 25RL78
		*25E78, *25EL78
1979	. . . . .	25R79, 25RL79
		*25E79, *25EL79
1980	. . . . .	25RCS, 25RLCS
		*25TECS, *25TELCS
1981	. . . . .	25RCI, 25RLCI
		25RWCI, 25RWLCI
		*25ECI, *25ELCI
		*25TECI, *25TELCI
1982	. . . . .	25RCN, 25RLCN
		25RWCN, 25RWLCN
		*25ECN, *25ELCN
		*25TECN, *25TELCN
1983	. . . . .	25RCT, 25RLCT
		*25ECT, *25ELCT
		*25TECT, *25TELCT
		25RWCT, 25RWLCT
1984	. . . . .	25RCR, 25RLCR
		*25TECR, *25TELCR
1985	20CRCO, 20CRLCO	25RCO, 25RLCO
	*20ECO, *20ELCO	*25ECO, *25ELCO
		*25TECO, *25TELCO
		25RWCO, 25RWLCO

*Electric start models.

Specifications

Hp/rpm	18/4000-5000
	20/4500-5500*
	25/4500-5500†
Bore:	
All models prior to 1977	2.500 in.
	(63.5 mm)
20 & 25 hp models after 1976	3.000 in.
	(76.2 mm)
Stroke	2.250 in.
	(57.15 mm)
Number of cylinders	2
Displacement:	
All models prior to 1977	22.0 cu. in.
	(361 cc)

Specifications (Cont.)

20 & 25 hp models after 1976	31.8 cu.in.
	(521 cc)
Spark plug — Champion:	
1969-1976	J4J
Electrode gap	0.030 in.
	(0.76 mm)
1977-1985	L77J4‡
Electrode gap	0.040 in.
	(1.0 mm)
Ignition type:	
1969-1976	Breaker Point
Breaker point gap	0.020 in.
	(0.51 mm)
1977-1985	CD
Carburetor make	Own
Idle speed (in gear)	650 rpm
Fuel:oil ratio	50:1§
Fuel pump:	
Discharge pressure at 600 rpm..............	1 psi
	(7 kPa)
Discharge pressure at 2500-3000 rpm	1.5 psi
	(10 kPa)
Discharge pressure at 4500 rpm..............	2.5 psi
	(17 kPa)

*1969-1972 Johnson 20 hp models are rated at 4000-5000 rpm.
†1969-1976 25 hp models are rated at 5000-6000 rpm.
‡A Champion L78V is recommended for 1985 models when used at sustained high speeds. Renew surface gap spark plug if center electrode is more than 1/32 inch (0.79 mm) below the flat surface of the plug end.
§On 1985 models, a 100:1 ratio can be used when Evinrude or Johnson outboard lubricant formulated for 100:1 fuel mix is used.

Maintenance

LUBRICATION

ENGINE. The engine is lubricated by oil mixed with the fuel. The fuel should be regular leaded or unleaded gasoline with a minimum pump octane rating of 86.

NOTE: On 1981 and later models, the manufacturer permits the above fuels to be used at a minimum pump octane rating of 67.

On models prior to 1985, recommended oil is Evinrude or Johnson 50/1 lubricant or a BIA certified two-stroke motor oil. The recommended fuel:oil ratio for normal operation and engine break-in is 50:1.

On 1985 models, a fuel:oil ratio of 100:1 can be used when Evinrude or Johnson outboard lubricant formulated for 100:1 fuel mix is used. When any other BIA certified two-stroke motor is used or during engine break-in, the recommended fuel:oil ratio is 50:1.

The manufacturer's recommended break-in period is defined as follows: For the first fifteen minutes of operation the engine should not exceed its slowest possible cruising speed. After fifteen minutes, slowly increase the engine speed to ½ throttle for the next 45 minutes of operation. During that 45 minutes, short full throttle accelerations (90 seconds) every five minutes are suggested. For the second hour, increase engine speed to ¾ throttle and periodically accelerate to full throttle. Run the engine at full throttle for 1 to 2 minutes before returning to ¾ throttle setting. Running the engine at or near full throttle for extended periods is not recommended until after 5 hours of operation.

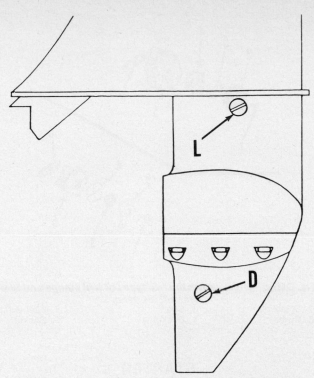

Fig. OM7-1—On models prior to 1985, view showing lower unit gearcase drain and fill plug (D) and oil level (vent) plug (L).

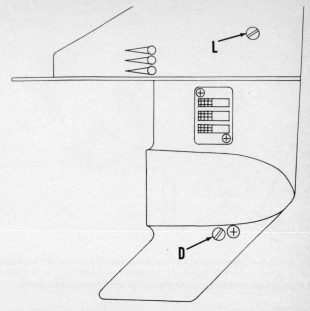

Fig. OM7-2—On 1985 models, view showing lower unit gearcase drain and fill plug (D) and oil level (vent) plug (L).

LOWER UNIT. The lower unit gears and bearings are lubricated by oil contained in the gearcase. The recommended oil is OMC Sea-Lube Premium Blend Gearcase Lube on models prior to 1977 and OMC HI-VIS Gearcase Lube on models after 1976. The gearcase oil level should be checked after every 50 hours of operation and the gearcase should be drained and filled with new oil every 100 hours or once each season, whichever occurs first.

The gearcase is drained and filled through the same plug port (D—Fig. OM7-1 or OM7-2). An oil level (vent) port (L) is used to indicate the full oil level of the gearcase and to ease oil drainage.

To drain the oil, place the outboard motor in a vertical position. Remove drain plug (D) and oil level plug (L) and allow the lubricant to drain into a suitable container.

To fill the gearcase with oil, place the outboard motor in a vertical position. Add oil through drain plug (D) opening with an oil feeder until the oil begins to overflow from oil level plug (L) port. Reinstall oil level plug (L) with a new gasket, if needed, and tighten. Remove oil feeder, then reinstall drain plug (D) with a new gasket, if needed, and tighten.

PIVOT POINTS AND SLIDES. Lubricate all pivot points and linkage slides with OMC TRIPLE-GUARD GREASE or a suitable equivalent every 60 days or more frequently if needed to keep the components operating freely and properly.

FUEL SYSTEM

Periodically inspect the fuel lines and connections for damage. Renew components if needed.

Keep the external surface of the carburetor clean and all connections and sealing surfaces tight.

FUEL FILTER. On some models, a fuel filter assembly is connected between the fuel supply line and the fuel pump inlet line. With the engine stopped, periodically unscrew fuel filter cover (1—Fig. OM7-3) from filter base (4) and withdraw filter element (2). Clean filter base (4) and filter element (2) in a suitable solvent and blow dry with clean compressed air. Inspect filter element (2). If excessive blockage or damage is noted, the complete fuel filter assembly must be renewed.

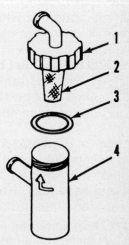

Fig. OM7-3—Exploded view of fuel filter assembly used on some models.
1. Cover
2. Element
3. Gasket
4. Base

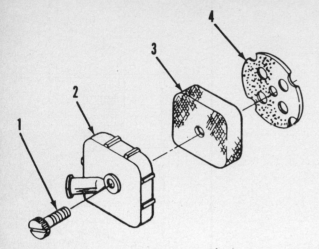

Fig. OM7-4—View showing fuel strainer (3) located behind fuel pump inlet cover (2). Screw (1) retains inlet cover (2) and gasket (4) seals between inlet cover (2) and the pump cover.

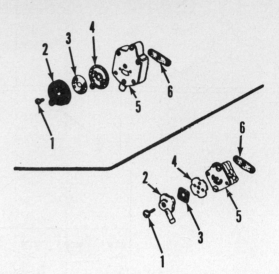

Fig. OM7-5—View shows the two types of fuel pumps and filter assemblies used.

1. Screw	3. Strainer	5. Fuel pump
2. Cover	4. Gasket	6. Gasket

Reassembly is reverse order of disassembly. Renew gasket (3) during reassembly.

A strainer (3—Fig. OM7-4) positioned behind fuel pump inlet cover (2) is used to filter the fuel prior to entering the fuel pump assembly. To inspect, remove screw (1) retaining inlet cover (2) and withdraw cover (2) with strainer (3). Clean strainer (3) in a suitable solvent and blow dry with clean compressed air. Inspect strainer (3). If excessive blockage or damage is noted, renew strainer. If needed, renew gasket (4).

FUEL PUMP. The fuel pump is operated by crankcase pressure changes from the up and down movement of the piston. When the crankcase pressure decreases (the piston is moving upward), the pump diaphragm is pulled toward the crankcase allowing fuel to enter the pump body and closing the discharge check valve. When the crankcase pressure increases (the piston is moving downward), the diaphragm is pushed outward discharging the fuel to the carburetor and closing the inlet check valve. This pulsating action provides continuous fuel flow. The check valves are used to prevent reverse flow of the fuel.

The fuel hoses must be connected according to fuel flow. The fuel tank supply line connects to the fuel pump inlet port and the line routed toward the carburetor assembly connects to the outlet port.

Shown in Fig. OM7-5 are the two types of fuel pump assemblies used. If fuel pump malfunction is noted, the fuel pump should be renewed as a complete assembly. Renew the mounting gasket and securely tighten the retaining screws.

NOTE: Fuel pump and engine malfunction will result if the fuel pump and all connections are not airtight.

STARTER

NOTE: Early type starters are equipped with one drive pawl (6 — Fig. OM7-6) and late type starters are equipped with two drive pawls (6). Service procedures are the same except where noted in the text.

When starter rope (2) is pulled, pulley (4) will rotate. As pulley (4) rotates, drive pawl (6) moves to engage the flywheel, thus cranking the engine.

When starter rope (2) is released, pulley (4) is rotated in the reverse direction by force from rewind spring (3). As pulley (4) rotates, the starter rope is rewound and drive pawl (6) is disengaged from the flywheel.

On later models, starter housing (1) is fitted with a starter lockout assembly to prevent starter engagement when the gear shift lever is in the forward or reverse position.

To overhaul the manual starter, proceed as follows: Remove the engine top cover. Remove the screws retaining the manual starter to the engine. Remove the starter lockout cable, if so equipped, at starter housing (1). Withdraw the starter assembly.

⚠WARNING

Care should be exercised when working with or around a coiled starter rewind spring as sudden uncoiling can cause injury. Safety eyewear and gloves are recommended.

Check pawl (6) for freedom of movement and excessive wear or damage of engagement area and

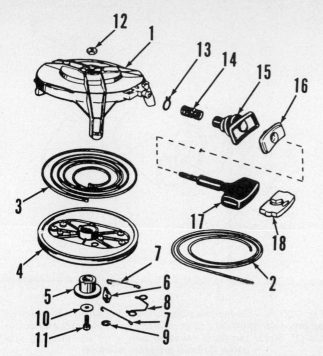

Fig. OM7-6 — Exploded view of manual rewind starter typical of early models. Later models are similar except drive pawls and associated parts located between pulley (4) and spindle (5) are not shown. Refer to text.

1. Housing	7. Links	13. Retainer
2. Rope	8. Spring	14. Spring
3. Rewind spring	9. Clip	15. Rope guide
4. Pulley	10. Washer	16. Cover
5. Spindle	11. Bolt	17. Handle
6. Drive pawl	12. Nut	18. Anchor

renew pawl if needed. If service to remaining starter components is not required, lubricate pawl with OMC TRIPLE-GUARD GREASE or Lubriplate 777 and return starter to service.

To disassemble starter, on early models, remove clip (9) and withdraw pawl (6), links (7) and friction spring (8). On all models, remove anchor (18) from handle (17) and detach starter rope (2) from anchor (18), then allow the rope to wind into the starter. Remove nut (12) and withdraw bolt (11), washer (10) and spindle (5). On late models, remove the two spring washers, friction ring, drive pawls and link assemblies and shim located between pulley (4) and spindle (5). On all models, carefully lift pulley (4) with starter rope (2) from housing (1). BE CAREFUL when removing pulley (4) to prevent possible injury from rewind spring (3). Note that later type starter uses spring plates above and below rewind spring (3). Remove starter rope (2) from pulley (4) if renewal is required. To remove rewind spring (3) from housing (1), invert housing so it sets upright on a flat surface, then tap the housing top to dislodge rewind spring (3).

Inspect all components for damage and excessive wear and renew if needed.

To reassemble, first apply a coating of OMC TRIPLE-GUARD GREASE or Lubriplate 777 to rewind spring area of housing (1). Install spring

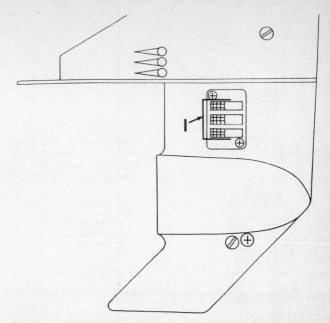

Fig. OM7-7 — On 1985 models, cooling system water inlet ports (I) are located on the port and starboard side of the lower unit.

plate in housing (1) if so equipped, then install rewind spring (3) in housing (1) so spring coils wind in a counterclockwise direction from the outer end. Make sure the spring's outer hook is properly secured over starter housing pin.

NOTE: Lubricate all friction surfaces with OMC TRIPLE-GUARD GREASE or Lubriplate 777 during reassembly.

With the exception of starter rope (2), complete the reassembly in the reverse order of disassembly. Make sure that pulley pin engages hook end in rewind spring (3). With bolt (11) installed through housing (1), spray bolt threads and nut (12) with OMC Locquic Primer and apply OMC Screw Lock on threads. Install nut (12) on bolt (11) and securely tighten.

With the starter assembly inverted, wind pulley (4) counterclockwise until rewind spring (3) is tight. Then allow pulley (4) to unwind ½ to 1 turn. Align starter rope hole in pulley (4) with rope guide in housing (1) and secure position. Thread starter rope (2) through pulley (4), housing (1), handle (17) and secure in anchor (18). Assemble anchor (18) to handle (17). Release pulley (4) and allow starter rope (2) to slowly wind into pulley (4).

NOTE: Do not apply any more tension on rewind spring (3) than is required to draw starter handle (17) back into the proper released position.

Remount manual starter assembly and install the starter lockout cable if so equipped.

COOLING SYSTEM

On 1984 and prior models, a port located on the bottom side of the antiventilation plate is used as

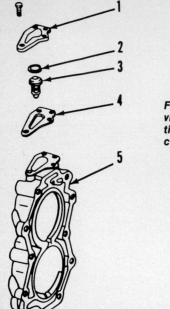

Fig. OM7-8—Exploded view showing the location of thermostat (3) in cylinder head (5) on models prior to 1977.

1. Cover
2. Seal
3. Thermostat
4. Gasket
5. Cylinder head

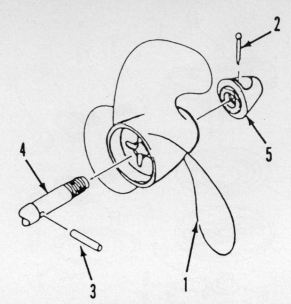

Fig. OM7-10—On models prior to 1985, propeller (1) is mounted on propeller shaft (4) and is retained by spinner (5) and cotter pin (2). Shear pin (3) is renewed only after withdrawing propeller (1) from propeller shaft (4).

the water inlet for the cooling system. The port must be kept clean of all foreign matter to ensure efficient operation of the cooling system.

On 1985 models, ports (I—Fig. OM7-7) located on the port and starboard side of the lower unit gearcase are used as the water inlets for the cooling system. The ports must be kept clean of all foreign matter to ensure efficient operation of the cooling system.

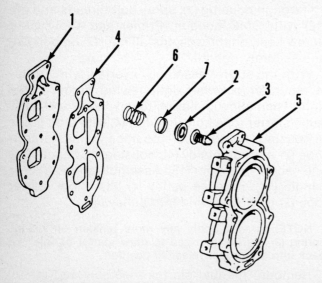

Fig. OM7-9—Exploded view showing the location of thermostat (3) in cylinder head (5) on models after 1976.

1. Cylinder head cover
2. Seal
3. Thermostat
4. Gasket
5. Cylinder head
6. Spring
7. Retainer

⚠CAUTION

Do not operate outboard motor unless the lower unit is immersed in water, otherwise, the water pump impeller will be damaged.

Thermostat (3—Fig. OM7-8 or OM7-9) positioned in cylinder head (5) is used to regulate engine operating temperature. Note that a thermostat that sticks or stays closed too long could cause engine overheating, resulting in poor engine operation and possible engine damage. A thermostat that opens too quickly or is stuck in the open position will cause the engine not to reach its recommended operating temperature range, resulting in possible engine malfunction and poor engine efficiency. The thermostat is calibrated to control the coolant temperature within the range of 145°-150°F (63°-66°C). If thermostat (3) malfunction is suspected, remove thermostat cover (1—Fig. OM7-8) located at the top of cylinder head (5) on models prior to 1977 and cylinder head cover (1—Fig. OM7-9) on models after 1976 to gain access to the thermostat.

Refer to the Outboard Motor Service Manual if more extensive service to the cooling system is required.

PROPELLER

Consult your local dealer or the manufacturer for the specifications pertaining to the standard

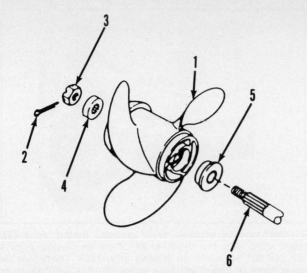

Fig. OM7-11—Exploded view showing propeller setup on 1985 models.

1. Propeller
2. Cotter pin
3. Nut
4. Thrust washer
5. Thrust bushing
6. Propeller shaft

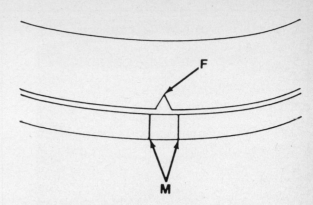

Fig. OM7-12—Ignition timing is correct if flywheel mark (F) is centered between timing marks (M) on magneto armature plate. Refer to text.

Apply OMC TRIPLE-GUARD GREASE to propeller shaft (6), then install thrust bushing (5), propeller (1) and thrust washer (4). Install nut (3) and tighten to 10 ft.-lbs. (13.6 N·m). Secure nut with a new cotter pin (2).

Tune-Up

IGNITION SYSTEM

Breaker Point Type

The standard spark plug is Champion J4J with an electrode gap of 0.030 inch (0.76 mm). The magneto breaker point gap should be 0.020 inch (0.51 mm) on used points and 0.022 inch (0.56 mm) on new points. The flywheel must be removed to service the breaker point assemblies and the condensers.

To check the ignition timing, proceed as follows: With the outboard motor properly mounted on a boat or a suitable test tank, immerse the lower unit. Connect a tachometer and set it on the appropriate range scale. Connect a suitable timing light to the top cylinder spark plug lead. Start the engine and adjust the speed control until the engine is running at 1000 rpm. Ignition timing is correct if flywheel mark (F — Fig. OM7-12) is centered between timing marks (M) on magneto armature plate. Repeat the previous procedure with the timing light connected to the bottom cylinder spark plug lead. If ignition timing is not correct, check and adjust breaker point gaps or renew breaker point assemblies as follows:

Remove the manual rewind starter assembly. To remove the flywheel, use a suitable flywheel holding tool and remove the securing nut and lockwasher with suitable tools. Remove the flywheel from the crankshaft end using a suitable puller assembly and suitable tools. Note flywheel key located in the crankshaft keyway.

propeller used on your model of outboard motor. Optional propellers are available. Select a propeller that will allow the engine at full throttle to reach maximum operating rpm range (refer to Specifications).

⚠️**WARNING**

Shift directional control lever to "NEUTRAL." Disconnect the spark plug leads and properly ground leads before performing any propeller service, otherwise, accidental starting can occur if propeller shaft is rotated.

To remove the propeller on models prior to 1985, remove cotter pin (2—Fig. OM7-10) and unscrew spinner (5). Withdraw propeller (1) from propeller shaft (4).

Inspect propeller (1) and shear pin (3) for damage and excessive wear and renew if needed. Apply OMC TRIPLE-GUARD GREASE to the propeller bore, then install propeller (1) on propeller shaft (4). Screw spinner (5) onto propeller shaft (4) and retain with a new cotter pin (2).

To remove the propeller on 1985 models, remove cotter pin (2—Fig. OM7-11) and nut (3). Withdraw thrust washer (4), propeller (1) and thrust bushing (5) from propeller shaft (6).

Inspect all components for damage and excessive wear and renew if needed.

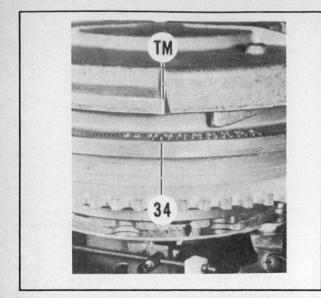

Fig. OM7-13—On manual rewind start models, timing mark (TM) should align with the flywheel 34° mark on models prior to 1982 and 30°-31° mark on models after 1981. Thirty-four (34) degree mark is identified. Turn screw (S—Fig. OM7-15) to adjust timing.

⚠ WARNING

Be sure suitable tools are used to remove the flywheel. Damage resultant from the misapplication of force or the use of incorrect tools may cause engine dmage, engine malfunction or personal injury.

Rotate the crankshaft until the breaker point contact surfaces are placed at their widest position. Using a suitable feeler gage, check and adjust the point set until 0.020 inch (0.51 mm) gap is obtained. Repeat the adjustment procedure on the other breaker point assembly.

NOTE: No service to the breaker point assemblies is recommended by the manufacturer. The manufacturer recommends cleaning the contact surfaces with alcohol only. A strip of bias tape should be used between contact surfaces to remove any foreign matter.

If needed, renew the breaker point assemblies and condensers. On a new breaker point assembly, point gap should be set at 0.022 inch (0.56 mm).

After adjustment, make sure the breaker point assemblies and condensers securing screws are properly tightened. Be sure the flywheel key is properly positioned in the crankshaft keyway, then reinstall the flywheel. Install the lockwasher then install and tighten flywheel securing nut to 40-45 ft.-lbs. (54-61 N·m). Remount the manual rewind starter assembly and check the ignition timing as previously outlined.

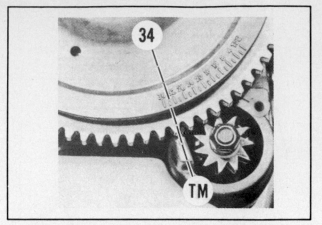

Fig. OM7-14—On electric start models, timing mark (TM) should align with the flywheel 34° mark on models prior to 1982 and 30°-31° mark on models after 1981. Thirty-four (34) degree mark is identified. Turn screw (S—Fig. OM7-15) to adjust timing.

CD Type

A capacitor discharge ignition (CDI) system is used. Refer to the Outboard Motor Service Manual for testing and servicing the CD ignition system. If engine malfunction is noted and the ignition system is suspected, make sure the spark plugs and all electrical wiring are in good condition and all electrical connections are tight before troubleshooting the CD ignition system.

The standard spark plug is Champion L77J4 with an electrode gap of 0.040 inch (1.0 mm). A Champion L78V is recommended for 1985 models when used at sustained high speeds. Renew surface gap spark plug if center electrode is more than 1/32 inch (0.79 mm) below the flat surface of the plug end.

IGNITION TIMING. To check the ignition timing, first mount the outboard motor on a boat or a suitable test tank and immerse the lower unit. Connect a suitable timing light to the top cylinder (No. 1) spark plug lead. Start the engine and adjust the speed control until the engine is running at full throttle. On manual rewind start models, timing mark (TM—Fig. OM7-13) should align with the flywheel 34° mark on models prior to 1982 and 30° - 31° mark on models after 1981. On electric start models, timing mark (TM—Fig. OM7-14) should align with the flywheel 34° mark on models prior to 1982 and 30°-31° mark on models after 1981. To adjust ignition timing on all models, turn timing stop screw (S—Fig. OM7-15). Each complete turn is equivalent to approximately one degree. Turning screw (S) clockwise retards the timing and counterclockwise advances the timing.

NOTE: Backfiring and popping may be due to improperly connected wiring. Refer to the Outboard Motor Service Manual for a wiring schematic of the ignition circuit.

Fig. OM7-15—View of ignition timing adjusting screw (S) on models with CD type ignition system.

Fig. OM7-17—To adjust speed control linkage on models prior to 1973, loosen throttle lever set screw and adjust throttle lever until the proper setting is obtained.

SPEED CONTROL LINKAGE

The speed control linkage rotates the armature plate to advance the ignition timing. The throttle cam attached to the bottom of the armature plate is used to open the carburetor throttle as the ignition is advanced. The throttle opening and ignition timing cannot be properly synchronized if the throttle cam and related components are worn or damaged in any way. Renew components if needed.

To synchronize speed controls, first remove the engine cover. Move the speed control from the stop position until the carburetor throttle just begins to open. At this point, the cam follower roller (Fig. OM7-16) should be centered between the marks on the throttle cam. If not, proceed as follows to adjust: On models prior to 1973, loosen set screw (Fig. OM7-17) and adjust throttle lever until the proper setting is obtained, then tighten set screw. On models 1973 through 1976, loosen bracket securing throttle link (15—Fig. OM7-20)

and adjust length of throttle link until the proper setting is obtained, then secure bracket. On all models after 1976, loosen throttle shaft screw (S—Fig. OM7-18) and adjust throttle lever until the proper setting is obtained, then tighten screw (S).

On models after 1976, the throttle control rod must be adjusted to allow the carburetor throttle plate to obtain full open position, but stop throttle plate movement at this point to prevent binding. To adjust, shift directional control lever to "FORWARD" gear, then advance throttle so throttle lever is against cylinder stop. Push throttle control rod (R—Fig. OM7-19) to full open position. Loosen collar (C) set screw, then move collar (C) so it is against pivot block (B). Tighten collar set screw.

Fig. OM7-16—Cam follower roller should be centered between the throttle cam marks just as the carburetor throttle opens. Refer to text.

Fig. OM7-18—To adjust speed control linkage on models after 1976, loosen throttle shaft screw (S) and adjust throttle lever until the proper setting is obtained.

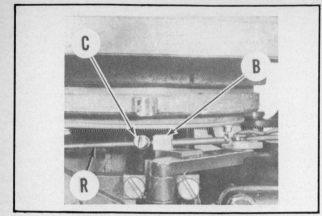

Fig. OM7-19—Collar (C) should touch pivot block (B) when throttle control rod (R) is in the full open position. Refer to text.

CARBURETOR

ADJUSTMENT. The carburetor is equipped with an adjustment needle for the low speed mixture. The initial setting of low speed mixture needle (5 — Fig. OM7-20) is 1 turn out from a lightly seated position. The mixture needle should be adjusted after the motor reaches normal operating temperature to provide the best operation at idle speed. Turning the needle clockwise leans the fuel mixture.

A nonadjustable high speed jet (23) is used to regulate the high speed air:fuel mixture. The orifice size of high speed jet (23) must be varied to adjust high speed air:fuel mixture. Consult your local dealer or the manufacturer for the standard size high speed jet (23) used on your model of outboard motor. Other jet sizes are available for adjusting the calibration for altitude or other special conditions.

Recommended idle speed is 650 rpm with the engine at normal operating temperature and in gear.

With the outboard motor properly mounted on a boat or a suitable test tank, immerse the lower unit. Start the engine and allow it to warm up to normal operating temperature. Shift into forward gear and place the speed control in the slow position (approximately 700-800 rpm). Adjust low speed mixture needle (5) until the highest consistent rpm is obtained. Note that high speed air:fuel mixture is adjustable only by varying the size of high speed jet orifice. After adjustment, stop the engine and turn low speed mixture needle (L) 1/8 turn counterclockwise. This is to prevent a too lean fuel mixture at low engine speeds. If so equipped, install low speed knob with pointer facing up.

The idle speed stop screw (Fig. OM7-22) should be adjusted to provide an idle speed of 650 rpm with the outboard motor in gear.

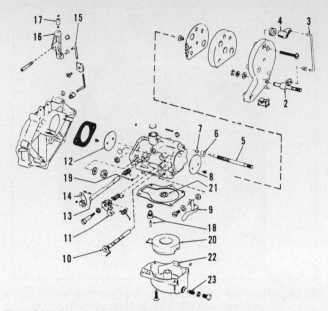

Fig. OM7-20—Exploded view of carburetor typical of all models. Link (15) is adjustable for speed control on models 1973 through 1976. Refer to text. Throttle lever (14) can be separated from shaft (13) on models prior to 1973.

2. Needle adjustment shaft (early models)	8. Choke plate	16. Follower
3. Link	9. Choke lever	17. Roller
4. Lever	10. Choke shaft	18. Needle & seat
5. Low speed mixture needle	11. Choke bellcrank	19. Pin
6. Retainer	12. Throttle plate	20. Float
7. Bushing	13. Throttle shaft	21. Nozzle gasket
	14. Throttle lever	22. Float bowl
	15. Link	23. High speed jet

OVERHAUL. Remove the engine's top cover. Disconnect any linkage that will interfere with the carburetor removal. Remove all components as needed to completely expose the carburetor. Clean all external surfaces and remove accumulated dirt and grease. Remove the two nuts retaining the carburetor and withdraw the carburetor.

With reference to Fig. OM7-20, disassemble the carburetor and note any discrepancies which must be corrected before reassembly. Remove all gaskets and set to the side for future reference.

Thoroughly clean all carburetor parts with a suitable solvent and inspect for damage and excessive wear.

NOTE: The manufacturer does not recommend submerging the parts in carburetor or parts cleaning solutions. An aerosol type carburetor cleaner is recommended. The float and other components made of plastic and rubber should not be subjected to some cleaning solutions. Safety eyewear and solvent resistant golves are recommended.

Blow dry with clean compressed air. If compressed air is not available, use only lint-free cloths to wipe dry.

With reference to Fig. OM7-20, reassemble the carburetor components with new gaskets. Note that the new gaskets should match up with those

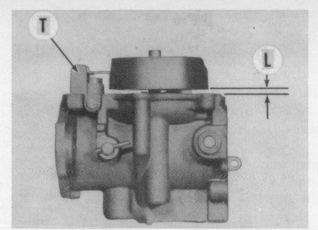

Fig. OM7-21—Float should be parallel to carburetor body for correct float level (L). Bend float tang (T) to adjust float level.

Fig. OM7-22 — Idle speed stop screw should be adjusted to provide an idle speed of 650 rpm with the outboard motor in gear.

removed. If not, check with your parts supplier to be sure you have the correct gasket set.

To determine the float level, invert the carburetor body as shown in Fig. OM7-21. With the fuel inlet needle closed, the float should be parallel (L) with the carburetor float bowl gasket surface. Adjust the float level by bending tang (T) on float (20 — Fig. OM7-20).

When reinstalling the carburetor, place a new gasket between the carburetor and the intake manifold. Securely tighten the retaining nuts. Complete reassembly in the reverse order of disassembly. Initially adjust low speed mixture needle (5) 1 turn out from a lightly seated position.

SEAGULL

BRITISH SEAGULL CO, LTD.
418 Ringwood Rd., Parkstone
Poole, England

IMTRA CORP.	INLAND MARINE CO.	SEAGULL MARINE
151 Mystic Ave.	79 E. Jackson St.	1851 McGaw Avenue
Medford, Mass. 02155	Wilkes-Barre, Pa. 18701	Irvine, Calif. 92705

Model Code	Year Produced	Engine Displacement
ENC	1985	6.18 cu. in. (101.3 cc)
EFPW	1984-1985	3.86 cu. in. (63.3 cc)
ENS	1983-1985	6.18 cu. in. (101.3 cc)
EFNR	1979-1984	6.18 cu. in. (101.3 cc)
EFPC	1979-1985	3.86 cu. in. (63.3 cc)
EFS	1979-1985	3.86 cu. in. (63.3 cc)
ESC	1979-1984	6.18 cu. in. (101.3 cc)
F	1969-1976	3.86 cu. in. (63.3 cc)
FP	1969-1979	3.86 cu. in. (63.3 cc)
FPC	1978-1979	3.86 cu. in. (63.3 cc)
FS	1978-1979	3.86 cu. in. (63.3 cc)
GF	1977-1978	3.86 cu. in. (63.3 cc)
GFP	1976-1979	3.86 cu. in. (63.3 cc)
GFPC	1978-1979	3.86 cu. in. (63.3 cc)
GFS	1969	6.18 cu. in. (101.3 cc)
SP	1969	6.18 cu. in. (101.3 cc)
SPC	1969	6.18 cu. in. (101.3 cc)
W	1969-1973	6.18 cu. in. (101.3 cc)
WP	1969	6.18 cu. in. (101.3 cc)
WPC	1969-1973	6.18 cu. in. (101.3 cc)
WS	1969-1979	6.18 cu. in. (101.3 cc)

Model Code	Year Produced	Engine Displacement
WSC	1978-1979	6.18 cu. in. (101.3 cc)
WSPC	1969-1979	6.18 cu. in. (101.3 cc)

Model designation may include suffix letter "L" to denote a long shaft model.

Specifications

ENGINE DISPLACEMENT

	3.86 Cu. In. (63.3 cc)	6.18 Cu. In. (101.3 cc)
Bore	1.77 in. (45 mm)	2.24 in. (57 mm)
Stroke	1.57 in. (40 mm)	1.57 in. (40 mm)
Displacement	3.86 cu. in. (63.3 cc)	6.18 cu. in. (101.3 cc)
Ignition type:		
Early models	Breaker Point	Breaker Point
Breaker point gap	0.020 in. (0.51 mm)	0.020 in. (0.51 mm)
Late models	CD	CD
Spark plug:		
Champion	British, 8 Com. American, D16	British, 8 Com. American, D16
Electrode gap—		
Magneto ignition	0.020 in. (0.51 mm)	0.020 in. (0.51 mm)
CD ignition	0.035 in. (0.9 mm)	0.035 in. (0.9 mm)
Carburetor make	See Text	See Text
Fuel:oil ratio	See Text	See Text

Maintenance

LUBRICATION

ENGINE. The engine is lubricated by oil mixed with the fuel. Recommended oil is Seagull Two-Stroke oil or a BIA certified two-stroke motor oil.

On models manufactured prior to 1978, the recommended fuel:oil ratio is 10:1, while the recommended fuel:oil ratio for models after 1977 is 25:1. Early GF and GFP series motors equipped with a Bing carburetor may use the 25:1 fuel:oil ratio. Early F and FP series motor may use the 25:1 fuel:oil ratio if equipped with a Villiers carburetor and the tapered needle is changed to a number 2 needle. Early WS and WSPC series motors may use the 25:1 fuel:oil ratio if equipped with an Amal carburetor and the power jet is changed to a number 40 power jet.

LOWER UNIT. The lower unit gears and bearings are lubricated by oil contained in the gear-

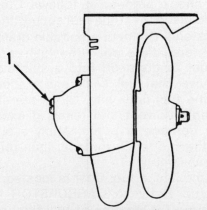

Fig. SG1-1 — View showing location of oil plug (1) in gearcase housing. Refer to text.

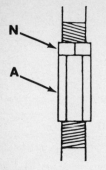

Fig. SG1-2—View showing adjustment nut (A) and locknut (N) used to adjust shift linkage on some models. Refer to text.

case. The recommended gear oil is SAE 90 on EF-NR and ENS models and SAE 140 on all other models. Gearcase oil level should be checked after every 15 hours of operation and the gearcase should be drained and filled at the end of each season. The gearcase is drained and filled through the same plug port.

To drain the oil, remove oil plug (1—Fig. SG1-1) from gearcase housing. Lay the motor with the plug opening down and allow the lubricant to drain into a suitable container.

To refill the gearcase on EFNR and ENS models, place the outboard motor in a vertical position. Add oil through plug opening until the oil begins to overflow. Allow the oil level to stabilize at the bottom of the fill port, then install oil plug (1) and tighten. DO NOT overfill gearcase.

To refill the gearcase on all other models, lay the motor with the plug opening up. Add oil through plug opening until oil level is just below plug opening, then install oil plug (1) and tighten.

FUEL SYSTEM

Periodically inspect the fuel tank and fuel lines for damage. Renew components if needed.

Keep the external surface of the carburetor clean and all connections and sealing surfaces tight.

On models with the fuel tank mounted adjacent to the power head, the fuel tank strainer should be inspected periodically for blockage and damage. To check, proceed as follows: Close the fuel cock and disconnect the fuel supply line from the fuel cock end. Connect a suitable drain hose to fuel cock end, then open the fuel cock and allow the fuel to drain off into a suitable container. Remove the fuel cock and inspect the strainer at the fuel cock end. Clean the strainer with a suitable solvent and renew if excessive blockage or damage is noted. Apply a suitable sealant on the fuel cock threads, then reinstall. Complete reassembly.

On some models, a fuel filter is located within the carburetor. Refer to CARBURETOR in the Tune-Up section for location of fuel filter on carburetors so equipped.

SHIFT LINKAGE

Some models are equipped with an adjustment nut (A—Fig. SG1-2) located between the upper and lower shift rods. Turning adjustment nut (A) will vary length of upper and lower shift rods, thus allowing adjustment for proper engagement of all gears.

To check shift linkage for proper adjustment, first place shift lever in the forward detent position. Check for proper engagement and propeller rotation by turning the propeller.

⚠ WARNING

Disconnect spark plug lead and properly ground lead before performing any propeller service, otherwise, accidental starting can occur if propeller shaft is rotated.

Check for proper engagement of neutral and reverse (if so equipped).

To adjust, loosen locknut (N) and turn adjustment nut (A) until proper engagement of forward, neutral and reverse (if so equipped) is obtained, then retighten locknut (N).

STARTER

To remove the starter on models with breaker point type ignition system, remove three cap screws at the base of flywheel cover (15—Fig. SG1-3) and withdraw the starter assembly. On models with CD type ignition system, remove the two screws retaining starter cover (1) to flywheel cover (15) and withdraw the starter assembly.

To disassemble, remove handle (6) from starter rope (5) end and allow the rope to slowly rewind into the starter. Remove clip (14), then withdraw components (7 through 13). Carefully lift pulley (4) with starter rope (5) from housing (1).

⚠ WARNING

Care should be exercised when working with or around a coiled starter rewind spring as sudden uncoiling can cause injury. Safety eyewear and gloves are recommended.

Inspect all components for excessive wear or any other damage and renew if needed. If rewind spring (3) is renewed, spring coils should wind in a counterclockwise direction from the outer end

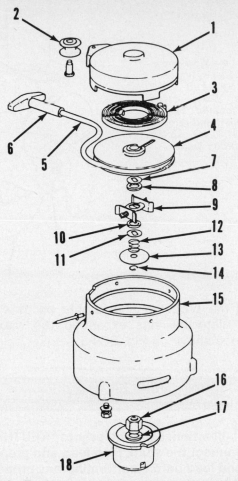

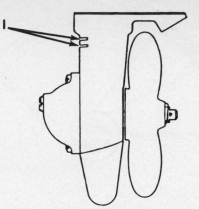

Fig. SG1-6 — Cooling system water inlet ports (I) are located on the front side of the lower unit.

Fig. SG1-3 — Exploded view of manual rewind starter typical of the type used on all models so equipped. Flywheel cover (15) is not used on some models.

1. Starter housing	10. Friction disc
2. Roller	11. Engaging disc
3. Rewind spring	12. Spring
4. Pulley	13. Washer
5. Starter rope	14. Clip
6. Handle	15. Flywheel cover
7. Engaging disc	16. Nut
8. Friction disc	17. Washer
9. Clutch unit	18. Starter cup

NOTE: Do not apply any more tension on rewind spring (3) than what is required to draw starter handle (6) back into the proper released position.

Remount manual starter assembly.

COOLING SYSTEM

Ports (I — Fig. SG1-6) located at the front of the lower unit are used as the water inlets for the cooling system. The ports must be kept clean of all foreign matter to ensure efficient operation of the cooling system.

⚠CAUTION

Do not operate outboard motor unless the lower unit is immersed in water, otherwise, the water pump impeller will be damaged.

---

when viewed from the flywheel side. Install and wind starter rope (5) on pulley (4) in a counterclockwise direction when viewed from the flywheel side.

NOTE: Lubricate all friction surfaces with a suitable water-resistant grease during reassembly.

Make sure pulley (4) properly engages rewind spring (3) during reassembly. Complete reassembly in the reverse order of disassembly.

With the starter assembly inverted, wind pulley (4) three complete turns counterclockwise and hold pulley so it cannot rotate. Feed starter rope (5) end through housing (1) and secure in handle (6). Release pulley (4) and allow starter rope (5) to slowly wind onto pulley (4).

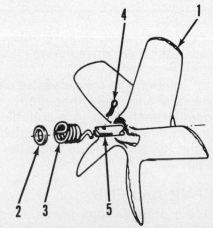

Fig. SG1-7 — Exploded view of propeller setup used on all models except EFNR and ENS.

1. Propeller	
2. Washer	
3. Drive spring	4. Cotter pin
	5. Propeller shaft

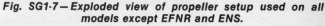

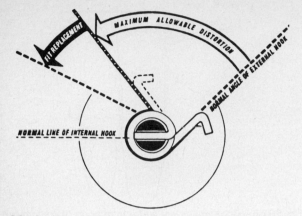

Fig. SG1-8—View showing distortion limits of propeller drive spring.

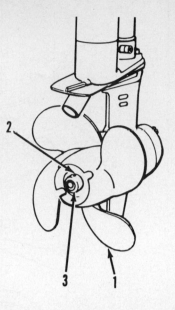

Fig. SG1-9— View showing propeller setup used on EFNR and ENS models. Note drive spring located behind propeller (1) and refer to Fig. SG1-8 for spring distortion limits.
1. Propeller
2. Pin
3. Collar

PROPELLER
All Models Except EFNR And ENS

All models are equipped with a propeller drive spring (3—Fig. SG1-7) which also cushions propeller (1). The drive spring should be renewed if spring distortion has exceeded the maximum allowance shown in Fig. SG1-8. Later models are equipped with a weedless type propeller which is also available as a replacement for early model propellers. Consult one of the British Seagull distributors listed at the front if the standard propeller is unknown or an optional propeller is desired.

> **⚠WARNING**
>
> **Shift direction control lever to "NEUTRAL." Disconnect the spark plug lead and properly ground lead before performing any propeller service, otherwise, accidental starting can occur if propeller shaft is rotated.**

To remove the propeller, remove cotter pin (4) and withdraw washer (2), drive spring (3) and propeller (1) from propeller shaft (5).

Inspect all components for excessive wear and any other damage and renew if needed.

Coat propeller shaft (5) with a suitable water-resistant grease. Install propeller (1), drive spring (3) and washer (2), then secure propeller with a new cotter pin (4).

Models EFNR And ENS

The standard propeller has four blades and a diameter of 9½ inches (241 mm) on Model EFNR and 10-5/8 inches (270 mm) on Model ENS. A drive spring is used to rotate the propeller as well as cushion the lower unit. The drive spring is located behind the propeller and should be renewed if spring distortion has exceeded the maximum allowance shown in Fig. SG1-8.

> **⚠WARNING**
>
> **Shift directional control lever to "NEUTRAL." Disconnect the spark plug lead and properly ground lead before performing any propeller service, otherwise, accidental starting can occur if propeller shaft is rotated.**

To remove the propeller, drive out pin (2—Fig. SG1-9) and withdraw collar (3) and propeller (1) from the propeller shaft.

Inspect all components for excessive wear or any other damage and renew if needed. Note the drive spring.

Coat the propeller shaft with a suitable water-resistant grease. Install propeller (1) and collar (3). Align collar holes with propeller shaft pin opening and drive in a new pin (2).

Tune-Up
IGNITION SYSTEM
Breaker Point Models

Two different breaker point type ignition systems have been used. The Villiers magneto (Fig. SG1-10) can be identified by the silver colored flywheel. The Wipac magneto (Fig. SG1-13) has a bronze flywheel. On both models, the flywheel can be removed as follows: Remove the flywheel nut, washer and starter pulley, then

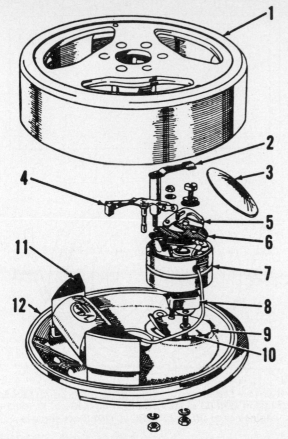

Fig. SG1-10 — *Exploded view of Villiers magneto assembly. Retainer (2) holds cover (3).*

1. Flywheel
2. Retainer
3. Cover
4 & 5. Breaker points
6. Insulator
7. Housing
8. Condenser
9. Gasket
10. Studs
11. Coil
12. Stator plate

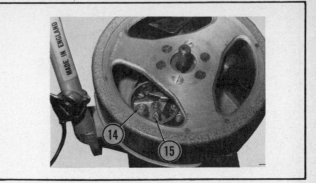

Fig. SG1-11 — *Breaker point lock screw is shown at (14) and eccentric adjuster cam at (15).*

breaker point cam is on the flywheel and the flywheel should be seated firmly on the crankshaft taper when adjusting the breaker point gap. Condenser (8 — Fig. SG1-10 and SG1-12) is retained in the housing by the shoulder on studs (10).

Ignition timing is fixed and not adjustable. Stator plate (12 — Fig. SG1-10) is retained on the crankcase with one screw (13 — Fig. SG1-16) which must engage hole in crankcase shoulder for correct ignition timing.

NOTE: The crankshaft top main bearing may be damaged if screw (13) is overtightened.

WIPAC. The breaker point gap should be 0.020 inch (0.51 mm) and can be adjusted through the opening in the flywheel. Breaker point lock screw is shown at (14 — Fig. SG1-14) and adjusting (cam) screw at (15). Breaker point cam is on the flywheel and the flywheel should be firmly seated on the crankshaft taper when checking point gap. The condenser is a molded unit with the coil and cannot be renewed separately.

Ignition timing is fixed and not adjustable. The stator plate is retained on the crankcase with one screw (13 — Fig. SG1-16) which should engage the recess in crankcase shoulder for correct timing.

reinstall flywheel nut finger tight. Remove the spark plug and turn the flywheel until the piston is at the bottom of its stroke. Suspend the outboard motor above the floor by holding the flywheel, then bump the flywheel nut until the flywheel is loose on the crankshaft taper.

NOTE: It is important to have the piston at the bottom of its stroke when bumping to prevent possible engine damage.

The stator plate should be marked, if removal is required, so the plate can be reinstalled in the original position. Note correct position of stator plate in Fig. SG1-15 if plate was not marked prior to removal. Securely tighten flywheel retaining nut.

Refer to the appropriate following paragraphs for servicing the breaker point assembly used.

VILLIERS. The breaker point gap should be 0.020 inch (0.51 mm) and can be adjusted through the opening in the flywheel after removing the starter pulley, flywheel cover and cover (3 — Fig. SG1-10). Breaker point lock screw is shown at (14 — Fig. SG1-11) and adjuster cam at (15). The

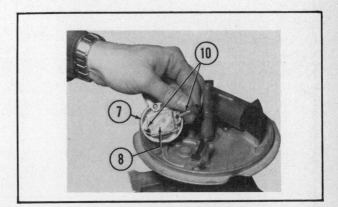

Fig. SG1-12 — *Condenser (8) is retained in housing (7) by shoulder on studs (10).*

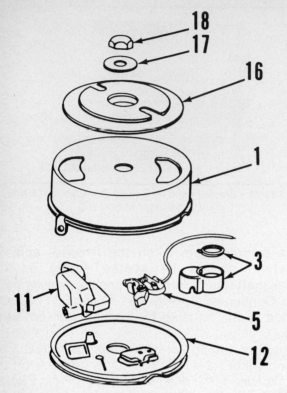

Fig. SG1-13 — Exploded view of Wipac magneto assembly. Condenser is molded inside coil (11).

1. Flywheel	12. Stator plate
3. Breaker point cover	16. Pulley plate
5. Breaker point assy.	17. Washer
11. Coil	18. Flywheel nut

Make certain that screw (13) is aligned with hole before tightening.

NOTE: The crankcase top main bearing may be damaged if screw (13) is overtightened.

CD Models

Outboard motors with the letter "E" at the beginning of the model code are equipped with a capacitor discharge ignition (CDI) system. Ignition timing is fixed and the only service required

Fig. SG1-14 — Breaker point lock screw is shown at (14) and eccentric adjusting cam at (15).

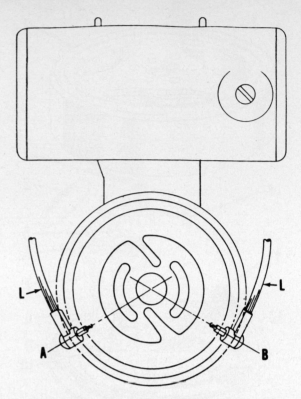

Fig. SG1-15 — The magneto stator plate must be installed so high tension lead (L) is located at (A) on 3.86 cu. in. (63.3 cc) engines or at (B) on 6.18 cu. in. (101.3 cc) engines.

is to renew damaged components. If engine malfunction is noted and the ignition system is suspected, make sure the spark plug and all electrical wires are in good condition and all electrical connections are tight before proceeding to troubleshooting the CD ignition system.

The standard spark plug is Champion 8 Com. (British) or D16 (American) with an electrode gap of 0.035 inch (0.9 mm).

SPEED CONTROL LINKAGE

The engine speed is controlled by the position of the throttle slide in carburetor throttle bore. A throttle lever mounted on the steering arm controls the operation of the throttle slide by way of a control cable. Make sure all components operate

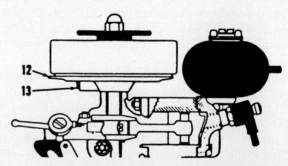

Fig. SG1-16 — View showing location of stator plate (12) retaining screw (13). Refer to text.

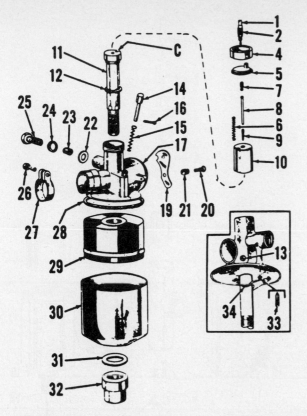

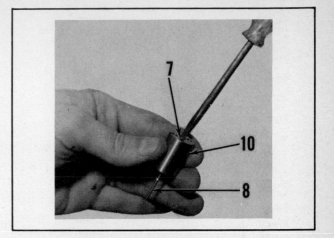

Fig. SG1-18—Mixture is adjusted by turning screw (7) on Villiers carburetor. Refer to text.

Fig. SG1-17—Exploded view of Villiers carburetor. Washer (22) has smaller inside diameter than washer (24).

1. Throttle cable
2. Cable adjuster
4. Cover retainer
5. Top cover
6. Throttle spring
7. Mixture adjusting screw
8. Taper needle
9. Needle spring
10. Throttle slide
11. Jet
12. Washer
13. Jet locking screw
14. Primer
15. Spring
16. Cotter pin
17. Body
19. Choke
20. Pivot screw
21. Spring washer
22. Fiber washer
23. Filter
24. Fiber washer
25. Banjo bolt
26. Clamp screw
27. Mounting clamp
28. Gasket
29. Float
30. Float bowl
31. Washer
32. Nut
33. Inlet needle
34. Lever

freely and properly. Renew any component that is excessively worn or damaged in any way.

CARBURETOR

Five different carburetors have been used. The Villiers concentric float chamber carburetor is shown in Fig. SG1-17. The Seamal with offset float chamber is shown in Fig. SG1-19. The Amal "Twin Jet" carburetor with removable float chamber is shown in Fig. SG1-20. The Amal "Concentric" carburetor is shown in Fig. SG1-21. The Bing carburetor is shown in Fig. SG1-22. Refer to the appropriate following paragraphs for servicing.

VILLIERS. **Adjustment.** Refer to Fig. SG1-17. The fuel mixture is adjusted by turning screw (7—Fig. SG1-18) in center of throttle slide (10). Normal setting is accomplished by turning screw (7)

until top of screw is flush with top of throttle slide (10), then turn screw (7) out ½ to 1 turn above flush. Turning screw (7) in will lean the fuel mixture. The fuel mixture should be adjusted to provide even running at high speed. Correct adjustment may cause idle mixture to be slightly rich.

Overhaul. To disassemble the carburetor, first disconnect the fuel line banjo fitting by removing bolt (25—Fig. SG1-17). Throttle slide (10) and associated parts can be withdrawn after removing nut (4). Carburetor can be separated from cylinder after loosening clamp screw (26). To remove jet (11), remove nut (32), washer (31), float bowl (30), float (29) and gasket (28). Then remove screw (13) and withdraw jet (11) from carburetor body (17).

Inspect all components for excessive wear and any other damage and renew if needed.

When reinstalling jet (11), make certain that screw (13) engages the cutaway (C) on top of jet (11). With fuel inlet needle lever (34) correctly shaped, the distance between top of float (29) and carburetor body (17) should be 7/32 inch (5.56 mm) with needle valve (33) seated.

SEAMAL. **Adjustment.** Refer to Fig. SG1-19. The fuel mixture is adjusted by location of clip (4) on needle (5). Moving the clip to a higher groove on needle (5) leans the mixture. Normal clip (4) position is in center groove. The fuel mixture should be adjusted to provide smooth even running at high speed. Correct adjustment may cause idle mixture to be slightly rich.

Overhaul. Disassemble the carburetor with reference to Fig. SG1-19. Clean components in a suitable solvent. Inspect all components for excessive wear and any other damage and renew if needed. Reassembly is the reverse order of disassembly. Secure inlet needle (15) to float (14) by attaching clip to top of float. Needle (15) should provide a tight seal against seat (16).

British Seagull

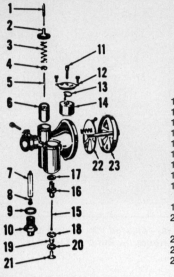

1. Cable
2. Top screw cap
3. Throttle spring
4. Clip
5. Needle
6. Throttle slide
7. Jet tube
8. Main jet
9. Gasket
10. Bottom nut
11. Primer
12. Float cover
13. Primer spring
14. Float
15. Inlet needle
16. Inlet seat
17. Gasket
18. Banjo fitting gasket (large hole)
19. Screen
20. Banjo fitting gasket (small hole)
21. Union bolt
22. Choke plate
23. Air intake cover

Fig. SG1-19 — Exploded view of Seamal carburetor.

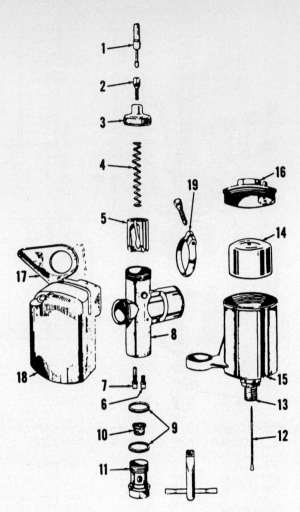

Fig. SG1-20—Exploded view of Amal "Twin Jet" carburetor.

1. Cable	11. Float chamber holding bolt
2. Adjuster	12. Fuel inlet needle
3. Top screw cap	13. Seat
4. Spring	14. Float
5. Throttle slide	15. Float bowl
6. Economy jet	16. Cover
7. Power jet	17. Choke
8. Body	18. Air intake
9. Gaskets	19. Clamp ring
10. Screen	

AMAL "TWIN JET." Refer to Fig. SG1-20. The fuel mixture is not adjustable. Disassemble the carburetor with reference to Fig. SG1-20. Clean components in a suitable solvent. Inspect all components for excessive wear and any other damage and renew if needed. Reassembly is the reverse order of disassembly. Observe the following during reassembly: Make certain that the short jet (6) is toward power head end of carburetor and longer jet (7) is toward inlet (18) end. Jets do not use gaskets. The slot on side of throttle slide (5) should correctly engage screw in side of carburetor body. Fuel inlet needle (12) should provide a tight seal against seat (13). Seat (13) is available only as part of float bowl (15) and should not be removed. The float bowl must be installed on the carburetor side opposite the fuel tank (nearest boat).

AMAL "CONCENTRIC." **Adjustment.** Refer to Fig. SG1-21 for an exploded view of Amal "Concentric" carburetor. High speed fuel mixture is controlled by main jet (18). Intermediate speed fuel mixture is controlled by taper needle (8) and position of clip (7) in needle (8) grooves. Normal position of clip (7) is in second groove from tapered end of needle (8). Moving clip (7) to a higher groove will lean fuel mixture while moving clip (7) to a lower groove will richen fuel mixture.

Overhaul. Disassemble the carburetor with reference to Fig. SG1-21. Float bowl (20) is attached to the carburetor body by screw threads. Fuel inlet valve seat is permanently fixed to carburetor body and is not renewable. Clean components in a suitable solvent. Inspect all components for excessive wear and any other damage and renew if

needed. Reassembly is the reverse order of disassembly. Be sure throttle slide groove properly engages pin in throttle slide bore of carburetor during throttle slide installation.

BING. **Adjustment.** Refer to Fig. SG1-22 for an exploded view of Bing carburetor used on some models. High speed fuel mixture is controlled by main jet (19). Intermediate speed fuel mixture is controlled by taper needle (9) and the position of clip (8) in needle (9) grooves. Normal position of clip (8) is in second groove from tapered end of needle (19). Moving clip (8) to a higher groove will lean fuel mixture while moving clip (8) to a lower groove will richen fuel mixture.

Overhaul. Disassemble the carburetor with reference to Fig. SG1-22. Float bowl (22) is attach-

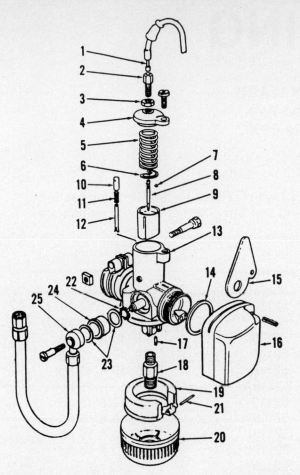

Fig. SG1-21 — Exploded view of Amal "Concentric" carburetor.

1. Throttle cable
2. Cable adjuster
3. Locknut
4. Cap
5. Spring
6. Retainer
7. Clip
8. Tapered needle
9. Throttle slide
10. Primer button
11. Spring
12. Primer rod
13. Body
14. Washer
15. Choke plate
16. Air intake
17. Inlet fuel valve
18. Main jet
19. Float
20. Float bowl
21. Float pin
22. Filter
23. Washer
24. Spacer
25. Fuel fitting

ed to the carburetor body by screw threads. Fuel inlet seat is permanently fixed to carburetor body and is not renewable. Clean components in a suitable solvent. Inspect all components for excessive wear and any other damage and renew if needed. Reassembly is the reverse order of disassembly. When installing needle retainer (7), position retainer end gap over "B" engraved on throttle slide (10). Be sure throttle slide groove properly engages pin in throttle slide bore of carburetor during throttle slide installation.

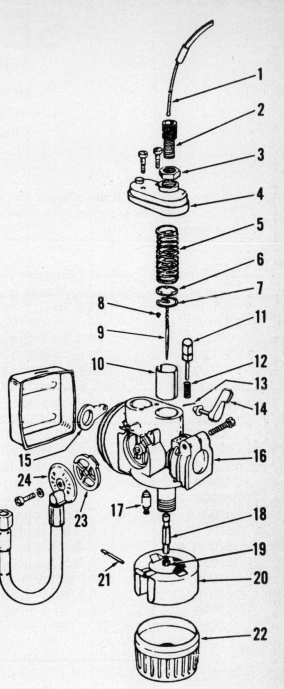

Fig. SG1-22—Exploded view of Bing carburetor used on some models.

1. Throttle cable
2. Cable adjuster
3. Locknut
4. Cap
5. Spring
6. Washer
7. Retainer
8. Clip
9. Tapered needle
10. Throttle slide
11. Primer button
12. Spring
13. Pin
14. Choke lever
15. Choke plate
16. Body
17. Fuel inlet valve
18. Jet holder
19. Main jet
20. Float
21. Float pin
22. Float bowl
23. Filter
24. Filter cover

SEA KING

MONTGOMERY WARD
619 W. Chicago Ave.
Chicago, Illinois 60607

Some Sea King motors were manufactured by Chrysler. Refer to the Chrysler section listed below for maintenance information. Sea King and Chrysler horsepower ratings are the same.

Sea King Model	Chrysler Model	Sea King Model	Chrysler Model
27009	9.9, 10 & 15 hp	52100	6 & 8 hp (1971-1977)
27020	20 hp (1969-1976)	52106	6 & 8 hp (1971-1977)
27209	9.9, 10 & 15 hp	52110	9.9, 10 & 15 hp
27220	20 hp (1969-1976)	52115	9.9, 10 & 15 hp
27400	6 & 8 hp (1971-1977)	52118	9.9, 10 & 15 hp
27406	6 & 8 hp (1971-1977)	52118A	9.9, 10 & 15 hp
27409	9.9, 10 & 15 hp	52119	9.9, 10 & 15 hp
27420	20 hp (1969-1976)	52119A	9.9, 10 & 15 hp
28920	20 hp (1969-1976)	52119B	9.9, 10 & 15 hp
28921	20 hp (1969-1976)	52119C	9.9, 10 & 15 hp
52000	6 & 8 hp (1971-1977)	52125	25 hp
52003	3.5 & 4 hp	52175	6 & 8 hp (1971-1977)
52004	3.5 & 4 hp	52179	7.5 hp
52004A	3.5 & 4 hp	52179A	7.5 hp
52004B	3.5 & 4 hp	52179B	7.5 hp
52004C	3.5 & 4 hp	52179C	7.5 hp
52004D	3.5 & 4 hp	52179D	7.5 hp
52006	6 & 8 hp (1971-1977)	52299	9.9, 10 & 15 hp
52010	9.9, 10 & 15 hp	52299A	9.9, 10 & 15 hp
52015	9.9, 10 & 15 hp	52299B	9.9, 10 & 15 hp
52025	25 hp		

SUZUKI

SUZUKI INTERNATIONAL, INC.
3251 E. Imperial Way
P.O. Box 1100
Brea, California 92621

SUZUKI DT2

NOTE: Metric fasteners are used throughout outboard motor.

Specifications

Hp/rpm	2/4500
Bore	41.0 mm
	(1.61 in.)
Stroke	37.8 mm
	(1.49 in.)
Displacement	50.0 cc
	(3 cu. in.)
Spark plug:	
NGK	BR5HS
Electrode gap	0.5-0.6 mm
	(0.020-0.024 in.)
Magneto:	
Breaker point gap	0.3-0.4 mm
	(0.012-0.016 in.)
Carburetor:	
Make	Mikuni
Model	VM-11-10
Idle speed	800-900 rpm
Fuel:oil ratio	50:1
Gearcase oil capacity	40 mL
	(1.35 oz.)

Maintenance

LUBRICATION

ENGINE. The engine is lubricated by oil mixed with the fuel. The fuel should be regular leaded or unleaded gasoline with an octane rating of 85-95. Recommended oil is Suzuki "CCI" or a BIA certified two-stroke motor oil. The recommended fuel:oil ratio for normal operation if 50:1. During engine break-in, the fuel:oil ratio should be increased to 30:1.

NOTE: Manufacturer's recommended break-in period is defined as follows: For the first five minutes of opera-tion the engine should not exceed its slowest possible cruising speed. After five minutes, slowly increase the engine speed, but do not exceed ¾ throttle for the first five hours of operation.

LOWER UNIT. The lower unit gears and bearings are lubricated by oil contained in the gearcase. The recommended oil is Suzuki Outboard Motor Gear Oil or a suitable SAE 90 hypoid outboard gear oil. The gearcase oil capacity is 40 milliliters (1.35 oz.). The gearcase should be refilled periodically and the lubricant renewed after every 50 hours of operation or more frequently if needed. The gearcase is drained and filled through the same plug port.

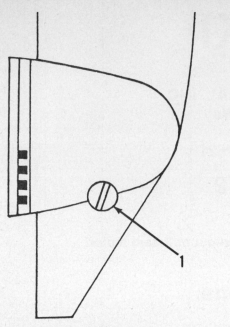

Fig. S1-1 — View showing location of the lower unit drain and fill plug (1). Refer to text.

To drain the oil, remove oil plug (1 — Fig. S1-1) from gearcase housing. Lay the motor with the plug opening down and allow the lubricant to drain into a suitable container.

To fill the gearcase with oil, lay the motor with the plug opening up. Add oil through plug opening until the oil begins to overflow, then reinstall oil plug (1) with a new gasket and tighten.

FUEL SYSTEM

Periodically inspect the fuel tank and fuel lines for damage. Renew components if needed.

After every 50 hours of operation, close the fuel valve and remove carburetor filter element (17 — Fig. S1-10). Clean filter element in a suitable solvent and blow dry with clean compressed air. Inspect filter element (17). If excessive blockage or damage is noted, renew element. If filter element damage is noted, carburetor float bowl (22) should be removed to thoroughly clean the fuel system.

Keep the external surface of the carburetor clean and all connections and sealing surfaces tight.

FUEL TANK. It may be necessary to remove the fuel tank for cleaning or for access to underlying engine components.

To remove the fuel tank, first remove the screws retaining the port and starboard engine covers and then withdraw the covers. Close the fuel valve and disconnect the fuel hose from the fuel valve outlet. Remove the screws retaining the fuel tank and withdraw.

Installation is reverse order of removal.

STARTER

When starter rope (2 — Fig. S1-2) is pulled, pulley (4) will rotate. As pulley (4) rotates, the drive pawl (5) moves outward to mesh with drive plate (9) and crank the engine.

When starter rope (2) is released, pulley (4) is rotated in the reverse direction by force from rewind spring (3). As pulley (4) rotates, the starter rope is rewound and drive pawl (5) is disengaged from drive plate (9).

The manual starter must be disassembled to renew starter rope (2) and internal starter components.

To overhaul the manual starter, proceed as follows: Remove the fuel tank as outlined in FUEL TANK paragraphs in the FUEL SYSTEM section. Remove the screws securing the manual starter to the power head and withdraw.

⚠WARNING

Care should be exercised when working with or around a coiled starter rewind spring as sudden uncoiling can cause injury. Safety eyewear and gloves are recommended.

To disassemble, untie starter rope (2) at handle (12) and allow the rope to wind into the starter. Invert the manual starter and remove cap screw (8), then withdraw plate (7), spring clip (6) and drive pawl (5). Lift pulley (4) with starter rope (2) from starter housing (1). BE CAREFUL when removing pulley (4) as rewind spring may be dislodged.

NOTE: Should pulley (4) not lift free from rewind spring (3), insert a suitable screwdriver blade through hole in pulley (4) to hold rewind spring (3) securely in housing (1).

Untie starter rope (2) and remove rope from pulley (4) if renewal is required. To remove rewind spring (3), use suitable hand protection and extract rewind spring (3) from housing (1). Allow rewind spring to uncoil in a safe area.

Inspect all components for damage and excessive wear and renew if needed.

To reassemble, first apply a coating of a suitable water-resistant grease to rewind spring area of housing (1). Install rewind spring (3) in housing (1) so spring coils wind in a counterclockwise direction from the outer end. Make sure the spring's outer hook is properly secured in starter housing. Wind starter rope (2) onto pulley (4) approximately 3 turns counterclockwise when viewed from the flywheel side. Direct remaining starter rope (2) length through notch in pulley (4).

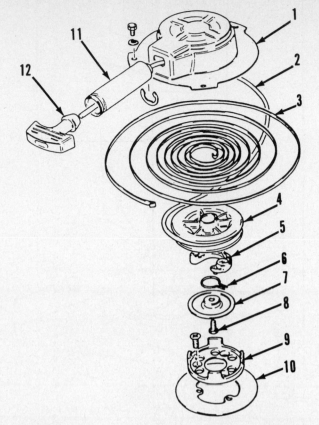

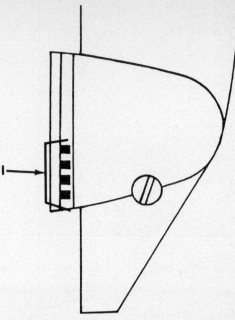

Fig. S1-3—Cooling system water inlet ports (I) are located on the starboard side of the lower unit gearcase.

Fig. S1-2—Exploded view of manual starter assembly.

1. Starter housing	5. Drive pawl	9. Drive plate
2. Starter rope	6. Spring clip	10. Cover plate
3. Rewind spring	7. Plate	11. Rope guide
4. Pulley	8. Cap screw	12. Handle

NOTE: Lubricate all friction surfaces with a suitable water-resistant grease during reassembly.

Assemble pulley (4) to starter housing making sure that slot in pulley drum properly engages hook end in rewind spring (3). Thread starter rope (2) through housing (1), rope guide (11) and handle (12) and secure. Install drive pawl (5), spring clip (6) and plate (7). Apply a suitable thread fastening solution on cap screw (8) threads and securely tighten. Turn pulley (4) 2-3 turns counterclockwise when viewed from the flywheel side, then release starter rope (2) from pulley (4) notch and allow rope to slowly wind onto pulley.

NOTE: Do not apply any more tension on rewind spring (3) than what is required to draw starter handle (12) back into the proper released position.

Remount manual starter assembly, then complete reassembly.

COOLING SYSTEM

Ports (I—Fig. S1-3) located on the starboard side of the lower unit gearcase are used as the water inlet for the cooling system. The ports must be kept clean of all foreign matter to ensure efficient operation of the cooling system.

⚠CAUTION

Do not operate outboard motor unless the lower unit is immersed in water, otherwise, the water pump impeller will be damaged.

PROPELLER

The standard propeller has three blades, a diameter of 188 mm (7-3/8 in.) and a pitch of 115 mm (4½ in.). Optional propellers are available. Select a propeller that will allow the engine at full throttle to reach maximum operating rpm range (4200-4800 rpm).

⚠WARNING

Remove spark plug lead and properly ground lead before performing any propeller service, otherwise, accidental starting can occur if propeller shaft is rotated.

To remove the propeller, remove cotter pin (2—Fig. S1-4) and withdraw propeller (1) from propeller shaft (4).

Inspect propeller (1) and shear pin (3) for damage and excessive wear and renew if needed.

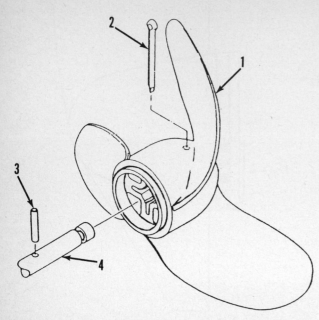

Fig. S1-4 — Propeller (1) is mounted on propeller shaft (4) and is retained by cotter pin (2). Shear pin (3) is renewed only after withdrawing propeller (1) from propeller shaft (4).

Apply a water-resistant grease to the propeller bore, then install propeller (1) on propeller shaft (4) and retain with a new cotter pin (2).

Tune-Up

IGNITION SYSTEM

The standard spark plug is NGK-BR5HS with an electrode gap of 0.5-0.6 mm (0.020-0.024 in.).

The breaker point gap should be 0.3-0.4 mm (0.012-0.016 in.) and can be inspected and adjusted through the opening in flywheel (4 — Fig. S1-5). To inspect and, if needed, adjust the breaker point gap, first remove the manual starter assembly as outlined in the STARTER section. Remove screws retaining drive plate (9 — Fig. S1-2) and cover plate (10) to flywheel (4 — Fig. S1-5), then withdraw components.

Inspect the breaker point surfaces for excessive wear, pitting and damage. If needed, renew breaker point assembly (5) and condenser (8) as outlined later in this section.

To clean the breaker point contact surfaces, use a point file or sandpaper with a grit rating of 400 to 600. After polishing, wipe the contact surfaces clean with a dry cloth and lightly grease the breaker point arm with a suitable lubricant.

Turn the flywheel until the breaker point contact surfaces are at their widest position. Reach through the flywheel opening with a feeler gage of the appropriate size and check the distance between the point surfaces. If the distance is not within the recommended limits, then loosen the point set securing screw and adjust the point set

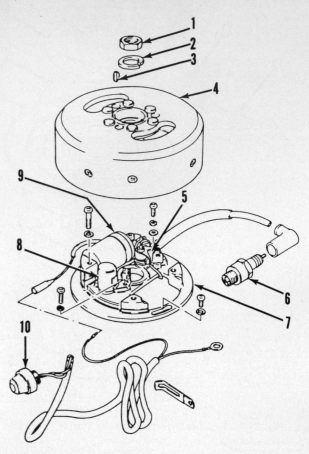

Fig. S1-5 — Exploded view of flywheel magneto unit.

1. Nut
2. Lockwasher
3. Flywheel key
4. Flywheel
5. Breaker point assy.
6. Spark plug
7. Magneto base plate
8. Condenser
9. Ignition coil
10. Engine kill switch

until the correct gap is obtained. Tighten the point set securing screw and recheck the breaker point gap. Repeat the adjustment procedure, if needed, until the correct breaker point gap is obtained.

To renew breaker point assembly (5) and condenser (8), proceed as follows: Using Suzuki flywheel holding tool (H — Fig. S1-6) or a suitable equivalent, remove securing nut (1 — Fig. S1-5) using suitable tools (T — Fig. S1-6). Remove flywheel (4 — Fig. S1-5) from crankshaft end using Suzuki puller assembly (P — Fig. S1-7) or a suitable equivalent and tools (T). Note flywheel key (3 — Fig. S1-5) located in crankshaft keyway.

⚠WARNING

Be sure suitable tools are used to remove the flywheel. Damage resultant from the misapplication of force or the use of incorrect tools may cause engine damage, engine malfunction or personal injury.

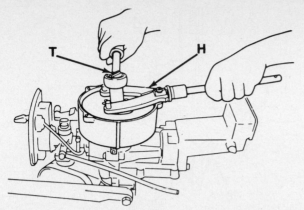

Fig. S1-6 — View showing the use of Suzuki flywheel holding tool (H) to prevent flywheel rotation during removal of flywheel securing nut (1 — Fig. S1-5) with suitable tools (T).

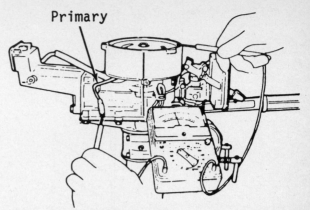

Fig. S1-8 — Connect ohmmeter leads as shown to measure the resistance in the primary side of the ignition coil. Refer to text.

With reference to Fig. S1-5, renew breaker point assembly (5) and condenser (8). Adjust the breaker point gap to the recommended setting as previously outlined. Make sure the securing screws are properly tightened. Be sure the flywheel key is properly positioned in the crankshaft keyway, then reinstall flywheel (4). Tighten securing nut (1) to 40-50 N·m (29-37 ft.-lbs.).

To obtain the correct ignition timing, first adjust breaker point assembly (5) to the proper point gap as previously outlined. Remove spark plug. Unplug wire at connector leading from magneto base plate (7) to engine kill switch (10). Use a point checker and attach the red tester lead to the wire coming from the magneto base plate (7). Connect the black tester lead to an engine ground.

NOTE: A suitable continuity tester can be used.

Install a dial indicator in the spark plug hole. Determine top dead center for the piston and zero the dial indicator for piston TDC. Slowly turn the flywheel clockwise while observing the point

checker meter. When the meter moves from "CLOSE" to "OPEN", stop turning the flywheel. Check the piston position reading on the dial indicator. The piston should be 0.804 mm (0.032 in.) BTDC. If not, remove flywheel (4) as outlined earlier. Loosen screws securing magneto base plate (7) and rotate until proper piston position is obtained when points "OPEN." Rotating magneto base plate (7) clockwise retards ignition timing, while rotating magneto base plate (7) counterclockwise advances ignition timing.

Ignition Coil. To check ignition coil (9 — Fig. S1-5), use a suitable ohmmeter. Connect one tester lead to a suitable engine ground, then connect the remaining tester lead alternately to the primary (Fig. S1-8) and secondary (Fig. S1-9) ignition coil leads. Resistance reading for primary circuit should be 0.9-1.22 ohms, while the secondary circuit resistance reading should be 5200-6900 ohms. Renew ignition coil (9 — Fig. S1-5) if the meter readings are not within the proper range.

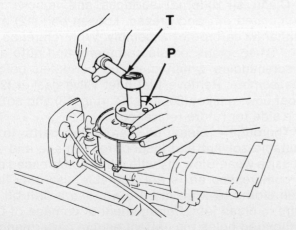

Fig. S1-7 — View shows flywheel (4 — Fig. S1-5) being removed from crankshaft end using Suzuki puller assembly (P) and suitable tools (T).

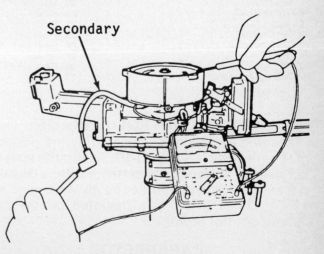

Fig. S1-9 — Connect ohmmeter leads as shown to measure the resistance in the secondary side of the ignition coil. Refer to text.

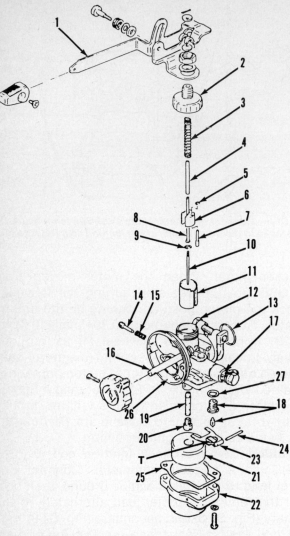

Fig. S1-10—Exploded view of carburetor.

1. Throttle control lever
2. Cap nut
3. Spring
4. Tube
5. Clip
6. Spring seat
7. Seat pin
8. Throttle rod
9. Clip
10. Jet needle
11. Throttle valve
12. Bolt
13. "O" ring
14. Idle speed screw
15. Spring
16. Choke assy.
17. Fuel filter
18. Fuel inlet valve
19. Main nozzle
20. Main jet
21. Float
22. Float bowl
23. Float arm
24. Float pin
25. Gasket
26. Carburetor body
27. Gasket

SPEED CONTROL LINKAGE

The engine speed is regulated by the position of throttle lever (1—Fig. S1-10). As throttle lever (1) is raised or lowered, the carburetor throttle valve (11) is operated via throttle rod (8). An engine kill switch (10—Fig. S1-5) is mounted on the carburetor control cover.

CARBURETOR

ADJUSTMENT. Standard carburetor is a Mikuni Model VM-11-10. Standard main jet (20—Fig.

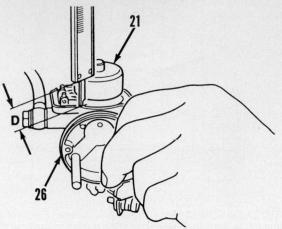

Fig. S1-11—Invert carburetor body (26) and measure the distance (D) from the body surface (without gasket) to float (21) base to determine float level. Refer to text.

S1-10) size is #95 for normal operation. Preliminary positioning of clip (9) in jet needle (10) is the third notch from the top. Inserting clip (9) in a higher notch will lean mid-range mixture while inserting clip in a lower notch will richen mid-range mixture. Recommended idle speed is 800-900 rpm with engine at normal operating temperature.

Properly mount the outboard motor on a boat or a suitable test tank and immerse the lower unit. Connect a tachometer and set it on the appropriate range scale. Start the engine and allow it to warm up to normal operating temperature. Position the throttle control lever (1) to the complete closed position, then adjust the engine idle speed screw (14) until the engine is idling at 800-900 rpm.

OVERHAUL. Remove all components as needed to remove control panel and expose carburetor assembly. Close fuel valve and remove all external components that will interfere with carburetor removal.

Clean all external surfaces and remove accumulated dirt and grease. Loosen bolt (12) and withdraw carburetor assembly. With reference to Fig. S1-10, disassemble carburetor and note any discrepancies which must be corrected before reassembly. Remove fuel inlet valve gasket (27), float bowl gasket (25) and "O" ring (13) and set to the side for future reference.

Thoroughly clean all carburetor parts in a suitable solvent and inspect for damage and excessive wear. Blow dry with clean compressed air. If compressed air is not available, use only lint-free cloths to wipe dry. Do not use a drill bit or wire to clean jets. Enlargement or damage of the calibrated holes may affect engine performance.

With reference to Fig. S1-10, reassemble the carburetor components with new gaskets. Note that the new gaskets should match up with those removed. If not, check with your parts supplier to be sure you have the correct gaskets.

To determine the float level, invert the carburetor body (26—Fig. S1-11) and measure the distance (D) from the body surface (without gasket) to the base of float (21). The distance should be 19-21 mm (0.75-0.83 in.). Adjust the float level by bending tang (T—Fig. S1-10) on float arm (23).

When reinstalling the carburetor, place a new "O" ring (13) inside the carburetor bore, then install the carburetor on crankcase half spigot end. Lightly push the carburetor towards the crankcase half until the "O" ring is properly seated against the spigot end. Tighten bolt (12) until the carburetor retaining clamp is tight. Be sure the carburetor is in a vertical position. Completely reassemble the engine with the exception of the starboard engine cover. Perform final carburetor adjustments as described in ADJUSTMENT section.

SUZUKI DT9.9 AND DT16

NOTE: Metric fasteners are used throughout outboard motor.

Specifications

	DT9.9	DT16
Horsepower	9.9	16
Bore	56 mm	59 mm
	(2.20 in.)	(2.32 in.)
Stroke	52mm	52 mm
	(2.05 in.)	(2.05 in.)
Number of Cylinders	2	2
Displacement	256 cc	284 cc
	(15.6 cu. in.)	(17.3 cu. in.)
Spark plug:		
NGK	B6HS	B7HS
Electrode gap	0.6-0.7 mm	0.6-0.7 mm
	(0.024-0.027 in.)	(0.024-0.027 in.)
Magneto:		
Breaker point gap	Breakerless	Breakerless
Carburetor:		
Make	Mikuni	Mikuni
Model	BV24-16	BV24-19
Idle speed (in gear)	600-650 rpm	600-650 rpm
Fuel:oil ratio	50:1	50:1
Gearcase oil capacity	220 mL*	220 mL*
	(7.44 oz.)	(7.44 oz.)

*Gearcase oil capacity is 200 milliliters (6.76 oz.) on models with through-the-propeller exhaust.

Maintenance

LUBRICATION

ENGINE. The engine is lubricated by oil mixed with the fuel. The fuel should be regular leaded or unleaded gasoline with an octane rating of 85-95. Recommended oil is Suzuki "CCI" or a BIA certified two-stroke motor oil. The recommended fuel:oil ratio for normal operation is 50:1. During engine break-in, the fuel:oil ratio should be increased to 30:1.

NOTE: Manufacturer's recommended break-in period is defined as follows: For the first five minutes of operation the engine should not exceed its slowest possible cruising speed. After five minutes, slowly increase the engine speed, but do not exceed ¾ throttle for the first five hours of operation.

LOWER UNIT. The lower unit gears and bearings are lubricated by oil contained in the gearcase. The recommended oil is Suzuki Outboard Motor Gear Oil or a suitable SAE 90 hypoid out-

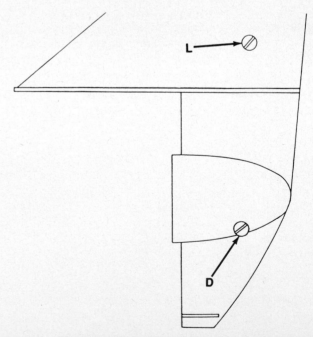

Fig. S2-1—View showing lower unit drain and fill plug (D) and oil level (vent) plug (L) on models with an integral exhaust outlet in the lower housing.

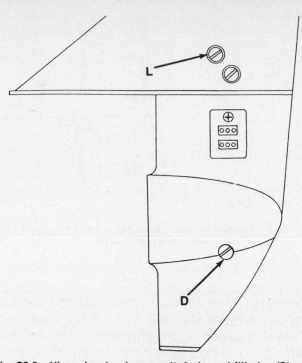

Fig. S2-2—View showing lower unit drain and fill plug (D) and oil level (vent) plug (L) on models with through-the-propeller exhaust.

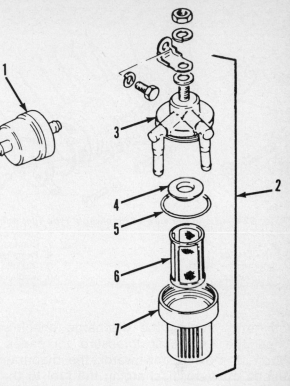

Fig. S2-3—View showing a disposable type fuel filter (1) and an exploded view of a cup type fuel filter assembly (2).

1. Disposable type fuel filter	4. Gasket
	5. "O" ring
2. Cup type fuel filter assy.	6. Filter element
3. Filter base	7. Cup

board gear oil. The gearcase oil capacity on models with an integral exhaust outlet in the lower housing is 220 milliliters (7.44 oz.) and on models with through-the-propeller exhaust is 200 milliliters (6.76 oz.). The gearcase should be refilled periodically and the lubricant renewed after every 50 hours of operation or more frequently if needed. The gearcase is drained and filled through the same plug port (D—Fig. S2-1 or Fig. S2-2). An oil level (vent) port (L) is used to indicate the full oil level of the gearcase and to ease oil drainage.

To drain the oil, place the outboard motor in a vertical position. Remove drain plug (D) and oil level plug (L), and allow the lubricant to drain into a suitable container.

To fill the gearcase with oil, place the outboard motor in a vertical position. Add oil through drain plug (D) opening with an oil feeder until the oil begins to overflow from oil level plug (L) port. Reinstall oil level plug (L) with a new gasket, if needed, and tighten. Remove oil feeder, then re-install drain plug (D) with a new gasket, if needed, and tighten.

FUEL SYSTEM

Periodically inspect the fuel lines and connections for damage. Renew components if needed.

Keep the external surface of the carburetor clean and all connections and sealing surfaces tight.

FUEL FILTER. A fuel filter assembly is connected between fuel tank supply line and fuel pump inlet line. After every 50 hours of operation, or more frequently if needed, check the condition of filter element (1 or 6—Fig. S2-3). Stop the engine and remove the engine cover.

On disposable type filter element (1), remove the filter element and blow through the filter inlet side with low air pressure and note the resistance. A minimal amount of resistance should be noted. If not, filter assembly should be renewed.

On cup type fuel filter assemblies (2), unscrew fuel filter cup (7) from filter base (3) and withdraw filter element (6), "O" ring (5) and gasket (4). Clean cup (7) and filter element (6) in a suitable solvent and blow dry with clean compressed air. Inspect filter element (6). If excessive blockage or damage is noted, renew element. If needed, renew "O" ring (5) and gasket (4).

Reassembly is reverse order of disassembly.

FUEL PUMP. The fuel pump is operated by crankcase pressure changes from the up and down movement of the piston. When the crankcase pressure decreases (the piston is moving upward), the pump diaphragm is pulled toward the crankcase allowing fuel to enter the pump

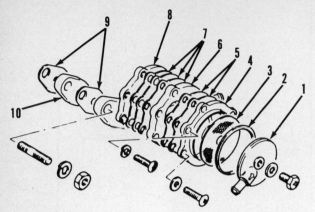

Fig. S2-4—Exploded view of diaphragm type fuel pump.

1. Inlet cover
2. Gasket
3. Filter screen
4. Upper body
5. Pump valves
6. Lower body
7. Diaphragm set
8. Pump base
9. Gaskets
10. Insulator block

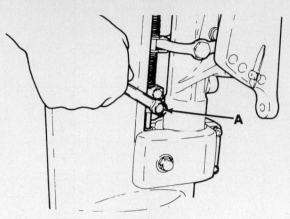

Fig. S2-5—Adjustment cap screw (A) is used to adjust shift linkage. Refer to text.

body and closing the discharge check valve. When the crankcase pressure increases (the piston is moving downward), the diaphragm is pushed outward discharging the fuel to the carburetor and closing the inlet check valve. This pulsating action provides continuous fuel flow. The check valves are used to prevent reverse flow of the fuel.

The inlet port is identified with an arrow on inlet cover (1—Fig. S2-4). The arrow indicates the fuel flow direction. The fuel hoses must be connected accordingly.

To overhaul, first remove the engine's top cover and disconnect the fuel tank supply hose at the outboard motor connector. Disconnect the fuel hoses at the fuel pump inlet and discharge nozzles and label if needed. Remove securing nuts and lockwashers, then withdraw fuel pump assembly.

With reference to Fig. S2-4, disassemble the fuel pump assembly. Inspect all components for damage and excessive wear and renew if needed. Clean filter screen (3) with a suitable cleaning solvent.

With reference to Fig. S2-4, reassemble the fuel pump assembly with new gaskets. Mount the fuel pump assembly on the crankcase with new gaskets and securely tighten the retaining nuts.

NOTE: Fuel pump and engine malfunction will result if the fuel pump and all connections are not airtight.

Complete reassembly.

SHIFT LINKAGE

Direction of propeller rotation is determined by the position of the gear shift lever. The gear shift lever actuates gearcase components using shift linkage consisting of an upper and lower shift rod connected by an adjustment bracket. The notched end of the lower shift rod controls the movement of the dog clutch on the propeller shaft. The positioning of the dog clutch on the propeller shaft determines whether forward, neutral or reverse directional movement is selected.

To adjust, loosen cap screw (A—Fig. S2-5) enough to allow lower shift rod to slide freely in adjustment bracket. Place shift lever in reverse detent position and lower shift rod in reverse position. Push down on adjustment bracket only with enough force to remove any slack in the linkage, then tighten adjustment cap screw (A). Check adjustment by turning propeller.

⚠️**WARNING**

Remove spark plug leads and properly ground leads before performing any propeller service, otherwise, accidental starting can occur if propeller shaft is rotated.

Make sure neutral and forward properly engage. If not, repeat adjustment procedure.

STARTER
Overhead Type

When starter rope (4—Fig. S2-6) is pulled, pulley (3) will rotate. As pulley (3) rotates, the drive pawl (5) moves outward to mesh with starter cup (19) and crank the engine.

When starter rope (4) is released, pulley (3) is rotated in the reverse direction by force from rewind spring (2). As pulley (3) rotates, the starter rope is rewound and drive pawl (5) is disengaged from starter cup (19).

The manual starter must be disassembled to renew starter rope (4) and internal starter components.

To overhaul the manual starter, proceed as follows: Remove the engine's top cover. Remove the screws securing the manual starter to the power head and withdraw.

⚠ WARNING

Care should be exercised when working with or around a coiled starter rewind spring as sudden uncoiling can cause injury. Safety eyewear and gloves are recommended.

To disassemble, untie starter rope (4) at handle (18) and allow the rope to wind into the starter. Invert the manual starter and remove cap screw (12), lockwasher (11), flat washer (10), drive plate (9), spring (7) and spacer (8). Withdraw drive pawl (5) and return spring (6). Lift pulley (3) with starter rope (4) from starter housing (1). BE CAREFUL when removing pulley (3) to prevent possible injury from rewind spring (2).

Untie starter rope (4) and remove rope from pulley (3) if renewal is required. To remove rewind spring (2), use suitable hand protection and extract rewind spring (2) from housing (1). Allow rewind spring to uncoil in a safe area.

Inspect all components for damage and excessive wear and renew if needed.

To reassemble, first apply a coating of a suitable water-resistant grease to rewind spring area of housing (1). Install rewind spring (2) in housing (1) so spring coils wind in a counterclockwise direction from the outer end. Make sure the spring's outer hook is properly secured in starter housing. Wind starter rope (4) onto pulley (3) approximately 3 turns counterclockwise when viewed from the flywheel side. Direct remaining starter rope (4) length through notch in pulley (3).

NOTE: Lubricate all friction surfaces with a suitable water-resistant grease during reassembly.

Assemble pulley (3) to starter housing making sure that slot in pulley drum properly engages hook end in rewind spring (2). Thread starter rope (4) through housing (1), rope guide (17) and handle (18) and secure. Install drive pawl (5), return spring (6), spacer (8), spring (7) and drive plate (9). Apply a suitable thread fastening solution on cap screw

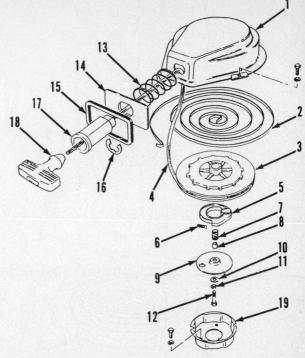

Fig. S2-6—Exploded view of overhead type manual starter.

1. Housing		
2. Rewind spring	8. Spacer	14. Plate
3. Pulley	9. Drive plate	15. Grommet
4. Starter rope	10. Flat washer	16. Clip
5. Drive pawl	11. Lockwasher	17. Rope guide
6. Return spring	12. Cap screw	18. Handle
7. Spring	13. Spring	19. Starter cup

(12) threads, then install cap screw (12) with flat washer (10) and lockwasher (11) and securely tighten. Turn pulley (3) 2-3 turns counterclockwise when viewed from the flywheel side, then release starter rope (4) from pulley (3) notch and allow rope to slowly wind onto pulley.

NOTE: Do not apply any more tension on rewind spring (2) than what is required to draw starter handle (18) back into the proper released position.

Remount manual starter assembly, then complete reassembly.

Gear Type

When starter rope (14—Fig. S2-7) is pulled, starter reel (13) will rotate. As starter reel (13) rotates, starter pinion (3) will rotate upward to engage flywheel gear and crank the engine.

When starter rope (14) is released, starter reel (13) is rotated in the reverse direction by force from rewind spring (11). As starter reel (13) rotates, starter pinion (3) will disengage the flywheel gear and return to the relaxed position.

The manual starter must be disassembled to renew starter rope (14) or any other internal starter component.

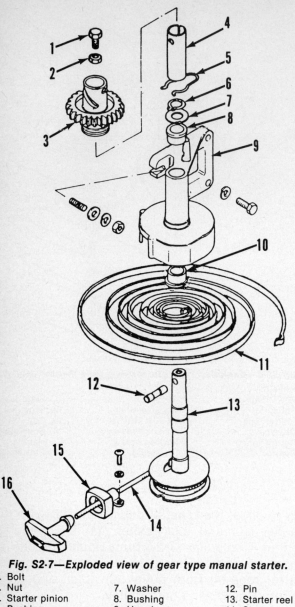

Fig. S2-7—Exploded view of gear type manual starter.

1. Bolt
2. Nut
3. Starter pinion
4. Bushing
5. Spring clip
6. Snap ring
7. Washer
8. Bushing
9. Housing
10. Bushing
11. Rewind spring
12. Pin
13. Starter reel
14. Starter rope
15. Rope guide
16. Handle

To overhaul the manual starter, proceed as follows: Remove the engine's top cover. Untie starter rope (14) at handle (16) and allow the rope to wind into the starter. Remove the nut and three cap screws securing the manual starter to the power head and withdraw the assembly.

⚠ WARNING

Care should be exercised when working with or around a coiled starter rewind spring as sudden uncoiling can cause injury. Safety eyewear and gloves are recommended.

Loosen jam nut (2) and unscrew bolt (1), then using a suitable punch, drive out pin (12). Slide starter pinion (3) with spring clip (5) from starter reel (13). Remove snap ring (6) and washer (7), then withdraw starter reel (13) from housing (9). BE CAREFUL when removing starter reel (13) as rewind spring (11) may become dislodged from housing.

Untie starter rope (14) and remove rope from starter reel (13) if renewal is required. To remove rewind spring (11), use suitable hand protection and extract rewind spring (11) from housing (9). Allow rewind spring to uncoil in a safe area.

Inspect all components for damage and excessive wear and renew if needed.

To reassemble, first apply a coating of a suitable water-resistant grease to rewind spring area of housing (9). Install rewind spring (11) in housing (9) so spring coils wind in a clockwise direction from the outer end. Make sure the spring's outer hook is properly secured in starter housing. Completely wind starter rope (14) onto starter reel (13) in a clockwise rotation when viewed from the bottom side.

NOTE: Lubricate all friction surfaces with a suitable water-resistant grease during reassembly.

Insert starter reel (13) into housing (9). Make sure inner hook end of rewind spring (11) properly engages notch at base of starter reel (13). Install washer (7) and snap ring (6), then place starter pinion (3) with spring clip (5) on shaft. Make sure spring clip (5) is centered over lug on housing (9). Install pin (12) and secure in position with bolt (1) and nut (2). Thread rope through starter housing (9), rope guide (15) and handle (16) and secure. If more tension is needed on rewind spring (11) to return handle (16) to the proper released position, hook starter rope (14) in starter reel pulley notch and rotate pulley one complete turn clockwise when viewed from the bottom side. Release starter rope (14) from pulley notch and allow rope to slowly wind onto pulley.

NOTE: Do not apply any more tension on rewind spring (11) than what is required to draw starter handle (16) back into the proper released position.

Remount manual starter assembly, then complete reassembly.

COOLING SYSTEM

Ports (I—Fig. S2-8) located on the port side of the lower unit gearcase are used as the water inlet for the cooling system on models with an integral exhaust outlet. Ports (I—Fig. S2-10) located on the port and starboard side of the lower unit

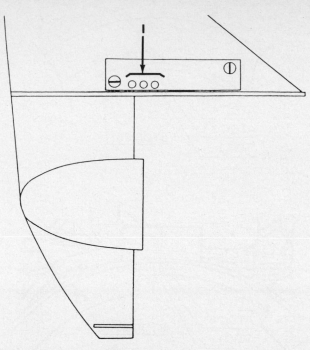

Fig. S2-8—Cooling system water inlet ports (I) are located on the port side of the lower unit gearcase on models with an integral exhaust outlet.

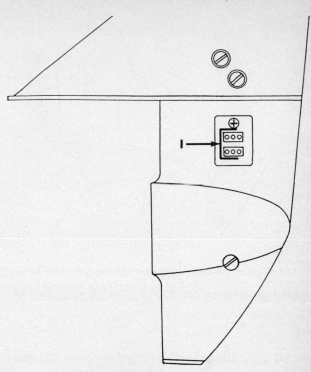

Fig. S2-10—Cooling system water inlet ports (I) are located on the port and starboard side of the lower unit gearcase on models with through-the-propeller exhaust.

gearcase are used as the water inlets for the cooling system on models with through-the-propeller exhaust. The ports must be kept clean of all foreign matter to ensure efficient operation of the cooling system.

⚠CAUTION

Do not operate outboard motor unless the lower unit is immersed in water, otherwise, the water pump impeller will be damaged.

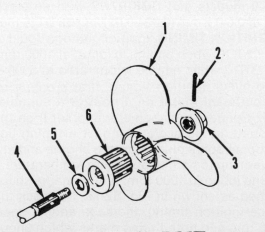

Fig. S2-9—On models with an integral exhaust outlet, stopper (5), thrust hub (6) and propeller (1) are mounted on propeller shaft (4) and retained by propeller spinner (3) and cotter pin (2).

PROPELLER
Models With Integral Exhaust Outlet

The standard propeller has three blades and a diameter of 225 mm (8⅞ in.). Standard propeller has a pitch of 205 mm (8⅛ in.) on DT9.9 models and 230 mm (9 in.) on DT16 models. Optional propellers are available. Select a propeller that will allow the engine at full throttle to reach maximum operating rpm range (4500-5500 rpm on DT9.9 models and 5200-5700 rpm on DT16 models).

⚠WARNING

Remove spark plug leads and properly ground leads before preforming any propeller service, otherwise, accidental starting can occur if propeller shaft is rotated.

To remove the propeller, remove cotter pin (2—Fig. S2-9) and unscrew propeller spinner (3). Withdraw propeller (1), thrust hub (6) and stopper (5) from propeller shaft (4).

Inspect all components for damage and excessive wear and renew if needed.

Apply a water-resistant grease to the propeller shaft splines, then install stopper (5), thrust hub

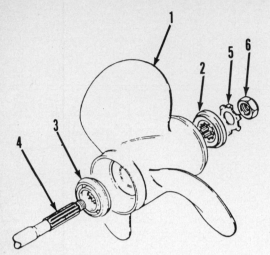

Fig. S2-11—On models with through-the-propeller exhaust, stopper (3), propeller (1) and spacer (2) are mounted on propeller shaft (4) and retained by lockplate (5) and nut (6).

(6) and propeller (1) on propeller shaft (4). Install propeller spinner (3) and a new cotter pin (2).

Models With Through-The-Propeller Exhaust

The standard propeller has three blades and a diameter of 235 mm (9¼ in.). Standard propeller has a pitch of 203 mm (8 in.) on DT9.9 models and 230 mm (9 in.) on DT16 models. Optional propellers are available. Select a propeller that will allow the engine at full throttle to reach maximum operating rpm range (4500-5500 rpm on DT9.9 models and 5200-5700 rpm on DT16 models).

> ### ⚠ WARNING
>
> **Remove spark plug leads and properly ground leads before performing any propeller service, otherwise, accidental starting can occur if propeller shaft is rotated.**

To remove the propeller, straighten tabs on lockplate (5 – Fig. S2-11) and use suitable tools to remove nut (6). Withdraw lockplate (5), spacer (2), propeller (1) and stopper (3) from propeller shaft (4).

Inspect all components for damage and excessive wear and renew if needed.

Apply a water-resistant grease to the propeller shaft splines, then install stopper (3), propeller (1) and spacer (2). Install a new lockplate (5) if needed. Install nut (6), then bend tabs of lockplate (5) to secure nut (6) in place.

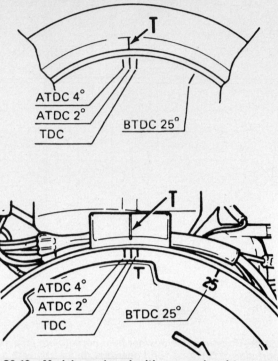

Fig. S2-12—Models equipped with an overhead type manual starter have timing marks shown in top view while models equipped with a gear type manual starter have timing marks shown in bottom view.

Tune-Up

IGNITION SYSTEM

On all models a capacitor discharge ignition (CDI) system is used. Refer to Outboard Motor Service Manual for testing and servicing the CD ignition system. If engine malfunction is noted and the ignition system is suspected, make sure spark plugs and all electrical wiring are in good condition and all electrical connections are tight before troubleshooting the CD ignition system.

The standard spark plug is NGK-B6HS with an electrode gap of 0.6-0.7 mm (0.024-0.027 in.) on DT9.9 models and NGK-B7HS with an electrode gap of 0.6-0.7 mm (0.024-0.027 in.) on DT16 models.

IGNITION TIMING. Ignition timing should occur at 2° ATDC when engine is idling at 1000 rpm and 25° BTDC when engine is operated at 5000 rpm.

To check ignition timing, first properly mount the outboard motor on a boat or a suitable test tank. Connect a tachometer and set it on the appropriate range scale. Connect a timing light to the upper spark plug. Start the engine and allow it to warm up to normal operating temperature. With engine idling at 1000 rpm, timing marks should be aligned as shown in Fig. S2-12. To check full advance ignition timing, increase engine speed to 5000 rpm and note timing marks which should indicate 25° BTDC. Reposition control ring stop (3 – Fig. S2-13) to adjust ignition timing.

Illustrations Courtesy Suzuki

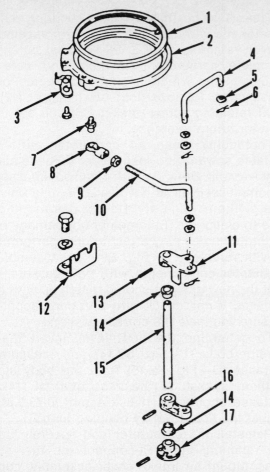

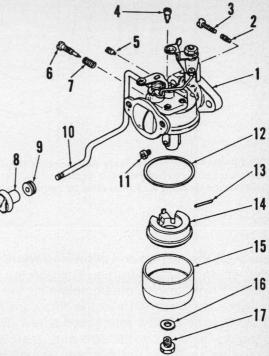

Fig. S2-13—Exploded view of speed control linkage.

1. Bushing
2. Speed control ring
3. Control ring stop
4. Carburetor link rod
5. Washer
6. Hairpin clip
7. Ball stud
8. Ball socket
9. Nut
10. Stator link rod
11. Linkage connector
12. Cable mounting
13. Pin
14. Bushing
15. Shaft
16. Lever
17. Pulley

Fig. S2-14—Exploded view of Mikuni BV24 type carburetor.

1. Body
2. Spring
3. Idle speed screw
4. Pilot jet
5. Air jet
6. Idle mixture screw
7. Spring
8. Choke knob
9. Bushing
10. Choke actuating rod
11. Main jet
12. Gasket
13. Float pin
14. Float
15. Float bowl
16. Gasket
17. Bowl retaining screw

SPEED CONTROL LINKAGE

The speed control handle components are connected by cables to pulley (17—Fig. S2-13). The pulley movement is transferred by linkage to rotate the stator assembly and actuate the carburetor throttle so the ignition timing is advanced as the throttle opens.

To synchronize ignition and throttle control linkage, first make sure the ignition timing has been correctly adjusted as outlined in the previous IGNITION SYSTEM section. When the twist grip is moved completely against the high speed stop, the carburetor throttle should be fully opened. MAKE SURE that the carburetor throttle does not reach the full open position before the ignition timing is fully advanced.

To adjust speed control linkage, proceed as follows: With twist grip in the complete closed position, the carburetor throttle should be completely closed. Remove ball socket (8) from ball stud (7). Force control ring stop (3) against boss on cylinder block. Loosen nut (9) and adjust ball socket (8) on stator link rod (10) until ball socket (8) will slide over ball stud (7) without moving stator assembly. Tighten nut (9) and reconnect components.

CARBURETOR

ADJUSTMENT. Standard carburetor is a Mikuni Model BV24-16 on DT9.9 models and a Mikuni Model BV24-19 on DT16 models. Standard main jet (11—Fig. S2-14) size is #92.5 on DT9.9 models and #117.5 on DT16 models for normal operation. Preliminary adjustment of idle mixture screw (6) is 1-1½ turns out from a lightly seated position for DT9.9 models and 1¾-2¼ turns out from a lightly seated position for DT16 models. Recommended idle speed is 600-650 rpm in gear with engine at normal operating temperature.

With the outboard motor properly mounted on a boat or a suitable test tank, immerse the lower unit. Remove engine top cover. Connect a tachometer and set it on the appropriate range

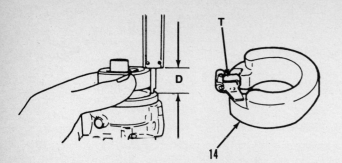

Fig. S2-15—*Invert carburetor body and measure the distance (D) from the body surface (without gasket) to float (14) base to determine float level. Adjust level by bending tang (T).*

scale. Start the engine and allow it to warm up to normal operating temperature. Position the throttle control twist grip to the complete closed position. Place the gear shift in the "Forward" position. Adjust the engine idle speed screw (3) until the engine is idling at 600-650 rpm, then adjust idle mixture screw (6) until smooth engine operation is noted. Readjust the engine idle speed screw (3) until the recommended idle speed is obtained.

Reinstall engine top cover.

OVERHAUL. Remove engine's top cover. Remove screw retaining air intake outer cover. Remove the two cap screws securing the air intake to the carburetor. Remove the choke knob and detach throttle linkage from carburetor. Disconnect the fuel tank supply hose at the outboard motor connector. Disconnect the fuel supply hose at the carburetor inlet. Clean all external surfaces and remove accumulated dirt and grease. Remove the two nuts securing the carburetor and withdraw the carburetor assembly.

With reference to Fig. S2-14, disassemble the complete carburetor assembly and note any discrepancies which must be corrected before reassembly. Remove float bowl gasket (12) and bowl retaining screw gasket (16) and set to the side for future reference.

Thoroughly clean all carburetor parts in a suitable solvent and inspect for damage and excessive wear. Blow dry with clean compressed air. If compressed air is not available, use only lint-free cloths to wipe dry. Do not use a drill bit or wire to clean jets. Enlargement or damage of the calibrated holes may affect engine performance.

With reference to Fig. S2-14, reassemble the carburetor components with new gaskets. Note that the new gaskets should match up with those removed. If not, check with your parts supplier to be sure you have the correct gaskets.

To determine the float level, invert the carburetor body (1—Fig. S2-14) and measure the distance (D—Fig. S2-15) from the body surface (without gasket) to the base of float (14). The distance should be 18.5-20.5 mm (0.73-0.81 in.). Adjust the float level by bending tang (T).

Reinstall the carburetor and securely tighten the retaining nuts. Reconnect the fuel supply hose. Mount air intake cover assembly, connect carburetor linkage and install choke knob. Initially, adjust idle mixture screw (6—Fig. S2-14) 1-1½ turns out from a lightly seated position for DT9.9 models and 1¾-2¼ turns out from a lightly seated position for DT16 models. Perform final carburetor adjustments as described in ADJUSTMENT section.

SUZUKI DT20 AND DT25

NOTE: Metric fasteners are used throughout outboard motor.

Specifications

	DT20	DT25
Hp	19.8	25
Bore	64 mm	68 mm
	(2.52 in.)	(2.68 in.)
Stroke	61.5 mm	61.5 mm
	(2.42 in.)	(2.42 in.)
Number of cylinders	2	2
Displacement	396 cc	447 cc
	(24.16 cu. in.)	(27.28 cu. in.)
Spark plug:		
NGK	B7HS	B7HS
Electrode gap	0.6-0.7 mm	0.6-0.7 mm
	(0.024-0.027 in.)	(0.024-0.027 in.)
Breaker point gap	Breakerless	Breakerless
Carburetor:		
Make	Mikuni	Mikuni
Model	BV28-22	BV32-28
Idle speed (in gear)	600-650 rpm	600-650 rpm
Fuel:oil ratio	50:1	50:1
Gearcase oil capacity	380 mL	380 mL*
	(10.14 oz.)	(12.84 oz.)

*Gearcase oil capacity is 300 milliliters (10.14 oz.) on models with through-the-propeller exhaust.

Maintenance

LUBRICATION

ENGINE. The engine is lubricated by oil mixed with the fuel. The fuel should be regular leaded or unleaded gasoline with an octane rating of 85-95. Recommended oil is Suzuki "CCI" or a BIA certified two-stroke motor oil. The recommended fuel:oil ratio for normal operation is 50:1. During engine break-in, the fuel:oil ratio should be increased to 30:1.

NOTE: Manufacturer's recommended break-in period is defined as follows: For the first five minutes of operation the engine should not exceed its slowest possible cruising speed. After five minutes, slowly increase the engine speed, but do not exceed ¾ throttle for the first five hours of operation.

LOWER UNIT. The lower unit gears and bearings are lubricated by oil contained in the gearcase. The recommended oil is Suzuki Outboard Motor Gear Oil or a suitable SAE 90 hypoid outboard gear oil. The gearcase oil capacity on DT25 models with through-the-propeller exhaust is 300 milliliters (10.14 oz.). The gearcase oil capacity on DT20 models and DT25 models with an integral exhaust outlet in the lower housing is 380 milliliters (12.84 oz.). The gearcase should be refilled periodically and the lubricant renewed

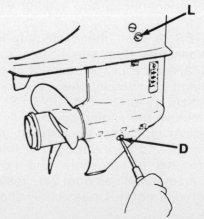

Fig. S3-1—View showing lower unit drain and fill plug (D) and oil level (vent) plug (L) on models with through-the-propeller exhaust.

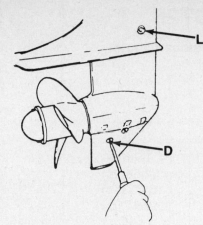

Fig. S3-2—View showing lower unit drain and fill plug (D) and oil level (vent) plug (L) on models with an integral exhaust outlet in the lower housing.

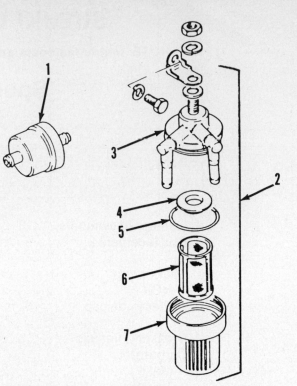

Fig. S3-3 — View showing a disposable type fuel filter (1) and an exploded view of a cup type fuel filter assembly (2).

1. Disposable type fuel filter
2. Cup type fuel filter assy.
3. Filter base
4. Gasket
5. "O" ring
6. Filter element
7. Cup

after every 50 hours of operation or more frequently if needed. The gearcase is drained and filled through the same plug port (D—Fig. S3-1 or Fig. S3-2). An oil level (vent) port (L) is used to indicate the full oil level of the gearcase and to ease oil drainage.

To drain the oil, place the outboard motor in a vertical position. Remove drain plug (D) and oil level plug (L) and allow the lubricant to drain into a suitable container.

To fill the gearcase with oil, place the outboard motor in a vertical position. Add oil through drain plug (D) opening with an oil feeder until the oil begins to overflow from oil level plug (L) port. Reinstall oil level plug (L) with a new gasket, if needed, and tighten. Remove oil feeder, then reinstall drain plug (D) with a new gasket, if needed, and tighten.

FUEL SYSTEM

Periodically inspect the fuel lines and connections for damage. Renew components if needed.

Keep the external surface of the carburetor clean and all connections and sealing surfaces tight.

FUEL FILTER. A fuel filter assembly is connected between fuel tank supply line and fuel pump inlet line. After every 50 hours of operation, or more frequently if needed, check the condition of filter element (1 or 6—Fig. S3-3). Stop the engine and remove the engine cover.

On disposable type filter element (1), remove the filter element and blow through the filter's inlet side with low air pressure and note the resistance. A minimal amount of resistance should be noted. If not, filter assembly should be renewed.

On cup type fuel filter assemblies (2), unscrew fuel filter cup (7) from filter base (3) and withdraw filter element (6), "O" ring (5) and gasket (4). Clean cup (7) and filter element (6) in a suitable solvent and blow dry with clean compressed air. Inspect filter element (6). If excessive blockage or damage is noted, renew element. If needed, renew "O" ring (5) and gasket (4).

Reassembly is reverse order of disassembly.

FUEL PUMP. The fuel pump is operated by crankcase pressure changes from the up and down movement of the piston. When the crankcase pressure decreases (the piston is moving upward), the pump diaphragm is pulled toward the crankcase allowing fuel to enter the pump body and closing the discharge check valve. When the crankcase pressure increases (the piston is moving downward), the diaphragm is pushed outward discharging the fuel to the carburetor and closing the inlet check valve. This pulsating action provides continuous fuel flow. The check valves are used to prevent reverse flow of the fuel.

The inlet and outlet port is identified with arrows on cover (1—Fig. S3-4). The arrows indicate fuel flow direction. The fuel hoses must be connected accordingly.

To overhaul, first remove the engine's top cover and disconnect the fuel tank supply hose at the

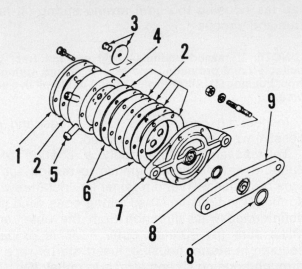

Fig. S3-4—Exploded view of diaphragm type fuel pump assembly.

1. Cover	4. Outer body	7. Inner body
2. Diaphragm set	5. Fuel outlet	8. "O" rings
3. Check valve	6. Gaskets	9. Insulator block

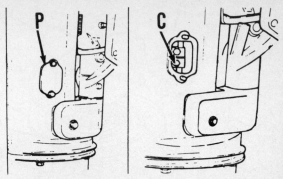

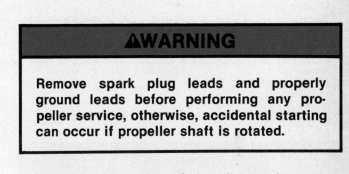

Fig. S3-5—View of drive shaft housing showing location of shift linkage cover plate (P) and shift linkage adjustment cap screw (C).

outboard motor connector. Disconnect the fuel hoses at the fuel pump inlet and outlet nozzles and label if needed. Remove securing nuts and lockwashers, then withdraw fuel pump assembly.

Scribe reference marks on cover (1), outer body (4) and inner body (7). With reference to Fig. S3-4, disassemble the fuel pump assembly. Inspect all components for damage and excessive wear and renew if needed.

With reference to Fig. S3-4, reassemble the fuel pump assembly with new gaskets. Be sure reference marks on cover (1), outer body (4) and inner body (7) align. Mount the fuel pump assembly on the crankcase with new "O" rings (8) and securely tighten the retaining nuts.

NOTE: Fuel pump and engine malfunction will result if the fuel pump and all connections are not airtight.

Complete reassembly.

SHIFT LINKAGE

Direction of propeller rotation is determined by the position of the gear shift lever. The gear shift lever actuates gearcase components using shift linkage consisting of an upper and lower shift rod connected by an adjustment bracket. The lower shift rod is connected to a shifting yoke which actuates the dog clutch cradle resulting in the movement of the dog clutch on the propeller shaft. The positioning of the dog clutch on the propeller shaft determines whether forward, neutral or reverse directional movement is selected.

To adjust, remove cover plate (P—Fig. S2-5) then loosen cap screw (C) enough to allow

lower shift rod to slide freely in adjustment bracket. Place shift lever in reverse detent position and lower shift rod in reverse position. Push down on adjustment bracket only with enough force to remove any slack in the linkage, then tighten adjustment cap screw (C). Check adjustment by turning propeller.

> ## ⚠WARNING
>
> **Remove spark plug leads and properly ground leads before performing any propeller service, otherwise, accidental starting can occur if propeller shaft is rotated.**

Make sure neutral and forward properly engage. If not, repeat adjustment procedure.

STARTER
Overhead Type

When starter rope (3—Fig. S3-6) is pulled, pulley (6) will rotate. As pulley (6) rotates, the three drive pawls (10) move apart thus meshing with starter pulley (22) and cranking the engine.

When starter rope (3) is released, pulley (6) is rotated in the reverse direction by force from rewind spring (4). As pulley (6) rotates, starter rope (3) is rewound and drive pawls (10) are disengaged from starter pulley (22).

The manual starter must be disassembled to renew starter rope (3) and internal starter components.

To overhaul the manual starter, proceed as follows: Remove the engine's top cover. Remove the screws retaining the manual starter to the engine, then withdraw the starter assembly.

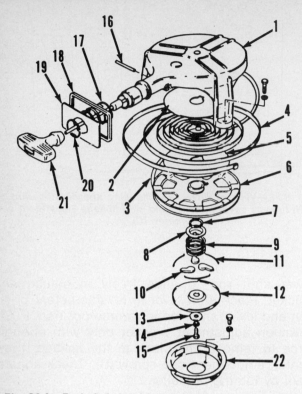

Fig. S3-6—Exploded view of overhead type manual starter.

1. Housing	9. Spring	16. Pin
2. Retainer	10. Pawl	17. Spring
3. Starter rope	11. Clip	18. Grommet
4. Rewind spring	12. Drive plate	19. Plate
5. Retainer	13. Flat washer	20. Snap ring
6. Pulley	14. Lockwasher	21. Handle
7. Washer	15. Cap screw	22. Starter pulley
8. Spring guide		

⚠WARNING

Care should be exercised when working with or around a coiled starter rewind spring as sudden uncoiling can cause injury. Safety eyewear and gloves are recommended.

To disassemble, invert starter housing and turn pulley (6) until pulley notch aligns with rope outlet in housing (1). Pull starter rope (3) up to engage notch in pulley (6) and allow pulley to slowly unwind clockwise until tension is removed from rewind spring (4). Press on drive plate (12) to ease in removal of cap screw (15), lockwasher (14) and flat washer (13). Remove drive plate (12), clips (11), pawls (10), spring (9), spring guide (8) and washer (7). Untie starter rope (3) at pulley (6) and withdraw. Lift pulley (6) from housing (1). BE CAREFUL when removing pulley (6) so as not to dislodge rewind spring (4) in housing (1). To remove rewind spring (4) from housing (1), invert housing so it sets upright on a flat surface, then

tap the housing top until rewind spring (4) falls free and uncoils.

NOTE: If rewind spring (4) will not fall free, use suitable hand protection and extract rewind spring (4) from housing (1). Allow rewind spring to uncoil in a safe area.

Inspect all components for damage and excessive wear and renew if needed.

To reassemble, first apply a coating of a suitable water-resistant grease to rewind spring area of housing (1) and retainer (2). Install rewind spring (4) in housing (1) so spring coils wind in a counterclockwise direction from the outer end. Make sure the spring's outer hook is properly secured in starter housing. Insert starter rope (3) through housing (1) and attach to pulley (6).

NOTE: Lubricate all friction surfaces with a suitable water-resistant grease during reassembly.

Assemble retainer (5) and pulley (6) to starter housing making sure that slot in pulley drum properly engages hook end in rewind spring (4). Install washer (7), spring guide (8), spring (9), pawls (10), clips (11) and drive plate (12). Apply a suitable thread fastening solution on cap screw (15) threads. Install cap screw (15) with flat washer (13) and lockwasher (14) and securely tighten. Direct starter rope (3) length through notch in pulley (6). Turn pulley (6) 3-4 turns counterclockwise when viewed from the flywheel side, then release starter rope (3) from pulley (6) notch and allow rope to slowly wind onto pulley.

NOTE: Do not apply any more tension on rewind spring (4) than what is required to draw starter handle (21) back into the proper released position.

Remount manual starter assembly, then complete reassembly.

Gear Type

When starter rope (16 — Fig. S3-7) is pulled, starter reel (13) will rotate. As starter reel (13) rotates, starter pinion (4) will rotate upward to engage the flywheel gear and crank the engine.

When starter rope (16) is released, starter reel (13) is rotated in the reverse direction by force from rewind spring (11). As starter reel (13) rotates, starter pinion (4) will disengage the flywheel gear and return to the relaxed position.

The manual starter must be disassembled to renew starter rope (16) and internal starter components.

To overhaul the manual starter, proceed as follows: Remove the engine's top cover. Untie starter rope (16) at handle (17) and allow the rope to wind into the starter. Remove the cap screws

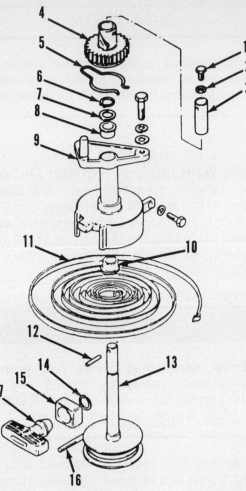

Fig. S3-7—Exploded view of gear type manual starter.

1. Bolt	7. Washer
2. Nut	8. Bushing
3. Bushing	9. Housing
4. Starter pinion	10. Bushing
5. Spring clip	11. Rewind spring
6. Snap ring	12. Pin

13. Starter reel
14. Snap ring
15. Rope guide
16. Starter rope
17. Handle

securing the manual starter to the power head and withdraw the assembly.

⚠ WARNING

Care should be exercised when working with or around a coiled starter rewind spring as sudden uncoiling can cause injury. Safety eyewear and gloves are recommended.

Loosen jam nut (2) and unscrew bolt (1), then using a suitable punch, drive out pin (12). Slide starter pinion (4) with spring clip (5) from starter reel (13). Remove snap ring (6) and washer (7), then withdraw starter reel (13) from housing (9). BE CAREFUL when removing starter reel (13) as rewind spring may become dislodged from housing (9).

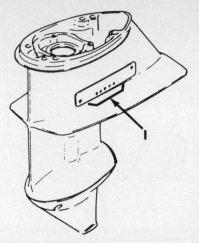

Fig. S3-8—Cooling system water inlet ports (I) are located on the port side of the lower unit gearcase on models with an integral exhaust outlet.

Untie starter rope (16) and remove rope from starter reel (13) if renewal is required. To remove rewind spring (11), use suitable hand protection and extract rewind spring (11) from housing (9). Allow rewind spring to uncoil in a safe area.

Inspect all components for damage and excessive wear and renew if needed.

To reassemble, first apply a coating of a suitable water-resistant grease to rewind spring area of housing (9). Install rewind spring (11) in housing (9) so spring coils wind in a clockwise direction from the outer end. Make sure the spring's outer hook is properly secured in starter housing. Completely wind starter rope (16) onto starter reel (13) in a clockwise rotation when viewed from the bottom side.

NOTE: Lubricate all friction surfaces with a suitable water-resistant grease during reassembly.

Insert starter reel (13) into housing (9). Make sure inner hook end of rewind spring (11) properly engages notch at base of starter reel (13). Install washer (7) and snap ring (6), then place starter pinion (4) with spring clip (5) on shaft. Make sure spring clip (5) is centered over lug on housing (9). Install pin (12) and secure in position with bolt (1) and nut (2). Thread rope through starter housing (9), rope guide (15) and handle (17) and secure. If more tension is needed on rewind spring (11) to return handle (17) to the proper released position, then hook starter rope (16) in starter reel pulley notch and rotate pulley one complete turn clockwise when viewed from the bottom side. Release starter rope (16) from pulley notch and allow rope to slowly wind onto pulley.

NOTE: Do not apply any more tension on rewind spring (11) than what is required to draw starter handle (17) back into the proper released position.

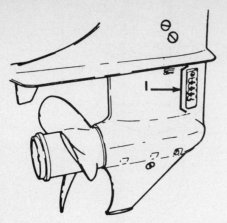

Fig. S3-9—Cooling system water inlet ports (I) are located on the port and starboard side of the lower unit gearcase on models with through-the-propeller exhaust.

Remount manual starter assembly, then complete reassembly.

COOLING SYSTEM

Ports (I—Fig. S3-8) located on the port side of the lower unit gearcase are used as the water inlets for the cooling system on models with an integral exhaust outlet. Ports (I—Fig. S3-9) located on the port and starboard side of the lower unit gearcase are used as the water inlets for the cooling system on models with through-the-propeller exhaust. The ports must be kept clean of all foreign matter to ensure efficient operation of the cooling system.

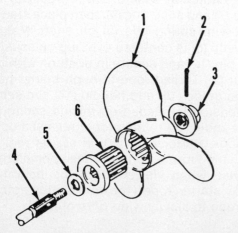

Fig. S3-10—On models with an integral exhaust oulet, stopper (5), thrust hub (6) and propeller (1) are mounted on propeller shaft (4) and retained by propeller spinner (3) and cotter pin (2).

> ### ⚠CAUTION
>
> Do not operate outboard motor unless the lower unit is immersed in water, otherwise, the water pump impeller will be damaged.

PROPELLER
Models With Integral Exhaust Outlet

The standard propeller has three blades, a diameter of 225 mm (8⅞ in.) and a pitch of 255 mm (10 in.). Optional propellers are available. Select a propeller that will allow the engine at full throttle to reach maximum operating rpm range (5200-5700 rpm).

> ### ⚠WARNING
>
> Remove spark plug leads and properly ground leads before performing any propeller service, otherwlse, accidental starting can occur if propeller shaft is rotated.

To remove the propeller, remove cotter pin (2—Fig. S3-10) and unscrew propeller spinner (3). Withdraw propeller (1), thrust hub (6) and stopper (5) from propeller shaft (4).

Inspect all components for damage and excessive wear and renew if needed.

Apply a water-resistant grease to the propeller shaft splines, then install stopper (5), thrust hub (6) and propeller (1) on propeller shaft (4). Install propeller spinner (3) and a new cotter pin (2).

Models With Through-The-Propeller Exhaust

The standard propeller has three blades, a diameter of 235 mm (9¼ in.) and a pitch of 230 mm (9 in.). Optional propellers are available. Select a propeller that will allow the engine at full throttle to reach maximum operating rpm range (5200-5700 rpm).

> ### ⚠WARNING
>
> Remove spark plug leads and properly ground leads before performing any propeller service, otherwise, accidental starting can occur if propeller shaft is rotated.

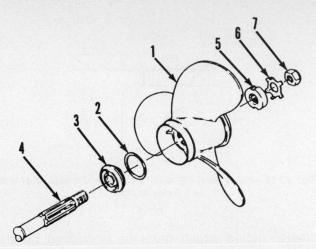

Fig. S3-11—On models with through-the-propeller exhaust, stopper (3), washer (2), propeller (1) and spacer (5) are mounted on propeller shaft (4) and retained by lockplate (6) and nut (7).

To remove the propeller, straighten tabs on lockplate (6—Fig. S3-11) and use suitable tools to remove nut (7). Withdraw lockplate (6), spacer (5), propeller (1), washer (2) and stopper (3) from propeller shaft (4).

Inspect all components for damage and excessive wear and renew if needed.

Apply a water-resistant grease to the propeller shaft splines, then install stopper (3), washer (2), propeller (1) and spacer (5). Install a new lockplate (6) if needed. Install nut (7), then bend tabs of lockplate (6) to secure nut (7) in place.

Tune-Up

IGNITION SYSTEM

A capacitor discharge ignition (CDI) system is used. Refer to Outboard Motor Service Manual for testing and servicing the CD ignition system. If engine malfunction is noted and the ignition system is suspected, make sure spark plugs and all electrical wiring are in good condition and all electrical connections are tight before troubleshooting the CD ignition system.

The standard spark plug is NGK-B7HS with an electrode gap of 0.6-0.7 mm (0.024-0.027 in.).

SPEED CONTROL LINKAGE

The engine speed is regulated by the position of the carburetor throttle shaft. The throttle shaft position is controlled by twist grip (3—Fig. S3-12) via control cables (11) and adjoining linkage.

CARBURETOR

ADJUSTMENT. Standard carburetor is a Mikuni Model BV28-22 on DT20 models and a Mikuni Model BV32-28 on DT25 models. Standard main jet (8—Fig. S3-13) size is #130 on DT20 models and

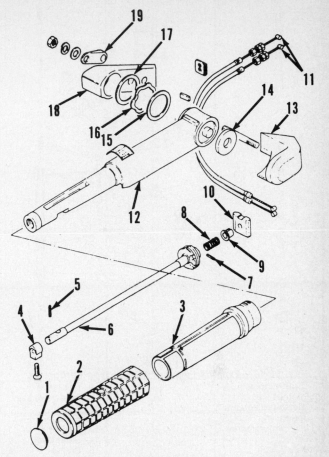

Fig. S3-12—View of steering handle speed control components.

1. Cap		
2. Rubber grip	8. Spring	14. Spacer
3. Twist grip	9. Bushing	15. Washer
4. Stopper	10. Wire protector	16. Wave washer
5. Pin	11. Control cables	17. Washer
6. Handle rod	12. Steering handle	18. Block
7. Pin	13. Cover	19. Spacer

#160 on DT25 models for normal operation. Preliminary adjustment of idle mixture screw (5) is 1½-2 turns out from a lightly seated position for DT20 models and 1¼-1¾ turns out from a lightly seated position for DT25 models. Recommended idle speed is 600-650 rpm in gear with engine at normal operating temperature.

With the outboard motor properly mounted on a boat or a suitable test tank, immerse the lower unit. Remove engine top cover. Connect a tachometer and set it on the appropriate range scale. Start the engine and allow it to warm up to normal operating temperature. Position the throttle control twist grip to the complete closed position. Place the gear shift in the "Forward" position. Adjust the engine idle speed screw (3) until the engine is idling at 600-650 rpm, then adjust idle mixture screw (5) until smooth engine operation is noted. Readjust the engine idle speed screw (3) until the recommended idle speed is obtained.

Reinstall engine top cover.

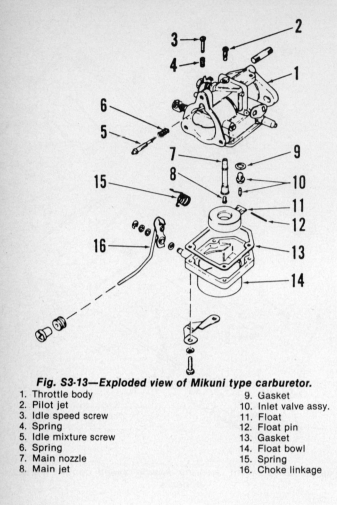

Fig. S3-13—Exploded view of Mikuni type carburetor.

1. Throttle body
2. Pilot jet
3. Idle speed screw
4. Spring
5. Idle mixture screw
6. Spring
7. Main nozzle
8. Main jet
9. Gasket
10. Inlet valve assy.
11. Float
12. Float pin
13. Gasket
14. Float bowl
15. Spring
16. Choke linkage

OVERHAUL. Remove engine's top cover. Remove air intake outer cap. Bend tabs of air intake lockplate away from heads of securing cap screws, then remove the three cap screws securing the air intake to the carburetor. Remove the choke knob and detach throttle linkage from carburetor. Disconnect the fuel tank supply hose at the outboard motor connector. Disconnect the fuel supply hose at the carburetor inlet. Clean all external surfaces and remove accumulated dirt and grease. Remove the two nuts securing the carburetor and withdraw the carburetor assembly.

With reference to Fig. S3-13, disassemble the complete carburetor assembly and note any

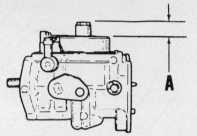

Fig. S3-14—Float level (A) should be 10.4-12.4 mm (0.41-0.49 in.). Refer to text.

discrepancies which must be corrected before reassembly. Remove float bowl gasket (13) and inlet valve gasket (9) and set to the side for future reference.

Thoroughly clean all carburetor parts in a suitable solvent and inspect for damage and excessive wear. Blow dry with clean compressed air. If compressed air is not available, use only lint-free cloths to wipe dry. Do not use a drill bit or wire to clean jets. Enlargement or damage of the calibrated holes may affect engine performance.

With reference to Fig. S3-13, reassemble the carburetor components with new gaskets. Note that the new gaskets should match up with those removed. If not, check with your parts supplier to be sure you have the correct gaskets.

To determine the float level, invert the carburetor body (1 — Fig. S3-13) and measure the distance (A — Fig. S3-14) from the base of the main jet to the base of the float. The distance should be 10.4-12.4 mm (0.41-0.49 in.). Adjust the float level by bending float tang.

Reinstall the carburetor with a new gasket and securely tighten the retaining nuts. Reconnect the fuel supply hose. Mount air intake assembly, connect throttle linkage and install choke knob. Initially adjust idle mixture screw (5 — Fig. S3-13) 1½-2 turns out from a lightly seated position for DT20 models and 1¼-1¾ turns out from a lightly seated position for DT25 models. Perform final carburetor adjustments as outlined in ADJUSTMENT section.

TOHATSU

TOHATSU U.S.A.
1211 Avenue of the Americas
New York, NY 10036

TOHATSU 3½ HP

NOTE: Metric fasteners are used throughout outboard motor.

Specifications

Hp/rpm..3.5/4750
Bore..47 mm
(1.85 in.)
Stroke..43 mm
(1.69 in.)
Displacement..74.6 cc
(4.5 cu. in.)
Number of cylinders..1
Spark plug:
  NGK...B7HS
  Champion...L81Y
  Electrode gap...................................0.6-0.7 mm
(0.024-0.027 in.)
Breaker point gap...............................0.3-0.4 mm
(0.012-0.016 in.)
Ignition timing...Fixed
Carburetor:
  Make...TK
  Model...K13PA-1A
Idle speed..................................1100-1300 rpm
Fuel:oil ratio...50:1
Gearcase oil capacity................................90 mL
(3 oz.)

Maintenance

LUBRICATION

ENGINE. The engine is lubricated by oil mixed with the fuel. Recommended oil is Tohatsu outboard motor oil or a BIA certified two-stroke motor oil. The recommended fuel:oil ratio for normal operation is 50:1. During engine break-in, the fuel:oil ratio should be increased to 20:1 for a period of 10 operating hours.

LOWER UNIT. The lower unit gears and bearings are lubricated by oil contained in the gearcase. The recommended oil is Tohatsu gear oil or a suitable EP 80 outboard gear oil. The gearcase oil capacity is 90 milliliters (3 oz.). The gearcase should be refilled after every 50 hours of operation and the lubricant renewed after every 200 hours of operation or more frequently if needed. The gearcase can only be drained and filled after removing propeller (1—Fig. T1-1), water pump housing cover (5), impeller (7) and water pump housing (9).

To remove components to drain and/or fill gearcase, proceed as follows: Remove cotter pin (2) and withdraw propeller (1) from propeller shaft (4). Remove shear pin (3), then remove cap screws (6) and withdraw water pump housing cover (5). Ex-

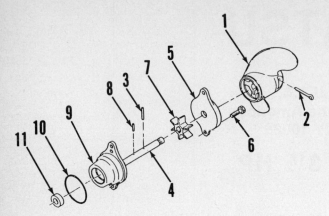

Fig. T1-1—Exploded view showing outer gearcase components. Text outlines removal of components for draining and/or filling gearcase.

1. Propeller
2. Cotter pin
3. Shear pin
4. Propeller shaft
5. Cover
6. Cap screw
7. Impeller
8. Pin
9. Water pump housing
10. "O" ring
11. Seal

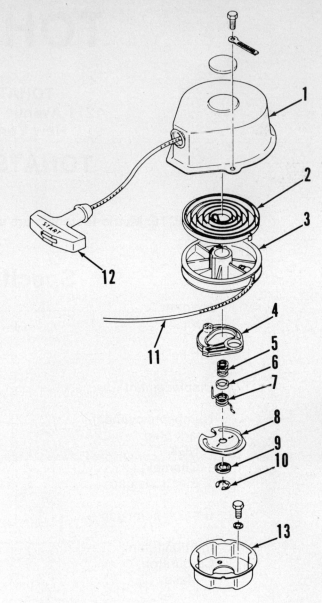

Fig. T1-2 — Exploded view of manual starter assembly.

1. Housing
2. Rewind spring
3. Pulley
4. Ratchet
5. Spring
6. Sleeve
7. Return spring
8. Friction plate
9. Thrust washer
10. Clip
11. Starter rope
12. Handle
13. Starter pulley

tract impeller (7) and pin (8) from propeller shaft (4). Remove water pump housing (9).

Drain and/or fill gearcase as needed. Renew any components if needed. Reverse disassembly prodecure for reassembly. Securely tighten cap screws (6) and install a new cotter pin (2).

FUEL SYSTEM

Periodically inspect the fuel tank and fuel lines for damage. Renew components if needed. After closing the fuel valve, occasionally remove the carburetor float bowl drain plug and allow the fuel to drain off into a suitable container. Inspect fuel for any foreign matter. If an excessive amount of foreign matter is found, extensive cleaning of the fuel system is needed.

Keep the external surface of the carburetor clean and all connections and sealing surfaces tight.

Refer to CARBURETOR in the Tune-Up section for checking float bowl fuel level.

STARTER

When the starter rope (11 — Fig. T1-2) is pulled, pulley (3) will rotate. As pulley (3) rotates, ratchet (4) moves to engage with starter pulley (13), thus cranking the engine.

When starter rope (11) is released, pulley (3) is rotated in the reverse direction by force from rewind spring (2). As pulley (3) rotates, the starter rope is rewound and ratchet (4) is disengaged from starter pulley (13).

The manual starter must be disassembled to renew starter rope (11) and internal starter components.

To overhaul the manual starter, proceed as follows: Remove the screws retaining the engine port and starboard side covers, then withdraw covers. Remove the screws retaining the manual starter assembly to the power head and withdraw.

⚠**WARNING**

Care should be exercised when working with or around a coiled starter rewind spring as sudden uncoiling can cause injury. Safety eyewear and gloves are recommended.

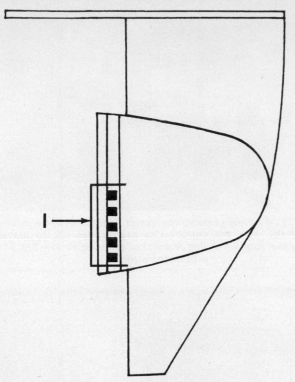

Fig. T1-3 — Cooling system water inlet ports (I) are located on the starboard side of the lower unit gearcase.

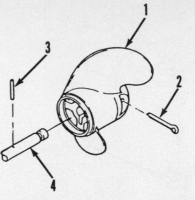

Fig. T1-4 — Propeller (1) is mounted on propeller shaft (4) and is retained by cotter pin (2). Shear pin (3) is renewed only after withdrawing propeller (1) from propeller shaft (4).

To disassemble, untie starter rope (11) at handle (12) and allow rope to wind into the starter. Invert the unit and remove clip (10), then withdraw thrust washer (9), friction plate (8), return spring (7), sleeve (6), spring (5) and ratchet (4). Remove pulley (3) while being careful not to dislodge rewind spring (2). Remove starter rope (11) from pulley (3) if renewal is required. If rewind spring (2) must be removed, care must be used to prevent spring from uncoiling uncontrolled.

Reassembly is the reverse order of disassembly. Apply a water-resistant grease to rewind spring area of starter housing (1). Install rewind spring (2) with coils wrapped in a counterclockwise direction from outer spring end. Wrap starter rope (11) around pulley (3) in a counterclockwise direction when viewed from the bottom side. Install pulley (3) in starter housing (1) making sure pulley properly engages rewind spring (2). Thread rope end through starter housing (1) and secure on handle (12).

NOTE: Lubricate all friction surfaces with a suitable water-resistant grease during reassembly.

Install ratchet (4) so ratchet tooth points counterclockwise when viewed from the bottom side. Assemble remaining components. Apply tension to rewind spring (2) by engaging starter rope (11) in pulley (3) notch and turning pulley counterclockwise, then release starter rope (11) from pulley notch.

NOTE: Do not apply any more tension on rewind spring (2) than is required to draw starter handle (12) back into the proper released position.

Check starter action, then remount manual starter assembly and engine side covers to complete reassembly.

COOLING SYSTEM

Ports (I-Fig. T1-3) located on the starboard side of the lower unit gearcase are used as the water inlets for the cooling system. The ports must be kept clean of all foreign matter to ensure efficient operation of the cooling system.

⚠CAUTION

Do not operate outboard motor unless the lower unit is immersed in water, otherwise, the water pump impeller will be damaged.

PROPELLER

The standard propeller has two blades, a diameter of 180 mm (7 in.) and a pitch of 166 mm (6½ in.).

⚠WARNING

Remove spark plug leads and properly ground leads before performing any propeller service, otherwise, accidental starting can occur if propeller shaft is rotated.

To remove the propeller, remove cotter pin (2 — Fig.T1-4) and withdraw propeller (1) from propeller shaft (4).

Illustrations Courtesy Tohatsu

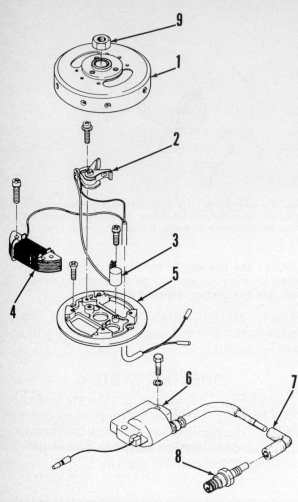

Fig. T1-5 — Exploded view of flywheel magneto unit.

1. Flywheel
2. Breaker point assy.
3. Condenser
4. Exciter coil
5. Magneto base plate
6. Ignition coil
7. Spark plug boot
8. Spark plug
9. Nut

Inspect propeller (1) and shear pin (3) for damage and excessive wear and renew if needed.

Apply a water-resistant grease to the propeller bore, then install propeller (1) on propeller shaft (4) and retain with a new cotter pin (2).

Tune-Up

IGNITION SYSTEM

The standard spark plug is NGK B7HS or Champion L81Y with an electrode gap of 0.6-0.7 mm (0.024-0.027 in.).

The breaker point gap should be 0.3-0.4 mm (0.012-0.016 in.) and can be inspected and adjusted through the opening in flywheel (1 — Fig. T1-5). To inspect and, if needed, adjust the breaker point gap, first remove the screws retaining the engine port and starboard side covers, then withdraw covers. Remove the screws retaining the manual starter assembly to the power head

Fig. T1-6 — View showing the use of Tohatsu flywheel holding tool (H), with the correct size cap screws (C), to prevent flywheel rotation during removal of securing nut (9 — Fig. T1-5) with suitable tools (T).

Fig. T1-7 — Remove flywheel (1 — Fig. T1-5) from crankshaft end using Tohatsu puller assembly (P), correct size cap screws (C) and suitable tools (T).

and withdraw. Remove the screws and lockwashers securing starter pulley (13 — Fig. T1-2) to flywheel (1 — Fig. T1-5) and withdraw.

Inspect the breaker point surfaces for excessive wear, pitting and damage. If needed, renew breaker point assembly (2) and condenser (3) as outlined later in this section.

To clean the breaker point contact surfaces, use a point file or sandpaper with a grit rating of 400 to 600. After polishing, wipe the contact surfaces clean with a dry cloth and lightly grease the breaker point arm with a suitable lubricant.

Turn the flywheel until the breaker point contact surfaces are at their widest position. Reach through the flywheel opening with a feeler gage of the appropriate size and check the distance between the point surfaces. If the distance is not within the recommended limits, loosen the point set securing screw and adjust the point set until the correct gap is obtained. Tighten the point set securing screw and recheck the breaker point gap. Repeat the adjustment procedure, if needed, until the correct breaker point gap is obtained.

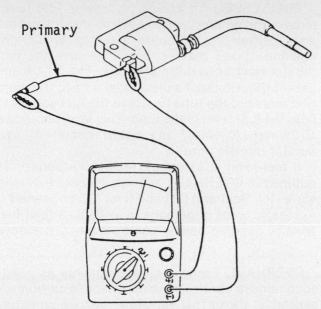

Fig. T1-8 — Connect ohmmeter leads as shown to measure the resistance in the primary side of the ignition coil. Refer to text.

To renew breaker point assembly (2) and condenser (3), proceed as follows: Using Tohatsu flywheel holding tool (H — Fig. T1-6) or a suitable equivalent and the proper size cap screws (C), remove flywheel securing nut (9 — Fig. T1-5) using suitable tools (T — Fig. T1-6). Remove flywheel (1 — Fig. T1-5) from crankshaft end using Tohatsu puller assembly (P — Fig. T1-7) or a suitable equivalent, cap screws (C) and tools (T). Note flywheel key located in crankshaft keyway.

⚠ WARNING

Be sure suitable tools are used to remove the flywheel. Damage resultant from the misapplication of force or the use of incorrect tools may cause engine damage, engine malfunction or personal injury.

With reference to Fig. T1-5, renew breaker point assembly (2) and condenser (3). Adjust the breaker point gap to the recommended setting as previously outlined. Make sure the securing screws are properly tightened. Be sure the flywheel key is properly positioned in the crankshaft keyway, then reinstall flywheel (1). Tighten securing nut (9) to 39.2-44.1 N·m (29-33 ft.-lbs.).

Magneto base plate (5) is fixed to the engine with tapered screws and no timing adjustment is possible other than varying the breaker point gap between the recommended limits of 0.3-0.4 mm (0.012-0.016 in.). Breaker point contacts should open when piston is 18°-20°BTDC or 1.2-2.0 mm

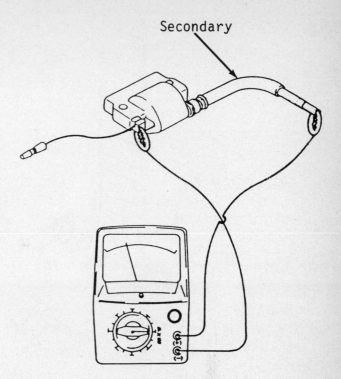

Fig. T1-9 — Connect ohmmeter leads as shown to measure the resistance in the secondary side of the ignition coil. Refer to text.

(0.047-0.079 in.) BTDC. A suitable degree wheel on the flywheel or a dial indicator in the spark plug hole may be used to verify piston position when breaker point contacts open.

Ignition Coil. To check ignition coil (6 — Fig. T1-5) located on the side of the engine cylinder, use a suitable ohmmeter. Connect one tester lead to the coil's metal laminations, then connect the remaining tester lead alternately to the primary (Fig. T1-8) and secondary (Fig. T1-9) ignition coil leads. Resistance reading for primary circuit should be 0.81-1.09 ohms while the secondary circuit resistance reading should be 4250-5750 ohms. Renew ignition coil (6 — Fig. T1-5) if meter readings are not within the proper range.

SPEED CONTROL LINKAGE

The engine speed is regulated by the position of throttle lever (12 — Fig. T1-10). As throttle lever (12) is raised or lowered, the carburetor throttle slide (9) is operated via throttle wire (1). An engine kill switch is mounted on carburetor control cover.

CARBURETOR

ADJUSTMENT. Standard carburetor is a TK Model K13PA-1A. Standard main jet (19-Fig. T1-10) size is #88 for normal operation. Preliminary positioning of clip (7) in jet needle (8) is one of the middle grooves. Inserting clip (7) in a higher notch will

---

Tohatsu 3½ Hp

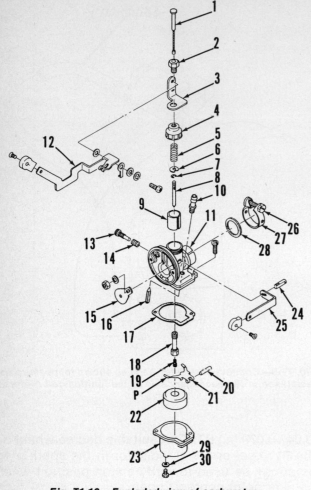

Fig. T1-10 — Exploded view of carburetor.

1. Throttle wire
2. Guide screw
3. Bracket
4. Cap
5. Spring
6. Retainer
7. Clip
8. Jet needle
9. Throttle slide
10. Fuel inlet
11. Body
12. Throttle lever
13. Idle speed screw
14. Spring
15. Choke plate
16. Fuel inlet valve
17. Gasket
18. Needle jet
19. Main jet
20. Float arm pin
21. Float arm
22. Float
23. Float bowl
24. Shaft
25. Choke lever
26. Cap screw
27. Clamp
28. Gasket
29. Gasket
30. Drain plug

lean mid-range mixture while inserting clip in a lower notch will richen mid-range mixture. Recommended idle speed is 1100-1300 rpm with engine at normal operating temperature.

Properly mount the outboard motor on a boat or a suitable test tank and immerse the lower unit. Connect a tachometer and set it on the appropriate range scale. Start the engine and allow it to warm up to normal operating temperature. Position the throttle control lever to the complete closed position, then adjust the engine idle speed screw (13) until the engine is idling at 1100-1300 rpm.

FUEL LEVEL. To check carburetor fuel level, remove the engine port and starboard side covers and position the outboard motor in an upright position. Close the fuel valve. Remove the carburetor float bowl drain plug (30 – Fig. T1-10) and gasket (29). Connect a clear vinyl tube to the drain port and hold the tube up. Open the fuel valve and note the fuel level in the tube. Fuel level should be 20-22 mm (0.79-0.87 in.) below center of carburetor throttle bore.

If fuel level is incorrect, remove carburetor as outlined in OVERHAUL section. Inspect fuel inlet valve (16), float arm (21) and float (22) and renew if excessive wear or damage is evident. Adjust fuel level by bending pads (P) on float arm (21) evenly.

OVERHAUL. Remove all components as needed to remove control panel and expose carburetor assembly. Close fuel valve and remove all external components that will interfere with carburetor removal.

Clean all external surfaces and remove accumulated dirt and grease. Loosen cap screw (26 – Fig. T1-10) and withdraw carburetor assembly. With reference to Fig. T1-10, disassemble carburetor and note any discrepancies which must be corrected before reassembly. Remove all gaskets (label if needed for later reference) and set to the side.

Thoroughly clean all carburetor parts in a suitable solvent and inspect for damage and excessive wear. Blow dry with clean compressed air. If compressed air is not available, use only lint-free cloths to wipe dry. Do not use a drill bit or wire to clean jets. Enlargement or damage of the calibrated holes may affect engine performance.

With reference to Fig. T1-10, reassemble the carburetor components with new gaskets. Note that the new gaskets should match up with those removed. If not, check with your parts supplier to be sure you have the correct gasket set.

When reinstalling the carburetor, place a new gasket (28) inside the carburetor bore, then install the carburetor on spigot end of crankcase half. Lightly push the carburetor towards the crankcase until the gasket is properly seated against spigot end. Tighten cap screw (26) until the carburetor retaining clamp (27) is tight. Be sure the carburetor is in a vertical position. Verify carburetor fuel level as outlined in the FUEL LEVEL section and note if fuel level adjustment is needed. Remove carburetor and adjust pads (P) of float arm (21) evenly until proper setting is obtained. Completely reassemble the engine with the exception of the engine side covers. Perform final carburetor adjustments as outlined in ADJUSTMENT section.

Illustrations Courtesy Tohatsu

TOHATSU 5 HP

NOTE: Metric fasteners are used throughout outboard motor.

Specifications

Hp/rpm 5/5000
Bore . . . . .52 mm
(2.04 in.)
Stroke . . . . .43 mm
(1.69 in.)
Displacement . . . . .91 cc
(5.5 cu. in.)
Number of cylinders 2
Spark plug:
  NGK B7HS
  Champion L81Y
  Electrode gap . . . . .0.6-0.7 mm
(0.024-0.027 in.)
Breaker point gap . . . . .0.3-0.4 mm
(0.012-0.016 in.)
Ignition timing (BTDC) . . . . .See Text
Carburetor:
  Make . . . . .TK
  Model R14F-2A
Idle speed . . . . .1100-1200 rpm
Fuel:oil ratio 50:1
Gearcase oil capacity . . . . .80 mL
(2.7 oz.)

Maintenance

LUBRICATION

ENGINE. The engine is lubricated by oil mixed with the fuel. Recommended oil is Tohatsu outboard motor oil or a BIA certified two-stroke motor oil. The recommended fuel:oil ratio for normal operation is 50:1. During engine break-in, the fuel:oil ratio should be increased to 20:1 for a period of 10 operating hours.

LOWER UNIT. The lower unit gears and bearings are lubricated by oil contained in the gearcase. The recommended oil is Tohatsu gear oil or a suitable EP 80 outboard gear oil. The gearcase oil capacity is 80 milliliters (2.7 oz.). The gearcase should be refilled after every 50 hours of operation and the lubricant renewed after every 200 hours of operation or more frequently if needed. The gearcase is drained and filled through the same plug port (D—Fig. T2-1). An oil level (vent) port (L) is used to identify the full oil level of the gearcase oil and to ease oil drainage.

To drain the oil, place the outboard motor in a vertical position. Remove drain plug (D) and oil level plug (L) and allow the lubricant to drain into a suitable container.

To fill the gearcase with oil, place the outboard motor in a vertical position. Add oil through drain plug (D) opening with an oil feeder until the oil begins to overflow from oil level plug (L) port. Reinstall oil level plug (L) with a new gasket, if needed, and tighten. Remove oil feeder, then reinstall drain plug (D) with a new gasket, if needed, and tighten.

FUEL SYSTEM

Periodically inspect the fuel tank and fuel lines for damage. Renew components if needed. After closing the fuel valve, occasionally remove the carburetor float bowl drain plug and allow the fuel to drain off into a suitable container. Inspect fuel for any foreign matter. If an excessive amount of foreign matter is found, extensive cleaning of the fuel system is needed.

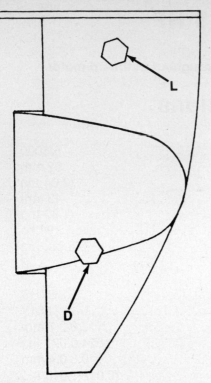

Fig. T2-1—View showing lower unit gearcase drain and fill plug (D) and oil level (vent) plug (L).

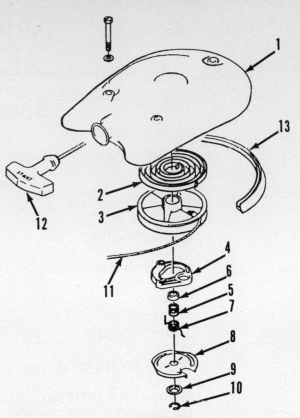

Fig. T2-2—Exploded view of manual starter assembly.

1. Starter housing		
2. Rewind spring	6. Sleeve	10. Clip
3. Pulley	7. Return spring	11. Starter rope
4. Ratchet	8. Friction plate	12. Handle
5. Spring	9. Thrust washer	13. Seal

Keep the external surface of the carburetor clean and all connections and sealing surfaces tight.

Refer to CARBURETOR in the Tune-Up section for checking float bowl fuel level.

FUEL TANK. It may be necessary to remove the fuel tank for cleaning or for access to underlying engine components. The manual starter is attached to the top of the fuel tank. The fuel tank assembly serves as the top engine cover.

To remove the fuel tank, first remove the three cap screws retaining the manual starter, then withdraw the starter assembly. Remove carrying handle, rear cover and any other component that will interfere with removal of engine port and starboard side covers. Remove screws retaining engine side covers and withdraw covers. Close fuel valve and disconnect fuel hose, then remove the four cap screws securing the fuel tank and withdraw fuel tank.

Installation is reverse order of removal.

SHIFT LINKAGE

Directional control is selected by the position of a gear shift lever. The lever operates an upper and lower shift rod connected by a clevis pin and bracket. The tapered end of the lower shift rod controls the movement of the dog clutch on the propeller shaft. The positioning of the dog clutch on the propeller shaft determines whether for-

ward, neutral or reverse directional movement is selected.

No adjustment of the linkage is provided. Should improper engagement or disengagement be noted, examination of components for damage and excessive wear must be performed.

STARTER

When starter rope (11—Fig. T2-2) is pulled, pulley (3) will rotate. As pulley (3) rotates, ratchet (4) moves to engage with the starter pulley, thus cranking the engine.

When starter rope (11) is released, pulley (3) is rotated in the reverse direction by force from rewind spring (2). As pulley (3) rotates, the starter rope is rewound and ratchet (4) is disengaged from the starter pulley.

The manual starter must be disassembled to renew starter rope (11) or any other internal starter component.

To overhaul the manual starter, proceed as follows: Remove the three cap screws retaining the manual starter, then withdraw the starter assembly.

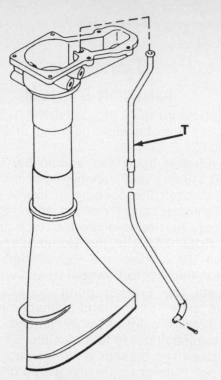

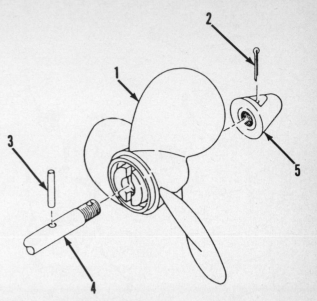

Fig. T2-3 — Water tube (T) directs cooling water from the aft of the antiventilation plate to the engine mount plate, thus cooling the engine crankcase and exhaust port.

Fig. T2-4 — Propeller (1) is mounted on propeller shaft (4) and is retained by spinner (5) and cotter pin (2). Shear pin (3) is renewed only after withdrawing propeller (1) from propeller shaft (4).

⚠ **WARNING**

Care should be exercised when working with or around a coiled starter rewind spring as sudden uncoiling can cause injury. Safety eyewear and gloves are recommended.

To disassemble, untie starter rope (11) at handle (12) and allow rope to wind into the starter. Invert the unit and remove clip (10), then withdraw thrust washer (9), friction plate (8), return spring (7), sleeve (6), spring (5) and ratchet (4). Remove pulley (3) while being careful not to dislodge rewind spring (2). Remove starter rope (11) from pulley (3) if renewal is required. If rewind spring (2) must be removed, care must be used to prevent spring from uncoiling uncontrolled.

Reassembly is the reverse order of disassembly. Apply a water-resistant grease to rewind spring area of starter housing (1). Install rewind spring (2) with coils wrapped in a counterclockwise direction from outer spring end. Wrap starter rope (11) around pulley (3) in a counterclockwise direction when viewed from the bottom side. Install pulley (3) in starter housing (1) making sure pulley properly engages rewind spring (2). Thread rope end

through starter housing (1) and secure on handle (12).

NOTE: Lubricate all friction surfaces with a suitable water-resistant grease during reassembly.

Install ratchet (4) so ratchet tooth points counterclockwise when viewed from the bottom side. Assemble remaining components. Apply tension to rewind spring (2) by engaging starter rope (11) in pulley (3) notch and turning pulley counterclockwise, then release starter rope (11) from pulley notch.

NOTE: Do not apply any more tension on rewind spring (2) than is required to draw starter handle (12) back into the proper released position.

Check starter action, then remount manual starter assembly to complete reassembly.

COOLING SYSTEM

The engine cylinder and cylinder head are air-cooled by the flywheel fan. Make sure that the flywheel cooling fins and the cylinder fins are unobstructed. To prevent possible overheating, do not attempt to run the engine for an extended period without the engine covers in place.

The engine crankcase and exhaust port areas are cooled by water directed at the engine mount plate. Cooling water is directed by a water tube (T — Fig. T2-3) from the aft of the antiventilation plate to the engine mount plate. Water pressure is obtained from water forced past the propeller. The water tube must be kept clean of any blockage.

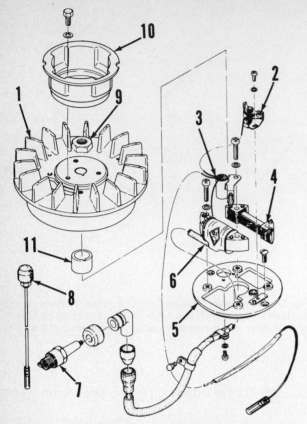

Fig. T2-5 — Exploded view of flywheel magneto unit.

1. Flywheel
2. Breaker point assy.
3. Condenser
4. Lighting coil
5. Magneto base plate
6. Ignition coil
7. Spark plug
8. Engine kill switch
9. Nut
10. Starter pulley
11. Breaker point cam

PROPELLER

The standard propeller has three blades, a diameter of 188 mm (7-13/32 in.) and a pitch of 157 mm (6-3/16 in.).

⚠️WARNING

Shift directional control lever to "NEUTRAL." Remove spark plug leads and properly ground leads before performing any propeller service, otherwise, accidental starting can occur if propeller shaft is rotated.

To remove the propeller, remove cotter pin (2 — Fig. T2-4) and unscrew propeller spinner (5). Withdraw propeller (1) from propeller shaft (4).

Inspect propeller (1), propeller shaft (4) and shear pin (3) for excessive wear and renew if needed.

Apply a water-resistant grease to the propeller bore, then install propeller (1) on propeller shaft (4)

and retain with propeller spinner (5) and a new cotter pin (2).

Tune-Up

IGNITION SYSTEM

The standard spark plug is NGK B7HS or Champion L81Y with an electrode gap of 0.6-0.7 mm (0.024-0.027 in.).

The breaker point gap should be 0.3-0.4 mm (0.012-0.016 in.) and can be inspected and adjusted through the opening in flywheel (1 — Fig. T2-5). To inspect and, if needed, adjust the breaker point gap, first remove the fuel tank as outlined under FUEL TANK in the Maintenance section. Remove the screws and lockwashers securing starter pulley (10) to flywheel (1) and withdraw.

Inspect the breaker point surfaces for excessive wear, pitting and damage. If needed, renew breaker point assembly (2) and condenser (3) as outlined later in this section.

To clean the breaker point contact surfaces, use a point file or sandpaper with a grit rating of 400 to 600. After polishing, wipe the contact surfaces clean with a dry cloth and lightly grease the breaker point arm with a suitable lubricant.

Turn the flywheel until the breaker point contact surfaces are at their widest position. Reach through the flywheel opening with a feeler gage of the appropriate size and check the distance between the point surfaces. If the distance is not within the recommended limits, loosen the point set securing screw and adjust the point set until the correct gap is obtained. Tighten the point set securing screw and recheck the breaker point gap. Repeat the adjustment procedure, if needed, until the correct breaker point gap is obtained.

To renew breaker point assembly (2) and condenser (3), proceed as follows: Reinstall starter pulley (10). Using Tohatsu flywheel holding tool (H — Fig. T2-6) or a suitable equivalent, remove securing nut (9 — Fig. T2-5) using suitable tools (T — Fig. T2-6). Remove flywheel (1 — Fig. T2-7) from crankshaft end using Tohatsu puller assembly (P) or a suitable equivalent with suitable tools (T). Note flywheel key located in crankshaft keyway.

⚠️WARNING

Be sure suitable tools are used to remove the flywheel. Damage resultant from the misapplication of force or the use of incorrect tools may cause engine damage, engine malfunction or personal injury.

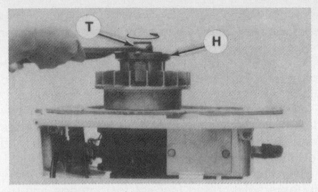

Fig. T2-6 — View showing the use of Tohatsu flywheel holding tool (H) to prevent flywheel rotation during removal of securing nut (9 — Fig. T2-5) with suitable tools (T).

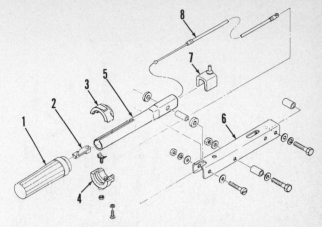

Fig. T2-8 — View of speed control linkage components.

1. Twist grip	5. Steering handle
2. Slider	6. Handle bracket
3. Upper retainer half	7. Cushion
4. Lower retainer half	8. Control cable

With reference to Fig. T2-5, renew breaker point assembly (2) and condenser (3). Adjust the breaker point gap to the recommended setting as previously outlined. Make sure the securing screws are properly tightened. Be sure the flywheel key is properly positioned in crankshaft keyway, then reinstall flywheel (1). Tighten flywheel securing nut (9) to 59-78 N·m (43-57 ft.-lbs.).

Magneto base plate (5) is fixed to the engine with tapered screws and no timing adjustment is possible other than varying the breaker point gap between the recommended limits of 0.3-0.4 mm (0.012-0.016 in.). Breaker point contacts should open when piston is 27°-31° BTDC or 2.9-3.7 mm (0.114-0.146 in.) BTDC. A suitable degree wheel on the flywheel or a idal indicator in the spark plug hole may be used to verify piston position when breaker point contacts open.

SPEED CONTROL LINKAGE

The engine speed is regulated by the position of the carburetor throttle slide (6 — Fig. T2-9). Throttle slide (6) is controlled by twist grip (1 — Fig. T2-8) via control cable (8). An engine kill switch (8 — Fig. T2-5) is used to stop engine operation.

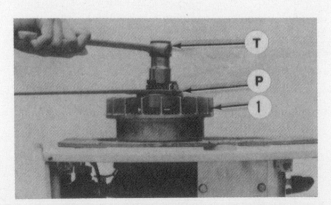

Fig. T2-7 — Remove flywheel (1) from crankshaft end using Tohatsu puller assembly (P) and suitable tools (T).

CARBURETOR

ADJUSTMENT. Standard carburetor is a TK Model R14F-2A. Standard main jet (22 — Fig. T2-9) size is #90 for normal operation. Preliminary positioning of clip (4) in jet needle (5) is in the middle groove. Inserting clip (4) in a higher notch will lean mid-range mixture while inserting clip in a lower notch will richen mid-range mixture. Recommended idle speed is 1100-1200 rpm with engine at normal operating temperature.

Properly mount the outboard motor on a boat or a suitable test tank and immerse the lower unit. Connect a tachometer and set it on the appropriate range scale. Start the engine and allow it to warm up to normal operating temperature. Turn the twist grip to the complete closed position, then adjust the engine idle speed screw (8) until the engine is idling at 1100-1200 rpm.

FUEL LEVEL. To check carburetor fuel level, remove the engine port and starboard side covers and position the outboard motor in an upright position. Close the fuel valve. Remove the carburetor float bowl drain plug (26 — Fig. T2-9) and gasket (27). Connect a clear vinyl tube to the drain port and hold the tube up. Open the fuel valve and note the fuel level in the tube. Fuel level should be 17.5 mm (0.69 in.) below center of carburetor throttle bore.

If fuel level is incorrect, remove carburetor as outlined in OVERHAUL section. Inspect fuel inlet valve (18), float arm (20) and float (23) and renew if excessive wear or damage is evident. Adjust fuel level by bending pads (P) on float arm (20) evenly.

OVERHAUL. Remove air intake cover half (33 — Fig. T2-9), filter element (32) and inner cover

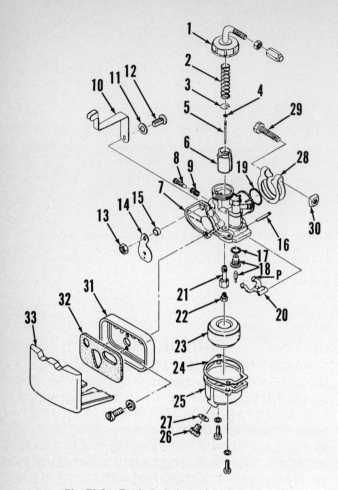

Fig. T2-9 — Exploded view of carburetor.

1. Cap	12. Special screw	23. Float
2. Spring	13. Locknut	24. Gasket
3. Retainer	14. Choke plate	25. Float bowl
4. Clip	15. Sleeve	26. Drain plug
5. Jet needle	16. Float pin	27. Gasket
6. Throttle slide	17. Gasket	28. Clamp
7. Body	18. Fuel inlet valve	29. Bolt
8. Idle speed screw	19. "O" ring	30. Nut
9. Spring	20. Float arm	31. Inner cover half
10. Choke lever	21. Needle jet	32. Filter element
11. Washer	22. Main jet	33. Outer cover half

half (31). Close fuel valve and remove all external components that will interfere with carburetor removal.

Clean all external surfaces and remove accumulated dirt and grease. Loosen bolt (29) and withdraw carburetor assembly. With reference to Fig. T2-9, disassemble carburetor and note any discrepancies which must be corrected before reassembly. Remove all gaskets (label if needed for later reference) and set to the side.

Thoroughly clean all carburetor parts in a suitable solvent and inspect for damage and excessive wear. Blow dry with clean compressed air. If compressed air is not available, use only lint-free cloths to wipe dry. Do not use a drill bit or wire to clean jets. Enlargement or damage of the calibrated holes may affect engine performance.

With reference to Fig. T2-9, reassemble the carburetor components with new gaskets. Note that the new gaskets should match up with those removed. If not, check with your parts supplier to be sure you have the correct gasket set.

When reinstalling the carburetor, place a new "O" ring (19) inside the carburetor bore, then install the carburetor on spigot end of intake manifold. Lightly push the carburetor towards the intake manifold until the gasket is properly seated against spigot end. Tighten bolt (29) until the carburetor retaining clamp (28) is tight. Be sure the carburetor is in a vertical position. Verify carburetor fuel level as outlined in the FUEL LEVEL section and note if fuel level adjustment is needed. Remove carburetor and adjust pads (P) on float arm (20) evenly until proper setting is obtained. Completely reassemble the engine with the exception of the engine side covers. Perform final carburetor adjustments as outlined in ADJUSTMENT section.

TOHATSU 8 AND 9.8 HP

Note: Metric fasteners are used throughout outboard motor.

Specifications

	8 Hp	9.8 Hp
Hp/rpm	8/6000	9.8/5000
Bore	45 mm	52 mm
	(1.77 in.)	(2.04 in.)
Stroke	43 mm	43 mm
	(1.69 in.)	(1.69 in.)
Displacement	137 cc	183 cc
	(8.4 cu. in.)	(11.2 cu. in.)
Number of cylinders	2	2
Spark plug:		
NGK	B7HS	B7HS
Electrode gap	0.6-0.7 mm	0.6-0.7 mm
	(0.024-0.027 in.)	(0.024-0.027 in.)
Breaker point gap	0.3-0.4 mm	0.3-0.4 mm
	(0.012-0.016 in.)	(0.012-0.016 in.)
Ignition timing (BTDC)	23½-26½°	23½-26½°
Carburetor:		
Make	TK	TK
Model	PA17C-4	PA17C-4
Idle speed (in gear)	1100-1200 rpm	1100-1200 rpm
Fuel:oll ratio	50:1	50:1
Gearcase oil capacity	185 mL	185 mL
	(6.25 oz.)	(6.25 oz.)

Maintenance

LUBRICATION

ENGINE. The engine is lubricated by oil mixed with the fuel. Recommended oil is Tohatsu outboard motor oil or a BIA certified two-stroke motor oil. The recommended fuel:oil ratio for normal operation is 50:1. During engine break-in, the fuel:oil ratio should be increased to 20:1 for a period of 10 operating hours.

LOWER UNIT. The lower unit gears and bearings are lubricated by oil contained in the gearcase. The recommended oil is Tohatsu gear oil or a suitable EP 80 outboard gear oil. The gearcase oil capacity is 185 milliliters (6.25 oz.). The gearcase should be refilled after every 50 hours of operation and the lubricant renewed after every 200 hours of operation or more frequently if needed. The gearcase is drained and filled through the same plug port (D—Fig. T3-1). An oil level (vent) port (L) is used to indicate the full oil level of the gearcase and to ease oil drainage.

To drain the oil, place the outboard motor in a vertical position. Remove drain plug (D) and oil

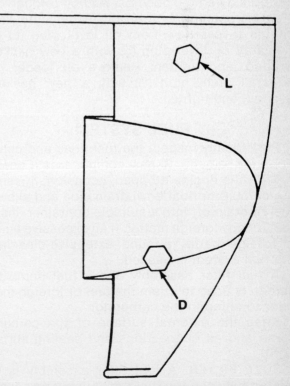

Fig. T3-1 — View showing lower unit gearcase drain and fill plug (D) and oil level (vent) plug (L).

Illustrations Courtesy Tohatsu

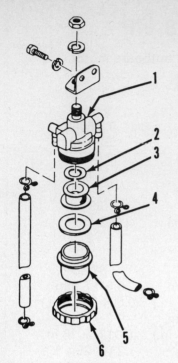

Fig. T3-2 — Exploded view of fuel filter assembly and related components.

1. Filter base
2. Gasket
3. Filter element
4. Gasket
5. Cup
6. Cup retainer

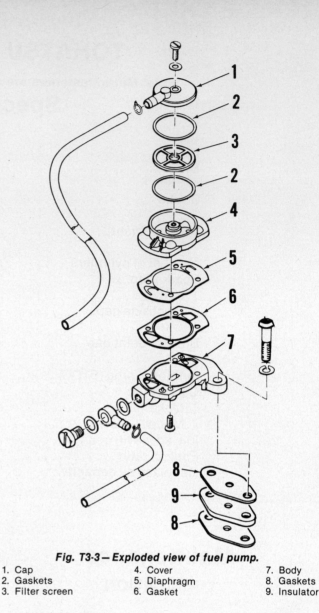

Fig. T3-3 — Exploded view of fuel pump.

1. Cap
2. Gaskets
3. Filter screen
4. Cover
5. Diaphragm
6. Gasket
7. Body
8. Gaskets
9. Insulator

level plug (L) and allow the lubricant to drain into a suitable container.

To fill the gearcase with oil, place the outboard motor in a vertical position. Add oil through drain plug (D) opening with an oil feeder until the oil begins to overflow from oil level plug (L) port. Reinstall oil level plug (L) with a new gasket, if needed, and tighten. Remove oil feeder, then reinstall drain plug (D) with a new gasket, if needed, and tighten.

FUEL SYSTEM

Periodically inspect the fuel lines and connections for damage. Renew components if needed.

With the engine stopped, occasionally remove the carburetor float bowl drain plug and allow the fuel to drain off into a suitable container. Inspect fuel for any foreign matter. If an excessive amount of foreign matter is found, extensive cleaning of the fuel system is needed.

A fuel filter assembly and a fuel pump filter screen is used to strain the fuel of foreign matter prior to entering the carburetor.

Keep the external surface of the carburetor clean and all connections and sealing surfaces tight.

FUEL FILTER. A fuel filter assembly is connected between the fuel tank supply line and the fuel pump inlet line. With the engine stopped, oc-

casionally unscrew the cup retainer (6 — Fig. T3-2) from filter base (1) and withdraw cup (5), gasket (4), filter element (3) and gasket (2). Clean cup (5) and filter element (3) in a suitable solvent and blow dry with clean compressed air. Inspect filter element (3). If excessive blockage or damage is noted, renew element.

Reassembly is reverse order of disassembly. Renew gaskets (2 and 4) during reassembly.

FUEL PUMP. A diaphragm type fuel pump is mounted on the starboard side of the upper cylinder. The fuel pump is operated by crankcase pressure changes from the up and down movement of the piston.

The fuel must enter cap (1 — Fig. T3-3) inlet nozzle and be discharged through nozzle mounted to body (7). The hoses must be connected accordingly.

To overhaul, first remove the engine top cover and disconnect the fuel tank supply hose at the outboard motor connector. Disconnect the fuel hoses at the fuel pump from the inlet and discharge nozzles and label if needed. Remove securing cap screws and withdraw fuel pump assembly.

With reference to Fig. T3-3, disassemble the fuel pump assembly. Inspect all components for damage and excessive wear and renew if needed. Clean filter screen (3) with a suitable cleaning solvent.

With reference to Fig. T3-3, reassemble the fuel pump assembly with new gaskets. Mount the fuel pump assembly to the crankcase with new gaskets (8) and securely tighten the retaining cap screws.

NOTE: Fuel pump and engine malfunction will result if the fuel pump and all connections are not airtight.

Complete reassembly.

SHIFT LINKAGE

Direction control is selected by the position of a gear shift lever. The lever operates an upper and lower shift rod connected by an adjustment nut (A — Fig. T3-4). The tapered end of the lower shift rod controls the movement of the dog clutch on the propeller shaft. The positioning of the dog clutch on the propeller shaft determines whether forward, neutral or reverse directional movement is selected.

To check shift linkage for proper adjustment, first place shift lever in reverse detent position. Check for proper engagement and propeller rotation by turning the propeller.

⚠WARNING

Remove spark plug leads and properly ground leads before performing any propeller service, otherwise, accidental starting can occur if propeller shaft is rotated.

Check for proper engagement of neutral and forward.

To adjust, loosen locknuts (N) and turn adjustment nut (A) until proper engagement of reverse, neutral and forward is obtained, then retighten locknuts (N).

NOTE: Upper locknut (N) has left-hand threads.

STARTER

When starter rope (3 — Fig. T3-5) is pulled, pulley (30) will rotate. As pulley (30) rotates, drive pawl

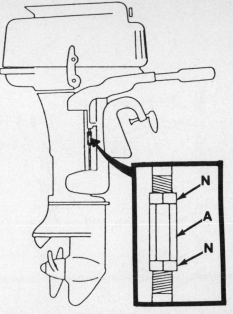

Fig. T3-4 — Loosen locknuts (N) and turn adjustment nut (A) to alter length of upper and lower shift rod. Adjust nut (A) until proper engagement of reverse, neutral and forward is obtained, then retighten locknuts (N). Note that upper locknut (N) has left-hand threads.

(27) moves to engage the starter pulley, thus cranking the engine.

When starter rope (3) is released, pulley (30) is rotated in the reverse direction by force from rewind spring (20). As pulley (30) rotates, the starter rope is rewound and drive pawl (27) is disengaged from the starter pulley.

A starter lockout assembly is used to prevent starter engagement when the gear shift lever is in the forward or reverse position.

To overhaul the manual starter, proceed as follows: Remove the engine top cover. Remove the screws retaining the manual starter to the engine. Remove starter lockout rod (16) from rod keeper (15). Withdraw the starter assembly.

⚠WARNING

Care should be exercised when working with or around a coiled starter rewind spring as sudden uncoiling can cause injury. Safety eyewear and gloves are recommended.

Check pawl (27) for freedom of movement and excessive wear or damage of engagement area. Renew or lubricate pawl (27) with a suitable water-resistant grease if needed.

To disassemble, remove clip (28) and withdraw pawl (27) and pawl springs (25 and 26). Untie starter rope (3) at anchor (1) and allow the rope to

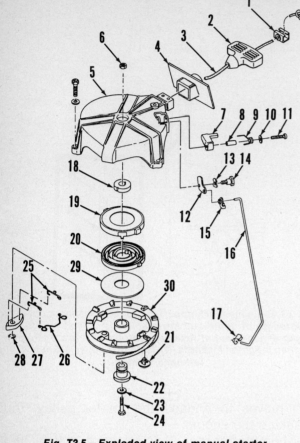

Fig. T3-5 — Exploded view of manual starter.

1. Anchor	11. Screw	21. Spring case stop
2. Handle	12. Cam	22. Spindle
3. Starter rope	13. Wave washer	23. Washer
4. Rope guide	14. Shoulder screw	24. Bolt
5. Starter housing	15. Rod keeper	25. Spring
6. Nut	16. Rod	26. Spring
7. Starter lock	17. Rod keeper	27. Pawl
8. Sleeve	18. Spring guide	28. Clip
9. Spring	19. Spring case	29. Washer
10. Washer	20. Rewind spring	30. Pulley

wind into the starter. Remove bolt (24), washer (23) and spindle (22). Carefully lift pulley (30) with starter rope (3) from housing (5). BE CAREFUL not to dislodge rewind spring (20) when removing pulley (30). Remove starter rope (3) from pulley (30) if renewal is required. If renewal of rewind spring (20) is required, use extreme caution when removing rewind spring (20) from spring case (19).

Inspect all components for damage and excessive wear and renew if needed.

To reassemble, first apply a coating of a suitable water-resistant grease to rewind spring area of spring case (19). Install rewind spring (20) in spring case (19) so spring coils wind in a counterclockwise direction from the outer end. Make sure the spring's outer hook is properly secured. Wind starter rope (3) onto pulley (30) 2-3 turns counterclockwise when viewed from flywheel side. Direct remaining starter rope (3) length through notch in pulley (30).

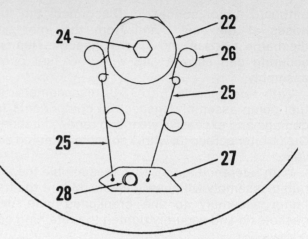

Fig. T3-6 — Drawing showing proper installation of starter pawl (27) and springs (25 and 26). Refer to Fig. T3-5 for complete identification of parts.

NOTE: Lubricate all friction surfaces with a suitable water-resistant grease during reassembly.

Assemble pulley (30) to starter housing making sure that pulley hub properly engages inner hook of rewind spring (20). Install spindle (22), washer (23) and bolt (24). Apply a suitable thread fastening solution on bolt (24) threads and install nut (6) and securely tighten.

Thread starter rope (3) through starter housing (5), rope guide (4), handle (2) and anchor (1) and secure with a knot. Turn pulley (30) 2-3 turns counterclockwise when viewed from flywheel side, then release starter rope (3) from pulley notch and allow rope to slowly wind onto pulley.

NOTE: Do not apply any more tension on rewind spring (20) than is required to draw starter handle (2) back into the proper released position.

Install springs (25 and 26), pawl (27) and clip (28) as shown in Fig. T3-6. Remount manual starter assembly. Reconnect starter lockout rod (16—Fig. T3-5) to rod keeper (15) and check for proper operation of starter lockout assembly.

Complete reassembly.

COOLING SYSTEM

A water pump located in the lower unit circulates water through the power head. Water temperature is regulated by a thermostat located in the top of the cylinder head.

⚠ CAUTION

Do not operate outboard motor unless the lower unit is immersed in water, otherwise, the water pump impeller will be damaged.

Illustrations Courtesy Tohatsu

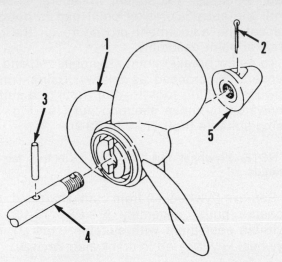

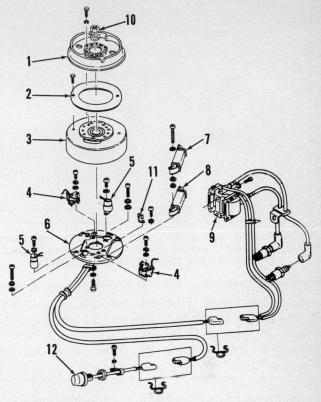

Fig. T3-7 — Propeller (1) is mounted on propeller shaft (4) and is retained by spinner (5) and cotter pin (2). Shear pin (3) is renewed only after withdrawing propeller (1) from propeller shaft (4).

If cooling system problems are encountered, first check the water inlet for material which may be blocking the inlet.

If the thermostat is believed faulty, remove the engine top cover then remove the thermostat cover on top of the cylinder head for access to the thermostat. The thermostat should begin opening at 50°-54°C (122°-129°F) and be fully open at 65°C (149°F). Thermostat valve opening at maximum opening temperature should be 3.0 mm (0.118 in.).

If the water pump must be inspected, refer to the Outboard Motor Service Manual.

PROPELLER

The standard propeller has three blades on all models. Propeller on standard 8 hp models has a diameter of 220 mm (8-21/32 in.) and a pitch of 197 mm (7¾ in.), while propeller on long-shaft 8 hp models has a diameter of 230 mm (9-1/16 in.) and a pitch of 152 mm (5-63/64 in.). Propeller on 9.8 hp models has a diameter of 230 mm (9-1/16 in.) and a pitch of 220 mm (8-21/32 in.).

⚠WARNING

Shift directional control lever to "NEUTRAL." Remove spark plug leads and properly ground leads before performing any propeller service, otherwise, accidental starting can occur if propeller shaft is rotated.

Fig. T3-8 — Exploded view of ignition system components.
1. Starter pulley
2. Flywheel cover
3. Flywheel
4. Breaker point assemblies
5. Condensers
6. Magneto base plate
7. Upper cylinder low voltage coil
8. Lower cylinder low voltage coil
9. Ignition coils
10. Nut
11. Lubricator
12. Engine kill switch

To remove the propeller, remove cotter pin (2 — Fig. T3-7) and unscrew propeller spinner (5). Withdraw propeller (1) from propeller shaft (4).

Inspect propeller (1), propeller shaft (4) and shear pin (3) for damage and excessive wear and renew if needed.

Apply a water-resistant grease to the propeller bore, then install propeller (1) on propeller shaft (4) and retain with propeller spinner (5) and a new cotter pin (2).

Tune-Up

IGNITION SYSTEM

The standard spark plug is NGK B7HS with an electrode gap of 0.6-0.7 mm (0.024-0.027 in.).

The breaker point gap should be 0.3-0.4 mm (0.012-0.016 in.) and can be inspected and adjusted through the opening in flywheel (3 — Fig. T3-8). Two breaker point assemblies (4) and two condensers (5) are used. To inspect and, if needed, adjust the breaker point gap, first remove the engine's top cover. Remove the screws retaining the manual starter to the engine and withdraw the

Tohatsu 8 & 9.8 Hp

Fig. T3-9 — View showing the use of Tohatsu flywheel holding tool (H) to prevent flywheel rotation during removal of securing nut (10 — Fig. T3-8) with suitable tools (T).

starter assembly. Remove the cap screws and lockwashers securing starter pulley (1) and flywheel cover (2) to flywheel (3) and withdraw.

Inspect the breaker point surfaces for excessive wear, pitting and damage. If needed, renew breaker point assemblies (4) and condensers (5) as outlined later in this section.

To clean the breaker point contact surfaces, rotate the flywheel until the breaker point contact surfaces are accessible through the opening in flywheel (3). Use a point file or sandpaper with a grit rating of 400 to 600. After polishing, wipe the contact surfaces clean with a dry cloth and lightly grease the breaker point arm and lubricator (11) with a suitable lubricant.

Turn the flywheel until the breaker point contact surfaces are at their widest position. Reach through the flywheel opening with a feeler gage of the appropriate size and check the distance between the point surfaces. If the distance is not within the recommended limits, loosen the point set securing screw and adjust the point set until the correct gap is obtained. Tighten the point set securing screw and recheck the breaker point

gap. Repeat the adjustment procedure, if needed, until the correct breaker point gap is obtained. Repeat the adjustment procedure on the other breaker point assembly.

To renew breaker point assemblies (4) and condensers (5), proceed as follows: Using Tohatsu flywheel holding tool (H — Fig. T3-9) or a suitable equivalent, remove securing nut (10 — Fig. T3-8) using suitable tools (T — Fig. T3-9).

NOTE: Flywheel nut (10 — Fig. T3-8) has left-hand threads.

Remove flywheel (3) from crankshaft end using Tohatsu puller assembly (P — Fig. T3-10) or a suitable equivalent with suitable tools (T). Note flywheel key located in crankshaft keyway.

⚠WARNING

Be sure suitable tools are used to remove the flywheel. Damage resultant from the misapplication of force or the use of incorrect tools may cause engine damage, engine malfunction or personal injury.

With reference to Fig. T3-8, renew breaker point assemblies (4) and condensers (5). Adjust the breaker point gap to the recommended setting as previously outlined. Make sure the securing screws are properly tightened. Be sure the flywheel key is properly positioned in the crankshaft keyway, then reinstall flywheel (3). Install lockwasher and tighten securing nut (10) to 59 N·m (43 ft.-lbs.).

To obtain the correct ignition timing, first adjust both breaker point assemblies (4) to the proper point gap as previously outlined. Remove both spark plugs. Use a point checker and attach the red tester lead to the blue wire coming from the magneto base plate (6) (top cylinder low voltage coil lead). Attach the black tester lead to an engine ground.

NOTE: A suitable continuity tester can be used.

Slowly turn the flywheel clockwise until the tester's pointer moves from "CLOSE" to "OPEN", then note flywheel timing mark. The flywheel timing mark (U — Fig. T3-11) should be aligned with mark (I) on manual starter mounting base. If not, the flywheel must be removed as outlined earlier and the magneto base plate (6 — Fig. T3-8) adjusted until proper alignment of timing marks (U and I) is obtained.

Fig. T3-10 — Remove flywheel (3 — Fig. T3-8) from crankshaft end using Tohatsu puller assembly (P) and suitable tools (T).

Illustrations Courtesy Tohatsu

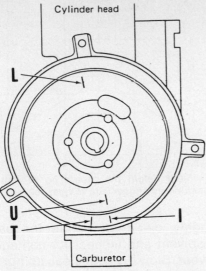

Fig. T3-11—Drawing showing location of timing marks on flywheel and manual starter mounting base.

I. Ignition mark
L. Lower cylinder mark
T. TDC mark
U. Upper cylinder mark

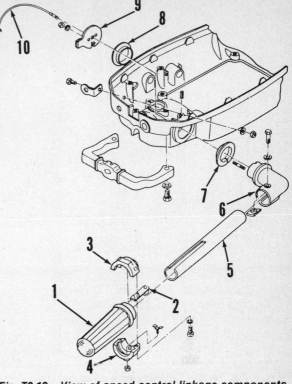

Fig. T3-12—View of speed control linkage components.

1. Twist grip
2. Slider
3. Upper retainer half
4. Lower retainer half
5. Steering handle
6. Handle bracket
7. Outer grommet
8. Inner grommet
9. Handle stop
10. Control cable

After top cylinder ignition timing has been checked and adjusted as needed, and the flywheel has been properly remounted, check bottom cylinder ignition timing.

Attach the point checker's red tester lead to the black wire coming from magneto base plate (6). Make sure the black tester lead remains attached to engine ground. Bottom cylinder breaker point contacts should open when timing mark (L) is aligned with mark (I) on manual starter mounting base. Adjust bottom cylinder ignition timing by varying bottom cylinder breaker point gap between the recommended limits of 0.3-0.4 mm (0.012-0.016 in.).

Complete reassembly.

SPEED CONTROL LINKAGE

The engine speed is regulated by the position of the carburetor throttle slide (8—Fig. T3-13). Throttle slide (8) is controlled by twist grip (1—Fig. T3-12) via control cable (10). An engine kill switch (12—Fig. T3-8) is used to stop engine operation.

CARBURETOR

ADJUSTMENT. Standard carburetor is a TK Model PA17C-4. Standard main jet (26—Fig. T3-13) size is #92 for normal operation. Preliminary positioning of clip (6) in jet needle (7) is in the middle groove. Inserting clip (6) in a higher notch will lean mid-range mixture while inserting clip in a lower notch will richen mid-range mixture. Preliminary adjustment of idle mixture screw (14) is 1 turn out from a lightly seated position on 8 hp models and ¾ turn out from a lightly seated position on 9.8 hp

models. Recommended idle speed is 1100-1200 rpm with engine in gear and at normal operating temperature.

With the outboard motor properly mounted on a boat or a suitable test tank, immerse the lower unit. Connect a tachometer and set it on the appropriate range scale. Start the engine and allow it to warm up to normal operating temperature. Position the throttle control twist grip to the complete closed position. Place the gear shift lever in the "Forward" position. Adjust the engine idle speed screw (9) until the engine is idling at 1100-1200 rpm, then adjust the idle mixture (14) until smooth engine operation is noted. Readjust the engine idle speed screw (9) until the recommended idle speed is obtained.

OVERHAUL. Remove engine top cover. Remove screws retaining air intake cover half (33—Fig. T3-13), filter element (32), inner cover half (31) and spacers (24), then withdraw. Disconnect the fuel tank supply hose at the outboard motor connector. Disconnect the fuel supply hose at the carburetor inlet. Disconnect all linkage that will interfere with carburetor removal. Clean all external surfaces and remove accumulated dirt and grease. Remove the two nuts securing the carburetor and withdraw the carburetor assembly.

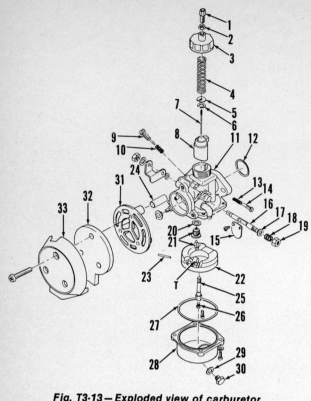

Fig. T3-13 — Exploded view of carburetor.

1. Cable adjuster
2. Nut
3. Cap
4. Spring
5. Retainer
6. Clip
7. Jet needle
8. Throttle slide
9. Idle speed screw
10. Spring
11. Body
12. Gasket
13. Spring
14. Idle mixture screw
15. Choke plate
16. Choke shaft
17. Washer
18. Spring
19. Nut
20. Gasket
21. Fuel inlet valve
22. Float
23. Float pin
24. Spacer
25. Needle jet
26. Main jet
27. Gasket
28. Float bowl
29. Gasket
30. Drain plug
31. Cover half
32. Filter element
33. Cover half

With reference to Fig. T3-13, disassemble the complete carburetor assembly and note any discrepancies which must be corrected before reassembly. Remove all gaskets (label if needed for later reference) and set to the side.

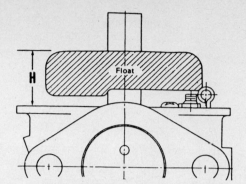

Fig. T3-14 — Float height (H) should be 15 mm (0.59 inch) measured as shown with the gasket removed.

Thoroughly clean all carburetor parts in a suitable solvent and inspect for damage and excessive wear. Blow dry with clean compressed air. If compressed air is not available, use only lint-free cloths to wipe dry. Do not use a drill bit or wire to clean jets. Enlargement or damage of the calibrated holes may affect engine performance.

With reference to Fig. T3-13, reassemble the carburetor components with new gaskets. Note that the new gaskets should match up with those removed. If not, check with your parts supplier to be sure you have the correct gasket set.

To determine the float level, invert carburetor body (11) and measure height (H — Fig. T3-14) of float (22 — Fig. T3-13) from surface of carburetor body (without gasket) to top of float. Float height (H — Fig. T3-14) should be 15 mm (0.59 in.) and is adjusted by bending tang (T — Fig. T3-13).

When reinstalling the carburetor, place a new gasket (12) between carburetor and intake manifold. Securely tighten the retaining nuts. Reconnect fuel supply line and carburetor linkage. Install air intake cover assembly and retain with screws. Initially adjust idle mixture screw (14) 1 turn out from a lightly seated position on 8 hp models and ¾ turn out from a lightly seated position on 9.8 hp models.

TOHATSU 12, 15 AND 18 HP

NOTE: Metric fasteners are used throughout outboard motor.

Specifications

	12, 15 Hp	18 Hp
Hp/rpm	12/5000	18/5500
	15/5500	
Bore.........................	55 mm	60 mm
	(2.165 in.)	(2.362 in.)
Stroke	52 mm	52 mm
	(2.047 in.)	(2.047 in.)
Displacement.................	247 cc	294 cc
	(15.07 cu. in.)	(17.94 cu. in.)
Number of cylinders	2	2
Spark plug:		
NGK......................	B7HS	B7HS
Electrode gap	0.6-0.7 mm	0.6-0.7 mm
	(0.024-0.027 in.)	(0.024-0.027 in.)
Ignition type	CD	CD
Ignition timing (BTDC)...........	*17°	25°
Carburetor make	TK	TK
Idle speed (in gear).............	800-850 rpm	800-850 rpm
Fuel:oil ratio	50:1	50:1

*Full advance ignition timing is 25° BTDC on 15 hp models.

Maintenance

LUBRICATION

ENGINE. The engine is lubricated by oil mixed with the fuel. Recommended oil is Tohatsu outboard motor oil or a BIA certified two-stroke motor oil. The recommended fuel:oil ratio for normal operation is 50:1. During engine break-in, the fuel:oil ratio should be increased to 20:1 for a period of 10 operating hours.

LOWER UNIT. The lower unit gears and bearings are lubricated by oil contained in the gearcase. The recommended oil is Tohatsu gear oil or a suitable EP 80 outboard gear oil. The gearcase should be refilled after every 50 hours of operation and the lubricant renewed after every 200 hours of operation or more frequently if needed. The gearcase is drained and filled through the same plug port (D—Fig. T4-1). An oil level (vent) port (L) is used to indicate full oil level of the gearcase and to ease oil drainage.

To drain the oil, place the outboard motor in a vertical position. Remove drain plug (D) and oil level plug (L) and allow the lubricant to drain into a suitable container.

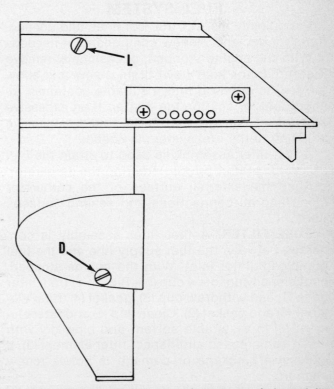

Fig. T4-1—*View showing lower unit gearcase drain and fill plug (D) and oil level (vent) plug (L).*

Illustrations Courtesy Tohatsu

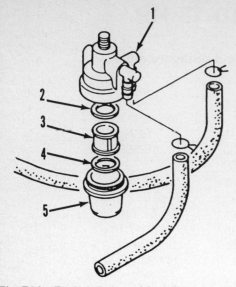

Fig. T4-2—Exploded view of fuel filter assembly.

1. Filter base
2. Gasket
3. Filter element
4. Gasket
5. Cup

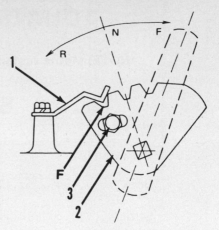

Fig. T4-3—Adjustment of shift lever. Refer to text.

F. Forward groove
1. Detent arm
2. Stopper plate
3. Cap screw

To fill the gearcase with oil, place the outboard motor in a vertical position. Add oil through drain plug (D) opening with an oil feeder until the oil begins to overflow from oil level plug (L) port. Reinstall oil level plug (L) with a new gasket, if needed, and tighten. Remove oil feeder, then reinstall drain plug (D) with a new gasket, if needed, and tighten.

FUEL SYSTEM

Periodically inspect the fuel lines and connections for damage. Renew components if needed.

With the engine stopped, occasionally remove the carburetor float bowl drain screw and allow the fuel to drain off into a suitable container. Inspect fuel for any foreign matter. If an excessive amount of foreign matter is found, extensive cleaning of the fuel system is needed.

A fuel filter assembly is used to strain the fuel of foreign matter prior to entering the carburetor. Keep the external surface of the carburetor clean and all connections and sealing surfaces tight.

FUEL FILTER. A fuel filter assembly is connected between the fuel supply line and the fuel pump/carburetor inlet. With the engine stopped, occasionally unscrew cup (5—Fig. T4-2) from filter base (1) and withdraw cup (5), gasket (4), filter element (3) and gasket (2). Clean cup (5) and filter element (3) in a suitable solvent and blow dry with clean compressed air. Inspect filter element (3). If excessive blockage or damage is noted, renew element.

Reassembly is reverse order of disassembly. Renew gaskets (2 and 4) during reassembly.

FUEL PUMP. The fuel pump is an integral part of the carburetor. Refer to CARBURETOR in the Tune-Up section for fuel pump overhaul.

NOTE: The fuel pump assembly may be overhauled without carburetor removal.

SHIFT LINKAGE

Direction control is selected by the position of a gear shift lever. The lever operates an upper and lower shift rod connected by a sleeve and spring pins. The tapered end of the lower shift rod controls the movement of the dog clutch on the propeller shaft. The positioning of the dog clutch on the propeller shaft determines whether forward, neutral or reverse directional movement is selected.

To check shift linkage for proper adjustment, first place shift lever in reverse detent position. Check for proper engagement and propeller rotation by turning propeller.

⚠WARNING

Remove spark plug leads and properly ground leads before performing any propeller service, otherwise, accidental starting can occur if propeller shaft is rotated.

Check for proper engagement of neutral and forward.

To adjust, first place lever stopper plate 2—Fig. T4-3 in forward (F) detent position. Loosen cap screw (3) and rotate the shift lever until proper engagement is obtained, then retighten cap screw (3). Check for proper engagement of neutral and reverse. If proper adjustment cannot be obtained, check all shift linkage components for damage and excessive wear and renew if needed.

STARTER

When starter rope (12—Fig. T4-4) is pulled, pulley (14) will rotate. As pulley (14) rotates, drive pawl (21) moves to engage the starter pulley, thus cranking the engine.

When starter rope (12) is released, pulley (14) is rotated in the reverse direction by force from rewind spring (13). As pulley (14) rotates, the starter rope is rewound and drive pawl (21) is disengaged from the starter pulley.

A starter lockout assembly is used to prevent starter engagement when the gear shift lever is in the forward or reverse position.

To overhaul the manual starter, proceed as follows: Remove the engine top cover. Remove the screws retaining the manual starter to the engine. Remove starter lockout rod (27) from rod keeper (26). Withdraw the starter assembly.

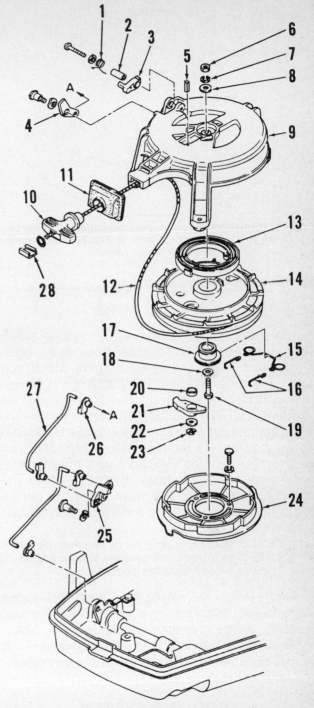

Fig. T4-4 — Exploded view of manual starter assembly.

1. Spring	11. Rope guide	
2. Spacer	12. Starter rope	21. Pawl
3. Starter lock	13. Rewind spring	22. Washer
4. Cam	14. Pulley	23. Clip
5. Spring pin	15. Spring	24. Starter pulley
6. Nut	16. Links	25. Reverse throttle
7. Lockwasher	17. Spindle	stop
8. Washer	18. Washer	26. Rod keeper
9. Starter housing	19. Bolt	27. Rod
10. Handle	20. Bushing	28. Anchor

⚠WARNING

Care should be exercised when working with or around a coiled starter rewind spring as sudden uncoiling can cause injury. Safety eyewear and gloves are recommended.

Check pawl (21) for freedom of movement and excessive wear or damage of engagement area. Renew or lubricate pawl (21) with a suitable water-resistant grease if needed.

To disassemble, remove clip (23) and withdraw washer (22), pawl (21), pawl spring (15) and links (16). Detach starter rope (12) at anchor (28) and allow the rope to wind into the starter. Remove bolt (19), washer (18) and spindle (17). Carefully lift pulley (14) with starter rope (12) and rewind spring (13) from starter housing (9). BE CAREFUL not to dislodge rewind spring (13) when removing pulley (14). Remove starter rope (12) from pulley (14) if renewal is required. If renewal of rewind spring (13) is required, use extreme caution when removing rewind spring (13) from pulley (14).

Inspect all components for damage and excessive wear and renew if needed.

To reassemble, first apply a coating of a suitable water-resistant grease to rewind spring area of pulley (14). Install rewind spring (13) in pulley (14) so spring coils wind in a counterclockwise direction from the inner end. Make sure the spring's inner hook is properly secured. Wind starter rope (12) onto pulley (14) 2-3 turns counterclockwise when viewed from flywheel side. Direct remaining starter rope (12) length through notch in pulley (14).

NOTE: Lubricate all friction surfaces with a suitable water-resistant grease during reassembly.

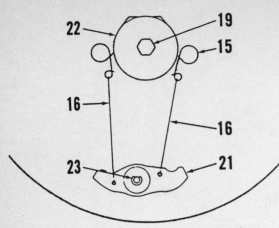

Fig. T4-5 — Drawing showing proper installation of starter pawl (21), spring (15) and links (16). Refer to Fig. T4-4 for complete identification of parts.

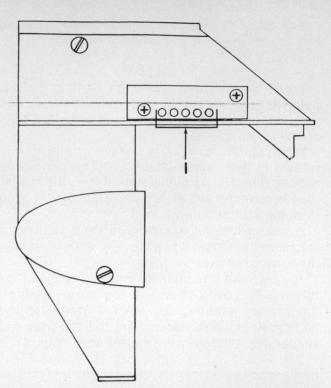

Fig. T4-6 — Cooling system water inlet ports (I) are located on the port side of the lower unit.

Assemble pulley (14) to starter housing making sure rewind spring's (13) outer hook end properly engages pin (5) in starter housing (9). Install spindle (17), washer (18) and bolt (19). Apply a suitable thread fastening solution to bolt (19) threads and install nut (6) and securely tighten.

Thread starter rope (12) through starter housing (9), rope guide (11), handle (10) and anchor (28) and secure. Turn pulley (14) 2-3 turns counterclockwise when viewed from flywheel side, then release starter rope (12) from pulley notch and allow rope to slowly wind onto pulley.

NOTE: Do not apply any more tension on rewind spring (13) than is required to draw starter handle (10) back into the proper released position.

Install links (16), spring (15), pawl (21), washer (22) and clip (23) as shown in Fig. T4-5. Remount manual starter assembly. Reconnect starter lockout rod (27) to rod keeper (26) and check for proper operation of starter lockout assembly.

Complete reassembly.

COOLING SYSTEM

A water pump located in the lower unit circulates water through the power head. Water temperature is regulated by a thermostat located in the top of the cylinder head.

If cooling system problems are encountered, first check water inlet (I — Fig. T4-6) for material which may be blocking the inlet.

If the thermostat is believed faulty, remove the engine top cover then remove the thermostat cover on top of the cylinder head for access to the thermostat. The thermostat should begin opening at 50°-54°C (122°-129°F) and be fully open at 65°C (149°F). Thermostat valve opening at maximum opening temperature should be 3.0 mm (0.118 in.).

If the water pump must be inspected, refer to the Outboard Motor Service Manual.

PROPELLER

The standard propeller has three blades on all models. Various propeller diameters and pitches are available. Select a propeller that will allow the engine at full throttle to reach maximum operating rpm range (4500-5300 rpm for 12 hp models and 4750-5500 rpm for 15 and 18 hp models).

⚠CAUTION

Do not operate outboard motor unless the lower unit is immersed in water, otherwise, the water pump impeller will be damaged.

⚠WARNING

Shift directional control lever to "NEUTRAL." Remove spark plug leads and properly ground leads before performing any propeller service, otherwise accidental starting can occur if propeller shaft is rotated.

Illustrations Courtesy Tohatsu

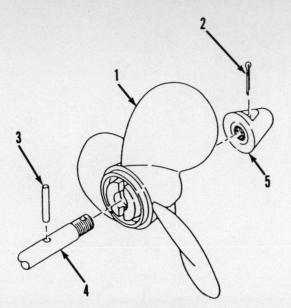

Fig. T4-7 — Propeller (1) is mounted on propeller shaft (4) and is retained by spinner (5) and cotter pin (2). Shear pin (3) is renewed only after withdrawing propeller (1) from propeller shaft (4).

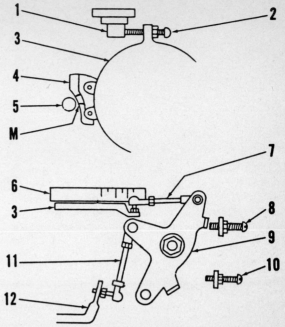

Fig. T4-8 — Drawings of speed control linkage. Refer to text for adjustment.

1. Reverse speed stop	
2. Reverse speed stop screw	8. Full advance stop screw
3. Speed control ring	9. Bellcrank
4. Throttle cam	10. Idle speed ignition stop screw
5. Throttle roller	
6. Stator plate	11. Link
7. Link	12. Speed control shaft

To remove the propeller, remove cotter pin (2 — Fig. T4-7) and unscrew propeller spinner (5). Withdraw propeller (1) from propeller shaft (4).

Inspect propeller (1), propeller shaft (4) and shear pin (3) for damage and excessive wear and renew if required.

Apply a water-resistant grease to the propeller bore, then install propeller (1) on propeller shaft (4) and retain with propeller spinner (5) and a new cotter pin (2).

Tune-Up

IGNITION SYSTEM

On all models a capacitor discharge ignition (CDI) system is used. Refer to the Outboard Motor Service Manual for testing and servicing the CD ignition system. If engine malfunction is noted and the ignition system is suspected, make sure spark plugs and all electrical wiring are in good condition and all electrical connections are tight before troubleshooting the CD ignition system.

The standard spark plug is NGK B7HS with an electrode gap of 0.6-0.7 mm (0.024-0.027 in.).

IGNITION TIMING. To adjust ignition timing, disconnect lower link (11 — Fig. T4-8). Measure length of upper link (7) from back of locknut to center of bent end as shown in Fig. T4-9. Length should be 47 mm (1-55/64 in.) and is adjusted by loosening locknut (N) and turning link end (D). Rotate bellcrank (9 — Fig. T4-8) so it contacts maximum advance screw (8) and note which timing mark on stator plate (6) is aligned with crankcase and cylinder block mating surface. Maximum ad-

vance ignition timing is 17° BTDC for 12 hp models and 25° BTDC for 15 and 18 hp models. Turn maximum advance screw (8) to adjust timing. Rotate bellcrank (9) so it contacts idle speed ignition timing screw (10). Ignition timing should be 0°-2° ATDC at idle. Turn idle speed ignition timing screw (10) to adjust timing. Reconnect lower link (11). Proceed to the following SPEED CONTROL LINKAGE section.

SPEED CONTROL LINKAGE

Check and adjust, if needed, the ignition timing as outlined in the previous IGNITION SYSTEM section. With twist grip (1 — Fig. T4-10) in the released position, bellcrank (9 — Fig. T4-8) should

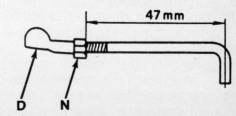

Fig. T4-9 — Length of speed control link (7 — Fig. T4-8) should be 47 mm (1-55/64 in.) when measured as shown. Loosen locknut (N) and turn link end (D) as required.

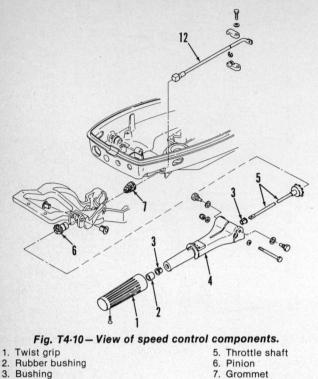

Fig. T4-10 — View of speed control components.

1. Twist grip
2. Rubber bushing
3. Bushing
4. Steering handle
5. Throttle shaft
6. Pinion
7. Grommet
12. Speed control shaft

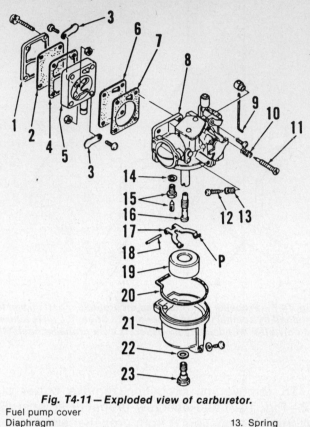

Fig. T4-11 — Exploded view of carburetor.

1. Fuel pump cover
2. Diaphragm
3. Check valve
4. Gasket
5. Pump body
6. Diaphragm
7. Gasket
8. Carburetor body
9. Rod
10. Spring
11. Idle mixture screw
12. Idle speed screw
13. Spring
14. Gasket
15. Fuel inlet valve
16. Main nozzle
17. Float lever
18. Float pin
19. Float
20. Gasket
21. Float bowl
22. Gasket
23. Main jet

be touching ignition stop screw (10). With twist grip (1—Fig. T4-10) held in the full throttle position, bellcrank (9—Fig. T4-8) should be touching ignition stop screw (8). If not, adjust length of link (11) to synchronize twist grip and bellcrank.

Position gear shift lever in reverse and turn twist grip (1—Fig. T4-10) towards full throttle. Speed control rotation should stop when centerline of carburetor throttle roller (5—Fig. T4-8) aligns with the first mark (M) on throttle cam (4). Adjust reverse throttle stop screw (2) to align roller (5) centerline with mark (M).

CARBURETOR

ADJUSTMENT. Standard main jet (23—Fig. T4-11) size is #86 for 12 hp models, #110 for 15 hp models and #108 for 18 hp models under normal operation. Preliminary adjustment of idle mixture screw (11) is 1½ turns out from a lightly seated position for 12 hp and 15 hp models, and 1¼ turns out from a lightly seated position for 18 hp models. Recommended idle speed is 800-850 rpm in gear with engine at normal operating temperature.

With the outboard motor properly mounted on a boat or a suitable test tank, immerse the lower unit. Connect a tachometer and set it on the appropriate range scale. Start the engine and allow it to warm up to normal operating temperature. Position the throttle control twist grip to the com-

plete closed position. Place the gear shift lever in the "Forward" position. Adjust the engine idle speed screw (12) until the engine is idling at 800-850 rpm, then adjust the idle mixture screw (11) until smooth engine operation is noted. Readjust the engine idle speed screw (12) until the recommended idle speed is obtained.

OVERHAUL. The fuel pump is an integral part of the carburetor. The fuel pump assembly may be overhauled without overhauling the complete carburetor. If the fuel pump is to be overhauled without carburetor removal, proceed as follows: Remove the engine top cover and disconnect the fuel supply hose at the outboard motor connector. Disconnect the fuel supply hose at the carburetor/fuel pump inlet.

With reference to Fig. T4-11, disassemble the fuel pump assembly. Inspect all components for damage and excessive wear and renew if needed. Clean components as needed with a suitable cleaning solution. Blow dry with clean compressed air. If compressed air is not available, use only lint-free cloths to wipe dry. Be careful when handling check valves (3). Make sure all passages are clear of any obstructions.

With reference to Fig. T4-11, reassemble the fuel pump assembly with new gaskets. Securely tighten the retaining screws.

NOTE: Fuel pump and engine malfunction will result if the fuel pump and all connections are not airtight.

Complete reassembly.

Refer to the following for complete carburetor overhaul: Remove engine top cover. Remove the screws retaining air intake cover and disconnect choke linkage from carburetor choke lever during cover removal. Disconnect the fuel tank supply hose at the outboard motor connector. Disconnect the fuel supply hose at the carburetor/fuel pump inlet. Clean all external surfaces and remove accumulated dirt and grease. Remove the two nuts securing the carburetor and withdraw the carburetor assembly.

With reference to Fig. T4-11, disassemble the complete carburetor assembly and note any discrepancies which must be corrected before reassembly. Remove all gaskets (label if needed for later reference) and set to the side.

Thoroughly clean all carburetor parts in a suitable solvent and inspect for damage and excessive wear. Blow dry with clean compressed air. If compressed air is not available, use only lint-free cloths to wipe dry. Do not use a drill bit or wire to clean jets. Enlargement or damage of the calibrated holes may affect engine performance.

With reference to Fig. T4-11, reassemble the carburetor components with new gaskets. Note that the new gaskets should match up with those

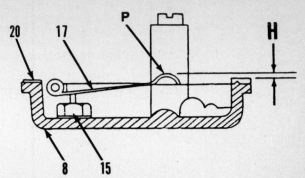

Fig. T4-12—With carburetor body (8) inverted, float lever pads (P) height (H) above gasket (20) should be 2 mm (0.079 in.) with a good inlet valve (15) installed. Bend arms of float lever (17) evenly to adjust.

removed. If not, check with your parts supplier to be sure you have the correct gasket set.

To determine the float level, invert carburetor body (8—Fig. T4-12) and measure height (H) of float lever pads (P) with a good inlet valve (15) and gasket (20) installed. Float lever height (H) should be 2 mm (0.079 in.) and is adjusted by bending the arms of float lever (17) evenly until pads (P) are at the proper height.

When reinstalling the carburetor, place a new gasket between the carburetor and the intake manifold. Securely tighten the retaining nuts. Reconnect the fuel supply hose. Install air intake cover and connect choke linkage during installation, then secure air intake cover with retaining screws. Initially adjust the idle mixture screw (11—Fig. T4-11) 1½ turns out from a lightly seated position for 12 hp and 15 hp models, and 1¼ turns out from a lightly seated position for 18 hp models.

Perform final carburetor adjustments as outlined in ADJUSTMENT section.

TOHATSU 25 HP

NOTE: Metric fasteners are used throughout outboard motor.

Specifications

Hp/rpm 25/5000
Bore . . . . .66 mm
(2.60 in.)
Stroke. . . . . .58 mm
(2.28 in.)
Displacement . . . . .397 cc
(24.23 cu. in.)
Number of cylinders 2
Spark plug:
  NGK B7HS
  Electrode gap . . . . .0.6-0.7 mm
(0.024-0.027 in.)
Ignition type . . . . .CD
Ignition timing (BTDC) . . . . .25°
Carburetor:
  Make. . . . . .Keihin
  Model. 1000-286-00
Idle speed (in gear) . . . . .1000-1100 rpm
Fuel:oil ratio. 50:1

Maintenance

LUBRICATION

ENGINE. The engine is lubricated by oil mixed with the fuel. Recommended oil is Tohatsu outboard motor oil or a BIA certified two-stroke motor oil. The recommended fuel:oil ratio for normal operation is 50:1. During engine break-in, the fuel:oil ratio should be increased to 20:1 for a period of 10 operating hours.

LOWER UNIT. The lower unit gears and bearings are lubricated by oil contained in the gearcase. The recommended oil is Tohatsu gear oil or a suitable EP 80 outboard gear oil. The gearcase should be refilled after every 50 hours of operation and the lubricant renewed after every 200 hours of operation or more frequently if needed. The gearcase is drained and filled through the same plug port (D—Fig. T5-1). An oil level (vent) port (L) is used to indicate the full level of the gearcase oil and to ease oil drainage.

To drain the oil, place the outboard motor in a vertical position. Remove drain plug (D) on the port side and oil level plug (L) on the starboard side, and allow the lubricant to drain into a suitable container.

To fill the gearcase with oil, place the outboard motor in a vertical position. Add oil through drain plug (D) opening with an oil feeder until the oil begins to overflow from oil level plug (L) port.

Reinstall oil level plug (L) with a new gasket, if needed, and tighten. Remove oil feeder, then reinstall drain plug (D) with a new gasket, if needed, and tighten.

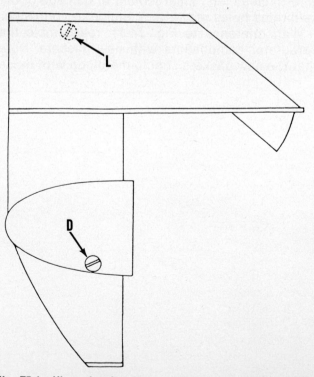

Fig. T5-1 — View showing lower unit gearcase drain and fill plug (D) located on port side and oil level (vent) plug (L) located on starboard side.

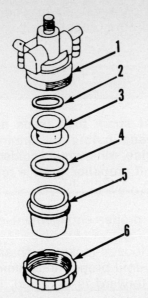

Fig. T5-2 — Exploded view of fuel filter assembly.

1. Filter base
2. Gasket
3. Filter element
4. Gasket
5. Cup
6. Cup retainer

FUEL SYSTEM

Periodically inspect the fuel lines and connections for damage. Renew components if needed.

With the engine stopped, occasionally remove the carburetor float bowl drain plug and allow the fuel to drain off into a suitable container. Inspect fuel for any foreign matter. If an excessive amount of foreign matter is found, extensive cleaning of the fuel system is needed.

A fuel filter assembly is used to strain the fuel of foreign matter prior to entering the carburetor.

Keep the external surface of the carburetor clean and all connections and sealing surfaces tight.

FUEL FILTER. A fuel filter assembly is connected between the fuel tank supply line and the fuel pump inlet line. With the engine stopped, occasionally unscrew the cup retainer (6—Fig. T5-2) from filter base (1) and withdraw cup (5), gasket (4), filter element (3) and gasket (2). Clean cup (5) and filter element (3) in a suitable solvent and blow dry with clean compressed air. Inspect filter element (3). If excessive blockage or damage is noted, renew element (3).

Reassembly is reverse order of disassembly. Renew gaskets (2 and 4) during reassembly.

FUEL PUMP. The fuel pump is operated by crankcase pressure changes caused by the up-and-down movement of the piston. When the crankcase pressure decreases (the piston is moving upward), the pump diaphragm is pulled toward the crankcase allowing fuel to enter the pump chamber and closing the discharge check valve.

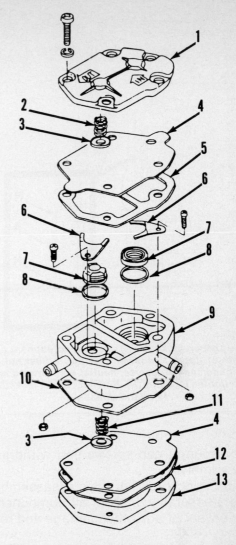

Fig. T5-3 — Exploded view of fuel pump assembly.

1. Cover
2. Spring
3. Spring seat
4. Diaphragm
5. Gasket
6. Retainer
7. Check valve
8. Gasket
9. Body
10. Gasket
11. Spring
12. Gasket
13. Plate

When the crankcase pressure increases (the piston is moving downward), the diaphragm is pushed outward discharging fuel to the carburetor and closing the inlet check valve. This pulsating action provides continuous fuel flow. The check valves are used to prevent reverse flow of the fuel.

A spring is used to load the diaphragm, thus allowing the diaphragm to respond more quickly to crankcase pressure changes.

The inlet port is identified as "IN" and the discharge port is identified as "OUT." The fuel hoses must be connected accordingly.

To overhaul the fuel pump, first remove the engine's top cover and disconnect the fuel tank supply hose at the outboard motor connector. Disconnect the fuel hoses at the fuel pump inlet and discharge nozzles and label if needed.

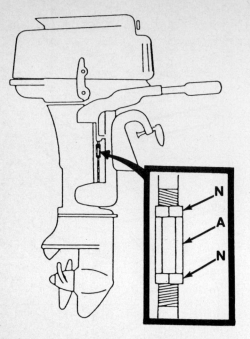

Fig. T5-4 — Loosen locknuts (N) and turn adjustment nut (A) to alter length of upper and lower shift rod. Adjust nut (A) until proper engagement of reverse, neutral and forward is obtained, then retighten locknuts (N). Note that upper locknut (N) has left-hand threads.

Remove securing cap screws and withdraw fuel pump assembly.

With reference to Fig. T5-3, disassemble the fuel pump assembly. Inspect all components for excessive wear or any other damage and renew if needed.

With reference to Fig. T5-3, reassemble the fuel pump assembly with new gaskets. Coat fuel pump mounting gaskets with a nonhardening type gasket sealer making certain that passage in center is not plugged with gasket sealer. Mount the fuel pump assembly to the crankcase and securely tighten the retaining cap screws.

NOTE: Fuel pump and engine malfunction will result if the fuel pump and all connections are not airtight.

Complete reassembly.

SHIFT LINKAGE

Direction is determined by the position of the gear shift lever. The lever operates an upper and lower shift rod connected by an adjustment nut (A — Fig. T5-4). The tapered end of the lower shift rod controls the movement of the dog clutch on the propeller shaft. The positioning of the dog clutch on the propeller shaft determines whether forward, neutral or reverse directional movement is selected.

To check shift linkage for proper adjustment, first place shift lever in reverse detent position.

Check for proper engagement and propeller rotation by turning the propeller.

⚠WARNING

Disconnect spark plug leads and properly ground leads before performing any propeller service, otherwise, accidental starting can occur if propeller shaft is rotated.

Check for proper engagement of neutral and forward.

To adjust, loosen locknuts (N) and turn adjustment nut (A) until proper engagement of reverse, neutral and forward is obtained, then retighten locknuts (N).

NOTE: Upper locknut (N) has left-hand threads.

STARTER

When starter rope (2 — Fig. T5-5) is pulled, pulley (9) will rotate. As pulley (9) rotates, the three drive pawls (12) move apart thus meshing with the starter pulley and cranking the engine.

When starter rope (2) is released, pulley (9) is rotated in the reverse direction by force from rewind spring (7). As pulley (9) rotates, starter rope (2) is rewound and drive pawls (12) are disengaged from the starter pulley.

The manual starter must be disassembled to renew starter rope (2) and internal starter components.

To overhaul the manual starter, proceed as follows: Remove the engine top cover. Remove the screws retaining the manual starter to the engine, then withdraw the starter assembly.

⚠WARNING

Care should be exercised when working with or around a coiled starter rewind spring as sudden uncoiling can cause injury. Safety eyewear and gloves are recommended.

To disassemble, untie starter rope (2) at handle (1) and allow the rope to wind into the starter. Invert the unit and press on drive plate (15) to ease in removal of cap screw (18), lockwasher (17) and flat washer (16). Remove drive plate (15), pawls

Illustrations Courtesy Tohatsu

(2) onto pulley (9) 2-3 turns counterclockwise when viewed from flywheel side. Direct remaining starter rope (2) length through notch in pulley (9).

NOTE: Lubricate all friction surfaces with a suitable water-resistant grease during reassembly.

Assemble pulley (9) with washer (8) to starter housing (5) making sure that rewind spring's (7) inner hook end properly engages pulley (9).

Thread starter rope (2) end through housing (5), rope guide (4) and grommet (3), then secure rope end in handle (1) with a knot. Turn pulley (9) 2-3 turns counterclockwise when viewed from flywheel side, then release starter rope (2) from pulley notch and allow rope to slowly wind onto pulley.

NOTE: Do not apply any more tension on rewind spring (7) than is required to draw starter handle (1) back into the proper released position.

Install washer (10), spring seat (11) and friction spring (13). Install pawls (12) and pawl return springs (14). Hook drive plate (15) in return springs (14) and rotate drive plate (15) as needed to install. Press on drive plate (15) and install flat washer (16), lockwasher (17) and cap screw (18).

Remount manual starter assembly and install engine top cover to complete reassembly.

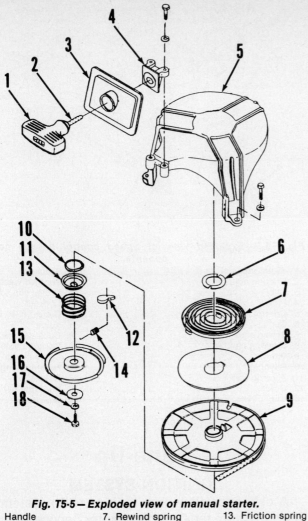

Fig. T5-5 — Exploded view of manual starter.

1. Handle	7. Rewind spring	13. Friction spring
2. Starter rope	8. Washer	14. Return spring
3. Grommet	9. Pulley	15. Drive plate
4. Rope guide	10. Washer	16. Flat washer
5. Starter housing	11. Spring seat	17. Lockwasher
6. Washer	12. Pawl	18. Cap screw

(12), return springs (14), friction spring (13), spring seat (11) and washer (10). Lift pulley (9) with starter rope (2) and washer (8) from starter housing (5). BE CAREFUL not to dislodge rewind spring (7) when removing pulley (9). Remove starter rope (2) from pulley (9) if renewal is required. To remove rewind spring (7) from housing (5), invert housing so it sets upright on a flat surface, then tap the housing top until rewind spring (7) falls free and uncoils. Note washer (6).

Inspect all components for damage and excessive wear and renew if needed.

To reassemble, first apply a coating of a suitable water-resistant grease to rewind spring area of housing (5). Install washer (6), then install rewind spring (7) in housing (5) so spring coils wind in a counterclockwise direction from the outer end. Make sure the spring's outer hook is properly secured in housing (5). Wind starter rope

COOLING SYSTEM

A water pump located in the lower unit circulates water through the power head. Water temperature is regulated by a thermostat located in the top of the cylinder head.

⚠CAUTION

Do not operate outboard motor unless the lower unit is immersed in water, otherwise, the water pump impeller will be damaged.

If cooling system problems are encountered, first check the water inlet for material which may be blocking the inlet.

If the thermostat is believed faulty, remove the engine top cover then remove the thermostat cover on top of the cylinder head for access to the thermostat. The thermostat should begin opening at 50°-54°C (122°-129°F) and be fully open at 65°C (149°F). Thermostat valve opening at maximum opening temperature should be 3.0 mm (0.118 in.).

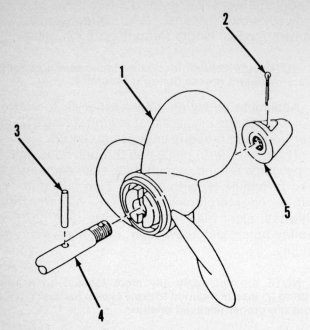

Fig. T5-6 — Propeller (1) is mounted on propeller shaft (4) and is retained by spinner (5) and cotter pin (2). Shear pin (3) is renewed only after withdrawing propeller (1) from propeller shaft (4).

If the water pump must be inspected, refer to the Outboard Motor Service Manual.

PROPELLER

The standard propeller has three blades. Various propeller diameters and pitches are available. Select a propeller that will allow the engine at full throttle to reach maximum operating rpm range (4800-5500 rpm).

⚠️WARNING

Shift directional control lever to "NEUTRAL." Disconnect spark plug leads and properly ground leads before performing any propeller service, otherwise, accidental starting can occur if propeller shaft is rotated.

To remove the propeller, remove cotter pin (2—Fig. T5-6) and unscrew propeller spinner (5). Withdraw propeller (1) from propeller shaft (4).

Inspect propeller (1), propeller shaft (4) and shear pin (3) for damage and excessive wear and renew if needed.

Apply a water-resistant grease to the propeller bore, then install propeller (1) on propeller shaft (4) and retain with propeller spinner (5) and a new cotter pin (2).

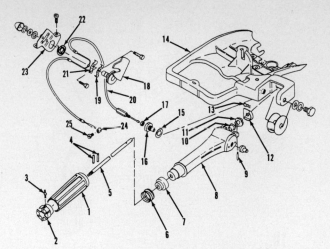

Fig. T5-7 — Exploded view of speed control linkage components.

1. Twist grip
2. Friction adjuster
3. Clip
4. Pins
5. Control shaft
6. Spring
7. Spring seat
8. Steering handle
9. Pin
10. Bushing
11. Throttle cam
12. Guide
13. Clip
14. Bracket
15. Toothed washer
16. Drilled cap screw
17. Locknut
18. Cable pulley & guide
19. Cable retainer
20. Control cable
21. Cable clamp
22. Return spring
23. Bracket
24. Wire retainer
25. Screw

Tune-Up

IGNITION SYSTEM

A capacitor discharge ignition (CDI) system is used. Refer to the Outboard Motor Service Manual for testing and servicing the CD ignition system. If engine malfunction is noted and the ignition system is suspected, make sure spark plugs and all electrical wiring are in good condition and all electrical connections are tight before troubleshooting the CD ignition system.

The standard spark plug is NGK B7HS with an electrode gap of 0.6-0.7 mm (0.024-0.027 in.).

SPEED CONTROL LINKAGE

The engine speed is regulated by the position of the carburetor throttle shaft. The throttle shaft position is controlled by twist grip (1—Fig. T5-7) via control cable (20) and adjoining linkage. An engine kill switch is used to stop engine operation.

CARBURETOR

ADJUSTMENT. Standard main jet (4—Fig. T5-8) size is #155 under normal operation. Preliminary adjustment of idle mixture screw (1) is 1⅛ turns out from a lightly seated position. Recommended idle speed is 1000-1100 rpm in gear with engine at normal operating temperature.

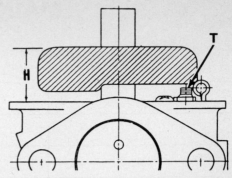

Fig. T5-9—Float height (H) with carburetor inverted should be 18 mm (0.71 in.) and is adjusted by bending float tang (T).

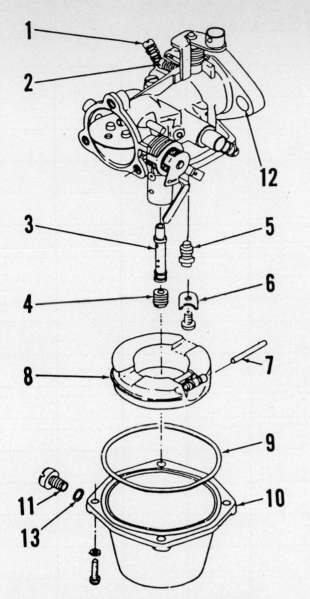

Fig. T5-8 — Exploded view of carburetor.

1. Idle mixture screw
2. Idle speed screw
3. Nozzle
4. Main jet
5. Fuel inlet valve
6. Inlet valve retainer
7. Float pin
8. Float
9. Gasket
10. Float bowl
11. Drain screw
12. Carburetor body
13. Gasket

With the outboard motor properly mounted on a boat or a suitable test tank, immerse the lower unit. Connect a tachometer and set it on the appropriate range scale. Start the engine and allow it to warm up to normal operating temperature. Position the throttle control twist grip to the complete closed position. Place the gear shift lever in the "Forward" position. Adjust the engine idle speed screw (2) until the engine is idling at 1000-1100 rpm, then adjust idle mixture screw (1) until smooth engine operation is noted. Readjust the engine idle speed screw (2) until the recommended idle speed is obtained.

OVERHAUL. Remove engine top cover. Remove screws retaining air intake cover assembly. Disconnect the fuel tank supply hose at the outboard motor connector. Disconnect the fuel supply hose at the carburetor inlet. Disconnect all linkage that will interfere with carburetor removal. Clean all external surfaces and remove accumulated dirt and grease. Remove the two nuts securing the carburetor and withdraw the carburetor assembly.

With reference to Fig. T5-8, disassemble the complete carburetor assembly and note any discrepancies which must be corrected before reassembly. Remove gasket (9) and drain screw gasket (13) and set to the side for future reference.

Thoroughly clean all carburetor parts in a suitable solvent and inspect for damage and excessive wear. Blow dry with clean compressed air. If compressed air is not available, use only lint-free cloths to wipe dry. Do not use a drill bit or wire to clean jets. Enlargement or damage of the calibrated holes may affect engine performance.

With reference to Fig. T5-8, reassemble the carburetor components with new gaskets. Note that the new gaskets should match up with those removed. If not, check with your parts supplier to be sure you have the correct gasket set.

To determine the float level, invert carburetor body (12) and measure height (H — Fig. T5-9) of float (8 — Fig. T5-8) from surface of carburetor body (12) (without gasket) to top of float (8). Float height (H — Fig. T5-9) should be 18 mm (0.71 inch) and is adjusted by bending float tang (T).

When reinstalling the carburetor, place a new gasket between carburetor and intake manifold. Securely tighten the retaining nuts. Reconnect fuel supply line and carburetor linkage. Install air intake cover assembly and retain with screws. Initially adjust idle mixture screw (1 — Fig. T5-8) 1⅛ turns out from a lightly seated position. Perform final carburetor adjustments as outlined in ADJUSTMENT section.

MAINTENANCE LOG

NOTES

NOTES

NOTES

NOTES

NOTES

NOTES

NOTES

NOTES